ISBN 978-0-265-59968-6
PIBN 10873559

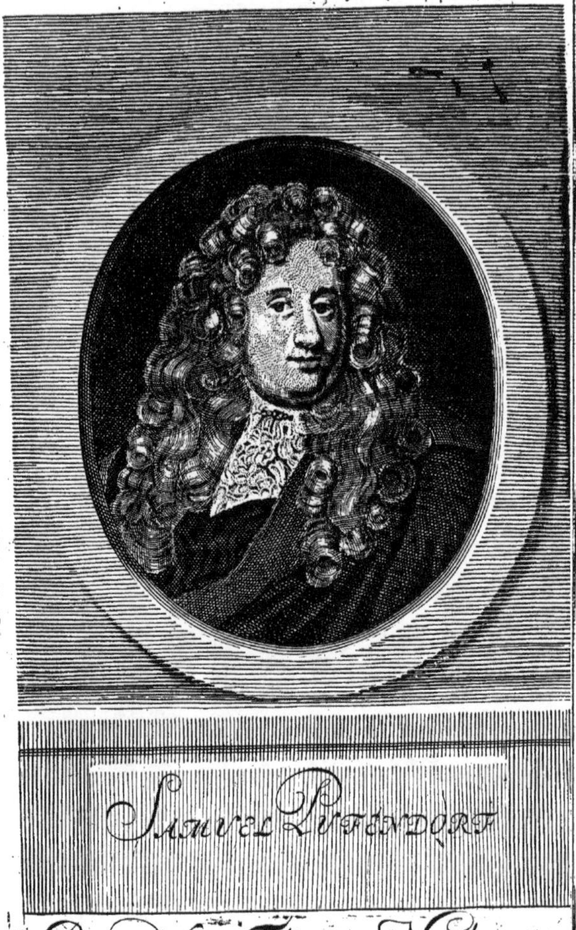

Printed for Thomas Newboroug
and Daniel Midwinter

INTRO
HIST
Of
Kingdom
EUR
By SAMUEL
Counsellor of State
Made English from
An APPENDIX
ing an Introd
pal Sovereign
Venice,
Printed for Dan.
Maurice Atkins
yard. MDCCXI

AN
INTRODUCTION
TO THE
HISTORY
Of the Principal
Kingdoms and States
OF
EUROPE.

By *SAMUEL PUFFENDORF*,
Counsellor of State to the late King of *Sweden*.

Made English from the Original High-Dutch.

The Seventh Edition Corrected and Improved.

WITH
An APPENDIX never Printed before, containing an Introduction to the History of the Principal Soveraign States of *ITALY*; particularly *Venice*, *Modena*, *Mantua*, *Florence* and *Savoy*.

LONDON:
Printed for *Dan. Midwinter* at the *Three Crowns*; and *Maurice Atkins* at the *Golden Ball*, in St. *Paul's* Church-yard. MDCCXI.

AN

INTRODUCTION

TO THE

HISTORY

Of the Principal

Kingdoms and States

OF

EUROPE.

MDCCII.

To His Excellency

CHARLES

DUKE of

SHREWSBURY,

His Majesty's Principal Secretary of State; Knight of the most Noble Order of the Garter, &c. *And one of the Lords Justices of* England.

SIR,

I Should scarce have had the Boldness to prefix your great Name to this Book, had I not been fully persuaded that the extraordinary Worth of my Author would strongly plead for me to your Excellency's Generosity. For, since my Intention was, that the *Sieur Puffendorf*'s Introduction to the History of *Europe* should appear in no leſs Luſtre in this Kingdom, than it has heretofore done in moſt parts of *Europe*; I could not, without injuring a Perſon ſo famous for his Learning, and the Rank he bears in one of the Northern Kingdoms, ſubmit his Treatiſe to the Protection of any other Perſon than your Excellency, whoſe judging Power is ſo univerſally acknowledg'd: If it endures this Teſt, it muſt paſs current in this Nation. The high Station in which you are now plac'd by the Choice of the Wiſeſt and Braveſt of Kings, having put your Merits above the Praiſes of a private Perſon; I ſhall rather Admire than pretend to enumerate them, wiſhing, that as your Actions have hitherto been moſt Effectual in preſerving your Country's Liberty, ſo your Counſels may for the future prove as fatal to the *French*, as the Swords of your glorious Anceſtors in former Ages. Thus recommending my ſelf to your Excellency's Protection, I beg leave to Subſcribe my ſelf,

Your Excellency's

moſt devoted Servant,

J. Crull, M. D.

THE
Author's Preface
TO THE
READER.

THAT History is the most pleasant and useful Study for Persons of Quality, and more particularly for those who design for Employments in the State, is well known to all Men of Learning. It is therefore requisite, that young Gentlemen should be exhorted to apply themselves betimes to this Study, not only because their Memory is then vigorous, and more capable to retain what they learn, but likewise in regard it may be concluded, that he who has no Relish for History, is very unlikely to make any great Progress in the Way of Knowledge. It is a common Custom, indeed, both in publick and private Schools, to read to their Scholars some ancient Historians; and there are a great many who employ several Years in reading Cornelius Nepos, Curtius, Justin *and* Livy, *but never so much as take into their Consideration the History of later Times. 'Tis true, and it cannot be deny'd, but that we ought to begin with the ancient Historians, they being equally useful and pleasant; but to neglect the History of later Times is a notorious piece of Indiscretion, and want of Understanding in those to whom the Education of Youth is committed; for I lay down this as a Principle, That we are to study those Things in our Youth, which may prove useful to us hereafter, when we come to riper Years, and apply our selves to Business. Now I cannot, for my life, apprehend what great Benefit we can expect to receive from* Cornelius Nepos, Curtius, *and the first Decad of* Livy, *as to our Modern Affairs, tho' we had learn'd them by heart, and had, besides this made a perfect* Index *of all the Phrases and Sentences that are to be found in them: Or if we were so well vers'd in them, as to be able to give a most exact account, how many Cows and Sheep the* Romans *led in Triumph when they had conquer'd the* Æqui, *the* Volsci, *and the* Hernici. *But what a considerable Advantage it is to understand the Modern History as well of our Native Country, as of its neighbouring Nations, is sufficiently known to such as are employ'd in State-Affairs. But after all it is not so easie a matter to acquire this Knowledge, partly because those Histories are com-*

mes ; part-
'd in the
so that he
this Study,
tages. To
ty, I did
ome young
mpendium
'd to have
vith intent
those Hi-
provement.
fallen into
to fear,
her would
s happen'd
ted, have
nd Know-
notwith-
revise the
d it some-
h it, such
us Copy to
I hope the
upon this
sen of ad-
the Appre-
en, whom
ind, as it
they might
earch into
vertise the
History of
each

each Kingdom from its own Historians, so a great difference is to be found in those several Relations, which concern the Transactions of some Nations that were at Enmity; it being a common Observation, that the respective Historians have magnify'd those Actions which prov'd Favourable to their Native Country, as they have lessen'd those that prov'd Unfortunate. To reconcile and decide these Differences, was not my Business. But, to give a clearer Insight into the History of each Country, I have added such Observations as are generally made concerning the good and bad Qualifications of each Nation, without offering either to Flatter or Undervalue any; as also, what concerns the Nature, Strength, and Weakness of each Country, and its form of Government: All which I thought might be an Inducement to young Gentlemen when they Travel or Converse with Men of greater Experience in the Affairs of the World, to be more inquisitive into those Matters. What I have related concerning the Interest of each State, is to be consider'd as relating chiefly to that Time when I compos'd this Work. And tho' I must confess that this is a Matter more suitable to the Capacity of Men of Understanding than of young People, yet I could not pass it by in silence, since this is to be esteem'd the Principle, from whence must be concluded, whether State-Affairs are either well or ill managed. I must withal mention one thing more, which may serve as an Instruction to young Men; viz. *That*

The Author's PREFACE.

That the Interest of Nations may be divided into the Imaginary and the Real Interest. The first I understand to take place, when a Prince judges the Welfare of his State to consist in such things as cannot be perform'd without disquieting and being injurious to a great many other States, and which these are oblig'd to oppose with all their Power: As for Example, The Monarchy of Europe, *or an universal Monopoly; such things being the Fuel with which the whole World may be put into a flame.* Num si vos omnibus imperare vultis, sequitur ut omnes servitutem accipiant? If you would be the only Masters of the World, doth it thence follow, that all others should tamely lay their Necks under your Yoke? *The Real Interest may be subdivided into Perpetual and Temporary. The former depends chiefly on the Situation and Constitution of the Country, and the natural Inclinations of the People; the latter, on the Condition, Strength, and Weakness of the neighbouring Nations; for as those vary, the Interest must also vary. Whence it often happens, that whereas we are, for our own Security, sometimes oblig'd, to assist a neighbouring Nation, which is likely to be oppressed by a more potent Enemy; at another time we are forced to oppose the Designs of those we before assisted; when we find they have recover'd themselves to that degree, as that they may prove Formidable and Troublesome to us. But seeing this Interest is so manifest to those who are vers'd in State-Affairs,*

that

that they can't be ignorant of it; one might ask, How it oftentimes happens, that great Errors are committed in this kind against the Interest of the State. To this may be answer'd, That those who have the Supreme Administration of Affairs, are oftentimes not sufficiently acquainted with the Interest both of their own State, and of their Neighbours; and yet being fond of their own Sentiments, will not follow the Advice of understanding and faithful Ministers. Sometimes they are misguided by their Passions, or by Time-serving Ministers and Favourites. But where the Administration of the Government is committed to the Care of Ministers of State, it may happen, that these are not capable of discerning it, or else are led away by a private Interest, which is opposite to that of the State; or else, being divided into Factions, they are more concern'd to ruin their Rivals, than to follow the Dictates of Reason. And for this Reason, some of the most exquisite parts of Modern History consists in knowing the just Character of the Person who is the Sovereign, or of the Ministers, which rule a State; their Capacity, Inclinations, Caprices, Private Interests, Manner of proceeding, and the like; since upon this depends, in a great measure, the good and ill Management of a State. For it frequently happens, That a State, which in it self consider'd is but weak, is made to become very considerable by the good Conduct and Vigilance of its Directors; whereas a powerful State, by the ill Management of those that sit at the Helm, oftentimes declines apace. But as the Knowledge of these Matters appertains properly to those who are employ'd in the Management of Foreign Affairs, so it is mutable, considering how often the Scene is chang'd at Court. Wherefore it is better learn'd from Experience and the Conversation of Men well vers'd in these Matters, than from any Books whatsoever. And this is what I thought my self oblig'd to premise in a few Words, before I entred upon the Body of the Work.

THE

THE

CONTENTS.

The Contents of the Appendix.

Books

Books Printed for Dan. Midwinter.

NAvigantium atque Itinerarium Bibliotheca; or a compleat Collection of Voyages and Travels into all the Parts of the World. Consisting of above 1400 of the most Antient Writers; with many Maps and Cuts. In 2 Large Vol. *Folio.*

Dr. *Harris's Lexicon Technicum*; or an Universal English Dictionary of Arts and Sciences. In 2 Vol. *Folio.*

Cosmographia in 4 Books. By *Peter Heylin*, D. D. *Folio.*

Britannia Illustrata: or Views of several of the Queen's Places; as also of the Principal Seats of the Nobility and Gentry of *Great Britain*, Curiously Engraven on 80 Cop. Plates, *Fol.*

The *Dutch Gardiner*; or the *Compleat Florist*, containing the most Successful Method of Cultivating all sorts of Flowers; the Planting, Dressing, and Pruning of all manner of Fruit-Trees. Together with a particular Account of the Nursing of Lemon and Orange Trees in Northern Climates. Written in *Dutch* by *Henry Van Oosten*, the *Leyden* Gardener. Translated into *English*. The Second Edition, with great Amendments. 8*o*.

Magnæ Britaniæ Notitia, or the Present State of *Great Britain*: with divers Remarks upon the Antient State thereof. By *John Chamberlayne* Esq; The 23*d*. Edition. In 2 Parts, 8*o*.

Mathesis Juvenilis; or a Course of Mathematicks. By *Jo. Christ. Sturmius*, with Cuts, in 3 Vol. 8*o*.

Missellanies by the Late Lord Marquis of *Hallifax*. 8*o*.

Mechanick Exercises; or the Doctrine of Handy-Works, *&c.* to which is added Mechanick Dialing. By *Joseph Moxon*. The 3*d*. Edition 8*o*.

Letters to a Nobleman from a Gentleman Travelling through *Holland*, *Flanders* and *France*, &c. 8*o*.

Reflections on Ridicule; or what it is, that makes a Man Ridiculous, and means to avoid it, *&c.* In 2 Vol. 8*o*.

Plutarch's Morals by way of Abstract, done from the *Greek*. 8*o*.

Esop Naturaliz'd: Being a Collection of Fables from *Esop*, *Locman*, *&c.* The 3*d*. Edition, with the Addition of above 50 New Fables. 8o.

Glossographia Anglicana Nova; or a Dictionary Interpreting such hard Words of whatever Language as are at Present used in the *English* Tongue. 8o.

The Practice of Physick, Reduced to the Antient way of Observations, *&c.* By *G. Baglivi*, M. D. 8*o*.

Books

ROyal *Cookery*; or the Compleat Court Cook, containing the Receipts in all the Particular Branches of Cookery now in Use in the Queen's Palaces of St. *James's*, *Kensington*, *Hampton Court* and *Windsor*, with near Forty Figures, Curiously Engraven on Copper, of the Magnificent Entertainments at Coronations, Instalments, Balls, Weddings, *&c.* at Court. Also Receipts for Making Soupes, Jellies, Bisques, Ragooes, Pattys, Tanzies, Forced Meats, Cakes, Puddings, *&c.* by *Patrick Lamb*, Esq; near 50 Years Master Cook to their Late Majesties King *Charles* the Second, King *James* the Second, King *William* and Queen *Mary*, and to Her Present Majesty Queen *Anne*; to which are added Bills of Fare for every Season of the Year.

The Life of *Elfred* the Great. By Sir *John Spelman*, Knight, from the Original Manuscript in the *Bodleian* Library, with Considerable Additions, and several Historical Remarks, by the Publisher *Thomas Horne*, M. A. *Oxford* Printed for *Maurice Atkins*, at the *Golden Ball* in St *Paul's* Church-Yard, *London*.

Essays upon several Moral Subjects; Part the First upon *Prid*, upon *Cloaths*, upon *Dweelling*, upon *General Kindnesses*, upon the *Office of a Chaplain*, upon the *Weakness of Humane Reason*. Part the Second, of *Fame*, of *Musick*, of the *Value of Life*, of the *Spleen*, of *Eagerness* of *Desire*, of *Entertainment*, of *Books*, of *Confidence*, of *Envy*, of the *Aspect*, against *Despair*, of *Covetousness*, of *Liberty*, of *Old Age*, or *Pleasure*. Part the Third, of *Pain*, *Revenge*, *Authors*, *Power*, *Infancy* and *Youth*, of *Riches*, *Poverty*, *Whoredom*, *Drunkenness*, *Usury*, an *Apostate*, *Solitude*. Part the Fourth, of *Goodness*, *Honesty*, *Religious Temper*, *Lying*, *Fortitude*, *Flattery*, *Theft*, *Peace*, the *Resurrection*. By *Jeremy Collier*, M. A. In 3 Vol. 8o.

Antonini Iter Britanniarum, Commentariis Illustratum *Thoma Gale*, S. T. P. nuper Decani *Ebor*; Opus Posthumum revisit, Auxit, Edidit *R. G.* Accessit Anonimi Ravennatis Britanniæ Chorographia cum Autographo Regis Galliæ, Mss. & codice Vaticano collata Adjiciuntur Conjecturæ Plurime cum nominibus Locorum Anglicis, quotquot iis Assignari Potuerint.

Thirteen Sermons on several Practical Subjects. By *Thomas Gregory*, M. A. late of *Wadham* College in *Oxford*.

Animadversions upon the First Part of Mr. *Richard Johnson's* Grammatical Commentaries, with a Copy of a Letter Writ to Mr. *Johnson*, after that which he calls his Defence, by Mr. *Edward Leeds*, Master of the Free-School in *Bury*.

The Original and Right of Tiths, for the Maintenance of the Ministry in a Christian Church, Truly Stated, to which is Annexed the Draught of a Bill, Prepared to have been Offered to the Parliament, in the Reign of King *William* and Queen *Mary*, *Ann.* 1691. for the Restraining of Pluralities of Benifices, with Cure of Souls: with the Reasons for the said Bill. By *Humphrey Prideaux*, D. D. Dean of *Norwich*. AN

JCTION
HE
ORY
HE
ns and States
'ROPE.

'. I.

:s, and more especially
: Ruines of which arose
ind States.

ımon Senſe, imagines, that pagation of Mankind, there vernments as are among us For in thoſe Times every to any Superiour Power, ıd Servants, as a Sovereign.) me, that even to the time Magiſtracy, nor any civil vernment was lodged only For it is ſcarce to be ima- centiouſneſs, and the Con- both Humane and Divine, vhere the Power of Magi- : And it is obſervable, that ment were conſtituted, we neral did run into the ſame ighty was oblig'd to purge the

The moſt an- cient State of Mankind.

the World by an universal Punishment; though the Root of the Evil was remaining as well after, as before the Deluge. However 'tis likewise probable, that for a considerable time after the Deluge, this separate Paternal Government continued in the World.

The Original of civil Societies.

§. 2. But the Reason why Fathers of Families left this separate way of Living, and joyned in a mutual civil Society, seems to be, that among the Neighbouring Families, sometimes Quarrels us'd to arise, which being often decided by Force, drew along with them very great Inconveniencies; to prevent which, it was thought necessary, for the Preservation of Peace and Quietness among Neighbours, to leave the Decision of such Matters to the Judgment of some of the wisest and most considerable among them. Besides, upon the increase of Mankind, the Insolence and Violence of dissolute Men, became so remarkable and notorious, that a small handful of ill Men combining together, could with the greatest ease oppress and ruine a single Man with his Wife and Children: And to guard off such Injuries, the Neighbours that lived so near, as to be able to assist one another in case of necessity, did enter into a Society mutually to defend themselves against their common Enemies. That they might do this with the better success, the supream Government of the Society was committed to him, who appeared most considerable for his Wisdom and Valour. It is also very probable, that such as by common Consent sought out new Habitations, chose a Leader, who both in the Expedition, and in the Country they possessed themselves of, had the chief Direction of Affairs. And this Office of a Judge, Head or Leader, degenerated by degrees, into that sort of Government that *Aristotle* calls *Heroical*; which indeed is nothing else but a *Democracy* presided over by one of the Citizens, who has a Power rather to advise than to command the rest. Now this seems to be the most ancient Form of *Republicks*: For the Fathers and Masters of Families could not so soon forget their Liberty, as not to reserve to themselves a share in the Government, by which their Consent was necessary at least in all Affairs, that were to be decreed in the Name of the whole Society.

At what time the first States were constituted.

§. 3. But at what time precisely these Societies were first instituted, and which of them is to be esteemed the most

most Ancient, is not easie to be determined; for tho' commonly the *Assyrian* Empire is taken for the first Monarchy, yet it is not from hence to be concluded, that the same was the first civil Society; since it is evident, that this Empire acquired its greatness by swallowing up lesser States. And those Wars which the *Assyrian* Kings waged against other States, do abundantly testifie, that besides the *Assyrian*, there were other civil Societies even at that Time in the World. Upon this Head it is to be observ'd, that as no humane Affairs come immediately to Perfection, so were the first Institutions of civil Society very simple and imperfect, till by Degrees all the parts of the Supreme civil Power, together with such Laws and Constitutions as were requisite for the maintaining of a civil Society, were settled and instituted. The first Commonwealths were likewise very small, and their Territories of a very little Extent, so that it was easie for the Citizens to assemble, either to consult upon Matters of Importance, or to defend themselves against a foreign Power. It is evident out of History; that the deeper you search into the most ancient Times, the more separate small Commonwealths you will meet withal; from the coalition of which great Empires in process of time did arise, some uniting by common Consent, and others being subdued by the more powerful.

The first States were very small and imperfect.

§. 4. Among these great Empires, the *Assyrian* is commonly reckoned the most Ancient; the reason of which may probably be, that those Parts were sooner, and more inhabited than other Places, which being later possessed had fewer Inhabitants, and those scattered at greater distances one from another. Add to this that these earlier and more numerous Inhabitants had a greater support of Riches and Laws, than the latter who were perpetually imployed in Agriculture. So that the *Assyrians* might without much difficulty overcome one small Commonwealth after another, and by subduing some, make way, for an entire Conquest over the rest, that had not then learned the Advantage of a joint Power and Confederacy. The vast Armies with which *Ninus* and *Semiramis* (the first Founders of this Monarchy) over-power'd far distant Nations, make the common Chronologies very doubtful: But to settle this is not to our present Purpose. 'Twill be of more use to take Notice, by what means the

The *Assyrian* Empire.

Kings of this vast Empire did bridle the conquered Nations; and indeed two of their Measures are very remarkable. The first was, That intending to imprint an extraordinary Character of their Persons upon the Minds of the People, they always kept themselves very close in their Palaces, and being seldom to be seen by any but their nearest Servants, they never issued out Orders, or answered their Subjects Petitions but by them. By this means, they inspired the Vulgar People, with the Thoughts, that they were in some Degree above the Humane Race. The second was, That every Year they us'd to draw a certain number of Soldiers out of each Province, and these being quartered in and about the Place of their Residence, and commanded by such a one as was thought most faithful, they struck Terror both into the Subjects at Home and the neighbouring Nations Abroad. This Army was again disbanded every Year, and another drawn out of the Provinces, that the General being thus deprived of an opportunity to gain the Affection of the Soldiers, might not be in a Condition to invade the Empire.

By what means this Empire was maintained.

Its Fall.

The Ruin of this Empire under *Sardanapalus*, is not so much to be ascribed to his Effeminacy, as to this, That the Kings allowed too much Power to the Governors of Provinces of so vast an Extent. These grew at last too powerful for the Kings themselves, who being lulled asleep by Voluptuousness (the Effects of Peace and Plenty) did not, as they used to do formerly, by great Actions, endeavour to maintain their Authority among the People. Out of the Ruins of the *Assyrian* Empire two new Kingdoms were erected; *Arbaces* taking upon himself the Sovereignty of *Media*, where he was Governor, as the Governor of *Babylon* did the same in his Province; both which were afterwards re-united under the *Persian* Monarchy.

The *Persian* Empire.

§. 5. *Cyrus* the first Founder of the *Persian* Empire, did, besides what formerly belonged to *Media* and *Babylon*, also conquer a great part of the Lesser *Asia*. This Prince, besides other remarkable Constitutions, did wisely throw in this, as a most necessary one to preserve the Peace of his Empire; that in all Provinces, where he sent his Lords Lieutenants, he appointed Governors of the Fortresses chosen out of the Commons, who being not under the Jurisdiction of the Lords Lieutenants, had their dependance immediately on the King. These therefore living in continual

By what means it was maintained.

tinual

tinual Emulation and Jealousies, served as a Bridle to on- The Lords Lieutenants, without the assistance of the Governors of the Fortresses, were not in a Capacity to mutiny against the King; and the Governors having a watchful Eye upon all their Attempts and Intrigues, gave constant Notice of the same to the King. On the other Hand, from the Governors of the Fortresses nothing was to be feared, because, being of mean Condition and a very limited Power, they were not capable of making any great Factions, or drawing any considerable Party after them. *Cambyses* annexed *Egypt* to the *Persian* Empire. But whenever the Kings of *Persia* attempted to extend their Conquests farther, it always proved fruitless. *Cambyses* did in vain attack the *Æthiopians*, as *Darius Hystaspes* did the *Scythians*: And *Xerxes* was shamefully beaten by the *Greeks*. But the following Kings, *Artaxerxes Longimanus*, *Darius Nothus*, and *Artaxerxes Mnemon* manag'd their Affairs with more Wisdom against the *Greeks*, whom they did not attack; but leaving them at rest, they quickly saw intestine Wars kindled among them, wherein they so well knew how to play their Game, that by always affording Assistance to the weaker side, they rather protracted than finished these intestine Wars, till the *Greeks*, quite tired and exhausted, were obliged to accept of such Conditions of Peace as were projected by the *Persians*; by vertue of which, each City being declared free and independent of one another, *Greece* was disabled thereafter to undertake any thing of Moment. But after all, *Macedon* an obscure Nation of *Greece*, prov'd the Ruin of the *Persian* Monarchy, through a defect of Policy in their Kings, in not making early Opposition to the growing Power of *Philip*, by raising powerful Enemies in *Greece*, against him and his Son *Alexander*; which for great Sums of Money they might easily have done, and thus have cut out so much work for these two War-like Princes at home, that they could not have had leisure so much as to have entred on the thoughts of invading *Persia*: In the same manner as formerly the *Persians* had obliged *Agesilaus* quickly to return into *Greece*. But being over secure in their own strength, and despising others, they drew upon themselves their own Destruction.

The vain Attempts of their Kings to enlarge the Empire.

Their Fall.

§. 6. *Greece* was in ancient Times divided into a great many petty Common-wealths, every one of those being

Greece.

Govern'd by its own peculiar Laws. Among those [illegible] Athens. process of Time, *Athens* grew most Famous [illegible] Citizens, for Ingenuity, Eloquence, the Knowledge of Arts and Sciences, and civiliz'd Manners, surpassed all the rest; and their Glory encreas'd exceedingly after they had signaliz'd themselves so bravely against the *Persians*. After this, by adding the Harbour of *Pyreum* to their City, they made it very commodious for Shipping, and acquir'd such vast Riches, that by their Naval Strength they subdu'd the Isles of the *Ægean* Sea and the Coast of the Lesser *Asia*. But elated with Success, and thereupon offering hard usage to their Subjects and Confederates, they drew upon themselves the hatred of their Allies: And after they once attempted to be sole Masters of *Greece*, the *Peloponnesians*, and others, headed by the *Spartans* (who above all bore a particular Emulation and Envy to the *Athenians*) united together to chastise the insolence of *Athens*. Yet the *Athenians* behav'd themselves so bravely, that the War was carried on for a considerable Time with near equal Success, till at last being vanquish'd in a Battle in *Sicily*, they also lost their whole Fleet on the Coast of *Thrace*. Then the *Lacedæmonians* becoming Masters of *Athens* constituted thirty Governors, who tyranniz'd most cruelly over such of the Citizens of *Athens* as surviv'd the Storming of their City; yet *Thrasibulus* having expell'd the same, with the Assistance of some of the banish'd *Athenians*, restor'd the City to its former Liberty. After this, though the *Athenians* recover'd themselves a little, yet were they never able to arrive at the former Grandure of their Common-wealth; and being afterwards too forward in making Head against *Philip*, they were severely chastiz'd by him. It was therefore the immoderate Ambition of the *Athenians*, and their desire of conquering more than they were able to defend, which occasion'd their Ruin. For the number of the Citizens of *Athens* did not much exceed ten thousand, and they rarely receiving others as Citizens among them, great Cities and Provinces could not be kept in Obedience by such a number; and so with one unfortunate Blow their whole Power was struck down without Recovery. For considering that such Cities are better fitted for their own Defence, than for making Conquests upon others, it is more adviseable for them to mind the Advantage of their own Trade, than to inter-meddle too much in Foreign Affairs; and

and rather to secure their own Walls, than to invade their Neighbours. Next to *Athens*, *Lacedæmon* was famous in *Greece*, the Citizens of which, by the Constitutions and rigorous Discipline introduc'd by *Lycurgus*, seem'd to be most fitly qualify'd for warlike Atchievements. While this City had no powerful Neighbour to contest withal, it was strong enough to defend its Liberty against the neighbouring Common-wealths. And the *Spartans*, as long as they, according to their Laws and Institutions, despis'd Riches, had no great occasion to invade others. But as soon as they began to aim at higher Matters, they found by Experience, that it was a quite different Case to conquer wide extended Kingdoms, and to preserve a small Republick. For having had the good Fortune of subduing *Athens*, they fell into the same Folly which had been the ruin of the *Athenians*; and not satisfied with the attempts of conquering *Greece*, and the *Asiatick* Sea Coasts, had the Presumption to invade *Persia* under the Conduct of *Agesilaus*. But it was easie for the King of *Persia* to find out means to punish their Insolence, by causing a Diversion to be made by the *Greeks*, that envied the Success of the *Spartans*, so that they were quickly obliged to recal *Agesilaus* to defend themselves at home. Not long after, their Fleet being beaten by *Conon*, *Epaminondas* defeated their Army by Land in the Battle of *Leuctra*; whereby they were so weakened, that they were scarce able to defend their own Walls. Next to these two Cities, *Thebes* was for a while Famous, through the Valour and Wisdom of *Epaminondas*, who knew so well how to Head his Country-men, that they humbled the *Spartans*, and, as long as he liv'd, were the most flourishing State of *Greece*. But after his Death, this City return'd to its former State; and making Head against *Philip*, was severely humbled by him, and quite destroy'd by his Son *Alexander*.

Sparta.

Thebes.

§. 7. *Macedon* was before the times of *Philip* an inconsiderable Kingdom, and so expos'd to the Incursions of its Neighbours, that it was scarce able to defend it self; this Nation being then esteem'd the most despicable of *Greece*. But by the Military Vertue of two Kings, it made such a considerable Figure, that it conquer'd a great Part of the World. The perplex'd Circumstances of the neighbouring Nations of *Macedon* at that time, and the good Conduct of *Philip*, whereby he so settled the Kingdom at home,

Macedon.

The Politick Conduct and great Actions of *Philip*.

home, that it quickly became the Head of all *Greece*, gave the firſt opportunity to lay the Foundation of this Monarchy. For on one ſide it had for its Neighbours, the *Thracians*, *Triballians*, and *Illyrians*, very barbarous Nations, and given to Robbery; which were eaſily kept in awe by a neighbouring, wiſe, and brave King. On the other ſide, was *Greece* and its Cities, which, tho' they were much fallen from their ancient Glory, yet, were all together ſtill too hard for the *Macedonians*. Againſt theſe he made uſe of this Artifice, That by ſetting them together by the Ears among themſelves, he ſo weakned them with inteſtine Wars, that they were afterwards not able to hold out long againſt him. And becauſe *Philip* us'd only to attack one of thoſe Cities at a time, and the reſt were not forward enough unanimouſly to prevent his growing Greatneſs, he was upon a ſudden, before they were aware of it, grown too ſtrong and potent for them all. *Philip* ſeem'd particularly endow'd with great Qualifications for this Enterprize. For beſides the Vivacity of his Spirit, he was puſh'd on by an extraordinary Ambition to make himſelf Famous by great Actions. What real Vertues were wanting in him, he endeavour'd to ſupply with pretending to the ſame; and tho' he did nothing without a fair pretence, yet did he never ſtick at any thing, provided he could obtain his Ends, and was never ſparing in Promiſes or Oaths, if he thought he could thereby deceive ſuch as he intended to overcome. He was an abſolute Maſter of his Paſſions, and knew how to conceal and diſguiſe his Deſigns, how to ſet Friends together by the Ears, and by pretending Friendſhip to both Parties, to deceive them by vain Hopes. He had likewiſe a flattering, deceitful, crafty way of Speaking and Converſing, and ſo knew how to inſinuate himſelf with every Body; how to Diſcourſe ſeriouſly, and to break a Jeſt with equal Dexterity; and as for Money, he made no other uſe of it, than to advance his Deſigns. He was a moſt experienc'd Warriour, and had made the *Macedonians* ſuch excellent Soldiers, that the *Macedonian* Phalanx, firſt invented by him, was terrible even to the *Romans*. And in regard he was always at the Head of his Armies, continually exercis'd his Soldiers, and punctually paid them, there were no better Soldiers in his Days than the *Macedonians*. When arriv'd at ſo high a pitch of Greatneſs, that he was choſen by the common Conſent of *Greece*, their General against the *Persians*, and when busie in making Preparations for the Expedition, he was barbarously murder'd, leaving his Son *Alexander* the Glory of pursuing it.

§. 8. The whole Compass of History does scarce afford a more famous and glorious Expedition, than that of *Alexander* the Great, in which, with about thirty thousand Men, he conquer'd so vast and potent Kingdoms, and by his victorious Arms, extended his Empire from the *Hellespont* to the *Indies*. If we enquire into the Causes of such uncommon and happy Progresses; it is undeniable that, next to the Providence of God Almighty, who has put bounds to all Kingdoms upon Earth, the incomparable Valour of *Alexander* himself had a great share in the same; who having an Army of chosen Men, fell upon his Enemies Army with such dispatch and Vigour, that it was impossible for any new levied Forces of the *Barbarians*, tho' never so numerous, to resist him. In the next place *Darius* committed a grand Mistake, when he offer'd Battle to *Alexander*; it being evident, that the *Persians* never were equal to the *Greeks* in pitch'd Battles. Besides this, the *Persians* having liv'd for a considerable Time in Peace, had few experienc'd Soldiers among them; so that the greater the number was of such undisciplin'd Soldiers, the sooner were they brought into disorder at the Time of Battle. *Darius* was ignorant of that great Art of protracting the War, and endeavouring, by posting himself advantageously, and cutting off the Provisions from his Enemies, to take off the Edge of *Alexander*'s Fury. And because he had neglected to give him a Diversion at home, with the Assistance of the *Greeks*, who envied his Greatness, no other Event could reasonably be expected, than what afterwards followed. *Alexander the Great.*

§. 9. But the untimely Death of *Alexander* robb'd both his Children and the World of the Fruits of his Victories. For not only his Children being young lost their Father's Kingdom; but the fatal Wars carried on after his Death betwixt his Generals, brought the conquer'd Nations under great Calamities, who else would have been in hopes to have changed their Kings for a much better and greater Prince. 'Tis true, it seem'd to be next to an impossibility, that these so suddenly conquer'd Countries should *He dies young.*

ſo ſoon be united in one Kingdom; ſince a firm Union betwixt ſo many Nations could not be eſtabliſhed without a ſingular Prudence of their Supreme Head, and a conſiderable Time. Beſides, we find, that a ſudden Greatneſs is rarely laſting, there being no leſs Ability required to maintain, than to acquire a thing of this Nature. The Conqueſts therefore of *Alexander* being of ſo vaſt an Extent, that the ſmall numbers of his *Macedonians* was by no means ſufficient to keep them in awe, and to make thoſe Provinces dependant on the *Macedonian* Empire; there was no other way to maintain ſuch vaſt Conqueſts, but to treat the conquer'd Nations in the ſame manner with his native Subjects, and not to oblige them to depart from their ancient Laws and Cuſtoms, or to turn *Macedonians*; but rather for him to turn *Perſian*, that the conquer'd might not be ſenſible of any other change, but what they found in the Perſon of their King. *Alexander* underſtood this very well; and accordingly he not only uſed himſelf to the *Perſian* Cuſtoms and Habit, but likewiſe married the deceaſed King's Daughter, and had a *Perſian* Guard about him. Thoſe Writers who cenſure *Alexander*'s Conduct in this matter, only betray their own Indiſcretion. However to ſettle a right Underſtanding betwixt the Conquerors and Conquered, required a conſiderable Time; to effect which, *Alexander* ſeemed to be the fitteſt Man in the World, as being endowed with a more than ordinary Valour, Magnanimity, Liberality and Authority. If he had left a Son behind him not unworthy of ſo great a Father, the *Perſian* Throne would queſtionleſs have been entailed upon his Family.

Great Troubles after the Death of *Alexander*.

§. 10. The Death of *Alexander* the Great was the occaſion of long and bloody Wars: For the Army, puff'd up with the Glory of its great Actions, eſteemed no Body worthy of the ſupream Command; and the Generals refuſing to obey one another, were grown too potent to live as private Perſons. 'Tis true, *Aridæus* had the Name of King; but this poor Man wanted both Authority and Power to bridle the Ambition of ſo many proud and great Men. So that ſpur'd on by the hopes, ſome of obtaining the whole Empire, ſome of getting a conſiderable ſhare, they waged a moſt bloody and long War among themſelves, till their number was reduced to a few, from a great many, who firſt pretended to the Empire. Five

the Sovereign Dominion or [illegible] the Title of Kings, and *Lysimachus*, *Antigonus*, *Seleucus* and *Pto*[illegible] viz. *Cassander*, three last transmitted their Kingdoms to their [illegible] the So that only three Kingdoms remain'd in the Power of the *Macedonians*; viz. That of *Syria*, *Egypt* and *Macedon*; That part of the *Persian* Empire which lay Easterly beyond the River *Euphrates*, being again become a vast new Kingdom under the Name of the *Parthian* Empire. The above-mentioned three Kingdoms were afterwards swallowed up by the *Romans*, and of these the Kingdom of *Macedon* was the first, as lying nearest to *Italy*. For the *Romans*, after having subdued all *Italy*, began to extend their Conquests beyond the Seas; and perceiving that *Philip*, an active King, bid fair for the Conquest of all *Greece*; they did not think it adviseable to let him grow more powerful, he being so near to them, that in Time he might easily prove troublesome to *Italy*. They entring therefore into a League with the same Cities of *Greece*, which were Attack'd by *Philip*, under that pretence made War upon *Philip*; and having driven him back into *Macedon*, restored Liberty to all *Greece*. By which means the *Romans* at the same Time divided their Strength, and gain'd their Affections: At length they Conquer'd *Perseus*, and with him the Kingdom of *Macedon*: Then they turn'd their Arms against *Syria*, and took from *Antiochus* the Great, all that part of *Asia* which extends as far as Mount *Taurus*. And though this Kingdom held out for a while after, yet being miserably torn to pieces by the Dissentions, which were risen in the Royal Family, it Surrendred it self to *Tigranes*, King of *Armenia*. But he being Conquered by *Pompey*, the whole was made a Province of the *Roman* Empire. *Egypt* at last could not escape the Hands of the *Romans*, after the Emperor *Augustus* had defeated *Cleopatra* and her Gallant *Mark Anthony*.

The Fall of the Macedonian Empire.

§. 11. Before we come to *Rome*, we must say something of *Carthage*; this City having long contested with *Rome* for the Superiority, so that the *Roman* Government did not think it self well secured, as long as it was in being. This City, though it was rather fitted for Trade than War; yet having acquired vast Riches by its Traffick, and being vastly encreased in Power and Inhabitants; it not only forced the next adjacent Countries in *Africa* to

Carthage.

to pay them Tribute, but also occasioned the Wars betwixt *ly, Sardinia* and *Spains*; the Two First they maintain'd them and ordinary Resolution and Valour, but in the Third they were brought to utter Deſtruction. If they had avoided to meddle with the *Roman* Affairs, they might in all probability have been able for a great while to defend their Liberty. Ambition therefore was the chief cauſe of their Ruin, ſince the Conſtitution of their Government was ſuch, as being adapted for Trade, did not require any great Poſſeſſions, except a few Lands for the uſe of their Citizens, and ſome Sea-Ports in *Spain* and *Sicily*, for the conveniency of Commerce and Shiping. But the Conqueſts of large Countries were more hurtful than profitable to them. For thoſe Generals who Commanded their Armies abroad, proved at laſt dangerous to them, thinking it below themſelves, after ſo much Glory and vaſt Riches obtained, to be put in the ſame Rank with their Fellow Citizens. Beſides, the Inhabitants of this City, were not ſo well fitted for Land-ſervice; ſo that they being obliged to fill up their Armies with Mercenary Soldiers, rais'd out of ſeveral Nations, theſe were a vaſt and certain Charge to them, the hopes of the Benefit remaining uncertain. And further, the ſtedfaſtneſs and faithful Obedience of Mercenary Soldiers is always precarious, and the Conquer'd Places could ſcarce be truſted to thoſe whoſe Faith might eaſily be bought by Money. After their firſt War with the *Romans*, they Experienced, almoſt to their utter Ruin, how dangerous it is to wage War altogether with Foreign and Mercenary Soldiers. And therefore they could not poſſibly hold out againſt the *Romans*, who fought with a much greater Conſtancy for their Native Country, than theſe Foreign Mercenaries did for their Pay. 'Twas a Capital Errour in the *Carthaginians*, that they did not take care in Time, ſo to eſtabliſh their Power at Sea, that they needed not to have feared any thing from the *Romans* that way: But after they had once let the *Romans* become Maſters at Sea, they could not but expect them one Time or other at their City-gates. At the Time when *Hannibal* had ſuch prodigious Succeſs againſt the *Romans*, it proved alſo a fatal Neglect in them, that they did not timely ſend freſh Supplies to Re-inforce him, ſo that he might have proſecuted the War to the Deſtructi-

on

on of *Rome*. For after they had once given leisure to the *Romans* to recollect themselves, they, mindful of their former Danger, never rested till they had razed *Carthage* to the Ground.

§. 12. 'Twill be worth while to trace the Commonwealth of *Rome* back to its Original, because none ever yet equal'd it in Power and Greatness, and because young Students are first Entred and best Read in the *Roman* History. This City was perfectly made for War, from whence she first had her Rise, and afterwards her Fall. Its first Inhabitants were a sorry Rabble of Indigent People, the very Dregs of *Italy*, ignorant of what belonged to Commerce, and not expert in any Handy-craft Trade. For the carrying on of the first, *Rome* was not commodiously Situated; and the latter was at that Time unknown in *Italy*. That small parcel of Ground which at first they possess'd themselves of, was not sufficient to maintain a considerable Number of People; nor was there any vacant Ground in the Neighbourhood, which could be Tilled for their Use. If therefore they would not always remain Beggars, nothing was left them but their Swords, wherewith to cut out their Fortune. And truly *Rome* was nothing else but a Den of Wolves, and its Inhabitants always thirsting after their Neighbour's Goods and Blood, and living by continual Robberies. It was then necessary for a City, under these Circumstances, to keep up a constant Stock of Valiant Citizens. To effect this the better, *Romulus* commanded, that no Child should be kill'd, except such as were very Deformed; which barbarous Custom was then very common among the *Grecians*. Besides this, he ordered that all Slaves at *Rome* should have, together with their Liberty, the Privilege of the City; from whom afterwards descended great Families, their Posterity being ambitious by great Deeds, to Efface the Memory of their base Original. But above all, one thing did mightily contribute towards the Increase of *Rome*: Namely, that *Romulus* did not suffer the Men to be put to the Sword, in such Places, as were taken by force by the *Romans*, nor would let them be sold for Slaves; but receiving them into *Rome*, granted them the same Privileges with the rest of the Citizens. The *Roman* Writers give this for one Reason, why *Athens* and *Sparta* could not maintain their Conquests so long as *Rome* did; for they

Rome a War-like City.

By what means *Rome* became so populous.

they seldom Naturalized Strangers; whereas *Romulus* frequently used to receive those as Citizens of *Rome* in the Evening, with whom he had fought in the Morning. For War cannot be carried on without a good Stock of Men; nor can Conquests be maintain'd without a considerable number of Valiant Soldiers, upon whose Faith the Government can rely in case of an Attack. But that the Conquer'd Places might not be left destitute of Inhabitants, and *Rome* might not be crouded with too much Rabble, from many conquer'd Places he transplanted only the most opulent and the bravest of the Inhabitants to *Rome*, filling up their Places with the poorest of the *Roman* Citizens; who settling a continual good Correspondence betwixt the Conquer'd and the *Romans*, served also for a Garrison in these Places. By these means, the most Valiant and Richest Inhabitants of the Neighbouring Countries were drawn to *Rome*, and the poorest among the *Romans* obtained thereby, in those Places, large Possessions. But although Necessity gave an Edge to the *Roman* Valour, 'twas not that alone that made them so Warlike a People; for the Courage of their Kings, who instructed them in Military Affairs, and hardn'd them to Dangers, had a great share in it; though the thing rightly consider'd, it is not always adviseable, to lay the Foundation of a State upon Military Constitutions; since the Changes of War are uncertain, and so it is not for the Quiet of any State that Martial Tempers should prevail too much in it. Accordingly we find peaceable Times did never agree with the *Romans*; and as soon as they were freed from the Danger of Foreign Enemies, they sheath'd their Swords in one another's Bowels.

Several other Military Institutions.

§. 13. There were likewise other things worth our Observation, which did greatly advance the Military Affairs of *Rome*. One of the chiefest was, That their King *Servius Tullius*, upon a Survey and Valuation of the People, ordered, that only the most able and wealthy Citizens should do Service as Soldiers, and Equip themselves either with light Arms or compleat Armour, according to their Ability: And, whereas formerly every Body, without Distinction, was obliged to serve the Publick in the Wars at his own Charge; the poorer sort were afterwards never made use of, but upon extraordinary Occasions. And though Riches do not make a Man the more Valiant,

ant, yet was it but reasonable, (since every Body was obliged to serve without Pay) that those, who were scarce able to maintain themselves, should be spared as much as could be. And besides this, the Wealth of the former was a Pledge of their Fidelity. For he that has nothing to lose but his Life, carries all along with him, and has no such strict Obligation to face Death; not to mention, that he may easily be brought to desert his own Party, if he meets with a prospect of a better Fortune among the Enemies. On the contrary, a wealthy Man fights with more Zeal for the Publick Interest; because in defending That, he secures his own, and is not likely to betray his Trust: For if he Deserts, he leaves his Possessions behind him, with uncertain Hopes of a recompence of his Treachery from the Enemy. And, though this Custom grew out of Fashion under the Emperours, yet in lieu of that, they always kept part of the Soldiers Arrears behind, to insure their Fidelity; for these were never paid, till they were Disbanded. It is also remarkable, that, though the *Romans* were often Signally beaten in the Field, yet did they never dispair or accept of any disadvantageous Conditions of Peace, except what they did with *Porsenna*, and the *Gauls* call'd the *Senones:* To the first they were fain to give Hostages, upon Condition, that they should not make any Iron Work, except what was requisite for Tilling the Ground. Of which shameful Peace, the *Roman* Historians have cautiously avoided to speak in their Writings. And the *Gauls* were within an Inch of having put a Period to the very Being of *Rome*, if they had not been bought off with Money, to Raise the Siege of the *Capitol*, when reduced to the utmost extremity by Famine. For what is related, that *Camillus* coming up just at the Time of the weighing out of the Gold, drove the *Gauls* from the *Capitol*, some look upon as a Fabulous Relation. Upon all other occasions they always bore their publick Misfortunes with an extraordinary Constancy. For, notwithstanding that *Hannibal* in the second *Punick* War had reduced them to the last Extremity, yet there was not a word of Peace mentioned at *Rome*. And when their Generals by *Claudius* found *Numantia* had agreed to shameful Articles with the Enemies, they chose rather to deliver up the Generals to the Enemies, than to Ratifie the Treaty. In like manner they us'd commonly to have but a small regard for, and rarely to redeem such as surrender'd them-

themselves to the Enemy, to teach thereby the *Roman* Soldiers to expect no Deliverance but from their own Swords. As this Custom oblig'd the Soldiers to fight till the last; so did their Constancy stand them in great stead among other Nations. For he that shows himself once fearful of his Enemy, must expect to be attacked by him, as often as opportunity presents it self.

Of the Religion of the Romans. §. 14. 'Twill likewise be of use to touch a little upon the Religion of the ancient *Romans*, which, tho' derived from the *Greeks*, yet the *Romans* knew much better how to accommodate it to the advantage of their State. Thus it was from the very beginning a constant Rule at *Rome*, not to begin any publick Affairs of Moment, without good Presages: Because that the Event of Things is commonly supposed to happen according to the Approbation of the Gods: And therefore such as think themselves assured of the good Will of the Gods, undertake and effect Things with a greater Courage. These Augurims or Indications were commonly taken from Birds: Which is a very ancient Superstition, taking its rise from an Opinion of the *Heathens*, that the Gods having their Place of Residence immediately above the Region of the Air, made use of the Creatures of the next adjoyning Element for their Interpreters. Moreover, these Indications were thought particularly useful, because they were at hand at all times, and the Motions and Chirping of the Birds might be variously interpreted according to the Exigency of the Times, and the Affairs of the State. The cunning Augurs or Sooth-sayers made use of these Predictions from the flight of Birds, to inspire the ignorant Multitude either with Hope or Despair, Valour or Fear, according as it seem'd most suitable and convenient to the publick Affairs. And accordingly *Cato* the Elder, who was an Augur himself, did not stick to say; *He wonder'd how one Augur, meeting another, could forbear laughing, since their Science was built upon so slight a Foundation.* What the *Romans* call'd Religion, was chiefly instituted for the Benefit of the State, that thereby they might the better be able to rule the Minds of the People, according to the Conveniencies and Exigencies of the State, quite in another manner, than the Christian Religion does, which is instituted for the Benefit of the Soul, and the future Happiness of Mankind. For which Reason, there were no certain Heads or Arti-

cles

cles of Religion among the Romans, whence the People might be instructed concerning the Being and Will of God, or how they should regulate their Passions and Actions so as to please God: But all was wrap'd up in outward Ceremonies, viz. What sort of Sacrifices were to be made, what Holidays and publick Games were to be kept, &c. For the rest, the Priests were unconcern'd, as to what the People believ'd or disbeliev'd of Divine Matters; or whether after this Life the Vertuous and Wicked were to expect Rewards according to their respective Merit or Demerit; or, whether the Souls perish'd together with the Bodies. For we see, that the Heathens have spoken very dubiously concerning these Matters, and the wisest of them have taken these things for Inventions calculated to keep the People in awe. But in their Ceremonies they were most exact, performing them with great Pomp and outward Shew, and rarely admitting of the least Alteration to be made in the same. All this was instituted to please the Humour of the Multitude, who are most moved with those things, which dazle the Eyes, and strike strongly on the Senses. With this view their Temples and Sacrifices were not only extraordinary Magnificent, but the Priests also were chosen out of the most Noble Families, which serv'd to raise the Veneration of the People, that commonly judge of the Value of things, according to the quality of such as are employ'd about them. But besides this, there was another Mystery in it: For, in regard they made use of their Religion only as an Instrument of State, to make the People pliable to the Intentions of their Rulers; it was by all means Necessary that such Priests should be made use of, as understood the Interest of the State, and sate in Person at the Helm of the Common-wealth. On the contrary, if the meaner sort had been employ'd as Priests, they might easily, out of Ambition, have, with the Assistance of the People, rais'd a Faction contrary to the Governors, since the Multitude commonly depends on those of whose Sanctity they have an Opinion; or else out of Ignorance of the publick Affairs and the present Exigencies they might chance to influence the People in another Manner, than was consistent with the present State of Affairs.

§. 15. After Rome had been govern'd for Two Hundred Forty and Two Years by Kings, another Form of

The Expulsion of their Kings, and the Erection of a new Form of Government.

Government was introduc'd, *Sextus Tarquin*, the King's Son, having at that time ravish'd *Lucretia*. Whether *Junius Brutus* had sufficient Reason, upon this Account, to expel the King, may very well admit of Dispute. For on one side the Fact was most abominable, and of such a Nature, that a brave Man would rather venture at any Thing, than bear such an Affront. And there are a great many Examples, of Princes, who, to satisfie their brutish Lusts, have violated the Chastity of their Subjects Wives and Daughters, and thereby lost both their Lives and their Crowns. But on the other hand, it is to be consider'd, that a Fact, tho' never so Criminal, committed by a Son, without the Knowledge and Consent of his Father, ought not to be prejudicial to the Father and Family; much less could it be a pretence to depose a King from a Throne, which he lawfully possess'd; especially, since to take Vengeance of Criminals belongs only to the King, and not to the Subjects. Indeed *Brutus* and *Collatinus* would have had Reason to complain, after the King had denied them just Satisfaction for the Fact committed by his Son, or if he had in any way approv'd of the same. But it is commonly observ'd, that in Revolutions things are seldom carry'd according to the true Rules of Justice. And as there is commonly some Injustice committed at the first Settlement of a new Form of Government; so Ambition and Envy, cover'd with pretences of the Faults and Male-Administration of the Prince, are the true Motives of Dethroning him. But not to insist further upon this, it is certain, that Kingly Government could not be durable at *Rome*: For such States as are comprehended in one great City are more fit for an *Aristocratical* or *Democratical* Form of Government; whereas a Monarchy is fittest to be erected in Kingdoms, where the Subjects are dispers'd in a considerable Tract and Extent of Land. The true Reason of this is, That Mankind in general, politically consider'd, is like wild unruly Creatures, ready upon all Occasions to shake off the Bridle of Civil Obedience, as often as Matters do not suit with their Humours. Besides, such Men cannot be kept in Obedience without the Assistance of other Men. From whence it may rationally be concluded, why a King, who commands only over one great populous City, is immediately in danger of losing all, as soon as his Subjects are disgusted at him, or another can insinuate himself into their Favour, except he is fortify'd with a strong Guard of Foreigners, and a considerable Fort; though these Remedies are very odious, and oftentimes very uncertain. For when in such a Government the Prince comes to be odious, the Hatred is quickly communicated to all his Subjects, as living close together, and having consequently an opportunity of uniting themselves easily against him. But where the Subjects of a Prince live at a distance from one another, it is easie for him to keep so many of them inclin'd to his side, as are sufficient to suppress the mutinous Party. And for the same Reason, they are not so much to be fear'd, as being not able to meet so soon, and to unite themselves in one Body. But it is more especially very dangerous to command over Subjects living in one Place, of a fiery Temper, and exercis'd in Arms. For common sense tells us, that he who will controul another, ought to have more force than that other. In the mean while, this is most certain, that this Alteration of the Government mainly contributed towards the encrease of *Rome*; it being not credible, that under the Monarchical Government it could have arrived to that Greatness; partly, because the Kings would have been oblig'd for their own Security to suppress, in some measure, the Martial Spirit of their Citizens; partly, because the Negligence or Incapacity of some Kings must needs have prov'd disadvantageous to the Common-wealth.

§. 16. Above all, it is worth our Consideration, by what means the *Roman* Empire, which extended it self over so considerable a part of the World, was destroy'd, and became a Prey to the *Northern* Nations, after it had been broken by its own intestine Troubles. The Causes of which we will enquire into from their first beginning. The People of *Rome*, then, being naturally of a fierce and Martial Spirit, and enclos'd together within the Walls of one City, their Kings had no way left to secure their Obedience, but by gaining their Affections with the Gentleness and Moderation of their Government, since they had not sufficient Power to balance the Forces of so vast a City. Accordingly, we find the first six Kings kept the People in Obedience, rather by their Clemency and gracious Government, than by Fear. But as soon as *Tarquin* the Proud began to oppress the People with new Impositions, and by that means alienate the Hearts of his Subjects from

Reasons of the fall of the *Roman* Greatness.

him; it was easie for *Brutus* under pretext of the Fact committed upon *Lucretia*, to stir up the discontented People, and to shut the City Gates against the King. But as all sudden Changes of Government, that are brought about before Things have been maturely consider'd, and all Emergencies provided against, are commonly accompany'd with great Defects: So was this at *Rome*, where some things were admitted, and others left undone; not so much because they conduc'd to the advantage and safety of the State, but because the present Juncture of Affairs would not suffer them to be otherwise. There were also many Oversights committed in the beginning, which left a Gap open for future Evils and Troubles. It seems evident, that *Brutus* and his Associates, after they had expell'd *Tarquin*, did intend to introduce an *Aristocratical* Form of Government: For it is scarce credible, that they being Noble-men, would, at the Peril of their Lives, have expell'd *Tarquin* on purpose to subject themselves to the Government of the common People: But because no Wise Man is willing to exchange his present Condition with another, without hopes of amending the same; therefore the chief Authors of this Revolution were oblig'd, not only to render the Kingly Government odious to the People, but also by Mildness and Concessions to make the People in love with the new Government. For, if the common People had not been made sensible of the Benefit they received from the Government of the Nobility, they might easily have open'd the Gates again to *Tarquin*. Upon this Consideration, *Valerius Publicola*, strove to please and humour the People in many things, particularly in lowering the Rods or *Fasces* (the Ensigns of Authority) before them, and allowing appeals to the People, as a tacit Confession that the Supreme Power of *Rome* did belong to them. It was by all means requisite, if the Noble-men did intend to maintain the new acquir'd Authority, to have a particular Care of these two Things. First, To take heed that they did not exasperate the common People with their Pride; And, Secondly, To find Means to maintain the poorer sort, that they might not be forced to seek for Remedies against their Poverty and Debts by disturbing the Publick. But neither of these were sufficiently regarded by the Nobility. There being at that time no written Laws at *Rome*, and the Nobility being in Possession of all publick Offices, Ju-

The Defects of the *Roman* Common-wealth.

stice

ſtice was oftentimes adminiſtred according to Favour and Affection, the poorer ſort being often, though unjuſtly, oppreſſed by the more powerful. And becauſe the Citizens were obliged to ſerve in the Wars at their own Charge at that time, when little Spoil was to be got, they were thereby miſerably exhauſted; ſo that the poor had no other Remedy left them but to borrow Money from the Richer ſort. Theſe uſed ſuch as were not able to ſatisfie their Creditors in ſo barbarous a manner, by Impriſoning, laying them in Chains, and other Cruelties, that the Commons, quite put into Deſpair, unanimouſly retired out of the City; neither could they be perſwaded to return, before the Senate had agreed to conſtitute Magiſtrates, called *Tribunes of the People*, who were to protect the Commons, and ſcreen them from the Power of the Nobility.

§. 17. This was the Original and Cauſe of the Diviſion of the *Romans* into two Factions, *viz.* One of the Nobility, and the other of the common People: The continual Jealouſies of which did afterwards miniſter perpetual Fewel for Civil Diſſentions. It ſeem'd at firſt ſight but equitable and of no great Conſequence, that the Commons might have for their Heads ſome, who could upon all occaſions protect them from the Oppreſſion of the Nobility: But in this the Nobles did commit a grand Errour, that they allowed to the common People, which made the major part of the City, a Protection independant of the Senate; making thereby the Body of the Common-wealth as it were double-headed. For the *Tribunes*, ſpurr'd on by Ambition, and Hatred, which is common in the *Plebeians*, againſt the Nobility, were not ſatisfied with affording their Protection to the People againſt the Inſults of the Nobility; but were always endeavouring to be equal in Power with the Senate, and even to Inſult it upon occaſion. And Firſt of all, by their continual Conteſts they obtained a Priviledge for the Commons to intermarry with the Nobles; afterwards they forced the Nobility to conſent that one of the Conſuls ſhould be choſen out of the Commonalty. They took upon themſelves the Power of a Negative Voice, ſo as that no Decree of the Senate could paſs into a Law without their Conſent: Nay they went further, and pretended, without the conſent of the Senate, to make Laws, and to exer-

Two Factions in *Rome.*

The Efforts of the *Tribunes.*

exercise the other Acts of Sovereign Authority. The Senate, 'tis true, to divert and employ the People, continually engag'd them in one War or another, that they might not have leisure to contrive any thing against the Government. This, though it did very well for a while, and the Power and Territories of *Rome* were mightily thereby encreased, yet did arise from thence some other Inconveniences, which did not a little contribute towards the Indisposition of the State. For whereas the conquer'd Lands ought to have been given to the poorer sort of the People, by which means the City would have been freed from a great many needy Citizens; the Nobles under pretence of Farming the same, took them into their own Possession; and what with these Revenues, and the great Booty which fell in the Wars to their share, as being Commanders in Chief, the Riches of the Nobles increased prodigiously; whereas a great many of the *Plebeians* had scarce wherewithal to maintain themselves. The Commonalty being for these Reasons extreamly dissatisfied with the Senate, there were not wanting some of the Nobility, and others, of an ambitious Spirit, who having taken distaste at some Transactions of the Senate, did, under pretence of maintaining the Liberties of the People, make a considerable Party among them, though, in effect, their chief aim was, with the Assistance of the *Plebeians*, to carry on their ambitious Designs. Those being by force opposed by the Senate, it came quickly to a Civil War, and they sheath'd their Swords in each other's Bowels.

Citizens too Powerful.

§. 18. In the mean time, partly by the vast Increase of the *Roman* Empire, partly by the Inadvertency of the Senate, another Evil had taken root, *viz.* That vast and rich Provinces, together with great Armies, were committed to the Government of some of the *Roman* Citizens, and that for several Years. From which, as it created in them an Aversion to a private Life, so it gave 'em an opportunity to have whole Armies at their Devotion. It is not adviseable for any State whatsoever to let any of its Citizens mount to that degree of Power. For he that has a potent Army at his Devotion, will scarce be able to resist the Temptation, but will be apt to attempt to make himself Sovereign. It is evident, that the Ambition and great Power of *Marius*, *Sylla*, *Pompey* and *Cæsar* spurr'd them on, by Intestine Wars, to suppress the Liberty of their

their Native Country; and after *Rome* was shatter'd, to introduce a new form of Government. There was scarce any remedy left against this Evil, after the Citizens had once laid aside the respect due to the Senate and the Laws, and the Soldiers had tasted the Sweets of the Booty got by Civil Commotions. From thence it was, that this Common-wealth, when just arrived to the pitch of its Greatness, did of necessity slip into the worst sort of Monarchies, where the Army exercis'd Sovereign Authority. *Augustus* was the first Founder of this Monarchy, which he by his wise and long Reign, seem'd to have establish'd pretty well: And truly this new introduc'd form of Government, did for a while promise very fair, since *Augustus* assumed only the Title of Prince, and maintaining the Senate, and the rest of the great Officers in their Stations, took upon himself no more than the administration of Military Affairs. But in effect, this Monarchy was not founded so much upon the consent of the Senate and People, as upon the Power of the Soldery, by whose assistance it was introduc'd and maintain'd. And because the ancient Nobility could not brook to be commanded by one single Person, and was always for recovering its former Liberty, the Emperours left no Stone unturn'd either to diminish, or quite to extinguish the Splendour of the ancient Nobility; so that within the space of 200 Years very few were left; and their room was supplied with new Favourites of the Emperours, who were willing to submit themselves to their Commands.

The Constitution of the *Roman* Monarchy.

§. 19. But the instability and tottering State of this Monarchy, was owing to the Army: For as soon as the Soldiers had once learn'd this Secret, that they being the Supporters of the Monarchy, could dispose of the Empire at Pleasure, and that the Senate and People were now empty Names; not only the Emperours were oblig'd with double Pay and great Presents to purchase their Favour; but they also began to kill such Emperours as they did not like, and to fill up their room with such as could obtain their Favour. And in regard one Army claim'd the same Prerogative as well as the other, not only the *Pretorian* Bands that guarded the Person of the Emperour, but the other Armies, which were posted on the Frontiers, presum'd upon the like Insolence. Hence came nothing but Misery and Confusion in the *Roman* Empire, the Life of each

The *Roman* Monarchy could not be of a long continuance.

each Emperour depending on the Will of the covetous and unruly Soldiers, so that no Emperour was sure to leave the Empire to his Posterity. Oftentimes the bravest Princes were murther'd, and in their room others set up of the meanest Rank and Capacity. Oftentimes two or more were declared Emperours, who used to make horrid slaughters among the Citizens in deciding their Titles to the Empire. And this was the Reason why not only very few of the ancient Emperours died a natural Death, but even the Power of this vast Empire was impair'd to that degree by these intestine Wars, that it appear'd no otherwise than as a Body without its Nerves. *Constantine* the *Great* did also hasten its fall, when he transferr'd the Imperial Court from *Rome* to *Constantinople*, and sent away the Veterane Legions which guarded the Frontiers of the Empire, along the *Danube* and the *Rhine*, to the Eastern Parts; upon which the Western Provinces, destitute of their Guards, became a prey to other Nations. Besides this, *Theodosius* divided the Empire betwixt his two Sons, giving to *Arcadius* the *Eastern*, to *Honorius* the *Western* parts; which division did not a little contribute towards the destruction of the Empire. The *Western* parts became a prey to the *Germans* and *Goths*, who about that time came in prodigious numbers to change their poor Habitations for the pleasant and rich Provinces of the *Romans*. *England* the *Romans* left of their own accord, as being not in a capacity to defend it against the *Scots*, and having occasion for their Troops to defend *France*, *Spain* fell to the share of the *West Goths*. The *Vandals* settled themselves in *Africa*. The *Goths*, *Burgundians* and *Francks* divided *France* betwixt them. *Rhætia* and *Noricum* were conquer'd by the *Suevians* and *Bavarians*. A great part of *Panonia* and *Illyricum* was possessed by the *Huns*. The *Goths* settled a Kingdom in *Italy*, and did not think *Rome*, the Mistress of the World, worthy to be made the place of Residence of the *Gothick* Kings.

The Imperial Seat in *Constantinople*.

§. 20. Though the *Western* parts of the *Roman* Empire fell to the share of Foreign Nations, yet the *Eastern* Provinces, the Capital City of which was *Constantinople*, continued untouch'd for a great many hundred Years after. But this *Eastern* Empire was neither in Power nor Splendour to be compar'd to the Ancient *Roman* Empire. And *Agathias* the Vth. says, That *whereas heretofore the* Roman

Forces

Forces consisted of 645000 *Men, the same did amount in the times of* Justinian *scarce to* 150000. 'Tis true, under the Reign of this *Justinian*, the Empire began to recover something of its former Power, *Belisarius* having destroy'd the Empire of the *Vandals* in *Africa*, as *Narses* did that of the *Goths* in *Italy*, these Nations being then infeebled by Effeminacy, and overcome with the deliciousness of a plentiful Country, and a temperate Climate: Yet did it again decrease by degrees, the neighbouring Nations taking away, some one piece, some another: Nay, the Emperours were partly in fault themselves, some of them being sunk in Pleasures, and grown quite effeminate; others involv'd in continual Divisions, and destroying each other. One part was subdu'd by the *Bulgarians*. The *Saracens* conquer'd *Syria*, *Palestine*, *Egypt*, *Cilicia*, and other neighbouring Countries, and ravaging the rest, besieged *Constantinople*; which City was once taken by Count *Baldwin* of *Flanders*, but his Forces were obliged to quit it not long after. The City also of *Trebisond*, with the neighbouring Countries, withdrawing from the rest of the Empire, set up an Emperour of their own. At last the *Turks* entirely sunk this Empire, for they not only conquer'd most of the Provinces of the *Saracens*, but after that swallow'd up the Remnants of the *Eastern* Empire of *Constantinople*. *Greece* having before withdrawn itself from the Obedience of the Emperours, was govern'd by its own petty Princes; making thereby, the Conquests of the *Turks* over them the easier; till, at last, the City of *Constantinople* being taken by Storm by the *Turks*, was afterwards made the place of Residence of the *Ottoman* Emperors. *Anno* 1453.

CHAP. II.

Of the Kingdom of SPAIN.

The ancient State of Spain.

SPAIN was in ancient Times divided into a great many States, independent of one another, which was at that time the condition of most other Countries of *Europe*. But, this multiplicity or partition of Principalities, expos'd this otherwise War-like Nation to the inroads of Foreign Enemies. To this may be added, That the *Spaniards* had but

but few good and experienced Generals, under whose Conduct they might easily have resisted the Power of their Enemies. For not to mention how the *Celts* pass'd out of *Gaul* into the next adjacent parts of *Spain*, who being mixt with the *Iberians*, were from thence-forward called *Celtiberians*; neither how the *Rodians* built *Roses*, the Citizens of *Zante Saguntum*, the *Phœnicians*, *Cadiz*, *Malaga*, and other Cities; the *Carthaginians*, above all the rest, immediately after the first *Punick* War with the *Romans*, began to conquer a great part of *Spain*. And for this Reason, in the second *Punick* War, the *Romans* sent their Forces into *Spain*, where they fought so long with the *Carthaginians*, till at last, *Scipio*, afterwards sirnam'd the *African*, made a great part of it a *Roman* Province; the other parts were subdu'd by degrees, till at last *Augustus* entirely subduing the *Cantabrians*, who liv'd next to the *Pyrenean* Mountains, joined all *Spain* to the *Roman* Empire, under the protection of which it was peaceably govern'd for a considerable time, except that the *Spaniards* now and then were suck'd in by the Eddy of the Civil Wars of the People of *Rome*.

West *Goths* conquer *Spain*.

§. 2. But the *Western* parts of the *Roman* Empire declining, the *Vandals*, *Suevians*, *Alani* and *Silingi* made an Inrode into *Spain*, and after many bloody Battels fought, divided it between them; which Conquests nevertheless they did not enjoy long; for the *Vandals* passing over into *Africa*, the *Alani* were quite routed by the *Suevians*, who, having also subdu'd the *Silingi*, were in a fair way of becoming Masters of all *Spain*, if they had not been prevented by the *West Goths*. But the *Goths*, after they had under the Conduct of their King *Alarick*, ransack'd *Italy* and *Rome* itself, settled themselves upon the adjoining Confines of *Spain* and *France*, in the Reign of King *Athaulpus*, making *Narbonne* the Seat of their Kings, who at first had under their Jurisdiction *Catalonia* and *Languedock*, but soon after extended their Power over *Spain*. Among these King *Euric* was particularly renown'd, who took from the *Romans* all the other Provinces of *Spain*, except *Gallicia*, which remained under the Power of the *Suevians*. He also conquer'd several Provines in *France*. But *Clodoveus*, King of the *Franks*, having defeated *Alaric* the Son of *Euric*, retook from the *Goths*, what they had conquer'd before in *France*. Under the Reign of *Agila* and *Athanagildus*, the

Romans,

Romans, who had before rescu'd *Africa* from the hands of 554.
the *Vandals*, retook part of *Spain*; but were dispossess'd of
most of it, under the Reign of *Levigildis*, who likewise 572.
extirpated the *Suevians* in *Gallicia*. Under the Reign of 586.
his Son *Recaredus*, the Empire of the *Goths* was arriv'd to
its highest pitch of greatness, as comprehending not only
some neighbouring Provinces of *France*, and a part of
Mauritania, but also all *Spain*, except a small part possess'd as yet by the *Romans*; of which they were afterwards dislodged by King *Suinthila*. King *Wamba* subdu'd 646.
the Rebels in *France* with great success, and beat the Fleet 677.
of the *Saracens*, who much infested those Seas; but under
Witiza the *Gothick* Empire began to decline from their
ancient Valour, the *Goths* being much degenerated; and
under the Reign of *Roderic* it was quite extinguish'd. The
King himself contributed greatly to its sudden downfal;
for having ravish'd a certain Court Lady call'd *Cava*, the
Daughter of Count *Julian*, Governour of that part of *Mauritania* or *Barbary*, which belong'd to the *Goths*, and of that
Tract of *Spain* which lies near the Streights of *Gibraltar*;
he, in resentment of this Affront, first stirr'd up a great
many of the King's Subjects against him, and afterwards
perswaded the *Saracens* to pass out of *Africa* over into
Spain. These to try their Fortune, first pass'd over with
a small number, but quickly encreasing by continual Supplies of Men sent from home, they easily defeated King
Roderic's raw and undisciplin'd Troops. After this Success the traiterous *Julian*, understanding that *Roderic* in- 713.
tended to bring into the Field the whole Forces of his Kingdom, which consisted of 100000 Men, brought more *Saracens* over into *Spain*, who being joined with the rest, did
in a most memorable Battle intirely rout that numerous
Multitude of undisciplin'd and ill arm'd Soldiers, who
were surpriz'd to see one of their own Party call'd *Oppas*,
with the Troops under his Command, go over to the Enemy, and fall upon them, in Conjunction with the Forces
of *Julian*. Thus it was, that their Empire sunk, for in
this one Battle fell the whole Power and Splendour of the
Goths, which had been famous in *Spain* for three hundred
Years; *Roderic* himself being kill'd in the Fight, so that
the *Goths* being without a Head were quite dispers'd, and 714.
all the great Cities, partly by force of Arms, partly upon
Articles, fell into the Hands of the Enemy within the
space of three Years. Only *Asturia*, *Biscay*, part of *Gallicia*,

The Ruin of the Gothick Empire in Spain.

The Saracens conquer Spain.

cia, and some Countries adjacent to the *Pyranean* Mountains, remain'd under the *Goths*, rather, because the Enemies did not think it worth their while to dislodge them of those mountainous, uncultivated and craggy Places, than that the *Goths* trusted to their own Strength to defend themselves against them. These parts prov'd likewise a Sanctuary to such Christians as had escap'd the Sword of the Enemy. But all the rest of *Spain* was inhabited by the *Saracens* and *Jews*.

The Kings that rescued *Spain*. *Pelagius*. 726. §. 3. The first that attempted to rescue *Spain* from this Tyranny, was *Pelagius*, who (as 'twas said) was descended from the Race of the *Gothick* Kings. This Man being chosen King, rally'd the sorry remains of the unfortunate Nation; and having drawn together an Army, obtained a signal Victory over the *Moors*; and in the mean while that the *Saracens* were weakening their Strength in *France*, took from them the City of *Leon*, and several others. His Son *Favila*, who succeeded him, did nothing worth mentioning. (*Favila*. *Alfonso* I.) But *Alfonso* the Catholick re-took several Places from the *Moors*, and reigned till the Year 757. His Son *Froila*, in Imitation of the Father valiantly defended his Kingdom, vanquishing the *Moors* in a great Battle. (*Froila*.) He died in the Year 768. But his Successor *Aurelius* made a shameful Peace with the *Moors*, by vertue of which he was oblig'd to give them a yearly Tribute of a certain number of Virgins. (*Aurelius*.) He died in the Year 774. In like manner, his Successor *Silo*, did no memorable Action, and died in the Year 783. (*Silo*.) After him reigned *Alfonso* the Son of *Froila*, whom *Mauregatus* outed of his Kingdom; and to fix himself on his new purchas'd Throne, implor'd the Aid of the *Moors*, promising them a yearly Tribute of 50 Noble Virgins, and as many Girls of a mean Extraction. (*Alfonsus* II.) He died in the Year 788. His Successor *Veremundus* did nothing Praise-worthy, except that he restor'd *Alfonso*, surnamed *the Chaste* from Exile; (*Veremundus*. 791. *Alfonsus* III.) who refusing to pay the scandalous Tribute of the Virgins to the *Moors*, gave them several signal Defeats: But having no Children, he made an Agreement with *Charles the Great*, that he should assist him in driving the *Moors* out of *Spain*; in recompence of which, he was to be his Heir in the Kingdom of *Spain*. In pursuance of this Treaty, he sent his Son *Bernard* with a puissant Army into *Spain*, but the *Spaniards* not liking the Contract, as being not willing to be under the Com-

mand

mand of the *French*, made an Insurrection, and falling upon the *French* near *Ronceraux*, just as they were entring into *Spain*, entirely routed them; in which Battle the Famous *Rowland* was slain. Thus it is related by the *Spanish* Historians, but the *French* do not agree with them in the Relation. *Alfonso* died in the Year 844, whose Successor *Ramirus* most gloriously usher'd in the *Spanish* Liberty. *Ramirus.* For the *Moors* demanding the Tribute according to the Agreement made with *Mauregatus*, he defeated them in a bloody Battle, but could take but few of their strong Holds, being diverted partly by intestine Commotions, partly by an Inroad the *Normans* made upon him. He died in the Year 851. After him succeeded his Son *Ordonius*, *Ordonius II.* who reigned with great applause, and was celebrated for his Valour and Moderation; He obtained a Victory over the *Moors*, and took some of their strong Holds. He died in the Year 862; and his Son and Successor *Alfonso*, *Alfonso III.* surnamed *the Great*, fortunately overcame the Rebels at home, and the *Moors* abroad. But by laying too heavy Impositions upon the People, he drew the hatred of a great many upon himself, and was thereupon dethroned by his Son *Garsias*. This King with Valour and Success *Garsias.* attack'd the *Moors*, but dy'd soon after. His Brother *Ordonius* II. was likewise Victorious against the *Moors*, *910. 913.* transferring the Seat of the *Spanish* Kings from *Oviedo* to *Leon*. He died in the Year 923. But besides this Kingdom of *Oviedo*, there were several other Soveraignties in *Spain*. For *Garsias Semenus* erected a new Kingdom in *The Origin of the Kingdoms of Navarre and Arragon.* *Navarre*; and *Aznar*, Son of *Eudo*, Duke of *Aquitain*, having taken several Places from the *Moors*, took upon himself, with the Consent of the before-mention'd *Garsias*, the Title of Earl of *Arragon*. *Lewis* also, Son of *Charles the Great*, taking *Barcelona*, constituted a Governor there, whose Name was *Bernard*, a *French-man*, from whom descended the Earls of *Catalonia*. About the time of the above mention'd Kings, there were in like manner several Earls or Governours of *Old Castile*, who acknowledg'd the foresaid Kings for their Sovereigns. These Earls being once suspected by King *Ordonius*, he call'd them together; who appearing, were all kill'd by his Order. Wherefore the Old *Castilians*, under the Reign of his Son *Froila*, a *Froila II.* cruel Tyrant, separating from the Kingdom of *Leon*, chose Two Governours, under the Name of *Judges*, who were to administer all Civil and Military Affairs.

But

But this Form of Government did not last long among them.

Alfonso IV. §. 4. After the Death of *Froila*, *Alphonso* the IVth. obtained the Kingdom; under whose Reign *Ferdinand Gon-*
salvo, Earl of *Castile*, perform'd great Things both against
the *Moors*, and against *Sanctius Abarca*, and his Son *Gar-*
sias, Kings of *Navarre*, whom he vanquish'd. But *Al-*
phonso himself being unfit to govern the Kingdom, sur-
Ramirus II. rendred it to his Brother *Ramirus*; who, with the Assi-
931. stance of the before-mention'd *Ferdinand*, beat the *Moors*
in several Places. He died in the Year 950, and was suc-
Ordonius III. *Sanctius.* ceeded by his Son *Ordonius*, a valiant Prince, who did
955. not Reign long, leaving the Kingdom to his Brother *San-*
ctius Crassus. This *Sanctius* was dethron'd by *Ordonius*,
surnam'd the Wicked; but *Ordonius* in his turn, was in
like manner dispossessed of the Throne by the help of the
Moors. It is said, that by certain Articles made betwixt
Sanctius and *Ferdinand*, Earl of *Castile*, it was agreed,
965. that *Castile*, after that time, shou'd not be oblig'd to ac-
Ramirus III. knowledge any dependance on the Kings of *Leon*. He
967. was succeeded by *Ramirus*, who, in his Minority, was
under Womens Tuition; and when grown up, prov'd
very useless to the Publick. For under his Reign, partly
by Civil Commotions, partly by Inroads made by the
Moors, the Kingdom was considerably weakned, and in
great danger of losing more, several Places being taken
Veremund II. from the *Christians*. Under *Veremund*. II. also, the *Moors*
982. did considerable Mischief in those Parts, taking and plundering, besides a great many others, the City of *Leon*; to
which Misfortunes the Civil Commotions did greatly
contribute. But at last *Veremund* entring into a Confederacy with the King of *Navarre*, and *Garsias* Earl of *Ca-*
Alfonso V. *stile*, forc'd the *Moors* out of his Kingdom. To him suc-
999. ceeded his Son *Alphonso* V. under whose Reign there were
great intestine Commotions in *Castile*, by vertue of which
the *Moors* were encourag'd to attack it with such Vigour,
that they overthrew *Garsias*, and took him Prisoner; whose
Son *Sanctius* reveng'd himself afterwards upon the *Moors*.
After this, great Dissentions being arisen among the *Moors*,
their Empire was divided into several Parts, each Governour of a Province assuming the Name of King. *Alphonso*
Veremund III. was succeeded by his Son *Veremund* III. under whose
1015. Reign there happen'd a great Revolution in *Spain*; for

Garsias,

Garsias, Earl of *Castile*, being upon the Point of being marry'd to the King's Sister at *Leon*, was there barbarously murther'd by some of his Vassals. *Castile* thereupon falling to *Sanctius*, King of *Navarre*, who had marry'd the Sister of *Garsias*, he took upon him the Title of King of *Castile*. This *Sanctius*, surnamed *Major*, wag'd War with *Veremund*, who had no Children, taking from him, by force of Arms, a considerable part of the Kingdom. Whereupon a Peace was concluded, by which it was agreed, that *Sanctius* should keep what he had taken before; but, that his Son *Ferdinand* should Marry *Sanctia*, the Sister of *Veremund*, she being Hieress to her Brother, and to succeed him in the Kingdom of *Leon*. In this manner was *Leon*, *Navarre*, and *Castile*, united in one House: But in the mean time while *Sanctius Major* was in the Field against the *Moors*, a great Disaster happen'd at home. He had particularly recommended to the care of his Queen a very fine Horse, which *Garsias*, her eldest Son had a mind to have, and would have obtain'd it from his Mother, if the Master of the Horse had not oppos'd it, telling them, That his Father would be mightily displeas'd at it. The Denial wrought so upon the Son, that he accus'd his Mother of committing Adultery with the Master of the Horse. The Matter being examin'd, the King's natural Son *Ramirus*, proffer'd to justifie the Innocence of the Queen in a Duel with *Garsias*; and the King being much perplex'd and at a loss what to resolve upon, a Priest did at last enforce the Confession of the Calumny cast upon the Queen from *Garsias*; whereupon *Garsias* was declar'd incapable of succeeding his Father in *Castile*, which descended to him by the right of his Mother; and *Ramirus* obtain'd the Succession to the Kingdom of *Arragon* as a recompence of his Fidelity. This *Sanctius Major* died in the Year 1035.

Castile made a Kingdom.

Sanctius III. *Major*.

§. 5. All the Provinces of *Spain*, possess'd by the Christians, being thus join'd in one House, it seem'd an easie matter to root out the *Moors* divided among themselves, and to restore *Spain* to its former State, if the Provinces had but continued under one Head. But the Division made by *Sanctius Major* occasion'd most bloody and pernicious Wars. This *Sanctius* had four Sons: To the Eldest, *Garsias*, he left *Navarre* and *Biscay*; to *Ferdinand*, *Castile*; to *Gonsalvo*, *Suprarbe* and *Ripagorsa*; and to *Ramirus* his

The pernicious Division of *Spain*.

his natural Son, *Arragon*; giving to each of them the Title of *King*. These being all ambitious to be equal in Power and Greatness to their Father, and thinking their Bounds too narrow, fell quickly together by the Ears. For whilst *Garsias* was gone in Pilgrimage to *Rome*, *Ramirus* endeavour'd to make himself Master of *Navarre*; but the other returning home, drove him out of *Arragon*. There arose also a War betwixt *Ferdinand* of *Castile*, and his Brother-in-law *Veremund*, King of *Leon*; wherein the latter being slain in Battle, *Ferdinand* became Master of *Leon*, which indeed did by right of Succession belong to him. He took also from the *Moors* a great part of *Portugal*. After the Death of *Gonsalvo*, the third Son of *Sanctius Major*, *Ramirus* made himself Master of his Territories; and at the same time attempted to recover, by force of Arms, *Arragon* from the King of *Navarre*. Not long after, *Ferdinand* of *Castile*, and *Garsias* of *Navarre*, wag'd War together, about a certain Tract of Ground, and *Garsias* was slain in a Battle. By his Death *Ramirus* got an opportunity of recovering *Arragon*. At last *Ferdinand*, surnamed *the Great*, died in the Year 1065, dividing the Empire, to the great detriment of *Spain*, among his three Sons. The eldest, *Sanctius*, had *Castile*; *Alfonso*, *Leon*; *Garsias*, *Gallicia*, and a part of *Portugal*; with the Titles of *Kings*. *Sanctius* waged War with *Ramirus* of *Arragon*, whom he slew in a Battle, but was beaten back again by *Sanctius*, Son of *Ramirus*, and King of *Navarre*. Afterwards, having driven *Alfonso* out of his Territories and taken *Garsias* Prisoner, he took Possession of the Territories belonging to his Brothers, but was slain in the Siege of *Camora*, which City he endeavour'd to take from his Sister. Then *Alfonso* his Brother, who had hitherto dwelt with the *Moorish* King of *Toledo*, made himself Master of *Castile* and *Leon*: And took from the *Moors*, besides some other Places, the City of *Toledo*, which was in those Days esteem'd impregnable. But the *Moors* in *Spain* having receiv'd fresh Reinforcements out of *Africa*, got new Courage, and falling upon the *Christians*, defeated them in two Battles; but *Alfonso* got an entire Victory over them, and obliged the *Moorish* King of *Corduba* to pay him a yearly Tribute. Nevertheless, he was afterwards beaten in a Battle fought with the *Moors*, where he lost his only Son, *Sanctius*, whose Death he reveng'd soon after upon them. He died in the Year 1109. *Urraca* his Daughter was

Heir-

Mary. *Ferdinand* the Great. 1038. 1045. 1053. *Sanctius* III. 1067. *Alfonso* VI. 1073. 1085. *Alfonso* VII. 1109.

Heiress to the Kingdom, she being Married to *Alfonso* King of *Arragon*; which Marriage, under pretence of too near a Consanguinity, and Adultery committed by the Queen, was afterwards dissolved. But, *Alfonso* pretending still to keep *Castile* as the Dowry of the Queen, it caused great intestine Wars and Divisions. For *Alfonso* VIII. Alfonso VIII. Son of *Urraca* by *Raymond* of *Burgundy*, her first Husband, who had come out of *France* to assist her Father in the Wars against the *Moors*, was proclaim'd King of *Castile*, 1118. in the mean while that *Alfonso* of *Arragon* was busied in taking, besides some other Places, the City of *Saragossa* from the *Moors*. At last a Peace was concluded betwixt *Arragon* and *Castile*. Afterwards *Alfonso* of *Castile* made 1122. War against the *Moors* with great Success, taking from them divers Places of Note. But *Alfonso* of *Arragon* being 1134. slain in a Battle fought with the *Moors*, and leaving no Children behind him, those of *Navarre* chose for their King, *Garsias*, who was of the Race of their former Kings: But the *Arragonians* conferr'd the Crown upon *Ramirus*, Brother to the deceased King, who had formerly been a Monk. *Alfonso* of *Castile*, in Opposition to both, pretending to have a Right to these Kingdoms conquer'd a great part of them, causing himself, with the Consent of *Pope Innocent* II. who was supposed to do it in spite to the *German* Emperours, to be proclaimed Emperour of *Spain*. But this difference was likewise compos'd at last, it being agreed that *Ramirus* should give his only Daugh- 1137. ter, together with the Kingdom, to *Raymond* Earl of *Barcelona*, by which means *Catalonia* and *Arragon* were United. Then *Alfonso* entring into a Confederacy with the Kings of *Navarre* and *Arragon*, attack'd the *Moors* again, and took from them the City of *Almeria*, which in those Days was a great Sea-port and Harbour for Privateers. *Raymond* took from the *Moors*, *Tortosa*, *Lerida*, and other strong Holds. *Alfonso* died in the Year 1157.

§. 6. The same *Alfonso* left to his Son *Sanctius*, *Castile*; Sanctius IV. and to *Ferdinand*, *Leon* and *Gallicia*. *Sanctius*, who did nothing remarkable, except that he beat twice those of *Navarre*, died in the Year 1158, leaving his Son *Alfonso* Alfonso IX. IX. a Child of four Years of Age. During the time of his Minority, there were great Disturbances in *Castile*, occasion'd partly by the Divisions among the Nobility, partly by the Wars with *Ferdinando* of *Leon*, and *Sanctius* of

Navarre, who took several Places from the *Castilians*. But coming to his riper Years, he extricated himself, though not without great Difficulty, out of those Troubles. In the War against the *Moors*, which all the *Spanish* Kings were most intent upon, he suffered extreamly; so that he was oblig'd to make a Truce with them, because the Kings of *Navarre* and *Leon* at the same time fell upon him. At last there was a Confederacy made betwixt these Kings, with a certain Agreement, how such Places should be disposed of as should be taken from the *Moors*. Accordingly, in the Year 1210, a most memorable Expedition was undertaken against the *Moors*, in which were a great many Foreigners, that came to Signalize themselves; but many of them being soon tired out, returned home. At that time was fought the famous Battle of *Losa*, where 200000 *Moors* being slain, they lost all their Strength. In this Battle *Sanctius* King of *Navarre*, broke first thro' a Chain which surrounded the *Moorish* Army, and in Memory of the Action he afterwards bore a Chain with an Emerald in his Shield. In this War was taken from the *Moors* besides other Places, the City of *Calatrava*, and the King of *Leon* took *Alcantara*. *Alfonso* died in the Year
Henry. 1214, leaving behind him his Son *Henry*, whose Minority occasion'd great Disturbances in the Kingdom; he died
1217. without Issue in the Year 1217. He had two Sisters, the Eldest, *Blanch*, was married to *Lewis* VIII. Son of *Philip Augustus*, King of *France*: The second, *Berengaria*, was married to *Alfonso*, King of *Leon*. The Crown descended by Right of Succession to the Eldest, and her Heirs: But out of the hatred the States bore to Foreigners, they
Ferdinandus Sanctius. conferr'd the Kingdom upon *Ferdinand*, Sirnamed *the Holy*, Son of *Berengaria*, who with all speed imaginable, possess'd himself of it, before he could be prevented by his Father; surmounting all the Difficulties which were rais'd against him, partly by his Father, and partly by some of the Nobility. It is related by some, That *Blanch* was not the Eldest Sister, and that some of the *Castilian* Noblemen disputed *Berengaria*'s right to the Crown, upon the Plea that the Pope had declared her Marriage with *Alphonso* void, and their Children illegitimate, as being
1230. too near in Blood. By the Death of *Alfonso*, *Leon* and *Castile* were re-united under *Ferdinand*, at what time the
1232. *Moors* suffered extreamly in their Affairs. King *James* of *Arragon* took from them *Majorca*, in the Year 1230. *Mi-*

norca in the Year 1232. Yvica in the Year 1234. The City and Kingdom of Valencia in the Year 1238. Ferdinand took from them, besides other Places in the Year 1230, Merida and Bajadoz. In the Year 1236, the City and Kingdom of Corduba: In the Year 1240, Murcia surrendered it self to the Protection of Castile. 1240. In the Year 1243, Sevile, and the greatest part of Andaluzia. 1248. But whilst he was making Preparations to carry the War into Africa, he died in the Year 1252.

§. 7. The History of the next insuing Years is full of intestine Troubles and Divisions. Alfonso X. Alfonso, 'tis true, was famous in foreign Countries for his Wisdom and great Skill in Astronomy, insomuch that it is reported of him he used to say, *That if God had advised with him at the time of the Creation of the World, the World would have been made more uniform*; yet he was unfortunate at home, and hated by his Subjects. The first occasion of which was, that being desirous to fill his Treasury, which was exhausted, he caus'd the Current Coin to be diminished, which inflamed the price of every thing; and whilst to prevent this, he set certain Rates on all Commodities, this occasioned a general Scarcity of all things, the People not being willing to sell at his Rates. He was by some of the 1256. Electors chosen Roman Emperour: But because his Children were then very young, and great Divisions arose among his Nobles, he delayed for a great many Years to go thither, and to receive the Imperial Crown; till in the Year 1275, a fancy took him all on a sudden, to go and take Possession of the Empire, though Rudolph of Habsburgh was already got into the Imperial Throne. But his Journey was ended in Provence, he returning from thence home by the Persuasion of the Pope, who afterwards excommunicated him, and obliged him also to renounce the Title of Emperour. After the Death of Ferdinand his eldest Son, Sanctius the younger Brother aim'd at the Succession, though Ferdinand had left Children behind him. This raised a Jealousie betwixt the Father and Son; and thereupon the Son rose in open Rebellion against his Father, being assisted by the major part of the States; which Commotion however ceased with the Death of Alfonso. Under the Reign of this King many Battles were fought 1284. against the Moors with various Success. Sanctius V. In the Year of his Accession to the Throne, viz. 1284, happened the Si- The Sicilian Vespers.

 cilian

cilian Vespers, by which means *Peter* King of *Arragon*, obtained the Kingdom of *Sicily*. He died in the Year
Ferdinand IV. 1295. During the time of the Minority of his Son *Ferdinand* IV. the Kingdom of *Castile* was overwhelm'd with Trouble. After he came to Age, he undertook an Expedition against the *Moors*, taking from them *Gibraltar*; and
1312. died in the flower of his Age. Under the Reign of this
1297. King, *James* King of *Arragon* was presented with the Kingdom of *Sardinia*, by the Pope, who pretended to have a right of disposing of it; and those of *Pisa* being then in Possession of the same, were afterwards beaten out
1324. *Alfonso* XI. by the *Arragonians*. The Minority of *Alfonso* XI. was in like manner full of Troubles. At that time the *Moors* had again received a great Reinforcement out of *Africa*, and yet the *Castilians* obtain'd a most signal Victory over them in the Year 1340, in which Battle, 'tis said, 200000 were slain on the side of the *Moors*, and but 25000 *Spaniards*. Upon this *Algezire* was taken, and a Peace concluded with the King of *Granada*, under Condition that he should be
1350. Tributary to *Castile*. This King died in the Siege of *Gibraltar*, which he had lost before. His Son *Peter*, sirna-
Peter the Cruel. med *the Cruel*, reigned very tyrannically. He drew the Hatred of most of his Subjects upon himself by parting from his Queen *Blanch*, whom he afterwards caused to be murdered tho' innocent, for the sake of a Concubine. This occasion'd a Plot against him, which he suppressed with a great deal of Bloodshed. In the mean while a War arose betwixt him and *Peter* IV. King of *Arragon*, who assisted the Rebels in *Castile*, who had set up for their King, *Henry* the King's Brother, begotten on a Concubine called *Eleonora Gusman*: With him also joined a great many *French* Voluntiers: So that falling upon *Peter*
1366. of *Castile*, he forced him to flee into *Aquitain*. But he having raised there a considerable Army, returned into *Spain*, defeated *Henry*, and obliged him to flee to *France*; but did not desist from his Tyranny, whereby he quite lost the Affection of his Subjects: And *Henry* having gathered another Army in *France*, returned to *Castile*; where
1359. being assisted by the *Castilians*, he vanquished *Peter*, and in the fight killed him with his own Hands.

Henry II. §. 8. From the Race of this *Henry* II. sirnamed *the Bastard*, sprang afterwards Princes that proved very weak. *Henry* himself did at first labour under great Difficulties,

the

the neighbouring Nations attacking him every where; yet he surmounted them, and at last made a Peace with them all upon honourable Terms. He died in the Year 1379. His Son *John* endeavoured to obtain the Crown *John* II. of *Portugal*, upon the Death of *Ferdinand* its King, whose Daughter he had married. But the *Portuguese*, out of a hatred to the *Castilians*, set up for their King, *John* natural Son to *Peter* King of *Portugal*, who maintained himself against the *Castilians*, routing them near to *Aliumbaret*; which Victory the *Portuguese* boasted mightily of in their Histories. *Castile* was at that time in great Danger, the *English* siding with the *Portuguese*, under the Duke of *Lancaster*, who having married the Daughter of *Peter*, sirnamed *the Cruel*, pretended to the right of the Crown of *Castile*, and accordingly assumed the Title and Arms: But the Business was at last composed, by marrying the Daughter of the *English* Duke to the Prince of *Castile*; after which a Peace was likewise concluded with *Portugal*. *John* died by a fall from his Horse *Ann.* 1390. His Son *Henry* III. was a sickly Prince, under whose Minority great 1390. *Henry* III. Divisions arose in the Kingdom. During the time of his Reign he did nothing remarkable, except that he restored the Revenues which the Nobles had alienated from the Crown. He died in the Year 1407, leaving behind him *John* II. a Child of two Months old. The Tuition of *John* II. this Prince was, besides his Mother, committed to *Ferdinand* his Uncle, to whom the States offered the Kingdom, which he generously refusing to accept of, he obtained afterwards the Crown of *Arragon*. This King being under the Tuition of his Mother, grown very Effeminate, and only addicted to Voluptuousness, having no Genius nor Inclination for publick Business, committed the whole Management to his Favourite *Alvarez de Luna*, an ambitious Man; which occasioned great Jealousies in his Nobles against him. *John* taking his Favourite's part against the Nobility, an open War ensued betwixt them, the Rebels being headed by his own Son, and the City of *Toledo* declaring against the King. At last the King tired out of protecting *Alvarez* with the many Inconveniences, cut this Favourit's Head off, but died himself the next Year. 1453. Under the Reign of this King a War broke out betwixt the *Spaniards* and those of *Granada*, wherein the first signalized themselves to their great Advantage. In the Year 1420, King *Alfonso* of *Arragon* was adopted by *Joan*

Queen of *Naples*; but a Difference arising betwixt *Joan* and *Alfonso*, she declared the said Adoption void and null, receiving in his stead *Lewis* Duke of *Anjou*; which afterwards occasioned bloody Wars betwixt *France* and *Spain*: But at last *Alfonso* got the upper Hand, making himself Master of *Naples*, and leaving the same to his natural Son
1442. *Henry* IV. *Ferdinand*. In the Kingdom of *Castile*, *John* II. was succeeded by his Son *Henry* IV. the Plague and Scandal of the *Spanish* Nation. Being incapable of begetting Children, to remove the Suspicion, he hir'd one *Bertrand Curva*, who for this Service was made Earl of *Ledesma*, to lie with the Queen; who having brought forth a spurious Daughter called *Joan*, *Henry* caused her to be proclaimed Heiress to the Crown. What confirmed this Crime the more, was, that the Queen afterwards had another Bastard begotten by another Person. To wipe off the Affront, and to exclude *Joan* from the Succession of the Crown, the Nobles of *Spain* entered into an Association; and putting the Image of *Henry* upon a Scaffold, they there formally accused him, and afterwards, having taken off his Ornaments, threw his Image from the Scaffold, proclaiming at the same time *Alfonso*, Brother of *Henry*, their King. From hence arose most dismal intestine Wars, which occasioned bloody Battles. During
1468. these Troubles *Alfonso* died. About the same time *Ferdinand* Son of *John* II. King of *Arragon*, whom his Father had declared King of *Sicily*, proposed a Marriage with *Isabella*, *Henry*'s Sister, to whom the rebellious *Castilians* had offered the Crown, and forced *Henry* to confirm her right to the same; whereupon the Nuptials were celebra-
1469. ted, but privately: Yet would *Henry*, by making this Concession void, have afterwards set up again the Title of *Joan*, whom he had promised in Marriage to *Charles* Duke of *Aquitain*, Brother to *Lewis* XI. King of *France*: But he dying suddenly, *Henry* at last was reconciled to *Ferdinand* and *Isabella*, and died in the Year 1472.

Ferdinand the Catholick and *Isabella*. The Kingdom of *Castile* and *Arragon* united.

§. 9. From this match of *Ferdinand* (whom the *Castilians* call the Vth, or *the Catholick*) with *Isabella*, sprang the great Fortune and Power of *Spain*; for in his Reign it arrived to that pitch of Greatness, which ever since has made it both the Terrour and the Envy of *Europe*. This *Ferdinand* met with some obstacles at the beginning of his Reign, the States of *Castile* having limited his Power within too narrow Bounds: And *Joan*, the late King *Henry*'s supposed Daughter, having contracted a match with *Alfonso* King of *Portugal*, he entring *Castile* with a puissant Army, caused her to be proclaimed Queen; but the *Portuguese* being soundly beaten, the whole Design vanished, and *Joan* retiring to a Monastery, the civil Commotions were totally suppress'd. *Ferdinand*'s next Care was to regulate such Disorders as were crept into the Government in the former Reigns; with which view he caused that Law-book to be compiled, which from the City of *Toro*, where it was first Published, is called *Leges Tauri*. In the Year 1478, the famous *Spanish* Inquisition was first instituted by him against the *Moors* and *Jews*, who having once professed themselves Christians, did afterwards return to their Idolatry and Superstitious Worship. This Court of Inquisition is esteemed an inhumane and execrable Tribunal among other Nations, and carries the greatest Injustice with it, in ordering the Children to bear the Guilt of their Parents, and not permitting any one to know his Accusers in order to clear himself against them: But the *Spaniards* ascribe to this Inquisition, the Benefit they enjoy of one Religion, the variety of which has brought great Inconveniencies upon other States. However, 'tis certain, That tho' by those Means Men may be forced to a feigned Conformity, and obliged to shut their Mouths, yet they are not the proper Instruments for inspiring the Minds of Men with sincere Piety. After *Ferdinand* had ordered his Affairs at home, and upon the Death of his Father, taken upon him the Government of *Arragon*, he undertook an Expedition against the *Moors* of *Granada*, which lasted ten Years, wherein the *Spaniards* were routed near *Malaga*, but quickly revenged themselves upon their Enemies, taking from them one Place after another, till at last they besieged the City of *Granada* with 50000 Foot and 12000 Horse; and having forced the King *Boabdiles* to a surrender, they put an end to the Kingdom of the *Moors* in *Spain*, after it had stood there for above 700 Years. And to prevent the possibility of their ever encreasing again in *Spain*, King *Ferdinand* banished 17000 Families of *Jews* and *Moors* out of *Spain*, by which means, the Kingdom was at the same time despoiled of vast Riches, and of a great number of Inhabitants. After this he took from them *Mazalquivir*, *Oran*, *Pennon de Velez*, and *Mellilla*, situated upon the Coast of *Barbary*.

The first beginning of the *Spanish* Inquisition.

1497.

1481.

1483.

Granada taken.

1492.

He likewise made use of this opportunity to teach his Nobles, who were grown over powerful, their due Respect and Obedience to the King, and took upon himself the Sovereign Disposal of all the *Spanish* Orders of Knighthood, which were grown to that excess of Riches and Power in *Spain*, that they were formidable to its Kings. Much a-

1494. *America* discover'd.

bout the same time *Christopher Columbus*, a *Genouese*, discovered *America*, after his Offers had been refused by the Kings of *Portugal* and *England*; and after he had been seven Years solliciting at the Court of *Castile* for a Supply to undertake the Voyage: At last 17000 Ducats were employed in equipping three Vessels, out of which Stock such prodigious Conquest and Riches have accrued to *Spain*, that ever since it has aimed at the universal Monarchy of *Europe*. How easily the *Spaniards* conquered these vast Countries, and with what Barbarity they used the Inhabitants, is too long to be related here. Not long after a War was kindled betwixt *Spain* and *France*, which has been the occasion of inspeakable Miseries in *Europe*, these two warlike Nations being now freed from that Evil which had hitherto diverted them from medling with Foreign Affairs, the *French* having rid themselves from the *English*, and the *Spaniards* from the *Moors*. For when

1494. The first rise of the War betwixt *France* and *Spain*.

Charles VIII. King of *France* undertook an Expedition against the Kingdom of *Naples*, *Ferdinand* did not judge it for his Interest, to let the *French*, by conquering this Kingdom, become Masters of *Italy*; especially, since by marrying his Daughter he was in Alliance with *England*, *Portugal* and the *Netherlands*, and the then Kings of *Naples* descended from the House of *Arragon*: And tho' *France* lately entered with him into a Confederacy, by vertue of which the *French* gave up *Roussilion* to *Spain*, hoping thereby to bring over *Ferdinand* to their Party; nevertheless, when he perceived that by all his Intercessions he could not disswade him from undertaking this Expedition, he entered into a Confederacy with the Pope, the Emperor, *Venice* and *Milan*, against *France*. At the same time, he sent to the Assistance of the *Neapolitanes*, *Gonsalvus Ferdinand de Cerdua*, afterward sirnamed *the Grand Captain*, under whose Conduct the *French* were beat out of the *Neapolitan* Territories, whilst he himself made an inroad into *Languedoc*. In the Year 1500 the *Moors* living in the Mountains near *Granada* rebelled, and were not without great Difficulty appeased. Afterwards an Agreement was made

made betwixt *Ferdinand* and *Lewis* XII. King of *France*, to take joint Possession of the Kingdom of *Naples*, under the pretence of making War from thence against the *Turks*; which being soon conquered by their joint Power, they divided it according to their Agreement. But each of them coveting this delicious Morsel for himself, they fell at Variance and came quickly to Blows, *Gonsalvus* routed the *French*, near *Carinala*, took the City of *Naples*, beat them again near the River *Liris* or *Girigliano*, and taking *Cajeta*, drove the *French* a second time out of the Kingdom of *Naples*: But *Gonsalvus* was not rewarded by *Ferdinand* according to his Merits, for *Ferdinand* being jealous of his great Power, undertook a Journey in Person to *Naples*, on purpose to bring *Gonsalvus* handsomely away from thence; and taking him along with him into *Spain*, he treated him ill for his great Deserts. In the mean time 1504. died the Queen *Isabella*, which occasioned some Differences betwixt *Ferdinand* and his Son-in-law *Philip* the *Netherlander*; *Ferdinand* pretending, according to the last Will of *Isabella*, to take upon him the Administration of *Castile*. And to maintain his Claim the better, he entered into a Confederacy with *France*, by marrying *Germana de Foix*, Sister to *Lewis* XII. hoping thereby to obtain a powerful Assistance, in case *Philip* should come to attack him; But *Philip* coming into *Spain*, and taking upon him the Administration of the Government in the Name of his Lady *Joan*, *Ferdinand* retired into *Arragon*. However, *Philip* died soon after, and Queen *Joan*, tho' disturbed in her Senses, undertook the Administration, but some of the Nobility opposing her, the Government was conferr'd upon *Ferdinand*, after his return from *Naples*, notwithstanding the Emperour *Maximilian* pretended to it, in the right of his Grandson *Charles*. In the Year 1508, *Ferdinand* entered into a Confederacy against the *Venetians*, whereby he regained the Cities of *Calabria*, *Brindisi*, *Otranto*, *Trano*, *Mola* and *Polignano*, which the *Venetians* had formerly obtained for some Services done to the *Neapolitans*. But as soon as *Ferdinand* perceived that the *Venetians* were like to be swallowed up by the Emperor and *France*, the Pope and he left the Confederacy, thinking it more convenient to preserve the State of *Venice*; since by adding the Territories of *Venice* to those of *Milan*, which were then possessed by the *French*, these would have grown too powerful in *Italy*. Hence arose a War, in which

John

John d'Albert, King of *Navarre*, taking part with the *French*, was upon the Instigation of *Ferdinand* excommunicated by the Pope; under which pretext *Ferdinand* took an opportunity to possess himself of that part of the King-

1512. dom of *Navarre*, which lies on the *Spanish* side of the *Pyrenean* Mountains; and which since that time the *French* have in vain endeavoured to recover. In the Year 1510 the *Spaniards* took *Bugia* and *Tripoli* upon the Coast of *Barbary*; but were routed in the Island of *Zerbi*. This wise King died in the Year 1516.

Ferdinand conquer'd Navarre.

Charles.

§. 10. To him succeeded his Grandson by his Daughter, *Charles*, the fifth Emperor of that Name, who, with the Assistance of the Cardinal *Ximenes*, immediately took upon himself the Administration of the Government, his Mother, to whom the same belonged, being uncapable of exercising it. This Prince, who, since *Charles* the Great, was the most potent Prince that hath been in *Europe*, spent the greatest part of his Life in Travels and Wars. In the very beginning of his Reign, there were some Commotions in *Spain*, which were soon appeased. *John d'Albert* also made an Inrode into the Kingdom of *Navarre*, in hopes to recover it, but was quickly repulsed. But with the *French*, during his whole Life, he waged continual Wars. For, though in the Year 1516, he made a League with King *Francis* I. whereby the Daughter of *Francis* then under Age was promised to him in Marriage; yet was this Tie not strong enough to keep down the Animosity of these two emulous Princes. *Charles* flush'd with the great Success of his House, had always in view his Motto, *Plus ultra.* On the other hand, *Francis*, surrounded every where by so Potent a Prince, opposed his Designs with all his Might, fearing, lest his Power should grow too strong

1519. both for him and all the rest of *Europe*. *Charles* obtain'd a most particular Advantage, when the Imperial Dignity was conferr'd upon him; to obtain which was for himself, or somebody else, *Francis* had labour'd with all his Might, but in vain. Upon this, their Emulation flam'd out into open War, in which the *French* lost *Tournay* and St. *Amant*, but beat the *Imperialists* from before *Mezeres*. At the same time *Charles*, took up a Resolution upon the Instigation of Pope *Leo* X. to dispossess the *French* of *Milan*; upon the Plea that *Francis* had neglected to receive this Dutchy in fief of the Empire; and accordingly he beat the

Wars betwixt Charles and France.

the *French* near *Bicoque*. *Fonterabie* also, which the *French* had taken by Surprize, was retaken from them by force. It prov'd withal very disadvantageous to the *French*, that the Constable *Charles* of *Bourbon* sided with the Emperor; and entring *Provence*, besieg'd *Marseilles*; which nevertheless he was forc'd to quit, as soon as *Francis* march'd with all his Forces that way into *Italy* to recover the *Milaneze*. In this Expedition *Francis* took the City of *Milan*, but at the Siege of *Pavia* was attack'd by the *Imperial* General, who totally routed his Army, and having taken him Prisoner, carry'd him into *Spain*. The King himself was in part the occasion of this loss, in having sent a great part of his Army towards *Naples* and *Savona*; especially considering that those who remain'd with him, were mostly *Italians*, *Swiss* and *Grisons*, who did not perform their Duty in the Battle; and that most of his Generals were of Opinion, their best way was to avoid the hazard of a Battle, by retiring under the City of *Milan*. The *French* met with equal bad success in the Diversion they endeavour'd to give the Emperour, by the help of *Charles* Duke of *Gelderland*, and the *Friselanders*: For these were at that time worsted by *Charles*'s Forces. There were some that advis'd *Charles* to set *Francis* at Liberty without any Ransom, and by this Act of Generosity to oblige him for ever: But he follow'd the Counsels of such as advised to make Advantage of so great a Prisoner. Accordingly he tied him up to very hard Terms; which *Francis* refusing to accept of, fell, through Discontent, into a dangerous fit of illness; upon which *Charles* himself went to visit and comfort him; though he was advis'd to the contrary by his Chancellor *Gattinara*, who alledg'd, that such a visit, where he did not intend to promise the Prisoner his Liberty, would rather seem to proceed from Covetousness, and fear of losing the Advantange of his Ransom, than from any Civility or good Inclination towards him. And this Sickness was the real Cause, why at last the Treaty, concerning his Liberty, which had been so long on Foot, was finish'd, the Emperour fearing that his Discontent might plunge him into another Sickness, or Death it self. In the mean time, the prodigious Success which attended the Emperour, raised no small Jealousie among other Princes; and by the Instigation of Pope *Clement* VII. three Armies were rais'd to maintain the Liberty of *Italy*. To prevent this Storm, and especially to withdraw the Pope

1524. 1525.

from

from the Confederacy, the Emperor's Generals march'd directly against *Rome*, which they took by Storm (where *Charles* of *Bourbon* was slain) and for several Days together plunder'd the City, and committed great Outrages. The Pope himself was besieg'd in the Castle of St. *Angelo*; and *Charles*, at the same time that the Pope was block'd up by his own Forces, caus'd Prayers to be said in *Spain* for 40 Days together, for his Deliverance. At last, punish'd by Famine, he was forc'd to surrender, and to renounce the above mention'd League. The Conditions on which *Francis* had obtain'd his Liberty, were, That *Francis* should surrender the Dukedom of *Burgundy*; renounce the Sovereignty over *Flanders* and *Artois*; quit all his pretences upon *Naples* and *Milan*; marry the Emperor's Sister *Eleonora*; and give his two Sons as Pledges for the performance of these Articles. But as soon as he got into his own Kingdom, he protested against the Treaty, which was extorted from him during his Imprisonment: And making a League with the Pope, *England*, *Venice*, the *Suiss* and *Florence*, sent an Army into *Italy* under the Command of *Odet de Foix*, Lord of *Lautrée*. This occasion'd very gross Words between these two Princes, insomuch that they gave one another the Lie, and a Challenge pass'd betwixt them; but *Lautrée*, who had at first great Success, being destroy'd with his Army by Sickness in the Siege of *Naples*, a Peace was at last concluded at *Cambray*, in the Year 1529, by vertue of which, *Francis* paid for his Sons 2550000 Rixdollars, renounc'd his Pretensions to *Flanders*, *Artois*, *Milan*, and *Naples*, and married *Eleonora*, Sister to the Emperor; from which Marriage, if a Son should be Born, he was to be put in Possession of the Dukedom of *Burgundy*. In the Year 1530, *Charles* was Crown'd by Pope *Clement* VIII. at *Bononia*; where the Pope stipulated with the Emperor, that the Common-wealth of *Florence* should be made a Principality: And accordingly the said City was by force obliged to admit this Change; *Alexander de Medicis* being constituted their first Duke, to whom the Emperor married his Natural Daughter *Margaret*. In the same Year the Bishop of *Utrecht* resign'd the Soveraignty of that City, and the Province of *Over-yssel*, into the Hands of *Charles*: And soon after the Provinces of *Gelderland*, *Zutphen*, *Groningen*, *Twente* and *Drente* fell also into his Hands. In the Year 1535, he went with a puissant Army into *Africa*, took *Tunis* and *Goletta*, restoring the King-

Rome taken by *Charles* V. 1527.

A Peace made at *Cambray*.

Kingdom of *Tunis* to *Muleassa*, who had been outed before by *Haradin Barbarossa*: But in *Goletta* he left a Garrison. In the Year 1537, another War broke out betwixt *Charles* and *Francis*: For the latter could not digest the loss of *Milan*; and being advised by the Pope, that when-ever he intended to attack *Milan*, he should first make himself Master of *Savoy*; and *Francis Sforza* dying at the same time; he fell upon *Charles* Duke of *Savoy*; and under pretence, that he defrauded his Mother of her Dowry, drove him quite out of *Savoy* and conquer'd a great part of *Piedmont*. But the Emperor, who was resolved to annex the Dutchy of *Milan* to his Family, came to the Assistance of the Duke of *Savoy*, and at the Head of his Army, entring *Provence*, took *Aix*, and some other Places; but his Army being much weakned with Sickness and want of Provisions, he was forced to retire again. In the *Netherlands*, the *Imperialists* took St. *Paul* and *Monstrevil*, killing great Numbers of the *French*. But through the Mediation of Pope *Paul* III. a Truce of 10 Years was 1538.
concluded at *Nissa* in *Provence*; after which these two Princes had a friendly interview at *Aigues Mortes*. And the very next Year, the Emperor, contrary to the Advice of his Friends, ventur'd to take his way through the very Heart of *France*, travelling the shortest way with all possible speed to compose the Disorders, which were arisen at *Ghent*. But before that he had, by the Contestable *Anna Mmtmorency*, cajolled *Francis* into a belief, that he would restore to him the Dutchy of *Milan*, which however he never intended to perform. In the Year 1541, he undertook an Expedition against *Algiers* in *Africa*, at the latter end of the Year, against the Advice of the Pope, and others of his Friends, who persuaded him to stay till next Spring. He there Landed his Army with good Success; but a few Days after, such prodigious Storms and Rains dispersed his Ships, and spoiled the Fire-locks of the Soldiers, that the Emperor was obliged, with the loss of one half of his Army, to return into *Spain*. The Year 1542.
after that, *Francis* broke with him again, accordingly *William* Duke of *Cleves* entring *Brabant* on one side, the Duke of *Orleans* on the other side, took *Luxemburgh* and some other Places. The *Dauphin* besieg'd *Perpignan*, but was oblig'd to raise the Siege: The famous Pirate *Barbarossa*, did, by the Instigation of *Francis*, great Mischief on the Sea-coasts of *Calabria*, destroying *Nissa* in *Provence* by

Fire. *Charles* seeing himself attack'd at once in so many Places, setting aside the Differences which were arisen about the Divorce betwixt *Henry* of *England* and his Aunt *Catharine*, made a League with *Henry* King of *England*; wherein it was agreed, That the Emperor should force his way through *Campaigne*, whilst *Henry* enter'd into *Picardy*; that so they might, by joining their Forces, ruin the whole Power of *France*. Thereupon the Emperor, with an Army of 50000 Men, beat the Duke of *Cleves* in the *Netherlands*, forcing him to surrender *Guelderland*; and after having recover'd the Places in *Luxemburgh*, taken before by the *French*, enter'd into *Campaigne*, taking by force *Lygny* and *Disier*. *Francis* kept with his Army on the other side of the River *Marne*, and not daring to fight the *Imperialists*, contented himself to ravage the Country they were to march through, in order to cut off their Provisions. Nevertheless the *Imperial* Army found a sufficient quantity at *Espernay* and *Chasteau Thirry*. After this *Charles*, not receiving that Assistance from the King of *England* which he expected, and having lost a considerable in *Italy*, near *Carizola*, from the *French*, made a Peace with *Francis* at *Crespy*, in the County of *Valois*. Then *Charles* undertook to reduce the *Protestants*, entring, for that Purpose, into a League with Pope *Paul* III. and this War he carried on with such Success, that without much Trouble he broke them, making their chief Heads, the Elector of *Saxony* and Landgrave of *Hesse*, Prisoners. The Emperor made use of great Policy, in fomenting Divisions betwixt Duke *Maurice* and his Cousin, the Elector of *Saxony*: And refusing to fight with them at first, he thereby protracted the War, foreseeing that a Confederacy under so many Heads would not last long. At the same time *Francis* and *Henry* VIII. were both of them lately dead, who else would questionless, have oppos'd his Design of oppressing the *Protestants*, in order to make himself absolute Master of *Germany*: Nay the very Heads of the *Protestant* League very much contributed to their own Misfortune, as having let slip several opportunities, especially at first, before the Emperor had rightly settled his Matters, when they might have done him considerable Mischief. But after all, *Charles* was no great gainer by these Victories, for that he us'd the Conquer'd, with too much Rigour, keeping the Captive Princes in too close an Imprisonment. He also disobliged *Maurice* Elector of

Peace made at *Crespy*. 1544. *Charles* wages War against the *Protestants* in *Germany*. 1547.

Saxony

Saxony, after his Father-in-law the *Landgrave* of *Hesse* had, through his Persuasion, surrender'd himself to the Emperor. The Elector therefore being persuaded by the Prayers of his Children and others, who remonstrated to him, That through his Means their Religion and Liberty were in danger of being lost, he fell unawares upon *Charles*, whom, under favour of the Night and a Fog, he forc'd to retire from *Inspruck*. After this Exploit a Peace was concluded by the Mediation of King *Ferdinand* at *Passaw*, in which the *Protestant* Religion was establish'd. In the mean while *Henry* II. King of *France*, coming to the Assistance of the *Protestants*, had taken *Metz*, *Toul* and *Verdun*. The Emperor again attackt *Metz* with great Fury, but being fain to leave it after a considerable loss sustain'd, he discharg'd his Fury upon *Hesden* and *Tervanne*, which he levell'd with the Ground. In *Italy* the *Imperialists* took *Siena*, which afterwards *Philip* II. gave to *Cosmo* Duke of *Tuscany*, reserving to himself the Sovereignty and some Sea-ports. At last, *Charles* tir'd with the Toils of the Empire, and the Infirmities of his Body, resign'd the *Imperial* Crown to his Brother *Ferdinand*, who would not Consent that the same should come to his Son *Philip*. But to *Philip* he gave all his Kingdoms and Territories, except those in *Germany* (which fell to *Ferdinand*'s share) reserving to himself only a yearly Allowance of 100000 Ducats. He had made a little before, a Truce of five Years with *France*, which was soon broke by the Sollicitation of the Pope, who endeavour'd to turn the Family of *Colonna* out of their Possessions; and they being upheld by the *Spaniards*, the *French* sided with the Pope. But this War prov'd very unfortunate to the *French*, for being routed at St. *Quintins*, they lost that City, and the Mareschal *de Thermes* was also soundly beaten near *Gravelin*. At last a Peace was concluded at *Chateau en Cambrasis*, by virtue of which, the *French* were oblig'd to restore all they had taken in *Italy*: And thus were all those Provinces lost in one Moment, for the Conquest of which *Charles* and *Henry* had shed so much Blood. But under-hand it was agreed, That both the King of *Spain* and *France* should endeavour to root out the Hereticks (as they call'd them) which succeeded afterwards very ill both in *Spain* and *France*. In the Year before this, *viz*. 1558, died *Charles* in the Convent of St. *Justus* in *Spain*, where he spent his last Days in quiet. His last Will and Testament (tho' never

[Margin notes: 1550. — Treaty at *Passaw*. — 1554. — Abdication of *Charles*. — Peace betwixt *Spain* and *France*, 1559. — *Charles* dies.]

ver so Rational) was so far from being pleasing to the Inquisition, that it wanted but little of having been burnt as Heretical. And his Father Confessor and the rest of the Monks in that Convent, who had been present, were forc'd to undergo the severe Judgment of that Court.

Philip II. §. 11. In the Reign of *Philip* II. the greatness of the *Spanish* Monarchy began to be at a stand; neither had its Kings the same Success, as formerly, to get vast Kingdoms by Marriages. For from the match of *Philip* and *Mary* Queen of *England*, came no Children. And truly, in my Opinion, the *Spanish* Greatness receiv'd the first shock at the time, when *Charles* V. surrender'd his Dominions in *Germany* to his Brother *Ferdinand*, and afterwards had him elected King of the *Romans*; by which means the Power of this House was divided, and the Imperial Crown separated from the *Spanish* Monarchy. *Charles* would fain have afterwards persuaded *Ferdinand* to transfer the Succession of the Imperial Crown upon *Philip*; but he influenced by his Son *Maximilian* to keep what he had got, would in no ways part with it. Besides, he was much belov'd by the *Germans*, whereas they had an Aversion against *Philip*; who being a meer *Spaniard*, did not so much as understand the *German* Tongue: And *Ferdinand* and his Successors prov'd very good Princes, who were not fond of the *Spanish* Methods of Governing. But that which gave the greatest shock to the *Spanish* Greatness, was the Commotions in the *Netherlands*. The reason why this Evil grew incurable, was, that *Philip* being over fond of his ease, would rather sit still in *Spain*, than by his Presence endeavour to stem the current before it became too rapid; tho' his Father did not think it too much, to venture himself at the Discretion of *France* his Rival, to appease the Tumults arisen only in the City of *Ghent*. Another reason was, That he took the most violent Course, by sending the Duke of *Alva*, a cruel Man, among the *Netherlanders*, who being us'd to a mild sort of Government, were thereby put into Despair; especially when they were inform'd, that the Inquisition had declar'd Criminal, not only those who were guilty of the Rebellion, and pulling down the Images, but even all such Catholicks as had not made Resistance against them. Besides this, the *Spaniards* were much hated by the *Netherlanders*, not only by reason of the great Diversity of the Man-

Manners of these Nations, but likewise upon the account that the latter had been in great esteem with *Charles* V. whose humour suited mightily with their Customs. On the contrary, *Philip* only encourag'd the *Spaniards*, who having an extraordinary conceit of their own Abilities, and taking the *Netherlanders* for Cowards, did not think they had Courage enough to oppose their Designs. The *Spaniards* were well pleas'd to see the *Netherlanders* tumultuous, hoping the King would, upon that score have an opportunity to clip their ample Privileges, and by making them all alike obtain an absolute Dominion over them: This done, they hoped to make these Countries their Armory and Store-house, from whence they might with more ease invade *France* and *England*, and raise the *Spanish* Monarchy to the highest degree of Greatness. But the *Netherlanders*, were resolv'd not to part with their Liberty, nor to be treated as a conquer'd Nation. The neighbouring Princes also, but especially *Elizabeth*, Queen of *England*, took the opportunity of these Troubles to empty the vast Treasures of *Spain*, and to exhaust its Strength. In like manner the *Protestant* Princes also of *Germany*, who hated the *Spaniards*, were glad of this opportunity, and assisted the Prince of *Orange* upon all occasions. And the Emperors thought it more convenient to be quiet and to please the *Germans*, than to be too forward to assist their Cousins. These Commotions in the *Netherlands* occasion'd a War betwixt *Philip* and *Elizabeth*, Queen of *England*, in which she not only afforded Assistance to the *Netherlanders*, but with the *English* Privateers did considerable mischief to the *Spanish West India* Ships; and the famous *Francis Drake* plunder'd the very Southern Coast of *America*. On the other side, *Philip*, by supporting the Rebels in *Ireland*, prov'd very troublesome to Queen *Elizabeth*. At last *Philip* resolved with one stroak to sink the whole Strength of *England*; to which purpose he was equiping a great Fleet for several Years together, which he call'd *the Invincible*, the like being never seen before those Times. The Fleet consisted of 150 Sail of Ships, which carry'd 1600 great pieces of Brass Cannon, and 1050 of Iron; 8000 Seamen, and 20000 Marines, besides Volunteers; the Charge amounted daily to 30000 Ducats, but the whole Expedition came to twelve Millions of Ducats. At the same time the Pope *Sixtus* V. excommunicated Queen *Elizabeth*, adjudging her Kingdom to *Philip*. But

War with England.

all these Preparations came to nothing, the greatest part
The *Spanish* Armado destroy'd. of this Fleet being destroy'd, partly by the *English* and
Dutch, partly by Tempests in the *German* Ocean; so that
few return'd home, and those that did were very much
shattered; and in fine the loss was so universal, that there
was scarce a Noble Family in *Spain* but went into Mourning
for the loss of some Friend or another. But the magnanimity
and evenness of Temper that *Philip* shew'd upon
this occasion, was much to be admir'd, for he receiv'd
the bad News without the least Alteration, giving only
this Answer, *I did not send them out to fight against the*
1588. *Winds and Seas.* After that, the *English* and *Dutch* Fleets
being join'd, beat the *Spanish* Fleet near *Cadiz*, taking
1596. from the *Spaniards*, not only a great many Ships richly
Laden, but also the City of *Cadiz* it self; which nevertheless
was abandon'd by the *English* General, the Earl
of *Essex*, after he had plunder'd it: Neither did *Spain*
get any Advantage by having entangl'd it self in the Troubles,
and (as it was call'd) *the Holy League*, made in
France. *Philip*, 'tis true, propos'd to himself to have met
with a fair opportunity, by excluding the *Bourbon* Family,
to annex the Crown of *France* to his House, or by raising
Divisions in that Kingdom to assist one of his Creatures in
obtaining that Crown; but by the Courage and good
Fortune of *Henry* IV. all these Measures were broke, and
he declaring himself a Catholick, took away the Foundation
whereupon the League was built. By this turn,
Philip suffer'd extreamly in his Affairs; for in the mean
time that he sent the Duke of *Parma*, Governor of the *Netherlands*,
to the Assistance of the League in *France*, the
Confederate *Netherlanders* had leisure given them to put
themselves and their Affairs in a good posture. Besides,
1594. *Henry* IV. after reducing most of *France*, declar'd War
against *Philip*; the Count *de Fuentes* took *Cambray* in the
Year 1595, and the next Year the Arch-Duke *Albert* master'd
Calais. On the other side, *Henry* recover'd *Fere*
from the *Spaniards*. In the Year 1597, the *Spaniards* took
Amiens by surprise, which *Henry* recover'd not without
Peace made at *Vervin*. great Difficulty. At last, a Peace was concluded in that
same Year betwixt *France* and *Spain* at *Vervin*; *Philip* waged
also several Wars against the *Turks*; for the Pyrate
1551. *Dragutes* had taken from the *Spaniards* *Tripoli*, after they
had been in Possession of it for forty Years. To retake
this, *Philip* sent a strong Army, which took the Isle of
Gerbis;

Gerbes; but being afterwards beaten by the *Turkish* Fleet, he lost, together with the Island, 18000 Men and 42 Ships. 1560. In the Year 1566 *Maltha* was besieg'd by the *Turks* during the space of four Months, but was reliev'd by *Philip*, who forced the *Turks* to raise the Siege with great loss. In the Year 1571, the Confederate Fleet of *Spain*, *Venice*, and other *Italian* States, under the Command of *Don John* of *Austria*, obtained a most signal Victory over the *Turkish* Fleet near *Lepanto*, whereby the *Turkish* Naval Strength was weaken'd to that degree, that they were never afterwards so formidable in those Seas, as they were before: Tho' indeed the *Spaniards* got no great Reputation in this War, for by their delays that considerable Island of *Rhodes* was lost before. In the Year 1573 *Don John* of *Austria* passed with an Army into *Africa*, to retake *Tunis*, which succeeded so well, that he forced the City, and added a new Fortification to it: But in the Year next following, the *Turks* sent a puissant Army thither, and retook the City, its Fortifications being not quite perfected; as also *Goletta*, which was but sorrily provided with Necessaries, tho' lost indeed by the unskilfulness and Cowardice of the Governor; so that the whole Kingdom of *Tunis*, to the great Prejudice of the Christians, fell into the Hands of the *Turks*. At home *Philip* was at War with the *Marans* of *Granada*, who rebelling against him, were supported by the *Algorines*, and could not be subdu'd but with great difficulty; and if the *Turks* had been quick enough in giving them timely Assistance, it might have prov'd very dangerous to *Spain*. This Rebellion did not end till the Year 1570, after it had continu'd for three Years. 1562. There were also some Commotions among the *Arragonians*; who pretended to take part with *Anthony Perez*, who stood upon the Privileges of the Kingdom of *Arragon*, to avoid the Indictment laid against him, for having, upon the King's Orders, privately murther'd *Escovedo*, an intimate Friend of *Don John* of *Austria*. By laying this Indictment, *Philip* intended at once to purge himself of the Infamy of the Fact, and to be revenged upon *Perez*, who had been unfaithful to him in some Love Intrigue. And tho' this did not much redound to the Honour of *Philip*, yet by this he took an opportunity to retrench the Privileges of the *Arragonians*. In the Year 1568, *Philip* caus'd his Son *Charles* to be kill'd, upon the pretence, that he had endeavour'd to kill his Father; and not long after, the

Queen *Isabella*, *Charles*'s Step-mother, died, not without Suspicion of having been Poison'd. But a great many are of Opinion, that some Love Intrigues were the occasion of their Death, which is the more probable, because the said *Isabella* being intended for the Bride of *Charles*, had been taken by the Father in spite of his Son. *Henry* King of *Portugal* dying, there were several Pretenders to that Crown, among whom was *Philip* (as being born of *Isabella*, *Emanuel* King of *Portugal*'s Daughter) who maintain'd his Right by the Sword; and by the Conduct of the Duke of *Alva* conquer'd the Kingdom, forcing *Anthony*, the Bastard, who had caus'd himself to be proclaim'd King, to fly into *England*, and from thence into *France*, where he died an Exile in *Paris*: Only the Island of *Tercera* held out for some time longer, which the *French* intending to relieve, were totally routed by the *Spaniards*. And thus *Philip* became Master both of the *East* and *West-Indies*, the two greatest Mines of Riches in the World. Nevertheless, the *French*, *English*, and *Hollanders*, had found out a way to ease him of these prodigious Revenues. For *Philip*, just before his Death, did confess, That the War with the *Netherlands* only, had cost him 564 Millions of Ducats. And truly, it is very probable, that trusting to his vast Riches he was thereby prompted to his ambitious Designs, and to undertake more than prov'd beneficial to him. He died in the Year 1598.

Portugal falls to *Spain*. 1579.

1595.

Philip III.

§. 12. *Philip* the III's Father had left him the Kingdom in Peace with *France*, but the *Dutch* War grew every Day the heavier upon the *Spaniards*. The *Spaniards* did hope, that after *Philip* II. in his latter Days had married his Daughter *Clara Eugenia* to *Albert* Arch-Duke of *Austria*, giving her the *Netherlands* for a Dowry, the *Dutch* would become more pliable, and re-unite themselves with the rest of the Provinces in the *Netherlands*, as having now a Prince of their own, and being freed from the *Spanish* Yoak that was so odious to them. But in regard the *Hollanders* did by no means like this Bait, and at the Siege of *Ostend* gave a taste to the *Spaniards*, both of their Strength and their firm Resolution to stand it out, the *Spaniards* resolved to make Peace with them; especially since the *Hollanders* had found out the way to the *East-Indies*, where they made great Progress. Besides *France* enjoying a peaceable Government under *Henry* IV. and encrea-

sing

sing in Power, it was fear'd, That if the *French* should fall, with fresh Forces, upon *Spain*, which was then tir'd out and exhausted by this tedious War, it might prove fatal to *Spain*. Add to this, that *Spain* fed themselves with vain Hopes, that the fear of a foreign Enemy ceasing, the *Hollanders* in time of Peace might fall into Divisions among themselves; or at least, that Peace and Plenty might abate their Courage. The *Spaniards* gave sufficient Proof of their eagerness for a Peace with *Holland*, by setting the Treaty on foot in the *Hague*, by sending among others, *Ambrosius Spinola* himself, thither as Ambassador, and by granting and allowing them the *East-India* Trade. Whereas the *Hollanders* carried it very high, and would not bate an Ace of their Proposal. At last, a Truce for 12 Years was concluded with *Holland*. The next insuing Year, *Philip* banish'd out of *Spain* 900000 *Marans*, the Off-spring of the ancient *Moors*, who had profess'd themselves Christians only for a Shew, and intended to raise a Rebellion, for which end they had under-hand crav'd Assistance from *Henry* IV. In the same Year the *Spaniards* took the Fortress of *Arache*, situated on the Coast of *Africa*; as they had likewise possess'd themselves before of the Harbour of *Final* near *Genoua*. In the Year 1619, the *Valteline* revolted from the *Grisons*; and the *Spaniards* sided with the former, in hopes to annex them to the Dukedome of *Milan*. But *France* taking part with the *Grisons*, the Business was protracted for a great many Years, till at last matters were restor'd to their former State. This difference did rouse up all *Italy*, and the Pope himself took part with the *Grisons*, tho' *Protestants*, assisting them in the recovery of the *Valteline*. The War breaking out in *Germany*, the *Spaniards* sent *Ambrose Spinola* from the *Netherlands* into the *Palatinate*, part of which was subdu'd by them. *Philip* III. died in the Year 1621.

Truce with *Holland*. 1609.

1602.

§. 13. His Son *Philip* IV. at the very beginning of his Reign made great Alterations in the Court, sending away the Creatures of the Duke *de Lerma*, the Favourite of his Father: But the Duke foreseeing what was likely to befal him, did timely obtain a Cardinal's Cap, fearing the King should aim at his Head. With the beginning of the Reign of this King, the Truce with *Holland* being expir'd, the War was re-kindled, in which *Spinola* was forc'd to raise the Siege of *Bergen-op-Zoom*, because *Christian* Duke

Philip IV.

of *Brunswick*, and General *Mansfield*, having before rout-
1622. ed the *Spaniards* near *Fleury*, came to the Assistance of the
Hollanders. *Pieter Heyn* surpriz'd the *Spanish* Silver Fleet,
1628. with a Booty of 12 Millions of Gilders. At the same time
the *Hollanders* made a Settlement in *Brasile*, taking the City of *Olinda*. In the Year 1629, the *Spaniards*, in hopes to make a considerable Diversion, and to put the *Dutch* hard to it, made an Inrode into the *Velaw*, and took *Amersfort*, whilst the *Hollanders* were busied in the Siege of *Bois le Duc*: But the *Hollanders* taking *Wesel* by Surprize, they were oblig'd to retreat with all speed over the River *Yssel*, for fear their retreat should be cut off by the *Dutch*. In the Year 1639, a great Fleet was sent out of *Spain* into the Channel, under the Command of *Don Oquendo*, which was destroy'd by *Martin Tromp*, in the *Downs*, in the very sight of the *English*. What the Intention was of sending so great a Fleet this way, was not generally known at that time; but afterwards it was divulg'd, that the same was intended against *Sweden*, and that there were 20000 Men ready in *Denmark*, which, as soon as this Fleet should have appear'd before *Gothenburg*, were to have join'd them and enter'd *Sweden*. Afterwards the War was protracted, but most to the disadvantage of the *Spaniards*, till the Year 1648; when the *Spaniards* concluded a Peace with the *Hollanders* at *Munster*, declaring them a free People, renouncing all their Pretences over them, and leaving to them all the Places which they had taken from them. *France* did its utmost to hinder the Conclusion of this Peace, at least so long, till that Kingdom might also make a Peace with *Spain*; but the *Hollanders* did not think it adviseable to stay their Leisure, fearing, that if *Spain* was brought too low, the *French* would thereby be enabled to swallow up the *Netherlands*, and become their immediate Neighbours, which they foresaw would prove fatal to their State. *Spain* also perceiving, that the *Dutch* were not to be overcome by force, was willing to agree to those Conditions, being glad to be rid once of so troublesome an Enemy, that they might have the more leisure to be even with *France* and *Portugal*. It is reported, that this War cost the *Spaniards* above One thousand five hundred Millions of Ducats. In the Year 1628, *Vincent* II. Duke of *Mantua* dying, the Emperor endeavour'd to exclude *Charles* Duke of *Nevers*, he being a Frenchman born, from the Succession of that Dukedom, under pretence of having neg-

neglected some Acknowledgment of Entrance due upon it, as being a Fief of the Empire. At the same time the *Savoyards* took the opportunity to renew their Pretensions upon *Montferrat*; and the *Spaniards*, in hopes of getting something in the Fray, besieg'd *Casal*. On the other side, the *French* espous'd the Cause of the Duke of *Nevers*, rais'd the Siege of *Casal*, and put the Duke into Possession of the Dukedom of *Mantua*; which did much weaken the Reputation of the *Spaniards* in *Italy*. In the Year 1635, the *French* declared War against *Spain*, under pretence, that they had taken Prisoner *Philip Christopher* Elector of *Treves*, he being under the Protection of the King of *France*, and that they had dispossess'd the *French* Garrison of *Treves*, and possess'd themselves of that City; but the true Reason was, that it was tho't high Time to bridle the Ambition and Power of the House of *Austria*, which after the Battle of *Nordlingen*, and the Peace concluded at *Prague*, was grown very formidable; and that *France* being well settled at home, began to be in a very flourishing Condition. So the *French*, after they had beat the Prince *Tomaso* near *Avennes*, enter'd the *Netherlands* with a great Army, but the Success did not answer Expectation; the *Dutch* especially being unwilling, that *France* should make any considerable Conquests on that side: Neither did the *French* gain any thing in *Italy*. The Year after that, the Prince of *Conde* was forc'd to raise the Siege of *Dole*; and the *Spaniards* entring *Picardy* fill'd *Paris* it self with Terror and Confusion. *Gallas* the *Imperial* General, endeavour'd to enter *Burgundy* with his Army, but did not gain much Ground. In the Year 1637, the *Spaniards* lost *Landresi*. The next Year they were forc'd to retire from before *Leucate* with great Loss; but the Prince of *Conde*, on the other hand, had the like ill fortune before *Fonterabia*. In 1639.
1639, The *Spaniards* beat the *French* soundly near *Thionville*, but lost *Hesdin*, *Salses* and *Salins*; and in the Year following, the strong City of *Arras*, being likewise routed near *Casal*, after they had attempted in vain with all their Strength to oblige the Earl of *Harcourt* to raise the Siege of *Turin*. In the same Year the *Catalonians* revolted, after a long Discontentment; for their first Dissatisfaction had been owing to the Pride of the Duke *d'Olivarez*, the King's Favourite, against whom they had made great Complaints, but were still severely oppress'd by him. These Discontents encreased afterwards, when the

Catalonia rebels.

Catalonians endeavouring the Relief of *Salses*, were beaten, and pretending they were not duly assisted by the *Castilians*, left the Army and marched home. The Duke taking this opportunity, represented them very ill to the King, and caused their Priviledges to be considerably diminished, and their Country to be oppress'd with the quartering of Soldiers. This put them in open Rebellion, and *Barcelona* beginning first, they drove the *Spaniards* out of *Catalonia*. Then they implor'd the Aid of *France*, and at last, put themselves under the Protection of that Kingdom: And it was Eleven Years before the *Spaniards* could quite recover *Catalonia*: Then indeed the intestine Commotions in *France* presented them with a fair
1651. opportunity; for *Barcelona*, being not timely reliev'd, was forc'd to surrender to the *Spaniards*. But the revolt of the

Portugal falls off from Spain. 1640.

Portuguese gave a greater shock to the *Spaniards*: *Philip* II. tho' he conquer'd this Kingdom, yet had always endeavour'd by mildness, and by preserving their Privileges, to mitigate the hatred that the *Portuguese* bore to the *Castilians*, which was grown to that height, that the Priests used to insert in their Prayers, *That God would be pleased to deliver them from the* Castilian *Yoak*: But after his Death the *Spanish* Ministers had not been so careful, by maintaining their Privileges, to retain the Affection of the *Portuguese*, but rather had treated them as a conquer'd Nation;
1636. which so exasperated the *Portuguese*, that as soon as they saw *Spain* begin to decline, immediately some Places in *Portugal* rebell'd, but were soon after reduc'd to their former Obedience. Thereupon the *Spaniards* thought it adviseable, that to bridle this People, nothing could be more proper, than by employing the Nobles as well as the Commoners in the Wars, to purge off the superfluous ill Humours of the Nation. In the mean while the *Catalonians* falling into Rebellion, the *Portuguese* Nobles were order'd to go into the Field, which they did not well relish; having besides this, some other reasons to be dissatisfy'd with the *Spaniards*: And, for as much as the *Portuguese* had a great Affection for the Duke of *Braganza*, the *Spaniards* try'd all ways to entice him to come to Court, and fancying they had cajoll'd him sufficiently with fair Promises, invited him very courteously to go in Person with the King into the Field; which Invitation, nevertheless, he knew how to decline very dextrously. At last the *Portuguese* Nobility being hard press'd to serve

in the Expedition against the *Catalonians*, which they would in no ways consent to, unanimously agreed to shake off the *Castilian* Yoak, and secretly sounded the Inclinations of the Duke of *Braganza*. As soon as he, upon the perswasions of his Lady, had resolv'd to accept of the Crown, they broke loose, and surprising the Garrison in the City of *Lisbon*, the Palace and the Fort, seiz'd the Ships, kill'd the Secretary of State *Vasconcello*, and proclaim'd the Duke of *Braganza* King, under the Name of *John* IV. purging the whole Kingdom within eight days of the *Castilians*, and that with the loss only of two or three Persons. Which may serve as a remarkable instance to convince the World, how easily a Kingdom is lost, where the Peoples Inclination is averse to the supreme Head. Thus the *Spanish* Monarchy received a signal Blow, and its Power being divided into several Channels, it could not act effectually on all sides. They also lost *Perpignan*; tho' the *French* could not go further into *Spain*, for the Prince of *Conde* besieg'd *Lerida* in vain, *Ann.* 1647. The Prince *Monaco* driving the *Spanish* Garrisons out of his Territories, put himself under the protection of *France*, *Ann.* 1641. There happen'd likewise a most dangerous Rebellion at *Naples*, the Head of which was a poor Fisherman, whose Name was *Massanello*; who might have put the whole Kingdom into a Flame, if the *French* had been at hand to give him timely assistance; but by the prudent management of the Governour, the Earl of *Ogante*, the Tumult was appeased. *Spain* then being forc'd to quench the Flames on all sides, it could not be so mindful of *Holland*, which was the most remote; having all hands full, to resist the dangers threatning them nearer home. And indeed the *Spaniards* had the good fortune to reduce, as we said before, *Catalonia*, and to drive the *French* out of *Piombino* and *Porto Longone*: But the *English* took from them the Island of *Jamaica* in the *West-Indies*. At last *France* being re-established in its former Tranquillity, the *Spaniards* thought it most convenient to make Peace with that Crown: Which was concluded betwixt the two great Ministers of State, the Cardinal *Mazarini* and *Don Lewis de Haro*, in the *Pyrenean* Mountains: By vertue of which *France* got *Roussilion*, and several considerable places in the *Netherlands*. *Spain* having thus concluded a Peace with all the rest of its Neighbours, it began to make

Duke of Braganza *proclaimed King of* Portugal.

1642.

1647.

Massanello's *Rebellion at* Naples, 1647.

The Pyrenean *Treaty.*

make War in earnest against *Portugal*. In pursuance of which the *Spaniards* entred *Portugal* with a great Force, taking from the *Portuguese* several places; but withal were at several places soundly beaten. The Battle near *Entremos* where *Don Juan*, and that near *Villa Viciosa*, where *Caracena* received a fatal Defeat, are most famous; *Philip* IV. died in the Year 1665.

1662. 1665.

Charles II. §. 14. He had for his Successour his Son *Charles* II. a Child of Four Years of Age, who, under the Tuition of his Mother, negligently prosecuted the War against *Portugal*, and at last, by the Mediation of *England* was forc'd to make a Peace with that Crown, renouncing his right to the same; because the *French* at that time made a grievous havock in the *Netherlands*. For tho *Mary Teresia*, Daughter of *Philip* IV. at the time when she was married to the King of *France*, had renounced all her right of Succession to her paternal Inheritance, yet the *French* taking the opportunity of their flourishing Condition, and the decayed State of *Spain* (*England* and *Holland* being then engaged in a War with one another, who else could not have seen the *Netherlands* devoured by them) they entred *Flanders* with a vast Army, using among other things, for a pretence, that which in *Brabant* is called *Jus devolutionis*, by which the real Estates of private Persons, fall to the Children born during the time of the first Marriage, when the Father Marries again. The *French* took in this War, without much resistance, a great many considerable Cities and Forts, *viz*. *Charleroy*, *Tournay*, *Lisle*, *Doway*, *Oudenarde*, and some others; they conquered also the whole *Franche Compte*, which hastened the Peace betwixt *England* and *Holland*, and occasioned the *Triple Alliance*, as it is called, made betwixt *England*, *Sweden* and *Holland*, for the preservation of the *Spanish Netherlands*. In the following Year *France* made a Peace with *Spain* at *Aix la Chapelle*, restoring to *Spain* the *Franche Compte*, but keeping what Places they had taken in *Flanders*. But when *Holland*, in the Year 1672, was attack'd by the *French*, *Spain* sided with the *Dutch*, knowing that the loss of the *United Provinces* must draw after it that of the *Spanish Netherlands*: So it came again to an open War, in the very beginning of which *Spain* lost *Burgundy* once more. The rebellious People of *Messina* threw themselves under the protection of *France*, but were afterwards

1668. *Peace with* Portugal. The Triple Alliance. *Peace made at* Aix la Chapelle, 1668.

deser-

defeated by them. France got also *Limburgh, Conde, Valenciens, Cambray, Ypres*; St. *Omer, Aeth* and *Ghent*: But a Peace was concluded at *Nimeguen*, by virtue of which France kept the *Franche Compte*, and most places taken in the *Netherlands*, restoring only to *Spain, Limburgh, Ghent, Cortryck, Oudenarde, Aeth* and *Charleroy*. *Peace made at Nimmeguen.*

§. 15. Having thus given a brief History of the Kingdom of *Spain*, 'twill not be improper to subjoin some Remarks concerning the Genius of the *Spaniards*, and the extent of their Territories; as also of the Strength and Weakness of this Kingdom, and its Condition with reference to its Neighbours. The *Spanish* Nation is commonly esteemed to be very wise, and to take remote prospects, throughly weighing a thing before they undertake it. But being over-cautious and dilatory in their Counsels, they often lose the opportunities of Action. The *Spaniards* are very firm and steddy in their Resolutions; and tho' they fail once in an Attempt, they will try their Fortune again, endeavouring to overcome its Frowns by their Constancy. They are very fit for War, and not only brave at the first Attack, but will also hold out till the last; their sober way of living, and spare Bodies qualify them to bear Hunger and Thirst, and to be very watchful: But this the *Spaniards* are extreamly blamed for, that they maintain their Gravity by high-flown Words and a proud Behaviour. Tho' this Gravity which appears so odious, is not so much the effect of their Pride, as of a melancholy Constitution, and an ill custom. Being naturally superstitious, they are in general, very zealous for the *Roman Catholick* Religion, and abominate all others. They are seldom fit for any Trade or Business where hard labour is required, such as Husbandry, or Handicraft Trades; so that these are chiefly managed among them by Foreigners. It is credibly reported, That in *Madrid* alone, there are above 40000 *Frenchmen*, being for the most part, Merchants, Artists, Handycrafts-men and Labourers, who go under the Name of *Burgundians*, to avoid the hatred, which the *Spaniards* naturally bear against the *French*. And such is the *Spanish* Pride, that tho' they think it below themselves to meddle with those trifles, yet they do not think much to be a poor Centinel in some Fort or other all their life time; the honour of the Sword, and hopes of becoming in time an Officer, making *The Nature of the Spaniards.*

making them amends for what hardship they endure. Their Pride, Covetousness and rigorous proceedings make them hateful to all that are under their Command; and these indeed are very unfit Qualifications for the maintaining of great Conquests. *Spain* being mightily exhausted of Men, and consequently incapable of raising great Armies within it self, is very unfit to maintain vast and distant Countries; for which several Reasons may be given. The Women here are not so fruitful as in the Northern parts, which is to be attributed to the heat of the Climate, and the constitution of their spare Bodies. And those parts which are remote from the Sea-shore, are not well peopled, for that some places are very barren, and produce nothing for the subsistence of Mankind. Whoring being publickly allowed of here; a great many of them will rather make shift with a Whore, than maintain a Wife and Children. Those who have taken upon them holy Orders or Vows of Chastity, of whom there is a great number, are obliged not to Marry. The Wars they have waged against so many Nations, but especially in *Italy* and the *Netherlands*, have swept off a great many *Spaniards*. A vast number having transplanted themselves into *America*, being fond of going to a place where they may with a small beginning come to live very plentifully. Before the discovery was made of *America*, *Ferdinand* the *Catholick*, had at once before the City of *Granada*, an Army of 50000 Foot and 20000 Horse, though *Arragon* did not concern it self in that War, and *Portugal* and *Navarre* were at that time, not united with *Castile*. To conclude; this Country was mightily dispeopled, when *Ferdinand*, after the taking of *Granada*, and *Philip* III. banished a great many thousands of *Jews* and *Marans* out of *Spain*; these setling themselves in *Africa*, retain to this day their hatred against the Christians, robbing their Ships in those Seas. Upon the whole; the *Spaniards* could never have made a Conquest of those vast Countries, by force of Arms, if the greatest part of them had not fallen into their Hands by easier ways.

The Constitution of the Spanish Countries.

§. 16. As for the Jurisdiction of this Nation; *Spain* is large enough in extent for the number of its Inhabitants, but it is not equally fertile, in all places; for the most remote parts from the Sea-coasts are many of them barren, and parch'd, and afford scarce any thing for the subsi-

subsistence of Men or Beasts: Whereas, nearer to the Sea-side, the Country is very fine and fruitful. There is abundance of Sheep here. They have also very fine and swift Horses, but scarce enough for their own use. This Kingdom is very well situate for Trade, having on the one side the Ocean, and on the other the Mediterranean, where they have most excellent Harbours. Their Native Product fit for Exportation is chiefly Wool, Silk, Wine, Oyl, Raisins, Almonds, Figs, Citrons, Rice, Soap, Iron, Salt, and such like. In former times the *Spanish* Gold Mines were very famous, but now a-days, neither Gold nor Silver, so far as I know, is digged in *Spain*: Some will alledge for a reason of this, That it is forbidden under severe Penalties, in order to keep it as a reserve in case of great extremity. But I am rather apt to believe, That these Gold Mines have been long ago quite exhausted by the Avarice of the *Spaniards*.

§. 17. The greatest Revenue of *Spain* comes from *America*, from whence, as from an inexhaustible Source, immense quantities of Gold and Silver are conveyed into *Spain*, and from thence into the other parts of *Europe*. At what time, and by whom this Country, which had been so long unknown to the *Europeans*, was first discovered, we have already mentioned. Though there are some who pretend, That *America* was discovered in the Year 1190. by one *Madoc*, Son to *Owen Gesneth*, a Prince in *Wales*, who made two Voyages thither; and having built a Fort in *Florida* or *Virginia*, or as others say, in *Mexico*, died in *America*: That this is the reason why in the *Mexican* Tongue abundance of *British* words are to be met withal: And the *Spaniards*, at their first coming into *America*, found the Reliques of some *Christian* Customs among the Inhabitants: From whence some infer, That if the first Discovery of a Country gives a good Title of Propriety to the Discoverers, *England* would have as good, if not a better Title to *America* than *Spain*: But it is not so evident, from whence *Spain* could claim a right of subduing that Country by force of Arms. For, what is alledged among other pretences, concerning the Bull of *Alexander* VI. wherein he granted those Countries to *Spain*, this does not only seem ridiculous to us, but even to those *Barbarians* themselves, who have ridicul'd it, saying, *The Pope must be a strange sort of a Man*,

The Spanish West-Indies.

Man, who pretended to give away that which was none of his own. However, some of the most conscientious *Spaniards* do not justifie what Cruelties their Country-men committed in the beginning against those poor People, of whom they killed, without any Provocation given, a great many hundred thousands: or destroy'd them by forcing them to undergo intolerable Hardships, and making the rest their Slaves: Tho' afterwards *Charles* V. being inform'd of this miserable Condition, order'd all the rest of the *Americans* to be set at liberty. The *Spaniards* are not Masters of all *America*; but only of the middle part of it, *viz.* The Kingdoms of *Peru* and *Mexico*, and those vast Islands of *Hispaniola*, *Cuba*, and *Porto Rico*; *Jamaica* having been taken from them by the *English*. These parts of *America* are now-a-days inhabited by five several sorts of People: The first are the *Spaniards*, who come thither out of *Europe*; these are put in all Offices: The second are call'd *Criolians*, who are born in *America* of *Spanish* Parents: These are never employ'd in any Office, as being ignorant of the *Spanish* Affairs, and too much addicted to love their native Country of *America*; wherefore the King is cautious in giving them any Command, fearing least they should withdraw themselves from the Obedience of *Spain*, and set up a Government of their own; especially considering that these *Criolians* bear an implacable hatred against the *European Spaniards*. For this Reason also the Governours are changed every three Years to remove the opportunity of strengthning their Interest too much; and after their return into *Spain*, they are made Members of the Council for the *Indies*, as being esteem'd the most proper to advise concerning the preservation of that Country. The third sort call'd *Metiffs*, who are born of a *Spanish* Father and an *Indian* Mother, are in no esteem among them. The fourth sort are the remnants of the ancient Inhabitants, of whom a great many are to be met with, especially in the Kingdoms of *Peru* and *Mexico*. The fifth sort are the *Moors*, or as the *Spaniards* call them *Negroes*, who being bought in *Africa*, are sent thither to do all sorts of drudgery. These are generally very handy, but very perfidious and refractory; so that they must always be kept under a strict hand. Such as are born of a *Negro* and an *Indian* Woman, are call'd *Mulats*. Upon the whole, that part of *America*, considering its bigness, is not very well stock'd

Several sorts of Inhabitants in the Spanish West-Indies.

ſtock'd with People, for that the *Spaniards* did in a moſt cruel manner root out moſt of its ancient Inhabitants: And, if I remember well, *Hieronymus Benzonus* ſays, *That all the Cities in* America, *inhabited by the* Spaniards, *joined together, were ſcarce to be compared, for number of People, with the Suburbs of* Milan: Yet there are ſome who talk largely concerning *Mexico, viz.* That it has betwixt 30 and 40000 *Spaniſh* Citizens, who are moſt of them very wealthy, inſomuch that it is reported, there are 18000 Coaches kept in that City. The *Spaniards* are not eaſily to be beaten out of *America*; becauſe moſt places in their poſſeſſion, are hard to come at, and it is very difficult to tranſport ſuch a number of Soldiers out of *Europe*, as can be ſufficient to attack any of theſe places: Beſides, the great difference of the Climate and Diet, could not but occaſion mortal Sickneſſes among them: But in *Peru* eſpecially, they are very well ſettled, there being ſcarce any acceſs by Land, and by Sea you are obliged to go round the South and remoteſt parts of *America*, or elſe to come from the *Eaſt-Indies*; both which are long Sea Voyages, which an Army can ſcarce undergo without running the hazard of being deſtroyed by Sickneſs. As for the Riches of *America*, 'tis true, the *Spaniards* at their firſt coming thither found no coined Gold or Silver, that being unknown in thoſe days to the Inhabitants; but an inconceivable quantity of Bullion, and abundance of Gold and Silver Veſſels made without Iron Tools, all which the *Spaniards* carry'd into *Spain*: But now a-days thoſe Rivers which formerly us'd to carry a Golden Sand, are almoſt exhauſted; and what is found there now is all dug up out of the Mines: Above all the Silver Mines of *Potoſi* in *Peru*, afford an incredible quantity of Silver, which is yearly, together with ſome other Commodities, tranſported into *Spain*: Tho' after all, a great part of this Silver belonging to *Italian*, *French*, *Engliſh* and *Dutch* Merchants, the leaſt part of it remains in *Spain*. In alluſion to which, when the *French* and *Spaniſh* Ambaſſadors at *Rome* quarrell'd about Precedency, and the latter, to repreſent his Maſter's Greatneſs, ſpoke very largely of the vaſt Riches of *America*, the *Frenchman* anſwered, *That all* Europe, *but eſpecially* Spain, *had been a conſiderable loſer by that, in regard it made every thing dear; That the* Spaniards *having employed themſelves in ſearching after the Treaſures of* America, *were thereby become*

Riches of America.

1563.

come Idle, and had dispeopled their own Country. So that it lay uncultivated: That the King of Spain *trusting to his great Riches, had begun unnecessary Wars. That* Spain *being the Fountain from whence vast Riches were derived to other Nations, received the least Benefit of all by them, since those Countries that furnished* Spain *with Soldiers and Commodities drew the Riches to themselves.* Formerly Emeraulds and Pearls were found in *America*, but that Stock is long since, by the Avarice of the *Spaniards*, quite exhausted. As *America* is the best Appendix of the *Spanish* Kingdom, so the *Spaniards* take all imaginable care to prevent its being separated from *Spain*. They make among other things, use of this Artifice, That they will not allow any Manufactury to be set up in *America*, so that the Inhabitants cannot be without the *European* Commodities, which they do not suffer to be transported thither in any other Ships but their own.

The Canary Islands. § 18. Besides *America*, the *Canary Islands* are in the possession of the *Spaniards*, from whence are exported great quantities of Sugar and Wine. It is credibly reported, That *England* alone imports above 13000 Pipes of Canary, at 20*l. per* Pipe. The Island of *Sardinia* (Sardinia.) also belongs to the *Spaniards*, which Isle is pretty large, but not very rich, its Inhabitants being for the most part *Barbarians*. The Isle of *Sicily* (Sicily.) is of much greater value, from whence great quantities of Corn and Silk are exported; but the Inhabitants are an ill sort of People, who must be kept under, according to the old Proverb, *Insulani quidem mali, Siculi autem pessimi.* To *Sicily* are annex'd the Isles of *Maltha* and *Goza*, which were given in Fief from *Charles* V. to the Order of the Knights of *Rhodes*. *Spain* has likewise a great part of *Italy* in its possession, *viz.* (Naples.) The Kingdom of *Naples*, the Capital City of which is scarce kept in awe by three Castles: The Sovereignty of *Siena*, and a great many strong Forts on the Sea-Coasts of *Tuscany*, viz. *Orbitello*, *Porto Hercule*, *Telamone*, *Monte Argentario*, *Porto Longone*, and the Castle of *Piombino*; (Milan.) besides the Noble Dukedome of *Milan*, which is the Paradise of *Italy*, as *Italy* is commonly called the Paradise of *Europe*: They have also the Harbour of *Final* upon the *Genoese* Coast. In the City of *Milan*, Trade and Manufactury flourishes extreamly, and this Dukedome is much valued by the *Spaniards*, because they have thereby a convenient Correspondence with the House of *Austria*. As long as *Burgundy* and the *Netherlands* were united, they might be compared to a Kingdom; but now *Burgundy* is lost, the Seven united Provinces have separated themselves from the rest of the *Netherlands*. In the *East-Indies* the *Philippine* Islands belonging to the *Spaniards*, the Capital City of which being *Manilla*, was taken by them in the Year 1565. But these Islands are so inconsiderable, that it has been often under debate, whether it were not most convenient to abandon them: However some *Indian* Commodities, which are brought from several places, and especially from *China*, to *Manilla*, are from thence transported to *New Spain* and *Mexico*, and by this means there is kept a constant Communication betwixt the *Spanish West* and *East-Indies*.

The Netherlands.

The Philippine Islands.

§ 19. From what has been said it is evident, that *Spain* is a potent Kingdom, which has under its Jurisdiction, rich and fair Countries, abounding with all Necessaries; and affording not only a sufficiency for the use of its Inhabitants, but a great overplus for Exportation. Add to this, that the *Spaniards* do not want Wisdom in managing their State Affairs, nor Valour to carry on a War. Nevertheless this vast Kingdom has its Infirmities, which have brought it so low, that it is scarce able to stand upon its own Legs. Their chief defect is the paucity of the Inhabitants; the number of which is sufficient either to keep in Obedience such wide Provinces, and those so averse to the *Spaniards*, or to make Head against a Potent Enemy: And this defect is not easily to be repaired out of those Countries which are under their Subjection; since it is the Interest of *Spain*, rather to check the Courage of these Inhabitants, for fear they should one time or another take Heart, and shake off the *Spanish* Yoak. And whenever they raise Soldiers in these Provinces, they cannot trust them with the defence of their Native Country, but are obliged to disperse them, by sending them into other Parts, under the command only of *Spaniards*. *Spain* therefore is scarce able to raise within it self a sufficient number of Soldiers for the Guard and Defence of its frontier Places: And accordingly whenever *Spain* happens to have War with other Nations, it is obliged to make use of Foreign mercena-

Strength and Weakness of Spain.

ry Troops; which is attended with this inconveniency, besides the immense Charge of hiring them, that the King is not so well assured of their Faith, as of that of his own Subjects. The want of Inhabitants is likewise one Reason, why *Spain* cannot now-a-days keep a considerable Fleet at Sea, which nevertheless is extreamly Necessary to support the Monarchy of that Kingdom. Another Weakness is, That the *Spanish* Provinces are mightily dis-join'd, as being sever'd by vast Seas and Countries: So that they cannot be maintain'd and govern'd without great difficulty; for the Governours of the Provinces being remote from the inspection of the Prince, he cannot take so exact an account of their Actions; and the oppressed Subjects want often opportunity to make their Complaints to the King; besides that, Men and Money are with great charge and danger sent out of *Spain* into these Provinces, without hopes of ever returning into the Kingdom. Their Strength cannot be kept together, for that they are thus obliged to divide their Forces. The more dis-joyn'd these Provinces are, the more frontier Garrisons are to be maintained. They are at the same time liable to be attack'd in a great many places at once, one Province not being able to assist another. Above all, *America* the Treasury of *Spain*, is parted from it by the vast Ocean, whereby their Silver Fleets are Subject to the hazard of the Seas and Pyrates. And if it happens that such a Fleet is lost, the whole Government must needs suffer extreamly by the want of it; the Inhabitants of *Spain* being so exhausted, as not to be able to raise sufficient Summs to supply the Publick Necessities. The King of *Spain* has this Prerogative, which he obtained from Pope *Hadrian* VI. that he has the disposal of all the Chief Church Benefices in his Kingdom; and he is also Head and Master of all the Ecclesiastical Orders of Knighthood in *Spain*: and because the Kings of *Spain* have hitherto professed themselves the most zealous Protectours of the Papal Chair and Religion, they have thereby so obliged the Zealots of the *Roman Catholick* Religion, and especially the *Jesuits*, that these have always been endeavouring to promote the Interest of *Spain*.

§. 20. *Lastly*, It remains, to consider what Conduct *Spain* observes in relation to its Neighbours, and what

Good

In what condition Spain is, in reference to its Neighbours, and especially to Barbary.

Good or Evil it may again expect from them. *Spain* lies opposite to the Coast of *Barbary*, on which it has several Forts, *viz.* *Pegnon de Velez*, *Oran*, and *Arzilla*; and 'twere their Interest to have also *Algiers* and *Tunis*. *Spain* has no occasion to apprehend any thing from that Coast, now that it has quite freed it self from the very Remnants of the *Moors*: And as for the Pyracies committed by those *Corsairs*, they're not so hurtful to *Spain*, as to other Nations, who traffique with *Spain*, *Italy* or *Turky*; for the *Spaniards* seldom export their own Commodities into the other Parts of *Europe*; these being exported by other Nations. The *Turks* seem to be pretty near to the Islands of *Sicily* and *Sardinia*, and to the Kingdom of *Naples*. Yet are they not so much fear'd by the *Spaniards*; the Sea which lies betwixt them being an obstacle against making a Descent with a considerable Army in any of those Parts; and if an Army should be landed, its Provisions, which must come by Sea, might easily be cut off: For in such a Case, all the States of *Italy* would be obliged to side with the *Spaniards* to keep this cruel Enemy from their Borders; and their Naval Strength joined together, much surpasses the *Turks* in every respect.

Turks.

From the *Italian* States, the *Spaniards* have little to fear, it being a Maxim with them, to preserve the Peace of *Italy*. Nevertheless this is most certain, That if *Spain* should endeavour to encroach upon the *Italian* States, they would unanimously oppose it; and if they should find themselves too weak to oppose their Designs, they might be easily wrought upon to call *France* to their Aid.

Italian States.

The Pope, perhaps, might be willing enough to be Master of the Kingdom of *Naples*, *Spain* holding the same in Fief of the Papal Chair. But the Pope wants Power to execute such a Design, and the rest of the States of *Italy* would not be forward to see so considerable a Country added to the Ecclesiastical State; and besides, the Pope's Kindred are more for gathering of Riches out of the present Ecclesiastical Revenues, than for bestowing the same upon an uncertain War. On the other side, *Spain* having found it very beneficial for its Interest, to pretend to the chief Protectorship of the *Roman* Religion, and being sensible that the Pope's good or bad Inclinations towards it, may either prove advantageous or disadvantageous, they have always endeavour'd, by all means, to keep fair with the Popes. *France*, on the contrary, having taken Part with the *Protestants*, whom *Spain*

The Pope.

and the House of *Austria* have sought to oppress, has demonstrated sufficiently to the *Roman* Court, that it is not so fond of that Religion. Upon this Consideration, the chief aim of the wisest Popes has been, to keep the Power of *Spain* and *France* in an equal Balance, that being the most proper Method to keep up the Authority and provide for the Security of the Popedom. It being the principal Maxim of the *Venetians*, to preserve their Liberty and State, by maintaining the Peace of *Italy*, *Spain* has no Reason to be jealous of them as long as it undertakes nothing against them. Besides, 'tis their Interest, as well as of all the other *Italian* States, that the *Spaniards* remain in Possession of *Milan*; for fear, if *France* should become Master of this Dukedom, it might thereby be put in a way to conquer all the rest of *Italy*. On the other side, if *Spain* should shew the least Inclination to attempt any thing against the Liberty of *Italy*, it cannot expect, but that the *Venetians*, if not by an open War, at least by their Counsels and Money, would oppose it. For the rest, this State endeavours to remain Neuter betwixt *France* and *Spain*, and to keep fair with both of them, as long as they do not act against her Interest. *Genoua* is of great Consequence to the *Spaniards*, upon which depends, in a great measure, the Security and Preservation of the *Milaneze*: With this view when *Charles* V. could not effect his Intention of building a Castle (being opposed therein by *Andreas Doria*) whereby he intended to oppress the *Genouese*, the *Spaniards* found out another way to make them dependent on their Interest, by borrowing vast Sums of Money from the *Genouese* upon the Security of the King's Revenues in *Spain*. Besides this, they are possess'd of the Harbour of *Final* on the Coast of *Genoua*, whereby they have taken away the Power from them of cutting off the Correspondence betwixt *Spain* and *Milan*. *Spain* has great reason to live in a good Correspondency with *Savoy*; for if that Prince should side with *France* against it, the *Milaneze* would be in immediate danger of being lost. It would be very pernicious for *Savoy*, if the King of *France* should become Master of *Milan*, since *Savoy* would be then surrounded on all sides by the *French*, it being easie for *Spain* to maintain a good Correspondence with *Savoy*. *Florence*, and the rest of the *Italian* Princes, have all Reason to be cautious how to offend *Spain*, yet, they would scarce suffer *Spain* to encroach upon any of them.

Venice. Genoua. Savoy. Florence.

It

It is alſo of Conſequence to the *Spaniards* to live in friendſhip with the *Swiſs*, partly becauſe they muſt make uſe of ſuch Soldiers as are liſted among them; partly becauſe they may be very ſerviceable in preſerving the *Milaneze*; and their Friendſhip is beſt preſerved by Money. But the *Swiſs* being of ſeveral Religions, *Spain* is in greater Authority with the *Roman-Catholick Cantons*, but *France* with the *Proteſtant Cantons*, which being the moſt potent, have either been-cajoll'd by fair Words, or Money, or out of Fear have conniv'd at the *French* becoming Maſters of the County of *Burgundy* in the laſt War, whereas formerly they us'd to take effectual care for its Preſervation. The *Hollanders* were before the Peace of *Munſter* the moſt pernicious Enemies to *Spain*; but ſince the concluſion of that Peace, there is no cauſe that *Spain* ſhould fear any thing from them, ſince I do not ſee any reaſon why theſe ſhould attack *Spain*, or endeavour to take any thing from them, as having enough to do to maintain what they have already got. And, if they ſhould attempt any thing againſt the *Weſt-Indies*, they would not only meet with great reſiſtance from the *Spaniards* there, but *France* and *England* would not eaſily ſuffer, that both the *Eaſt* and *Weſt-Indies*, ſhould be in poſſeſſion of the *Dutch*: And the *Dutch* are, for their own Intereſts, oblig'd to take care, that *France* by ſwallowing up the *Netherlands* may not become their next Neighbour on the Land, nor obtain any conſiderable Advantage againſt *Spain*. The Power of *Germany*, *Spain* may conſider as its own, as far as the ſame depends on the Houſe of *Auſtria*. And it is not long ago, ſince the States of *Germany* were perſuaded to take upon them afreſh the Guaranty of the Circle of *Burgundy*; whereby *Spain* hoped to have united its Intereſt with that of the *German* Empire againſt *France*; ſince, whenever a War happens betwixt theſe two Crowns, it is ſcarce poſſible, that this Circle ſhould eſcape untouch'd, it being the moſt convenient place where they may attack one another with vigour. *England* is capable of doing moſt damage to the *Spaniards* at Sea, and eſpecially in the *Weſt-Indies*: But *England* would be no great gainer by it, ſince they have a vaſt Trade with the *Spaniſh* Sea-ports, and their Trade in the *Levant* would ſuffer extreamly from the *Spaniſh* Privateers; not to mention that *Holland* could not look with a good Eye upon ſuch Conqueſts made by the *Engliſh*. *Portugal*, by itſelf cannot much hurt *Spain*, but in Conjunction with another Enemy, it is capable of

The *Swiſs*.

Holland.

Germany.

England.

Portugal.

making a considerable Diversion at home. But the *Porteguese* could not propose any considerable Advantages to themselves thereby; and it might easily happen, that *Holland* siding with *Spain* might take from thence an opportunity to drive the *Porteguese* quite out of the *East-Indies*.

France. Upon the whole, the King of *France* is the Capital and most formidable Enemy to *Spain*.

CHAP. III.

Of PORTUGAL.

The Origin of the Kingdom of Portugal. § 1. PORTUGAL, which comprehends the greatest part of that Province that the *Romans* call'd *Lusitania*, fell with the rest of *Spain*, under the last *Gothick* King *Roderick*, into the hands of the *Moors*, who were in possession of it for a long time; but in the Year 1093 *Alfonsus* VI. King of *Castile* and *Leon*, arming with all his Power to attack the *Moors*, and calling for, and craving the Assistance of Foreign Princes; among others, came one *Henry*, to signalize himself in this War, whose Pedigree is variously related by the Historians. For some will have him descended from the House of *Burgundy*, and a younger Son of *Robert* Duke of *Burgundy*, whose Father was *Robert* King of *France*, Son of *Hugh Capet*. Others derive his Pedigree from the *House* of *Lorain*, alledging, That the reason of his being called a *Burgundian* was, because he was born at *Besançon*. *Henry Earl of Portugal.* To this *Henry*, King *Alfonsus* VI. gave in Marriage his natural Daughter *Theresia*, as a reward of his Valour, assigning him for a Dowry, under the Title of an Earldom, all that part of *Portugal* which was then in the possession of the Christians; which comprehended that part of the Country, where are the Cities of *Braga*, *Coimbra*, *Viseo*, *Lamego*, and *Porto*; as also that Tract of Ground which is now called *Tralos Montes*; granting to him withal, a Power to conquer the rest of that Country, as far as to the River of *Guadiana*, and to keep it under his Jurisdiction; but upon these Conditions, that he should be a Vassal of *Spain*, repair to the Dyets of that Kingdom, and in case of a War, be obliged to serve with 300 Horse. *Henry* died in the Year 1112, leaving a Son whose name was

Alfon-

Alfonsus, being then very Young: His Inheritance was, *Alfonso* I. King of *Portugal.*
during his Minority, usurp'd by *Ferdinand Paiz*, Count of *Trastamara*, his Father-in-law, he having married his Mother. But as soon as he was grown up, he took up Arms against his Father-in-law, and beat him out of *Portugal*, but his Mother he put in Prison; and she calling to her Aid *Alfonsus* VII. promised to dis-inherit her Son, and to give him all *Portugal*. But *Alfonsus* of *Portugal* defeated the *Castilians* in a Battel, by which Victory he pretended 1126.
to have freed himself from the *Spanish* Subjection. This *Alfonsus* undertook an Expedition against King *Ismar*, who 1139.
had his Kingdom on the other side of the River *Tajo*, and being joined by the Forces of four other petty *Moorish* Kings, drew out against him. *Alfonsus* was then in his Camp near *Cabecas des Reyes* proclaimed King, in order to animate his Soldiers; and got a most signal Victory, taking the five Standards of those Kings, whence he put five Shields in *The Origin of the five Shields in the Arms of* Portugal.
the Arms of *Portugal*, and retained ever after the Title of King. He took afterwards a great many Cities from the *Moors*; and among the rest, with the assistance of the *Netherland* Fleet, the City of *Lisbon* in the Year 1147. This 1179.
Alfonsus was taken Prisoner near *Badajoz*, by *Ferdinand* King of *Egypt*, who gave him his Freedom without any other Ransom, than that he was to restore to him some Cities, which he had taken from him in *Gallicia*. After he had reigned very Gloriously, and greatly enlarged the limits of his Kingdom, he died in the 80th Year of his Age. 1185.

§ 2. To him succeeded his Son *Sanctius*, who built a *Sanctius* I.
great many Cities, and filled them with Inhabitants. He took from the *Moors* the City of *Selva*, being assisted in the Expedition, by a Fleet sent out of the *Netherlands* to the *Holy Land*. He was, during his whole Reign, always in Action with the *Moors*, and died in the Year 1212. After him reigned his Son *Alfonsus*, sirnamed *Crassus*, who did *Alfonsus* II.
nothing worth mentioning, but that, with the help of the *Netherlanders*, who went to the *Holy Land*, he took from the *Moors* the City of *Alcassar*. He died in the Year 1223. His Son *Sanctius*, sirnamed *Capellus*, succeeded him; who *Sanctius* II.
being very careless, and ruled by his Wife, was excluded from the Administration of the Government by the *Portuguese*, who conferr'd it on *Alfonsus* his Brother, and *Sanctius* died an Exile in *Toledo*; and married *Beatrice*, Daughter to *Alfonsus* X. King of *Castile*, with whom he had for a

Dowry the Kingdom of *Algarbia.* He reigned very laudably, and united a great many Cities to his Kingdom, and died in the Year 1279. The extraordinary Virtues of his
Dionysius. Son *Dionysius*, especially his Justice, Liberality and Constancy, are highly extoll'd by the *Portuguese*. He having also adorn'd the Kingdom with a great many publick Buildings, among which is the Academy of *Coimbra*, first founded by him. There is an old Proverb relating to him, used among the *Portuguese*. *El Rey D. Denys, qui fiz quanto quin*: King *Dionysius*, who did whatsoever he pleased. He
Alfonsus IV. died in the Year 1325. His Son *Alfonsus* IV. sirnamed the *Brave*, was very glorious for his Atchievements both in Peace and War; but he banished his Bastard Brother, who was greatly beloved both by his Father and the People; and caus'd *D. Agnas de Castro*, a very beautiful Lady, who was without his consent married to his Son *Pieter*, barbarously to be murther'd; which so exasperated *Pieter*, that he taking up Arms against the Father, did considerable Mischief, till at last the Business was compos'd. He died
Pieter. in the Year 1357. His Son *Pieter* was commonly call'd *The Cruel*, tho' some will have this rather to have been spoken to his Praise, as having been an exact observer of Justice, never sparing any Offender. He died in the Year
Ferdinand. 1368. His Son *Ferdinand* contended for the Kingdom of *Castile* with *Henry* the Bastard, who had murther'd his Brother *Pieter*, sirnam'd *The Cruel*, King of *Castile*. But he being too strong for him, he could not maintain his Pretensions, but was oblig'd to make Peace. However, the
1373. War broke out afresh again betwixt them. *Henry* made an inrode into *Portugal*; and finding no resistance, over-ran the greatest part of the Country. After the death of *Henry*, *Ferdinand* made a Peace with his Son *John*, but it was soon violated again by the *Portuguese*, who encouraged the Duke of *Lancaster*, that marry'd *Constantia* Daughter of *Pieter* King of *Castile*, to pretend to the Crown of *Castile*. This Duke came with a good Army into *Portugal*; but the *English* growing quickly weary of the War in *Spain*, and living very disorderly in *Portugal*, a Peace was concluded on both sides. At last *Ferdinand* marry'd his Daughter *Beatrice* to *John* of *Castile*, under condition, that such Children as were born of their Bodies, should succeed to the Kingdom of *Portugal*; which was afterwards the occasion of bloody Wars. This *Ferdinand* died in the Year 1383, being the last of the true Race of the Kings of *Portugal*.

§ 3. After

§ 3. After the Death of *Ferdinand*, great Troubles arose in *Portugal*, most of the *Portuguese* being unwilling to live under the Subjection of the *Castilians*, whom they mortally hated. 'Tis true, 'twas agreed on in the Articles of Marriage made betwixt the King of *Castile* and *Beatrice* Daughter of *Ferdinand*, That her Mother *Eleonora* should have the Administration of the Government in *Portugal*, till such Children as should be born of this Marriage should be of Age: But this *Eleonora* leaving all to the management of the Count of *Andeira*, her much suspected Favourite, she drew upon her self the hatred of the *Portuguese*. Thereupon *John* natural Son of *Pieter* King of *Portugal*, privately murther'd him, whereby he got both the Favour of the People, and encreas'd the hatred against the Queen Dowager: But some of the *Portuguese* being much dissatisfy'd at these Proceedings, begg'd the King of *Castile*, to take upon him the Crown of *Portugal*; which he might in all likelihood have obtain'd; but he being uncertain in his Resolutions, gave by his delays, time and opportunity to the adverse Party to strengthen it self. In short, coming without an Army into *Portugal*, his Mother-in-law resign'd to him the Government, but he found but an indifferent Reception among the *Portuguese*, who were very averse to him, because he us'd very rarely to speak or Converse with them. 'Tis true, a great many of the Nobility and some Cities sided with him; but most out of a hatred to the *Castilians*, chose for their Leader *John* the *Bastard*, a wise and brave Man, and much belov'd by the People. The *Castilians* thereupon besieged *Lisbon*, but their Army being for the most part destroyed by the Plague, they were oblig'd to leave it, without having got any Advantage. In the next ensuing Year, the *Portuguese* declared this *John* their King, who very courageously attack'd those places which had declared for the *Castilians*, and subdu'd the greatest part of them. The *Castilians* then entred with an Army into *Portugal*, but were entirely routed by this new King near *Aliubarotta*, which Victory is annually celebrated to this Day among the *Portuguese*. After this Battle, all the rest of the Cities did surrender themselves to the new King. The *Portuguese* calling to their aid the Duke of *Lancaster*, to whom they had promis'd the Crown of *Castile*, entered into that Kingdom with an Army: But the *English* having suffered extreamly by Sickness, the Duke of *Lancaster* thought

Interregnum.

Some call in the King of Castile.

1385.

John the Bastard.

thought it most convenient to conclude a Peace with the *Castilians*; whereupon it was agreed, That the Son of the King of *Castile* should marry his only Daughter *Catharine*, which he had by *Constantia*, Daughter to *Pieter* King of *Castile*. At the same time a Truce was made betwixt *Portugal* and *Castile*; but the War soon breaking out again, at
1399. last, an everlasting Peace was concluded betwixt both Kingdoms: So that *John* had the good fortune to maintain himself in the possession of the Crown of *Portugal*, and reigned with great Applause. After he was quietly settled in the Throne, he undertook an Expedition into *Africa*,
1415. and took the City *Ceuta*: And his Son first found out the
1420. Isle of *Madera*. This King died in the Year 1433, and left a Memory that is to this Day dear to the *Portuguese*.

Edward. § 4. His Son *Edward* was a very Vertuous Prince, but did not Reign long; for at that time, *Portugal* being over-run with the Plague, he got the Infection by a Letter, and died in the Year 1438. During his Reign, his Brothers undertook a most unfortunate Expedition into *Africa*; where being themselves taken Prisoners before *Tangier*, they promised to restore to the *Moors Ceuta* for a Ransom, leaving *Don Ferdinand* as a Hostage behind them. But the States of *Portugal* refusing to stand to the Contract, the
Alfonsus V. Hostage was forc'd to end his days in Prison. *Alfonsus* was but six Years old when his Father died, and his Tuition was committed to his Mother. But the States refusing to submit themselves to the Government of a Foreign Woman, conferr'd the Administration on *Don Pedro* Duke of *Coimbra*, Brother to King *Edward*: But he being falsly accused before the new King, was slain as he was going with some Troops to the King to justify himself. *Alfonsus* V. was else a very good Soldier and a brave Prince, under whose Reign the *Portuguese* took several places on the Coast of *Africa*, viz. *Tangier*, *Arcilla*, *Alcassar*, and some others. In his Reign good store of Gold was transported out of *Guinea* into *Portugal*, which he employ'd in coining of Crusadoes. After this, *Alfonsus* had great Contests with *Ferdinand* the *Catholick* and *Isabella*, there being a promise of Marriage made betwixt him and *Johanna*, the supposed Daughter of *Henry* IV. King of *Castile*; but, as it was reported, begotten in Adultery: But the Marriage was not consummated, she being *Alfonsus*'s Sisters Daughter; tho', at last, the Pope gave his Dispensation which he had refused

at

first. *Alfonsus* under this pretence, took upon himself the Title and Arms of *Castile*, surprizing several Cities, assisted by some of the Nobility of *Castile*, who sided with him; and *Lewis* XI. King of *France*, sent him some Auxiliaries: But these were not sufficient to enable him to undertake any thing of moment, so that *Ferdinand* retaking 1476. all the places from the *Portuguese*, routed them near *Toro* 1479. and near *Albuhera*; upon this, *Alfonsus* concluded a Peace with *Ferdinand*, wherein he renounced both *Castile* and the Bride *Johanna*, she being promised in Marriage to *John* Son of *Ferdinand*, who was then a Child: But she, perceiving that this was only done to elude her, went into a Nunnery. *Portugal* sustained considerable losses in this 1479. War, and *Alfonsus* died in the Year 1481, as it is supposed out of Grief, because he had lost the hopes of his Bride and the Crown of *Castile*. To him succeeded his Son *John* II. *John* II. against whom a most horrid Conspiracy was discover'd, for which *Ferdinand* Duke of *Braganza*, and *James* Duke of *Viseo*, lost their Lives, the latter being kill'd by the King's own Hand. This King *John* was the first who found *A Project of sailing to the* East-Indies. out the way to sail into the *East-Indies*, having not only ordered an exact Survey to be made of the *African* Coast, as far as to the *Cape* of *Good Hope*, but also sent some by Land into the *East-Indies*, to inform themselves concerning the condition of those Countries. He likewise built the Castle of *Mina* on the Coast of *Guinea*: But before this intended Voyage to the *East-Indies* could be begun, this King died in the Year 1495, leaving no Heirs behind him.

§ 5. *John* II. Was succeeded by his Cousin *Emanuel*, Son *Emanuel*. of *Ferdinand* Duke of *Viseo*, Grand-child of King *Edward*. With him contended for the Succession, the Emperor *Maximilian*, whose Mother *Eleonora* was a Daughter of King *Edward*: But the *Portuguese* declared *Emanuel*, who for his extraordinary Qualifications both of Body and Mind, was extreamly beloved by them. He, married *Isabella*, eldest Daughter of *Ferdinand* the *Catholick*, from which Marriage a young Prince was Born, whose name was *Michael*, who if he had liv'd, would have been Heir to all the *Spanish* Kingdoms, except that of *Navarre*. To please his Bride, Moors *and* Jews *banish'd* Portugal. he, by his Proclamation banished all the *Jews* and *Moors* out of *Portugal* by a prefix'd time, under Penalty, for all such as should stay behind, to be made Slaves for ever. Whereupon the *Moors* immediately retir'd into *Africa*; but from

the

the *Jews* they took their Children which were under the Age of fourteen, and Baptized them against their Will: And as for the old ones, they were so plagu'd and vex'd every where, and stop'd or hinder'd in their Journeys, that most, to be rid of these Vexations, and to avoid the danger of Slavery, were Baptized, retaining nevertheless, in their minds, their ancient Superstition. Under the Reign of this King, *Portugal* arrived to the highest pitch of its Greatness, the design of the *East-India* Voyage round *Africa*, which was projected by the former King, being now accomplished by *Vascus de Gama*, who first arrived at *Calicut*. As soon as the *Portuguese* began to draw into their Country the Trade of Spices, they were opposed, especially by the Sultan of *Egypt*, because formerly these Commodities used to be conveyed through *Egypt* to *Venice*, and from thence to other parts of *Europe*, from which both these Countries drew vast Profit. Upon this account, the *Venetians* stirred up the Sultan, sending him great store of Metal to make Canon of, and Shipwrights to build Ships; by which means they hoped to drive the *Portuguese* out of the *Indies*: But the *Portuguese*, who did not much trust the *Barbarian* Kings of the *Indies*, began to build Forts and Strong holds in the most convenient places; wherein they met with little opposition. Above all, the Duke of *Albuquerque* did mightily advance the Power of the *Portuguese* in the *Indies*, in taking the Cities of *Ormuz*, *Malacca*, *Cochin*, and *Goa*; the latter of which is the place of Residence of the *Portuguese* Governour in the *Indies*. And thus the *Portuguese* engrossed to themselves the whole Trade and Commerce of *Africa*, and the remotest parts of *Asia*, having possessed themselves of all the most commodious Ports and Places, not only on the *Western* side of *Africa*, in *Mauritania*, *Guinea*, *Congo*, *Angola*, in the Isle of St. *Thomas*, and some others, but also on the *East* side, in *Mozambique*, *Melinde*, *Mombazo*, *Zefala*, and from the mouth of the *Red-Sea*, as far as *Japan*; from whence incredible Riches were conveyed into *Portugal*. Besides all this, *Pieter Alvanus Capralis*, or as some will have it, *Americus Vespusius* discovered the Country of *Brasile* in *America*, whither the *Portuguese* sent 1500 several Colonies. And under the Reign of this King *Emanuel*, who died in the Year 1521, *Portugal* increased to that degree, that his Reign was called *The Golden Age*. After him reigned his Son *John* III. under whose Reign *Portugal* continued in the same flourishing

The first Sea-Voyage to the East-Indies, 1497.

The reason why the Venetians *opposed the* Portuguese *settling themselves there.*

The Progress of the Duke of Albuquerque *in the* East-Indies.

The discovery of Brasile *in* America.

John III.

ing Condition. This King sent *Francis Xavier*, and some other Jesuits, into the *East-Indies*, who were to settle the Christian Religion among the *Barbarians*. He died in the Year 1557. *The Jesuits sent to the Indies.*

§. 6. *John* III. Had for his Successor his Grandson *Sebastian*, a Child of three Years of Age, whose Tuition was committed to the Cardinal *Henry* his Uncle, because his Grandmother was not willing to take upon her the burden of the Government. Through the overforwardness of this young Prince, *Portugal* received such a blow, that it fell from the Pinacle of its Greatness: For some of his Court Favourites put this magnanimous and ambitious Prince upon such Enterprizes as far surpass'd both his Age and Power, and were in no ways suitable to the present juncture of Affairs; so that his whole Mind was bent upon Warlike Exploits, and how by Martial Exercises to revive the ancient Valour of his Subjects, which by Peace and Plenty, arising from their great Commerce, was of late much decayed. With this view he undertook an Expedition into the next adjacent parts of *Africa*, intending by light Skirmishes to try his Enemies. He proposed afterwards, a Voyage into the *Indies*, but his Council opposing it, it was agreed upon, that he should undertake an Expedition into *Africa*, and occasion presenting it self at that time; for that *Muley Mahomet*, King of *Morocco*, being banished by his Uncle *Muley Malucco*, crav'd the assistance of King *Sebastian*: Pursuant to this Resolution, notwithstanding the good Counsels of *Philip* King of *Spain*, and others, who dissuaded him from it, he in Person, with a great but undisciplin'd Army enter'd *Africa*, and advancing, against all Reason, too far into the Country, was oblig'd, in a disadvantageous place, to fight a much more numerous Army; the success of the Battel was answerable to the rash attempt; his Army, wherein was the flower of the Nobility of *Portugal*, being miserably routed, and all the Soldiers either cut to pieces or made Prisoners. This Battle is Famous for the fall of three Kings, *viz.* King *Sebastian*, the banish'd *Muley Mahomet*, and *Muley Malucco*, King of *Morocco*, who during the time of the Battle, died of a Fever. This happen'd in the Year 1578. To him succeeded his Uncle *Henry* the Cardinal, a very old Man, under whose Reign there happened nothing worth mentioning, but that perpetual Contests were set on foot concerning the Succession.

Sebastian. *His fatal Expedition into Africa.* *Henry.*

Succession. And he dying in the Year 1580, *Philip* II. King of *Spain*, thought it the most efficacious way, to dispute his Title to the Crown of *Portugal* with Sword in Hand; and perceiving that the *Portuguese*, out of the hatred they bear to the *Castilians*, were inclined to *Anthony* Son of *Lewis de Beya*, natural Son to King *John* III. He sent the Duke *de Alba* with a great Army into *Portugal*, who quickly chased away *Anthony*, and in few days became Master of the whole Kingdom, all being forced soon to submit, except the Isle of *Tercera*, which was not reduced till after the *French*, who came to its relief, were beaten. As the *Portuguese* did not, without great Reluctancy, bear the Government of the *Castilians*; so this Union with *Castile* proved very prejudicial to them afterwards. For *Philip*, intent upon the reducing of the *Netherlands*, thought that nothing could do it more effectually, than to stop their Trade and Commerce with *Spain* and *Portugal*: For hitherto the *Dutch* had traded no further, being used to fetch away their Commodities from thence, and to convey them into the more Nothern parts of *Europe*. Upon this Consideration *Philip* concluded, that if this way of getting Money were once stopp'd, they would quickly grow poor, and thereby be obliged to submit. But this design had a quite contrary effect; for the *Hollanders* themselves, being excluded from Trade with *Spain* and *Portugal*, try'd, about the end of the latter Age, to sail to the *East-Indies*. And as soon as they had once got Footing there, they greatly impair'd the *Portuguese* Trade, who hitherto had been the sole managers of it, and afterwards took from them one Fort after another. And the *English* with the Assistance of *Abbas*, King of *Persia*, forced from them the famous City of *Ormutz*. Nor was this all, for the *Hollanders* took from a great part of *Brasile*, and several places on the Coast of *Africa*; which the *Hollanders*, in all probability, would have had no reason to attempt, if *Portugal* had remained a Kingdom by it self, and had not been annexed to *Spain*.

Portugal united to Spain.

The Dutch sail to the East-Indies.

1620.

1630.

§. 7. But in the Year 1640, the *Portuguese* took occasion to shake off the *Spanish* Yoke. For *Philip* IV. then summoned the *Portuguese* Nobility to assist him in the War against the *Catalonians*, who had rebelled against him. And they being upon that design armed, and finding an opportunity to consult with one another, concerning those Troubles

The Portuguese shake off the Yoke of Spain.

bles in which *Spain* was involv'd at that time; they agreed to withdraw themselves from the Subjection of *Spain*, proclaiming for their King, the Duke of *Braganza*, who stiled himself *John* IV. whose Grandmother had stood in competition with *Philip* II. for that Crown. The *Spaniards* committed a gross mistake in this, that they did not in time secure the Duke, whom they knew to have a fair pretence to that Crown, to be extreamly beloved by that Nation, and to be in possession of the fourth part of the Kingdom. The *Spaniards* being at that time imbroiled in Wars with *France*, *Holland* and *Catalonia*; the *Portuguese* had leisure given them, to settle their Affairs. They made also a Peace with *Holland*, by virtue of which, both Parties were to remain in possession of what they had gotten. But this Peace did not last long; for those places which were in the possession of the *Hollanders*, in *Brasile*, revolted to the *Portuguese*, which the *Hollanders* looking upon as done by contrivance of the *Portuguese*, denounced War against them. And tho' they did not retake *Brasile*, yet did they take a great many other places from them in the *East-Indies*, viz. *Malacca*, the places on the Coast of the Isle of *Zeylon*, on the Coast of *Cormandel*, and on the Coast of *Malabar*, *Cochin*, *Cananor*, *Cranganor*, and some others; and if they had not clapt up a Peace with them, they would in all likelihood have also driven them out of *Goa* it self. *John* IV. died in the Year 1656, leaving the Kingdom to his Son *Alfonsus*, who was under Age, but the Administration of the Government was in the mean time lodged with his Mother. After the *Pyrenean* Treaty was concluded, from which *Portugal* was excluded by the *Spaniards*, it being besides stipulated with *France*, that they should not send any Assistance to the *Portuguese*, the *Spaniards* fell upon the *Portuguese* in good earnest: But these defended themselves bravely, and notwithstanding the Articles of the *Pyrenean* Treaty, the *French* King gave leave to the Earl of *Scombergh*, and a great many other *Frenchmen*, to enter into the Service of the *Portuguese*, who routed the *Spaniards* in several Encounters, but more especially near *Extremos* and *Villa Vitiosa*. At last, the *French* entring with a great Army into the *Netherlands*, the *Spaniards* were fain to conclude a Peace with the *Portuguese*, who were also glad to be once disentangl'd out of so tedious a War. By virtue of this Peace, *Spain* resign'd all its Pretensions upon *Portugal*. In the mean time *Alfonsus* was grown up, but

The Duke of Braganza *proclaim'd* King John IV.

A League betwixt Portugal *and* Holland.

A War breaks out betwixt them.

A Peace in 1661.

Alfonsus VI.

1666.

as *Don Pedro*'s Friends have represented him to the World, was neither fit to Rule, nor to Marry: However, he took the Administration of Affairs from his Mother, (who died soon after) and married a Princess of *Nemours*, descended from the House of *Savoy*; who having lived with him about sixteen Months, retir'd into a Monastery. *Don Pedro* having his Eye upon the Kingdom, brought the Nobility and People over to his Party, forced *Alfonsus* to surrender to him the Administration of the Kingdom, reserving for his Maintenance only the yearly Revenue of 270000 Livres, and the Palace of *Braganza*, with all its Appurtenances. *Don Pedro* would not take upon himself the Title of King, but chose rather to be call'd Regent of *Portugal*, in the name of his Brother *Alfonsus*. At the same time he married, with the Dispensation of the Pope, his Brother's Wife. And that *Alfonsus* might not be in a capacity of raising any Disturbances, he was carry'd Prisoner under a strong Guard, to the Island of *Tercera*.

1666. — *Don Pedro.*

The Humours of the Portuguese.

§ 8. It remains to say something of the Genius of the *Portuguese*, and the Strength and the Nature of the Country. The *Portuguese* are not inferiour to the *Spaniards* in Pride and Haughtiness, but fall short of 'em in Prudence and Caution, as being over-secure in Prosperity, and in time of Danger rash and fool-hardy. Where they get the upper-hand they are very Rigorous and Cruel. They are mightily addicted to be Covetous, and love Usury, and have hunted for Money in all corners of the World. Some will have them to be very Malicious, which they say is the Reliques of the *Jewish* Blood, which is intermingl'd with that of the *Portuguese* Nation. This Country in proportion to its extent, is very populous, as is evident by the number of *Portuguese*, that have settled themselves in *Brasile*, on the Coast of *Africa*, and in the *East-Indies*: Yet are they not in a capacity to raise a numerous Land Army without Foreign help, or to Man out a mighty Fleet of Men of War; for they have enough to do, to Garrison their Frontier Places well, and to keep Convoys for their Merchant Ships.

Fruitfulness of Portugal.

§ 9. As for the Countries which belong now-a-days to *Portugal*. The Kingdom of *Portugal*, by it self considered, is neither very large nor very fruitful, the Inhabitants living mostly upon Corn imported: Yet is the Country full of Cities and Towns, and has a great many commodious Seaports.

ports. The Commodities of the growth of *Portugal*, fit for Exportation, are Salt, of which a great quantity is from *Setubal* or St. *Hubes* transported into the Northern Countries: As also Oyl, some Wine, and all sorts of Fruit. The other Commodities brought from thence are first imported from the Provinces that belong to them. The Silver Mine called *Guadaldane*, is said to be of the yearly value of 178 Quentoes of Silver (each Quent being reckon'd to amount to 2673 Ducats, 8 Reals, and 26 Marvedoes.) Among the Colonies that now belong to *Portugal*, the chiefest is *Brasile*, being a long tract of Land in *America* extended all along the Sea-side, but very narrow, and famous for the wholsomness of the Air, and its fertility. Here abundance of Sugar is made, from whence arises the main Revenue of the Country, the *Portuguese* makeing use of the same in preserving those excellent Fruits that grow both in *Portugal* and *Brasile*. *Brasile* affords also Ginger, Cotten, Wool, Indigo and Wood for the Dyers. But in regard the Natives of this Country are naturally Lazy, and cannot by any ways be forced to hard Labour; the *Portuguese* buy upon the Coast of *Africa*, and especially in *Congo* and *Angola*, Negroes, whom they use for Slaves, buying and selling them in *Brasile*, as we do Oxen; and these are employ'd in all sort of hardships and drudgery. The Trade of the *Portuguese* on the *West* side of *Africa* is not now of any great consequence, since the *Hollanders* have interfer'd with them; and the places they are possess'd of on the *East* side of *Africa* only serve to enrich their Governours. What the *Hollanders* have left them in the *East-Indies* is of no small consequence to them; for *Goa* is a very large City, where there is a great Trade among People of all Nations: But the wiser sort do not approve of the *Portuguese* Government in the *East-Indies*; for the *Portuguese* there are given to Voluptuousness, and neglecting Military Affairs, are nevertheless so presumptuous, as to imagine, that with their haughty Carriage they can out-brave others. Hence it was that the *Hollanders* found it so easie to drive this Nation out of the greatest part of the *Indies*, where they were hated and contemn'd: Yet the *Portuguese* enjoy one Privilege which the *Dutch* have not, that they are allowed a free Trade with *China*, where they have the City of *Macoa* in an Island not far distant from the Continent; and they have so mis-represented the *Hollanders* with the *Chinese*, that hitherto, as far as I know, they have

Brasile. Africa. The East-Indies.

A horrible Perſecution raiſed on the Chriſtians of Japan, *and the occaſion of it.*

not been able to obtain a free Commerce with *China*. Formerly the *Portugueſe* had a great Intereſt in *Japan*, which was chiefly procur'd by means of the Jeſuits, who made it their buſineſs to convert the *Japoneſe* to the Chriſtian Religion. It is related that above 400000 of them were baptized, not without hopes, that all the reſt would at laſt have follow'd their Example. But about thirty Years ago the *Dutch*, by their Practices and Artifices, render'd the *Portugueſe* ſuſpected to the Emperor of *Japan*, having intercepted a Letter from the Jeſuits to the Pope, wherein they promis'd to bring, e're long, the whole Kingdom of *Japan* under the Obedience of the *Roman* See. The *Hollanders* interpreted this Letter in ſuch a ſence, as if the Jeſuits, with the aſſiſtance of the new Converts, did intend to dethrone the Emperor; telling him, that the Pope pretended to an Authority of diſpoſing Kingdoms at his pleaſure, and that the King of *Spain*, who was then Maſter of *Portugal*, was in great eſteem with him. The jealous *Japoneſe* were eaſily perſwaded hereof, when they conſider'd with what Reſpect and Kindneſs the Jeſuits were treated by the new Chriſtians; thoſe being alſo very ready to accept of what theſe good natur'd People offer'd them. And the Governours were ſenſible, and complain'd, that their uſual Preſents from the Subjects decreaſed daily, ſince the new Converts gave ſo much to their Prieſts. The *Hollanders* alſo ſhew'd the Emperor of *Japan* in a Map, how the Conqueſts of the King of *Spain* extended on one ſide as far as *Manilla*, on the other ſide as far as *Macao*, ſo that by ſubduing of *Japan*, he would have an opportunity of uniting his Conqueſts. This occaſion'd a moſt horrible Perſecution againſt the Chriſtians, the *Japoneſe* endeavouring by incredible Torments to overcome the Conſtancy of a Nation, which is naturally one of the moſt obſtinate. Neither did they ceaſe, till there was not one Chriſtian left in *Japan*; and the *Portugueſe* upon pain of Death, were for ever baniſh'd the Country. And the *Hollanders*, when afterwards they ſent any Ships to *Japan*, us'd to forbid their Subjects, to ſhew the leaſt appearance of Religious Chriſtian Worſhip, but if they were ask'd, *Whether they were Chriſtians*, to anſwer, *They were not, but they were* Hollanders. To *Portugal* belong alſo the Iſles call'd *Azores*, whereof *Tercera*, and the Iſle *Madera*, which are tolerably fruitful, are the Principal.

§ 10. From

§. 10. From what hath been said, it is apparent, that the welfare of *Portugal*, depends chiefly on their Commerce with the *East-Indies*, *Brasile* and *Africa*; 'Tis likewise manifest, that the Strength and Power of *Portugal* in comparison of the rest of the more potent States of *Europe* is not to be esteem'd such, as to be able to attack any of them, or gain any thing upon them. As for its Neighbours in particular; *Portugal* is adjacent to *Spain*, so that it is easie for the *Spaniards* to enter *Portugal*; yet is the Power of *Spain* not very dreadful to the *Portuguese*, partly, because the *Spaniards* cannot conveniently keep an Army of above 25000 Men on foot on that side, by reason of the scarcity of Provisions, and the like number the *Portuguese* can also bring into the Field; partly, because *Spain* cannot man out a considerable Fleet of Men of War wherewith to attack the *Portuguese* Provinces: Besides, *Portugal* in case of such an attack might certainly expect to be assisted either by the *French* or *English*, who, as much as in them lies, will not suffer *Spain* to become again Master of *Portugal*. Neither does it appear for the Interest of *Portugal*, upon the Instigation of *France* or some other Foreign Power, to engage it self without a pressing Necessity in a War with *Spain*, since it is not probable that it could, by that means, gain any thing considerable, but would only weaken it self without the hopes of any Advantage. *Portugal* has in all probability, not much to fear from *France*, they lying at a considerable distance from one another; besides that, the Naval Strength of *France* is not come, as yet, to that height, as to be in a Capacity to be hurtful to a Nation that has settled it self very securely in the *East* and *West-Indies*; and more especially, since these two Nations have not any pretensions on each other: Nay it rather concerns *France*, that *Portugal* may stand secure against *Spain* and *Holland*. The *Hollanders* have hitherto prov'd the most pernicious Enemies to *Portugal*, as being in a capacity not only to disturb their Trade on the Coast of *Portugal*, but also to prove very troublesome to them both in the *East* and *West-Indies*: And it seems that it would be no difficult matter for the *Hollanders*, by taking from the *Portuguese* the City of *Macao*, on the Coast of *China*, and some other places off the Coast of *Malabar*, quite to destroy their Trade in the *East-Indies*. But it is probable, that in case of a War betwixt the *Portuguese* and *Hollanders*, *England* would assist the

The Strength of Portugal.

How it stands with regard to Spain.

France.

To Holland.

the former against the latter, since it has not been without great Displeasure to the *English*, to see what progress the *Hollanders* have made in the *East-Indies*, whereby they have acquir'd such vast Riches, that they have bid defiance to *England*, and all the rest of *Europe*.

CHAP. IV.

Of ENGLAND.

The ancient State of England.

§ 1. IN Ancient Times, *Britain*, the bigest Island of the then known World, was not rul'd by one Prince, but divided into a great many petty States, each of them govern'd by its own King; but this multitude of petty Princes, as it caus'd great Divisions among them, so it expos'd them to the danger of being overcome by their Foreign Enemies. This Island was scarce known to the *Greeks* and *Romans* till *Julius Cæsar*'s time, who after he had conquer'd the greatest part of *France*, undertook an Expedition into *Britain*, hoping to meet there with great Booty and Riches. But he enter'd not very far into the Country, and after some Skirmishes with the Inhabitants, return'd again without leaving a Garrison, or exacting any Contributions. After this, *Britain* was not attack'd again by the *Romans*, till under the Reign of the Emperor *Claudius*, who bent his Arms against it in good earnest, and the Inhabitants being divided among themselves, he, without great difficulty, conquer'd part of it. At which time *Britain* was made a *Roman* Province, a constant Army being maintain'd there by the *Romans*, who by degrees conquer'd one part after another, tho' not without receiving some Defeats. At last, under the Rein of *Domitian*, *Julius Agricola* marched with his victorious Army through the whole Island, and giving a signal overthrow to the *Caledonians*, who are now call'd the *Scots*, subdu'd them; tho' the *Romans* could never entirely conquer the utmost parts of *Britain*, which are almost inaccessible. Wherefore, afterwards the Emperors *Adrian* and *Severus*, by building a Wall cross the Island from Sea to Sea, divided these inaccessible places from the *Roman* Province, hoping thereby to stop the Incursions of the Inhabitants. But the *Romans* never came into *Ireland*. After the *Britains* had been above 400 Years under subjection

The Romans *conquer* England.

to

to the *Romans*, the Northern Nations at that time over-running the Western parts of the *Roman* Empire, the *Romans* left this Island voluntarily, being oblig'd to recal their Legions in *Britain*, accompanied with some numbers of the British Natives, to make head against their Enemies upon the Continent.

§ 2. *Britain* being thus without an Army, and withal, mightily exhausted in its Strength, for that the *Romans* had made use of their young Men in their Wars, the *Picts* and *Scots*, from their barren Country, made an Inrode into the more plentiful Provinces, destroying all before them. The *Britains*, to make the better Head against them, had chosen one *Vortigern* for their King; but he perceiving himself to be no ways able to resist their Power; and Assistance being denied him from the *Romans*, called in the *Angles*. These *Angles*, or *Saxons*, under their Leaders *Hengist* and *Horsa*, coming with some thousands of Men to the assistance of the *Britains*, beat out the *Scots*. But being mightily taken with the Fruitfulness of the Country resolved to subdue it, and to lay the Yoak upon the *Britains*, who had called them in to deliver them from it. As soon as the *Britains* perceived what their Intention was, they endeavoured to drive them out of the Island: But these calling in a great many thousands of their Country-men to their assistance, conquer'd all *Britain*, except the Province of *Wales*, which being very Mountainous, they were not able to subdue. *Cadwallader* was the last King of the ancient *British* Race, who perceiving that he was by no means able longer to resist the Power of the *Saxons*, retired to *Rome*, into a Convent. 'Twas then that *Britain* received the Name of *Anglia* or *England*, from the *Angles*. *The Saxons come into Britain.*

§ 5. These *Saxons* erected seven Kingdoms, which however had not their beginning all at one time, but according as they had taken one part after another from the Inhabitants: At last they fell together by the ears among themselves, till one having swallow'd up another, all were united into one Kingdom; which, how it happened we will briefly relate. The first Kingdom then was that of *Kent*, which began in the Year 455, and during the Reigns of seventeen Kings, lasted till the Year 827, when it was subdued by the *West-Saxons*. The second was the Kingdom of *Sussex*, which began in the Year 488, and, *The Saxon Kings in England. The Saxon Heptarchy.*

under five Kings, lasted till the Year 601, when it was likewise made a Province by the *West Saxons*. The third was that of the *West Saxons*, which began in the Year 519, and lasted under nineteen Kings, 561 Years. The eleventh of these Kings, named *Ina*, did order, That each Subject that was worth ten Pence, should yearly give one Penny to the Pope of *Rome*, which Tax was called the *King's Alms*, and afterwards *Peter's Pence*. The fourth Kingdom was that of *Essex*, which began in the Year 527, and lasted, under fourteen Kings, till the Year 808, when it was also conquered by the *West Saxons*. The fifth was that of *Northumberland*, which began in the Year 547, and lasted, under three and twenty Kings, till the Year 926, when it was also brought under subjection by the *West Saxons*. The sixth Kingdom was that of the *Mercians*, which had its beginning in the Year 522, and lasted, under twenty Kings, till the Year 724, when it fell into the hands of the *West Saxons*. The seventh was that of the *East Angles*, which began in the Year 575, and lasted, under fifteen Kings, till the Year 928, when under its King *Athelstan*, it was united with the rest. But after *Egbert*, King of the *West Saxons*, had either subdued the rest, or forced their Kings to acknowledge him for their Supream Head, he and his Successors were henceforward called no more Kings of *Britain*, but of *England*. Under his Reign the *Danes* first entered *England*, as they continued to do under the following Kings, tho' in the beginning they were at several times bravely repulsed: Nevertheless they got footing, at last, in the Northern parts of *England*, where they lived for a while pretty quietly under the Protection of the Kings of *England*. But in the time of King *Ethelred*, who began his Reign in the Year 979, the *Danes* made inrodes into the Southern parts of *England*, forc'd the *English* to pay them great Sums of Money, ravished their Women, and committed such Outrages, that they got the Name of *Lord Danes*. And tho' the *English* conspired against the *Danes*, and cut them all off, yet the *Danish* King returned the next Year, and made prodigious havock among the *English*, their great Preparations which were made against the *Danes*, being by the Craft of the Traitor *Edrick* (notwithstanding *Ethelred* had made him Duke of *Mercia*, giving him his Daughter for a Wife) rendered ineffectual; so that *Ethelred* was obliged to leave his desolate Kingdom, and to retire into *Normandy*. *Sueno* the *Danish* King being kill'd

Peter's Pence.

The Kingdom of England.

828.

Danes *first come into* England.

1002.

kill'd with a Sword from an unknown Hand, while he was amusing himself with the Plunder of St. *Edmonds-bury* in *Suffolk*; *Ethelred* returned out of *Normandy* into *England*, and forc'd *Canute Sueno's* Son, to retire out of *England* into *Denmark*; but he returned quickly with a much greater Force, and *Ethelred* making all imaginable Preparations against him, died in the Year 1016; whose Son *Edmund*, sirnamed *Ironside*, did defend himself with great Bravery against the *Danes*, and might have obtained several Victories over them, if he had not been therein prevented by that Traitor *Edrick*. At last it was agreed, that both Kings should make an end of the War by a Duel, in which, tho' *Edmund* had the advantage of giving *Canute* a dangerous stroke, yet was he persuaded to finish the Combat, by dividing the Kingdom with the *Danes*; and was afterwards, as he retired privately to ease Nature, treachreously murthered by *Edrick*.

The Danes *driven out, but return again.*

King Edmund *treacherously murther'd.*

§ 4. After the Death of *Edmund*, *Canute* was Crown'd King of *England*. Having dispatch'd all that were left of the Royal Race, he, to ingratiate himself with the People, married *Emma*, the Widow of King *Ethelred*, sent most of his *Danes* home, and reigned with great applause. Some of his Parasites, who pretended to attribute to him something above a Humane Power, he redicul'd, by causing a Chair to be set near the Sea-side, commanding the Seas not to wet his Feet; but the Tide rolling on the Waves as usually, he told them, That from thence they might judge of what extent was the Power of all worldly Kings. He died in the Year 1035. His Son *Harald* succeeded, and was in allusion to his nimbleness sirnam'd *Harefoot*: He did nothing worth mentioning, but that he caus'd his Step-mother *Emma*, and her Sons, to be miserably murthered. He died in the Year 1039, leaving no Children behind him. After his death the great Men of the Kingdom call'd out of *Denmark*, *Hardiknut* his Brother, born of *Emma* and *Canute*, who was famous for nothing but his greedy Appetite, he being us'd to sit at Table four times a day. The *Danes* after his Death growing so despicable to the *English*, that the Government expir'd, after they had ravaged *England* for the space of 240, tho' they possess'd the Throne but 26 Years. After the death of *Hardiknut*, *Edward* sirnam'd the *Confessor*, Son of King *Ethelred* and *Emma*, Brother of *Hardiknut* on the Mother's side, who had

Canute, *the Dane, King of* England. 1017.

Hardiknut.

Edward *the Confessor.*

sought Sanctuary in *Normandy*, was called in to be King of *England*: He was Crown'd in the Year 1042, and to gain the Affection of the People, he remitted a Tax called *Danegild*, which had been constantly paid for forty Years last past. He reigned very peaceably, except, that he was now and then pestered with the *Irish* and *Danish* Pirates, whom, nevertheless, he quickly overcame. He was the first to whom was attributed that Virtue, which even to this Day the Kings of *England* are said to have, of healing by touching, that Disease which in *England* is call'd the
1066. King's Evil. He died without Children. He intended to have left the Kingdom to his Cousin *Edgar Atheling*, Grandson of King *Edmund Ironside*; but he being very young, *Harald*, Son of *Goodwin* Earl of *Kent*, who had the Tuition of *Edgar*, put the Crown upon his own Head, but did not enjoy it above nine Months, being slain in a Battle by *William* Duke of *Normandy*, whereby the Crown of *England* was transferred to the *Norman* Family.

William *the* Conquerour.

§ 5. This *William*, firnamed *the Conquerour*, was Son of *Robert* Duke of *Normandy*, descended from *Rollo*, a Dane, who about the Year 900, with a great number of his Country-men and *Norwegians*, fell into *France*, and ravaged the Country without resistance; upon which *Charles the Simple*, the then King of *France*, thought it the best way to set him at quiet, by puting him in possession of the Provinces of *Neustria*, which afterwards was called *Normandy*, and giving to him in Marriage his Daughter *Geisa*, upon condition that he should become a Christian. *Rollo* had a Son whose Name was *William*, firnam'd *Longsword*; whose Son was *Richard*, firnam'd *the Hardy*; who was the Father of *Richard* II. firnam'd *the Good*, who was succeeded by his Son *Richard* III. as he was by his Son *Richard* IV. But he dying without Issue, after him *Robert* became Duke of *Normandy*. This *Robert* was Father to *William the Conquerour*, whom he had by one *Arlotte*, a Furrier's Daughter, with whom, 'tis said, he fell in love, seeing her dance among other Maids in the Country, and afterwards married her. And notwithstanding this *William* was a Bastard, yet his Father made him his Successor, and got the Nobility to acknowledge him as such when he was but nine Years of Age, and died soon after. This *William* met with great Troubles and Dangers in his younger Years, which he had the fortune to overcome by his

Valour,

Valour, and acquired thereby great Reputation. After the death of *Edward the Confessor*, *William* understanding that *Harald* had made himself King, resolved to demand the Crown of *England*, as belonging to him by vertue of the last Will of King *Edward*, who, he pretended, had left the same to him, as an acknowledgment for the great Favours he had received from his Father *Robert*. There are others who say, That *Edward* did only promise this by word of mouth; and that *Harald* being then in *Normandy*, was forced to engage by Oath, to assist him in obtaining the Crown of *England*. It is possible, this was only made use of as a Pretence. But however it be, *William* landed without opposition with a great Army, compos'd of *Normans*, *French*, and *Netherlanders*, whilst the Fleet of *Harald* was sailed to the Northern Coast of *England*, to oppose his Brother and *Harald Harfager*, King of *Norway*, who had entered *England* on that side, and were both vanquished by him; but by this means he left an open Door for *William* to enter the Kingdom, and brought his Soldiers back much weakened and fatigu'd by their great Marches: Yet having re-inforced his Army as well as he could, he offer'd Battle to *William* near *Hastings* in *Sussex*; which Battle was fought on both sides with great obstinacy, till *Harald* being mortally wounded by an Arrow, the Victory and Crown of *England* remained to *William*. The *English* were at first extreamly well satisfy'd with his Government; partly because he left every one in possession of what was his own, and gave only the vacant Lands to his *Normans*; partly, upon the account of his being related to the former Kings of *England*. He was also very strenuous in securing himself, commanding all the Arms to be taken from the People, and to prevent Nocturnal Assemblies and Commotions, he ordered, That after the Bell had rung at Eight in the Evening, no Fire nor Candle should be seen in their Houses: Besides this, he built several Forts in the most commodious Places. Notwithstanding all these wise Precautions, he met with various Troubles. *Edgar Atheling*, with some of the Nobility, retir'd into *Scotland*; and assisted by the *Danish* Pirates, continually ravag'd the Northern Parts of *England*, burning the City of *York* it self, wherein all the *Normans* were put to the Sword; tho' indeed *William* expell'd them afterwards. His Son *Robert* also, endeavour'd to take from him *Normandy*, against whom his Father led a great Army, out

William conquers *England*.

October 14. 1066.

The Corfew Bell.

Edgar Atheling makes an attempt.

His Son *Robert* Rebels.

out of *England*, and the Father and Son encountring one another in the Battle, the first was dismounted by the latter; who discovering him to be his Father by his Voice, immediately dismounted, embrac'd, and begg'd pardon, and was reconciled to his Father. This King forced *Wales* to pay him Tribute; and King *Malcolm* of *Scotland* to swear Fealty to him. At last perceiving that his new conquer'd People would not be govern'd altogether by mildness, he began to act more severely, taking out of the Convents what Gold and Silver he could meet with; of which there had been great store conveyed thither, as into Sanctuaries. He imposed heavy Taxes, and appropriated to himself a great part of the Lands of *England*, which he gave unto others, reserving to himself out of them a yearly Revenue. He took upon him the Administration of the Goods and Possessions of all Minors, till they came to the twenty first Year of Age; allowing them only so much as was requisite for their Maintenance: He revis'd all their Privileges, introduc'd new Laws in the *Norman* Tongue; by vertue of which innovation a great many that did not understand that Language, fell under severe Penalties: He erected new Courts of Judicature, and employed great Tracts of Ground for the conveniency of his Hunting. This King introduced first the use of the long Bow in *England*, whereby he had chiefly obtained the Victory against *Harald*. At last, *Philip* I. King of *France*, by stiring up his Son *Robert* against him, endeavouring to raise Disturbances in *Normandy*, he went in Person over thither, where the Son was reconciled to the Father. But being obliged to keep his Bed at *Roan*, by reason of an Indisposition in his Belly, which was very gross, the King of *France* ridicul'd him; asking, *How long he intended to lie in?* To whom *William* sent this Answer, *That as soon as he could go to Church after his lying in, he had vow'd to sacrifice a thousand Torches in* France: and he was as good as his word; for he was no sooner recovered, but he invaded *France*, and burnt all wherever he came: But overheating himself in the Expedition, he fell ill and died, leaving by his last Will, to his eldest Son, *Normandy*; but to the second, called *William*, the Crown of *England*.

He acts as a Conqueror.

Robert rebels again.

1087.

§. 6. *William* II. Sirnam'd *Rufus*, met at first with some Disturbances, occasioned by his Brother *Robert*: But he appeased

William Rufus.

appeased him by promising to pay him yearly, the Sum of 3000 Marks, and that he should succeed him after his Death. The Nobles, he partly by fair means, partly by force, reduced to Obedience. This Rebellion prov'd very beneficial to the *English*, the Rebels being most of them *Normans*; wherefore the King afterwards rely'd more upon the *English*, as the most faithful. He waged War twice with *Malcolm* King of *Scotland*, whom he forced in the first to swear him Fealty, and in the last he killed both him and his eldest Son. He also subdued the Province of *Wales*. Among other Inventions to get Money, one was remarkable; for he summoned together 20000 Men, under pretence to go with them into *Normandy*; but when they were just a going to be shipp'd off, he caused Proclamation to be made, that every one who was willing to pay Twelve Shillings, should have leave to stay at home, unto which every Man of them readily consented. He was killed by a random shot in Hunting. To him succeeded his younger Brother *Henry*, who being present when the King died, seized upon his Treasures whereby he procured himself a great many Friends, so that he was prefered before *Robert* his elder Brother, who at that Time assisted in the taking of *Jerusalem*, which proved no less than the loss of a Crown to him. For *Henry*, the better to establish himself in the Throne, remitted not only several Taxes, which were laid upon the People by the former Kings, but also secured to his Interest the King of *Scotland*, *Edgar*, his most dangerous Neighbour, by marrying his Sister *Maud*. Notwithstanding this *Robert* landed a great Army in *England*, but *Henry* and *Robert*, by the Mediation of some Friends, and a Promise of a yearly Pension to be paid to *Robert*, were reconciled; which Pension *Henry* accordingly remitted to *Robert*. But afterwards repenting of what he had done, *Henry* was so exasperated against him, that he made a Descent in *Normandy* with a great Army, and vanquish'd him in a bloody Battle, wherein he took him Prisoner. He kept him not only a Prisoner all his Life-time, but at last, put his Eyes out, uniting *Normandy* to the Crown of *England*. But King *Lewis* of *France*, Sirnamed *Crassus*, being very jealous of the Greatness of *Henry*, undertook, with the Assistance of *Fulco* Earl of *Anjou*, and *Baldwin* Earl of *Flanders*, to restore unto *William*, Son of *Robert*, the Dukedom of *Normandy*; whereupon a bloody War ensued, which

1100. *Henry* I.

Robert makes a Descent in *England*.

Normandy annexed to the Crown of *England*.

was at last composed upon these Terms. That *William*, Son of *Henry*, should swear Fealty to *France*, for the Dukedom of *Normandy*. And it obtained afterwards as a Custom, that the King's eldest Son was called *Duke of Normandy*, as long as this Province was united to *England*. The new Duke of *Normandy* did also marry the Daughter of the Earl of *Anjou*: And *William*, Son of *Robert*, being then made Earl of *Flanders*, and endeavouring a second time to regain *Normandy*, was slain in that War. His Son *William*, being by the carelesness of a drunken Master of a Ship drowned at Sea, with a great many other Persons of Quality of both Sexes, as they were coming back from *Normandy* to *England*, he endeavoured to settle the Crown upon his Daughter *Maud*, and her Heirs, she being first married to the Emperour, *Henry* IV. by whom she had no Children, and afterwards to *Geoffery Plantagenet*, Son to *Fulk* Earl of *Anjou*. Her Father made the States of *England* take Oaths of Fealty to her in his Life-time. He died in the Year 1135, and with him ended the Male Race of the *Norman* Royal Family in *England*.

The *Norman* Race extinct.

Stephen.

§. 7. After the Death of *Henry*, *Stephen* Earl of *Boulogne*, *Henry*'s Sister's Son, did, by great Promises, obtain the Crown of *England*, notwithstanding that both he and the States had taken the Oaths to acknowledge *Maud* for their Sovereign, which they endeavour'd by a great many frivolous Pretences to prove to be of no force. The better to establish himself in the Throne, he gained the Affection of the States with Presents, and discharged the People of several Taxes, giving Authority to the Nobility to build fortify'd Castles, which afterwards prov'd very mischievous to him. He also married his Son *Eustace* to *Constantia*, the Daughter of *Ludovicus Crassus*, King of *France*. This King's Reign was clouded with continual Troubles. For the *Scots* at first, and afterwards a great many of his Nobles, confiding in their strong Castles, rais'd great Disturbances; yet he check'd the Insolence of the *Scots*, in giving them a signal overthrow. But his greatest Contest was with the Empress *Maud*, for she landing in *England* was received by a great many, and King *Stephen* in a Battle fought near *Chester*, was taken Prisoner. But she refusing to restore to the *Londoners*, King *Edward*'s Laws, they sided with her Enemies, and besieg'd her very closely in the City of *Oxford*, from whence

Maud makes War on him.

whence she narrowly escaped; and at the same time King *Stephen* got out of Prison. These Troubles continued till *Henry*, Son of *Maud*, came to the Nineteenth Year of his Age, who, being Lord of four large Dominions, as having inherited *Anjou* by his Father's, *Normandy* by his Mother's side, *Guienne* and *Poictou* by his Wife *Eleonora*, Daughter and Heiress of *William*, the last Duke of *Guienne*, he also endeavoured to obtain the Crown of *England*; for which Purpose he landed with an Army in *England*; and obtained his End without any great Opposition; for *Eustace*, King *Stephen*'s Son dying suddenly, an Agreement was made betwixt them, in which *Stephen* adopted him, and constituted him his Heir and Successor; and died not long after in the Year 1154. Thus *Henry* II. succeeded him, who, among other memorable Actions, demolished such fortified Castles of the Nobility and Bishops, as were built with Consent of King *Stephen*. After he had reigned near Eighteen Years in Peace and Quietness, he had a mind to have his Son *Henry* Crown'd, the better to secure the Succession, as Copartner with him in the Government; but he being married to *Margaret*, the Daughter of *Lewis* the younger King of *France*, this proved the Cause of great Disturbances afterwards. For some persuaded young *Henry*, That his Father having himself abdicated the Government, had by so doing committed the same to his Management. *France* envy'd that a King of *England* should have such vast Possessions in *France*; The *Scots* wish'd for nothing more, than to have an opportunity of committing Depredations in *England*. Wherefore the *French* and *Scots*, joining with young *Henry*, fell upon *Henry* II. all at one time, but were as vigorously repulsed by him; a Peace was concluded with *France*; *Adela*, Daughter of *Lewis* King of *France*, being promised in Marriage to *Richard*, second Son of *Henry*. But the old King opposed the Consummation of the Marriage betwixt her and his Son *Richard*. This so exasperated *Richard*, who, after the Death of his eldest Brother *Henry*, was now the next Heir to the Crown, that he made Head against his Father; and *Philip Augustus*, King of *France*, taking hold of this Opportunity, took the City of *Mons*. King *Henry* seeing himself, deserted by his Friends, Wife, and Children, died in a few Days of Grief. This *Henry* conquered *Ireland*, and united it to *England*, which he and his Successors governed under the Title of Lord's of *Ireland*,

Henry II.

His Son, with the *French* and *Scots* join in a War against him.

1189.

Ireland conquered.

Ireland, till the Time of *Henry* VIII. who after he had withdrawn himself from the Obedience of the Pope, to nettle him the more, assumed the Title of King of *Ireland*, because the Pope pretends to the sole right to bestow the Title of King in Christendom; wherefore the Pope, afterwards, to make his Pretence the more plausible, freely gave the same Title to *Mary* Queen of *England*. The same *Henry* had some Differences with *Thomas Becket* Archbishop of *Canterbury*, who pretended it was derogatory to the Glory of God, that the Priests, according to the King's Commands, should be subject to the Civil Judicatures.

Richard I. §. 8. *Richard* I. Who succeeded his Father *Henry* in the Kingdom, did, out of Zeal, undertake an Expedition into the *Holy Land*, with 35000 Men, being accompanied by *Philip Augustus*, King of *France*. In this War he took the Island of *Cyprus*, which he gave to *Guido Lusignanus*, who in Consideration thereof resigned his Right to *Jerusalem*; and in the Year 1192, he was present at the taking of *Ptolemais*, where the Standard of Duke *Leopold* of *Austria* being set up first, he pull'd it down again, putting his own in the Place. But when they were in great hopes of gaining *Jerusalem*, *Philip* returning home engaging himself by a solemn Oath, that he would not injure *Richard* in any of his Dominions. Not long after *Hugo*, Duke of *Burgundy*, followed his Example, which greatly encouraged *Saladin*: And *Richard* understanding that the *French* were fallen into *Normandy*, he also made a Peace with *Saladin*; and taking his way by Land *incognito*, was discovered in his Journey through *Austria*, where Duke *Leopold*, remembring the Affront done to him near *Ptolemais*, took him Prisoner, and delivered him to the Emperor, who after Fifteen Months Imprisonment, made him pay 100000 Pounds for his Ransom. Upon his return home, he found every thing in Confusion, the *French* having ravaged *Normandy*, and other Provinces belonging to him, his Brother had rais'd a Pretension to the Crown; but he oblig'd the latter to implore his Pardon, and beat the *French* back into their own Country. He died not long after, of a wound which he received in a Siege of some inconsiderable place in *France*. After his Death his Brother *John* took upon him the Crown of *England*, who was opposed by *Arthur* Earl of *Lesser Britany*, his elder Brother's Son; who

[Margin notes: He makes an Expedition into the *Holy Land*. — In his return he is taken Prisoner. — 1199. — *John*. His Nephew *Arthur* opposes him.]

who finding himself alone not strong enough, implor'd the Aid of the King of *France*, who was ready upon all Occasions to create Troubles in *England*. He took a great many Cities in *Normandy* and *Anjou*. Upon which King *John* was oblig'd to make a dishonourable Peace with him, giving in Marriage, to *Lewis*, King *Philip's* Son, *Blanch* Daughter of *Alfonsus*, King of *Castile*, and of his Sister *Eleonora*, to whom he gave as a Dowry, all the Cities which *Philip* had taken from him, except *Angiers*. Then he married *Isabella*, Daughter and Heiress of the Earl of *Angoulesme*, who was promised before to *Hugh* Earl of *Marche*. He, to revenge this Affront, join'd his Forces with the King of *France* and Prince *Arthur* of *Britany*, and fell into *Touraine* and *Anjou*. But King *John* falling upon him unawares, routed the Enemy, and took Prince *Arthur* Prisoner, who died not long after in Prison at *Roan*. But *Constantia*, the Mother of *Arthur*, address'd her Complaint to *Philip* King of *France*, whose Vassal King *John* was, on the score of such Provinces, as he was possess'd of in *France*; and thereupon the King of *France* summon'd King *John* to appear before him, and to answer for the Death of *Arthur*. But he not appearing, it was declar'd, that King *John* had forfeited what Fiefs he was possess'd of in *France*, and King *Philip* took from him *Normandy*, 316 Years after *Rollo* the *Norman* had conquer'd it. After that, the *French* attack'd also *Angiers*, where they were repulsed with great loss by King *John*, and thereupon a Truce was concluded betwixt them for two Years: During which time he routed the *Scots*, and suppressed the Rebels in *Ireland* and *Wales*. The Truce being expired, the War began afresh with *France*, and King *John's* Army being routed, he made another Truce with *France*. But this ill success had much diminished his Authority among his Nobles, who also hated him, because he had imposed heavy Taxes upon them; in resentment of which, they with joint Consent, demanded from him the Restitution of their ancient Privileges; but perceiving, that he only intended to give them fair Words for Deeds, they called to their Aid, *Lewis*, Son of *Philip* King of *France*, who landing with a great Army in *England*, was received with a general applause, and whilst King *John* endeavour'd to make Head against him, he died overwhelm'd with Care and Calamity.

The King of France dispossesses him of Normandy.

The Dauphin invited by the Barons, invades England.

1216.

§. 9.

Henry III.

§. 9. To him succeeded his Son *Henry* III. whose tender Age wrought Compassion on most, and extinguish'd the Hatred which had been conceived against his Father: And the Earl of *Pembroke*, to whose Tuition he was committed, having totally routed the *French* near *Lincoln*, and destroyed the *French* Forces at Sea, that were sent to their Assistance, *Lewis* renounced all his Pretensions to the Crown of *England*, and retir'd to *France*. This King's Reign was very long, and withal very troublesome, which was occasion'd chiefly by the great Concourse of Foreigners into *England*, who crept into all Places of Profit: For the Pope sent at one time 300 *Italians*, who being admitted into Church Benefices, did so lay about them, that their yearly Rents amounted to 60000 Marks of Silver, which was a greater Revenue than the Crown had at that time. And by reason of the Prodigality of the King, tho' he constantly burthen'd the People with Taxes, he was always in great want of Money. Add to this, that he married the Daughter of the Earl of *Provence*, who having abundance of poor Kindred, they enrich'd themselves out of the Treasury of the King. This caused, at last, an open War betwixt the King and the principal Men of the Kingdom, in which *Henry* resign'd to the King of *France*, all his Pretensions upon *Normandy*, *Anjou*, *Poictou*, *Touraine* and *Mons*, in Consideration of the Sum of 300000 Pounds paid him by the *French* King, and was himself taken Prisoner in the first Battle: But his Son, Prince *Edward*, gather'd another Army, and kill'd the General of the Rebels, *Simon Manfort* Earl of *Leicester*, by which means he rescued his Father; and suppressed the whole Rebellion. He did nothing worth mentioning abroad, except that he undertook two Expeditions into *France*, both which proved fruitless. He died in the Year 1273, and was succeeded by his Son *Edward*, who was at that time in the *Holy Land*; and tho' he did not come into *England* till a Year after his Father's Death, yet he took quiet Possession of the Crown. This King entirely united the Principality of *Wales* to the Crown of *England*, *Lyonel*, the last Prince of the former being slain in a Battle. Under his Reign also began a bloody War, and an implacable hatred was raised betwixt the *English* and *Scotch* Nations, which for 300 Years after caused abundance of Bloodshed betwixt both Nations. The occasion was thus: After the

The *Dauphin* is forced home again.

A War with the Barons.

He quits his Pretensions on *Normandy* for a sum of Money.

Edward I.

Death

Death of *Alexander* III. King of *Scotland*, who died without Heirs, there were several that pretended to the Crown of *Scotland*, wherefore King *Edward* took upon him the Arbitration of this Matter, and *John Baliol* Earl of *Galloway*, and *Robert Bruce*, were found to have the best Title to that Crown. But these two having contested for the same during the space of Six whole Years, *Edward* sent underhand to *Bruce*, telling him, That he would decide the Difference concerning the Crown of *Scotland* in favour of him, if he would swear Fealty to *England*, which *Bruce* refused. But *John Baliol* receiving the offer, was made King of *Scotland*. There was about that Time a capital Quarrel in *Scotland*, betwixt the Earl of *Fife* and the Family of *Albernethy*, who had kill'd the Earl's Brother, and *Baliol* King of *Scotland* had by Sentence absolved the latter. The Earl, therefore, appeal'd to the *English* Court, whither King *Baliol* was call'd to appear, and to sit with the King in Parliament: But as soon as this matter came under debate, *Baliol* was ordered to rise from his Seat, and to give an Account of what Sentence he had past. He pretended to answer by his Advocate, which being denied him, he was obliged to answer in Person from the same Place, where others used to plead their Causes: And this, both he and the *Scots* resented as so signal an Affront, that, no sooner was he returned home, but he renounced his Oath to King *Edward*, pretending the same to have been unjust, and that it was not in his Power to make such a Promise; and renewing the ancient Alliance with *France*, he denounced War against *England*. King *Edward*, thereupon, entered *Scotland* with an Army, took the best strong Holds, and forced the *Scots* and their King to swear Fealty to him; their King he sent a Prisoner into *England*, leaving a considerable Force in *Scotland*, which were, soon after beaten out of *Scotland* by the *Scots*, under the Conduct of a Gentleman of mean Fortune, whose Name was *William Wallis*. But King *Edward* soon returned, killed 40000 *Scots* in a Battle near *Torkirke*, and forced them to swear Fealty to him a third Time. Notwithstanding all these Oaths, *Robert Bruce*, who had been *John Baliol*'s Competitor, took upon him the Crown; King *Edward* had also had some Difference before with *France*. For some of his Subjects in *Aquitain*, having done considerable mischief by Privateering on the Coast of *Normandy*, King *Philip* Sirnam'd *the Handsome*, summoned *Edward* to ap-

The Causes of the Differences betwixt the *English* and *Scots*.

A War with *Scotland*.

1307.

appear at his Court as his Vassal, and to answer the [...] which *Edward* refusing to do, he declared all his Poss[...]ons that he held of the Crown of *France* to be forfeit[...] taking from him by force of Arms *Bourdeaux* and some [o]ther Places; against whom *Edward* enter'd into a Con[fe]deracy with the Earl of *Flanders* and the Emperor *A[dol]phus*. But coming into *Flanders* with an Army, and fin[d]ing every thing in Confusion and Disorder, he made Truce with King *Philip*, promising, That his Son *Edw[ard]* should marry *Isabella*, *Philip*'s Daughter.

With *France*.

Edward II. §. 10. To him succeeded his Son *Edward* II. who [in] the very beginning of his Reign, married *Isabella* Daugh[ter] of *Philip* Sirnamed *the Handsome*, with whom he had fo[r] Dowry *Guienne*, and the County of *Ponthieu*, the great[est] part whereof had been taken from his Father by [the] *French*. This King was very unfortunate in his Wars [a]gainst the *Scots*, and the *English* were continually beat[en] by them (except in *Ireland*, where they beat the *Scots* [who] had entred that Kingdom) so that *Edward* was [at] last obliged to make a Truce with them. He met [also] with great Disturbances at home, the great Men of [the] Kingdom pressing him without Intermission, to leave [to] their Mercy, his Favourites *Gaveston*, and after him, [the] *Spencers*, which he refusing to Consent to, they fell [into] open Rebellion, and proving unsuccessful, several of [the] Nobility paid with their Lives for it. But the Queen [pre]tending that the *Spencers* had alienated the King's [Love] from her, retir'd first into *France*, and from thence [into] *Hainault*, and returning with an Army, took the King [Pri]soner, and caused the *Spencers* to be executed. The [King] was carry'd from Place to Place, and heavily abus'd [du]ring his Imprisonment, having been forced before by [a] Parliament, to resign the Kingdom to his Son *Edward*. [At] last about six Months after his Deposition, he was mis[era]bly murther'd.

Unsuccessful in his War with *Scotland*.

His Troubles at home.

Edward III. §. 11. *Edward* III. was very young when the Cro[wn] was conferr'd upon him, so that the Administration of [the] Government, was, during his Minority, committed to [his] Mother, and managed under her chiefly by her Favou[rite] *Roger Mortimer*. At the very beginning of her Admi[ni]stration, she made a dishonourable Peace with *Scotla[nd]* whereby *Edward* renounc'd the Sovereignty and all [his]

Pre[...]

tensions upon that Kingdom; and the *Scots* renounced eir Title to *Cumberland* and *Northumberland*. This and me other matters laid to their Charge, was the reason hy, some Years after, the Queen was condemned to a rpetual Imprisonment, and *Mortimer* was hang'd. Af- rwards a most cruel War broke out betwixt *England* d *France*; for *Lewis*, *Philip* and *Charles*, all three Sons *Philip*, sirnamed the *Handsome*, dying without Issue, *dward* pretended a Right to the *French* Crown, as being e late King's Sister's Son; alledging, That if his Mother, being a Woman, might be thought incapable of go- erning the Realm, the same ought not to be prejudicial him, as being a Man. But *Philip de Valois*, notwith- anding he was a degree farther off, as being the late ing's Father's Brother's Son, prevailed with the States, ho under pretence of the *Salick* Law, and out of the ha- ed they bore to a Foreign Sovereign, as well as their re- ard to the Solicitations of *Robert* Earl of *Artois*, set him pon the Throne. *Edward* being afterwards summon'd y *Philip* to come in Person, and to do Homage for the ukedom of *Aquitain*, went thither in Person, at a time hen he was but young, and *England* full of intestine ommotions, notwithstanding this seemed to be very rejudicial to his Pretensions: And King *Edward* appear- ig in the Church at *Amiens* with the Crown upon his lead, his Sword and Spurs on, was ordered to lay them side, and to take the Oath upon his Knees; which so xasperated *Edward*, that *France* afterwards felt the Effects f it. Not long after, *Edward Baliol*, Son of *John Baliol*, nade Pretensions to the Crown of *Scotland* against the oung King, being assisted by King *Edward*, notwith- anding King *David* of *Scotland* had married his Sister. During which Commotions the *English* recovered *Berwick* pon *Tweed*, and in one Battle killed 30000 *Scots*; where- pon *Edward Baliol* did Homage to the King of *England* or the Crown of *Scotland*. By this time King *Edward* eing come to his riper Years, upon the Instigation of *Ro- ert* Earl of *Artois*, undertook an Expedition into *France*, nd taking upon him the Title and Arms of *France*, re- ewed his Pretensions to that Crown. In this Expedition e entirely routed the *French* Fleet near *Sluys*, which was ent to hinder his Landing, and kill'd 30000 Marines. And after he had besieged *Tournay*, he made a Truce with hem for Twelve Months. In the mean while the *English* 1340.

His Pretensions to the *French* Crown.

He is successful against *Scotland*.

His Expedition into *France*.

were engaged in a War with the *Scots*; who, under t
Conduct of their former King *David*, had driven out
ward Baliol. The Truce being expir'd, the War began
fresh in *France*, where, among other Places, the *Eng*
took *Angoulesme*. King *Edward* himself came with a gr
Army into *Normandy*, and took, both there, and in *Pic*
The Battle near *Crecy*. *dy*, a great many Places from the *French*. At last a blo
Battle was fought betwixt them near *Crecy* in *Picar*
wherein the *English*, tho' but 30000 strong, fought aga
60000 *French*, killing 30000 upon the spot, among wh
were 1500 Persons of Quality. The next Day after 70
French were cut to pieces by the *English*, who, not kno
1346. ing what had happened the Day before, were upon th
March to the *French* Camp. In this Battle no Quar
was given on either side. Much about the same ti
King *David* of *Scotland* entered *England* with an Army
60000 Men, to make a Diversion in behalf of *France*; b
The *Scotch* defeated. he was defeated in a great Battle, and himself taken Pris
ner. The *English* had no less success the same Year
Britany and *Guienne*. In the next Year King *Edward* to
He takes *Calais*. the City of *Calais*, which he filled with *English* Inhabita
Prince *Edward*, Son to *Edward* III. whom his Father h
sent with an Army into *Guienne*, behaved himself very
1356. liantly, making great slaughter where-ever he came. Th
King of *France* drew out an Army against him of 600
Men, tho' the Prince was not above 8000 strong; a
upon this the King thinking he had catch'd the Bird in t
Net, would not accept of any Conditions, tho' never
advantageous. But Prince *Edward* having posted his M
betwixt Woods and hilly Vineyards, from thence so gall
the *French* Horse with his long Bows, that they being r
pulsed, put all the rest in Confusion; King *John* hims
was taken Prisoner, as also his youngest Son, and abo
The Battle near *Poictiers*. 1700 Persons of Quality were slain. This Battle w
fought about two Leagues from *Poictiers*. At last, af
King *Edward* had with three Armies over-run the great
A dishonourable Peace to *France*. part of *France*, a Peace was concluded by the Mediati
of the Pope, at *Bretagny*, not far from *Chartres*: The Co
ditions of this Peace were, That *England*, besides wha
had before in *France*, should be put in Possession of *Po*
ctou, *Zaintogne*, *Rochelle*, *Pais d' Aulnis*, *Angoumois*, *Per*
gord, *Limoisin*, *Quercy*, *Angenois*, and *Bigorre*, with an a
solute Sovereignty over the same; That the City of *Cala*
the Counties of *Oye*, *Guisnes* and *Ponthieu*, and three Mi
lio

ons of Crowns should be given as a Ransom for the King; nd that King *John* should give his three younger Sons, is Brother, and thirty other Persons of Quality, as Hoages, for the payment of the said Sums. But that on the ther side, the *English* should restore all the other Places which they had taken from the *French*, and renounce their Right and Title to the Crown of *France*. The Peace beng thus concluded, Prince *Edward*, to whom his Father ad given the Dukedom of *Aquitain*, restored *Peter* King f *Castile* to his Kingdom. But in his Journey, the Soliers being very mutinous for want of Pay, he levy'd an xtraordinary Tax upon his Subjects, which they comlaining of to the King of *France*, he summoned the Prince o appear before him; who answered, He would suddenly ppear with an Army of 60000 Men; whereupon *Charles* V. King of *France*, declar'd War, pretending, that the romised Sovereignty, at the last Peace, was void, beause the Prince had not fulfilled the Articles of the same, nd had committed Hostilities against *France*. But whilst rince *Edward* was busie in making great Preparations aainst *France*, he died suddenly, and with him, the *English* good Fortune; for the *French* took from them all the Dukedom of *Aquitain*, except *Bourdeaux* and *Bayonne*. The King was so troubled at the loss both of so brave a on and his Conquests in *France*, that he died within Ten Months after his Son.

Another War with *France*.

1377.

§. 12. To him succeeded *Richard* II. Son of that brave Prince *Edward*, and being but Eleven Years of Age when e came to the Crown, was despised by the *French*, who urnt several Places on the *English* Coast. At the same me the *Scots* made an Inrode into *England*, and the War eing carried on with various Fortune, after several Trues expired, a Peace was at last concluded. There were lso great intestine Commotions in the Kingdom under his King's Reign: For in *Kent*, and other neighbouring ounties, there was an Insurrection of the Rabble, occaioned by the Insolence of one of the Receivers of the Poll Tax: This Rabble's Intention was to have murther'd both he Nobility and Clergy, except the *Mendicant* Fryars; ut they were soon restrained by the King's Valour. However there were continual Discontents betwixt the King and the Lords, the King being resolved to rule acording to his Pleasure, and to maintain his Favourites

Richard II.

A Peace with *France*.

Troubles at home.

against the Lords, who were for removing his Favourites, and bringing his Royal Power into a more narrow Compass by the Authority of the Parliament. But tho was the King's Custom, as soon as the Parliament was dissolv'd, to reverse all that was concluded upon before, yet once the Parliament got him at an Advantage, when it forc'd him to permit most of his Favourites to be either kill'd or banish'd; and oblig'd him by an Oath to Promise, That he would administer the Government according to the Advice of his Lords. Not long after, a Conspiracy among the Lords against him was discovered, and a great many of them paid for it with their Heads. In fine, the King seemed then to have master'd his Enemies; but was, nevertheless ruin'd at last, which was occasion'd thus: *Henry* Duke of *Lancaster* accused the Duke of *Norfolk*; as if he had spoken ill of the King, and the latter giving the Lie to the former, they challenged one another, but the Duel was prevented by the King's Authority, who banished them both out of the Kingdom. *Henry* of *Lancaster* retired into *France*, and raised there a Faction against the King, by inviting all dissatisfied Persons to join him, who promised to set him on the Throne of *England*. He landed but with a few in *England*, but at a time, as King *Richard's* ill Fortune would have it, when he was in *Ireland*; and the Wind proving contrary, he could not have notice of his Enemies Arrival in *England* till six Weeks after, which gave them opportunity and leisure to strengthen their Party. The King also committed a great Errour, for that he afterwards, against his Promise, tarry'd so long in *Ireland*, which was the cause, that such Forces as were brought together by his Friends, whom he had sent before, were again dispersed before his arrival in *England*. Coming afterwards in Person into *England*, he was made Prisoner. *Henry* of *Lancaster* calling immediately hereupon a Parliament, a great many Things were objected to *Richard*, and he was declared to have forfeited the Crown. But before this Resolution was Published, he resigned of his own accord, and was not long after barbarously murthered in Prison.

The occasion of his Ruin.

Henry Duke of *Lancaster* invades *England*,

1399.

§. 13. Thus *Henry* IV. of the House of *Lancaster* came to the Crown, he being after the Deposition of King *Richard* declared King by the Parliament; tho' if the Pretensions

Henry IV. of the House of *Lancaster*.

tensions of *Henry*, together with the Power of the Parliament, be duly examined, the Title of *Henry* IV. to the Crown of *England*, will be found to have a very ill Foundation. For what some pretend, that *Edmund*, from whom the House of *Lancaster* descended, was the eldest Son of *Henry* III. and that he being very deformed, was obliged to give way to his Brother *Edward* I. is rejected as a frivolous Fable by the *English* Historians. This King laboured under great Difficulties at the beginning of his Reign, all which he at last overcame; for the Design of the *French* to restore *Richard*, ended with his Death. And a Conspiracy of some Lords against him was discovered, even before *Richard* died. The *Scots*, who made War on him, got nothing but Blows. The *Welshmen* also, in hopes of having met with an opportunity to shake off the *English* Yoke, joined with a discontented Party out of *England*, and rebelled against him; but before they could join all their Forces, the King came suddenly upon them, and routed them in a bloody Battle, wherein, 'tis said, the King kill'd six and thirty with his own Hands. Yet the discontented Party did not rest, but entered into a third Conspiracy against him, which was soon discovered. A great many of them retired afterwards into *Scotland*, where they stirred up the *Scots* against *England*, but they got nothing but Blows again for their Pains. This King died in the Year 1413.

He had great Difficulties, which he surmounted.

§. 14. After him reigned his Son *Henry* V. who in his younger Years did not Promise much; but after he came to the Crown, shew'd himself one of the most valiant Kings the *English* ever had. And as he was very aspiring and ambitious, so he thought he could not meet with a better opportunity of gaining Glory, than by entring into a War with *France*, and reviving the ancient Pretensions upon that Crown. Accordingly he sent his Ambassadors to *Charles* VI. to lay claim to that Crown, and to make this Proposal to him, That if he would resign to him the Crown of *France*, he would marry his Daughter *Catharine*. But it being an unusual thing for Princes to part with a Crown so tamely, the next way was to try their Fortune by Arms. So *Henry* entered *France* with an Army, took *Harfleur*, and obtained afterwards a most signal Victory near *Agincourt* in *Picardy* against the *French*, who (according to the

Henry V.

He invades *France* to prosecute his Claim of the Crown.
The Battle near *Agincourt.*

English Historians) were six times stronger than the *English.* Ten Thousand of the *French* were killed upon the Spot, as many taken Prisoners, and not above some Hundreds slain of the *English*: Yet at that time *Henry* did not pursue his Victory. But not long after, the *French* Fleet being first beaten by the *English* near *Harfleur*, *Henry* made a second Descent upon *France*, taking one place after another in *Normandy*, and at last the City of *Roan* it self:

1419. He met with very little opposition in *France* at that time, because all was in confusion at the *French* Court, the King, *Charles* VI. being not in his right Wits, and the Queen being fallen out with her Son, the Dauphin, who had taken from her all her Jewels and Money, alledging, That they might be better employ'd upon the Soldiery: Which was the reason that the Queen siding with *John* Duke of *Burgundy*, promoted him to the place of chief Minister of *France*; and he was more intent to maintain his private Interest and Greatness, against the Dauphin, than to make Head against the *English*. An Interview was proposed to be held betwixt the two Kings, but the effect of it was frustrated by the cunning of the Dauphin, who gave the Duke hopes of an entire Reconciliation betwixt them two. For *Monterau* being named for the place where the Duke and the Dauphin should meet, the Duke of *Burgundy* was there (questionless, by instigation of the Dauphin) miserably murther'd. Thereupon his Son, Duke *Philip*, being resolv'd to revenge his Fathers Death, declared openly for the *English*. and by his Mediation obtain'd, That King *Henry* should marry the Princess *Catharine*, and during the life of his Wife's Father, administer the Government in his name, but after his death, should succeed him in the Throne. The

1420. Nuptials were afterwards celebrated at *Troyes* in *Champaigne*, After the Treaty had been confirm'd by solemn Oaths on both sides, it was also ratified by the three Estates assembled in *Paris*, where the Dauphin was summoned to appear, to answer concerning the death of the Duke of *Burgundy*: But he not appearing, Sentence was given against him, that he should for ever be banished out of *France*. There were at that time some who design'd to make him away, and he was forced to go from place to place, but his common place of Residence was *Bourges*, upon which they us'd to call him, by way of ridicule, *The King of* Bourges. In the mean time the *English* took one place after another from him. At

The Administration of *France* to be in *Henry* during *Charles's* life, and after his death the Crown to descend to him.

t last, King *Henry* being upon his March to raise the Siege f the City of *Cosne* on the *Loire*, which was then besieged y the *Dauphine*, fell sick in his Journey thither, and being arry'd to *Bois de Vicennes*, there died in the flower of his Age 1422. nd Felicity, leaving the Administration of *France* to his rother the Duke of *Bedford*, and the Administration of *ngland* to his second Brother, the Duke of *Gloucester*.

§ 15. To him succeeded his Son *Henry* VI. a Child of *Henry* VI. ight Months old; who, after he was grown up, degene- ated from his Fathers Martial Valour, and by his ill ma- agement, lost what his Father had got, eclipsing thereby he *English* Glory. He was after the Death of *Charles* VI. who died not long after *Henry* V. proclaimed King of *France* Proclaim'd n *Paris*. In opposition to him, the Dauphin, *Charles* VII. King of lso declared himself King of *France*; with whom sided *France*. he bravest among the *French*, and a great many *Scots* were ent to his assistance. But *Philip* Duke of *Burgundy*, and *ohn* Duke of *Britany*, kept to the Confederacy with the *nglish*, which was renewed at that time. And then they egan to fall upon one another with great Fury: For the *rench* received a signal Defeat near *Crevant* in *Burgundy*, nd were again soundly beaten near *Verneuil*. In the Year 1425 the *French* besieged St. *Jaques de Beuveron* with Forty 1422. housand Men; and the Garrison being reduced to great 1424. extremity, prayed with a loud Voice to St. *George* of *Salis- bury*: Upon which the Besiegers hearing the name of *Salis- bury* very frequently among the Besieged, suppos'd that the Earl of *Salisbury* was coming to raise the Siege; whereat the *French* were so terrify'd, that they run away for fear of his Name. This is certain, that the *English* for a while were Masters wherever they came; but before *Orleans* the career of their Fortune was first stopp'd. For, though du- ring that Siege they beat the *French*, who came to cut off their Provisions, (which Battle is commonly call'd, *The Battle of the* Flemmings) and the City would have surren- der'd it self to the Duke of *Burgundy*, which the *English* would not accept of; yet they not only lost in that Siege the brave Earl of *Salisbury*, but were beaten from before the place by the *French*, who were animated and encouraged The Maid of by a Maid called *Joan*, that was born in *Lorrain*. This *Orleans*. Maid did several great Exploits against the *English*, and led her self in Person, King *Charles* to his Coronation in *Rheims*. At last she was taken Prisoner by the *English* in

an

an Encounter, who carried her to *Roan*, where they burnt her for a Witch. However the *English* perceiving that after the Coronation of *Charles*, a great many Cities sided with him, they called over their King *Henry* out of *England*, and crowned him King of *France* in *Paris*. About the same time a Truce was concluded by Mediation of the Pope, for six Years, but it lasted not long; for the *French*, during the time of the Truce, possess'd themselves of several places, which they brought over to their side by cunning Insinuations, pretending That any thing gained without open violence, did not violate the Truce. And King *Charles*'s Maxim was, *Not to fight with the* English, *but to strive to get Advantages over them rather by Policy than open force*. But that which gave a great blow to the *English*, was, That the Duke of *Burgundy* having taken a distaste at the *English* upon some slight occasion, was reconcil'd to King *Charles*. For the purpose, there were some small Differences arisen betwixt the Duke of *Bedford*, and the Duke of *Burgundy*; to compose which, a meeting was appointed at St. *Omer*: But the time being near at hand, a Dispute arose, which of them should appear there first, it being supposed, that he who should come first, did thereby yield the Precedency to the other; wherefore the Duke of *Bedford* refused to come first, alledging, That he being Regent of *France*, ought not in that Quality to give preference to a Vassal of *France*. But the Duke of *Burgundy* stood upon his right of being Sovereign of the place where they were to meet; so that the meeting being set aside, the Duke of *Burgundy* broke quite off with the *English*, and afterwards assisted King *Charles* against them. The death of the Duke of *Bedford* proved another Misfortune to the *English*: For the Duke of *Somerset* and the Duke of *York*, both pretended to his Post; and tho' the latter did obtain it, yet did the first always thwart his Designs, so that before the new Regent arrived, *Paris*, which had been seventeen Years in the possession of the *English*, and a great many other Cities, surrender'd to King *Charles*. But after all, the Duke of *Gloucester* beat the Duke of *Burgundy* before *Calais*, making great havock in *Flanders*, *Artois*, and *Hainault*; and the brave *Talbot* did considerable mischief to the *French*. But when afterwards, by a Truce made with *France*, the Fury of the War ceased for a little time, there was a Foundation laid in *England* for Intestine Commotions. The King had promised Marriage to the Daughter of the Earl of *Armagnac*,

1432. He was Crowned in *Paris*.

The *English* decline in *France*.

The Duke of *Burgundy* leaves the *English* and is reconcil'd to *Charles*.

1435.

1436.

The occasion of the Troubles in *England*.

nac, to prevent which, the French King had made both the Earl and his Daughter Prisoners. The Earl of Suffolk, who was then Ambassador in France, did propose thereupon, without having received any Instructions to that purpose from the King, a Match betwixt the King and Margaret Daughter of Rene, Duke of Anjou, and King of Naples and Sicily, and afterwards persuaded the King to ratifie the same. This Match was mightily opposed by the Duke of Glocester, the King's Uncle, who alledged, That her Father had only the bare Titles of King and Duke, and that besides this, great Injury was done thereby to the first Bride, viz. to the Daughter of the Count of Armagnac. Notwithstanding this, the Match went forward, and to obtain the Bride of the French, Anjou and Maine were given them as a Recompence. The King being thus led away by the Queen and his Favourites, her first design was to revenge her self upon the Duke of Gloucester, whom she accused of Male-Administration, and after she had got him committed to Prison, caused him privately to be murther'd. The death of so innocent a Man did afterwards fall heavy upon the King: For the French, not long after, took from them all Normandy, the English by reason of a Rebellion in Ireland, not being in a capacity to send thither speedy and sufficient Relief. They were also beaten out of Aquitain, so that they had nothing left them in France, but Calais, and some neighbouring Places; neither could they, afterwards, ever get footing again in France. This sudden loss was occasioned by the carelesness of the English Garrisons, that were not provided with able Governours, as also by the Pride of the English, for which they were become hateful to the French Subjects: But the chief cause was, Richard Duke of York, who had underhand raised intestine Commotions in England: For he being sensible of the King's Weakness, and how ill satisfy'd the People were with the Queen's Management of Affairs, hoped, by fomenting and raising Troubles in the Kingdom, to make way for himself to obtain the Crown; and this he did, because he had the best right to the Crown, being descended by his Mother's side, from Lionel Duke of Clarence, third Son of King Edward III. whereas Henry was descended from John of Gaunt, fourth Son of the said Edward III. but publickly he profess'd, That his Intention was only to remove from the King's Person his pernicious Favourites, and especially the Duke of Somerset. Having therefore got an Army on Foot, he fought with

1449. The English driven out of France.

The occasion of this sudden loss.

with the King's Forces, in which Battle the Duke of *Somorset* was slain, and the Duke of *York* was thereupon declared Protector of the King's Person and the Kingdom. But this Agreement did not last long, for things came quickly again to an open War, wherein the Duke of *York* being worsted, was forc'd to fly into *Ireland*. But not long after the Earl of *Warwick* beat the King's Army, and taking him Prisoner, the Duke of *York* was again declared Protector of the King and Kingdom, and lawful Heir of the Crown; upon condition that *Henry* should retain the Title of King during his Life. But Matters did not remain long in this condition: for the Queen, who was fled into *Scotland*, marched with a great Army against the Duke of *York*, who was kill'd in the Battle, and all the Prisoners were put to the Sword. But his Son, in conjunction with the Earl of *Warwick*, raised another Army, and marching up to *London*, the young Duke of *York* was there proclaimed King 1466. by the Name of *Edward* IV.

Edward IV. of the House of *York*.

§. 16. Thus *Edward* IV. came to the Crown, but could not maintain it without great difficulty: For *Henry* had got together a very powerful Army in the *North*, against whom *Edward* fought the most bloody Battle that was ever fought in *England*, there being 36796 Men killed upon the spot, because *Edward* knowing his Enemies to be superiour in number, had order'd, not to give Quarter to any of them: After which Battle *Henry* retir'd into *Scotland*, from whence he returned with another Army, and being again defeated, with much ado got safely into *Scotland*. But returning again incognito into *England*, he was taken Prisoner and committed to the *Tower*. This Prince would have made a better Priest than a King of such a Nation, that was distracted by the Animosities of several Factions. But the Tragedy did not end here: The King had sent the Earl of *Warwick* into *France* to conclude a Match betwixt him, and *Bona* the Daughter of *Lewis* Duke of *Savoy*. But the King having in the mean time suddenly married *Elizabeth*, the Widow of *John Gray*; the Earl was so dissatisfy'd at it, that he declared for King *Henry*; and having brought over to his Party the Duke of *Clarence*, the Brother of King *Edward*, he fell on a sudden upon *Edward*, and took him Prisoner; but by the carelesness of his Keepers he escaped not long after. And tho' an Agreement was then made betwixt them, yet was it of no long continuance; for the

A bloody Battle betwixt *Edward* and *Henry*.

Earl

Earl of *Warwick*'s Forces were routed soon after, and he forced to fly into *France*. As soon as he had recovered himself a little, he returned into *England*, where he was so well received, that he forced King *Edward* to fly into the *Netherlands* to *Charles* Duke of *Burgundy*: And King *Henry*, after he had been nine Years a Prisoner in the *Tower*, was again set upon the Throne. But *Edward* having received some Assistance from the Duke of *Burgundy*, returned again into *England*; and perceiving that but few came in to him, he made an Agreement with King *Henry*, which he confirm'd with a solemn Oath, That he would not undertake any thing against him, but be contented with his own Estate: Yet notwithstanding his Oath, he underhand gathered what Forces he could. Upon which, the Earl of *Warwick* marched towards him; but the Duke of *Clarence*, being reconciled to his Brother King *Edward*, went over with all his Forces to him. This gave a signal blow to the Earl of *Warwick*, who being now not strong enough to oppose him, was forced to let him march up to *London*, where he was joyfully received by the *Londoners*, to whom, as 'tis said, he owed much Money, and was very acceptable to their Wives; but King *Henry* was committed again to the *Tower*. Then King *Edward* attack'd the Earl of *Warwick*, where a bloody Battle was fought, the Victory seeming, at first, to incline on the Earl's side: But some of the Earl's Troops, by reason of a thick Fogg, charg'd one upon another, which lost him the Battle, he remaining, with a great many other Persons of Quality, slain in the Field. There happened also this misfortune, that King *Henry*'s Lady and his Son *Edward*, having got together very considerable Forces in *France*, could not come time enough to his assistance, as being detain'd by contrary Winds; and coming afterwards into *England*, she was taken Prisoner, and her Son kill'd; and King *Henry* himself was murthered by the hand of the bloody Duke of *Gloucester*. *England* being thus restor'd to its Tranquility at home, *Charles*, Duke of *Burgundy*, who was in hopes of reaping Advantage by a War betwixt *England* and *France*, stirr'd up King *Edward* against *Lewis* XI. King of *France*. But King *Lewis*, who was not ignorant how mischievous the Confederacy of *England* and *Burgundy* might prove to him, endeavour'd to soften the *English* King with fair Words, and to render the Duke of *Burgundy* suspected to him, which had the design'd effect with *Edward*, who considered

Henry taken out of Prison and set on the Throne.

Edward returns into *England*.

Henry a second time Prisoner, 1471, and murther'd by the Duke of *Gloucester*.

sidered with himself, That *Charles* Duke of *Burgundy* had not sent him the promised Succours for the Siege of *Nuys*: So that the Peace was easily concluded, the *French* making very liberal Presents to the *English*. To confirm this Peace, King *Lewis* proposed an Interview betwixt him and *Edward* at a certain place, where he, without making any further difficulty, appeared first in Person, and bestowed a good quantity of Wine upon the *English* Soldiers. And so *Edward* made an inglorious return to *England*, leaving the Duke of *Burgundy* to fret in vain. But he behaved himself better against the *Scots*, to whom he did considerable mischief. In the mean time the Duke of *Gloucester* had rid himself of his elder Brother, the Duke of *Clarence*, with intent to advance himself one step nearer to the Crown. At last King *Edward* being now resolved to enter again into a War with *France* (since King *Lewis* made a very slight account of what he had promised in the last Peace, after he was once rid of his Enemy) he fell sick, and died in the Year 1483.

Edward V. § 17. After the death of *Edward* IV. his Son *Edward* V. a Child of eleven Years of Age was proclaimed King, but scarce enjoyed this Title ten Weeks. For his Uncle *Richard*, Duke of *Gloucester*, the most bloody and wicked Man that ever the World beheld, immediately made it his business to set the Crown upon his own Head. With this view, he first of all secured to himself the Tuition of the King's and his Brother's Persons, by making away their most trusty Friends. Afterwards, by the help of some impudent Priests, he got it spread abroad, That *Edward* IV. was born in Adultery, and that consequently the Crown did of right belong to himself, as being the most like his Father. At last, the Duke of *Buckingham* insinuated to the Lord Mayor of *London*, That the Crown ought to be offered to *Richard*; and his Proposal being approved by the Acclamations of a few Villains set on for that purpose, it was divulged, That the People had conferr'd the Crown upon *Richard*. Having by these Intrigues obtained the Crown, *Richard* III. got himself proclaimed King; and being Crowned, he caused the innocent King *Edward* V. and his Brother, to be miserably murther'd. But soon after his Coronation, a difference arose betwixt him and the Duke of *Buckingham*, who had been chiefly instrumental in helping him to the Crown. Upon which *Buckingham* leaving the Court, began to make a Party against the King, with an

Richard III.

1483. Murthers his Nephews.

an intention to set the Crown upon the Head of *Henry* Earl of *Richmond*, who was then an Exile in *Britany*. And though the Duke of *Buckingham*'s Plot was discovered, and he beheaded, yet was not the design stopt; for the Earl of *Richmond* set sail with a great Fleet out of *Britany*, but being driven by contrary Winds on the Coast of *Normandy*, he sought Aid of *Charles* VIII. King of *France*, which he readily granted him. A great many *English* also, went over and swore Allegiance to him, he promising them upon Oath, that he would marry the Princess *Elizabeth*, Daughter of *Edward* IV. But *Henry* was within an Ace of being delivered up to *Richard* by the Treachery of one *Pieter Landois*, Treasurer of the Duke of *Britany*, who had received a great Sum of Money from *Richard* for undertaking it, for which reason he was afterwards hang'd by his Master's order. *Richard* had also an intention of marrying the Princess *Elizabeth*, and therefore had privately made away his former Lady, but was obliged to delay the Consummation of the Match, by reason of the approaching danger from *Henry*: Who to prevent this intended Match, did in all hast sail out of *France*, and landing in *Wales*, was kindly received by most. Not long after he gave Battle to *Richard* at *Bosworth*, where Sir *William Stanley*, with some thousands of Men, went over to *Henry*; and *Richard* himself was slain in the Field, his Crown being immediately put upon *Henry*'s Head in the very Field of Battle, he was proclaimed King with great applause. 1485.

He murthers his Wife.

Henry Earl of *Richmond* invades *England*.

§ 18. Hitherto *England* had been miserably torn to pieces by the fatal and bloody Wars betwixt the Houses of *York* and *Lancaster*, the first whereof bore a White, the latter a Red Rose in their Shields. For *Henry* IV. of the House of *Lancaster*, drove *Richard* II. from the Throne; *Edward* IV. of the House of *York* dethroned again his Grandson *Henry* VI. And *Henry* VII. of the House of *Lancaster* took from *Edward* the IVth's Brother, *Richard* III. both his Crown and Life. This King *Henry* marrying the Daughter of *Edward* IV. united the Red and White Roses, and by his singular Wisdom, did again settle the State of the Kingdom. Yet was he not altogether free from Disturbances at home. For first of all, one *Lambert Symnel*, Son to a Baker, taking upon him the Name and Person of *Edward* Earl of *Warwick*, caused himself to be proclaimed King in *Ireland*. This Imposture was first contriv'd by a Priest,

Henry VII.

He united the White and Red Roses.

Lambert Symnel.

and encouraged by *Margaret*, the Widow of *Charles* Duke of *Burgundy*, Sister to *Edward* IV. who, to spite *Henry*, gave them all the Assistance she could. This *Symnel* transported an Army out of *Ireland* into *England*, but was routed by *Henry*; and being taken Prisoner, was made a Turnspit in the King's Kitchin. In the Year 1491, *Henry* undertook an Expedition against *France*, and besieged *Bologne*. But the Emperor *Maximilian* failing in his promises of giving him Assistance, he in consideration of a good Sum of Money, made a Peace with *France*. In the mean time, *Margaret* Dutchess Dowager of *Burgundy*, had set up another Imposture, whose Name was *Perkin Warbeck*. He pretended to be *Richard*, a younger Son of King *Edward* IV. and knew so well how to act his part, that he got a considerable Party in *Ireland*. From thence he went to *Paris*, where he was very well received, *France* being then engag'd in a War with *England*: But a Peace being concluded betwixt them, he retir'd to the Dutchess *Margaret*'s Court. From thence he returned into *Ireland*, and afterwards came into *Scotland*, where being splendidly received by that King, he was married to one of his Kinswomen, and enter'd *England* with a considerable Army. This business might have prov'd very dangerous to *England*, since there were, at the same time, great Tumults in *England*, arisen about some new Taxes. But the Rebels were beaten, and the *Scots* oblig'd to retire with great loss into *Scotland*. The *Scots* made thereupon a Peace with *England*, promising, among other things, not to uphold, by any ways, the Imposture *Perkin*, who fled from thence into *Ireland*, and so came into *Cornwall*, where he caused himself to be proclaimed King: But perceiving that few came over to his side, and the King's Forces coming upon him; he took Sanctuary in a Church, and surrender'd himself to the King, who committed him a Prisoner to the *Tower*; but he having twice made an attempt to escape, was at last hang'd according to his Demerits. In the Year 1501, a Marriage was concluded betwixt *James* IV. King of *Scotland*, and *Margaret* the Daughter of *Henry*, which afterwards united *England* and *Scotland* under one King. *Arthur* also, eldest Son of *Henry*, married *Catharine*, Daughter of *Ferdinand the Catholick*. But the Prince dying a few Weeks after the Wedding, in the sixteenth Year of his Age, and *Henry* being unwilling to give back the Dowry, and desirous to maintain the new Alliance with *Ferdinand*, married

He makes an Expedition into *France*.

Perkin Warbeck.

He marries his Daughter *Margaret* to the King of *Scotland*.

married the said *Catharine* to his second Son *Henry*, who was then but twelve Years of Age, having obtained a Dispensation for that effect from Pope *Julius* II. under pretence that there had been no carnal knowledge betwixt them; which afterwards proved the cause of great Alterations. This King is reckoned among the wisest of his Age, and the only thing which is reprehended in him, is, that he had a way, by false Accusations against the rich, to squeeze great Sums of Money from them. He died in the Year 1508.

§ 19. *Henry* VIII. Immediately upon his first accession to the Throne, celebrated the Nuptials with his Brother's Widow, more to fulfil his Father's Will, than out of his own Inclination; yet as long as he liv'd with her in Wedlock he govern'd the Realm very laudably, and in the Court nothing was seen but Plays and Diversions. As to his Transactions abroad, upon the persuasions of Pope *Julius* II. and *Ferdinand the Catholick*, he entered into a Confederacy with them against *France*, which Confederacy was pretended to be made for the Defence of the Holy See. *Ferdinand* also put him in hopes of recovering *Guienne*; and accordingly *Henry* sent an Army into *Biscay*, to fall in conjunction with the *Spaniards* into *Guienne*. But *Ferdinand* having rather his Eye upon *Navarre*, and being negligent in sending timely Succours to the *English*, they returned home without doing any thing. In the Year 1513. *Henry* entered *France* with a great Army, where he lost his time in the taking of *Terouane*, and *Tournay*; the former of which he levell'd with the Ground in spight of all the Attempts of the *French* to relieve it; and *Tournay* was redeemed by *Francis* I. with a good Sum of Money. But at that time *Henry* did not pursue his Advantage, partly out of carelesness, incident to young Men, partly, because he had carried on this War, not so much for his own Interest, as in favour of the Pope; and so returned into *England*. During the absence of *Henry*, *James* IV. King of *Scotland*, upon instigation of the *French* invaded *England*, but received a signal Defeat, himself being kill'd in the Battle. In the Year next ensuing, *Henry* perceiving that his Father-in-law *Ferdinand* did only impose upon him, concluded a Peace with *France*, giving his Sister *Mary* in marriage to King *Lewis* XII. In the Year 1522, *Henry* again denounced War against *Francis* I. and sent considerable Forces into *France*, which, nevertheless, both in the

Henry VIII.

He enters into League with *Ferdinand* and the *Pope*. 1512.

His Expedition against *France*.

A second.

An Invasion of the *Scots*.

He makes a second War against *France*.

same and the next Year did nothing of moment; and the *Scots*, on the other side, obtained not any Advantages against the *English*. But after *Francis* was taken Prisoner near *Pavia*, tho' it appeared that *Henry* had then met with a fair opportunity to give a great blow to *France*, more especially, since he had before prepared a Fleet, which lay ready to make a Descent into *Normandy*, yet he left *Charles* and made Peace with *France*. And *Charles*, after he thought he had obtained his aim, did not make any great account of *England*, leaving the Princess *Mary* Daughter of *Henry*, to whom he had promised Marriage, for the Princess of *Portugal*, whom he married. And whereas he used formerly to write to the King with his own Hand, and subscribe himself, *Your Son and Trusty Friend*; he now caused his Letters to be writ by his Secretary, subscribing only his Name, *Charles*. And truly it seem'd very necessary for *Henry* to keep a little in the Balance, and not to incline too much either to *Spain* or *France*. Tho' a great many are of opinion, that Cardinal *Woolsey* had a great Hand in this business, who was no great Friend to *Charles* V. because he had not promoted him to the Papal Dignity, and had denied him the Archbishoprick of *Toledo*, of which he put him in hopes at first; but however it be, *Henry* at that time saved *France* from an imminent danger. After he had lived very peaceably and well with his Queen for the space of Twenty Years, he began to have a scruple of Conscience, Whether he could lawfully live in Wedlock with his Brother's Widow; which Scruple he pretended was raised in him first by the President of *Paris*, who was sent to treat concerning a Marriage betwixt *Mary* Daughter of *Henry*, and the Second Son of *Francis*. Some say, that he being weary of her, was fallen in love with *Anna Bullen*, and found out this way to be rid of her. Yet this seems not so probable to some, since he did not marry the said *Anna Bullen* till three Years after he pretended to the Scruple of Conscience; whereas the heat of Love does not usually admit of such Delays. Some will have it, that Cardinal *Woolsey* rais'd this scruple first in him, on purpose to nettle *Charles* V. and to please *Francis* I. in hopes, after this Divorce, to make up the Match betwixt *Henry* and the Dutchess of *Alenson*, Sister of *Francis*. But however it be, the business was brought before the Pope, who gave a Commission to the Cardinal *Campegius*, to enquire, in Conjunction with *Woolsey*, into the matter. 'Tis said,

The Divorce of *Henry* VIII.

That

That the Pope was willing to gratifie *Henry*, and for that purpose had sent a Bull to *Campegius*, but with this Caution, to keep it by him till further order. But when he afterwards saw *Charles* V. prove so successful, he durst not venture to do any thing that might displease him, wherefore he order'd *Campegius* to burn the Bull, and to delay the Business to the utmost. The Queen also refused to answer to their Commission, but appealed to the Pope in Person; besides, *Charles* V. and his Brother *Ferdinand* had protested against this Commission. At the same time *Woolsey* perceived, that the King was fallen in love with *Anna Bullen*, which being likely to prove prejudicial to his Authority, he perswaded the Pope underhand, not to give his Consent to this Divorce. *Henry* being informed what Intrigues the Cardinal was carrying on against him, humbled the greatness of this haughty Prelate, who died in the Year next following in great Misery. And *Henry* being made sensible, that the Pope regarded more his own Interest than the Merits of the Cause, he forbid, that any Body should henceforward appeal to *Rome*, or send thither any Money for Church Benefices. He therefore sent to several Universities in *France* and *Italy* to desire their Opinions in this Matter, who all unanimously agreed in this, that such a Marriage was against the Laws of God; and having once more, by his Ambassadours, solicited the Pope, but in vain, to decide the Matter, the King had the same adjudged in Parliament, and divorced himself from her, but conversed with her in a very friendly manner ever after till her Death, bating, that he did not Bed with her from the time when this Scruple first arose. Some Months after he was married to *Anna Bullen*, by whom he had *Elizabeth*, who was afterwards Queen. *Anno* 1535 the King caused himself to be declared *Supream Head of the Church of* England, abrogating thereby all the Pope's Authority in that Kingdom, and *John Fisher* Bishop of *Rochester*, and *Thomas Moor* the Lord Chancellour, refusing to acknowledge him as such, it cost them their Heads. But after all *Henry* would never receive the Doctrine of *Luther* or *Zwinglius*, but continued in the *Roman* Communion. *Henry* had formerly published a Book under his Name against *Luther* in favour of the Pope, for which he acquired the Title of *Defender of the Faith*: Which Title the Kings of *England* retain to this Day. But *Luther* setting aside all the Respect due to a King, writ

The fall of *Woolsey*.

1532.

He marries *Anna Bullen*.

He abrogates the Pope's Supremacy.

an Answer to it, full of unmannerly Heat, and bitter Reflections. However because he esteemed the Monks as a sort of People that were not only useless, but also such as depending on the Pope, might prove very pernicious to him at home, he gave free leave to all Monks and Nuns to go out of the Convents and Nunneries; and by degrees converted unto his own use the Revenues of all the Nunneries and Convents, Colleges and Chappels, as also those of the order of the Knights of St. *John* of *Jerusalem*; tho' indeed he employed some part of them in erecting six new Episcopal Sees, and Cathedral Churches, and to the advancing of Learning in the Universities. A great part also he gave away or sold for little Money to great Families, intending thereby to oblige them for the future to maintain the alterations he had made. It is reported that these Church Revenues which were so reduced, did amount yearly to 186512 *l.* or as some others will have it, to 500752 *l.* He also abolished the superstitious Worship of Images, and made some other alterations in Religious Worship, so that, in effect, he laid the Foundation of the Reformation. Nevertheless *England* was at that time in a miserable condition; for a great many *Roman* Catholicks, that would not acknowledge the King for the Supream Head of the *English* Church were executed: And a great many more Protestants received the same Punishment, because they would not own the Corporal presence of the Body of Christ in the Sacrament; tho' this effusion of Blood was not so much caused by the King, as by the Bishops, who had first brought in use such rigorous Laws, and now executed them with as much severity. In the Year 1543, a War broke out with the *Scots*, who making an Inrode into *England* were beaten by a few *English*; which did grieve King *James* V. to that degree, that he died for trouble, leaving behind him one only Daughter *Mary*, whom *Henry* would have engaged to his Son *Edward*, in order to unite the two Kingdoms; and in effect the Business was like to have succeeded very well, if the Archbishop of St. *Andrews* had not opposed it. *Henry* also entered into a League with the Emperor against *France*, wherein it was agreed, to join their Armies of 80000 Foot, and 22000 Horse near *Paris*, to plunder that City, and to ravage the whole Country as far as the *Loire*. But neither of them acted according to the Agreement, for *Henry* wasted his time in the Siege, and taking of *Bologne*, which he after-

Monasteries demolished.

Protestants and Papists executed.

War with *Scotland*.

He enters into a League with the Emperor against *France*.

afterwards, by the Peace concluded in the Year 1546, promised to restore to *France* within the space of eight Years, in consideration of the Sum of 800000 Crowns to be paid him for the same; which was performed accordingly under *Edward* VI. Neither do I believe, that *Henry* was in good earnest by ruining the *French* to give such great advantages to *Charles* V. After his Divorce with *Catharine* of *Arragon*, he was very unfortunate in his Marriages; for *Anna Bullen* was beheaded for Adultery and Incest, tho' some are of opinion, that it was more the Protestant Religion than the Crime which proved fatal to her. It is certain, that the Protestant Princes of *Germany* did so resent this matter, that whereas they intended to have made *Henry* the Head of their League, they afterwards would hold no correspondency with him. After *Anna Bullen*, he married *Jane Seymour*, Mother to *Edward* VI. who died in Child-bed. Then he married *Anna* of *Cleves*, whom he also pretending I know not what bodily infirmity in her, quickly dismiss'd. The fifth was *Catharine Howard*, who was beheaded for Adultery. The sixth *Catharine Parre*, Widow of the Lord *Latimer*, who out-lived him. *Henry* died in the Year 1547.

1550.

Anna Bullen beheaded.

His other Wives.

§ 20. *Edward* VI. was nine Years of age when he came to the Crown, during whose Minority his Uncle the Duke of *Somerset* had the administration of Affairs. His first design was to force the *Scots* to agree to a Match betwixt *Edward* and their young Queen *Mary*, in order to which he fell into *Scotland*, and routed them near *Muscleborough* in a bloody Battle. Nevertheless he miss'd his aim, for the *Scots* sent their Queen into *France*, who was there married to the Dauphin, afterwards King of *France* by the Name of *Francis* II. Under this King *Edward* the Reformed Religion was publickly established in *England*, and the Mass quite abolished, which occasioned great Disturbances in the Kingdom, that were nevertheless happily suppress'd. In the Year 1550 there was a Peace concluded betwixt *England*, *France*, and *Scotland*; and *Boulogne* was restored to the *French*. But King *Edward* falling sick, the Duke of *Northumberland*, who had before destroyed the Duke of *Somerset*, perswaded King *Edward*, under pretence of setling the Protestant Religion, to exclude by his last Will and Testament his two Sisters, *Mary* and *Elizabeth* (for of the Queen of the *Scots* they made but little account at that

Edward VI.

time) from the Succession of the Crown, and to settle it upon *Jane Grey*, Daughter of the Duke of *Suffolk*, whom he had by *Mary* Daughter of *Henry* VII. which afterwards proved fatal both to *Jane*, and to the Author of this Project. For after the death of *Edward*, the Duke of *Northumberland* caused *Jane* to be proclaimed Queen in the City of *London*; but *Mary*, eldest Sister of *Edward*, did immediately lay claim to the Crown in her Letters to the Privy Council: And Letters proving ineffectual, they began to come to blows: But most of the Nobility, unto whom *Mary* promised not to make any alteration in Religion, did side with her; and a part of the Army and Fleet, most of the Privy Counsellours, and the City of *London*, taking her part, proclaimed her Queen. Nay, *Northumberland* himself, who knew very well how to go with the tide, did proclaim *Mary* Queen in *Cambridge*; notwithstanding which, he afterwards lost his Head.

1553. Lady *Jane Grey* proclaimed Queen.

Mary. § 21. Queen *Mary* caused the *Roman* Catholick Religion and Mass, which were abolished in her Brother's time, as also the Pope's Authority to be restored in *England*. She us'd the Protestants very hardly, of whom a great many were punished with death; but was not able to restore the Church Revenues, for fear of exasperating the greatest Families, who had them in their possession. The Pope also sent Cardinal *Poole*, to reunite the Kingdom to the Holy See of *Rome*. This Queen *Mary* was married to *Philip*, Son of *Charles* V. who was afterwards King of *Spain*, but under these Conditions, that she should have the sole disposal of all Offices and Revenues of the Kingdom; and if a Son was born, he should, besides the Crown of *England*, inherit *Burgundy* and the *Netherlands*; *Don Carlos*, who was born of a former Wife, should be Heir of *Spain* and all the *Italian* Provinces; and in case he died without Issue, this should also inherit his Part. But no Children came of this Marriage, *Mary* being pretty well in Years; for she was thirty Years before proposed in Marriage to *Charles*, *Philip*'s Father. And there were some, who being dissatisfyed at this Match, raised Tumults: Among whom was the Duke of *Suffolk*, Father of *Jane*, who had hitherto been a Prisoner in the *Tower*; but she and her Husband *Guilford*, and her Father, paid with their Heads for it. It was within an ace but that *Elizabeth*, who was afterwards Queen, had also undergone the same fate, if

Restores Popery.

Marries *Philip* of *Spain*.

Lady *Jane*, &c. beheaded.

Philip

Philip and the *Spaniards* had not interceded for her, not out of any Affection to her Person, but because they knew, that after her, the next Heir to the Crown of *England*, was *Mary* Queen of *Scotland*, who being married to the Dauphin of *France*, they feared, lest by this means *England* and *Scotland* might be united with *France*. Among other Articles in the Marriage Contract of Queen *Mary*, it was agreed, that she should not be obliged to engage her self in the Wars which her Husband, *Philip*, should carry on against *France*: Notwithstanding which, when *Philip* afterwards was engaged in a War with *France*, she sent to his Assistance some of her best Forces, who by their Bravery chiefly obtained the Victory near St. *Quintin*; for which reason *Philip* gave the City to be plundered by the *English*. *Henry* II. King of *France*, taking hold of this opportunity, assaulted the City of *Calais*, under Command of the Duke *de Guise*, which not being well Garrisoned, he took in a few days, and obliged all the Inhabitants to quit the City, and to leave behind them all their Gold, Silver, and Jewels. He also took afterwards the two Castles of *Guisnes* and *Hammes*, and so drove the *English* quite out of *France*. Not long after this Loss, Queen *Mary* died.

The reason why *Philip* interceded for the Lady *Elizabeth*.

The Battle of St. *Quintin*.

Calais lost.

1558.

§ 22. *Elizabeth*, who after the death of her Sister was unanimously proclaimed Queen, maintained her Authority, and governed with great Prudence and Glory, in the midst of a great many threatning dangers, to the very end. In the beginning *Philip* endeavoured by all means to keep *England* on his side; for which reason he proposed a Marriage betwixt *Elizabeth* and himself, promising to obtain a Dispensation from the Pope, which was nevertheless opposed by the *French* in the Court of *Rome*. *Elizabeth* was very unwilling to disoblige so great a Prince, who had well deserved of her; but on the other side, the same scruple which had caused her Father to be divorced from *Catharine* of *Arragon*, by a parity of reason, did remain with her; she considered, especially, that the said Divorce must needs be esteemed unjust, if the Pope's Dispensation was allowed of; since it had been alledged as a Fundamental Reason of the said Divorce, that the Pope had no Power to dispense in any cases which were contrary to God's Law: She resolved therefore not to have any further concerns with the Pope, and to give a friendly refusal to *Philip*. Then she, by an act of Parliament, constituted the *Prote-*

Elizabeth.

Philip desires her in Marriage.

stant Episcopacy, yet not at once, but by degrees. She took away from the *Papists* the free exercise of their Religion, and under several Penalties and Fines obliged every one to frequent the Protestant Churches on *Sunday*. Every body also was obliged by a solemn Oath to acknowledge her the Supream Governour in *England* even in Spiritual Matters; which Oath was, among 9400, who were possess'd of Church Benefices, taken by all, except 189 who refused it, and among them were fourteen Bishops. She kept stedfast to the established Episcopal Church Government, tho' she met with great opposition from two sorts of People, *viz. Papists* and *Puritans*. The latter having conceived a great hatred against Episcopacy, and all other Ceremonies which had the least resemblance of Popery, were for having every thing regulated according to the model of *Geneva*. Tho' their number increased daily, yet the Queen kept them pretty well under. But the *Papists* made several attempts against her Life and Crown; for her envious Enemies did erect several Seminaries or Schools for the *English* Nation in foreign Countries; *viz.* at *Douay*, at *Rheims*, at *Rome* and *Valedolid*; all which were erected for the Instructing of the *English* Youth in these Principles, *viz*, That the Pope had the Supream power over Kings, and as soon as a King was declared a Heretick by him, the Subjects were thereby absolved from their Allegiance due to him; and that it was a meritorious work to murder such a King. Out of these Schools Emissaries and Priests were sent into *England*, whose business was there to propagate the *Roman* Catholick Religion; but more especially, to instruct the People in the above mentioned Doctrines. To these associated themselves some Desperado's, who, after Pope *Pius* V. had excommunicated the Queen, were frequently conspiring against her life. But most of them got no other advantage by it, than to make work for the Hangman, and occasioned that the *Papists* wer stricter kept than before. *Mary* also Queen of *Scotland*, rais'd abundance of Tumults against Queen *Elizabeth*; she being the next Heiress to the Crown of *England*, did, with the assistance of the Duke of *Guise*, endeavour to have Queen *Elizabeth* declared by the Pope Illegitimate (which the *Spaniards* underhand opposed) and both she and the *Dauphin* assumed the Arms of *England*; which attempt proved afterwards fatal to Queen *Mary*. For *Elizabeth* sided with the Earl of *Murray*, natural Brother of

Papists and *Puritans*.

Foreign Seminaries.

Queen

Queen *Mary*, whose main endeavour was to drive the *French* out of *Scotland*, and to establish there the *Protestant* Religion; both which he effected with the assistance of Queen *Elizabeth*. This Queen *Mary* returning after the death of *Francis* II. into *Scotland*, was married to her Kinsman *Henry Darnley*, one of the handsomest Men in *Britain*, by whom she had *James* VI. But her Love to him grew quickly cold; for a certain *Italian* Musician, whose name was *David Ritz*, was so much in favour with the Queen, that a great many perswaded *Henry*, that she kept unlawful company with him. *Henry* being animated, with the assistance of some Gentlemen, pulled *David Ritz* out of the Room, where he was then waiting upon the Queen at Table, and killed him immediately. Soon after this the King was murthered, as was supposed by the Earl of *Bothwell*, who was afterwards married to the Queen. The Earl of *Murray*, and some others, gave out that this Murther was committed by the instigatation of the Queen, and *George Buchanan*, a Creature of the Earl's, does boldly affirm the same in his Writings. Yet there are some, who say, that the Calumnies as well concerning *David Ritz*, as concerning the Death of *Henry Darnley*, were raised against the Queen by the Artifices of the Earl of *Murray*, in order to defame and dethrone her. But however it be, there was an insurrection made against the Queen and *Bothwell*, whom she married, was forced to fly the Land (who died in *Denmark* some Years after in a miserable condition.) and she being made a Prisoner, made her escape in the Year 1568. But the Forces which she had gathered being routed, she retired into *England*, where she was made Prisoner again. There she entered into a Conspiracy against Queen *Elizabeth*, with the Duke of *Norfolk*, whom she promised to marry, hoping thereby to obtain the Crown of *England*. But the Plot being discover'd, the Duke was made a Prisoner, but was afterwards released. And being again discovered to have afresh pursued his former design, paid for it with his Head 1572. Queen *Mary* was confined to a more close Imprisonment. Several Conspiracies were formed upon that, for her escape, but they were all detected before they took effect. Nay, several Treaties were set on foot to procure her Liberty, but no sufficient security could be given to Queen *Elizabeth*. Wherefore Queen *Mary* growing at last impatient, and being overcome by ill Counsellours, entered into a Conspiracy with *Spain*, the

The Queen of *Scots* married *Bothwell*, who murthered her Husband.

She was made a Prisoner in *England*.

Pope,

Pope, and the Duke of *Guise* against *Elizabeth*: Which Plot having been long carried on privately, did break out at last, and some Letters of her own hand writing having been produced among other matters, a Commission was
1586. granted to try the Queen; by vertue of which she received Sentence of Death; which being confirmed by the Parliament, great application was made to the Queen for Execution, which Queen *Elizabeth* would not grant for a great while, especially, because her Son *James* and *France* did make great intercessions in her behalf. At last the *French* Embassador *d' Aubespine*, having suborned a Ruffian to murther Queen *Elizabeth*, her Friends urged vehemently to hasten the Execution, which she granted and signed the Warrant, commanding nevertheless, Secretary *Davidson* to keep it by him till farther order: But he advising thereupon with the Privy Council, it was ordered,
1587. that Execution should be done upon her immediately.
Beheaded. Queen *Elizabeth* seemed much concerned thereat, and removing *Davidson* from his place. King *James* also was grievously exasperated, and some of his Friends advised him to joyn with *Spain* and to revenge his Mother's death, But Queen *Elizabeth* found a way to appease his Anger, and there was ever after a very good understanding betwixt them to the very last. The Duke of *Guise* and his party were great Enemies to Queen *Elizabeth* in *France*,
Queen *Elizabeth* assists the *Huguenots*. and she, on the other hand, assisted the *Huguenots* with Men and Money, who surrendered into her Hands as a Pledge, *Havre de Grace*; but her Forces were obliged to quit it the next Year. Neither could she ever get *Calais* restored to her, tho' in the Peace concluded at *Chasteau en*
1559. *Cambresis*, it was promised to her. With *Henry* the IVth. she lived in a good understanding, sending frequently to his assistance both Men and Money. But with *Spain* she was at variance upon the account of the Rebellious *Netherlanders*, to whom she not only granted a safe retreat in her Country, and Harbours, but also assisted them, first underhand, and afterwards openly both with Men and Money, they having surrender'd unto her as a Pledge,
The Sovereignty of the *Netherlands* twice offer'd her. *Flushing*, *Brill* and *Ramesken*: But she would never accept of the Sovereignty of the *Netherlanders*, which being twice offered her, she refused it as often, out of weighty and wise Considerations. She sent, however, the Earl of *Leicester*, her Favourite, thither as Governour, who did not acquire much Reputation; but having by his Supine negligence

ligence put things rather into confusion, he was recalled in the Second Year. She likewise did great damage to the *Spaniards* on their Coasts, and in the *West-Indies*, by Sir *Francis Drake* and others, and the Earl of *Essex* took from them *Cadiz*, but quited it immediately after. On the other side, *Spain* was continually busie in raising Commotions and Conspiracies against her. And forasmuch as the *Spaniards* were of Opinion, that *England* might be sooner conquered than the *Netherlands*, and that the latter could not be subdued without the other, they equipp'd a Fleet which they called the *Invincible Armado*, wherewith they intended to invade *England*. Which Fleet, to the immortal Glory of the *English* Nation, being partly destroyed by them, and partly miserable torn in Pieces by Storms, did return home in a very miserable condition. However *Spain* gave constant support to the Rebels in *Ireland*, who were very troublesome to Queen *Elizabeth*, tho' they were generally beaten by her Forces, except in the Year 1596, when they soundly beat the *English*. Upon which the Queen sent thither the Earl of *Essex*, who did nothing worth mentioning. And after his return, the Queen giving him a severe Reprimand, and ordering him to be kept a Prisoner, he was so exasperated at it, that tho' he was reconciled to the Queen, he endeavoured to raise an Insurrection in *London*, which cost him his Head. Tho' the *Spaniards* were twice repulsed and driven out of *Ireland* with considerable loss, yet the Rebellion lasted till the very end of her Life. Neither could a Peace be concluded betwixt her and the *Spaniards*, as long as she lived. For tho' a Treaty was appointed to be held at *Boulogne*, by the Mediation of *Henry* IV. yet it was immediately broke off, because the *English* disputed Precedency with the *Spaniards*. This Queen could never be brought to a fixt Resolution to marry, tho' her Subjects did greatly desire it, and she had great Offers made her: Amongst whom were, besides, *Philip*, *Charles* Archduke of *Austria*, *Eric* King of *Sweden*, the Duke *d'Anjou*, and his Brother the Duke *d'Alenson*, the Earl of *Leicester*, &c. It was her custom not to give a flat denial to such as sued for her in Marriage, but she used to amuse them with hopes, whereby she made them her Friends: For she treated with *Charles* Archduke of *Austria* for seven Years together; and with the Duke of *Alenson* she went so far, that the Marriage Contract was made, but she had got it so drawn, that a way was found to elude it afterward. Under her Reign the

[Margin notes: 1595. — The *Armado* defeated. — *Essex* beheaded. — 1600.]

the *English* Trade was first established in *Turkey* and the *East Indies*; the finest Coin, as also the Manufactury of Serges and Bays, was setled in *England* about the same time. This Queen also brought first into Reputation the *English* Naval Strength, which she was so jealous of, that, tho' she supported the *Netherlanders* against the *Spaniards*, yet would she never consent that the *Netherlanders* should so augment their Sea Forces, as that thereby they might be able to contest with *England* at Sea. This Maxim, which seemed so necessary for *England*, was not regarded by King *James*, he being a Lover of Peace. And King *Charles* I. having always his Hands full with his Rebellious Subjects, was not in a capacity to observe it; by which means it came to pass that the *Dutch* Power at Sea, could neither by *Cromwell*, nor by *Charles* II. be brought down again. This most glorious, and by her Subjects extreamly beloved Queen, died in the Year 1602, having before appointed *James* VI. King of *Scotland*, for her Successor.

She was jealous of her Power at Sea.

James I.

§ 23. After the Death of *Elizabeth*, *James* VI. King of *Scotland*, was with an unanimous applause proclaimed King of *England*. His Title to this Crown was derived from *Margaret* Daughter of *Henry* VII. who was married to *James* IV. King of *Scotland*; whose Son *James* V. left one only Daughter, who was Mother of *James* VI. He at first shewed himself pretty favourable to the *Papists*, fearing, least they might in the beginning of his Reign raise some Commotions against him. Notwithstanding which, immediately after his Coronation, the Lord *Cobham*, *Gray*, and others, entred into a Conspiracy against him: Their main design was, to root out the Line of *James*, and put in his place the Marchioness *d' Arbelle*, she being also descended from the abovesaid *Margaret* Daughter of *Henry* VII. This Lady was after the death of *James* IV. married to *Archibald Douglass*, by whom she had *Margaret*, who was married to *Matthias* Earl of *Lenox*; and this *Arbella* being the Daughter of *Charles Lenox*, the third Son of this Earl, was, by the intercession of *Spain*, to have been married to the Duke of *Savoy*, and by this means the Popish Religion was again to be introduced into *England*: But the whole Plot being discovered, the Ringleaders were punished, yet not with that Severity as the heinousness of their Crime did deserve; tho' in the Year next insuing, all the Jesuits and Popish Priests were, by a severe Proclamation, banished

Cobham's Conspiracy. 1603.

out

out of *England*. In the Year 1605, some Popish Miscreants hired a Vault under the Parliament House, which being fill'd with a great many Barrels of Gunpowder, they intended to have blown the King, the Prince, and the whole Parliament into the Air. But this Hellish Design was very oddly discovered; for one of the Accomplices, by a Letter that was obscurely written, and delivered by an unknown person to a Footman of the Lord *Mounteagle*, did intreat him not to come the next day into the Parliament-House: Which causing a suspicion in the King, all the Vaults were searched, and the Powder found. Hereupon the Parliament made an Act, *That all Subjects, by a solemn Oath, should acknowledge* James *for their lawful Sovereign; And that the Pope had no Authority to dethrone Sovereigns, or to absolve Subjects from their Allegiance.* He concluded a Peace with *Spain*, and was afterwards one of the Mediators of the Truce made betwixt *Spain* and *Holland*. His Son-in-law, the Elector of *Palatine*, being banished out of his Territories, he assisted him only with sending of Ambassadors, and proposing of an Agreement, all which the *Spaniards* rendered ineffectual. His Son, Prince *Charles*, was sent into *Spain* to marry the Infanta, where the Marriage Contract was concluded and confirmed by Oath, but the Nuptials were deferred till the next Year, the *Spaniards* being willing to gain time, and to see how things would be carried on in *Germany* for the House of *Austria*. But when, after the Prince's Return into *England*, the *English* would needs have the Restitution of the Elector *Palatine* inserted in the Articles, the Match was broke off; and tho' the Parliament voted a Subsidy to be employed towards the restoring of the Elector *Palatine*, yet the design came to nothing. Under this King there was a period put to the Differences and Wars betwixt *England* and *Scotland*, which had hitherto not a little impair'd the Native Felicity of that most beautiful Island. And that nothing of jealousie might remain betwixt these two Nations about precedency in the Royal Title, he introduced the Name of *Great Britain*, which comprehends both the Kingdoms. There was also set on Foot a Treaty to unite both Kingdoms into one Body; but it did not succeed, because the *Scots* would not come in as a conquered Province to the *English*. Under this King's Reign, Colonies were established in *Virginia*, *Bermudos*, and *Ireland*; by which means the *English* have extended their Dominions; but there are some who believe

The Powder Plot.

1604.

1626.

Foreign Plantations.

believe that this has weakened the *English* at home, and that in all probability, it would have been more profitable for *England* to have employed those People in Manufactury and Fishing of Herrings, which produce such vast Riches to the *Dutch* in the very sight of the *English*. Yet some are also of Opinion, that it is good for the publick repose, that the unruly Multitude do not grow too numerous in *England*. The *East-India* Trade was also greatly promoted at that time, but the *English* could not come there in competition with the *Dutch*, these having been beforehand with them. This King died in the Year 1625.

Charles I. § 24. His Son *Charles* I. succeeded him, who, after the *Spanish* Match was broke off, married *Henrietta* Daughter of *Henry* IV. He equipp'd out a great Fleet against the *Spaniards*, and landed his Men near *Cadiz*, but being repulsed with loss, returned without doing any thing; and all Commerce was prohibited betwixt *Spain* and *England*. He also broke with *France*; and the *French* Merchants being ill treated by the *English*, all Commerce was in like manner prohibited betwixt these two Nations. The *English* thereupon endeavoured to send Aid unto the City of *Rochelle*, and landing in the Isle of *Rhee*, besieged the Fort of St. *Martin*, which being valiantly defended by one *Toyras*, the *English* were repulsed with great loss. In the Year next insuing, they undertook to relieve *Rochelle*, but in vain. Whereupon *Charles* concluded a Peace with *France* in the Year 1629, and in the next Year with *Spain*: And thus ended a War against two Kings, whose joint Forces he was not able to cope with. Under this King arose very violent Divisions betwixt him and the Parliament, which produced a most strange Revolution in that Kingdom. It will be very well worth our while, to enquire a little more narrowly into the true causes thereof. That wise Queen, *Elizabeth*, held it for a constant Maxim, to oppose the overgrown power of *Spain* with all her might, especially at Sea, whereby she weakened *Spain*, and not only enriched her Subjects, but also exercised them in Sea Affairs, wherein consists the chief Strength and Security of this Kingdom: With this view she always kept a good correspondence with all such as were Enemies of the House of *Austria*; she assisted *France* against the Designs of the *Spaniards*, favoured the Protestant Princes in *Germany*, and upheld the *Dutch* against the *Spaniards*, partly to weaken such a formidable

1626. War with *Spain*.

War with *France*.

A Peace concluded with both.

Causes of the intestine Commotions in *England*.

midable Neighbour, and partly upon the account that she looked upon the *Netherlands* as a remote Frontier or out-work of her Kingdom, and the Bulwark of its safety; in which the slow but hot Blood might ferment, and as it were overboil, before it got room to spread further, to affect the inward parts of the Body, and breed intestine disorders. But King *James* took quite another course, and perceiving that the *United Provinces* were grown strong enough, not only to support themselves against *Spain*, but also to dispute the Dominion of the *Narrow Seas* with *England*, he left them to themselves, and concluding a Peace with *Spain*, established a lasting Tranquility at home, for his Inclinations were more for Books than Arms. And as Subjects in general are apt to follow the Inclinations of their Sovereigns, so the People laid aside all Warlike Exercises, and fell into such Weaknesses and Vices, as are commonly the Product of Plenty and Peace: And the King hoped, when these Nations applyed themselves only to Trade and Commerce, they would become effeminate, and when thus enervated with Luxury and Ease, would be diverted from having any thoughts of opposing his Authority. He likewise made it his main endeavour to unite the Minds of the *Scots* and *English*, by Naturalizing the *English* in *Scotland*, and the *Scots* in *England*, and by joyning the great Families by Marriages: But he was more especially careful of establishing one Form of religious Worship in both Kingdoms. For tho' there was no great difference in the Articles of Faith, yet the Ceremonies and Church Government were very different. For Queen *Elizabeth*, when she established the Protestant Religion, retained many Institutions and Ceremonies, which were anciently used in the Primitive Church, and continued by the Papists afterwards; she maintained also the Authority of the Bishops, but withal such as was subject to the Royal Power; as taking this Constitution to be most suitable to a Monarchy, considering that the Bishops had some dependance on the King, and had their Votes in Parliament. And it used to be the saying of King *James*, *no Bishops, no King*. But this Constitution did not agree with those of the Reformed Religion in *Holland*, *Switzerland*, and *France*, partly because these two Nations were used to a Democratical Liberty, and therefore lov'd an Equality in the Church Government as well as the State; partly because they had suffered equally from Kings and Bishops, and

The different Conduct of Queen *Elizabeth* and King *James* as to the State.

The occasion that were taken from Religion.

and therefore both were equally hated by them. These would not allow of any Superiority among the Clergy, but constituted the outward Church Government by Presbyteries, Classes and Synods; neither would they admit any of the Ancient Ceremonies, believing that the Protection of the Reformed Religion did consist in not having so much as any thing, tho' never so indifferent, common with the Papists. Now according to this Form was the Church of *Scotland* established; and the number of such as were of the same Opinion increased daily in *England*, who were commonly called Presbyterians or Puritans. And the Capriciousness of those who were of several Sentiments proved the more dangerous, because these Nations being of a melancholy temper used to adhere stedfastly to their Opinions so as not to be removed from them. King *James* being besides a great Enemy of the Puritans, thought to have found out a way to suppress them in *Scotland*, by inserting it among the Royal Prerogatives, which were to be confirmed by the Parliament of *Scotland*, *That he had the supream Power both in Spiritual and Temporal Affairs, in the same manner in* Scotland *as in* England. By this means he hoped to model, without any great difficulty, the Church of *Scotland* according to that of *England*. And tho' this Proposition was opposed by a great many in the Parliament of *Scotland*, yet the King's Party prevailed, and a new Form of Church Government was established in *Scotland*. But the King had no sooner turned his back, and was returned into *England*, but the common People made an Insurrection against the Bishops in *Scotland*, who began to introduce there the Ceremonies of the Church of *England*.

The Conduct of *Charles* I.

§ 25. Tho' King *Charles* I. was of a more Warlike temper than his Father, yet was he obliged, tho' against his Will, according to the Maxims of his Father, to preserve Peace abroad, to avoid the danger of being obliged to depend on the capricious Humours of his Subjects. And forasmuch as he had a great dislike of the Power of the common People, and bore an Hereditary hatred to the Temper and Principles of the Puritans, all his Thoughts were bent to find out ways how to secure himself from the danger of both. In regard the King could not impose any extraordinary Taxes without the consent of the Parliament, *Charles* chose rather to controul his own Inclinations, which were bent for War, than to fawn upon the Parliament; in hopes that

that their strength and authority which cramp'd the Regal Power extreamly, would dwindle and sink of it self, if they were not called together for a considerable time. It is supposed, that the Lord Treasurer *Weston* confirm'd him in this Opinion, as fearing to be called to an account by the Parliament. The Parliament used anciently to provide a certain yearly Revenue for the King, towards maintaining his Court, and the dignity of his Person; and the King on his part used out of that to maintain a Fleet to secure the Commerce of the Kingdom: But this Revenue was not hereditary to the next Successor. The first Parliament which was called by *Charles* I. settled the Customs, as part of his Revenue; but when he afterwards dissolved the same against the Opinion of the Malecontents, even the Revenue thus granted began to be called in question. For King *James* had left above 1200000 *l.* Debts, which were since encreas'd by *Charles* to 400000 *l.* more, which Money was expended in the War against *France* and *Spain*; it was therefore not visible, how he could extricate himself out of these Debts without the assistance of a Parliament, since he could not levy any Taxes upon the Subjects; and to force them to pay any, was beyond his Power, he having no Forces on Foot but the Militia of the Kingdom: And it was impossible to bring in such a Foreign Force as could be supposed to be able to make Head against the dissatisfyed People. Notwithstanding all this, the King pursued his Resolution, and having ask'd the Opinion of Men skill'd in the Law, who told him, *That it was allowable for the publick benefit, to levy Money by his own Authority*; he imposed several new Taxes, whereby he augmented his yearly Revenue from 500000 *l.* to 800000 *l.* Further, he laid a Tax upon every House for maintaining a Fleet, which amounted to 300000 *l.* Add to all this, that he revived a Title to the Forests and Woods, that in ancient Times were part of the Regal Possessions; and being grub'd up, were turned into Arable and Pasture Fields: Now, by the revival of this claim almost all the Estates in the Country came to be of disputed Titles; insomuch that the County of *Essex* alone, was forced to buy off the Suit commenced upon this Head, with the sum of 300000 *l.* Sterling. And the other Counties had been served the same way, if the Commotions that soon after insued, had not prevented it. These and such other Practices caused great dissatisfaction among the Subjects against the King: Besides, the King held a strict hand over the Puritans, (the blame of which fell in a great measure upon *William Laud*, Archbishop of *Canterbury*, who was zealous for the Church.) This was by the Puritans interpreted as if the King was resolved by depressing of them, to introduce Popery. To insinuate this into the Multitude, abundance of Libels and scurrilous Papers were scattered abroad against the King and the Bishops; and Commissioners being appointed to enquire into them, the People were rather exasperated than appeased by their Severity.

Troubles in *Scotland* and *England*. § 26. Both Nations being therefore full of Discontents, the Flame first broke out in *Scotland*: For, the King endeavouring to root out Puritanism there, to establish the Authority of the Bishops, and an Uniformity in Religion, he ordered a Church Liturgy to be composed, abrogating all Presbyteries, Classes and Provincial Synods, and enjoining every one, under severe Penalties, to conform to the same; there was a general Insurrection raised by that
1637. Party in *Scotland*. There was also another reason; for, at the time of the first Reformation, the Revenues of a great many Church Benefices were appropriated to the use of the Crown, but without any remarkable advantage; for they were let out, for the most part, to younger Brothers of Noble Families. These having found the benefit of them, had, by getting from time to time the Survivorship, continued the same in their Families, and kept them as their
1567. own Propriety. Nay, they did more than this; for during the Minority of King *James* VI. they had obtained the Titles of Lordships for some of the most considerable of these, or for some of the lesser Benefices joyned together. King
1617. *James* afterwards perceiving, that thereby they had bound him up from rewarding such with these Benefices as deserved well of him, would have recalled the beforesaid Grants; but met with such opposition in the Nobility, that he de-
1633. sisted from it. But *Charles* undertook the business effectually, employing the said Revenues towards the augmenting of the Salaries of the Clergy. Those therefore who had been losers by this Revocation, joyning with such Ministers as were mortal Enemies of the *Liturgy*, did, with all their might, help to stir up the Rebellion. *David Lesly* also, who had been a Commander under the King of *Sweden* in the *German* Wars, and having refused to serve under *John Banniers* there, was returned into his Native Coun-

try,

try, in hopes to make his advantage of these Troubles. He put himself at the Head of the Rebellious Party, and by perswading the Nobility, that the King intended to take away their ancient Privileges, stirred up a great many against the King. These Rebels to make a fair show to the common People, made use of the Religious Cloak of Conscience, ordering a Directory to be compos'd by the Ministers quite opposite to the former *Liturgy*. They thereupon entered into an Association, confirm'd by a solemn Oath, that they would maintain the same against all, even the King himself. This Association was called *The Covenant*; which being subscribed by the greatest part of the Nobility and Clergy, a Council was constituted, unto whom was committed the Supream direction of their Affairs. To suppress these Commotions, the King sent the Marquis of *Hamilton* into *Scotland*, who dealing mildly with them, only encouraged the adverse Party: For the King calling a Parliament in hopes to remedy these Disorders, the Covenant was by its Authority confirmed, the Episcopal Authority quite abolish'd, and Puritanism established in defiance of the Royal Authority. There being then no other way left to reduce the Rebellious Party to Obedience, but force, and the King being in want both of Money and a sufficient number of faithful Subjects, he was forced to make some use of the *Papists* to obtain both, wherefore he did not only raise an Army, wherein were some *Papists*, but also was assisted by them with some Sums of Money, all which, however, was in no ways sufficient to supply the want of the King; and a Supply being demanded from the Subjects, very few, except the King's Servants and Officers, were for contributing any thing. At last it being divulged, that a great many thousand *Irish* Papists and *Germans* were ready for the King's Service, to try, whether by this way the Subjects could be frighted out of some Money, it served only to exasperate the Minds of the People. Yet the King's Forces might in all probability have been successful against the *Scots*, if they had fallen upon them immediately. But because these had leisure given them, they did not only settle a Correspondency with *France* and *Holland*, from whence they were supplyed with Money and Ammunition; but also sent their Deputies into *England*, who knew so well there to represent the state of their Affairs, that the King, being persuaded by the *English*, made a dishonourable Agreement with them: Which

The Scotch Covenant.

nevertheless did not last long, the Court being ashamed of the Agreement, and the *Scots* not trusting the King. The King in the mean while intercepted a Letter, wherein the *Scots* had sollicited for some Officers and Money to be sent them from *France*; this he hoped might prove an Inducement to the *English* to oppose the Treachery of the *Scots*, and to furnish him with some Supplies, of which he stood in great need at that time. Accordingly he called a Parliament, where the Letter was read, but to no great purpose, the Members of the House of Commons being most of them Puritans, who were great Friends of the *Scots*, so that the Parliament was a little while after dissolved by the King's Authority. The King had caused to be made Prisoner in *London*, the *Scotch* Commissioner, who had subscribed the above-mentioned Letter; whereupon the *Scots* took up Arms, and took the Castle of *Edinburgh*. The King having with great difficulty, for want of Money, got together an Army, went in person against the *Scots*; but a Party of his Army endeavouring to force their passage was beaten back with loss, which augmented the Discontents of his Subjects, the Soldiers for want of Pay, being to be maintained by those Counties where they were quartered. Besides this, ten thousand Men, which were raised by the Parliament in *Ireland* for the King's Service, were forced to be disbanded for want of Pay. There was then no other remedy left, but to make a Truce with the *Scots*, and to call a new Parliament in *England*, which began to sit in *November*, in the Year 1640.

A Letter intercepted, wherein the *Scots* desire Succour from *France*.

The Parliament is factious, and favours the *Scots*.

§ 27. But in the Session of this Parliament, the Ulcer which had been long gathering in the Minds of the People broke out: For the Parliament, in lieu of assisting the King against the *Scots*, entered into a Confederacy with them, promising a monthly Subsidy towards the maintaining of the *Scotish* Army, which was to be ready at the *English* Parliament's command. Then they began to reform the State, to clip the King's Authority, to punish his Ministers and Servants, and to take away the Bishops, and the Liturgy, and fall upon Papists. The better to obtain their Aim, they forced the King to consent that he would not dissolve the Parliament till all such as were criminal were punished, and the State were entirely reformed; in a word, that they should have the Liberty to sit as long as they pleased: Which, in effect, put an end to the Royal Authority. To try

The Parliament of *England* directly oppose the King.

try the King's Patience, and their own Strength, they brought the Earl of *Strafford*, Lord Deputy of *Ireland*, to his Tryal, who, notwithstanding he made a good Defence, and the King did his utmost to preserve his beloved and faithful Minister, yet the Rabble of *London*, then encouraged by the House of Commons, making an Insurrection, he received Sentence of Death in the House of Lords. And the King refusing to sign the Warrant for his Execution, was obliged thereunto, partly by the Importunity of the Parliament, partly by the Insurrection of the Rabble of the City of *London*. Then the rest of the King's Ministers went to rack, some of them saving themselves by flight, some being imprisoned. The Bishops were excluded from the House of Lords. The Star-chamber, the Authority of the Privy-Council, and the High Commission Court, were suppress'd. The Customs and Power over the Fleet were taken away from the King. These and many other things, which proved very prejudicial to him, the King was forced to grant them, in hopes thereby to heal the ulcerated Minds of the People. He went also in person into *Scotland*, where he granted them all what they could desire. About the same time a horrid Conspiracy broke out among the *Irish* Papists, who pretended to maintain the Popish Religion, and to redress some Grievances by force of Arms, which occasioned afterwards a most cruel Slaugther. At last it came to an open Rebellion: For 1642. the Parliament not ceasing to encroach daily more and more upon the Royal Authority, the King resolved to assert his Authority; accordingly he summoned five Members of Parliament, whom he accused as Traitors, and Authors of all the Differences: And the House of Commons taking their part, the King went into the House accompanied with some Officers, and in his Words and his Gesture justly resented their Behaviour: But they taking Anger without Power to be vain, did not much matter it. And an Argument that it really was so, was the King's sudden Lenity, and condescending to answer their Expectations. Thereupon the House of Commons stirred up the neighbouring Counties, and especially the *London* Apprentices, who made such an Insurrection, that the King, not thinking himself safe in *London*, retired into the Country. And the Parliament ordered all the Governours of the Sea-ports, not to obey the King's Commands. It was certainly a great Error in the King, that in such troublesome times he had not taken

The Rebellion begins.

Their Behaviours.

care to secure to himself the Sea-ports, by which means he might have hoped for some Assistance from abroad. For, when the King intended to possess himself of the Fort and Harbour of *Hull*, he was not admitted; so that there was nothing left, but that the Parliament had not as yet taken from the King the disposal of Offices. But for the rest, it was evident that their Intention was, to abolish totally the Royal Power, and to introduce a Democracy. And after the King had once given his Assent to the exclusion of the Bishops from the House of Lords, where they had six and twenty Votes, and the rest of the King's Friends had once absented themselves from both Houses, it was easie for the remainder quite to abolish the Authority of the House of Lords. Thus after there had been long contests by Words and Writings betwixt both Parties, the King now, as well as the Parliament, began to arm themselves. And the King having several times, at first, beat the Parliament Forces, the Parliament stirred up the *Scots*, entring with them into a Confederacy. Whereupon the *Scots* came with a considerable Force to the Assistance of the Parliament, which turned the Scale, the King's Forces being routed near *York*, and he obliged, for want of Men and Money, to give himself up to the Protection of the *Scots*; who nevertheless did surrender him to the *English* for the Sum of 400000 *l.* upon condition that he should not be abused by them. The King was afterwards carried Prisoner from place to place for a considerable time.

The King made a Prisoner.

The Independents become Masters.

§ 28. By these means the Puritains or Presbyterians, under the pretext of Religion, overthrew the Royal Power. But that they could not enjoy their unjust and usurped Power, was occasioned by a certain Sect that called themselves *Independents*, because they would not depend on any certain form of Faith or Worship, or Spiritual or Temporal Constitutions, nor acknowledge any of the same, whereby they opened a Door for all sorts of Fanaticks, to come under their Protection. These under pretence of a particular holy Zeal, not only got a great sway in the Parliament, and made Head against any peaceable accommodation, proposed by others; but also by their cunning insinuating way crept into the chief Civil and Military Employments: For, in the place of the Earl of *Essex*, *Thomas Fairfax* was made General, and *Oliver Cromwell* Lieutenant-General of the Army, the last of which was the Head

of

of the Independents, a sly and cunning Fox. And out of this party all vacant places were supplyed in Parliament. The Presbyterians therefore perceiving that the Independents began to be very strong in the House, and that most Military Employments were in their Hands, proposed in the House, That one part of the Army should be sent into *Ireland*, that some Forces only should be kept in *England*, and the rest be disbanded. *Cromwell* made use of this Motion to stir up the Soldiers, telling them, that they were likely to be disbanded without Pay, or else to be starved in *Ireland*. Thereupon the Soldiers entered into an Association among themselves, taking upon them not only the Military, but also all the Civil Power: They took the King from the Parliament into their own Custody, pretending they would give him his liberty, and made themselves Masters of the City of *London*, and acted in every thing at discretion. For they quickly after broke off the Treaty with the King; and a great many of the Subjects, who were not able to bear their Tyranny, taking up Arms, were dispersed by *Cromwell*, who also beat the *Scots* that were come into *England* to the Assistance of the King, making their General *Hamilton's* a Prisoner. But during the absence of *Cromwell*, the Parliament had re-assumed the Treaty with the King, and the business was carried on so far, that there was no small hopes of an Accommodation; when the Soldiers, headed by *Ireton*, Son-in-law to *Cromwell*, broke off the Treaty, taking Prisoners such Members of the House as did oppose them: So that there were not above forty Members left in the Parliament, and those that were, either Officers, or at least Favourers of the Army. These decreed, *That no Treaty should be set on foot for the future with the King; that the Supream Power was to be lodged in the People, which was represented by the House of Commons; but the Regal Power, and the Authority of the House of Lords, should be quite abolished.* Then they ordered a Court of 150 Persons to be erected, by whose Authority the King was to be summoned, sentenced and punished, notwithstanding that the generality of the People, look'd upon this Court as an abominable thing; some Presbyterian Ministers cryed out aloud against it in the Pulpits, the *Scots* protested against it, and the *Dutch* Ambassadors, and other Princes, did their utmost to oppose it. Before this Court, were sat, among the rest, a great many of very mean Extraction, the King was accused of High Treason, Tyranny, and of all

The King is sentenced to Death, and Executed.

all the Murthers and Roberies committed since the beginning of these Troubles. And the King, as in Justice he ought to do, bravely refusing to acknowledge its Authority, was sentenced to be beheaded, though there were but 67 of these pretended Judges present, the rest abominating the Fact, had absented themselves, among whom was *Fairfax.* In fine, the King after being cruelly and ignominiously abused by the Soldiers, was beheaded with an Axe upon a Scaffold erected for that purpose before *Whitehall*.

1648.

Ireland conquered.

§. 29. After the Death of the King, the outward shew of the Supream Power was in the Parliament, but in effect it was lodged in the Generals of the Armies. Their first Design was, to banish the King's Son, and the whole Royal Family, and to suppress all such as adhered to him. *Cromwell* was sent into *Ireland*, where the Royal Party was as yet pretty strong, which Island was reduced in the Space of one Year by *Cromwell's* good Fortune and Valour. In the mean while the *Scots* had proclaimed *Charles* II. tho under very hard Conditions, their King; and he arriving there safely out of *France*, whither he had gone for shelter, was Crowned King of *Scotland*. The Parliament thereupon recall'd *Cromwell* out of *Ireland*, and having made him General (for they had deposed *Fairfax*, whom they mistrusted) sent him into *Scotland*, where he beat the *Scots* several times, but especially gave them an entire defeat near *Leith*, taking, among other places, the Castle of *Edinboreugh*, which had been hitherto esteemed impregnable. The King in the mean while having gathered a flying Army, entered *England*, in hopes that a great many *English* would join with him: But he was deceived in his hopes, very few coming to him; and *Cromwell* overtaking him with his Army near *Worcester*, his Forces were routed and dispersed; so that he was forced to change his Cloaths in his flight, and after a great many dangers, was miraculously saved, and escaped by the help of a Merchant Ship into *France*. The King being thus driven out of the Island, the *Scots* were entirely subdued under the Conduct of General *Monk*, who was sent thither by *Cromwell*, and having imposed upon them very hard Conditions, according to their deserts, intirely subjected them to the *English*. This done, the Parliament began to take into consideration how to disband part of the Army, and to quarter the rest in the several Counties. But *Cromwell* dismiss'd that Parliament,

Charles II. routed.

The *Scots* conquered.

which

which had been the cause of so much trouble, and constituted a new Parliament consisting of 144 Members, most of them Fanaticks and Enthusiasts; among whom, *Cromwell* had put a few cunning Fellows, who being entirely devoted to his Service, did make the rest dance after his Pipe. These having first let the silly Wretches go on in their own way, till by their phantastical Behaviour they had made themselves ridiculous and hated by every body, then offer'd the Supream Administration of Affairs to *Cromwell*; who having accepted of the same under the Title of *Protector*; selected a Privy Council, wherein were received the Heads of the several Sects. Thus they who had shown so much aversion to the Royal Power, hatched out a Monarch of their own, who, without controul, ruled the three Kingdoms of *England*, *Scotland* and *Ireland* at pleasure. *Cromwell* to have a fair pretence to keep on foot his Sea and Land Forces, which were the foundation of his Power, began a War with the *Dutch*, who seemed to dispise this new Monarch. But Fortune was so favourable to *Cromwell* in this War, that he took above 1700 Merchant Men from the *Dutch*, and beat them in five Sea Engagements, in the last of which the *Dutch* lost *Martin Tromp*, and twenty seven Men of War. The *Hollanders* then were obliged to beg for Peace, and to accept of such Conditions as were proposed to them; among which, one was, *That the Province of* Holland *should exclude the Prince of* Orange *for ever, from succeeding in his Fathers Place.* Another was, *That they should not longer entertain the banished King* Charles II. *in their Territories.* Which some alledge as a reason, that he was always ready afterwards to revenge himself upon them, tho' at his return into the Kingdom, they endeavoured with abundance of flattery to make amends for the former affront. It is very likely also, that the King was suspicious, that the *Dutch* had fomented the Differences betwixt his Father and the Parliament. *Cromwell* acquired so much Glory by this War, that most Princes sent their Ambassadors to him, as if he had been a lawful Sovereign, and desired his Friendship. He was no less fortunate in discovering several Plots which were made against him: For which purpose he entertained his spies every where, even near the King's Person; having besides this a cunning way to draw the People over to his Party, and to suppress such as envyed his Fortune. He sent also a Fleet into the *Mediterranean*, wherewith he curb'd the Pirates on the

Cromwell made Protector.

1652.

1660.

the Coast of *Barbary*. Another was sent into the *West-Indies*, on Board of which he sent such Soldiers and Officers as he had a mind to have out of the way, as being useless to him at home. In the *West-Indies* his Designs against St. *Domingo* and *Hispaniola* miscarried; but *Jamaica* he took from the *Spaniards*, notwithstanding that a great many of his Men were taken off by Sickness: And he did considerable Mischief to the *Spaniards*, by ruining their Silver Fleet. He sent some Auxiliary Troops to the *French* in *Flanders*, who, in recompence, surrendered to him *Dunkirk*. He died in the Year 1658, having been as great and formidable as ever any King of *England*. He was a great Master in the Art of Dissimulation, knowing how to make his Advantage of Religious Pretences, with which view he gave Liberty of Conscience to all Sectaries, and by that means he not only got their Favour, but by dividing the People into several Opinions, prevented their easily joining against him.

King *Charles* II's Restoration.

§. 30. After the Death of *Cromwell*, this unlawful and violent Form of Government could not be of long Continuance: For though his Son *Richard* succeeded him in the Protectorship (this was the Title used by *Cromwell*, who refused the Name of King) yet was he no ways capable to bear such a weight. Wherefore he was soon deposed by the Parliament, which being divided within it self, *Monk*, who was then Governour of *Scotland*, took this opportunity, and marching with an Army out of *Scotland* into *England*, possessed himself of the City of *London*, dissolved the Military Parliament, and recall'd King *Charles*
1660. II. into his Kingdom. This King restored the ancient Form of Government in the Kingdom both in Spiritual and Temporal Matters, for his Subjects were ready to gratifie him in most respects, as having been taught by Experience, *That the Frogs who despised to have a Block for their King, got afterwards a Stork for their Master.* This King, who judged that the Greatness of *England* did chiefly depend on the Dominion of the Seas and Commerce, which was disputed by no Body but by the *Dutch*, did, in all probability, bend all his Thoughts that way, *viz.* How to make these proud Merchants more pliable, his hopes being grounded upon what he had seen *Cromwell* do against them. Wherefore he began a War with *Holland*, which was carried on at first with equal losses on both sides;

War with *Holland*. 1665.

sides; But the English at last taking a Resolution to tire out the Dutch without coming to an Engagement, they ventured at a bold stroke, and to the great dishonour of the English entered the River Thames, firing some Ships at Chatham. This obliged the King to make a Peace with them by the Mediation of Sweden, tho' the great success of the French Arms in Flanders may probably have contributed a great deal towards it. Yet it seems as if ever since he had kept up a Resolution of revenging himself upon them, he being also again exasperated by the Rabble in Holland, who affronted him afterwards. He therefore in the Year 1672 attacked the Dutch at Sea, whilst the King of France made War against them by Land. But this War did not succeed according to his Expectation; for the Dutch did not only take from the English a great number of Merchant-ships, but also the English could not master the Dutch in any of the Sea-fights, partly, because the French would not fall on in good earnest, partly, because the Dutch acted very circumspectly, not giving any opportunity to the English to make a Descent either on Holland or Zealand. It is possible that the King's Intentions may perhaps have been frustrated by some Intrigues at home. And because the English Nation began to grow 1674. very jealous of the great Successes of France, the King was obliged to make a separate Peace with Holland, and afterwards was received as a Mediator betwixt the Parties then engaged in War against one another.

§. 31. The English Nation is very populous and fruitful. There are some who have reckoned, that in England are 9913 Parishes, and in each Parish 80 Families, which make 793040 Families, and seven Persons reckoned to each Family amounts to 5551280 Souls, among which number may be supposed to be above a Million of Men capable of bearing Arms. This Nation is very fit to settle Colonies in Foreign Countries, because the English, as soon as they are in the least settled in a Place, they quickly marry, and remain there for their Life-time. Whereas other Nations, if they go into far distant Countries, go only with an intent to get a little Money, which they afterwards love to spend in their Native Country. The English are also Couragious, and Brave, not fearing Death. For in former Times their Land-forces were much Superiour to the French, and ever since the Times of Queen *Constitution of the English Nation.*

Eliza-

Elizabeth, when they first began to apply themselves in earnest to the Sea, they have not been inferiour in Naval Skill and Courage to any Nation in the World, except that the *Dutch* may be compared with them in Sea-Affairs. But this is to be observed of the *English* Valour, that they commonly are very Furious and Brave at the beginning, but great Hardship, Famine, and other Inconveniences they are not so well able to endure with Patience, as being us'd to live in great Ease and Plenty in their own Country. Wherefore *Maurice* Prince of *Orange* us'd to put the *English*, that were sent to his Assistance, upon desperate Enterprizes, before (as he us'd to say) they had digested the *English* Beef. They are also very dextrous in Woollen and Silk Manufacturies, which they learned chiefly from the *Dutch*; but after all, they are somewhat Proud and Lovers of Ease; and spend every Day some Hours in walking and smoaking Tobacco, which is the reason that they do not so much Work as otherwise they might; and yet they expect to be paid for their idle Hours as well as the rest: Which is the reason why they sell their Wares at a higher rate than others, and that they envy such *French* Handicrafts-men, who live among them, and are seldom diverted from their daily Labour by any Pleasures. Their being generally of a melancholy Temper, makes them very Ingenious, and when they apply themselves to any Science, they make great Progress in it, if they hit the right Way. But by the same Rule, because there happens often to be an ill mixture of this melancholy Temper, abundance of *Fanaticks* and *Enthusiasts* are to be found among them, who having formed to themselves Opinions from ill grounded Principles, adhere so stedfast to them, that they are not by any ways to be removed from them. And accordingly there is not any Nation under the Sun, where more different and more absurd Opinions are to be met with in Religion than in *England*. The loose sort of People are addicted to Thieving and Robbing upon the High-way, so that the Hangmen are always imployed in *England*. This Nation loves to eat and drink extremely well: Tho' there are some who will have it, that the *English* got their way of drinking so plentifully from the *Netherlanders* in the Wars of the *Low Countries*, and from thence brought that ill Custom over into *England*, which before, they say, was not in use there. Their own Histories are sufficient Evidences, that they have been always inclined to Rebellion and intestine Commotions. So that their Kings can never be secure, except they keep a watchful Eye over the restless Spirit of the People.

§. 32. The *Scots* are good Land Soldiers, and can endure hardship, which they have from the barrenness of their Native Country. They are very Revengeful, and intestine Broils among the Noble Families were formerly very common among them: For it was a Custom, that each Family used to select one for the Head of the Family, unto whom they almost paid more respect than to the King himself, and if any one of the Family had received an Injury, he made complaint thereof to the Head of his Family: And if the Head of the same Family did resolve to revenge the Injury, the whole Family, under the Conduct of their Head, fell upon the Family of the Aggressor with Fire and Sword. Which abominable Custom King *James* VI. did endeavour to abolish. Further, they are easily stirred up to Rebellion, and very obstinate in defending their Opinions to the utmost. Their fruitfulness in Children makes them seek other Countries, since their Country can scarce maintain them all at home. There is another Reason also to be given for this, which is the right of the First-born, whereby the eldest Son is Heir of all the real Estate of his Father, the rest of the Brothers being obliged to be satisfied with their share in the Personal Estate. These then being obliged to advance themselves as well as they can, apply themselves either to the Wars or Study: Wherefore most Ministers in *Scotland* are said to be younger Brothers of good Families. But in *England* it is no shame for the younger Brothers of such Families to be Merchants. In former Times, before *Scotland* and *England* were united under one King, the *Scotch* Soldiers were in great Esteem, because the *French* made constantly use of them in their Wars, and at home they were always pickeering with the *English*: But afterwards they grew careless of Warlike Exercises; and especially when *Cromwell* subdued them, their ancient Glory was quite obscured. The *Scots* are also very Ingenious, and well vers'd in the Latin Tongue. And at that Time when all Liberal Sciences were suppressed in *Europe* by a long Barbarism, the same were kept up in *Scotland*, which furnished several other Nations with Learned Men, who

Constitution of the *Scotch* Nation.

instruct-

instructed them in these Sciences. But as the *Scots*, who live in the low Countries, on the South-side, are well civiliz'd, so those who inhabit the Mountains, who are called *Highlanders*, as also the Inhabitants of the *Orkney* and Western Islands, are very rough and unciviliz'd.

Of the *Irish.* §. 33. The *Irish* are commonly esteemed to be a fool-hardy and ill sort of People; very Lazy, yet pretty Hardy in undergoing the Fatigues of War. They are very obstinate, and never to be bent from their Opinion. After *Ireland* was conquered by King *Henry* II. abundance of *English* settled themselves in that Kingdom, whose numbers increased from Time to Time to that Degree, that scarce the fourth Part of the Island remains in the Possession of the ancients Inhabitants. And as most of the *Irish* adhere to the *Popish* Religion, they not only rebelled several Times under Queen *Elizabeth*, but also under the Reign of King *Charles* I. at the Instigation of their Priests, entered into a most horrid Conspiracy against the *English* living among them; of whom, 'tis said, they murthered 200000 within the Space of six Months. But when the *English* had recollected themselves, they again killed about 100000 of them. *Cromwell* had once a mind to have rooted out the whole Nation, as being quite incorrigible, and past hopes of any amendment. With which view he sent some Thousands to serve the King of *Spain*, in a Military Capacity, under Condition, that none of them should return into the *English* Dominions. In fine he omitted nothing to Plague them, so that they are become a miserable Nation.

The Condition of *Great-Britain.* §. 34. As for the Countries subject to the King of *England*. The Kingdom of *England* is a pleasant Rich and Fertile Country, abounding in every thing, either for the Necessity or Pleasures of Mankind, except Oyl and Wine, and such other Commodities as do not grow in the other Parts of *Europe*. They have great numbers of very fine Horses, and good Cattle, especially the best Sheep of all *Europe*, which make the best Part of the native Riches of *England*, bearing so good a sort of Wooll, that an incredible quantity of the best Cloth is made in *England*, and from thence every Year transported into Foreign Parts. These Sheep feed in great Flocks in the Country without so much as a Shepherd, there being no Wolves to be met with in *England*; the reason of which, as 'tis reported, is, that King *Edgar*, about the Year 940, ordered a certain number of Wolves to be paid by the Prince of *Wales* to him as a yearly Tribute; by which means the Wolves were quite destroyed in *England*: Tho' it is also very probable, that the great *English* Mastiffs have been very instrumental in this Point, it being certain, that for Fierceness and Strength they surpass all the rest in the World. A great quantity also of Lead, but especially of the finest Tin, is to be found in *England*, which surpasses in Goodness all other in that kind. The *Sea* likewise is very profitable to the *English*, affording great Quantities of Fish, which are daily catch'd by the Inhabitants. Tho' by the Negligence and Laziness of the ancient *English*, who did not apply themselves industriously to Fishing, they have lost a great Part of that Advantage. The *Netherlanders* indeed, from ancient Times, have made use of this Advantage, and got vast Riches by the Fishery of Herrings and Cods, giving only a small Gratuity to the *English*, in Case they have Occasion to dry their Nets on their Shores; though oftentimes the *English*, envying the *Netherlanders*, will force them to pay more than ordinary, which has several Times served as a colour for a War betwixt both Nations. But the Sea is extreamly advantageous to *England* upon another Account, for thereby the *English* being separated from their Neighbouring Nations, cannot easily be attacked; whereas they may easily invade others: And in regard this Island is situated almost in the very middle of *Europe*, in a narrow Sea, where all Ships which either go East or Westward must pass by; and withal is naturally accommodated with a very deep Coast and commodious Harbours, it lies most convenient for Commerce and Trade, which the *English* carry on in most Parts of the World, and the *Dutch* hitherto have been the only Obstacle, that they are not become Masters of the whole Trade of the World. For it proves very disadvantageous to the *English*, that they love to eat and drink well, and that in great quantity, and by reason of their Love of Ease, they are fain to employ double the number of Seamen in their Ships, of what the *Dutch* do; and besides, they will not be contented with a small Gain: Whereas the *Dutch* live very sparingly, never refuse the Penny, and therefore are easier to be dealt with than the *English*. The *English* import a great deal

of

of raw Silk into *England*, which being wrought in the Country, mightily encreases their Riches. In the same manner they do now with their Woollen Manufactury; whereas before the Times of *Henry* VIII. they used to transport most of their Wooll into the *Netherlands*, where it was wrought, and turn'd to the great Advantage of those Cities. But this King perceiving that his own Subjects might as well make the same Benefit of it, he set up the Woollen Manufactury in his Kingdom, which encreased prodigiously, afterwards, when at the Time of the Troubles in the *Netherlands*, a great many of these Weavers settled in *England*. Add to all this, that the Riches of *England* also are, as it seems, not a little encreased, for that it is not permitted there to any Body to carry any Gold or Silver of their own Coin out of the Land, except it be perhaps to the value of Ten Pound Sterling for a Traveller. But *Scotland* does not come near *England*, neither in Fertility nor Riches, having no Commodities fit for Exportation, except Salt-Fish, Salt, Lead, and Coals. The Western and *Orkney* Islands also produce nothing but Fish. *Ireland* abounds in Cattle, and especially in Sheep; tho' the *Irish* Wooll is not so fine as the *English*; but for the rest, it is a fertile and plentiful Country. In *America* belong to the *English* Crown, the Islands of *Bermudos*, *Virginia* and *New-England*, and some of the *Caribby Islands*, whither the *English* have sent their Colonies, and have also begun to settle themselves on the Continent of *Guinea*. The Product of these Countries is chiefly Tobacco, Sugar, Ginger, Indigo, and Cotton. They have also a Colony in the Island of *Jamaica*, from whence the *English* Buccaneers and Privateers do great mischief to the *Spanish West-Indies*. For it is a Custom with the *English*, that tho' they are at Peace with the *Spaniards* in *Europe*, they do them, nevertheless, all the Mischief they can in the *West-Indies*. Lastly, The *English* are likewise possessed of some Places in the *Banda Islands*, and thereabouts, in the *East-Indies*, which are of no small Consequence to them.

The Form of the Government in *England*.

§ 35. The Constitution of the Government of *England* is chiefly remarkable for this, that the King cannot act at Pleasure, but in some matters is to take the advice of the Parliament. By this Name is to be understood the Assembly of the Estates of *England*, which is divided into the Higher and the Lower House. In the first sit the Bishops and

and the Lords, in the latter the Deputies of the Cities, and of the 52 Counties or Shires, into which the whole Kingdom of *England* is divided. The first Origin of the Parliament as 'tis related, was this. The former Kings of *England* granted great Privileges to the Lords, by whose assistance they had conquered the Country and kept the common People in obedience. But these, in conjunction with the Bishops, growing too head strong, proved very troublesome, especially to King *John* and *Henry* III. wherefore, to suppress their Insolence, *Edward* I. took part with the Commons. And whereas formerly, out of each County or Shire, two Knights and two Citizens were only called, to represent their Grievances, which having been debated by the King and the House of Lords, they used to receive an Answer, and to be sent home again; this King *Edward* call'd together the Commons by themselves, and consulted with them concerning the publick Affairs. This House, after it was once established, did extreamly weaken the Authority of the Lords, and in process of time did not a little diminish the Regal Power; for ever since that time the Rights of the People have been maintained with an high hand, the House of Commons imagining, that the Sovereignty was lodged among them; and if the Kings refused to gratifie them in their Requests, they used to grumble at their proceedings. And because the Power of the Parliament is not so much established by any ancient Laws as Precedents and Customs, this is the reason why it is always very jealous of its Privileges, and always ready to make out of one single Precedent a Right belonging to it ever after. This Parliament the King is obliged to call together as often as any extraordinary Taxes are to be levyed (for the Parliament assigned the King, at first, for his ordinary Revenue, 1200000 *l. per An.* which has been considerably augmented since) or any old Laws are abrogated, or new ones to be made, or any alteration to be made in Religion. For concerning these matters the King cannot decree any thing without consent of the Parliament. The Parliament used also to take into consideration the state of the Kingdom, and to present their Opinion to the King; yet is the same of no force till approved of by the King. It often calls in question the Ministers of State with reference to the Administration of publick Affairs, and inflicts punishment upon them, with the King's approbation. And it is a common Rule in *England*, that whatever is committed against the Constitutions of the Realm, is done by the Ministers and Officers; for the King, they say, does never amiss, but his ill Counsellors, which indeed is not altogether contrary to Truth. But if the Parliament should pretend to transgress its bounds, the King has power to dissolve it.

The Power and Strength of *England*.

§ 36. If we duly consider the Condition and Power of *England*, we shall find it to be a powerful and considerable Kingdom, which is able to keep up the Balance betwixt the Christian Princes in *Europe*; and which depending on its own Strength, is powerful enough to defend it self. For because it is surrounded every where by the Sea, none can make any attempt upon it, unless he be so powerful at Sea, as to be able entirely to ruine the Naval Force of *England*. And if it should happen that the *English* Fleet were quite defeated, yet would it prove a very hard task, to transport thither such an Army as could be supposed to be superiour to so powerful a Force as the *English* Nation is able to raise at home. But *England* ought to take especial care, that it fall not into civil Dissentions, since it has often felt the effects of the same, and the Seeds of them are remaining yet in that Nation; which chiefly arises from the difference in Religion, and the head-strong temper of this Nation, which makes it very fond of Novelties. Nevertheless a Wise and Courageous King may easily prevent this Evil, if he does not act against the general Inclination of the People, maintains a good Correspondence with the Parliament; and as soon as any Commotions happen, takes off immediately the Ring-leaders. Lastly, *England* and *Scotland* being now comprehended in one Island, whose chiefest Strength lies in a good Fleet, it is evident, that this King need not make any great account of such States as either are remote from the Sea, or else are not very powerful in Shiping. Wherefore as the King of *England* takes no great notice of *Germany*, (except as far as it relates to *France* or *Spain*) of *Poland* and other such like States; so it is easie for him to curb the Pirates on the *Barbary* Coast: *England* has nothing to fear from *Portugal*, and this must rather hope for Assistance from *England* and *Holland* against *Spain*.

With relation to other States.

To the Northern Crowns.

The Naval Strength of the Northern Crowns, *England* need not be jealous of, as long as the same is divided. Indeed it cannot be for the Interest of *England*, if one of those Kings should become absolute Master of the

East

East Sea, or they should be fain to depend on the Discretion of the *Dutch*. Since the Naval Strength of *Spain* is mightily decayed, *England* need not fear any thing from thence: Yet does it not seem to be the Interest of *England* to fall out with that Kingdom, considering what a vast Trade the *English* have into *Spain*; for *Spain* either consumes the *English* Commodities at home, or else exchanges them for Silver, by sending them into *America*. There are some who have computed, that in case of a War with *Spain*, the *English* would lose in Effects above thirty Millions: And besides this, their Trade into the *Levant* and other places, would be greatly endangered by the Privateers of *Biscay*, *Majorca*, and *Minorca*. Tho' the Land Forces of *France* are now-a-days much superiour to the *English*, this Island, both for its bigness and Strength, making up not above a third part of *France*; yet the Naval Strength of *France* has hitherto not been able to come in competition with the *English*. It is the chiefest Interest of *England*, to keep up the Balance betwixt *France* and *Spain*, and to take a special care, that the King of *France* does not become Master of all the *Netherlands*; for it is visible, that thereby his power at Sea would be encreased to that degree, that he might enter on a design of being even with *England*, for what they have formerly done to *France*. *Holland* seems to be the only obstacle that the *English* cannot be sole Masters of the Sea and of Trade; tho' after all they have no reason to fear the *Dutch* by Land, but only at Sea, because the *Dutch* Land Forces are not so considerable, as to be able to undertake any thing of great Moment. Nevertheless, how desirous soever the *English* are to be sole Masters at Sea, it does not seem to be the interest of *England*, frequently to engage it self in Wars with *Holland*, it having been observed, that the *Dutch*, since the Wars with *England* are rather increased in Valour, Experience, and Power at Sea. And because other Nations are not likely to suffer that *Holland* should be swallowed up by the *English*, or that one Nation should have the Monopoly of *Europe*, it seems therefore the best method for the *English* to set some others upon their Backs, who may give them so much work, as thereby to give a check to their growing Greatness; and in the mean while, take care to establish their own Power at Sea, and their Commerce abroad.

To Spain.

To France.

To Holland.

CHAP. V.

Of FRANCE.

The most ancient State of *France*.

§ 1. IT appears from the Records of Antiquity, that *Gaul*, now called *France*, was always a very opulent and populous Country. For in ancient times the *Gauls* conquered a great part of *Italy*, where they made Settlements; and over-running *Greece* and the adjacent Countries, inhabited that part of the *Lesser Asia*, which was called from them *Gallia*, or *Gallo-Græcia*. But after all, this potent People ignorant of their own Strength and Power, were in no capacity to exert it sufficiently against other Nations, because they were not then under the Government of one Prince, but divided into a great many petty States, which were always at variance with one another. This contributed much to facilitate the Conquest of the *Romans* over them, who otherwise dreaded no Nation so much as the *Gauls*; and tho' the unparallel'd Valour of *Julius Cæsar* was chiefly instrumental in subduing this Nation, yet with ten Legions he had work enough to effect it in ten Years time. But as soon as the *Romans* had brought this fair Country under their Subjection, they employed all means to suppress the Martial Spirit of the Nation, and incline them to Sloth and Idleness, in which Design they succeeded here as well as elsewhere. For in civilizing and refining the Manners of the People that came under their Yoke, they at the same time rendered 'em more Effeminate, and less qualified for Warlike Exploits. After *Gaul* had been near 500 Years under the Dominion of the *Romans*, it fell, in the Reign of the Emperor *Honorius*, into the Hands of the barbarous Nations. For the *Goths*, after they had over-run *Italy*, setled themselves in *Gallia Narbonensis*, and the *Burgundians* conquer'd a considerable part of the rest. But at last the *Franks* entring this Kingdom, setled and maintained themselves in it, giving it the title of *France*, after their own Name. These *Franks* were for certain *Germans*, tho' some of our modern *French* Writers pretend to demonstrate, that this Nation was a Colony of the ancient *Gauls*, who being over-stocked with People at home, passed over the *Rhine*, and having setled a Colony in *Germany*, after several hundred of Years returned into their Native Country. But it is more probable, that the *Franks* are the

Gaul subdu'd by the *Romans*.

By the Barbarous Nations.

the same Nations that were formerly encompass'd by the Rivers *Mayn*, *Rhine*, *Weser*, and the Sea; and which in *Tacitus*'s time were called *Salii*, *Bructeri*, *Frisii*, *Angrivari*, *Chamari*, *Sigambri* and *Chatti*; and who having enter'd into a mutual Confederacy against the *Romans*, called themselves in defiance of their Power, *Franks*, or *a free People*, as not doubting to be able to defend their Liberty against them. And it is certain, that they did transplant the *German* Tongue into *France*, which was for a great while after in fashion among Persons of the best Quality, till at last they used themselves by degrees, to the Latin Tongue, formerly introduced by the *Romans*, which being corrupted by the *Germans*, produced the modern *French* Language. It is also evident, that the Race of the ancient *Gauls* was then not quite extinguish'd, but that both Nations were by degrees united in one, tho' with this difference, that the *Frankish* Families made up the Body of the Nation.

The Franks came out of Germany.

The Origin of the French Language.

§ 2. But let this be as it will, all Historians agree, that about the Year 424, the *Franks* chose for their King *Pharamond*, who established among them wholesome Laws and Constitutions; tho' most are of Opinion, that not this *Pharamond*, but his Son *Clodion*, sirnamed *Long-Hair*, invaded *Gaul*; who, after he had been several times repulsed by *Ætius* the *Roman* General, at last took *Artois*, *Cambray*, *Tournay*, and some other places as far as the River *Somme*, makeing *Amiens* his place of Residence. He died in the Year 447; but his Successor and Kinsman *Merovæus*, having, in Conjunction with the *Roman* General *Ætius* and *Theoderick* the King of the *West-Goths*, beaten *Attila*, the King of the *Huns* out of *France*, extended his Dominions as far as *Mentz* on one side, and on the other side conquer'd *Picardy*, *Normandy*, and the greatest part of the Isle of *France*. The *Romans* themselves contributed to this loss, for that they had not only in the Battle fought against *Attila*, lost a great many of their best Forces, but *Ætius* also being fallen into disgrace with the Emperor *Valentinian*, was by him murthered; which *Ætius* may be justly said to have been the last great Captain the *Romans* had; there being after his Death nobody left who could resist *Merovæus*. From this King sprang the first Race of the *French* Kings, which is called the *Merovingian* Family. He died in the Year 458. His Son *Childerick* was banish'd for his Lasciviousness, in whose stead one *Ægidius*, of the ancient Race of the *Gauls*, was

Pharamond the first King.

Clodion.

Merovæus.

Childerick.

set up for King. But *Childerick*, thro' the faithfulness of his Friend *Guinoman*, was, after an Exile of eight Years, recalled out of *Thuringia*, whither he had fled, and restored to his Throne; and thereupon drove back the *Britains* and *Saxons* that made at that time great havock in *France*. He also conquered that part which is now called *Lorrain*, and took *Beauvau*, *Paris*, and some other places near the Rivers of the *Oise*, and the *Seyne*. He died in the Year 481. His Son *Clouis*, or *Lewis*, having killed *Syagrius*, the Son of *Ægidius*, established the *French* Monarchy, and added great Territories to the Kingdom. This King fell in love with *Clotildis*, of the Royal Race of *Burgundy*, who promised to marry him if he would turn Christian; which, however, he afterwards delayed to perform, till the *Allemans*, who in order to get footing in *France*, entered that Kingdom, with whom he had a bloody Battle near *Zulick*; and perceiving the *French* began to fall into disorder, he thereupon vowed, *That if he obtained the Victory, he would be baptized*: Accordingly, having carried the Victory, he was baptized at *Rheims*, by St. *Reim*; and his Example the whole Nation of the *French* followed. This done, he overturned the Kingdom of the *Goths*, which they had established in *Languedock*, and united that Country with his Kingdom: He also conquered several petty Principalities, and some part of *Upper Germany*. He died in the Year 511.

Clouis I. — *Battle of Zulick.* — *496.*

§ 3. After the Death of *Clouis*, *France* received a signal blow, the Kingdom being divided among his four Sons; who, tho' they annexed the Kingdom of *Burgundy* to it, yet, by this Division, each of 'em weaken'd their own Hands, and administred Fuel to the following intestine Dissentions: Nay, this mad Itch of Partition did not stop here, for they subdivided the Kingdom again among their Sons, which occasioned most dismal Civil Commotions in *France*; these Kings endeavouring, as it were, to out-do one another in Iniquity; and among the rest the two Queens *Brunechildis* and *Fredegundis* are infamous for their monstrous Crimes. At last *Clotarius* II. after encountering many Difficulties, reuniting the divided Kingdom, did in some measure restore its ancient State. He died in the Year 628. But his Son *Dagobart* fell into the same madness; for he not only gave part of the Kingdom to his Brother *Albert*, but also divided his own share among his two Sons; neither did he do any thing for the Benefit of the Publick during

France is divided. — *Clotarius II.* — *614.* — *Dagobert.*

ring his Reign. From this time the *French* Kings quite degenerated from their ancient Valour, giving themselves over to Laziness and Debauchery: Upon which the Grand Mareschals of the Kingdom did by degrees assume the Power and Administration of publick Affairs. Among these, *Pepin* descended of the noble Family of *Austrasia*, had the Administration of Affairs during the Space of twenty eight Years, under several Kings. His Son *Charles Martel* succeeded his Father in his Power and Office, which he rather augmented after he was grown framous by his Martial Exploits, having expelled the *Saracens*, who about that time conquering *Spain*, fell also into *France*, and of whom he killed a vast number. This Man took upon himself the Title of Duke of *France*, so that nothing remained with the Kings but the bare Title and an empty Name, they being kept in the Country, and once a Year carried for a Show thro' the City to expose them to the View of the People like strange Creatures. At last, *Pepin* the younger, Son of this *Charles Martel*, (who died in the Year 751.) having brought the great Men of the Kingdom over to his Party, deposed King *Childerick* II. and having put him into a Convent, got himself Proclaimed King of *France*. This was readily approved by Pope *Zachary*, who being then alarmed with the growing Power of the *Longobards* in *Italy*, endeavour'd by all means to oblige the King of *France* to come to his Assistance. And thus the *Merovingian* Family loses the Crown of *France*.

Pepin.

Charles Martel, 714.

732.

Pepin proclaimed King.

The *Merovingian* Family loses the Crown.

751.

§ 4. *Pepin*, to convince the World that he was not unworthy of the Crown, undertook an Expedition against the *Saxons*, whom he vanquished in a great Battle. And he had likewise, under the Reign of the former Kings, undertaken several Expeditions into *Germany* with great Success, and subdued some of the Nations bordering upon the *Rhine*. Not long after, an opportunity presented it self to make himself famous in *Italy*. For *Aistulphus*, King of the *Lombards*, had proposed to himself the Conquest of all *Italy*, having expelled the Governours appointed by the *Grecian* Emperors, who were then called *Exarches*, out of *Ravenna*, and all other places that were under their Jurisdiction, and was ready to March directly against *Rome*; upon which Pope *Stephen* III. being in great fear of this Enemy, and not knowing where to find Assistance, crav'd Aid of *Pepin*, whom he at last perswaded to take his part

Pepin's Expedition.

He assists the Pope against the *Lombards*.

against *Aistulphus*. In this War *Pepin* recovered from *Aistulphus* all that he had before taken from the *Grecian* Emperors in *Italy*, the Revenue of which, 'tis said, he gave to the *Roman* See, reserving to himself, as it is very probable, the Sovereignty over these places. He gained by this Action the Reputation of being very Zealous; and by bestowing these Revenues upon the Holy Chair, got firm footing in *Italy*, and the advantage of swaying Matters there according to his Pleasure. He likewise made *Tassilo*, Duke of *Bavaria* his Vassal, and reduced the Duke of *Aquitain*. This *Pepin* died in the Year 768, leaving behind him two Sons, *Charles* and *Carolomannus*, who divided the Kingdom betwixt them. But *Carolomannus* dying quickly after, the whole Kingdom fell to *Charles*. This *Charles* was justly sirnamed *The Great*, as having carried the *French* Monarchy to the highest pitch of its Greatness, and none of his Successors having been able to attain to the like, tho' some of them have aim'd at it. For after routing *Desiderius*, the last King of the *Lombards*, who endeavoured to recover what was formerly taken from *Aistulphus*, he conquered the Kingdom, and brought it under his Subjection. Having routed *Tassilo*, who had taken upon him the Title of King of *Bavaria*, and having waged War against the *Saxons*, for the space of thirty two Years, whom he at last brought under his Obedience, obliging them to embrace the Christian Faith; he thereupon subdued all *Germany*, and there erected several Episcopal Sees and Monasteries, by the help of the Priests, to reform the barbarous Manners of this Savage People. He likewise subdued the *Sclavonians*, *Danes* and *Huns*, and took from the *Saracens* part of *Spain*, as far as the River *Iberus*, tho' his Forces, in their return home, were defeated near *Ronceval*; in which Action *Roland*, that celebrated Hero, lost his Life. This *Charles* was in the Year 800, at Christmas, being then at *Rome*, proclaimed Emperor by the People, by the Instigation of the Pope, in St. *Peter's* Church; tho' he gained nothing by this Title, unless it was the Sovereignty or Protection of the *Roman* Church, and the Patrimony of St. *Peter*, if both did not belong to him before; for all the rest he enjoy'd before under other Titles. He died in the Year 814.

Charles the Great.

774.

He is proclaimed Emperor of the Romans.

Lewis the Pious.

§ 5. After the death of *Charles the Great*, the *French* Monarchy began to decline again, because his Son *Lewis*, sirnamed *The Pious*, was more fit to be a Priest than a Soldier:

er. And it is certain, that so vast a Kingdom, where the new Conquests were not yet well setled, did require a Prince of a Military Spirit. And notwithstanding he had the good Fortune to force some of the Rebellious Nations to return to their Duty, yet he committed afterwards two fatal Over-sights, when in his Life-time he gave to his Sons the Titles of Kings, and divided the Kingdom betwixt them. The first of which proved pernicious to himself, the second to the Monarchy. For these impious and ungrateful Sons were not for staying for their Father's Death, but Rebelling against him, made him, after he was deserted by every body, their Prisoner. The Bishops who had been kept by him under strict Discipline, after they had condemned him, forc'd him to resign the Government. But the great Men of the Kingdom quickly repenting, restored him to his Throne, and he also pardoned his Sons. He died in the Year 840, having before his Death made a new Division of the Kingdom betwixt his Sons, the Effects of which appeared soon after to the World, when *Lotharius*, the elder Brother, who had likewise the Title of Emperor, attempted to dispossess his two Brothers of their Shares; upon which, the other two Brothers, *Lewis* and *Charles* entring into a Confederacy, forced him to divide the Monarchy with them, having first obtained a bloody Victory near *Fountenay*, not far from *Auxerre*, in which Battle were slain above 100000 Men, and among them the Flower of the *French* Nation. In this Partition *Germany* fell to the share of *Lewis* the second Brother, which ever since has continued separate from *France*, and has made a distinct Empire; and the youngest, or third Brother, *Charles*, sirnamed *the Bald*, got for his Portion the greatest part of *France*, *viz*, all the Country that lies betwixt the *Western Ocean* and the *Maese*: But the eldest Brother retained *Italy*, *Provence*, and all those Countries which are situated betwixt the *Scheld*, the *Maese*, the *Rhine*, and the *Saone*. Under the Reign of this *Charles the Bald*, the *Normans* (so they called the *Danes* and *Norwegians*) fell, with a considerable Force into *France*, making great Havock where-ever they came: And the Kingdom was weakened to that degree, by the late bloody Battles, and its being divided into so many Principalities (for the Sons of *Lotharius* had also shared their Father's Provinces among themselves) that it was not strong enough to dislodge these Robbers of its Dominions, but was obliged, under *Charles*, sirnamed *The Simple*, to give into their Possession

[Margin notes: He divides his Kingdom. — His Sons rebel. — 833. — *Lotharius.* — *Germany* disunited from *France*. — *Charles the Bald*. — The *Normans* make an Irruption into *France*.]

session the Province of *Neustria*, which they called after their Name, *Normandy*. The Sons of *Lotharius* dying without Issue, *Charles the Bald*, and the Son of *Lewis* King of *Germany*, shared their part betwixt them, out of which *Charles* got *Provence*, at last *Charles* obtained the Title of Emperor, and died in the Year 877. His Son *Lewis*, firnamed *Balbus*, succeeded him, who dying soon after, left the Kingdom to his two Sons, who were very young, *viz.* to *Lewis* III. and *Carolomannus*; and from them *Lewis* King of *Germany* took *Lorrain*. *Lewis* III. dying in the Year 882, as did *Carolomannus* in the Year 884. none was left but a Brother of theirs by the Fathers side, *viz.* the Son of *Lewis* firnamed *Balbus*, who being then a Child of five Years of Age, was afterwards called *Charles the Simple*. For at that time the Authority of the Kings of *France* had dwindled to that degree, that it was a common Custom to give them Sur-names according to the respective defects of Body or Mind that were obvious in them. During his Minority he was committed to the Tuition of his Cousin *Carolus Crassus*, who had likewise the Title of Emperor; but not long after, because he was very infirm both in Body and Mind, was deposed, and died in the Year 888. The Royal Authority being thus contemned, and nothing but Divisions found in the Kingdom, the great Men of the Kingdom mightily increased their own Power, so that, whereas they used formerly to be Governors of their Provinces under the King's Command, they now began to claim them as a Property belonging to themselves independent of the King. It is related by some, that the Kings at that time had nothing left but *Rheims* and *Laon* that they could really call their own; which Evil could not be totally suppress'd by the following Kings till several hundred Years after. After the Death of *Carolus Crassus*, *Eudo* Count of *Paris* got himself to be crowned King, and waged War with *Charles the Simple*, but died in the Year 888. However, *Charles the Simple* afterwards found another rival for the Crown. For *Rudolph* King of *Burgundy*, got himself to be crowned King of *France*, making *Charles the Simple* his Prisoner, who died during his Imprisonment. After the death of *Rudolph* (which happened in the Year 936) reign'd *Lewis* IV. firnamed *Outremer*, because he had, during the Imprisonment of his Father, sheltered himself in *England*. This King's Reign was full of intestine Commotions; he died in the Year 954. leaving for his Successor his Son *Lotharius*, who like-

877. *Ludovicus Balbus Ludov.* III. and *Carolomannus.*

Charles the Simple.

The decay of the royal Authority. The excessive Power of the Nobles.

Eudo Count of *Paris* crown'd King of *France*.

Rudolph of *Burgundy* crown'd King.

936. *Lewis Outremer.*

Lotharius.

likewise reign'd in continual Troubles till the Year 985, leaving behind him his Son *Lewis*, sirnamed *the Faint-hearted*, of whom the *French* Historians only say this, that he did nothing. He had for his Tutor and Administrator of the Kingdom, *Hugh Capet* Earl of *Paris*. After this Kings Death, his Uncle, the Son of *Lewis*, sirnamed *Outremer*, laid Claim to the Crown, but was disappointed in his Pretensions by the great Power of *Hugh Capet*. He afterwards endeavoured to maintain his Right by force of Arms, but was made a Prisoner, and dying in Prison, put an end to the *Carolingian* Race, or at least to its Inheritance of the Crown of *France*; which had been in its Possession for at least 236 Years. It is very remarkable, that this Family lost the Kingdom thro' the same Error by which the former lost it. For tho' this Family had by prodigious Conquests raised the Power of *France*, yet were the Conquests soon after, by the Divisions made of the Kingdom again, disunited, and even a considerable part quite separated from that Kingdom, and annexed to the *German* Empire. Besides this, by the Negligence of these Kings, and the excessive Power of the great Men in the Kingdom, *France* was reduced to a very low Condition.

Lewis the Faint-hearted.

987.

The *Carolingian* Family extinct.

§. 6. As *Hugh Capet*, the first Founder of the present Royal Family obtained the Crown, not so much by right of Succession, as by the Assistance of the chief Men of the Kingdom, who excluded the right Heir; so (as Story goes) he was obliged to sink a great many of the ancient Royal Prerogatives, and to confirm to the great Men of the Kingdom the Power of governing their Provinces, with the Titles of Dukes and Earls, under Condition that they should acknowledge themselves Vassals of the Kingdom, tho' not obliged to depend absolutely on the King's Commands: So that *France* at that Time was like a mishapen and weak Body. *Hugh*, in the mean time, reannexed to the Crown (which at that Time had scarce any thing left that could be called her own) the County of *Paris*, the Dutchy of *France*, all the extent of Land that lies betwixt the Rivers *Seyne* and the *Loire*, and the County of *Orleans*. Among the great Men of the Kingdom, the chief were the Dukes of *Normandy* (on whom also depended *Britany*) of *Burgundy*, of *Aquitain*, and of *Gascoigne*; the Earls of *Flanders*, *Champaign*, and *Toulouse*, the latter of which was likewise Duke of *Languedoc*: But the

Hugh Capet the first of the present Race.

the Counties of *Vienne*, *Provence*, *Savoy* and *Dauphinee*, belong'd to the Kingdom of *Arelat*, which was a part of the *German Empire*. Yet the ensuing Kings had the good Fortune to see all these Demi-Sovereign Princes laid aside, and their Countries reunited to the Crown of *France*. *Hugh* died in the Year 996, whose Son *Robert*, a Prince celebrated for his Vertue reigned very peaceably, and by an Hereditary Right possess'd the Dukedom of *Burgundy*, upon the Death of his Father's Brother. The Cruelty exercised by the Pope upon this King, is so remarkable, that we can't but take notice of it. The King having an Intention of marrying *Bertha*, of the House of *Burgundy*, which Match was esteemed very beneficial to his State; and the said *Bertha* standing with him in the fourth Degree of Consanguinity, and he having been Godfather to a Child of hers in her former Husbands Time: He desired, and obtained the Approbation of his Bishops, the said Marriage being in effect prohibited by the Canon Law. But the Pope from thence took occasion to Excommunicate the King and the whole Kingdom, which proved so mischievous, that the King was deserted by all his Servants, except three or four, and no Body would touch the Victuals that came from his Table, insomuch that it was thrown to the Dogs. He died in the Year 1033. The Reign of his Son *Henry* was in like manner not very famous, except that he waged some inconsiderable Wars with his Vassals. He presented his Brother *Robert* with the Dukedom of *Burgundy*, from whom sprang the Race of the Dukes of *Burgundy*, dignified with the Royal Blood. He died in the Year 1060. His Son *Philip* did nothing memorable; he was likewise Excommunicated by the Pope, upon the score of his Marriage, but at last obtained a Dispensation. Under the Reign of this King *Philip*, *William* Duke of *Normandy* conquered *England*. About the same time the first Expedition was undertaken into the *Holy Land*, which Extravagancy continued near 200 Years after. The Popes drew the most Benefit from these Expeditions, assuming to themselves an Authority not only to Command, but also to Protect all such as had listed themselves under the Cross. Besides, under this pretext, frequent Indulgencies were sent abroad into the World; and what was given towards the use of this War, was collected and distributed by their Legates. Indeed, the King of *France* and other Kings received thereby this Benefit, that

Robert.

The Pope Excommunicates him and his Kingdom.

Henry I.

Philip I.

William Duke of *Normandy* Conquers *England*. Expedition into the *Holy Land*.

that these Wars carried off a great many turbulent Spirits; and a great many of the Nobility used either to sell or else to Mortgage their Estates to raise Money for the Expedition; and if any of them happen'd to die in the Expedition, leaving no Heirs behind them, their Estates fell to the King: Nay farther, 'twas by this means that *that* prodigious number of People, wherewith *France* was over-stocked at that Time, was much lessened, whereby the Kings got an Opportunity to deal more easily with the rest. Nevertheless, when afterwards the Kings, either by Instigation of the Popes, or out of their own Inclination, undertook these Expeditions in their own Persons, they found the dismal Effects of it. For neglecting the Government of their own Kingdoms, all the Profit that accrued to them by so doing was, that the best of their Subjects were led to the Slaughter; for it was impossible to maintain these Conquests, as long as they were not Masters of *Egypt*; whereas, if that Kingdom had been made the Seat of the intended Empire, and the Store-house of the War, a Kingdom might have been established, which would have been able to support it self by its own Strength. This King died in the Year 1108. His Son *Lewis*, sirnamed *The Fat*, *Lewis the Fat.* was always at variance with *Henry* I. King of *England*, and in continual Troubles with the petty Lords in *France*, who did him considerable Mischiefs from their strong Castles; yet he was too hard for them at last, and died in the Year 1137. His Son *Lewis* VII. sirnamed *The Younger*, under- *Lewis VII.* took, upon the Persuasion of St. *Bernhard*, an Expedition into the *Holy Land*; but this proved a fatal Expedition, for by the Defeat he received at *Pamphylia*, and the unsuccessless Siege of *Damascus*, which he was forced to quit, and the Fatigues of so great a Journey, among a barbarous, perfidious People; after he had ruined a great Army, he return'd with the wretched remains into *France*, without having done any thing answerable to such an Undertaking. *His unfortunate Expedition into the Holy Land.* But he committed the greatest Error, when he divorced himself from his Lady *Eleonora*, sole Heiress of *Aquitain* and *Poictou*; whether out of Jealousie or Tenderness of Conscience is uncertain, she being his Cousin in the third or fourth Degree. This *Eleonora* was immediately after married to *Henry* Duke of *Normandy*, afterwards King of *England*, the second of that Name, who, by this Match, annexed these fair Countries to the Crown of *England*. In fine, being kept in a continual alarm by his

petty

petty Vassals, but especially by *Henry* II. King of *England*; he died in the Year 1180.

Philip II. the *Conqueror.* §. 17. His Son *Philip* II. sirnamed *Augustus*, or *The Conqueror*, was at first engaged in a War against *Henry* II. King of *England*; from whom he took several considerable Places; which, however, he restored afterwards to his Son *Richard*, with whom he enter'd into a League to retake *Jerusalem* from the *Saracens*, pursuant to which, both the Kings went thither in Person with a considerable Force. Another Expedition to the *Holy Land.* But a Jealousie arising betwixt the two Kings, nothing was done worth mentioning; for *Richard* accused *Philip*, that he had an ill Design against him in *Sicily* in their Voyage; besides that, he had refused to consummate the before stipulated Match betwixt his Sister and *Richard*: Upon which, as soon as *Ptolemais* had been taken by their joint Forces, *Philip*, under pretence of Sickness, returned into *France*, leaving only with *Richard*, *Hugh* III. Duke of *Burgundy*, with some Troops, who envying *Richard*, hindred the taking of the City of *Jerusalem*, *Richard* after his return from that unfortunate Expedition, declared War against *Philip*, which was afterwards carried on by his Brother *John*. War betwixt *France* and *England.* In this War *Philip* had much the better of the *English*, for he took from them *Normandy*, and the Counties of *Anjou*, *Mayne*, *Touraine*, *Berry* and *Poictou*. At the same Time he took care to have the Earl of *Tholouse* excommunicated by the Pope, and ruined, for taking into his Protection the *Albigenses*. He likewise obtained a great Victory near *Bovines*, betwixt *Lisle* and *Tournay*, over the Emperor *Otho* IV. who being join'd by the Earl of *Flanders*, attack'd him with an Army of 150000 Men, whilst the King of *England* was to fall into *France* on the side of *Aquitain*. This King was so succesful in his Wars against *England*, that his Son *Lewis* was very near obtaining that Crown. 1223. And tho' he was drove out of *England*, yet after his Fathers Death, he pursued his Victories against the *English* in *France*, taking from them, among other Places, the City of *Rochelle*. But this *Lewis* VIII. *Lewis* VIII. did not Reign long, for he died in the Year 1226, leaving for Successor his Son *Lewis* IX. *Lewis* IX. sirnamed *The Holy*, during whose Minority, his Mother, *Blanch* of *Castile*, had the Supreme Administration of Affairs; and tho' some of the Nobility raised great Troubles against her, she subdued them all by her singular Prudence. In the Year 1244, the

the City of *Jerusalem* was ransack'd by some *Persians*, who
called themselves *Chorasmii*. *Lewis* being about the same
time dangerously ill, made a Vow, *That if he recover'd he
would undertake an Expedition against those Infidels*, which
he afterwards performed. But before his Departure, he
issued out a Proclamation throughout the Kingdom, intimating, that whoever had received any damage by his
Soldiers, should have Restitution made 'em, which was
performed accordingly. In this Expedition he took the
strong City of *Damiata*; but the overflowing of the River
Nile hindered him from taking *Grand Cairo*. After the
River was returned to its usual Bounds, he vanquished the
Enemy in two Battles; but they receiving new Reinforcements, cut off the Provisions from the *French*, who at the
same time were extremely pester'd with the Scurvy. The
King then resolved to retreat towards *Damiata*, but in
his March thither they Attack'd him, gave him a terrible
overthrow, and took him Prisoner, but released him again
for a Ransom of 400000 Livres, and the Restitution of
the City of *Damiata*. Thus he marched with the sorry
Remains of his Army, which from 30000 Men was
mouldered away to 6000, to *Ptolemais*, where, after he
had given what Assistance he could to the Christians, he
at last returned home. 'Twas in the Reign of this King 1254.
that *France* had the first opportunity to intermeddle in the
Affairs of *Italy*; and indeed this Kingdom never reaped
any great Benefit from their Pretensions that way. *Manfred*, natural Son of the Emperor *Frederick* II. having first
killed King *Conrad* his Brother, made himself King of
Naples and *Sicily*. But the Pope, on whom this Kingdom
depended as a Fief, being dissatisfied with *Manfred*, offered the same to *Charles* Earl of *Anjou*, Brother of *Lewis*
IV. King of *France*; and he accepting it, was crowned 1261.
at *Rome*, upon Condition that he should pay to the Pope
8000 Ounces of Gold, and make a yearly Present of a
White Horse as an acknowledgment; and if he was chosen Emperor, that he should not unite that Kingdom with
the Empire: The Pope being unwilling to have any one
more powerful than himself in *Italy*. *Charles* thereupon
vanquished *Manfred*, and having murthered him and his
Children, took Possession of the Kingdom. Then *Conra-
din*, Duke of *Swabia*, came with an Army to recover the
Kingdom, which was the Inheritance of his Ancestors;
and being routed in a Battle near the Lake of *Celano*, was 1268.
made

A third Expedition to the Holy Land without success.

The first Pretensions of the French upon the Kingdom of Naples.

made a Prisoner, and in the Year next following had his Head cut off at *Naples*, by the Instigation of the Pope, who being asked by *Charles*, *What he had best to do with his Prisoner?* answered, *Vita Conradini, mors Caroli*; *Mors Conradini, vita Caroli.* And as by the Death of this young Prince was extinguished the Noble Race of the Dukes of *Swabia*, so this *Charles* laid the first Pretensions of *France* to the Kingdom of *Naples*. In the mean while King *Lewis*, not satisfied with his former unfortunate Expedition against the Infidels, resolved to try his Fortune against *Tunis*, either because he found that this place lay very convenient for his Brother's Kingdom of *Sicily*, or because he hoped thereby to open a way for the Conquest of *Egypt*, without which, all the Expeditions into the *Holy Land* were like to prove ineffectual. But in this Siege he lost a great part of his Army by Sickness, and died himself there in the Year 1270. From the youngest Son of this *Lewis* IV. *viz.* from *Robert* Earl of *Clairmont* sprang the *Bourbon* Family, which now sways the Scepter of *France*.

An unfortunate Expedition of S. *Lewis*.

Philip the Hardy.

§ 8. His Son *Philip*, sirnamed *the Hardy*, succeeded him, under whose Reign that considerable Earldom of *Thoulouse* was united to the Crown of *France*, *Alfonsus*, Son of *Lewis* IX. who had married the only Heiress of this Country, happening to die without Issue, in an Expedition into *Africa*. In the Reign also of this King fell out the so much celebrated *Sicilian Vespers*, in which all the *French* were at one blow extirpated out of *Sicily*. The Business was thus. Some *French-men* had Ravished the Wife of *John* of *Prochyta*, born at *Salerno*, who enflamed with Revenge, sought for Aid from *Pieter* King of *Arragon*, hoping by his Assistance to drive *Charles* out of *Sicily*. At the same time the *Sicilians* were very averse to the *French*, who had committed great Outrages in that Kingdom; and Pope *Nicholas* V. lent a helping hand, as being apprehensive of the Power of *Charles*; as did also *Michael Paleologus* the *Constantinopolitan* Emperor, because *Charles* had made some Pretensions to that Empire. Upon the whole, *John*, disguised in a Monks Habit, travelled about from place to place, till he had brought his Design to perfection. It was next to a Miracle that the Design was not betray'd in three Years time, it having been so long a forming in several places. At last it was put in Execution, it being agreed upon, that on the

The *Sicilian Vespers*.

1282. second Holy-day in *Easter*, at that very time when the Bells

rung

rung in to the *Vespers*, all the *French* throughout the whole Kingdom of *Sicily* should be massacred at once, which was done accordingly within two Hours time with great Barbarity, no Person being spared in the Massacre. This done, *Pieter* King of *Arragon* possess'd himself of the Kingdom of *Sicily*. And tho' the Pope order'd the *Croisade* to be preached up against *Pieter*, and declared *Charles*, the second Son of *Philip*, King of *Arragon*, and this *Philip* marched with a great Army to put his Son in Possession, yet it all proved labour in vain, and *Philip* died in the Year 1285. His Son and Successor *Philip*, sirnamed *the Handsome*, upon some frivolous Pretences, began a War with the *English*, taking from them the City of *Bourdeaux*, and the greatest part of *Aquitain*, which however they soon after recovered by vertue of a Peace concluded betwixt them. Not long after he attacked the Earl of *Flanders*, who, by the Instigation of the *English*, had entred into a Confederacy with a great many Neighbouring Lords against him, and from whom he took most of his strong Holds. But the *Flemmings* being soon tired with the Insolencies committed by the *French*, cut in pieces the *French* Garrisons; whereupon the King sent an Army under the Command of *Robert* Earl of *Artois*, to reduce them to Obedience; but he was defeated near *Courtray*, there being 20000 *French* slain upon the Spot, which happened chiefly by this Misfortune, that the Cavalry putting on at full speed rode precipitantly into a Ditch. It is related that the *Flemmings* got above 8000 gilt Spurs as a Booty from the *French*. And tho' afterwards there were 25000 killed of the *Flemmings*, yet they quickly recollecting themselves, raised another Army of 60000 Men, and obliged the King, by a Peace made betwixt them, to restore them to their ancient State. This King *Philip* also, with consent of the Pope, suppress'd the rich Order of the Knights Templers, and died in the Year 1314. To him succeeded his three Sons, each in his turn, who all died without Issue, and without doing any thing of Moment. The eldest, *Lewis* X. sirnamed *Hutin*, died in the Year 1316; and his Brother *Philip*, sirnamed *the Tall*, had a Contest for the Crown with his deceased Brother's Daughter *Joan*, she being supported by her Mothers Brother, the Duke of *Burgundy*, but it was determined in favour of *Philip* by vertue of the *Salick* Law. Under this King the *Jews* were banished out of *France*, as being accused of poisoning the Fountains and Springs. He died in the Year 1322. To him succeeded the third Brother, *Charles* IV. sirnamed the *Handsome*, in whose Reign all the *Italians* and *Lombards*, who

Philip the Handsome. 1292.

He has ill success in *Flanders*.

1302.

1334.

He suppress'd the *Templers*.

Lewis X.

Philip the Tall.

Charles IV.

being Usurers, did exact upon the People, were banished the Kingdom. He commenced a War in *Aquitain* against the *English*, but these Differences were quickly composed by the Intercession of Queen *Isabella*, Sister of *Charles*. He died in the Year 1328.

Philip of Valois. His Title contested by *Edward* III. of *England*, and on what ground.

§ 9. After the Death of this King, *France* was for a great many Years together torn in pieces by very unfortunate and bloody Wars, which had almost proved fatal to this Kingdom: For a Contest arose about the Succession, betwixt *Philip of Valois*, *Philip the Handsom*'s Brother's Son, and *Edward* III. King of *England*, the above-mention'd *Philip the Handsom*'s Daughters Son. The former pretended a Right by virtue of the *Salick Law*, which excludes the Females from the Succession; But the latter, tho' he did not deny the *Salick Law*, made use of the plea, that this Law did not bar from the Succession the Sons born of the King's Daughters. And it was certain, that he was nearer akin to the deceased King than *Philip*, neither could any Precedent be brought where a Son of the King's Daughter had been excluded from the Succession to admit his Brother's Son. However the Estates of *France* declared for *Philip*, partly upon the perswasion of *Robert* Earl of *Artois*, and partly because they were unwilling to depend, as an accessory appendage upon *England*. And tho' King *Edward* put up this Affront at first, and came in Person to do Homage to *Philip* for his Provinces which he was possess'd of in *France*; yet not long after he began to show his Resentment. Besides, the States of *England* exhorted him not to let fall his just Pretensions tamely, and *Robert* Earl of *Artois*, *Philip*'s Cousin, being fallen out with him, for not consenting to reduce the County of *Artois*, stir'd up King *Edward* to undertake a War against *France*. In the mean time while *Philip* had defeated the *Flemmings*, who were risen in Rebellion against their Earl, to that degree, that of 16000 Men not one escaped the Sword. In the Year 1336. the *English* began to make War against *France*, which was carried on for some Years with equal Advantage on both sides, and was discontinued by several Truces; till at last *Edward* landed with an Army in *Normandy*, and out-braving the *French*, approach'd to the very Gates of *Paris*. But *Edward* making soon after his Retreat through *Picardy* towards *Flanders*, was overtaken by *Philip* near *Albeville*; where a bloody Battle was fought betwixt them. The *French* Forces being extreamly tir'd by a long March, gave the *English* an easie Victory. Besides, some *Genouese* Foot retreated immediately,

War with *England*.

Battle near *Crecy*.

diately, their Bows having been rendred useless by the rainy Weather; which the Duke d'Alenzon perceiving, and thinking it to have been done by Treachery, fell with a Body of Horse in among them, and so caused the first Confusion. And further, the English made use of four or five Pieces of great Brass Cannon against the French, which being never seen before in France, caused a great Terror in the French Army. This Victory is the more remarkable, because (according to the French Historians) the English were not above 25000 strong, whereas the French were above 100000. Out of which number 30000 Foot Soldiers were slain, and 1200 Horsemen, amongst whom was the King of Bohemia. This King, though he was blind, yet charged the Enemy on Horse-back betwixt two of his Friends, who had ty'd his Horse to theirs, and they were all three found dead together. The next day there was a great Slaughter made among some French Troops, who not knowing what had passed the day before, were on their March to joyn the French Camp. After this Battle, the English took Calais, Philip having in vain attempted its relief with 150000 Men. This unfortunate King, however, received this one Comfort, that the Dukedom of Dauphinee was annexed to the Crown of France, by the Gift of Hubert the last Duke, upon Condition, that the eldest Son of the Kings of France should always bear the Title of Dauphine. This Hubert having conceived a mortal hatred against the then Earl of Savoy, had before put himself under the Protection of France; but when afterwards by an unfortunate Accident he kill'd his only Son, he retir'd thro' grief into a Monastery, giving to the King of France the Possession of his Country. This King Philip also ransom'd and repossess'd himself of Roussilion and Montpelier, and was the first who imposed that so much abominated Tax in France upon Salt, called the Gabel, whereby the Subjects are oblig'd to pay for Salt and Sea-Water at so dear a rate. In allusion to which, King Edward used to call him in jest, *The Author of the Salick Law*. He died in the Year 1350.

The English take Calais. 1347.

Dauphinee annexed to France.

1349.

Philip introduced the Gabel.

§ 10. His Son and Successor, *John*, was yet more unfortunate in his Wars against the *English* than his Father. For the Truce being expir'd, the War began afresh, wherein Prince *Edward* made an Inrode with 12000 Men out of *Aquitain*, destroying all round about him; and King *John* intending to cut off his retreat, overtook him with all his Forces near *Maupertuis*, two Leagues from *Poictiers*. The Prince offer'd the King Satisfaction for the damage sustained, which

John unfortunate in his Wars against the English.

Battle near Poictiers.

he refusing to accept of, attack'd Prince *Edward* in his advantagious Post, he being surrounded with Hedges and Vineyards; but the *English*, by the help of their Bows soon broke through his Vanguard, and afterwards the whole Army, which consisted of 50000 Men, killing upon the Spot (as it is related by the *French* Historians) 6000 *French*, amongst whom were 1200 Gentlemen, and fifty Noblemen; and taking Prisoners, the King and his youngest Son; the three eldest having, by the counsel and direction of their Governour, sav'd themselves by flying upon the first break of the Army.

1356. During the Father's Imprisonment, *Charles*, the *Dauphine*, took upon him the Administration of Affairs, but the People which had been sorely oppress'd hitherto, being unwilling to obey it, caused great Disorders in the Kingdom. The Peasants rose up against the Nobility, and the Citizens of *Paris* made heavy Complaints. The Soldiers for want of Pay lived at Discretion, and made a miserable havock in the Country; *Charles* of *Navarre* added fuel to the Fire, in hopes to make his own Advantage by these troublesome Times, and did not stick to make pretensions to the Crown; yet Matters were composed with him at last. But the Estates of *France* refusing to accept of such Conditions as were proposed by the *English*, the King of *England* enter'd *France* with a great Army, and over-run the greatest part of it, but could not make himself Master of any fortify'd place. Then a Peace was concluded at *Bretigny*, a League from *Chartres*; by virtue of which the *French* were to surrender to the *English* besides what they were possess'd of before, *Poictou*, *Xaintonge*, *Rochelle*, *Pais d'Aulnis*, *Angoumois*, *Perigord*, *Limosin*, *Quercy*, *Agenois*, and *Bigorre*, with the Sovereignty over them; besides *Calais*, and the Counties *d'Oye*, *Guisnes*, and *Ponthieu*, and three Millions of Livers, as a Ransom for the King's Person. This Peace was very hard for *France*, and continued not long. King *John* forc'd by Necessity, was oblig'd to do another thing little becoming his Grandeur, for he sold his Daughter to *Galeace*, Viscount of *Milan*, for 600000 Crowns, giving her in Marriage to the said Viscount. This King presented his youngest Son *Philip*, sirnamed *the Hardy*, with the Dukedom of *Burgundy*, it being vacant by the death of the last Duke. From this *Philip* descended the famous Dukes of *Burgundy*, whose Territories, at last, devolved to the House of *Austria*. This King died in *England*, whether he was gone to make Satisfaction for his Son, who being a Hostage there had made his escape.

A dishonourable peace to *France*.

1364.

§ 11. King

§ 11. King *John* was succeeded by his Son *Charles* V. sirnamed *the Wise*, who prudently made amends for the rashness of his Grand-father and Father, by never engaging himself in Battles with the *English*, but protracting the War, and by secret Intrigues endeavouring to tire out their Courage. The disbanded Soldiers had mutiny'd, and were become so Insolent in their depredations, that no body durst oppose them. These he sent into *Spain*, where *Peter*, sirnamed *the Cruel*, and *Henry* I. contended then for the Crown of *Castile*: And their numerous force did so alarm the Pope, that in their March he presented them with 200000 Livres, and a good store of Indulgences, to divert them thereby from taking their way near *Avignon*. *Edward* Prince of *Wales* imbarqued also in this War, but got nothing by it but a sickly Body, and great want of Money. Upon which he pretended to lay a Tax upon his Vassals in *Guienne*, to pay off his Soldiers; but they complained thereof to the King of *France*; who having made all necessary preparations, and being inform'd that the Prince languished under a mortal Disease, summon'd him to appear in *Paris*, pretending, that the Peace made at *Bretigny* was of no force, since the *English* had not performed the Conditions, and had since that time committed Hostilities; and with that plea he insisted upon his former Right of Sovereignty over *Aquitain*. And Prince *Edward* having sent him a disdainful Answer, King *Charles* denounced War against the *English*. A great many Fast-days and Processions were kept by the King's Order in *France*; and the Priests made it their business to represent the Justice of the King's Cause, and the Injustice of the *English* to the People. By this way he insinuated himself into the Favour of the *French* that lived under the *English* Jurisdiction, and influenced his own Subjects to raise the larger Sums of Money. The Archbishop of *Tholouse* alone did, by his cunning and eloquent Perswasives, bring over to his Party above fifty Cities and strong Castles. The Constable *Bertrand du Guesclin* did also great mischief to the *English* with small Parties, and not only worsted them in several Rencounters, but beat them out of *Perigord* and *Limosin*: But in *Guienne* especially, the *English* Affairs were in a bad Condition, after the *Spanish* Fleet, which was sent to the assistance of the *French*, by *Henry*, King of *Castile*, had ruin'd the *English* Fleet near *Rochelle*. After which exploit *Poictiers* was taken from them, and *Rochelle* upon very advantageous Conditions, surrender'd it self to the King of *France*. And King *Edward* being detained by contrary Winds, and so unable to bring over timely Relief, *Xanitonge*, *Angoumois*, and

Charles the Wise.

He declares War against the *English*.

some other places followed the Example of the former. The *English*, not long after, with an Army of 30000 Men, marched from *Calais* cross the Country as far as *Guienne*, ravaging and plundering by the way where-ever they came; yet would *Charles* never hazard a Battle with them, but contented himself to annoy them with Skirmishes, in which he did them considerable Mischief. The Pope, in the mean time laboured hard to make Peace betwixt these two Crowns, but King *Edward* hapening to die about that time, King *Charles* took hold of this Opportunity, and attacking the *English* with five several Armies at one time, took all from them but *Calais*, *Bourdeaux*, and *Bayonne* in *Guienne*; and *Cherbug* in *Normandy*. The *English*, during the Minority of their King, being at the same time pester'd with the Plague, and the War with the *Scots*, were not in a Capacity to send sufficient Relief: Though after all *Charles* miscarried in his Enterprize against *Britany*. In the year 1379, the Emperor *Charles* IV. came to visit him in *Paris*, where he constituted the *Dauphin* a perpetual Vicar of the Empire in *Dauphinee*: And ever since, say the *French*, the *German* Emperors never did pretend to any thing in *Dauphinee*, or in the Kingdom of *Arelat*. He died in the Year 1380.

After the Death of *Edward*, *Charles* attacks the *English* with Advantage.

Charles VI.

§ 12. Now we are come to that most unfortunate Reign of *Charles* VI. At the very beginning of which one of the main occasions of Mischief to *France* was, that *Joan*, Queen of *Naples*, standing in fear of *Charles de Duraz*, did adopt *Lewis*, Duke of *Anjou*, declaring him Heir of that Kingdom. The Duke willingly accepting of her Offer, raised, on her behalf, an Army of 30000 Horse, applying to that use the Treasure left by *Charles* V. which he had got clandestinely into his Possession. With this Army he made himself Master of *Provence*, which then belong'd to *Joan*. And tho' in the mean time *Charles de Duraz* having kill'd *Joan*, had made himself Master of the Kingdom: the Duke of *Anjou*, nevertheless pursued his intended Expedition; but was by continual Marches, and the cunning of *Charles*, led about and tir'd to that degree, that he died in great Misery, very few of so great an
1384. Army having had the good fortune to return into *France*. The People also were generally much dissatisfy'd at the beginning: For those who had the Tuition of the King to curry Favour with the People, had promised an abatement of the heavy Taxes: But presently after the same being renewed, augmented, and devoured by the Courtiers, great Troubles and Insurrections arose, both in *Paris*, and other Places. In the

mean while, the *Flemings* had carried themselves insolently towards their Lord, and calling to his Assistance the *French*, they kill'd 40000 *Flemings*, together with their General *Arteville*. 1382. The general Dissatisfaction of the People was much increased afterward, when a great Sum of Money was employed upon an Expedition against *England*, which proving fruitless, both the Money and Men were lost. *Lewis* Duke of *Orleans*, Brother of this King *Charles*, married *Valentina*, the Daughter of *John Galeacius*, Viscount of *Milan*, upon this Condition, that he should receive immediately as a Dowry, not only a great Treasure of Money and Jewels, but also the County of *Ast*; and in case her Father should die without Issue, the whole Country should be devolved on *Valentina* and her Children, which Contract has not only furnished *France* with a pretension to *Milan*, but has likewise been the occasion of great Calamities. After this, another Misfortune happen'd to *France*; for the King, whose Brain was mightily weakned by Debaucheries in his younger Years, as he was travelling in *Britany*, fell into a sudden Distraction, caused partly by the great Heat, which was then in the Month of *August*; partly, because as 'tis reported, a tall black Man appear'd to him, who, stopping his Horse by the Bridle, said, *Stop King, whither will you go? You are betray'd.* Soon after, a Page falling asleep, let the Point of his Lance drop upon the Head-piece of him who rid just before the King, which the King being extreamly surpriz'd at, interpreted it as directed against him. And tho' this madness ceased afterwards, yet was his Understanding much impair'd, and the Fits would return by intervals. This unhappy Accident was the occasion of that fatal Contest concerning the Administration of the Kingdom (which the King was incapable of) betwixt *Lewis*, Duke of *Orleans*, the King's Brother, and *Philip*, Duke of *Burgundy*, his Uncle. The first claimed it on the account of Proximity of Blood; the latter on account of his Age and Experience. The latter was most approv'd of by the Estates, who declar'd him Regent; but the Duke of *Orleans*, by forming new Intrigues, still endeavour'd to make himself the Head of the Kingdom, which caused pernicious Factions in the Court. And though the Duke of *Burgundy* died, his Son, *John*, pursuing his Fathers Pretensions, the Hatred so increased betwixt both Parties, that notwithstanding an outside Reconciliation formerly made betwixt them, the Duke of *Burgundy* caus'd the Duke of *Orleans* to be murthered by some Ruffians, at Night, in the Streets of *Paris*. And though the Duke of *Burgundy*, after having made away his Rival, and forc'd a Par-

The first rise of the *French* Pretension upon *Milan*. 1389.

The King falls under an Alienation of Mind.

1404. The Duke of *Orleans* assassinated by the Duke of *Burgundy*. 1407.

don from the King, was now the only Man in the Court; yet were the Animosities betwixt the Duke of *Burgundy*, and the Sons of the murther'd Duke of *Orleans*, not extinguish'd thereby, which divided the whole Kingdom into two Factions, one siding with the *Burgundian*, the other with the Family of *Orleans*; and occasion'd barbarous Murthers, Devastations, and such other Calamities, which are the common Products of Civil Commotions. At last, the *Burgundian* Faction was brought very low by the King and his Party. But the *English* having a watchful Eye upon the intestine Divisions in *France*, landed in *Normandy* with a great Army, and took *Harfluer*: But being extreamly weaken'd, both in the Siege, and by Sickness, retir'd towards *Calais*. In the mean while the *French* had got together an Army, four times stronger than the *English*, which met them near *Agincourt*, a Village in the County of St. *Poll*, where a Battle being fought betwixt them, 6000 *French* were kill'd upon the Spot, and a great number taken Prisoners, among whom were a great many Persons of Quality. (The *English* Historians make this Defeat much greater; it being rarely to be observ'd, that the Historians of two Nations, who are at Enmity, agree in their Relations.) Yet the *English* being extreamly fatigued, could not pursue the Victory. However, the Invasion made by a Foreign Enemy did in no ways diminish the Intestine Divisions, but rather augmented them: For the Duke of *Burgundy* perceiving his Party in *France* to decline, began to favour the *English*; who, in the Year next following, landed again in *Normandy*, and had great Success. At last the Queen who had hitherto had a share in the Government, added fuel to the Fire: For the Constable *d'Armagnac* having now the sole Administration of Affairs, and being only balanc'd by the Authority of the Queen, took an opportunity, by the free Conversation of the Queen, to put such a Jealousie in the King's Head, that with the consent of *Charles* the *Dauphine*, she was banish'd the Court. Which so incens'd the Queen, that conceiving an implacable Hatred against her Son, she sided with the Duke of *Burgundy*, whose Party was thereby greatly strengthen'd. Thus commenc'd the Intestine Wars, wherein both Parties were so exasperated against one another, that they had little regard to the great Success of the *English*, who, in the mean time conquer'd all *Normandy*, and *Roan* itself. The *Dauphine* intending at one Blow to root out the Evil of these Intestine Commotions, cunningly invited the Duke of *Burgundy* to come to an Agreement with him; and in their second Interview at *Monterau*, caused him to be kill'd. But this stroke had a quite contrary

The English take advantage of these Troubles. 1415.

Battle of Agincourt.

1419. *The Duke of Burgundy assassinated.*

trary effect: For the generality of the Nation abominated the Fact, and the Queen took from hence an opportunity totally to ruin her Son, and to exclude him from the Succession. With this view, entring into a League with the murther'd Duke's Son, *Philip*, She concluded a peace with *Henry* V. King of *England*, by vertue of which, he was to marry *Catharine*, the Daughter of *Charles* VI. and during his Life to be Regent of *France*, and after his Death, to be put into the full Possession of the Crown of *France*; so that both the Crowns of *France* and *England* were to be united; only each Kingdom was to be ruled according to its own Laws. Besides this, a Sentence was pronounc'd against the *Dauphine* in *Paris*, that by reason of the Murther committed by him upon the Duke of *Burgundy*, he was declared incapable of the Crown, and that he should be banish'd the Kingdom for ever. He appeal'd from this Sentence to God and his Sword, and set his Court up at *Poictiers*, so that at that time there were in *France* two Governments and two Courts; but the Affairs of the *Dauphine* were in a very ill Condition, very few of the Provinces siding with him; those that did, were *Anjou*, *Poictou*, *Tours*, *Auvergne*, *Berry*, and *Languedock*, but all of them mightily exhausted of Money. But it was happy for him, that the brave King *Henry* V. died in the very Flower of his Age and good Fortune, as likewise did, not long after, *Charles* VI. whose Life (by the Infirmities of his Mind, being incapable of governing) had 1422. greatly obstructed the Welfare of the Kingdom.

§ 13. *Charles* VII. whom we have hitherto call'd *the Dauphine*, caused himself immediately after his Father's Death, to be proclaim'd King, with the Assistance of the bravest among the *French*, tho' indeed his Affairs at the beginning were under very ill Circumstances: For the Duke of *Bedford*, who was constituted Regent in *France*, having caused young *Henry* VI. of *England*, to be proclaim'd King of *France* in *Paris*, did in Conjunction with the Dukes of *Burgundy* and *Britany*, try all ways to expel him quite out of *France*. His Forces were several times miserably beaten by the *English*; the greatest part of the Cities abandon'd him. He was at last become so Poor, that he rarely could dine in Publick, and it was observ'd, that one time he had nothing for Dinner, but a piece of roasted Mutton, and a couple of Fowls. Besides this, most of the great Men about him being dissatisfy'd with the ambitious Proceedings of the Constable *Richmond*, had left the Court, and were driving on their own Intrigues. The only Comfort left to *Charles*, was, that there was a Misunder-

Charles VII.

Henry VI. of *England*, proclaim'd King of *France*.

Misunderstanding betwixt the English and the Duke of Burgundy, the only advantage Charles had left.

standing betwixt the *English* and the Duke of *Burgundy*; else if they had with their joynt Forces vigorously attack'd *Charles*, he, in all probability could not have held out against them. The occasion of the Misunderstanding happen'd thus; *Jaqueline*, Countess of *Hennegau*, *Holland*, *Zealand*, and *Friesland*, being divorc'd from her Husband, *John*, Duke of *Brabant*, a Cousin of the Duke of *Burgundy*, was married again to the Duke of *Gloucester*, Brother of *Henry* V. The Duke of *Burgundy* taking his Cousin's part, it caused great Heart-burning betwixt him and the Duke of *Gloucester*. And tho' the Duke of *Bedford* endeavour'd to appease them, yet from that time the Duke of *Burgundy* entertain'd a Grudge against the *English*; which encreased afterwards, when the *English* refused to put the City of *Orleans* into his Hands. This City being besieg'd by the *English*, was reduc'd to the utmost Extremity; the *French* that attack'd a Convoy which was going to the *English* Camp having been entirely beaten: Which Engagement is called *la journée des Haranes*, or, *the Battle of the Herrings*. *Charles*'s Affairs were then become so desperate, that he had resolv'd to retire into *Dauphinee*, when upon a sudden an unlook'd for help was sent him: For a Country Maid, born in *Lorraine*, whose Name was *Joan*, did in that juncture pretend that she was sent from God to relieve *Orleans*, and to see the King crown'd at *Rheims*. Both which she effected, striking thereby great Terror into the *English*; whereas, on the other side, the *French* being greatly incourag'd by this Success, saw their Affairs from henceforward mend every day. But this poor Wench following the Wars longer, as it seems, than she had in Commission, was taken Prisoner making a Sally out of *Campaigne*, and being deliver'd to the *English*, was with great dishonour burnt as a Witch at *Roan*. The *English* perceiving their Affairs not to go forward as formerly, resolved to give them new Life and Vigour, by bringing over the young King *Henry*, and having him crowned in *Paris*: And to keep fair with the Duke of *Burgundy*, they gave him the Counties of *Brie* and *Champaigne*; yet all this proved insufficient. So that the War being thus carried on for several Years only with light Skirmishes, and both Parties being tired out, a Treaty was at last propos'd by Mediation of the Pope at *Arras*; but the *English* rigorously insisting upon their Pretensions, which were very hard, they were deserted by the Duke of *Burgundy*, who made a separate Peace with *Charles* upon very advantageous Conditions. At the same time the *English* suffer'd an additional Misfortune in the Death of the Duke of *Bedford*, who hitherto had administred their Affairs in *France* with

The Maid of *Orleans*.

1431.

The *English* Power declines in *France*.

1435.

with great Prudence. After this, the Cities of *France* surrender'd one after another to *Charles*; and among the rest the City of *Paris*. But in regard the *English* had made miserable Havock throughout *France*, and the *French* Soldiers themselves being ill paid, had committed great Depredations, without any Order or Discipline, a great Famine ensu'd, and afterwards a violent Plague. It is related that the Wolves snatch'd the Children off the Streets of the Suburbs of St. *Anthony* in *Paris*. The War having been thus protracted for a considerable time, a Truce was concluded for some Years. The King to be rid of the Soldiers, sent them into *Alsace*, under pretence to disturb the Council at *Basil*. They killed at once 4000 *Swiss*; but having lost double the number, soon after returned home again. In the mean time, the *English* were degenerated from their former Valour, their Forces were extreamly diminish'd in *France*, and the Soldiers for want of Pay had given themselves over to Plunder and Robbery. They wanted good Officers, their Places of strength had but sorry Governors; and the *French* grew weary of the *English* Yoak. At home *England* labour'd under intestine commotions and the heat of faction; and withal suffer'd extreamly in being twice defeated by the *Scots*. *Charles* therefore having met with this Opportunity, resolved to beat the *English* at once out of *France*. He took, for a pretence of the War, that they had broken the Truce in invading *Britany*, and the *Scots*; and attacking them with great Vigour in several places at once, he drove them, within the space of thirteen Months, out of *Normandy*. The next Year after he master'd *Aquitain*; and the Year after *Bayonne*, the last place of all, surrender'd itself; so that the *English* had nothing left on the Continent of *France*, but *Calais* and the County of *Guines*. Soon after *Bourdeaux* revolted from the *French*, and sought for Aid of the *English*, but the brave *Talbot* being kill'd in an Engagement, it was retaken and reunited to the *French* Crown, after it had been 300 Years in the Possession of the *English*. Thus did this King reunite the mangled Kingdom, expelling the *English* out of its Bowels. Nevertheless he did not entirely enjoy the Fruits of his good Fortune, for he liv'd at variance with his Son, who for the space of thirteen Years came not to Court. And being at last persuaded, that a Design was formed against his Life, it so disturb'd him, that for fear of being poisoned, he starved himself.

[Margin: 1436. — He drives the *English* out of *France*, 1449. 1451. — 1453. — 1461.]

§ 14. To him succeeded his Son, *Lewis* XI. a cunning, resolute, and malicious Prince, who laid the first Foundation of

[Margin: *Lewis* XI.]

of the absolute Power since exercised by the Kings of *France*, whereas formerly the Royal Power was kept under by the Authority of the Great Men of the Kingdom. He began with reforming his Court and Ministers according to his Pleasure; Of which the Great Men forseeing the Consequence, enter'd into a League, which they call'd, *La Ligu du bien public, the League for the publick good*; by which they pretend to guard the Publick against the King's Arbitrary Proceedings. Among these were the Dukes of *Burgundy* and *Britany*, who endeavour'd by all means to keep the King within Bounds. In the Year 1465, *Charles*, the young Duke of *Burgundy*, enter'd *France* with an Army, and fought a Battle with the King near *Montleberry*, wherein the Advantage was near equal; but, because the King retreated a little backwards, the Night following, the Duke of *Burgundy* pretended to have gained the Victory, which put him upon those Enterprizes which afterwards cost him his Life. The King extricated himself with a great deal of Cunning out of this danger, for he released the Taxes, and with great Promises and fine Words appeas'd the People; all which, as soon as the danger was pass'd, he revok'd at pleasure. To dissolve this Faction, he made Divisions betwixt the most powerful; the bravest he brought over to his side by giving them particular Advantages; the rest he ruin'd by his Policy, especially by bribing their Friends and Servants. And being in great want of Money, he borrow'd great Sums of his Servants; and such as refused to lend, were put out of their Employments: Which, 'tis said, gave the first occasion of the Sale of Offices and Honours in *France*. But the Duke of *Burgundy* persisted in his Opposition, and in the Year 1468. hem'd him in at *Peronne*; and tho' *Lewis* with much ado got clear of the imminent danger, his conduct that upon other occasions had been very Politick was loudly censured. At last *Lewis* was rid of this his troublesome Enemy, who was kill'd by the *Swiss* near *Nancy*. *Lewis* taking advantage of the great Confusion, which was occasioned by the Death of the Duke in his Country, took Possession of the Dukedom of *Burgundy*, under pretext that the same was an Appanage, and brought over to his side the Cities situated on the River *Soam*, which had been under the jurisdiction of *Charles*. It was generally believ'd, that *Lewis*, by way of Marriage, might easily have annexed the whole Inheritance of this Duke unto *France*, if he had not conceived such an implacable hatred against this House, that he was resolved to ruin it. Two Years before the Death of the Duke of *Burgundy*, King *Edward* IV. of *England* landed with a

He reduces the excessive Power of the Nobility.

A League against him.

The King's politick Method.

The Original of selling the Offices of *France*.

Duke of *Burgundy* slain. 1477.

a great Army in France, whom Lewis with Presents and fair Promises persuaded to return home again: He united to the Crown Provence, Anjou, and Mons, having obtained the same by the last Will and Testament of Charles d'Anjou, Count de Maine, who was the last Male-Heir of the House of Anjou; notwithstanding that, Rene, Duke of Lorraine, Son of Yoland d'Anjou, pretended a Right to the same by his Mothers side. In his latter days he lived miserably, and grew ridiculous, being in continual fear of Death. He died in the Year 1483.

§ 15. His Son Charles VIII. had at the beginning of his Reign, his Hands full with the Duke of Britany, and was marching with an Army to unite that Province by main force to the Crown. But understanding that Maximilian of Austria, had got Anna, the only Heiress of this Dukedom, betroth'd to himself; the French King thought it no ways adviseable to let such a delicious Morsel fall to the share of the House of Austria; and accordingly obliged the Bride, partly by force, partly by fair words, to throw off Maximilian, and to be married to himself, whereby this Country was united to France. And tho' Henry VII. King of England, did not look with a favourable Eye upon the growing Power of France, and accordingly with a great Army besieged Boulogne, yet in consideration of a good Sum of Money, he was prevailed upon to return home again; especially, since Maximilian (who had received a double Affront from Charles, in not only taking his Bride from him, but likewise sending home his Daughter Margaret, that had been his contracted Bride) did not join his Forces with him according to Agreement. Maximilian took Arras and St. Omer, but being not able to go further, he consented that his Son Philip, Lord of the Netherlands, should make a Truce with Charles. On the other side, Charles gave to Ferdinand the Catholick, the Counties of Roussilion and Cardagne, some say, to engage him thereby not to oppose his intended Expedition against Naples. Others say, that Ferdinand corrupted Charles's Confessor, to persuade him, to restore that Country to its lawful Sovereign. France being thus by the Union with Britany become an entire Kingdom, it began to contrive how to obtain the Sovereignty over Italy. Charles had a Pretension to it, in regard the Right and Title of the Family of Anjou and Naples, had by the Death of the last Duke of Anjou and Earl of Provence, devolv'd to Lewis XI. and consequently to himself. But this young and fiery King received the greatest Encouragement from Lewis, sirnamed Morus, or the Black, Duke of Milan, who, having Tuition

Charles VIII.

Britany united to France, 1491.

An Expedition to Naples, and the Pretensions of it.

of

of his Nephew, *John Galeas*, the true Heir of this Dukedom, but a weak Prince, had under that pretence made himself Master of the same. This Duke fearing that he might be put out of Possession by *Ferdinand*, King of *Naples*, whose Son *Alphonso*'s Daughter *Isabella* was married to *John Galeas*, endeavour'd to give *Ferdinand* his Hands full, that he might not be at leisure to think of him; knowing that *Ferdinand* and his Son *Alphonsus* were much hated by their Subjects for their Tyranny and Impiety: Thereupon an Expedition was undertaken against *Naples*, which prov'd the occasion of continual Miseries to *Italy* for the space of forty Years.

1494. It seem'd to be fatal to *Italy*, that the wise *Italians* either could or would not prevent this Expedition, which had been projected two Years before.

Charles conquer'd *Naples*. *Charles* had at the beginning all the Success imaginable, for the *Italian* Troops were in a very ill Condition, and there being no body who durst oppose him, *Florence* and the Pope sided with him, the latter declaring *Charles* King of *Naples*. King *Alphonsus* stirr'd up by his own Conscience, abdicated himself, transfering all his Right and Title upon his Son *Ferdinand*: But his Forces being soon beaten and dispers'd, *Charles* made his solemn Entry into *Naples* with loud Acclamations. Immediately the whole Kingdom submitted to him, except the Isle of *Ischia*, and the Cities of

1495. *Brundisi* and *Gallipoli*. The Conquest of so fair a Kingdom, and that within five Months time, struck a Terror into the *Turkish* Emperor himself, at *Constantinople*, and even Greece was ready to Rebel as soon as the *French* should Land on that side. But the Face of Affairs was quickly changed; for the *French*, by their ill conduct, quickly lost the Favour of the *Neapolitans*: Besides, it was look'd upon as a thing of such Consequence by the rest of the Princes of *Europe*, that the Emperor, the Pope, King *Ferdinand* of *Arragon*, *Venice*, and *Milan*, enter'd into a Confederacy, to drive the *French* out of *Italy*;

The League of *Italy* against the *French*. *Charles* therefore fearing lest his Retreat might be cut off, took his way by Land into *France*, having left things but in an indifferent state of Defence in *Naples*. In his March he was met by the Confederate Army, near the River of *Taro*, where a Battle was fought, and tho' there were more kill'd on the Confederate side than of the *French*, yet he marched forward with such Precipitation, as if he had lost the Battle.

He loseth *Naples*. *Charles* was no sooner returned into *France*, but *Ferdinand* retook, without great Trouble, the Kingdom of *Naples*, to the great Dishonour of the *French*, who were not able to maintain themselves there a whole Year, and of whom very few return'd alive into *France*.

1498. Not long after *Charles* died without Issue.

§ 16. To

§ 16. To him succeeded *Lewis* XII. formerly Duke of *Orleans*, who, not to lose *Britany*, married *Anna*, Widow of the late King. He made War soon after on *Milan*, pretending a Right to that Dukedom by his Grand-mother's side, and having conquer'd the same within 21 days, *Lewis the Black* was forc'd to fly with his Children and all his Treasure into *Germany*. But the Inhabitants of *Milan* grew quickly weary of the *French*, their Free Conversation with the Women being above all intolerable to them, and therefore recall'd their Duke, who having got together an Army of *Swiss*, was joyfully receiv'd, and regain'd the whole Country, except the Castle of *Milan*, and the City of *Novara*. But *Lewis* sending timely Relief, the Duke's-*Swiss* Soldiers refus'd to fight against the *French*, so that the Duke endeavouring to save himself by flight in a common Soldiers Habit, was taken Prisoner, and kept ten Years in Prison at *Loches*, where he died. Thus the *French* got *Milan* again, and the City of *Genoua*. After so great Success, *Lewis* began to think of the Kingdom of *Naples*: To obtain which, he made a League with *Ferdinand the Catholick*, wherein it was agreed, that they should divide the Kingdom betwixt them, so that the *French* should have for their share *Naples*, *Terra di Lavoro*, and *Abruzze*; and the *Spaniards*, *La Puglia* and *Calabria*. Each of them got his share without any great trouble; *Frederick*, King of *Naples* surrendring himself to King *Lewis*, who allowed him a yearly Pension of 30000 Crowns. But soon after new Differences arose betwixt these two haughty Nations concerning the Limits; for the *French* pretended that the Country of *Capitanate* (which is very considerable for its Taxes paid for Sheep, which are there very numerous) did belong to *Abruzze*, whereas the *Spaniards* would have it belong to *Poville*. The *French*, at first, had somewhat the better; but as soon as *Gonsalvus de Cordova*, that cunning *Spaniard*, had broke their first Fury, and *Lewis* did not send sufficient Relief, they were as shamefully beaten again out of the Kingdom, as they had been before. *Lewis* endeavoured to revenge himself upon the *Spaniards* the next Year, but though he attack'd them with four several Armies, yet he could not gain any thing upon them: Wherefore he made a Peace with *Ferdinand*, and enter'd into an Alliance with him against *Philip*, Son in Law to *Ferdinand*, who having after the Death of *Isabella*, taken from him the Kingdom of *Castile*, was upheld by his Father *Maximilian*, and back'd by *Henry* King of *England*, whose Son had married his Wife's Sister. In the Year 1507. the City of *Genoua* rebell'd against

Lewis XII. 1499. He conquers *Milan*. He conquers *Naples*. 1501. Loses it again. 1503.

Lewis,

Lewis, but was soon reduc'd to her former Obedience. Then the War began afresh in *Italy* with the *Venetians*, who being too much addicted to Self-interest, had drawn upon themselves the hatred of all their Neighbours, having encroached upon every one of them; and *Lewis* especially attributed to them his loss of the Kingdom of *Naples*. To humble this proud State, a League was concluded at *Cambray*, betwixt the Emperor, the Pope, and the Kings of *France* and *Spain*. *Lewis* by entring into a Confederacy with his mortal Enemies, had more regard to his Passion than to his Interest, it being certain that he might upon all occasions have trusted to the Friendship of the *Venetians*. But now he was the first that fell upon them, and defeated them in a bloody Battle near *Giera d'Adua*, which caused such a Terror among them, that they left all what they had on the Continent, within 20 Days; and if *Lewis* had pursued his Victory whilst they were under this first Consternation, he might doubtless have put a period to their Greatness. But in the mean time that he marched backwards towards *Milan*, they got leisure to recover themselves; especially since the Emperor *Maximilian*, was not in earnest against them, and Pope *Julius* II. was reconciled to them. Nay, in the Year 1510, the Pope, *Ferdinand*, *Henry* VIII. and the *Swiss Cantons*, declar'd War against *Lewis*. For the Pope could not look with a good Eye upon the growing Power of *France* in *Italy*, *Ferdinand* feared lest *Lewis* might attack *Naples*; *Henry* being come lately to the Crown, was for making himself famous by so great an Undertaking; and the *Swiss* were set against *France*, for that *Lewis* had not paid them their old Arrears, and had refused to encrease their Pension, not because their Demands were extravagant, but because he would not be out-brav'd by them. In this War the *French* General, *Castro de Foix*, behaved himself very gallantly; for he relieved *Bononia*, beat the *Venetian* Army, killed 8000 of them in *Brescia*, and obtained a glorious Victory over the Confederate Army near *Ravenna*; in which Battle, nevertheless, this brave General being too hot in pursuing the Enemy, was unfortunately Slain. With his Death the *French* Affairs began to decline, and they were again forced to leave *Italy*. *Maximilian*, Son of *Lewis the Black*, was restor'd to his Dutchy of *Milan* by the help of the *Swiss*: The *Genouese* revolted, and made *Janus Fergosus* their Duke. *Ferdinand the Catholick* took from King *John* the Kingdom of *Navarre*, which the *French* in vain endeavoured to regain from the *Spaniards*.

But

The *Venetian* War.

Lewis joyns in the League against them, 1508.

1509.

A League against *Lewis*.

1512.

But *Lewis* being extreamly desirous to regain *Milan*, enter'd into a League with *Venice*, and retook most places of that Dukedom, and the City of *Genoua*. He besieg'd Duke *Maximilian* in the Castle of *Novara*, but the *Swiss* coming to the Assistance of the Duke, attack'd the *French* with incredible Fury in their Camp, and drove them quite out of the Dukedom, which was thus twice taken in one Month. Then *Lewis* was at once attack'd by the Emperor, *England*, and the *Swiss*; and if the *English* and the *Swiss* had join'd, *France* would have run a great Risque: But King *Henry*, instead of entring into the Heart of *France*, amus'd himself with the Siege of *Terouane*, where he defeated the *French*, that were come to its Relief, near *Guinegast*; this Battel was call'd, *The the Battel of the Spurs*, because the *French* made better use of their Spurs than their Swords. In short, after he had taken *Tournay*, he returned into *England*. The *Swiss*, who kept the Duke of *Tremovile* besieg'd in *Dijon* Castle, were bought off with 600000 Crowns, which were promised to them by the Duke without the King's Order, stipulating withal, that he should dismiss the Council of *Pisa*, and quit his Pretensions to the Dukedom of *Milan*. Which shameful Agreement the King refused to Ratify; and if the *Swiss* had not been more fond of the Ransom offer'd for the Hostages than their Blood, they had pay'd with their Lives for it. In the next insuing Year, *Lewis* made a Peace with the King of *England*, who gave him his Sister *Mary* in Marriage; and this young Lady, 'tis thought hasten'd the Death of the old King, which ensu'd in the beginning of the Year 1515. This King was so well belov'd by his People, that he was generally call'd, *The Father of the People*.

He conquers Milan *again.*

1513.

He is attack'd by several Prences at once.

§. 17. His Nephew, *Francis* I. succeeded him, who having made a League with *England*, the Arch-Duke *Charles*, and *Venice*, on a sudden invaded *Italy*, and took *Genoua*, and some other Places without great Opposition; but being encamp'd at *Marignano*, within a League of *Milan*, the *Swiss* unexpectedly fell upon him, and a bloody Fight ensu'd. The *Swiss* were at last repuls'd, and found that they could be beaten, having lost above 10000; but on the other hand, the *French* left 4000 of their best Men upon the Spot. After this Duke *Maximilian* surrender'd himself, and the whole Country, to

Francis I.

the King, on the Condition of an Annual Pension of 30000 Ducates to be paid him. Soon after the King treated with the *Swiss*, and in Consideration of a good Sum, brought them again into an Alliance with *France*. He made also an Agreement with Pope *Leo* X. by vertue of which the King was to have the Right of naming Bishops and Abbots, but the Pope to keep certain Profits out of the chiefest Church Benefices, in the Year 1518, he redeem'd *Tournay* from the *English* for a good Sum of Money. In the Year next insuing, after the Death of the Emperor, *Maximilian*, *Francis* employ'd all his Engines to be exalted to the Imperial Dignity; but the *German* Princes fearing lest the *French* should endeavour to humble them, and for some other Considerations, preferr'd before him *Charles* V. This proved the Occasion of great Jealousies betwixt these two Princes; for *Francis* being very sensible what great Advantages he had gain'd by the Imperial Dignity, put himself into a good Posture, to prevent his becoming Master of him, and all the rest of the Princes in *Europe*. This Jealousy broke at last out into an open War, *Francis* endeavouring to retake *Navarre* from the *Spaniards*, for effecting of which he had a fair Opportunity, whilst the Divisions in *Spain* were on foot. The *French* conquer'd that Kingdon in a few Days time; but being not careful enough to preserve it, as easily lost it again. Soon after the War was kindled in the *Netherlands*, occasion'd by *Robert Van de Marck*, Lord of *Sedan*, whom *Francis* took into his Protection. This *Robert* was so puft up with the *French* Protection, that he writ a Letter of Defiance to the Emperor, and fell into the Country of *Luxemburg*. But *Charles* quickly chastis'd this petty Enemy; and being persuaded that *Francis* had encouraged his Insolence, he took from him St. *Amand* and *Tournay*. The Business nevertheless might have been compos'd at the beginning, if the *French* had not insisted upon keeping *Fontarabia*, which in the mean time had been surpriz'd by them. But the hardest Task was in *Italy*, both the Emperor and Pope being willing to drive *Francis* out of *Milan*, and to restore *Francis Sforza*. And indeed they effected both with good Success; for the *French* Army was not timely supply'd with Money, and being, besides this, beaten near *Bicoque*, the *French* were again dispossess'd of *Milan* and *Genoua*. And on the other side they also lost

He aspires to the Empire.

In a few Days, he takes and loses the Kingdom of Navarre.

1521.

A War kindled in Italy.

The French *driven out of* Milan 1521.

Fontarabia,

Fontarabia. But what happen'd very ill to *Francis*, was, That the Constable, *Charles* of *Bourbon*, went over to the Emperor, the Reason of which was, That he had been for a while mightily kept under by the Queen Mother, the Chancellor *Duprat*, and Admiral *Bonnivet*. The first had commenc'd a Suit at Law against him, about the Dukedom of *Bourbon*, which he despaired to be able to maintain against so strong a Party, as believing that the King was under-hand concern'd in the Matter. The Duke of *Bourbon* therefore had agreed with the Emperor and the King of *England*, That they should divide the Kingdom of *France* betwixt them; the Kingdom of *Arelat*, and the Emperor's Sister being stipulated to the Duke of *Bourbon*. But the Design being discover'd, the Duke of *Bourbon* was forc'd to fly into *Italy*. Notwithstanding the *English* made an Inrode into *Picardy*, *Francis* sent again an Army into the *Milaneze*, under the Command of Admiral *Bonnivet*, which was beaten back with considerable loss by the Duke of *Bourbon*. This *Bonnivet* persuaded the King to go in Person into *Italy*, with this Prospect, That if Things succeeded well he should have the Glory of having been the Adviser, but if they succeeded ill, the Misfortune would be covered by the King's Person. *Francis* therefore went with a good Resolution into *Italy*, because he saw the Duke of *Bourbon*, who in the mean time having enter'd *Provence*, had besieg'd *Marseilles*, did retreat before him; and having laid Siege to *Pavia*, he for two Months together harrass'd his Army in that Siege. In the mean while the Imperialists drew their Forces together, and march'd against him (who was Encamp'd in the Parks) with an Intention, either to fight him, or to relieve *Pavia*. *Francis* engag'd with them in Battle, but was defeated and taken Prisoner. And thus the *French* were again driven out of *Italy*. *Francis* was carry'd into *Spain*, and us'd very hardly, so that he fell Sick for Grief; which hastened his Liberty, it being fear'd that he might die through Vexation. Upon this, *England* and the *Italian* Princes enter'd into a Confederacy to hinder the growing Power of *Charles*. The Conditions upon which he obtain'd his Liberty, we have touch'd upon in another place; but besides these, *Francis* gave his Parole of Honour, if the said Conditions were not fulfill'd, That he would return a Prisoner. But the wiser Sort did sufficiently foresee, that

The Duke of Bourbon *revolts to the Emperour.*

1524.

Francis *defeated at the Battle of* Pavia, *and taken Prisoner* 1525.

He is set at Liberty on hard Conditions, which he did not perform.

Francis would not perform the Agreement; and with that view *Gattinara*, the Chancellor, refused to Sign the Treaty, alledging, That *Charles* could get nothing else by this Treaty, but the implacable hatred of the *French*, and to be ridicul'd by every body, that he had been bubbled and disappointed in his covetous Designs. And *Francis* having obtain'd his Liberty after 13 Months Imprisonment, pretended, That what had been done was done in Prison, and contrary to his Coronation-Oath which he had taken at *Rheims*; That the Kingdom was not in his disposal, he having only the use of it for Life. The same was alledged by the Estates, and especially by the *Burgundians*, who would in no ways consent to be separated from the Crown of *France*. If *Charles* was so much for having *Burgundy*, he ought to have taken care to have been put into Possession of the same, before he set *Francis* at Liberty. As soon as *Francis* had got his Liberty, he made it his first Business to renew the League with *England* and the *Italian* States. And the new Treaty having proved fruitless, which was set on foot with the Emperor, both Kings denounced War against him. *Charles* afterwards accusing *Francis* of not having kept his Parole, the latter gave the first the Lye, sending him withal a Challenge, which Conduct was look'd upon by the World as very unbecoming the Grandeur of such Princes. *Francis* sent, after this, an Army into *Italy* under the Command of *Odet de Foix Lautree*, which having made considerable Progresses in the *Milaneze*, enter'd the Kingdom of *Naples*, and having taken a great many Places there, laid Siege to the Capital City it self. But the *French* Affairs received the first Shock there, when *Andrew Doria*, the Admiral, leaving the *French* side, went over to the Emperor, as being dissatisfy'd that the King had refus'd to confer upon him the Government of his Native City, *Genoua*, and to restore to the *Genouese*, *Savona*. This *Doria* is deservedly praised, for that, when he might have been Lord of his Native Country, he chose rather to procure its Liberty, which it enjoys to this Day. But *Doria* leaving the *French* side, was the occasion that the City of *Naples* could not be cut off of their Communication by Sea. And the Plague began to reign in the Army during this long Siege, which devoured the greatest part of it, and the General himself. Upon which the Remnants of the Army were miserably treated, the Officers

He with the King of England declare War against the Emperor.

He sends an Army into Italy.

being

being made Prisoners, and the Common Soldiers disarmed; and thereupon the *French* were also obliged to quit *Milan* and *Genoua*. At last, the Emperor having obtained his Aim, and *Francis* being very desirous to see his Children at Liberty again, a Peace was concluded betwixt them at *Cambray*, by Vertue of which, *Francis* pay'd two Millions of Ducats, as a Ransom for his Sons, and renounced the Sovereignty over *Flanders*, *Artois*, *Milan*, and *Naples*. And this was all the Benefit which this King and his Predecessors reapt from the *Italian* Wars. Nevertheless, some Years after the War began afresh, at which time *Francis* found a new way to make himself Master of the *Milaneze*, by first securing to himself the Dukedom of *Savoy*. With this Prospect he made Pretensions upon *Charles*, Duke of *Savoy*, about the Inheritance of his Mother, descended from the House of *Savoy*, fell upon him, and took most of his strong Holds. In the mean time died *Francis Sforza*, Duke of *Milan*, upon which the Emperor resolved to annex this Country to his House; but *Francis* could by no means digest the loss of it. Then *Charles* entered *Provence* in Person with an Army of 40000 Foot, and 16000 Horse, ransack'd *Aix*, and besieged *Marseilles*, which however he could not take, a third part of his Army being in a Months time swept off by Sickness. An Army of 30000 Men also enter'd *Picardy* from the *Netherlands*, which took *Guise*, but was beaten from before *Peronne*; tho' it afterwards took *S. Pol* and *Monstrevil*. *Francis* summoned the Emperor before him, as his Vassal, upon the score of *Flanders* and *Artois*, alledging, That the Sovereignty of these Provinces was inseparable from the Crown, and made an Alliance with the *Turks*. At last, by the Mediation of the Pope, the Truce which was the Year before made at *Nissa* in *Provence*, was prolong'd for nine Years, and these two great Rivals gave afterward one another a Visit at *Aigues Mortes*. And, when, in the Year next following the City of *Ghent* rebell'd, *Charles* had such a confidence in *Francis*, that he took his Journey through *France*, tho' *Charles* in the mean while had cunningly given *Francis* some Hopes of the Recovery of *Milan*; which however afterwards he would not acknowledge, for upon the Persuasions of the Constable, *Montmorency*, the King had not taken from him any Security under his Hand during his stay in *Paris*; which some alledge to

Peace made at Cambray, 1529.

1535. *The War breaks out afresh.*

The Truce prolong'd for nine Years.

be one Reason why *Montmorency* afterwards fell into Disgrace. But the Truce was broken again, under pretence, That the Governour of *Milan* had caused to be kill'd, *Cæsar Fregosus* and *Anthony Rinco*, the Ambassadors of *Francis*, as they were going along the River *Po* in their way to *Venice*, the first of whom was to have gone from thence to *Constantinople*. *Francis* thought to have met now with a fair Opportunity, because *Charles* had suffered a considerable loss before *Algiers*. He therefore attack'd the Emperor with five several Armies at once. But the strongest of all, which lay before *Perpignan*, did nothing; the second took some Places in the Country of *Luxemburgh*. The Emperor, *Solyman*, also made a great Diversion in *Hungary*, taking *Gran*, and some other Places. The great Pirate *Barbarossa*, arriv'd in *Provence* with his Fleet, but did more mischief than good to *France*. But *Charles*, on the other hand, made an Alliance with *Henry* VIII. who was dissatisfy'd with *Francis*, because he had taken part with the *Scots*, and would not renounce his Obedience to the Pope: And after he had beat the Duke of *Cleves*, who depended on the *French*, besieg'd *Landrecy* with a great Army, but to no purpose. In the mean time the *French* had obtain'd a most signal Victory over the Imperial Forces near *Cerisolles* in *Piedmont*. But the King could not prosecute his Victory, being oblig'd to recal his Troops, because the Emperor and *Henry*, King of *England*, had concerted to fall into *France*, with an Army of 80000 Foot and 22000 Horse; the first by the Way of *Champagne*, the second by the Way of *Picardy*. The Emperor took by the way *Luxemburgh*, lay six Weeks before *Disier*, got abundance of Provision in *Espernay* and *Chasteau Thierry*, which put the whole City of *Paris* into a great Consternation, and no small Danger seem'd to threaten that City, if King *Henry* had joyned his Forces in time, according to his Promise: But he losing his time in the Sieges of *Boulogne* and *Monstrevil*, *Charles* hearkened to a Peace, which was concluded at *Crespy*. By virtue of this Peace all the Places were restored, and the Emperor promised to the Duke of *Orleans*, the second Son of the King, either his or his Brother's Daughter in Marriage, and to give for her Dowry either *Milan* or the *Netherlands*; which was not performed, because the said Duke died the next Year. At the same time *Francis* made a Peace with *England*, stipulating, that

Francis breaks the Truce, 1542.

Peace concluded at Crespy, *1544.*

that he should have liberty to redeem *Boulogne* for a certain Sum of Money. He died in the Year 1547. 1546.

§. 18. To him succeeded his Son *Henry* II. to whom fell the Marquisate of *Saluzze*, as a Fief of *Dauphinee*, the last Marquiss, *Gabriel*, dying without Issue. He severely chastiz'd the City of *Bourdeaux*, which had rebell'd against him. In the Year next following he redeem'd *Boulogne* for a certain Sum of Money from the *English*. In the Year 1551, the Emperor being engag'd in a War against the *Turks*, and the *German* Princes being very jealous of his Greatness, *Henry* thought that a fit Opportunity to break with him. He began therefore in the *Netherlands* and *Piedmont*; and having made an Alliance with *Maurice*, Elector of *Saxony*, he marched with all his Army towards the *Rhine*, and surpriz'd by the way the Cities of *Metz*, *Toul*, and *Verdun*, and would have done the same with *Strasburgh*, if they had not been upon their Guard there. But the Elector of *Saxony* having made a Peace with the Emperor without including the King, and some Princes entreating him not to advance farther into the Empire, he marched back into the Country of *Luxemburgh*, where he took some places. The Emperor then besieged *Metz* with an Army of 100000 Men, but the Duke of *Guise* defended himself so bravely, that the Emperor was oblig'd to raise the Siege with great loss. To revenge this Affront, he attack'd *Terouene* in *Artois* with great Fury, and rased to the Ground that Fortress, which had proved hitherto so troublesome to the *Netherlands*. The same he did to *Hesdin*; both the Garrisons being put to the Sword. On the other side the *French* took *Siena* in *Italy*, and several places in the Island of *Corsica*, but were again beaten out of *Siena*, after they had been maul'd near *Marciano*. In the Year 1556, a Truce was concluded at *Vaucelles* near *Cambray*, the Emperor being desirous to leave the Kingdom to his Son (to whom he had resign'd the same) in Peace. But the Truce was scarce confirm'd by Oath, when the *French* broke it again, upon the Instigation of Pope *Paul* IV. who having some Differences with *Spain*, persuaded *Henry* to take his part. The Duke of *Guise* was thereupon sent into *Italy* with an Army, but did nothing worth mentioning. In the mean time King *Philip* had gathered an Army of 50000 Men, and having drawn *England* into

Henry II. 1548. 1549. 1550.

His Expedition into Germany, 1552.

1555.

A Truce between Charles V. *and* Henry II.

the War, he besieged St. *Quintin*, into which place the Admiral *Gasper Coligny*, had thrown himself. The Constable, *Montmorency*, advanced with an Army to the Relief of the Place, but he retreating again in sight of the Enemies, they fell upon him, and gave him a terrible Defeat. *France* had been then in the uttermost danger, if
1557. this Victorious Army had march'd directly towards *Paris*, and if the Enemies design upon *Lyons* had not miscarried. But King *Philip* feared lest the Duke of *Savoy*, who commanded his Army, might take this Opportunity to reconcile himself to *France* upon some advantageous Conditions; upon which apprehension he would not let him March on far into the Country, but took St. *Quintin* by Storm, and lost his Time in the taking of *Han, Castelet*, and *Noyon*. This gave leisure to the *French* to recollect themselves, upon which having recall'd the Duke of *Guise* out of *Italy*, they retook *Calais*, and those few other places which remained under the *English* thereabout, as likewise *Thionville* in the Year 1559. In the same Year a Project was set on foot, to unite the Kingdom of *Scotland* with *France*, by a Marriage betwixt Queen *Mary* and the *Dauphine*, *Francis*; but the Project miscarried, no Children being born of them. The Mareschal *de Termes*, who made an Inrode into *Flanders*, was soundly beaten near *Gravelingen*. At last a Peace was concluded at *Chasteau en Cambresis*, which prov'd very pernicious for *France*; because, for the Castle of *Chambray*, the Cities of *Han, Castelet*, and St. *Quintin*, there were not only 198 Places re-deliver'd to *Spain* and the Duke of *Savoy* restor'd; but also this Peace was partly the occasion of those Intestine Wars, which afterwards miserably tore in Pieces the Kingdom of *France*. It was then resolv'd in *France* not to intermeddle any more in the *Italian* Affairs, and to dissolve the Alliance with the *Turks*. After this Peace was concluded, *Henry* was kill'd in a Turnament, a Splinter of a broken Lance having got into his Eye; for the King had challeng'd the Earl of *Montgomery* to run against him with an open Vizor, and as soon as he was wounded he lost both his Senses and Speech, and died within 11 Days. By this Accident, the Wedding which he celebrated for his Sister *Margaret*, who was married to *Childebert Emanuel*, Duke of *Savoy*, was very mournfully consummated.

A Project to unite Scotland *with* France *miscarried.*

§. 19. He

§. 19. He was succeeded by his Son *Francis* II. under whose Reign the *French* Divisions began to break out with Fury in their own Bowels, which continued near 40 Years, whereas formerly the violent Heat of this Nation had been quell'd, partly by the Wars with the *English*, partly by the several Expeditions undertaken against *Italy*. With reference to the Causes of these Intestine Wars, it is to be observ'd, That after the House of *Valois* came to the Crown, the next in Blood were those of the House of *Bourbon*, which House had grown so Potent by the Riches, Power, and Authority of a great many brave Persons, which descended from it, that the Preceeding Kings were grown extreamly jealous of it. And tho' *Francis* I. at the beginning of his Reign did constitute the Duke of *Bourbon* Constable; yet being soon after convinced of the Reasons which had induc'd his Ancestors to keep under this House, he used all his Endeavours to humble the said *Charles* of *Bourbon*, who thereupon deserted to the Emperor, and was slain in the Storming of *Rome*. By his Death the House of *Bourbon* receiv'd a great blow, those who were left being look'd upon with a very ill Eye, tho' they kept themselves very quiet to extinguish the Suspicion and Hatred conceiv'd against them. The House of *Bourbon* being thus brought very low, the two Houses of *Montmorency* and *Guise* held up their Heads under the Reign of *Francis* I. The first was one of the most Ancient in *France*; the latter was a Branch of the House of *Lorraine*. The Head of the first was *Annas Montmorency*, Constable of *France*; of the latter, *Claude* Duke of *Guise*. Both of them were in great Favour and Authority with *Francis* I. but both fell into Disgrace at the latter end of his Reign, being banish'd the Court. It is related of *Francis*, that just before his Death he advised his Son, *Henry*, to consult with neither of them in his Affairs, since too great and too able Ministers proved often dangerous. Yet notwithstanding this, *Henry* II. received both *Annas Montmorency* and *Francis de Guise*, the Son of *Claude*, into his particular Favour; who quickly grew jealous of one another, the first taking much upon him because of his Experience in State Affairs, and Gravity: and the latter being puff'd up with the Glory of Martial Exploits, and the Applause of the People. The Authority of the Duke of *Guise* had receiv'd a mighty addition upon his repulsing *Charles* V. from

Francis II.

The Causes of the Intestine Wars of France.

1527.

The House of Guise *rises, and that of* Bourbon *declines.*

from before *Metz*, and taking *Calais*; whereas the unfortunate Battle fought near St. *Quintin*, and the ensuing dishonourable Peace, was very prejudicial to *Montmorency*. But the House of *Guise* got the greatest Advantage, when *Francis* II. married *Mary*, Queen of *Scotland*, whose Mother was Sister to the Duke of *Guise*: So that during the Reign of *Francis* II. the Duke of *Guise*, and the Cardinal, his Brother, were the Men that bore the greatest sway in the Kingdom; which extreamly exasperated *Montmorency*, and the two Brothers of *Bourbon*, viz. *Anthony*, King of *Navarre*, and the Prince of *Conde*, who would not bear to see themselves thus neglected. And tho' *Anthony*, was of a very modest Behaviour, watching only an Opportunity to regain his Kingdom of *Navarre* from the *Spaniards*, and having a sufficient Revenue out of his Country of *Bearn*, wherewithal to maintain himself; the Prince of *Conde* was ambitious, poor, and of a turbulent Spirit, as not being able to maintain his Grandeur without some considerable Employment. Besides this, he was continually stirr'd up by the Admiral *Gasper Coligny*, an ambitious, cunning, and sly Man; who, as his Enemies will have it, was very forward to Fish in troubled Waters; his Brother, *d'Andelot*, also being of a very wild and turbulent Spirit. These three only watch'd an Opportunity to raise Commotions in the Kingdom. Thus the great Men of the Kingdom were divided into these several Factions, at the Time when *Francis* II. began his Reign, a Prince scarce 16 Years old, weak both in Body and Mind, and therefore uncapable to Rule the Kingdom by himself.

Divisions about the Administration of the Government.

Several therefore pretended to have a Right to the Administration of the Government; those of *Bourbon*, as being the next Princes of the Blood; the House of *Guise*, as being nearly related to the Queen; and the Queen-Mother, *Catharine de Medicis*, the very Pattern of an aspiring and cunning Woman, hoped, That whilst the Princes were in Contest about the Administration of the Government, it would fall to her share with which view she always fomented the Divisions, by keeping up the Balance betwixt them. This *Catharine* first sided with the House of *Guise*, dividing the Administration of Affairs with them, so that she was to have the Supream Administration, the Duke of *Guise* was to manage the Military Affairs, and his Brother, the Cardinal, the Finances. This

Agreement

Agreement being made betwixt them, the Constable, under pretence of his old Age, was dismiss'd from Court, and the Prince of *Conde* sent as Ambassador into *Spain*. Those, who were thus excluded, had a meeting, to consider which way they might free themselves from these Oppressions, where it was resolv'd that the King of *Navarre* should intercede for them at Court; but he being put off with fair Words and empty Promises, set himself at rest. Thereupon *Conde* resolv'd to try his Fortune by force; but having not a sufficient Interest, *Coligny* advised him, he should side with the *Huguenots* (so they called in *France* those who profess'd the Protestant Religion) who laboured then under a severe Persecution, and wanted a Head, under whose Conduct they might obtain the free Exercise of their Religion: Besides that, they mortally hated the House of *Guise*, whom they supposed to be the Authors of their Persecution. The Business was thus concerted; That the *Huguenots* should assemble in private, and some of them by a humble Petition should request the free Exercise of their Religion at Court; which, if it should be refused, the rest should be at hand, to kill the *Guise* party, and to force the King to receive the Prince of *Conde* for his Chief Minister of State. The Execution of this Design was undertaken by a certain Gentleman, called *Renaudie*; but the Enterprize being deferr'd for some time, because the Court went from *Blois* to *Amboise*, it was discover'd, and thereby render'd impracticable, above 1200 that were taken, paying with their Lives for it; *Conde* was also sent to Prison, and was just upon the point of receiving Sentence of Death, when *Francis* II. after a very short Reign, died suddenly of an Ulcer in the Head, which caused great Alterations in the Affairs of the Kingdom. 1560.

§. 20. His Successor was his Brother, *Charles* IX. then scarce 11 Years old, whose Tuition his Mother *Catharine* took immediately upon her self, hoping to enjoy it quietly, whilst the Houses of *Bourbon* and *Guise* were engag'd in mutual Quarrels; and for that end she was very careful to uphold these Jealousies betwixt them. To find an Opportunity to set up the Prince of *Conde* and his Party thereby to balance the House of *Guise*, she pretended to be no Enemy to the Protestant Religion, by which means it became much in request at Court. To suppress the Charles IX.

Reformed

Reformed Religion, *Montmorency*, the House of *Guise*, and the Mareschal of St *Andrew*, join'd in a Confederacy, who calling themselves the *Triumvirate*, drew also the King of *Navarre* into their Party. After this, a Conference and Dispute was held betwixt some Divines of both Religions at *Poissy*, upon which the Royal Protection was by a Publick Edict, promis'd to the Protestant Religion: which from the Month is call'd, *The Edict of* January. This extreamly exasperated the *Triumvirate*, insomuch that in the very same Year the War commenc'd. The first occasion of it was given by some retaining to the *Guise* Faction, who in a small Town call'd *Vassay*, disturb'd the Protestants in the Exercise of their Religion; and a Quarrel arising thereupon, kill'd near threescore of them: Which was the first Blood shed in this Civil War; and from this time things went very strangely in *France*. In this first War the King of *Navarre* died of a Wound, which he received in the Siege of *Roan*. Near *Dreux* a bloody Battle was fought, where *Conde* at first had the Advantage, but his Soldiers falling to plundering, he was beat back again; and himself being made a Prisoner, and the Mareschal St. *Andrew* being kill'd by a Shot, 8000 Men were slain upon the Spot, and the Loss near equal on both sides. The Duke of *Guise* kept the Field; but was afterwards at the Siege of *Orleans*, treacherously murther'd by one *Poltrot*, with a Pistol-shot, who was suppo-sed to have committed the Fact by Instigation of *Coligny*. Soon after a Peace was made. It is related, that above 50000 *Huguenots* were slain in this War; on the other side, they took the Church-plate and Ornaments, which they turn'd into Money, and so it came to pass Silver was after this War more currant in *France* than before. However *Catharine* had persuaded her self, that both Parties were reduc'd to that Condition, that she could now handle them at pleasure. After the Peace was concluded, the *English* were presently dispossess'd of *Havre de Grace*, which the *Huguenots* had given them as an Acknowledgment for their Assistance. This Peace lasted no longer than till the Year 1576, when the *Huguenots* were persuaded, that at the Interview betwixt *Catharine* and the Duke of *Alva* at *Bayonne*, a League was set on foot for rooting out the Hereticks: And in effect, they were immediately after more severely dealt with, and, as it was reported, the Prince of *Conde* and *Coligny* were to be secur'd.

The Conference of Poissy.

1562.

The first Huguenot War.

1563.

secur'd. Upon this Apprehnsion the *Huguenots* began the Second War, during which, the Constable *Annas Montmorency*, being mortally wounded in an Engagement, he told a Monk, who at his last Hour was very troublesome to him; *He should let him be at quiet, since during the Time of 80 Years that he had liv'd, he had learn'd how to employ one quarter of an Hour in dying.* The *Huguenots* got great Reputation for Valour in this Engagement, they being much Inferiour to the other in Number. About the same time the City of *Rochelle* declar'd for the *Huguenots*, which afterwards for 60 Years together serv'd them for a secure Retreat. Then a second Peace was concluded, not with an Intention to keep it, but that each Party might find a better Opportunity to take Advantage of one another; nor were the Conditions ever fulfill'd. The War therefore was renewed in the same Year, during which the Prince of *Conde* was kill'd by a Shot in a Battle near *Jarnack*. After his Death, the *Huguenots* declar'd *Henry*, King of *Navarre*, the Son of *Anthony*, who afterwards was King of *France*, their Head, tho' in effect *Coligny* had the chief Management of Affairs. He in vain besieged *Poictiers*, in the Defence of which Place the young Duke of *Guise* gave the first Proofs of his Valour; he was also soundly beaten near *Moncontour*, where he lost 9000 Foot. He lost nevertheless nothing of his former Reputation, for he quickly recollected his broken Troops, and got together a great Army, being assisted by Queen *Elizabeth* with Money, and by the Counts *Palatine* with Soldiers. He directed his March towards *Paris*, whereupon a Peace was concluded to the great Advantage of the *Huguenots*, the four strong Cities, of *Rochelle*, *Montauban*, *Cognac*, and *Charite*, being given them for their Security: But the main design of this Peace was, that the King perceiving, that the *Huguenots* could not be suppress'd by Force, hop'd he might win them by Policy, and therefore endeavour'd by fair Words and great Promises to make them secure. The Admiral was caress'd at Court, and consulted withal about an Expedition to be undertaken against the *Spaniards* in the *Netherlands*. A Marriage was also concluded betwixt *Henry*, King of *Navarre*, and *Margaret*, the King's Sister, to which Wedding they invited the Chief of the *Huguenots*, with a Design to cut their Throats in *Paris*. And first of all the Admiral *Coligny*, as he was going

The Second War.

1568.

The third War.

The Prince of Conde *being slain, the King of* Navarre *is declar'd Head of the* Huguenots.

1570.

The Parisian Massacre.

going home from Court, was by some Villains, who were suborn'd by the Duke of *Guise*, shot with two Bullets through the Arm. Then it was agreed, That in the Year 1571, on the 24th of *August*, early in the Morning, when the Bells were ringing to Prayers, all the *Huguenots* should be massacred, except the King of *Navarre* and the young Prince of *Conde* : The Execution of this Enterprize the Duke of *Guise* had taken upon himself. The beginning of the Massacre was made with *Coligny*, who was ill of his Wounds; then it fell promiscuously upon the rest, the Fury of the Mob not ceasing till after seven Days slaughter. A great many other Cities of *France* follow'd the Example of *Paris*, so that within few Days near 30000 were miserably massacred. The King of *Navarre* and Prince of *Conde*, were forc'd to abjure the Reformed Religion. This was the so much celebrated *Parisian* Wedding, which *Gabriel Naude* would fain represent as a State's Trick, but that is, in my Opinion, a very gross way of arguing. Nevertheless the *Huguenots* did quickly recollect themselves, after the first Consternation was over, renewing the War with great Animosity and Revenge. During this War the King's Army besieged *Rochelle* near eight Months together, and having lost 12000 Men before it, News was brought, that the Duke of *Anjou* was elected King of *Poland*. Hence an Opportunity was taken to raise the Siege with some Reputation, and to make a Peace the fourth time with the *Huguenots*; by vertue of which, the Cities of *Rochelle*, *Montauban*, and *Nismes*, were given them for their Security. But soon after, in the next Year, the fifth War commenc'd; at which time a third Faction arose in *France*, which was call'd, *That of the Politicians*; they pretended, without having any regard to the Religious Differences, to seek the Publick Welfare, to have the Queen remov'd from the Administration of the Government, and the *Italians*, and the Family of *Guise* to be banish'd the Kingdom of *France*. The Heads of this Faction were the House of *Montmorency*, who intended, during these Troubles, to play their own Game: Though they were afterwards very instrumental in helping *Henry* IV. to the Crown. During these Troubles *Charles* IX. died, leaving no legitimate Issue behind him.

The Fourth War.

1573.

The fifth War.

§. 21. After

§. 11. After the Death of *Charles* IX. the Crown fell to *Henry* III. who was at that time in *Poland*, during whose absence his Mother *Catharine* govern'd the Kingdom, which was in a very confus'd Estate. He left *Poland* privately, and taking his way by *Vienna* and *Venice*, arriv'd safely in *France*. But after he had taken upon him the Administration of Affairs, he deceiv'd every body in those Hopes which were conceiv'd of him before. For being addicted only to his Pleasures and Idleness, he was led away by his Favourites, leaving the Chief Administration of the Kingdom to his Mother. The *Huguenots* Power encreas'd remarkably after the Duke of *Alenson*, the King's Brother sided with them, and *Conde* and the *Paltzgrave*, *John Casimir*, led an Army out of *Germany* into *France*; besides that, the King of *Navarre* found means to make his escape out of Prison. The fifth Peace was therefore concluded with the *Huguenots*, whereby they obtain'd very advantageous Conditions. About the same time a new Faction was set up, from the coalition of a great many small ones; this was call'd, *The Holy Union*, or *League*, which reduc'd *France* to the most miserable Condition that could be. The chief Promoter of it was *Henry* Duke of *Guise*, who, perceiving, that the great Authority which he had among the People, made him to be hated by the King, endeavour'd to make a Party of his own. He made use especially of the Priests and Common People of *Paris*; among whom the Name of the *Guises* was in great Veneration. He was encourag'd to undertake this Design, because the King was despised by all, and the Women by their Intrigues rul'd at Court. Besides this, he pretended, to be descended from the Race of *Charles the Great* which was excluded unjustly from the Crown by *Hugh Capet*. The Pretence of this League was the Catholick Religion; and there was a Draught made of it, which contain'd chiefly three things, *viz*. *The Defence of the Catholick Religion: The Establishment of* Henry III. *in the Throne: And the maintaining the Liberty of the Kingdom, and the Assembly of the States.* Those who enter'd into the League, promis'd to be obedient to such a Head or General as should be chosen for the Defence of it, all which was confirm'd by Oath. At the first setting up of the League the King conniv'd at it, hoping thereby the sooner to subdue the *Huguenots*; nay, he himself sign'd it at the Diet at *Blois*, declaring himself the

The Holy League.

1577. the Head of the League. Then the sixth War broke out against the *Huguenots*, but the King made Peace with them the same Year, notwithstanding that they were in a very ill Condition, neither was any thing done worth mentioning in this War. The War being ended, the King returning to his Pleasures, confounded great Sums of Money, and therefore laid new and heavy Impositions upon the People, and his Favourites grew very Insolent, which increas'd the Hatred against him, and at the same time the Respect and Love of the People to the Duke of *Guise*. At the same time, the Duke of *Alenson*, the King's Brother, declaring himself Lord of the *Netherlands*, *Philip*, King of *Spain*, was provok'd to revenge himself of the *French*, and uphold the League. In the Year 1579. the Seventh War was begun against the *Huguenots*, wherein also they succeeded very ill. Notwithstanding this the King made a Peace with them the next ensuing Year, as being unwilling they should be quite rooted out, for fear the League might prove too strong for himself. The *German* Horse were also much fear'd, and the Duke of *Alenson* was very forward to have the Peace concluded, that he might be at leisure to employ his Forces in the *Netherlands*. This Peace lasted five Years, during which time the Hatred against the King increas'd daily, because of the heavy Taxes which were devour'd by his Favourites. He further inlarg'd the contempt of the People by playing too much the Hypocrite, and affecting the severity of a Monastick Life. The *French* Glory was also much eclips'd, when the Duke of *Alenson* behav'd himself so ill in the *Netherlands*, and the *French* Fleet, which was sent to the Assistance of *Anthony the Bastard*, was totally ruin'd near *Tercera*. But the League grew very strong after the Death of the Duke of *Alenson*, the King's younger Brother, the King having no hopes of any Issue of his Body: Then it was that the Duke of *Guise* pro-pos'd to himself no less than the Crown, tho' for a Co-lour he set up the Cardinal of *Bourbon*, in order to exclude the King of *Navarre*. And because it was suspected that the King favour'd the King of *Navarre*, the Priests began to thunder in the Pulpits, and to make horrid Exclamations, that the Catholick Religion was lost: the Duke of *Guise* enter'd into a Confederacy with *Philip*, who was to furnish great Sums of Money under pretext of maintaining the Catholick Religion, and to assist the

The sixth War.

Spain enters the League.

The Seventh War.

Cardinal

Cardinal of *Bourbon* in obtaining the Crown; but in effect, this Intention was to uphold the Divisions in *France*, and so disable it to assist the *Netherlands*. Then the Leaguers began to break out into an open War; and having taken a great many Towns, oblig'd the King, in pursuance of their Demands, to forbid the Exercise of the Protestant Religion in *France*. And so began the Eighth War against the *Huguenots*, and if the King had been in earnest bent to ruin them, they would have been in a very ill Condition: For tho' the King of *Navarre* beat the Duke *de Joyeuse* near *Courtras*, yet did he not prosecute his Victory. And about the same time the Duke of *Guise* dispers'd the *German* and *Swiss* Forces, which under the Command of *Fabian de Dona* were marching to the Assistance of the *Hnguenots*. This Army, being destitute of a good Commander was miserably maul'd, and the rest sent home in a very shameful Condition. This Victory acquired the Duke of *Guise* great Applause and Favour among the People, and still lessen'd the Value of the King's Person; so that the Priests now did not stick to exclaim against the King in their Sermons, calling him a *Tyrant*. Thereupon the King having resolv'd with himself to punish the Heads of the League in *Paris*, they broke out into open Rebellion, and having sent for the Duke of *Guise* as their Protector, the King was oblig'd to leave *Paris* by Night: But the King perceiving that more Cities sided daily with the League, and despairing to overcome them by Force, took another Course to obtain his Ends, and made an Agreement with the Duke of *Guise*, with great Advantages on the Duke's and the Leaguers side: He pretended also to have forgotten all past injuries, on purpose to inveigle the Duke of *Guise*. And under those specious Pretences he got him to appear at the Assembly of the Estates at *Blois*. In the mean time the Duke of *Savoy* had taken from the *French* the Marquisate of *Saluzze*, the only Province left them in *Italy*: But the Estates, who were most of them Creatures of the Duke of *Guise*, being very urgent in their Demands, to have the King of *Navarre* declared incapable of the Crown, and the Duke of *Guise* to be made Constable, the King caus'd the Duke of *Guise* and his Brother the Cardinal, to be murther'd. This put the Members of the League into a Rage, and with the Assistance of the Priests, the King was in

1585. *The Eighth War.* *1587.* *The League force the King from* Paris. *1588.* *The Duke and Cardinal of* Guise, *assassinated by the King's Order at* Blois.

Paris publickly declar'd to have forfeited the Crown. Most of the great Cities of *France* being stirr'd up by the Example of the *Parisians* did the same, declaring the Duke *de Maine*, Brother to the Duke of *Guise*, Lieutenant-General of the State and Crown of *France*, and Supream Head of the League; who endeavour'd, but in vain, to surprize the King in *Tours*. The King being then overpower'd by the League; and at the same time, excommunicated by the Pope, was oblig'd to make an Agreement with the King of *Navarre*, and to make use of the *Huguenots*, and having got together a great Army, he march'd towards *Paris*, with a Resolution to reduce that City to Obedience by Force of Arms: But the day before the general Attack was to be made, one *James Clement* a *Dominican* Monk, brought a Letter out of the City directed to the King, which whilst he deliver'd, pretending to Whisper the King, he thrust a Knife into his Bowels, of which Wound he died the day following: The last of the House of *Valois*.

The King makes use of the Huguenots against the League.

Aug. 2. 1589

Henry IV.

§. 22. *Henry* IV. whom we have hitherto call'd *The King of* Navarre, and, who was the first of the House of *Bourbon*, did at the beginning of his Reign, meet with no less Difficulties than he had met with before. For, tho' he was Lawful Heir to the Crown, yet the Protestant Religion, which he profess'd, was no small Obstacle, for as long as he was addicted to that, the League, the Pope, and *Spain*, would questionless oppose him with all their might: On the other hand, if he chang'd his Religion he was in danger of losing the Assistance of the *Huguenots*, who had been steady to him: And besides it would have been very unbecoming, to have so publickly accommodated his Religion to his Interest. Notwithstanding this, immediately after the Death of *Henry* III. all the Great Men of the Army assembled together, promised him Obedience after several Contests, upon Condition that within six Months he would suffer himself to be instructed in the Catholick Religion. But because *Henry* would not be bound to any certain time, but only gave them some Hopes in general Terms, it was agreed, That the *Huguenots* should enjoy the free Exercise of their Religion, but that the Catholick Religion should be re-establish'd in all Cities, and the Revenues restor'd to the Clergy. But, the Members of the

His Difficulties on the account of his Religion.

League,

League, because the Duke of *Maine* at that time durst not take upon him the Title of King, proclaim'd the Cardinal of *Bourbon*, an antient decrepit Man, Uncle to King *Henry*, and who was then in Custody, their King, declaring the Duke *de Maine* Lieutenant-General of the Crown. The Leaguers made the strongest Party, having on their side the Common People, most of the great Cities, all the Parliaments, except that of *Rennes* and *Bourdeaux*, almost all the Clergy, *Spain*, the Pope, and the rest of the Catholick States, except *Venice* and *Florence*. But the Heads were not very unanimous, and the Duke *de Maine* had not Authority enough to keep them in Unity. On the King's side were almost all the Nobility, the whole Court of the deceas'd King, all the Protestant Princes and States, the old *Huguenot* Troops, who had done great Service to *Henry*, and would still have done more, if they had not mistrusted him, that he would Change his Religion. Each Party watch'd an Opportunity of surprizing one another, The Duke of *Maine* endeavouring to surprize the King near *Diep*, was bravely repuls'd which seemed to be ominous to the League. On the other hand, the King could not master *Paris*, tho' he had taken the Suburbs, But *Henry* was not only pester'd by the League, but also, for want of Money, was oblig'd to keep up his Party with fair Words and Promises. The *Spaniards* also began to intermeddle publickly in the Affairs of *France*, in hopes in this Juncture either to conquer the Kingdom, or to Divide it, or at least to Weaken it. But the Duke *de Maine* did under-hand oppose these Designs, being unwilling, that in case he could not be King himself, *France* should fall under the Subjection of *Spain*. In the Year 1590, *Henry* obtained a glorious Victory over the Duke *de Maine*, who had double the Number, near *Ivry*. Then he blocked up *Paris*, which was reduc'd to the greatest Extremity by Famine, but reliev'd by the Duke of *Parma*, Governour of the *Netherlands*. In the Year 1591. there arose a third Faction, the young Cardinal *Bourbon* making Pretensions to the Crown, but was very fortunately disappointed in his Aim by the King. Then Pope *Gregory* XIV. excommunicated *Henry*, exhorting all his Subjects to discontinue their Obedience, which Difficulty *Henry* did not surmount without great Troubles. The *Spaniards* also declared themselves more openly, *Philip* offe-

The Pope Excommunicates Henry.

ring his Daughter, *Isabella Clara Eugenia*, to be made Queen of *France*; which Proposal was mightily encouraged by the young Duke of *Guise*, he being then just escap'd out of Custody, as 'twas supposed, by connivance of the King, who presum'd, that thereby that Party might be divided, since he would certainly endeavour to oppose the designs of the Duke *de Maine*, his Uncle. After the Duke of *Parma* had rais'd the Siege of *Roan*, the *Spaniards* urg'd more and more, that the *French* would come to a Resolution concerning the setting up of another King. And in the Assembly of the Estates in *Paris*, which was held for that purpose, it was proposed, that *Isabella*, the Daughter of *Philip*, being born of a *French* Mother, should be declar'd Queen of *France*, and that she should have for her Husband, *Ernest*, Arch-Duke of *Austria*. But the *French* refusing to accept of a Foreigner for their King, *Charles*, Duke of *Guise*, was proposed as a Husband to *Isabella*. This Proposition relish'd very ill with the Duke of *Maine*, who thought himself so well deserving, that no body ought to be preferr'd before him; wherefore if he could not have the Crown, he was resolv'd the other should not have it, and accordingly employed all his Cunning, so that there was nothing determined in the Assembly, concerning this Proposition. The King however, plainly perceiv'd, That if he did not Change his Religion, his Affairs must needs grow worse, especially, since those Catholicks who hitherto had been of his Party did threaten to leave him, if he did not perform his Promise. He called therefore the Bishops together who instructed him in the Catholick Faith, and having received Absolution, he went to St. *Denys*'s Chappel to Mass. And that the People might taste the sweetness of Peace, and desire it, he made a Truce of three Months, which proved very successful, especially, since the fundamental Pretence, Namely, *Henry*'s being a Heretick, was now removed. *Vitry* and the City of *Meaux* were the first, that surrendred to the King in the same Year, upon very advantageous Conditions; *Aix*, *Lyons*, *Orleans*, *Bourges*, and other Cities, soon followed their Example. And to encourage the rest to do the same, the King caused himself to be Crowned and Anointed in *Chartres*, *Rheims*, being as yet in the Hands of the League. Not long after *Paris* was also surrendred by the Governour *Brissac*; and here the King was received with such joyful acclamations

Proposals about setting up another King.

1593.

The King Changes his Religion.

1593.

Several Cities surrendered to him.

of the People as if they had never been his Enemies, the *Spanish* Garrison being turn'd out with Ignominy, and the hissing of the Common People. Then all the rest of the Cities and Governours surrendred themselves to the King on very advantageous Conditions, which the King was willing to grant them, that he might once be put in quiet Possession of the Crown, and drive the *Spaniards* out of *France*. The young Duke of *Guise* submitted himself being made governour of *Provence*. Then *Henry* denounced War against *Spain*, not only to revenge himself for what Troubles they had created to him before, but also to please the *Huguenots*, and to root out of the People their Affection for the *Spaniards*. These were the Fruits *Philip* reapt for so many Millions, which he had bestowed in supporting the League. In the beginning of the same Year, a Knife was by a certain desperate Ruffian, called *John Castle*, thrust into the King's Mouth, whereby he lost one of his Teeth. It was the King's good Fortune that he just bowed himself, this Villain's Aim having been at his Throat: And because it was found out, that the Jesuits had been tampering with him, whose Principles withal were thought very dangerous, they were banish'd out of *France*, but some Years after restored again. Afterwards the Duke of *Nevers* being sent to *Rome* to obtain Absolution for King *Henry*, the same was granted by the Pope, who had been very averse hitherto to *Henry*; but perceiving that he would maintain his Crown in spight of him, was now for ingratiating himself with the King. Then the Dukes of *Maine*, and *Espernon*, and *Marseilles*, were received again into the King's Favour. But the War against *Spain* did not succeed to his wish. For tho' the King got some advantages over them in the *Franche Compte*, and beat the *Spaniards* out of *Han* in *Picardy*; yet on the other side, these took *Dourlans* and *Cambray*, the latter of which had been hitherto in the Possession of *Balagny* under *French* Protection; and in the Year 1596, they took *Calais* and *Ardres*. And tho' the King took from the *Spaniards* *Fere*, yet was that a very slender Compensation of his Losses. But there happened another great Misfortune; for the *Spaniards* in the Year after that took the City of *Amiens* by surprize, which was not retaken without great pains. In the Year 1598, the Duke of *Mercœur*, who hitherto had stood out resolutely in *Bretany*, did at last submit himself, hoping

1595.

The King assaulted and wounded by a Ruffian.

The Jesuits banish'd.

The Edict of Nants. thereby to obtain the said Dukedom. And to set the *Huguenots* at rest, the King published for their Security that famous Edict of *Nants*, as it is called, by vertue of which they have hitherto enjoyed the free Exercise of Religion. *The Peace of* Vervins. At last a peace was concluded betwixt *Henry* and the *Spaniards* at *Vervins*, stipulating that such places as were taken since the Year 1559, should be restored on both sides. A Peace being thus concluded, *Henry* resolved to be even with the Duke of *Savoy*, who under his Predecessors Reign had taken *Saluzze*, and during the Intestine Wars had raised great Troubles in *Dauphince* and *Provence*, and though the Duke came in Person into *France* and promised to the King to give him some other Places in exchange of the former, yet was he not in earnest, in hopes to be upheld by *Spain*, or that the Marshal *de Biron*, with whom he kept private Intelligence, should renew the Civil Commotions. *He takes from the Duke of* Savoy, *all that he possessed on this side the* Alpes. But the King fell upon him, and took from the Duke all what he was possess'd of on this side the *Alpes*. At last, by Mediation of the Pope, an Agreement was made; that the Duke should 1600. give to *France*, in exchange for *Saluzze*, *La Bresse*, *Bugey*, *Valromay* and *Gex*. The *Italian* Princes were very ill satisfied with this Peace, since there being no Door left for *France* to enter *Italy*, *Italy* was left to the Discretion of the *Spaniard*. But *Henry* being tired with so long and tedious a War, was resolved at last to enjoy the sweet Fruits of Peace after so many years Troubles. *The Conspiracy of the Marshal* de Biron. But soon after, a dangerous Conspiracy was discovered, contrived by the Marshal *de Biron*, who intended with the Assistance of the *Spaniards* to depose the King, and dismember the Kingdom, by setting up a great many Petty Principalities; having agreed with the rest, to have for his share the Dukedom of *Burgundy*. And refusing to accept of the King's Mercy, which he was willing to grant him in consideration of his great Deserts, he was condemn'd, 1602. and his Head cut off. The King being now at Peace, employed all his Thoughts how *France* might recover it self after such tedious Wars, and that good Constitutions might be established, but especially that his Revenues *He introduces Manufacturies.* might be encreased; He established for this purpose all sorts of Manufacturies, and especially that of Silk, (which afterwards drew great Riches into that Kingdom.) But even in the midst of Peace he was continually troubled with his Queen, who was enrag'd at his Mistresses; and the

the *Spaniards* were always plotting both against his Person and Crown. On the other hand, *Henry* had a design to oppose the growing Power of the House of *Austria*, by keeping it within the Bounds of *Spain*, and the Hereditary Countries in *Germany*. And 'tis said, that for that purpose he concerted Measures with the *Northern* Crowns, with *Holland*, with the Protestant Princes of *Germany*, with the Elector of *Bavaria*, the Duke of *Savoy*, the *Swiss*, and even the Pope himself. To put this Design in execution, he took the opportunity of the Differences which were then on foot concerning the Succession to the Country of *Juliers*, which, that it might not be devour'd by the House of *Austria*, he was resolved to prevent with all his might. This is certain, that his Preparations were greater than seem'd to be requisite only for the business of *Juliers*; for he had got 120000 Men of his own and auxiliary Troops together, and prodigious Sums of Money. The House of *Austria* on the other hand did not make the least Preparations, just as if it had fore-known the fatal Blow, which happen'd soon after. The Army was marching towards the *Netherlands*, and the King ready to follow in a few days, having caused the Queen to be Crowned and constituted her Regent during his Absence; When the King going along the Street in *Paris* in his Coach, which was fain to stop by reason of the great Crowd of People, was by a desperate Ruffian, whose name was *Francis Ravillac*, stabb'd with a Knife in his Belly, so that without uttering one Word he died immediately. There are some, who make no question of it, but that this Villain was suborn'd to commit this Fact, and that it was not done without the knowledge of the *Spaniards*, and the Queen her self. And so fell this Great Hero by the Hands of a profligate Wretch, after he had surmounted great Difficulties in ascending the Throne, and had got clear of above fifty several Conspiracies; which being, most of them contrived by the Priests against his Life, were all timely discovered. His Death proved very pernicious to the Kingdom, for that, during the Minority of his Son, the Power and interest of the Great Men, grew to a great height, and the *Huguenots* grew stiffer and more violent.

His design to put a stop to the growth of the House of Austria.

He is Assassinated by Ravillac. May 14. 1610.

§. 23. His Son, *Lewis* XIII. succeeded him, being scarce nine Years of Age, and under the Tuition of his Mother

Lewis XIII.

Mother *Mary de Medicis*, who endeavoured to preserve Peace abroad by Alliance, and at home by Clemency and Liberality towards the great Men of the Kingdom, who nevertheless several times raised Disturbances, whereby they made their own advantage, the Queen-Regent being not powerful enough to keep them in Obedience by force.

1617. As soon as the King had taken upon himself the Management of Affairs, he caused *Concini*, Marshal *d' Ancre*, who was born a *Florentine*, to be kill'd, he having been in great Power during the Queen's Regency, and by his Pride, Riches, and Power, drawn upon himself the hatred of the Subjects; so that by his Death the King hoped to appease the dissatisfied Multitude. The Queen-Mother was sent away from the Court to *Blois*, from whence she was carried off and set at Liberty by

1619. the Duke *de Espernon*. But these Commotions were at last appeased by bestowing liberal Presents among the Great Men. About the same time *Richelieu*, afterwards made a Cardinal, began to be in great Esteem at Court, who advised the King to establish his Authority, by extirpating the intestine Evils of *France*. He laid this down as a Fundamental Principle, that he should take from the *Huguenots* the Power of doing him any mischief, considering that such as were dissatisfied at any time, or that were of a Turbulent Spirit took always refuge, and were assisted by them. The first beginning was made in the King's Patrimonial Province of *Bearn*, where he caused the Catholick Religion to be re-establish'd. The *Huguenots* being greatly dissatisfied thereat, began to break out into Violence, whence the King took an opportunity to recover several Places from them, but sustained a considerable Loss in the Siege of *Montauban*, till at last Peace was made with the *Huguenots*, under Condition that they should demolish all their new Fortifications, except those of *Montauban* and *Rochelle*. In the Year 1625, Cardinal *Richelieu* was made Chief Minister of *France*, about which time also the second War with the *Huguenots* was ended; but this Peace did not last long, because the Citizens of *Rochelle* would not bear, that the Fortress called *Fort Lewis*, should be built just under their Noses. Thereupon *Richelieu* having taken a Resolution at once to put an end to this War by the taking of *Rochelle*, besieg'd it so close both by Sea and Land, that the *English* who had very ill Success in the Isle of *Rhee*, where they Landed, could

Richelieu *comes in play.*

Made Chief Minister of State.

bring

bring no Succours into the place. The Obstinacy of the besieg'd was at last over-come by Famine, there being not above 5000 left out of 18000 Citizens, for they had lived without Bread for thirteen Weeks. With this stroke the Strength of the *Huguenots* was broken, *Montauban* upon the Persuasion of the Cardinal having demolished its Works. At last the cunning Duke of *Roan* also made his Peace, after he had been sufficiently troublesome to the King in *Languedoc*, upon Condition that the Cities of *Nismes* and *Montpeller* should demolish their Fortifications, but enjoy the free Exercise of their Religion. And thus the Ulcer, which had settled it self in the very Entrails of *France*, was happily healed up. It is related by some that these Civil Wars devoured above a Million of People; that 150 Millions were employed in paying of the Soldiers; that 9 Cities, 400 Villages, 20000 Churches, 2000 Monasteries, 10000 Houses, were burnt or laid level with the Ground. Then *France* applied all their care towards Foreign Affairs. The King assisted the Duke of *Nevers*, in obtaining the Dukedom of *Mantua*, which belonged to him by Right of Succession, but whom the *Spaniards* endeavoured to exclude from the same, as being a *French-Man*. In this War the Siege of *Casal* is most famous, in the defence of which place, the *French* gave incredible Proofs of their Bravery. At last the Business was through the wise Management of the Popish Nuncio, *Mazarini*, (who then laid the first Foundation of his Future Greatness in *France*) composed, and the Duke of *Nevers* afterwards by the Treaty made at *Chierasco*, establish'd in the Dukedoms of *Mantua* and *Montferrat*. At the same time the King bought *Pignerol* of the Duke of *Savoy*, that so the *French* might not want a Door into *Italy*. *France* had also before taken part with the *Grisons* against the Inhabitants of the *Valteline*, who had revolted, being assisted by the *Spaniards*; whereby he prevented this Country from falling into the Hands of the *Spaniards*, and so Matters were restored to their former State. In the Year 1631. *France* made an Alliance with *Sweden*, allowing to that King a yearly Pension, to assist him in opposing the Greatness of the House of *Austria*. But when King *Gustavus Adolphus* began to be formidable on the *Rhine*, he took the Elector of *Treves* into his Protection, putting a Garrison into *Hermanstein*, (which nevertheless in the Year 1636, was forced to a surrender by Famine.) In the

Rochelle taken.

The Effects of the Civil Wars.

A War in Italy.

1628.

The first Occasion of Mazarini's Greatness.

How Pignerol came into the hands of the French.

The Queen-Mother raises Troubles. the mean time the Queen-Mother and the King's Brother, the Duke of *Orleans*, envying the Greatness of *Richelieu* had raised some Tumults. With them also sided *Montmorency*, who paid for it with his Head, and put an inglorious end to his Noble Family, which boasted to have been the first noble Family that embrac'd the Christian Religion in *France*. And though this business was afterwards Composed, the Queen-Mother being received into Favour again, yet was she so dissatisfied, because she could not Act according to her own will, that she retired into *Flanders*, and from thence into *England*, where she made some stay, and at last died in a very low Condition in *Cologne*. *The King takes Lorrain from that Duke.* In the Year 1633. the King took from the Duke of *Lorain* his Country, because he had declared himself for the Emperor. And when after the Battle fought near *Nordlingen*, the *Swedish* Affairs were in a
1634. very low Condition, and the House of *Austria* began to hold up its Head again, *France* broke out into open War with *Spain*, to balance the growing Power of the House of *Austria*. Alledging that the *Spaniards* had surprized the City of *Treves*, and taken the Elector Prisoner who was under *French* Protection. And then the War began in *Italy*, *Germany*, the *Netherlands*, and *Roussilion*, wherein the *French* got the better. The first Attack which the *French* made in the *Netherlands* did not succeed very well they being forced to raise the Siege of *Lovain* with great Loss. In the Year 1636, *Piccolomini* marched into *Picardy*, and *Galias* into *Burgundy*, but did nothing of Moment. On the other hand, the *French* raised the Siege of *Leucate* in *Roussilion*, and the brave Duke *Barnhard* of *Saxen-Weimar*, took the strong Fortress of *Brisac*. And after the Death of this Duke, which happened not long after, the King of *France* got possession of that Fortress and gain'd his Army with Money. Yet the *French* miscarried in the same Year before St. *Omar* and *Fontarabia*, before the last of which Places the Prince of *Conde* sustained a considerable Loss, In the same Year, on the 5th of *September*, *Lewis* XIV. was almost by a Miracle born of a Marriage, which had proved unfruitful for 20 Years before. In the Year 1639, the *French* were beaten before *Thionville*. In the Year 1640, they took *Arras*, and in the same Year *Catalonia*, revolting from *Spain*, threw it self under the *French* Protection. In the Year 1641, a great Misfortune hung over *Richelieu*'s Head, the Count

de Soissons

de Soissons having rais'd a dangerous Rebellion; but, he being killed in an Engagement wherein otherwise his Party had the better, his death established the Cardinal's Authority, and the Quiet of *France*. In the Year 1642, *Perpignan* was taken, at which Siege the King and *Richeliu* were both present. Monsieur *Cinqmars* did about that time first insinuate himself into the King's Favour, hoping thereby to undermine *Richelieu*. And the better to balance the Cardinal, he made some under-hand Intrigues with *Spain*. But the Cardinal having discover'd the Business, caused his Head to be cut off; as also *de Thou* the younger's, because he had been privy to the Business; tho' he had advised against it, but had not discover'd it. From the Duke of *Bouillon*, who had been also of the Cabal, he took for a Punishment, his strong Hold, *Sedan*. In the same Year *Richelieu* died, to his great good Fortune, the King being grown quite weary of him, notwithstanding he had laid the first Foundation of the Greatness of *France*, which is now so formidable to *Europe*. The King also died not long after. May 14. 1643.

§. 24. *Lewis* XIV. was but five Years of Age when he came to the Crown: his Mother, 'tis true, bore the Name of *Regent* of *France*; but in effect, the Cardinal *Julius Mazarini* had the chief Management of the Kingdom, which was then in a very flourishing Condition; but every body was for enriching himself out of the King's Purse during his Minority; and *Mazarini* was very liberal, thereby endeavouring to make them in love with his Government. But the Treasury being exhausted, there was a Necessity of laying new Taxes upon the People, which caused a great Dissatisfaction against the Government. Nevertheless for the first five Years every thing was pretty quiet at home, and War carried on abroad. At the beginning of this new Government the Duke of *Anguen* obtained a signal Victory against the *Spaniards* near *Rocroy*; after which he took *Thionville*; and *Gaston*, the King's Uncle took *Gravelin*. 1644. *Anguein* revenged the Loss which the *French* had sustained the Year before near *Dutlingen*, by beating the *Bavarians* near *Friburgh*, and taking *Philipsburg*. In the Year 1646. he beat the *Bavarian* Troops near *Nordlingen*, and afterwards took *Dunkirk*. But in the Year next following, he in vain besieged the City of *Lerida*. In the Year 1648

Lewis XIV.

Mazarini's Ministry.

Peace of Munster. a Peace was concluded at *Munster* in *Westphalia* betwixt the Emperor and *France*, by vertue of which the latter got the two Fortresses of *Brisac* and *Philipsburg*, the Country of *Puntgau*, and part of the *Upper Alsatia*. But as *France* by this Peace was freed from one Enemy, so on the other hand the intestine Commotions put a stop to its great Progresses. *The Intestine Commotions.* The chief Reason of these Troubles was that some envying *Mazarini* as being a Foreigner, they would by all means have him removed from the Helm; and this they sought with the greater Importunity, because they stood in no awe of the King, who was but a Child; nor of his Mother, she being an outlandish Woman. Some of the great Men also were for fishing in troubled Waters: but above all the rest the Prince of *Conde* would fain have been Master. The Cardinal was for bringing him over to his Party by a Marriage; but the Prince of *Conde* perceiving that the Cardinal was for maintaining his old Post, and would not depend on him, rejected the Offer, as unbecoming the Grandure of his House. There were also some Women of a restless Spirit concern'd in these Intrigues, among whom was Madam *de Longueville*, Sister of the Prince of *Conde*, Madam *Chevreuse*, *Mombazon*, and others. 1648. The first beginning was by slanderous Papers and Libels, which were daily dispers'd in *Paris*. There was also a certain Faction set up, who called themselves *The Slingers*, because *The Slingers.* they openly undertook to knock down the Cardinal, as *David* struck down the Giant *Goliah*, by the help of his Sling. The Heads of this Faction were the Duke of *Beaufort*, and *Guadi* the Archbishop of *Paris*, afterwards call'd the Cardinal *de Retz*. With this Party sided the Parliament of *Paris*, which did pretend to have a great Authority in opposition to the Cardinal's Administration at that time. The first Insurrection was made in *Paris*, occasion'd by the taking into Custody of one *Brauffel*, a Member of the Parliament; whereupon the King left the City. Yet the business was compos'd for that time, some Concessions being made to the mutinous Party. *The King forced to leave Paris, 1649.* But the Faction of the *Slingers* renewing their former Disturbances, the King left the City a second time. The Parliament having then publickly condemn'd the Cardinal, grew every day stronger, *Turenne*, who then commanded the *French* Army in *Germany*, having declar'd for that side; but he was fain to leave the Army, which was kept in Duty by the help of a good Sum of Money. And tho' Matters were afterwards reconcil'd a second time at St. Germains, yet the Design against *Mazarini* was not laid aside; the Prince of *Conde*, who had brought over the *Slingers* to his Party, not ceasing to stir them up against him. But forasmuch as they had a different Aim, for the *Slingers* were for totally pulling down of the Cardinal, but the Prince of *Conde* would only have humbled him, the Cardinal cunningly rais'd a Misunderstanding betwixt them, by setting the Prince of *Conde* against the *Slingers*. Whereupon the *Slingers* were reconcil'd with the Cardinal. The Cardinal taking hold of this Opportunity, caused the Prince of *Conde*, and his Brother, the Prince of *Conti*, and their Brother-in-law, the Duke of *Longueville*, to be taken into Custody. This was adding Fuel to the Fire, every body being dissatisfied at the Imprisonment of the Princes. The City of *Bourdeaux* openly rebell'd. The *Spaniards* upon this Occasion took from the *French*, *Piombino* and *Porto Longone* in *Italy*. The Arch-duke *Leopold* struck Terror into the City of *Paris* it self, on the side of the *Netherlands*. And tho' the Cardinal beat *Turenne* near *Rethel*, he being gone over to the *Spaniards*, yet the Hatred against him encreas'd daily, and the Faction of the *Slingers*, the Parliament and the Duke of *Orleans* were absolutely for having the Princes set at liberty. The Cardinal therefore perceiving that nothing was to be done by open Violence, resolved to avoid the Storm, by setting the Princes at Liberty. And he himself retired to *Bruel*, the Court of the then Elector of *Cullen*. Then he was by a Decree of the Parliament for ever banish'd the Kingdom of *France*. *Mazarini* being thus remov'd, the Prince of *Conde* began to disturb the publick Quiet with more freedom: Having engag'd himself with the *Spaniards*, and being gone to *Bourdeaux*, he began to make open War against the Government. And the *Spaniards* taking hold of this Opportunity, recover'd all *Catalonia*. Then the Queen recall'd the Cardinal, who having strengthen'd the King's Army by such Troops as he had got together, fought several times very briskly with the Prince of *Conde*. But perceiving that the Hatred which the Faction of the *Slingers* and the Parliament had conceived against him, did not diminish, he publickly declar'd, he was willing to leave the Kingdom, to re-establish the publick Quiet. Hoping by so doing,

The Imprisonment of the Princes.

1651.

The Cardinal banish'd France.

The Queen recalls him.

doing, to lay the Blame of the intestine Divisions upon the Prince of *Conde*: which Design prov'd successful; for thereby the Eyes of the People were opened, who now plainly perceiv'd, that the Cardinal sought the Good of the King and Kingdom, but the Prince of *Conde* his own Interest, *Dunkirk* and *Graveling* being lost in the Fray. The Prince of *Conde* therefore perceiving that he had lost the Favour of the People, retired with his Troops into the *Spanish Netherlands*. Then the Cardinal return'd to Court and ever after had the Administration of the chiefest Affairs of the Kingdom till his Death, without any farther Opposition. The City of *Paris* return'd to its due Obedience, the Faction of the *Slingers* was dissolv'd, the Duke of *Orleans* left the Court, *Retz* was taken into Cu-
1653. stody, and *Bourdeaux* forc'd to submit. In the Year next following, the *French* began again to make War on the *Spaniards*; they took *Mommedy* with great difficulty and loss of Men, and fortunately reliev'd *Arras*: but they were beaten with great Slaughter from before *Valentiennes* and *Cambray*.
1658. *France* having just made an Alliance with *Cromwel*, the joint Forces of *France* and *England* besieg'd *Dunkirk* under the Command of *Turenne*: And the Duke *John d'Austria* and Prince *de Conde*, who came with an Army to relieve it, being repulsed with great Loss, the City was taken and delivered to the *English*, from whom the King afterwards redeem'd it for four
1662. Millions. About the same time *Graveling* was also retaken.
The Pyrenæan Peace 1659. At last a peace was concluded between *France* and *Spain* near the *Pyrenæan* Mountains by the two chief Ministers of State, on both sides, *viz.* by *Mazarini* and *Don Lewis de Haro*; by vertue of which, *France* was to keep *Roussilion*, and the greatest part of the Places which were taken in the *Netherlands*; *Mary Theresa*, the Daughter of *Philip* IV. was to be married to the King, and the
The Death of Mazarini. Prince of *Conde* to be receiv'd into Favour again. In the Year next following died *Mazarini*, who, as 'tis said, left the King, among others, this Lesson, *That he should govern himself, and not trust entirely to any Favourite.* The first thing of moment which the King undertook, was to
1661. settle his Revenues in a good order. He began with the Lord High Treasurer *Fouquet*, whom he took into Custody, and made a strict Inquisition against all such as having had hitherto the Management of his Revenues, had enriched themselves therewith: which brought an

incredible Treasure into the King's Coffers. In the Year 1661: a Difference arose betwixt the *French* and *Spanish* Embassadors in *London*, about the Precedency at the solemn Entry made by Count *Nile Brake* the *Swedish* Embassador, where the *French* Embassador's Coach was put back by Violence. This might easily have prov'd the Occasion of a War, if the *Spaniards* had not given Satisfaction to the *French*, and agreed, *That where-ever there were any* French *Embassadors Resident, the* Spanish *should not appear upon any publick Occasions;* Which the *French* do interpret, as if the *Spanish* Ministers were always to give place to the *French* of the same Character. In the Year 1662, the King made an Agreement with the Duke of *Lorrain*, according to which he was to exchange his Dukedom for an Equivalent in *France*, and his Family to be the next in Right of Succession, if the Family of *Bourbon* should happen to fail: Which Agreement the Duke would fain have annull'd afterwards; but the King, who did not understand Jesting in such a point, forc'd him to surrender to him *Marsal*. In the same Year the Duke *de Crequi*, the *French* Embassador at *Rome*, was grosly affronted there by the *Corsi*-Guards, which the King resented so ill, that he took from the Pope the City of *Avignon*: But the Difference was compos'd by the Mediation of the grand Duke of *Tuscany* at *Pisa*, and the Pope was fain to send a splendid Embassy to give Satisfaction to the King. About the same time the *French* would have got footing at *Gigeri* on the Coast of *Barbary*, but were repuls'd with considerable Loss by the *Moors*. The King also sent some Troops to the Assistance of the Emperor against the *Turks*, who behaved themselves bravely in the Battle fought near St. *Gothard*, and contributed much to the Victory. Notwithstanding which, the Emperor clapt up a Peace with the *Turks*, fearing lest the King of *France* might make use of this Opportunity to fall into the *Netherlands*. But those Forces which were sent to the Assistance of the *Venetians* in *Candie*, did not acquire so much Glory as being too forward and hot in the first Onset, where they lost the Duke of *Beaufort*. In the Year 1665, the King of *France* kindled a War betwixt the *English* and *Dutch*, thereby to weaken their Naval Force, which was so formidable to him, and in the mean while to get leisure to conquer the *Netherlands*. In the Year 1667, he enter'd the *Netherlands* in Person, and took

A Dispute about Precedency between the French *and* Spanish *Embassadors.*

A Treaty with the Duke of Lorrain.

A Difference with the Pope

1664.

He attacks Flanders.

took *Charleroy*, *Lisle*, *Tournay*, *Doway*, *Courtray*, *Oudenarde*, and some other Places, pretending, that the *Netherlands* did belong to him in right of his Queen, by virtue of the *Right of Devolution*, in *Brabant*, notwithstanding that in the Marriage Contract she had renounc'd all her Title to it. He also conquer'd the Country of *Burgundy*, (*Franche Comte*) but after having demolish'd the Fortifications he restor'd it again, but kept those places which he had taken in the *Netherlands*, by virtue of the Peace concluded at *Aix la Chapelle*. The Triple Alliance, as it is call'd, made betwixt *Sweden*, *England*, and *Holland*, which was intended for the Preservation of the *Netherlands*, did greatly hasten this Peace; tho' *France* afterwards found out a way to draw the *English* Court from this Alliance, and to make them join with him in humbling the *Hollanders*, who were too proud. For tho' *France*, all along had been in the Interest of *Holland*, yet the King took it very ill, that the *Dutch* had made a Peace at *Munster* without including *France*, and that they had been so bold, as to undertake the Preservation of the *Netherlands*; and when afterwards the King put strong Garrisons into the conquer'd Places, they sent a Fleet upon his Coasts, as it were to brave him. The tripple Alliance also was displeasing to him, and some are of Opinion that the King of *England*, who had not forgot the Business at *Chatam*, and that the Peace concluded at *Breda* was not according to his Wishes, had engag'd himself in this Alliance, only to draw in the *Dutch* thereby, and so to exasperate the King of *France* against them. At last *France*, in Conjunction with *England*, made War on *Holland*, with prodigious Success at first; for he took three Provinces, *viz.* *Guelderland*, *Over-Yssel*, and *Utrecht*; besides that, he had already possess'd himself of some Passes leading into *Holland*: But his Confederate the Bishop of *Munster*, had not the same Success in the Siege of *Groningen*, and afterwards lost *Coeverden* again. And the *Dutch* had better cuccess at Sea where they behaved themselves bravely in four several Engagements, whereas the *French* Fleet, as the *English* say, did not engage heartily: Besides *England* grew jealous of the great Success of the *French*, which was one Reason why the Parliament did in a manner oblige the King to make a separate Peace with *Holland*, fearing that *France*, after *England* and *Holland* had destroy'd one another at Sea, might at last fall upon them.

Peace made at Aix la Chapelle, 1668

1667.

He invades Flanders, *1671.*

The

The Emperor and the Elector of Brandenbuagh endeavour'd, immediately at the beginning of the War, to give a Diversion to France, but to no great purpose, since they did nothing but ruine several Provinces in Germany, and drew Turenne with his Army thither, who ravag'd the Country, but especially Westphalia. The Elector of Brandenburgh made a Peace with France at Vossem, whereby he got the Restitution of his Strong-holds in the Dutchy of Cleves, but as soon as he got them into his Possession, he minded the Peace but little. In the Year next ensuing, France took the strong City of Maestricht, where the French shewed both their Bravery and Dexterity in attacking of Places. On the other hand, the Imperialists had good Success against Turenne, who pretended to oppose their March; for they trick'd him, and having marched to the Lower Rhine, in Conjunction with the Spaniards and Prince of Orange, took Bon: This, and the Loss of Narden, which the Dutch took, caus'd the French to leave Utrecht, and all the other Places in the United Provinces, except Grave and Maestricht: For it seem'd very difficult to maintain so many Garrisons, and at the same time to have a sufficient Army in the Field to oppose the Enemy; since it might easily have happen'd, that all Correspondency with these places in the United Provinces might have been cut off by the Enemy. Afterwards Spain and the whole German Empire declar'd against France, and a great many were of Opinion, that the joint Power of Spain, Holland, and Germany, would be sufficient to curb the French and to carry the Seat of the War into France it self; but this could not be effected. 'Tis true, the Germans did take from the French, Philipsburg; and beat them out of Treves, where Mareschal de Crequi receiv'd a Defeat. But on the other hand, the Germans were several times, especially near Sintsheim, and in Alsace, worsted by the French, and oblig'd to repass the Rhine. And in the Year 1675, there was a great Probability that it would not have gone very well with them on this side of the Rhine, if the brave Turenne had not been kill'd by an accidental Shot which oblig'd the French, who were ignorant of his Design, after a sharp Engagement, to retire on the other side of the Rhine. Upon the whole, Spain lost most by this War; for the Franche Compte was taken from them, Messina receiv'd voluntarily a French Garrison, and the Dutch Fleet which was sent

Maestricht taken by the French.

The Death of Turenne.

The Losses of the Spaniards in this War.

sent to the Assistance of the *Spaniards* in *Sicily*, got nothing but Blows, the brave Admiral *de Ruyter* being there slain; though afterwards the *French* quitted *Messina* on their own accord. Besides, the *French* took from them these Strong-holds; *Limburgh, Conde, Valenciennes, Cambray, Yper, St. Omer, Aire*, and several others. The Prince of *Orange* retook *Graves*, but in the Battle of *Seneff* and *St. Omer* he was worsted and sustained a considerable Loss before *Maestricht*. At last, *France* ended this War very gloriously for it self, restoring to *Holland* what it had taken from those *Provinces*, but keeping *Burgundy*, and a great many strong Places in the *Spanish Netherlands*. In *Germany*, in lieu of *Philipsburgh* it got *Friburgh*; and for the rest the *Westphalian* and *Copenhagen* Treaties were renewed, by vertue of which *Sweden* was restored to its own again.

Peace at Nimeguen, 1679.

The French Nation.

§. 25. To consider the *French* Nation, whose History we have briefly related, it must be observ'd, That it is swarming (if I may so speak) with People, and sow'd thick with Cities and Towns. Under the Reign of *Charles* IX. it is related, That above 20000000 of People paid the Poll Tax. Some say that *Richelieu* affirm'd, that, by Computation, *France* could bring into the Field 600000 Foot and 150000 Horse, provided every Man that was able to bear Arms did go into the Field. This Nation also has been always warlike: nevertheless, in former times it has been objected to them, That they were very brave at the first Onset; but after their first Fury was a little cool'd, their Courage us'd to slacken, if they met with a stout and brave Resistance: wherefore they us'd to make great Conquests, but seldom kept them very long. And after they had good Success, they us'd to grow careless, insult over the conquer'd, and put them to great Hardships under their Government. But in our late Wars they have shewn sufficiently, that they as little want Constancy at last, as Heat and Fury at first.

Full of Nobility.

There is a great number of Nobles in *France*, who make Profession of the Sword, and make no difficulty to expose themselves to any Hazards to gain Glory. In former times, the *French* Infantry was good for nothing, wherefore they always us'd to employ *Swiss* and *Scotch*; but now a-days, their Foot are very good, and in attacking of a Place, they are to be preferr'd before all other

ther Nations. This Nation hath always a great Veneration and Love for their King; and as long as he is able to maintain his Authority, is ready to sacrifice Life and Fortune for his Glory. The *French* are also brisk, forward, of a merry Constitution: as to their outward Appearance in their Apparel and Behaviour, they are generally very comely; and some other Nations, whose Temper is more inclined to Gravity, in attempting to imitate them, appear often very ridiculous, there being a vast Difference in these Matters, betwixt what is natural and what is affected. They are of a Genius fit to undertake any thing, whether it be in Learning, Trade, or Manufactures; especially in those things which depend more on Ingenuity and Dexterity than hard Labour. On the other side, the Levity and Inconstancy of the *French* is generally blam'd, which is easily to be perceiv'd in such of them as are young and unpolish'd. *Their Natural Qualities.*

§. 26. The Country which is possess'd by this potent Nation, is very conveniently situated, almost in the very midst of the Christian World; so that this King may conveniently keep Correspondence with them all, and prevent *Europe* from falling into the Hands of any one Prince. On the one side it has the *Mediterranean*, on the other the Ocean, and on both sides a great many good Harbours, and is well water'd with Rivers, besides that great Chanel with twelve Sluces, by which the present King has join'd the Rivers of *Garonne* and the *Aude*, and consequently the *Mediterranean* with the Ocean; which proves very beneficial for Trade. It is also very near of a circular Figure, and well compacted, so that one Province may easily assist another: On the side of *Spain*, the *Pyrenæan* Mountains; and on the *Italian* side the *Alps* are like a Bulwark to the Kingdom; but on the side towards *Germany* and the *Netherlands*, it lies somewhat open: For from the *Netherlands*, *Paris* it self has often been hard put to it. And this is the Reason why the *French* have been so eager in getting a good part of these into their Possession, in which they have been successful in the last War, and thereby have mightily strengthened their Frontiers; and for the same reason, they have made themselves Masters of *Lorrain*, to fortify themselves on the side of *Germany*; and by degrees to become Masters of the *Rhine*, the ancient Boundary of *Gaul*; which seems the *The Nature of the Country.* *Its Situation.*

the only thing wanting to the Perfection of *France*. Farther, *France* may be one of the most happy and most fruitful Countries, not only for the equal Temperature of its Climate, betwixt an immoderate Heat and an excessive Cold; but also, because it produces every thing which seems to be requisite for the Sustenance and Conveniency of Mankind. And its Product is not only sufficient for its Inhabitants, but also plentiful enough to be exported into Foreign Parts. The Commodities exported out of *France*, are chiefly Wine, Brandy, Vinegar, Salt, innumerable Sorts of Silks and Woollen Stuffs, and Manufactures, Hemp, Canvas, Linen, Paper, Glass, Saffron, Almonds, Olives, Capers, Prunello's, Chesnuts, Soap, and the like. Yet in *Normandy* and *Picardy* grow no Vines, but the common People drink Cyder. Scarce any Metals are to be found in *France*, and no Gold or Silver Mines. But this Want is supplied by the Ingenuity of the *French*, and the Folly of Foreigners: For, the *French* Commodities have drawn Fleets of their Money into *France*, especially since *Henry* IV. set up the Silk-Manufactury there. There are some who have computed, that *France* sells Stuffs *A-la-mode* yearly to Foreigners only, to the Value of 40000000 of Livres, Wine 15000000, Brandy 5000000, Salt 10000000, and so proportionably of other Commodities. Mr. *Forcy*, an *Englishman*, says, That about the Year 1669, the Commodities which were brought from *France* into *England*, exceeded what were carried from *England* to *France*, in Value 1600000 *lib. Sterl.* And it is notorious, that by help of such Commodities as they send into *Spain*, they get a great part of their *West-India* Plate-Fleet. But after all, Navigation does not flourish so much in *France* as it might. The reason seems to be, that the *French* Nation is not so much addicted to the Sea, and that other Nations have been before-hand with them in the *East* and *West-Indies*. Which is the reason, that the King, tho' he has above a 100 Capital Ships, yet cannot set out so great a Fleet hitherto as the *English* and *Dutch*. *France* has very few Plantations abroad, except what are in the *Caribby Islands*, the Isles called *Tartuges*, and on the North side of *Hispaniola*. They apply themselves also to fishing upon the great Sand-bank before *Newfound Land*, and catch in *Canada* and *New France* good store of Bevers. They have set several Projects on foot for carrying on the *East-*

Its Fertility.

Its Plantations.

India

India Trade, but without any great Success hitherto; the *Dutch*, who are so powerful there, opposing them with all their Might. Lastly, the great Strength of *France* may be judg'd of by this, that the Revenue of the Clergy, which is possess'd of two fifth parts, as it is said, of the Kingdom, amounts to 104 Millions and 500000 Crowns yearly. The King's Revenues are computed to amount now to 150 Millions of Livres, whereas in the last Age it did not amount to above 9 or 10 Millions; at the time of *Henry* IV. to 16 Millions, and in the Year 1639 to 77 Millions; which vast Difference is in part to be ascribed to the different Value of Money since those times, and the great Taxes which were imposed upon the Subjects: but without question the chief Reason is, that *France* since that time has found out new Ways to draw Money out of other Countries.

§. 27. As to the Form of Government of *France*, it is to to be observ'd, That anciently there were very potent Dukes, Earls, and Lords, in *France*, who tho' they were Vassals of the King, yet they us'd to pay no farther Obedience to him than was consistent with their own Interest, except the Kings were in a Condition to oblige them to it: But all these in process of Time, were set aside, and their Countries united to the Crown. Now-a-days the Dukedoms and Earldoms of *France* are nothing else but bare Titles annex'd to some considerable Estate without any Sovereignty or Jurisdiction. And whereas formerly certain Countries used to be assign'd to the King's Sons, whereof they bore the Title; now-a-days only a certain yearly Revenue is allotted them, with the Title of a certain Dukedom or Country, wherein perhaps they have not a foot of Ground. Indeed after the ancient Soveraign Dukedoms and Earldoms were abolish'd, some of the Great Men of the Kingdom took upon themselves great Authority in the Kingdom, but by the Policy of *Richelieu* and *Mazarini*, they were reduc'd to such a Condition, that now they dare not utter a Word against the King. The Assembly of the Estates (there being three of them, *viz.* The Clergy, Nobility, and the Citizens, these making up the third Estate) were also formerly in great Veneration, whereby the King's Power was much limited. But they having not been assembled since the Year 1614, their Authority is quite suppress'd.

The Government of France.

press'd. Those of the Reform'd Religion prov'd likewise very troublesome to the Kings of *France* as long as they were in a Condition to take up Arms, but with the loss of *Rochelle* they lost the Power of giving their Kings any Disturbance for the future. And tho' the King hitherto does not force their Consciences, yet he draws off a great many from that Party, by hopes of his Royal Favour and Preferments. Heretofore the Parliament of *Paris* us'd to oppose the King's Designs, under pretence that it had such a Right, that the King could not do any thing of great moment without its Consent; but this King hath taught it only to intermeddle with Judicial Business, and some other Concerns, which the King now and then is pleas'd to leave to its Decision. The *Gallick* Church also boasts of a particular Prerogative in regard of the Court of *Rome*, as having always disputed with the Pope some part of his Authority over her; and the King has the Nomination of the Bishops and Abbots; all which contributes much to the Strength and Increase of this Kingdom, if a wise and good King sits upon the Throne.

The Strength of France *with regard to* England.

§. 28. When we duly weigh the Power of *France* in comparison with its Neighbours, it is easily perceiv'd that there is not any State in Christendom which *France* doth not equal, if not exceed, in Power: 'Tis true, in former Ages the *English* reduc'd the *French*, but at that time they were possess'd of a great part of it themselves; there were then several Demi-Soveraign Princes; the *French* Infantry was then inconsiderable, and the *English* Bows were terrible to them. In the last Age *Spain* prov'd very troublesome to *France*, the *French* being not able to defend themselves against it, and being several times oblig'd to make Peace upon disadvantageous Conditions: But besides that, at that time the *French* Infantry was good for little, and the *Spanish* Nation was then at its heighth, whereas now the *Spanish* Nobility is more for Debauchery, Gaming, and such like Intrigues, than for acquiring Glory in War; they were then in full possession of all the *Netherlands*, and *Charles* V. had a great Advantage by being Emperor. *Italy* is neither willing nor powerful enough to hurt *France*; but these Princes are well satisfy'd if *France* does not pass the *Alps*, and disturb their Repose. The *French* are not powerful enough for the *Dutch* at Sea, if they have an Opportunity to make use of all their

To Spain. *To* Italy. *To* Holland.

Naval

Naval Strength; yet the *French* Privateers may do them considerable Mischief; wherefore I cannot see what Benefit *Holland* can reap from a War with *France*, without an absolute Necessity: For the *Dutch* Land-Forces gather'd out of all Nations, are not likely to do any great Feats against it. The *Swiss* also, neither can nor will hurt *France*, as being well satisfy'd if they can get *French* Money: Wherefore the *French* need not fear any thing from them, except they should make them desperate; in which Case, they might in Confederacy with others prove very troublesome. *Germany* seems to be the only Country, which alone might be able to balance *France*; for if these Princes were well united, they are able to bring more numerous Armies into the Field, and that in no ways inferior in Goodness to the *French*; and perhaps they might be able to hold it out with *France*. But considering the present State of *Germany*, it seems next to an Impossibility, that all the Members of the Empire should unanimously and resolutely engage themselves in a long War, and prosecute the same with Vigour: For it is not to be imagined that all of them should have an equal Interest in the War, and some of them must expect to be ruin'd, tho' the War in the main should prove successful; but if it should succeed otherwise, they must all be great Losers by it, without reprieve.

To the Swiss.

To Germany.

§. 29. But if it should be suppos'd, that *France* may be attack'd by a great many at once; it is to be consider'd, that it is absolutely against the Interest of some States to join themselves against *France*. For, as Affairs now stand, *Portugal* is not likely to join with *Spain*, *Sweden* with *Denmark*, *Poland* with the House of *Austria*, against *France*. Neither is it probable that the *Italian* Princes will be desirous to assist the Emperor and *Spain* in subduing *France*, except we suppose them to be willing to promote their own Ruin.

The Strength of France, *in regard of a Confederacy.*

CHAP. VI.

Of the United Provinces.

The Ancient State of the United Provinces.

§ 1. THat Country which is commonly call'd the *Netherlands*, or the *Lower-Germany*, was anciently comprehended, partly under *Gaul*, partly under *Germany*, according as they were situated, either on this or the other side of the *Rhine*, which was the ancient Boundary of these two vast Countries. That part which was situated on this side of the *Rhine*, was by *Julius Cæsar*, together with the rest of *Gaul*, reduc'd under the Obedience of the *Roman* Empire. Afterwards the *Batavi* and the *Zealanders* did also submit to the *Romans*; yet so, that they were rather esteemed Allies than Subjects. And when in the fifth Century, after the Birth of Christ, the *Franks* established a new Kingdom in *France*, these Provinces were at first united to it. But at the same time, when *Germany* was separated from *France*, most of them fell to *Germany*, few remaining with *France*. The Governors of these Provinces did, in process of time, under the Names of Dukes and Earls, make themselves Demi-Soveraigns, as did also other Princes of *Germany* and *France*; yet so, that it was a general Maxim among them, *To Rule the People with Mildness*. And for the Security of their Liberty, they us'd to grant them great Privileges, in the maintaining of which this Nation was always very forward. The Estates also, which consisted of the Clergy, Nobility, and Citizens, were always in great Authority, and would not easily suffer that any new Impositions should be laid upon the People without their Consent. These

The Division of the Seventeen Provinces.

Provinces according to the common Computation, are Seventeen in number; *viz.* Four Dukedoms, *viz. Brabant, Limburgh, Luxenburgh,* and *Guelderland:* Seven Earldoms, viz. *Flanders, Artois, Hainault, Holland, Zealand, Namur,* and *Zutphen*: Five Lordships, namely *Friesland, Malines, Utrecht, Over-Yssel,* and *Groningen. Antwerp* has the Title of a Marquisate of the *Roman* Empire. These Provinces were anciently ruled each by its Prince or Lord; but afterwards several of them were either by Inheritance, Marriages, or Contracts, united together, till most of them fell to the share of the House of *Burgundy*,

gundy, from whence they came to the House of *Austria*, by the Marriage of *Maximilian* I. who had marry'd *Mary*, the only Daughter of *Charles*, surnamed *The Hardy*; and were afterwards all united under *Charles* V. who govern'd them in Peace and Prosperity. 'Tis related, that he had once taken a Resolution to make them one Kingdom, which however he could not effect, their Laws and Privileges being so different, and they so jealous of one another, that none of them would remit any thing of their Pretences in favour of the rest. But the Reign of *Charles* V. over the *Netherlands*, proved so very fortunate, because he bore an extraordinary Affection to them, and they to him: For *Charles* was born at *Ghent*, educated amongst them, and liv'd a considerable time there. His Humour suited very well with theirs, he conversed with them in a friendly manner without Haughtiness, employing the *Netherlanders* frequently in his Affairs, whereby this Nation was in great esteem at his Court. But under the Reign of his Son, *Philip* II. these Provinces were torn in pieces by Intestine Commotions and Civil Wars, which occasion'd the Rise of a potent Commonwealth in *Europe*. This Republick having prov'd the Occasion of great Alterations, it is worth our while to enquire both into the Cause of these Commotions, and the Origin of this new Commonwealth.

The Union of the Seventeen Provinces.

Their Condition under Charles *V.*

§. 2. In the first place, 'tis manifest that *Philip* II. was much to be blam'd, as being partly himself the Cause of these Civil Troubles; for he being born in *Spain*, and educated after the *Spanish* Fashion, favour'd only the *Spaniards*, acting in every Step of his Conduct the part of a supercilious haughty *Spaniard*; which mightily alienated the Minds of the *Netherlanders*, especially after he resided altogether in *Spain*, and did not so much as honour the *Netherlands* with his Presence; thinking it perhaps below his Grandeur, that he who was Master of so great a Kingdom, and had such great Projects in his Head, should trouble himself much about the Affairs of the *Netherlands*. Tho', in all probability, these might have been kept in Obedience by his Presence; For his Father, the sooner to appease a Tumult which was only risen in the City of *Ghent*, did venture to take his Journey through *France*, and the Territories of King *Francis*, who was but lately reconcil'd to him. Moreover, *William* Prince of

The Cause of the Wars in the Netherlands *under* Philip *II.*

Orange,

William Prince of Orange. *Orange*, a crafty, through-pac'd, and ambitious Man, did not a little foment these Divisions: For when *Philip* had taken a Resolution to go into *Spain*, and to commit the Administration of the *Netherlands* to a Governour, this Prince was contriving how *Christina*, Dutchess of *Lorrain*, might be constituted Regent of the *Netherlands*, and how he, by marrying her Daughter, might bear the greatest Sway in the Government: But he miscarrying in both, because *Philip* constituted *Margaret* of *Parma*, Natural Daughter of *Charles* V. Regent of the *Netherlands*, and refus'd to give his Consent to the Match, was so dissatisfy'd thereat, that he resolv'd to shew what Strength he was Master of, when urged to Revenge. At the same time the Earls of *Egmont* and *Hoorn* were very much dissatisfy'd, as also a great many others, who being in great Esteem with the People, were all very jealous of the *Spaniards*. Besides, a great many of the Nobility were for a Change, partly out of Hatred to the *Spaniards*, partly because they were naturally of a turbulent Spirit, and were become Poor, and over Head and Ears in Debt, as having endeavour'd to outvy the *Spaniards* in Splendor at Court, and thereby spent more than their Incomes would allow of. The Clergy withal, was somewhat discontented, because *Philip*, having created several new Episcopal Sees, would have employ'd the Revenues of several Abbies for the Maintenance of them; which did not only dissatisfie such as were in present Possession of these Abbies, but others also, who were in hopes of them for the future: for the Abbots were chosen by a free Election of the Monks in each Monastery, but the Bishops were nominated by the King. But all this could not have furnish'd sufficient Fuel for so great a Flame, if Religion had not been an Ingredient, which proves most efficacious in disturbing the Minds of the Common-People, and always serves for a specious Pretence to such as are for Alterations in a State. There were great numbers in the *Netherlands*, who had relinquish'd the Roman Catholick Religion, some of them professing the *Augsburgh* Confession, some the Doctrine of the *Huguenots*, others falling into the Errors of the *Anabaptists*. Now *Charles* V. had by severe Proclamations and Punishments been very hard upon them, which had serv'd for nothing else than to exasperate the Minds of the People, and to promote the Itch after Religious Novelties.

Discontents of the Nobility and Clergy.

Change of Religion.

Where-

Wherefore it was the Opinion of *Mary*, Queen of *Hungary*, the Sister of *Charles* V. and then Regent of the *Netherlands*, *That they ought rather to be treated more mildly*: But *Philip* had taken a Resolution to root out by force this Heresie, as he call'd it; either out of a Zeal for the *Roman* Catholick Religion, or because he hop'd thereby to oblige the Pope, whose Favour he stood in need of at that time. In pursuance of this Resolution, he renewed his Father's Proclamation, and that with more Severity against these Hereticks; and to put them in Execution, he was for setting up a Court of Judicature, according to the Model of the *Spanish* Inquisition, the very Name of which was terrible to every body: And, in effect, this Inquisition is a very cruel Constitution, whereby the Life, Estate, and good Name of every Subject, is put into the Hands of unmerciful Priests, whose chief Glory is to be inhumane and rigorous in their Proceedings; and who have a Power to take up and punish any Person upon Suspicion only; and tho' a Man is wrongfully accus'd, he is not to know either his Accuser or Crime; nay, tho' he makes his Innocence appear, yet he seldom escapes without some Punishment. The *Netherlanders* were the more frightned, not only because in this Court, no Privileges, no Favour of the King, nor Intercessions, did avail; but also, because they knew themselves to be free-spoken, carrying, as it were their Hearts upon their Tongues, and that by way of Trade, they were oblig'd to be conversant with those of other Religions; whereas, on the other hand, it was natural and easie for an *Italian* or *Spaniard* to keep his Thoughts within himself. Some are of Opinion, That the *Spaniards* were glad to see that the *Netherlands* began the Fray, hoping thereby to get an Opportunity to force them to Obedience, and by suppressing their Liberty and Privileges to Rule over them at pleasure. They hoped that this Country might serve them one day for a Magazine, from whence they might conveniently attack *France*, *England*, and the *Northern* Kingdoms. However, 'tis most certain, that some Foreign Princes did administer Fuel to nourish and augment the Flame; especially *Elizabeth*, Queen of *England*, whose Intention was, by this means, to cut out so much Work for the *Spaniard*, that he might not be at leisure to think of Conquering others, his great Power being at that time become terrible to all *Europe*.

Spanish *Inquisition.*

Q. Elizabeth *fomented their Revolt;*

§. 3. Thus

§. 3. Thus the Seeds of Civil Commotions were sown
1559. in the Minds of the *Netherlanders*, about the time that *Philip* II. went into *Spain*; having so constituted the Government, that the supream Administration of Affairs should be in the Hands of the Regent and the Council of State; of which Council, besides the Prince of *Orange*, the Earl of *Egmont*, and others, was Cardinal *Granville*, a *Burgundian*, a wise Man, and much rely'd on by the King, who had given secret Instructions to the Regent to rule according to his Advice: but the *Netherlandish* Lords quickly perceiving that the whole Government was manag'd according to the Councils of the Cardinal, did sufficiently shew their Discontent in opposing what he mov'd; especially when the Cardinal press'd hard to execute the King's Commands concerning the Establishment of the Bishops, and rooting out of the new Religions, the *Netherlandish* Lords advising a Toleration of the same, and to deal more gently with the People. This rais'd a general Hatred against the Cardinal; whereupon the Prince of *Orange*, and the Earls of *Egmont* and *Hoorn* writ to the King, *That if he was not remov'd, it would be impossible to preserve the Peace of the* Netherlands: neither did they rest satisfy'd till *Philip* comply'd with their Demands. But in regard the Regent was, after the Remo-
1564. val of the Cardinal, sway'd by the President *Vigilius*, and the Earl of *Barlemont*, who in every respect follow'd the Footsteps of the Cardinal, this Satisfaction did not last long; for the old Discontents being renew'd, it was said, *That the Body of the Cardinal was remov'd from the Council, but his Spirit remain'd in it.* Thus the Divisions continu'd in the Council of State, nor could the Proclamations against the new Religion be put in Execution, because the People began more and more to oppose them. It was therefore with Consent of the Regent and Senate, agreed upon to send the Earl of *Egmont* into *Spain*, who was to give an Account to the King of the whole State of Affairs, and to see whether the King could find out another Remedy. The King receiv'd him very courteously as to his Person, but would not remit any thing from his Severity as to Religion. And imagining that the Cause why this Evil had taken so deep root, was the Mildness of the Regent, he caus'd his Proclamation to be renew'd, commanding withal, That the Council of *Trent* should be introduc'd in the *Netherlands*. Besides these Severities,

The Cardinal Granville.

Count Egmont *sent into* Spain.

ties, a Rumour was spread abroad, that *Philip* had agreed with *Charles* IX. at *Bayonne*, by all means and ways to root out the Hereticks; which was the Cause why it was resolv'd to oppose the King's Intentions. Some of the Nobility made the first Beginning, who enter'd into an Association (which they called, *The Compromise*) whereby they engag'd themselves to oppose the Inquisition, and to stand by one another, if any one should be molested for his Religion; but solemnly protested, That they had no other Aim by so doing, but the Glory of God, the Grandeur of the King, and the Peace of their Native Country. This Association was drawn up by *Philip Marnix*, Lord of *Aldegonde*, and subscrib'd by 400 Persons of Quality, among whom, the chiefest were *Henry* of *Brederode*, *Lewis* Earl of *Nassau*, Brother of the Prince of *Orange*, the Earls of *Culenburgh* and *Bergh*. These met at *Brussels*, and deliver'd a Petition to the Regent, wherein they desir'd, That the Proclamations issu'd forth touching Religion might be annull'd. The Regent answer'd them in courteous but general Terms, but promis'd nothing more than *That she would know the King's Pleasure in the Matter*. 'Tis said, that the Earl of *Barlemont*, who stood then near the Regent, did tell her, *That they were no ways to be fear'd, because they were only* Geusen *or Beggars*; which render'd the Name of the *Geusen* very famous afterwards, a Beggar's Pouch being made the Coat of Arms of that Confederacy. In the mean while abundance of Pamphlets were spread abroad, which did more and more exasperate the People. And because *Philip* had given but a very indifferent Reception to those Deputies which were sent into *Spain* to pray for a Mitigation of these Proclamations, and had refus'd to comply in the least with the Sentiments of the People, it came to an open Insurrection. So that the new Religion was not only publickly profess'd and taught in a great Concourse of People, but the Rabble also fell to plundering of Churches, and pulling down of Images. And tho' the Prince of *Orange*, and the Earl of *Egmont*, did what they could to appease this Tumult, yet the King conceiv'd a shrewd Suspicion, as if they had been at the bottom of it; which put them upon consulting their own Safety, but they could not, as yet come to any Resolution. In the mean time the Regent having rais'd some Troops, and endeavour'd either by Fear or fair Words, or any other Ways, to reduce

An Association of the Nobility.

1566.

Breaking of Images.

duce the diſſatisfy'd Party to Obedience, ſome of whom did by Submiſſion and other Services endeavour to be reconcil'd to the King. And this Deſign ſucceeded ſo well, that without any great Trouble, and the Puniſhment of a very few, the Country was reſtor'd to its Tranquility: Nevertheleſs becauſe it was rumor'd abroad, that a great Army was marching from *Spain* againſt them, a great many of the Inhabitants, and eſpecially of the Handycraft Trades, retired into the neighbouring Countries; nay, the Prince of *Orange* himſelf diſliking this Calm, retir'd into *Germany*.

§. 4. It was then the Advice of the Regent, that the King ſhould come in Perſon, without any great Force, into the *Netherlands*, and by his Preſence and Clemency endeavour entirely to heal the ulcerated Minds of the People. But he follow'd the Advice of the Duke of *Alva*, who adviſ'd to make uſe of this opportunity to bring the *Netherlands* under the Yoak, and to ſtrike terror into others. This Duke *d' Alva* march'd with a brave Army through *Savoy* and *Burgundy* into the *Netherlands*, and having immediately taken into Cuſtody the Earls of *Egmont* and *Hoorn*, whom he pretended to have been under hand the Authors of theſe Troubles, declared all thoſe guilty of High-Treaſon that had any hand in the Aſſociation, the Petition, and pulling down of the Images. And a Court was erected of twelve Judges, from which no Appeal was to be allow'd, where Judgment was to be given concerning theſe Matters. This Court was commonly call'd, *The Bloody Council*. Before this Court, the Prince of *Orange*, and ſome other Lords, who were fled, were ſummon'd to appear; and upon Non-appearance they were declar'd guilty of High-Treaſon, and their Eſtates confiſcated. The ſame Severity was us'd againſt others of leſs note. This caus'd ſuch a Terror among the Inhabitants that they left their Habitations in Troops. He caus'd alſo Citadels to be built in ſeveral great Cities, among which one of the chiefeſt was that of *Antwerp*. In the mean time, the Prince of *Orange* had drawn together conſiderable Forces in *Germany*, ſome of which, under the Command of *Lewis* his Brother, falling into *Frieſland*, beat the Count of *Arembergh*, the Governour of that Province. But ſoon after the Duke of *Alva*, having firſt caus'd the Earls of *Egmont* and *Hoorn* to be

The Duke of Alva.

1568.

The Earls of Egmont and Hoorn beheaded.

be beheaded, march'd against him in Person. Not long after the Prince of *Orange* fell with a great Army into *Brabant*, but was beaten back by the Duke of *Alva*, and his Forces dispers'd. The Duke of *Alva*, puff'd up with this great Success did not only cause a most magnificent Statue to be erected at *Antwerp*, in memory of what Glory he had acquir'd; but having also form'd a Design to Conquer the *Netherlands* with their own Money, he imposed a Tax upon them, of the hundredth Penny, to be paid of the whole Value of all Estates; and besides this, the twentieth Penny to be paid of all Immoveables, and the tenth of all Moveables as often as they were sold. This did exasperate the *Netherlands* to the utmost degree. And whilst the Duke of *Alva*, being in great want of Money, was busie in squeezing out these Taxes, and was upon the point of forcing the Inhabitants of *Brussels*, who refus'd to pay it, News was brought, That the banish'd *Netherlanders*, call'd *Sea-Geusen*, who were turn'd Privateers, and had about 24 Ships of indifferent Strength, had, under the Conduct of the Earl of *March*, taken the City of *Briel* in *Holland*; then most Cities of *Holland* out of a Hatred to the *Spaniards*, and the tenth Penny revolted from the *Spaniards*, except *Amsterdam* and *Schonhoven*, which remain'd for some time under the Obedience of *Spain*. It was a grand Mistake in the Duke of *Alva*, that during his Regency of four Years, he had not secur'd the Sea-Coasts. The revolted Places chose for their Governour the Prince of *Orange*, swearing to him Allegiance as the King's Stadtholder, as if they had only revolted from the Duke of *Alva*, and not the King. A great many Privateers then join'd from *France* and *England*, who within the space of four Months made up a Fleet of 150 Ships, who had their Rendezvouz at *Flushing*, and prov'd afterwards the greatest Annoyance that the *Spaniards* had. The Duke of *Alva* was not in a Condition to make timely Resistance to this Storm, because the Earl of *Bergh* had not only at the same time taken a great many Places in *Guelderland*, *Friesland*, and *Over-Yssel*; but also *Lewis*, Earl of *Nassaw*, had, with the Assistance of the *French*, surpriz'd *Mons*: Which City the Duke of *Alva* endeavoured to recover by Force of Arms; and the Prince of *Orange*, who with an Army newly rais'd in *Germany*, had made prodigious Havock in *Brabant*, endeavouring in vain to relieve it, retired into *Holland*: So that this City

Briel *taken* April 1.1571.

was

was surrender'd upon Articles to the Duke of *Alva*. He then try'd all ways to reduce the revolted Places to Obedience by Force, and among others pillag'd *Mechlin* and *Zutphen*, quite destroy'd *Naerden*, and took *Haerlem* after a tedious Siege, the Inhabitants of which City were most barbarously treated.

Duke of Alva *recall'd*.

§. 5. The Affairs of the *Spaniards* in the *Netherlands* being by the rigorous Proceedings of the Duke of *Alva* (who us'd to bragg, that during his Regency of six Years he had caus'd 18000 to be executed by the Hangman) put into Confusion, he was recalled in the Year 1573. *Lewis Requesenes* succeeded him, a Man of somewhat a milder Temper, but who had a very ill beginning of his Regency, the Fleet, which he had sent out to relieve *Middleburgh* being destroy'd before his Eyes, and the City surrender'd to the Prince of *Orange*: Yet the Prince also received a great Blow; for his Brother *Lewis*, who led an Army to his Assistance out of *Germany*, was routed near *Grave* upon the *Mockerhyde*, where he and his Brother *Henry* were slain in the Field. After this Victory, the *Spanish* Soldiers mutiny'd for want of Pay, and liv'd upon free Quarters in *Antwerp* till all was paid. Then the Siege of *Leyden* was undertaken, which was reduc'd to the utmost Extremity by Famine, till a Duke of the *Maese* was cut through, by which means and the help of a *North-West* Wind at Spring-Tide, the Country round about being put under Water, the *Spaniards*, after a great Loss sustained, were forc'd to leave it. In the Year next ensuing, the Emperor endeavoured by
1574. his Mediation to compose these Troubles, and a Meeting was held for that purpose betwixt the Deputies of both Parties at *Breda*, which prov'd fruitless. Then the *Spaniards* took *Zirickzee*, after a Siege of nine Months; but before the Place was taken, *Lewis Requesenes* died. After
1576. his Death the Council of State took the Administration of the Government into their Hands, which was approved by the King.

Lewis Requesenes *Governor*.

§. 6. In the mean time the Hatred of the *Netherlands* against the *Spaniards* was more and more inflam'd, especially after the Soldiers were grown so mutinous for want of Pay, and committed such great Outrages, that the Council of State declared them Enemies, giving leave to the Inhabitants to take up Arms against them. During which Disturbances, *Maestricht* and *Antwerp* were plunder'd by the *Spaniards:* Which dispos'd the rest to enter upon a Treaty with the Prince of *Orange* at *Ghent*, which contain'd, That the Provinces should be at Peace betwixt themselves; That the Proclamations issued forth during the Regency of the Duke of *Alva* should be annull'd, and the *Spaniards* sent out of the Country: Which Contract, tho' it was ratify'd by the King, yet he had taken a Resolution quickly to disunite them again. For this purpose, he constituted *Don John d' Austria*, his natural Brother, Governor of the *Netherlands*. The Prince of *Orange* forewarn'd the *Netherlanders*, That he ought not to be trusted; notwithstanding which, he was receiv'd by Plurality of Voices, but withal oblig'd to subscribe the Contract made at *Ghent*, and to send away the *Spanish* Soldiers. But the Prince of *Orange*, and the Provinces of *Holland* and *Zealand*, were not well satisfy'd with this Agreement; and the rest also quickly began to mistrust him. He gave them sufficient occasion to believe that their Jealousie was not ill grounded, when by Surprize, he made himself Master of the Castle of *Namur*, under Pretence to secure his Person against any Attempts; which so disturb'd the *Netherlanders*, that they took up Arms to drive him out of *Namur*. They also took all the Strong-holds, where any *German* Garrison was left, and demolish'd the Castles. And sending for the Prince of *Orange* to come to *Brussels* they constituted him Grand Bayliff of *Brabant*. This encrease of the House of *Orange* made some great Men envious, who form'd a Party to balance it; among whom one of the chiefest was the Duke of *Arshot*. Those called in *Matthew*, Arch-duke of *Austria*, whom they made Governor of the *Netherlands*, who coming with all speed, was likewise receiv'd by the Party of the Prince of *Orange*, under Condition that the Prince should be his Lieutenant, and he not do any thing without the consent of the Estates. On the other hand, *Alexander*, Duke of *Parma*, came with an Army out of *Italy*, to the Assistance of *Don John d' Austria*, who bringing with him a good number of old *Spanish* Troops, beat the Army of the Estates near *Gemblours*, and took *Louvain*, *Philippeville*, *Limburgh*, and several other Places. The Estates then finding themselves alone not strong enough, offer'd to put themselves under

The Treaty at Ghent.

Don John de Austria *made* *Governor.*

Arch-duke Matthew,

1577. Alexander *Duke of* Parma.

the Protection of *Henry* III. King of *France*; and he having refus'd to accept it, the same Offer was made to the Duke of *Alenson*, his Brother, who having accepted of it, came into the *Netherlands*: But could do nothing of moment, the Princes and great Men being so divided among themselves, that no body knew who was Master. There arose also a new Division among the Estates, when upon Request of those of the Reformed Religion, Liberty of Conscience was allow'd in the *Netherlands*; which was willingly consented to by those of *Ghent*, and others; but *Artois*, *Haynault*, and some other *Walloon* Cities, that were very zealous for the Catholick Religion, did oppose it with great Violence; and having by degrees separated themselves from the rest, set up a new Faction, who were call'd *The Male-Contents*. During these Troubles, *Don John d' Austria* died, leaving the Government to the Duke of *Parma*, who was confirmed in his Place by *Philip*. He began his Regency with the taking of *Maestricht*, and bringing over the *Walloon* Provinces, *viz.* *Artois*, *Haynault*, and the *Walloon-Flanders*, to the King's Party, by Capitulation.

Male-Contents.

The Duke of Parma.

The Union of Utrecht *the Foundation of the Commonwealth.*

§. 7. The Prince of *Orange* therefore perceiving that the Treaty of *Ghent* was quite broke, and that the great Men who envied one another, and the several Provinces that were of a different Religion, were scarce ever to be United; and at the same time being desirous to secure himself, and to establish the Protestant Religion; he got
1579. the Estates of the Province of *Guelderland*, *Holland*, *Zealand*, *Friesland*, and *Utrecht*, to meet. Here it was agreed, That they would defend one another as one Body; that they would consult concerning Peace and War, Taxes, and the like, with common Consent; and, that they would maintain Liberty of Conscience. This Union, made at *Utrecht*, (wherein afterwards *Over-Yssel* and *Groningen* were included) is the Foundation of the Commonwealth of the *United Netherlands*. At that time their Affairs were in so low a Condition, that they coined a Medal, wherein their State was represented by a Ship without Sails or Rudder, left to the Mercy of the Waves with this Inscription, *Incertum quo fata ferant*. The Fortune of the Prince of *Orange* absolutely depending now on this Union, he made it his business to hinder the Conclusion of the Treaty of a General Peace, which by the Mediation

diation of the Emperor was set on foot at *Cologne*, because a *General* Peace might easily have dissolved this *Particular* Union. And, because the Affairs of the *Netherlands* grew worse and worse every day, the *Spaniards* having taken one after another, the Cities of *Bois le Duc*, *Breda*, *Tournay*, *Valenciennes*, *Mechlin*, and others, and many of the great Men being gone over to the *Spanish* Party; the Prince of *Orange* on the other hand being well assured, that the *Spaniards*, one time or another, would revenge themselves upon Him and his Friends; and finding himself not in a Capacity to maintain the Cause against them, he persuaded the Estates of the *Netherlands* to renounce all Obedience to *Philip*, who had violated their Privileges confirm'd to them by Oath, and to make the Duke of *Alenson* their Sovereign, with whom he had under-hand made an Agreement, That the *United Provinces* should fall to his share. And, in effect, the Estates of *Holland*, *Zealand*, and *Utrecht*, were then for making the Prince of *Orange* their Soveraign, except the Cities of *Amsterdam* and *Gouda*; and questionless it would have been done afterwards, if his unexpected Death had not prevented it.

§. 8. The Duke of *Alenson* having obtained the Soveraignty, raised the Siege of *Cambray*, which was besieged by the *Spaniards*, and the next Year was at *Antwerp* proclaimed Duke of *Brabant*, and at *Ghent* Earl of *Flanders*. But his Power being confined within very narrow Bounds by the Estates, he, by the Advice of his Friends, resolved to make himself Absolute. He proposed to the Estates, That if he should die, without Issue, these Countries might be united with the Crown of *France*; which being denied him, he took a rash unaccountable Resolution, *viz.* by Surprize to make himself absolute Master of *Antwerp*, and some other Cities. For this purpose, several Thousands of *French* were already got privately into *Antwerp*, but were beaten out by the Citizens with considerable Loss. They made the like Attempts upon several other Places on the same day, which every-where miscarried, except at *Dendermond*, *Dunkirk*, and *Dixmuyde*. And thus the *French* having lost at once all their Credit, and the Affection of the *Netherlands*, the Duke of *Alenson*, full of Shame and Confusion, returned into *France*, where he died soon after. The *French* intermed-

The Duke of Alenson.

1581.

dling with the Affairs of the *Netherlands*, had brought with it another Evil; namely, That foreign Soldiers were again brought into the *Netherlands*, which was against the Agreement made with the *Walloons*. Then the Duke
1583. of *Parma* retook *Dunkirk*, *Newport*, *Winoxbergen*, *Menin*, *Alost*, and some other Places in *Flanders*, *Ypres* and *Bru-*
1584. *ges* did also submit. And in the same Year, the Affairs of the Estates received a great blow, by the Death of *William* Prince of *Orange*, who was stabb'd in his Palace at *Delft* by a *Burgundian*, whose Name was *Balthasar Gerhard*. By his Death, the *Netherlands*, being without a Head, were left in great Confusion.

Prince of Orange murthered.

§. 9. After the Death of Prince *William*, the Estates made *Maurice*, Son of the deceased, Stadtholder of *Holland*, *Zealand*, and *Utrecht*; and he being but 18 Years of Age, they constituted the Earl of *Hohenloe*, his Lieutenant. But the Soveraignty thy profered to the King of *France*, who being at that time involv'd in intestine Wars, was not at leisure to accept of it. The Duke of *Parma*, in the mean while, taking Advantage of this Juncture of Affairs, reduced *Antwerp* by Famine within a Twelvemonth's time; as also *Dendermond*, *Ghent*, *Brussels*, *Mechlin*, and *Nimeguen*, by Force. After the loss of *Antwerp*, the Estates, who were for submitting themselves to any body but the *Spaniards*, offered the Soveraignty over them to Qu. *Elizabeth*, which she refused to accept of: However, she enter'd into a more strict Alliance with them, by vertue of which she obliged her self to maintain a certain number of Soldiers at her own charge in the *Netherlands*; which, with all the other Forces of the Estates, were to be Commanded by an *English* General. And the Estates did Surrender to the Queen, as a Security for the Charges she was to be at, the Cities of *Flushing*, *Briel*, and *Rammekens*, or *Sceburgh* upon *Walchern*, which were afterwards (*Ann.* 1616.) restored to the Estates for
1586. the Sum of One Million of Crowns. The Queen sent *Robert Dudley*, Earl of *Leicester*, as General into *Holland*; who being arrived there, was made by the Estates their Governor-General, and that with a greater Power than was acceptable to the Queen: but he did no great Feats. For, not only the Duke of *Parma* took *Grave* and *Venlo*, and forced him from before *Zutphen*; but *Leicester* administer'd the Publick Affairs at a strange rate, to the great Dissatisfaction of the Estates, insomuch that they doubted

His Son, Prince Maurice, made Stadtholder.

The English Confederacy.

The Regency of the Earl of Leicester.

ed either his Capacity or his Integrity. Their Discontents were much augmented, after *William Stanley*, who was by the Earl of *Leicester* made commander in Chief in *Deventer*, betray'd that City to the *Spaniards*. The next Year the Earl of *Leicester* attempted the Relief of *Sluce* in *Flanders*, but to no purpose; and coming into *Holland*, where he by several unwonted and suspicious Proceedings augmented the Differences betwixt him and the Estates, he returned very ill satisfied into *Enland*; where, by Command of the Queen, he resign'd his Office of Governor.

§. 10. Hitherto the Affairs of the *United Netherlands* (whom henceforward we will call *Hollanders*) had been in a very ill Condition; but from this time forwards they began to mend a-pace, and became more settled. This was partly occasion'd by the Ruin of the two Provinces of *Brabant* and *Flanders*, which were reconciled to the King, upon Condition, that such as would not profess themselves *Roman Catholicks*, should leave the Country within a prefixt time; for a great many of these flocking into *Holland*, made its Cities very populous. Especially all the Traffick of *Antwerp* was transplanted to *Amsterdam*, which render'd that City very rich and potent at Sea. Besides, *Philip*, like those who will hunt two Hares with one Dog, did not only attempt to invade *England* with a great Fleet, but also sent in the very next Year the Duke of *Parma* with an Army to the Assistance of the League in *France*; both which proving fruitless, the *Hollenders*, had in the mean while leisure given them, to put themselves into a good Posture. Whereas the Duke of *Parma* had wisely advised the King, that he should with all his Power first subdue the *Hollanders*, before he engaged in another War. For *Maurice*, whom they had after the Departure of the Earl of *Leicester* made their Generalissimo both by Sea and Land, restored their lost Reputation, and did Wonders. His first Attempt was upon *Breda*, which he took by a Stratagem. In the Year next ensuing, he took *Zutphen*, *Deventer*, *Hulst*, and *Nimeguen*, And in the Year 1592. *Steenwyck* and *Coeverden*. In the same Year the Death of the brave Duke of *Parma* proved a great loss to the *Spaniards*. For the *Spanish* Soldiers growing mutinous every-where, did not a little advance the Progresses of the *Hollanders*. *Gertrudenburgh*

The State of Affairs in Holland *begins to mend.*

1588.

1590.

trudenbergh was taken in the sight of the *Spanish* Army.
1592. In 1592 *Groningen* was reduc'd whereby the *United Provinces* were made entire, and secured on this side of the *Rhine*. In the Year 1596, *Albert*, Arch-duke of *Austria*, arriv'd as Governor of the *Netherlands*, who began his Regency with the taking of *Hulst*. And because *Philip*, being oppressed with Debts, was fain to shut up his Exchequer; *Albert*, for want of Money, was not in a Capacity to undertake any thing of Moment the next Year, but was soundly beaten near *Tougenhout*. And after the Trade of the *Hollanders* with *Spain* and *Portugal*, whither they used to send their Ships under foreign Flags, had been quite cut off; whereby the *Spaniards* hoped the sooner to reduce them to Obedience; Necessity, and the desire of Lucre, taught them another way to obtain vast Riches. For by this means, the *Hollanders* were forced to try whether they could sail themselves into the *East-Indies*, and attempt to find out a nearer way thither by a *North* Passage. But this Design not succeeding, they took the common Course about *Africa*; and having with incredible Pains, in spite of all the Resistance made by the *Portuguese*, settled a Trade there, a great many Merchants and others, who knew no better way to employ their ready Money, erected several Societies to Trade into the *East-Indies*; All which were by vertue of a Patent granted by the Estates, formed into one Company, which did afterwards prodigiously encrease its Power in the *East-Indies*, and has conveyed unconceivable Riches into *Holland*. In the Year 1597. *Maurice* took *Rhineberg*, *Meurs*, and all the rest of those Places of *Over-Yssel*, which were yet in the Possession of *Spain*.

Arch-duke Albert, *Governor of the* Spanish Netherlands.

1602.

The East-India *Company*.

§. 11. In the Year 1598. the *Spaniards* found out another Decoy for the *Hollanders*. For it being generally pretended, that they would not live under *Spanish* Subjection, *Philip* found out this Artifice: He married his Daughter *Isabella Clara Eugenia* to *Albert* Arch-duke of *Austria*, giving unto her, as a Dowry, *Burgundy* and the *Netherlands*; but with this Condition, That the same should return to *Spain*, if no Heirs proceeded from this Match, which the *Spaniards* were very well assured of, the Princess being pretty well in Age; and besides this having been spoiled before by means of some Medicaments administred to her to prevent Conception. The

Isabella Clara Eugenia.

Netherland

Netherlands being then by this means, according to outward Appearance, freed from a foreign Subjection, as having got a Prince of their own it was hoped the *Hollanders* would the easier re-unite themselves with the other Provinces; because a Peace being lately concluded betwixt *France* and *Spain* at *Vervin*, the *Hollanders* had thereby lost their chief Confederate. But the *Hollanders* remained stedfast in their former Resolution, rejecting all Propositions of Peace made by the Emperor and the Arch-duke *Albert*. In the Year 1600, *Maurice* fell into *Flanders*, with an Intention to besiege *Newport*, but was met by *Albert*, where a bloody Battel ensued, and *Maurice* obtained a most glorious Victory, who was otherways always averse to Field-fights, and would never have resolved at that time to have ventured the whole Fortune of *Holland* upon the Issue of a Battel, if he had not been forced to it: Accordingly without attempting any thing farther, he returned into *Holland*. *Albert* then undertook the Siege of *Ostend*, during which, both sides did their utmost, till *Ambrose Spinola* forc'd the Place, the Besieged having no more room left to make any Retrenchments. 'Tis said, That the *Hollanders* lost within the Town above 70000 Men, and the *Spaniards* without a great many more. But in the mean time the *Spanish* Fleet under the Command of *Frederick Spinola* was destroy'd, and, *Rhinebergh*, *Grave*, and *Sluce*, taken by *Maurice*. In the Year 1605, *Spinola* retook from the *Hollanders*, *Lingen*, *Groll*, and *Rhinebergh*, and *Maurice* sustain'd some Loss before *Antwerp*. The last glorious Action in this War, was that of *James Hemskirke*, who burn'd the *Spanish* Fleet in the Harbor of *Gibraltar*, where he himself was kill'd. The *Spaniards* therefore finding it impossible to reduce *Holland* by Force, which they found increas'd in Strength by the War; and being at the same time jealous of *Henry* IV. and quite out of breath by this tedious War, they resolv'd to make an end of it at any rate. How desirous the *Spaniards* were of Peace, may easily be conjectur'd from hence, That *Albert* himself propos'd the Treaty to be at the *Hague*, and first sent *Spinola* himself thither as Ambassador, whereas the *Hollanders*, carry'd it very high, and were very resolute. The Business met with great difficulty, before it could be brought to the Conclusion of a Truce of 12 Years: The greatest Obstacle was, that the *Hollanders* urg'd it closely,

Battle near Newport.

Siege of Ostend, 1601

The Conquests on both sides.

That *Spain*, without any Exception, should declare them a free People; which the *Spanish* Ambassadors refusing to do, at last this Medium was found out, That *Spain* and the Arch-duke *Albert* did declare, they would treat with the *Netherlanders* as a free Nation. But they being still not satisfied with this, the President *Janin*, who was sent thither in behalf of *France*, answer'd, That the Word *As* could not add much to the Strength of *Spain*, nor diminish theirs; and that it was their Business to secure themselves and their State by Arms, and not by Words. So a Truce was concluded by vertue of which, both Parties kept what they were possess'd of, and the *Hollanders* maintain'd their Navigation into the *East-Indies*, which the *Spaniards* would fain have got from them. Now the chief Cause why the *Hollanders* at that time, when their Affairs were in so good a condition, consented to a Truce, seems to be, that they began to be jealous of *France*, for fear lest that King should snatch *Flanders* away upon a sudden, which must needs have prov'd their Ruine. Besides, being grown very powerful during this War, was likely to be troublesome to their Liberty. And this was the first Step which *Holland* made towards the Establishment of a free Common-wealth.

A Truce of 12 Years.

1609. §. 12. Soon after the Truce was concluded, the *Hollanders* were engaged in the Business concerning the Succession of the Country of *Juliers*; for the Emperor after the Death of the last Duke, being very desirous to annex these Countries unto his House, had sent the Arch-duke *Leopold* to make a Sequestration, who took the strong City of *Juliers*, but was beaten out again by the *Hollanders*, with the Assistance of the *French*. But a Difference arising afterwards betwixt the Elector of *Brandenburgh* and the Duke of *Newburgh*, who had at first made an Agreement betwixt themselves; and the Duke of *Newburgh*, having call'd to his Assistance *Spinola*, who took the City of *Wesel*: The *Hollanders* on the other hand sided with the Elector of *Brandenburgh*, and put Garrisons into *Rees* and *Emerick*, whereby the Country of *Cleves* was involved in the War of the *Netherlands*.

A Quarrel about the Dutchy of Juliers.

The Differences between the Remonstrants *and* Contra-Remonstrants.

§. 13. But there arose a more dangerous intestine Division in *Holland* betwixt the *Arminians* or *Remonstrants* and the *Contra-Remonstrants*, which Division, was partly occasi-

occasion'd by a State-jealousie, partly by Disputes among the Divines. We have said before, that Prince *William* did endeavour under-hand to be Soveraign over the United Provinces, which was prevented only by a very few Voices. After his Death, his Son *Maurice* pursued the same Design; but was opposed by the chief Men among them; who alledged, That their Labour was very ill bestowed, if in place of a great one, they should be brought under Subjection to a little Prince. Among those, one of the chiefest was *John* of *Olden Barneveldt*, Pensionary of *Holland*, who had been always for upholding the publick Liberty. However in regard the Authority of the Captain-General was more conspicuous during the War, *Maurice* endeavour'd to set aside the Treaty with *Spain*; and on the other hand, *Barneveldt* did, as much as he could, promote the Truce with *Spain*, knowing that in time of Peace the Authority of the Captain-General wou'd be diminish'd: Which Conduct of *Barneveldt*'s stuck so deep in *Maurice*'s Memory, that after, he took all Opportunities to be revenged. In the mean time *Arminius*, a Professor of Divinity in the University of *Leyden*, had defended several Propositions concerning Predestination, and some other Articles of that nature, with less Rigour than the rest of the Reform'd Churches had hitherto generally taught. His Opinion was, after his Death, oppos'd by one *Francis Gomarus*. This Dissention being spread abroad, most of the Clergy sided with *Gomarus*, but the chief States-men with *Arminius*. But considering the Generality of the People followed the Footsteps of the Clergy, *Maurice*, who after the Death of his elder Brother was become Prince of *Orange*, declar'd himself for the *Gomarists*. And there happening great Tumults in several Places, *viz.* at *Alkmaer*, *Leyden*, and *Utrecht*, the Prince took this opportunity to displace, up and down, such Magistrates as adhered to the *Arminians*. *Barneveldt*, *Hugo Grotius*, and some others, were under the same Pretext taken into Custody: The first, by a Sentence of the States-General, lost his Head in the 72d Year of his Age; *Grotius* was condemned to perpetual Imprisonment; out of which he afterwards made his Escape, by means of his Wife, who had shut him up in a Chest. And tho' at the Synod of *Dort* the Doctrine of *Arminius* was condemned as erroneous, yet this Violence of the Prince against a Man who had deserved

Afterwards manag'd by State-Policy.

1619.

deserved so well, was very ill resented by a great many: And these two Factions have ever since taken so firm Root there, that it is not improbable, but at last they may occasion the Ruin or Change of the State.

The Spanish *War renewed* 1621.

§. 14. But Dangers from abroad did afterwards appease these inward Dissentions: For, the time of the Truce being expir'd, the War began afresh with *Spain*. In the Year 1622, *Spinola* took *Juliers*, but was obliged to raise the Siege from before *Bergen-op-Zoom*; because the Count of *Mansfield* and *Christian* Duke of *Brunswick* having defeated the *Spanish* Army near *Fleury*, march'd to the Assistance of the *Hollanders*. To revenge this Affront, *Spinola* besieg'd *Breda*; and Prince *Maurice* having in vain endeavour'd to raise the Siege, and besides this, his Attempt upon the Castle of *Antwerp* having proved unsuccessful, he fell into a deep Melancholly, and died; *Breda* being not long after forc'd, by Famine, to surrender it self. To Prince *Maurice* succeeded, in the Stadtholdership, and all the other Offices that had been in his Possession, his Brother *Frederick Henry*, who took *Groll*. In the Year 1626, *Pieter Heyn* took the *Spanish* Silver-Fleet; and in the Year next ensuing, the Prince took *Bois le Duc*. During this Siege, the *Spaniards* made an Inroad into the *Velaw*, hoping thereby to give the *Hollanders* a Diversion; and indeed they were put into a great Consternation. But the *Hollanders* on that very Day, surprised the City of *Wesel*; which oblig'd the *Spaniards* to repass the River *Yssel* as fast as they could: And from that time forward the *Spaniards* despair'd of ever reducing *Holland* under their Obedience. In the Year 1630, the *Hollanders* got first footing in *Brasile*. In the Year 1631, they surprised some Thousands of *Spaniards* near *Bergen-op-Zoom*, who were gone out in Shallops upon some secret Enterprize. In 1632, the Prince took *Venlo*, *Ruremond*, *Limburg*, and *Maestricht*; and *Pappenheim* endeavouring to relieve the last, was soundly beaten. In the Year 1633, the Prince took *Rhineberg*; but the Year after that, the *Spaniards* took *Limburgh*. An Offensive Alliance was made betwixt *France* and *Holland*, wherein they shar'd the *Netherlands* betwixt them: But this Alliance prov'd fruitless, the *Hollanders* being very well satisfy'd, that this Design did not succeed, for they were glad not to have the *French* for their Neighbours on the Land-side. However,

Prince Maurice *dies*, 1625.

Prince Frederick Henry I.

A League Offensive between France *and* Holland. 1635.

ever, the *Spaniards* surpriz'd *Shenkenschantz*, which the *Hollanders* retook not without great trouble. In the Year 1637, the Prince retook *Breda*; but the *Spaniards*, *Venlo*, and *Ruremond*. In the Year 1638, the *Hollanders* were soundly beaten near *Callo*; but in the Year 1639, *Martin Tromp* entirely destroy'd the *Spanish* Fleet, which lay in the *Downs*, and was intended to attack *Sweden*, in Conjunction with the *Danes*. In the Year 1644, *Ghent*, and in the Year after that *Hulst* was taken by *William* II. who had succeeded his Father: It is thought he might also have taken *Antwerp*, if the Province of *Zealand* and *Amsterdam* had not oppos'd it, as being grown powerful out of its Ruins. At last, a Peace was concluded at *Munster*, betwixt *Spain* and *Holland*, wherein it was declar'd a free Commonwealth, to which *Spain* should, for the future make no Pretensions whatsoever. And though *France* and the Prince opposed this Peace with their utmost Endeavours yet the *Hollanders* consider'd, that the *Spaniards* having granted all that they could desire, the Cause of the War ceas'd: Besides they fear'd that *Spain* might be brought too low, and *France* grow too powerful; and the Province of *Holland* was considerably indebted. Thus *Holland* ended this tedious War with great Reputation, but the *Spaniards* with great Dishonour, having withal quite enervated themselves: Tho' this is observable that as long as the *Hollanders* were engag'd in the War against *Spain*, they were favour'd by every body except the *Spanish* Party; but immediately after the Peace was concluded, both *France* and *England*, by whom they had been hitherto upheld, gave manifest Proofs of their Jealousie of them.

1636.

Prince William II.

Peace concluded at Munster, 1648.

§. 15. But the *Hollanders* could not enjoy Peace very long; for soon after *Brasile* rebell'd against them, submitting it self to the *Portuguese*; which prov'd very disadvantageous for the *West-India* Company: But the *East-India* Company reap'd great Advantage from it; for this having occasion'd a War with *Portugal*, which lasted till the Year 1661, the *Hollanders* took from the *Portuguese* almost all the Places which they were possess'd of in the *East-Indies*. In the Year 1650, a remarkable Dissention arose in *Holland*, which might have prov'd the Cause of great Calamities. For, the War with *Spain* being now at an end, some of the States and especially the Province of *Holland*, were of Opinion, that to ease the

War with Portugal.

Division in Holland.

the Publick, their Forces should be diminish'd; which the People oppos'd, under pretence that it would not be advisable to be without an Army, as long as *France* and *Spain* were engaged in a War. And the States being divided concerning this Business, it was agreed upon by the Majority of the States-General, who were great Friends to the Prince, that the Prince should visit in Person the Cities, to try whether he could convince the Magistrates in this point: Against this petition'd some of the Cities in *Holland*, and especially *Amsterdam*, fearing that if the Prince should come in Person to them, he might, by changing the Magistrates, and other Alterations, do something which might prove prejudicial to their Liberty. The Prince, dissatisfy'd at these Proceedings, reply'd, That this was done to affront him and his Officers, and therefore desir'd that Reparation should be made him: but the Cities insisted upon their former Resolution, alledging, that it was according to their Privileges. Then the Prince took into Custody six of the States of *Holland* whom he suppos'd to be chiefly against him (among whom the chiefest was the Sieur *de Witt*, Burghermaster of *Dort*) whom he sent all together Prisoners to the Castle of *Louvestein*. He also privately order'd some Troops to march towards *Amsterdam*, to surprize that City; but some of these Troops having lost their way in the Night-time, the Design was discover'd by the *Hamburgher* Post Boy: And the *Amsterdammers* perceiving that the Prince intended to force them to a Compliance, open'd their Sluces, and put the Country round about it under Water. At last the Business was agreed, and the Prince had this Satisfaction given him, That the Sieur *Bicker* Burghermaster of *Amsterdam* was depos'd, and the Prisoners in the Castle of *Louvestein* were set at liberty, upon condition that they should be discharg'd from their Places. But this Business was likely to have been the occasion of more Troubles, if the Prince had not died soon after. Soon after his Death, *viz.* in the Year 1650, on the 14th Day of *November*, his Princess was brought to Bed of *William* III. In the Year 1651, the United Provinces held a grand Assembly, where they renew'd the Union, being now destitute of a Governour.

De Witt and others made Prisoners by the Prince.

The Birth of Prince William III.

§. 16. Not long after the *Hollanders* were engag'd in a heavy War with the *English* Parliament, which at the begin-

War with the English Parliament.

beginning being very ambitious of their Friendship, sent one *Dorislaw* to the *Hague*; who before he had his publick Audience, was murther'd by some *Scots* who were all mask'd. And the Parliament having receiv'd no Satisfaction upon this account, began to look with an ill Eye upon them; which they little regarded, till *Cromwel* had reduc'd the *Scots*. And tho' the Parliament sent other Ambassadours to the *Hague*, yet the *Dutch* were not very forward, but were for protracting the Treaty, till the Ambassadors having been affronted by the Rabble, departed dissatisfy'd: Whereupon the Parliament, by way of Reprisal, declar'd, That no Commodities should be transported into *England*, except on *English* Bottoms; and the *English* Privateers began to fall every where upon the *Dutch* Merchant Ships. The *Hollanders*, who were not very unanimous among themselves, resolved at last to try first whether the Business might be compounded by fair means, and if that did not succeed, to begin the War in good earnest; and for this purpose Ambassadors were sent into *England*. *Tromp* in the mean while was sent out with a Fleet, to secure their Commerce; and meeting with the *English* Admiral *Blake*, and refusing to strike, a bloody Engagement ensu'd, which ended with equal Loss on both Sides. The *Hollanders* pretended that this had happen'd by Accident; both Parties however, made great Preparations for War, and fought twice, the Advantage remaining on the *English* side, tho' they were afterwards beaten near *Leghorn*. But in the last Engagement the *Hollanders* having lost their Admiral *Tromp*, and seven and twenty Men of War, they were oblig'd to conclude a Peace with *Cromwel*, which was very advantageous and glorious on his side, they being among other Articles oblig'd, for the future, never to make any one of the House of *Orange* their Stadtholder. It was then observ'd, that the *Dutch* Ships were not large enough; which Error the *Hollanders* corrected afterwards. In the next Year the *Hollanders* growing jealous of the great Success of the *Swedes* against *Poland*, and being desirous to prevent the *Swedes* from becoming Masters of *Prussia*, they stirr'd up the King of *Denmark* against them. But the *Danes* being worsted in this War, the *Hollanders* sent a Fleet to relieve *Copenhagen*, which was besieg'd by the *Swedes*: Upon which a bloody Battle was fought in the *Oresound*, betwixt the *Swedish* and *Dutch* Fleets, wherein the *Hollan-*

A Peace, 1654.

Differences with Swedeland.

ders

ders lost two Admirals, but nevertheless gain'd their point in relieving *Copenhagen*. And in the next Year they also bore their share in the Battle of *Funen*, 'till at last a Peace
1660. was concluded before *Copenhagen*, to the small Satisfaction of the *Danes*, who accused the *Hollanders*, that they had not shewn due Vigour in assisting them against the *Swedes*. But the Truth of the Matter was this; The *Hollanders* were afraid that *England* and *France* might declare for *Sweden*, and under that *Pretence* fall upon 'em; besides that, they thought it their Interest not to let *Denmark* grow too powerful.

The Second War with England, 1665.

§. 17. *Holland* was then for a few Years at Peace, till a bloody War broke out betwixt them and the *English*, who could not but think the flourishing Trade and great Power of the *Hollanders* at Sea, to be very prejudicial to them. *France* blew up the Coals, being desirous to see these two mighty States weaken one another's Power. In this War the *English* had the Advantage in the first and third Engagements, but the *Hollanders* in the second: But the *English*, at last being willing to save Charges, resolved only to infest the *Hollanders* by their Privateers, and not to equip a Fleet; which the *Hollanders* taking an Advantage of, ventur'd to enter the River of *Thames*, and landing near *Chatham*, burnt several Ships in the Harbour. This oblig'd *England* to make a Peace with them, which was by Mediation of the Crown of *Sweden* concluded at *Breda*.

England *and* France *declare War with* Holland.

§. 18. At last, in the Year 1672, a prodigious Storm fell upon *Holland*, which at first threatned its Ruin; *France* attacking it by Land, and *England* by Sea. It was surprizing to see how the *French*, in a few days time took the Provinces of *Guelderland*, *Over-Yssel*, and *Utrecht*, which occasion'd so general a Consternation, that some are of Opinion, they might have taken *Amsterdam* it self, if they had immediately gone towards it, whilst the first Consternation lasted. Some lay the Fault upon *Rochford*, who having received Orders to make an Attempt upon that City, tarried two days at *Utrecht* which he bestow'd in receiving of Complements, the *Amsterdammers* getting thereby time to take a Resolution for their Defence. It serv'd also for a great Encouragement to the *Hollanders*, that the Bishop of *Munster* was forc'd to rise from before

Gronin-

Groningen, he having, together with the Elector of Cologn, taken the French side. In the Year next ensuing, the French took Maestricht from the Hollanders. But the Hollanders having behav'd themselves bravely in four Sea Engagements, and the Parliament of England being become very jealous of France, a separate Peace was, by the Mediation of Spain, concluded betwixt Holland and England. The Emperor and Spain having then declar'd for Holland, the French King took his Garrisons out of all the conquer'd Places (having first exacted from them great Contributions) except Naerden and Grave, which were retaken by Force. Thus the Hollanders got all their Places again except Maestricht; Rhinebergh which belonged to the Elector of Cologne being restor'd to him and the Country of Cleves to the Elector of Brandenburgh. This War restor'd the Prince of Orange to the same Dignity with his Ancestors, and that under better Conditions than when in their Possession: For the common People, who always favour'd the House of Orange, being put quite into a Consternation by the prodigious Success of the French and being persuaded, that this Misfortune was occasion'd by the Treachery of some who sat at the Helm, and that no body but the Prince could restore the decay'd State; raised Tumults in most Cities, which the Prince was forc'd to appease, by deposing the former Magistrates, and putting in their room such as he knew where Favourers of himself. In one of these Tumults Cornelius and John de Witt, two Brothers were miserably murther'd by the Rabble in the Hague; tho' a great many are of Opinion, that both of 'em, especially the last, who had so long sat at the Helm, had deserv'd better of his native Country. Tho' the Prince had been not a little instrumental in appeasing the Commotions, whereby Holland was put in a condition to recover it self, yet he was not so succesful in his War again France; for, he receiv'd a considerable Loss near Seneffe; he was repuls'd before Maestricht; and endeavouring to relieve St. Omer, he was defeated by the French; and the Dutch Fleet which was sent to the Relief of Sicily had no great Success. At last their Fear, that through long War their Liberty might be endanger'd by the Prince, influenc'd them to make a separate Peace with France, by Virtue of which Maestricht was restor'd to the Hollanders.

The De Witts murther'd.

1677. 1676. 1677.

§. 19.

The Constitution. §. 19. The Seven Provinces of the *United Netherlands* are fill'd with a prodigious number of People; there being some who have computed that in the Province of *Holland*, the Number amounts to two Millions and five hundred Thousand. And unto this vast number of People, is to be attributed their Industry, increase of Trade, and great Riches; for in a Country which is not the most fruitful, and where every thing is very dear, they must else of necessity perish by Famine. Most of the Inhabitants were transplanted thither out of other Countries; out of *France* during the times of the Civil Commotions; out of *England* under the Reign of Queen *Mary*; out of *Germany* during those long Wars there; but chiefly out of the other Provinces of the *Netherlands*, at the time of their revolting from *Spain*. These Strangers were invited into this Country by its convenient Situation, the Liberty of Religion and the Government; by its extraordinary Constitutions and Conveniences for Trade and Correspondence in all Parts; and at last, by the great Reputation which the States gain'd by their wise Management at home, and the Success of their Arms abroad. And in regard every body, who either brings some Means along with him, or has learn'd something to maintain himself withal, finds a good Reception in *Holland*; even those who are prosecuted in other Places find a certain Refuge in this Country.

Their Genius. *Charles* V. us'd to say of the *Netherlands*, *That there was not a Nation under the Sun, that did detest more the Name of Slavery, and yet, if you did manage them mildly and with Discretion, did bear it more patiently.* But the Rabble here is very bad, it being their common Custom to speak ill and despicably of their Magistrates as often as things do not answer Expectation. The *Hollanders* are very unfit for Land-service, and the *Dutch* Horse-men are strange Creatures; yet those who live in *Guelderland*, and upon the Borders of *Westphalia*, are tolerably good. But at Sea they have done such Exploits that they may be compar'd with any Nation in the World. And the *Zealanders* are esteem'd more Hardy and Venturous than the *Hollanders*. They are also generally very parsimonious, not much addicted to the Belly, it being not the Custom here to spend their yearly income, but to save every Year an Overplus. This saving way of living upholds their Credit, and enables them to bear such heavy Taxes without being ruin'd by them. They are very fit for all sorts of Manufactury,

factury, and very much addicted to Commerce, not refusing to undergo any Labour or Danger, where something is to be got; and those that understand Trade deal very easily with them. They are very punctual in every respect, pondering and ordering a thing very well before they begin it. And there is scarce any Nation in the World so fit for Trade as the *Dutch*; this being very praise-worthy in them, that they always choose rather to get somewhat by their own Industry, than by Violence or Fraud. But above all, the great Liberty which they enjoy, is a great Encouragement for Trade. Their chiefest Vice is Covetousness, which however is not so pernicious among them, because it produces in them Industry and Good-husbandry. There are a great many who have been amaz'd at the great Conduct which has appear'd in the Management of their Affairs, notwithstanding that the *Hollanders* in general are rarely of extraordinary Wit or Merits. For which some alledge this as a Reason, That a cold Temper and Moderation of Passions are the fundamental Qualifications of a good Statesman.

§. 20. The seven *United Provinces* are not very large in Extent as being but one Corner of *Germany*; but they are fill'd up with so considerable a Number of beautiful, large, and populous Cities, that no other Place of the same Bigness is to be compar'd to it. Besides the seven Provinces they are possess'd of some Cities in *Flanders* and *Brabant*, viz. *Hulst*, *Sluce*, *Ardenburgh*, *Bois le Duc*, *Maestricht*, *Breda*, *Bergen-op-Zoom*, *Grave*, and some others. They also keep a Garrison in *Embden*, thereby to secure the River of *Embs*. The Country in general is more fit for Pasture than Tilling, for it produces scarce so much Corn as is sufficient for the fifth part of its Inhabitants. But this Want is made up by the Industry of the Inhabitants, and the great Conveniency of so many Rivers, and the Seas fit for Fishing and Navigation. The Herring Fishery, and that of Codds, brings in vast Riches to them; and some *English* have computed, That the *Hollanders* sell every Year 79200 Last (which makes 138400 Tuns) of Herrings, which amount to the value of 1372000 *l. Sterl.* not including what is transported into *Spain*, *Italy*, and *France*, and what is consumed at home. But their Shipping and Commerce is of much greater Advantage to them, which flourishes there to that degree, *The Nature of the Country.* *Of their Shipping and Commerce.*

that some are of Opinion, That in *Holland* are more Ships than in all other Parts of *Europe.* Besides, *Holland*'s Situation in the midst of *Europe* makes it very fit for Trade, so that it sends its Ships with great Conveniency into the *East* and *Western* Seas; and the Commodiousness of those vast Rivers of the *Rhine, Maese, Elbe, Weser,* and *Embs,* draws the Commodities out of *Germany,* and in exchange for these, vends Manufactures of *Holland*: For *Holland* has in regard, especially of the *Rhine* and the *Maese,* a great Advantage in its Trade before *England,* tho' this, on the other hand, has better Harbours and a deeper Coast: And because *Holland* is at the latter end of the Year commonly overflown with Waters, which makes the Air very thick and foggy, Nature has been kind to this Country, in that about that time the Wind blows much *Easterly,* which disperses the Vapours, refreshes the Air, and renders it wholesome; but from hence it is that their Harbours are often shut up with Ice for three Months together, whereas they are always open in *England.* The *Hollanders* trade almost into every Corner of the World, and have been very careful to erect Fortresses and Colonies in far distant Countries. But above all, their *East-India* Company has vastly encreas'd her Trade and Riches: for this Company has extended her Trade from *Basora,* which is situated near the great Bay of *Persia,* at the very Mouth of the River *Tigris,* all along a prodigious Tract of rich Ground near the Sea-side as far as to the utmost Parts of *Japan*; she stands there in Confederacy with many Kings, and with many of them has made Treaties of Monopolies, and is possess'd of a great many Strong-holds in those parts. The Capital City there is *Batavia* in *Java Major,* where the Governour General keeps a Court like a King, under whose Jurisdiction are the other places. The Company is Sovereign Mistress over all these Countries, the chiefest of which are the *Isles* of *Molocca* and *Banda, Amboina, Malacca,* the Coast of the Island of *Zeilon, Paliacatta, Musulapatan, Negapatan* upon the Coast of *Cormandel, Cochin, Cananor* and *Cranganor* upon the Coast of *Malabar,* and several more. Whether they have a free Trade in the *East-Indies* with *China,* I cannot affirm, tho' it is certain that the *Chinese* drive a great Trade with them in *Batavia*; but in *Japan* they have the whole Trade alone, no *Portugese* being permitted to come there. This Company is able to set

East India *Company.*

ſet out a Fleet of betwixt 40 and 50 Capital Ships, and to raiſe an Army of 30000 Men. The firſt Funds of this Company did amount to 60 Tuns of Gold, which in the ſpace of 6 Years, deducting all the Charges and Dividends made to the Owners, was encreas'd to 300 Tuns of Gold. The Fund of the *Weſt-India* Company was 80 Tuns of Gold, and flouriſh'd extreamly at the beginning, but ruin'd it ſelf by making too great Dividends, and not keeping a Fund ſufficient for the carrying on of the War againſt *Spain*. Beſides, thoſe concern'd in this Company were more eager after Conqueſts than Trade; and when *Braſile* revolted they receiv'd a capital Blow: Yet they are poſſeſs'd in *Guinea* of the Caſtle *del Mina*; and, if I am not miſtaken, of *Loanda* in *Angola*, and ſome other Places, as alſo ſome of the *Caribby Iſlands*, and of *New Holland* in the *Northern* Parts of *America*. They have alſo lately begun to erect ſome Colonies in *Guiana*, and on the great River of *Orenoquo*. Some of the moſt curious have obſerv'd, that a great many things concurr in *Holland* for the promoting of Trade, which are not to be met with all together in any other Country; particularly, the great Quantity of People, the Conveniency and Security of the Country, the ſmall Intereſt which is paid for Money, which ſhews the great Superfluity of ready Money; the Severity us'd againſt Thieves, Cheats, and Bankrupts; the Bank of *Amſterdam*, the great Numbers of Convoys, and moderate Cuſtoms: And to this, That they are ſo exact and regular in their way of Trading; That the Magiſtrates are generally Merchants, or at leaſt, ſuch as have an Intereſt in Commerce; That they are Maſters in the *Eaſt-Indies*; and, That by reaſon of the Frugality and induſtry of the Inhabitants, far more Commodities are Exported than Imported. To this purpoſe it is obſervable, That tho' the *Hollanders* are Maſters of the Spice in the *Indies*, yet they uſe them leaſt of all themſelves. They have alſo the greateſt ſhare in the Silk-trade in Perſia, and yet they cloath themſelves in Woollen Cloth, generally ſpeaking. Nay, they ſell their fine Cloths abroad, and ſend for coarſer out of *England* for their own uſe. They ſell their delicious Butter, and ſend for other out of the *North* of *England* and *Ireland* for their own uſe. *French* Wine and Brandies are the chiefeſt Commodities which are conſumed here; yet even when they make a Debauch, they are not over-laviſh.

The Weſt-India Company.

Strength and Weakness of this Commonwealth.

§. 21. From what has been said, it is manifest that the Strength of this Commonwealth is founded upon Trade and its Naval Force, which is absolutely necessary to maintain the former: nor is there any Country so stock'd with good Seamen, for the fitting out of a great Fleet. But on the Land-side, where the Country cannot be under Water, it is not near so strong. For tho' they do not want Money to raise an Army of Foreigners, yet it is not always advisable for a Common-wealth to rely only upon such as have no other Tye but their Pay, since they may easily prove unfaithful, or else misled by the General, assist him in over-turning the Liberty of the State. And it has been in regard of this that some have advised that the Provinces of *Holland* and *Zealand* should separate themselves from the rest, and only endeavour to strengthen themselves betwixt the *Maese*, the *Rhine*, and *South-Sea*; and in case of Necessity, by opening of their Sluces, put the Country under Water; but for the rest, only endeavour to strengthen themselves at Sea: But to examine this Proposition, is not now my Business. There are several Inconveniences that proceed from the very Form of the Government of this State: For, to speak properly, these seven Provinces do not make up one entire Common-wealth, but there are seven Commonwealths, which by the Union at *Utrecht* are join'd into one Confederacy, and have their Deputies constantly residing at the *Hague*; whose Business it is to take care of such Affairs as concern the whole Union; and if any thing of moment is to be decreed, they send to the several Provinces, and according to the Approbation of these they make their Decrees: these Deputies are called the States-General. Nay, it seems that each Province is rather a Confederacy than one City or Commonwealth, because the several Members of each Province do treat with one another like Confederates, and not like one Body, where one is superiour to the other, or the Majority of Votes determines a Business. For even in the Provincial Assemblies a great many things cannot be determined by the Plurality of Votes, but every Member's Consent is required. Which shews, that these Provinces and Cities are not united by so strong a Tye, as those who are govern'd by one Soveraign, except as far as Necessity obliges them to keep together. And the great Cities are fill'd with Rabble; which if once put in motion, uses to make strange work

Form of Government.

among them. It is therefore the great Care of the Magistrates, that they are kept in constant Employment to get Bread, for Famine would quickly be the occasion of great Tumults here. There is also a Jealousie betwixt *Holland* and the other Provinces; the latter pretending to some Prerogative, as being the most Powerful, and contributing most to the Publick; whereas the others are for maintaining their Liberty and Equality. All the rest of the Cities are especially jealous of *Amsterdam*, because this City draws abundance of Trade from the rest, and puts them in apprehension, as if she were ambitious to domineer over them. But the greatest Irregularity happens in their Constitution, by means of the Prince of *Orange*, who having the Favour of the Common People, of the Land-Soldiers and the Clergy, (for the Clergy hate the *Arminians*, who being of the *Barnefeldt* Faction, are Enemies of the Prince) seems to endanger their Liberty. Wherefore the chief Men in the Cities, to whom belongs the Magistracy there, possess their places in continual Fear, except they will be pliable to the Prince of *Orange*; whose Interest is also inconsistent with that of the State, because no Land-War can be advantageous for *Holland*: whereas in time of War, his Authority is much greater than otherwise, especially considering that their Army is foreign and mercenary. And therefore, according to this Form of Government, scarce a firm Peace can be establish'd at home. It may easily happen that the Prince may aspire to be their Soveraign. And when the Province of *Guelderland* did offer to him the Soveraignty, he gave them to understand, That if all the rest were of the same Opinion they should have no occasion to look for him behind the Wine-pipes, as the *Jews* did for *Saul*; yet the wiser sort are of Opinion, that he would reap no great Benefit from this Soveraignty, since it would be scarce possible to keep so many great Cities in Obedience against their Will: For Cittadels and Garrisons would prove the Ruin of Trade, which never flourishes where absolute Power controuls the Subject. Wherefore it seems more adviseable for the Prince to be satisfied with what Power he has, it being certain that if he knows how to manage the Humour of the People he is almost able to do what he pleases. It has been a great Dispute, whether it be for the Advantage of these *Netherlands* to have a Governour-General. Those who are for the Affirmative

Prince of Orange.

1675.

Whether it is their Advantage to have a Sovereignty.

tive alledge, That this Country having been from ancient Time under the Jurisdiction of a limited Soveraignty, has been used to that Form of Government; That it conduces to the outward Splendour of the Common-wealth, and to uphold the Authority of the Magistrates in the Cities; That thereby Factions and Tumults are kept under and suppressed. That thereby are prevented a great many Inconveniences in executing any Designs of moment, which are incident to an Aristocratical and Democratical State; *viz.* Slow and divided Counsels in Consultations, Delays in Executions, and the divulging of secret Designs: all which we will leave undetermin'd here.

Other Defects of the Commonwealth.

This is also to be esteem'd one of the Weaknesses of this Commonwealth, that so great a number of Inhabitants cannot be maintain'd by the Product of the Land, but must get their Bread from abroad, and by the help of Foreigners. Wherefore the certain Ruin of this Commonwealth is at hand, whenever its Trade and Navigation should be stopt; which however is not altogether impossible to happen. The Difference of Religion is commonly reckoned among the Weaknesses of a State. But some make this one of the main Pillars of the flourishing Condition of *Holland*, because it contributes greatly to the Populousness, Strength, and Encrease of this State. The Reformed Religion is here the Establish'd Religion, all the rest being only tolerated: The *Papists* are connived at; but at the same time the State keeps a strict Eye over them, for fear the Priests, who all depend on the Pope, should enter into a Correspondency with *Spain*. Yet it is rarely seen in *Holland*, that one Subject hates the other, or prosecutes him upon the Score of Religion. It is also very inconvenient for the Inhabitants, that all sorts of Victuals are sold at so excessive a Rate; the Reason of which is, That the greatest Revenues of *Holland* are raised by way of Excise upon these Commodities; and it is a common Saying that before you can get a Dish of Fish ready dress'd upon your Table at *Amsterdam*, you have paid above 30 several Taxes for it. And notwithstanding all these heavy Impositions, the State is much in Debt. There are some also who pretend, that the Traffick of the *Dutch* dwindles; for which they alledge several Reasons; *viz.* That since the Peace concluded at *Munster*, other Nations have likewise applied themselves to Trade: That the Price of the *East-India* Commodities falls every Year,

and yet the Charges of the Company encrease daily. For whereas formerly five or six *East India* Ships coming home yearly were reckon'd very considerable, now eighteen or twenty return; which so overstocks them with these Commodities, that they are obliged to lay them up in their Warehouses for a considerable time, before they can vent them without Loss. They alledge also, That Corn has been of late Years so abundant in *France, Spain, Italy*, and *England*, that the *Hollanders* have not sent much of it into these Parts, it being their Custom to fetch Corn from the *East-Sea*, where they vent, in exchange of it, most of their Spices: that the great Addition of Fortifications and sumptuous Buildings to the City of *Amsterdam*, have taken up a great Quantity of Ready-money, which might have been better employ'd in way of Trade; and, that Luxury and Debauchery gains ground dayly in that City. In fine, the Reason why the *Hollanders* had such ill Success in the Beginning of the last War, seems to be, that by their great Eagerness for Gain and Trade, their Martial Heat was almost extinguish'd; and that after the Peace concluded at *Munster*, being not apprehensive of any Invasion by Land, they only applied themselves to strengthen their Power at Sea, and dismissing their best Officers, supplied their Places with their own Relations; whose Motto was *Peace and a good Government*. For in the time of the War with *England* they 1665.
dismiss'd the *English* veterane Troops; and in the Year 1668, the *French* Troops; both which were the Flower of their Armies, which of necessity must, by this means, have been reduc'd into a very ill Condition, since the Prince of *Orange* had no more concern with them. Besides this, they thought themselves very secure, not imagining that *France* would either dare or be able, to attempt a Conquest over them, as long as they were sure, that the Emperor and *Spain* would side with them: neither did they imagine that the *English* would join with the *French* against them. And at least they hoped they would beat the *English* out of the Sea before *France* should be able to take three or four Places. They relied upon the old way of making War, when a whole Campaign was taken up with the Taking of one Place, and when whole Books were composed of the taking of *Groll*, or the War of *Ghent*. It is also believed, that some of the *Hollanders* were not sorry that they had no great Success

by Land, hoping thereby to bring into Discredit the Conduct, and to diminish the Authority of the Prince, whom they had been obliged to make their Captain-General against their Will.

The Neighbours of Holland.

§. 22. As for the Neighbours of *Holland*, and what it has to fear or to hope from them; it seems that the *English* are the most dangerous Neighbours to the *Hollanders*, as being the only Nation that have been formidable to them hitherto, in opposing their Pretensions to the Dominion of the Seas and Trade; a Nation who are extreamly dissatisfied, that this new Commonwealth, which, when it was in a very tottering Condition, was powerfully upheld by them, has now been before-hand with them in the *East-Indies*, and daily spoil their Markets almost every-where. For because an *English-man* is naturally proud, and loves to live well, whereas a *Hollander* minds nothing so much as his Gain, being satisfied with an indifferent share, nor spends any thing idly; a *Hollander* can sell cheaper than an *English-man*, and Strangers will always rather deal with the first than the last. It is therefore, in all probability, the chief Interest of *Holland*, not to irritate *England*, and rather allow them some Ceremonial Prerogatives at Sea, such as Striking, and the like; but withal to strengthen their Power at Sea, that in case *England* should really contest with them for the Trade and Fishing, they may be able to make head against them. The *Hollanders* must also, as much as is possible, endeavour to encourage the same sort of Manufacture, as is in *England*, and either to make these Commodities better, or at least to sell them cheaper, in order to get the Advantage from them. The *Hollanders* ought to stand in great fear of *France* on the Land-side, especially since that King is their great Enemy, having opposed for a considerable time all their Designs. It is therefore very necessary to be in a good posture on the Land-side, and to keep fair with the Princes of *Germany*, who else would permit the *French* to march through their Territories, or else perhaps join with them. They must endeavour the Preservation of the *Spanish Netherlands*, which they ought to consider as their Frontier, and such a Frontier as obliges *Spain* always to side with *Holland* against *France*. They must take care to be provided with good Officers, and to put the Province of *Holland* into a better posture of

England. *France.*

Defence

Defence on the side of *Guelderland*. It is not easie to be supposed that *England* and *France* will join again against *Holland*; besides that this may be prevented by the *Hollanders*. It is the Interest of *Holland*, to take care that the Naval Strength of *France* do's not encrease too much, and to prevent, as much as in them lies, that, they do not settle a Trade in the *East-Indies*. And as *France* draws the Riches of all *Europe* to its self by its Manufactures, so the *Hollanders* must try to imitate them, and furnish other Nations with the like. From *Spain*, *Holland* need to fear nothing either by Sea or Land, since they were so much enervated by the *Belgick* War. Nay, it is their common interest now, that they cultivate a mutual good Understanding, to stop the Progress of the *French* in the *Netherlands*: And the *Spaniards* have scarce any thing left them from which the *Dutch* could have any Prospect of Benefit, as being not in a Capacity to conquer or to maintain the *West-Indies*. And though the *Hollanders* may be very troublesome to the *Spanish* Silver Fleets, yet the *Spanish* Privateers may, on the other hand, do them considerable mischief. *Portugal* has no Pretensions against *Holland*, and it ought most to stand in awe of the *Hollanders*, because these would be glad of an opportunity to take from the *Portuguese*, *Brazil*, and what they have left in the *East-Indies*; and, in effect, they want not Strength to execute such a Design upon occasion given. *Holland* being obliged to fetch their Bread from the *Baltick*, the Coasts of which are (as 'twere) the Granary of *Holland*, they have all along taken care that neither of the *Northern* Kings should be Master alone of the *East-Sea*; which Balance is the easier kept now, since the *Sound* is divided betwixt *Sweden* and *Denmark*. And it is notorious enough what Game they have play'd with these two Kings. For the rest, it is the general interest of *Holland* to keep fair with all other Princes, in order to maintain a free Commerce every-where. And in those Places where they cannot Trade alone, it is the Interest of the *Hollanders*, either by Goodness or Cheapness of their Commodities, and an easie Deportment, to endeavour to draw the chief Benefit of Trade to themselves. For this is the easier and less odious way to heap up Riches, than if they should attempt publickly to wrest the Foreign Trade from all other Nations; since it would prove impossible for them alone to maintain a general Monopoly.

Spain.

Portugal.

The Northern *Crowns*.

CHAP.

CHAP. VII.

Of the SWITZERS.

The first Original of this Common-wealth.

§. 1. THE Countries which are possess'd now by the *Switzers* belonged formerly to the *German* Empire; but their uniting in one Commonwealth, was occasion'd thus: The three small Counties of *Ury*, *Switz*, and *Under-Walden*, which commonly are call'd the three *Forest Towns*, enjoy'd very ancient Privileges, which they pretended to have been granted them by the Emperour *Lewis*, sirnamed the *Pious*; yet so, that the Emperour used to send thither a Judge or Vicar, who had the supreme Jurisdiction in criminal Affairs. There were also some Monasteries in those Countries, which, tho' they enjoy'd particular Privileges, yet did they not interfere with the Liberty of the People. But there lived a great many Noblemen among them, who by degrees getting the Ascendant over the common People, incroach'd upon their Liberty, especially during the Differences betwixt the Emperors and the Popes, when the Nobility us'd to side with the Pope, but the Commonalty with the Emperor. These Divisions betwixt the Nobility and the People grew very high at the time of the great Interregnum, which happen'd after the Death of the Emperor *Frederick the Second*;
1560. and breaking out into an open War, the whole Nobility was driven out of the Country; but by the Emperor *Rodolphus*'s Authority, a Reconciliation was made betwixt them, and the Nobles were restored to their Estates. Thus did these Countries enjoy their former Liberty, till the Reign of *Albert* I. who having conceived a Hatred against them, because they had sided with his Rival *Adolphus* of *Nassaw*, was very desirous to annex them to his Hereditary Countries; the Monasteries therefore, and a great many of the Nobility, having, upon his Desire, submitted themselves to the Jurisdiction of the House of *Austria*, the same was also proposed to the three abovementioned Places; who refusing his Proposition, he set over them imperial Judges or Vicars, who, contrary to the ancient Custom, began to reside in strong Castles, and having first try'd by Persuasives to bring them over to the House of *Austria*, afterwards when they found their labour

bour lost that way, grew very burthensome to the People by their Oppressions; neither were the Petitions made against them by the Commonalty any ways regarded by the Emperor; nay the Judge of *Under-Walden*, whose Name was *Geisler*, was become so extravagant, that he set his Hat upon a Pole in the Market-place of *Altorf*, commanding that every body should pay the same respect to his Hat as to himself; in order to make a tryal of their Obedience. And among others, one *William Tell* having often pass'd by without paying the Respect demanded, he forc'd him to shoot with an Arrow through an Apple, which was placed upon his only Son's Head: However, *Tell* having luckily, and by the kind direction of Providence, hit the Apple without hurting his Son, he was thereupon ordered to Prison; but making his Escape, work'd the People into an implacable Hatred of the Judges.

The first Union of the Swiss.

§. 2. There were at that time three Men of great Authority among them, *viz.* *Werner Stauffacher* born in *Switz*, *Walter Furst* born in *Ury*, and *Arnold* of *Melchthale* born in *Under-Walden*: These enter'd into an Association, whereby it was agreed among them to rid themselves of this Tyranny, and to restore their ancient Liberty. A great many more have enter'd afterwards into the same Association, an Agreement was made betwixt them, That in the Year 1308, on the first day of *January*, they should surprize these Judges in their strong Castles, and drive them out of the Country. This Confederacy was made in the Year 1307, on the 17th of *October*; and being afterwards put in execution in the Year 1308, on the first Day of *January*, the three Cities abovementioned entred into a Confederacy for ten Years, for the mutual Defence of their ancient Liberties. In the Year 1315, *Leopold* Arch-duke of *Austria*, Son of *Albert* I. marched with an Army of 20000 Men to force them to Obedience; against whom they marched out with 13000 Men, and whilst the *Austrian* Forces were marching betwixt a Lake and inaccessible Mountains, some of the *Switzers*, by rowling down upon them, and throwing great heaps of Stones among them, put the Enemy in Confusion, whilst the rest fell upon them and entirely defeated them near *Morgarten*. Then these three Places renewed their Confederacy; and having confirmed it by solemn Oaths, they agreed

The Battle near Morgarten.

agreed it ſhould continue for ever. This was done at *Brun* in the Year 1320, on the 7th of *December.* And this is the firſt beginning of that Commonwealth, the Confederates of which us'd to call themſelves *Edytſgenoſſen* (which ſignifies ally'd by Oath) but Strangers call them in general *Switzers*, from that one Place called *Switz.*

The firſt deſign of this Confederacy. §. 3. Neverthelefs the firſt Intention of this Confederacy was not to ſeparate themſelves from the *German* Empire, but only to maintain their ancient Privileges; tho' by degrees they began to adminiſter their own Affairs at home without ſending their Deputies to the Dyets of the Empire; and the *Switzers*, were not, till in the Year 1648, *viz.* in the *Weſtphalian* Peace, declared quite independant from the *Roman* Empire. The Emperor *Lewis* IV. confirmed the abovementioned Confederacy, and in 1320 ſent them a new Imperial Vicar or Judge, unto whom after having receiv'd new Aſſurances to be maintained in their Privileges, they did Homage in the Name of the Emperor. But the following Emperors gave them full power to chooſe Judges among themſelves, granting them the ſupreme Juriſdiction both in Civil and Criminal Affairs. In the Year 1332 *Lucern*, and in the Year 1351 *Zurick* entred into this Confederacy. *Lucern* was formerly under the Juriſdiction of the Houſe of *Auſtria*. *Zurick* which is the chiefeſt of the Confederacy, was formerly a free Imperial City. Immediately after, *Glaris*, and in the Year 1352, *Zug* and *Bern*, were united with the former. The *Switzers*, after this time, engaged in heavy Wars with the Houſe of *Auſtria*, and in 1386 ſlew *Leopold* Arch-duke of *Auſtria*, with a great many Nobles, in the Battle near *Sempach*. *Battle near Sempach.* In the Year 1444, the *Switzers* gave another Proof of their Valour; for the *Dauphine* of *France*, afterward call'd *Lewis* XI. marching with a great Army to diſturb the Council then held at *Baſil*, was attack'd by 1900 *Switzers* with ſuch fury, that tho' they all fell in the Enterprize, yet did they ſtrike ſuch a Terror into the *French*, that they quickly retreated homewards.

Wars with Charles Duke of Burgundy. §. 4. In the Year 1476 the *Switzers* were engag'd in a War againſt *Charles* Duke of *Burgundy*, the latter being ſtirr'd up by *Lewis* XI. who was for keeping his hands full and buſily employed. Againſt him *Rhene* Duke of *Lorrain*, and the Biſhops of *Stratsburgh* and *Baſil*, made an an Alliance with the *Switzers*. The Emperor *Frederick* III. taking hold of this opportunity to gratifie the implacable Hatred that his Family bore to the *Swiss*, commanded them to fall upon the Duke of *Burgundy*, who then was an Enemy of the Empire: And having afterwards made a Peace with the Duke without including the *Switzers*, hop'd they would be severely chastis'd by this brave Prince: but things happen'd quite contrary to his Expectation; for the *Switzers* defeated the Duke in three great Battels, first near *Granson*, afterwards near *Murten*, where the Duke had an Army of one hundred thousand Men, and at last near *Nancy* in *Lorrain*, where the Duke himself was killed. By these Victories the *Switzers* gained great Reputation. In the Year 1481, *Friburgh* and *Soluthurn*; in the Year 1501, *Basil* and *Shaftshausen*, and last of all *Appen-Zell*, were united with this Confederacy. The whole Body then of the *Swiss* Confederacy is composed of thirteen Commonwealths, called Cantons; among these *Zurick*, *Bern*, *Lucern*, *Zug*, *Basil*, *Friburgh*, *Soluthurn*, and *Shaftshausen*, are Cities; *Uri*, *Switz*, *Under-walden*, *Glaris*, and *Appen-Zell*, are Countries, where a good number of Towns and Villages are to be met withal. The *Switzers* have also some other Confederates, *viz.* the Abby and City of *St. Gall*, the *Grisons*, the *Vallesins*, the Cities of *Rotweil*, *Munthusen*, *Bienne*, *Biel*, *Geneva*, and *Newburgh*, on the Lake. There are also retaining to them several Cities and some Countries, which are either subject to the whole Confederacy, or to some particular Commonwealths. *Their Allies.*

§. 5. The *Switzers* were likewise oblig'd to fight against the Emperor *Maximilian* I. for their Liberty; he having stirr'd up the *Swabian League* against them, hoping by this way to chastise them. But the *Switzers*, for the most part got the better of their Enemies, till, through the Mediation of *Lewis* Duke of *Milan*, a Peace was made betwixt them. Not to relate here some intestine Commotions among them, they have done great Actions abroad, under the Conduct of other Nations, and more especially under the *French*. For *Lewis* XI. having, whilst he was *Dauphin* sufficiently tryed their Valour in the Engagement near *Basil*, sought by all ways, after he was King, to make use of the *Swiss* in his Wars; wherefore he allowed them a certain yearly Pension; And his Son *Some other Wars of the* Switzers. 1499.

Charles

Charles VIII. made use of the *Switzers* with good Success in his Expedition against *Naples*; for the *Italians*, when they saw the *Switzers* make such a prodigious Havock among them by the help of their Battle-Axes and large Back-Swords; they were so surpriz'd at it, that they counted the former Wars nothing in comparison of this, and look'd upon the *Switzers* more like some Monsters than Soldiers. *Lewis* XII. also employed the *Switzers* in his Service in his *Italian* Wars, tho' they lost great part of their Reputation there. For the *Switzers* which were listed in the Service of *Lewis Maurus* Duke of *Milan*, refusing to fight against their Countrymen that were in the *French* Army, thereby betray'd this Prince into the hands of the *French*.

The Wars with France. §. 6. But in the Year 1510, the *Switzers* left the *French* Service; for the time of Agreement with *France* being expired, they demanded a larger Pension, which *Lewis* XII. refused to pay them, thinking it unbecoming the Grandeur of a King to be imposed upon by these Highland Peasants (as he used to call them.) He having therefore dismissed them, took into his Service some of the *Grisons* and *Germans* in their stead. But this proved very disadvantageous to *France*; for they listed themselves under Pope *Julius* II. and did great Service against *France*. They attack'd the *French*, who were much more numerous, with such Fury, near *Novara*, that after a bloody
1513. Fight they not only routed them, but quite beat them out of *Italy*. Afterwards they fell into *Burgundy*, and besieged the City of *Dijon*, where the Duke of *Tremouille* was obliged to make a very dishonourable Agreement with them, and was glad to send them home with fair Promises of great Sums of Money; and if he had not stop'd their Progress, they would certainly have put *France* into the utmost Danger, the King of *England* being at the same time fall'n into *France* on the other side.
1515. The *Switzers* attack'd *Francis* I. in his Camp near *Marignano*; the Fight lasted two Days, and after a great deal of Bloodshed on both sides, the *Switzers* retired in good order. Upon which Consideration *Francis* I. in the Year next following gained their Friendship by a great Sum of Money; whose Example the succeeding Kings have followed ever since. Their ancient Reputation is much diminished of late Years, partly because

they

they are not altogether ſo furious now, partly becauſe other Nations have found out a way to bring their Infantry into a better condition. And beſides this, thoſe great Back-Swords which the *Swiſs* us'd to handle with ſo much dexterity by the extraordinary Strength of their Arms, are quite out of uſe in *Europe.*

The nature of the Soil.

§. 7. As to the Nature and Quality of the Countries, which are inhabited by the *Switzers,* they are very indifferent; for in the mountainous parts ſcarce any thing elſe but Paſture Grounds are to be met withal; and tho' the Valley and flat Country produces Corn and Wine in conſiderable Quantities, yet among ſo vaſt a number of Inhabitants there appears no great Plenty, for that foreign Commodities cannot be imported without great difficulty; and what is deficient in the native Soil, is not repaired by Traffick and Manufacturies. 'Tis therefore accounted a common Calamity among the *Switzers,* if once in ſome Years the Plague does not come among them, to rid them of ſo many ſuperfluous Mouths. Yet they enjoy this Benefit by the Situation of their Country, that, by reaſon of the high Mountains and narrow Paſſages, it is almoſt inacceſſible, eſpecially on the *Italian* ſide, and in the midſt of the Country; for ſome of the outward parts are of a very eaſie acceſs.

The Genius of this Nation.

§. 8. The *Switzers* pretend to be downright honeſt and true to their Word; and indeed, they are generally ſimple and plain-dealing, without any great Cunning or By-deſigns; but they are courageous, and ſoon provoked to Wrath. They are ſtedfaſt in their Reſolutions, from whence they don't eaſily recede; their Valour, Conſtancy, Tallneſs, and Strength of Body, has ſo recommended them to a great many Princes, that they chooſe their Guards among them; and the King of *France* maintains a conſiderable number of *Swiſs* Foot Soldiers. They are very forward to fight but not to undergo any other Hardſhip or Labour: They expect to have their Pay duly; if that fail, they return home as faſt as they can: from whence comes the Proverb, *Mo Money, no Swiſs.* They do not love to bear Hunger or Hardſhip in other Countries, becauſe they have enough of that at home: It is one of the Articles of Agreement made with *France,* That the Crown ſhall never have leſs than 6000 at a time in

Pay,

Pay, and that these are not to be separated, to the end that in case these Articles should not be perform'd, they may be in capacity to assist one another: They also never will be employ'd in any Sea-Service.

Their strength and weakness. §. 9. The main Strength of this Confederate Commonwealth consists in the Number of its Inhabitants; for the City of *Bern*, which has the greatest Territories, pretends alone to be able to send into the Field 100000 fighting Men. And it is not to be questioned, but that, if they had been ambitious of making Conquests, at that time when their Glory was at the highest pitch, or had not wanted Conduct, they might easily have brought under their Subjection the *Franche Compte*, and a great part of *Lombardy*; but the Reason why they did not aim at Conquests, was partly their Inclination, which did not prompt them to encroach upon their Neighbours, partly the Constitution of their Government, which seems to be unfit for great and sudden Enterprizes: for each Canton by it self considered is a Democracy, the highest Power being lodged in the *Guildes*; and it is certain, that such as are of little Understanding and Experience, are always very positive in their Opinions, and suspicious of all Mankind: And the whole Confederacy is altogether adapted for their common Defence, and for the maintaining of a firm Union betwixt themselves. The difference of Religion is also a main Obstacle among them, some of them being Roman Catholicks, but most Protestants, and both Parties great Zealots in their Religion: Wherefore it seems a hard task to make them all truly unanimous, except forc'd by the Necessity of a common Danger. And in this Democratical Government it is not to be supposed, that one Man can have sufficient Authority to sway the rest; and to stir them up to any great and sudden Enterprize. And this slowness of their publick Councils is such a check upon their natural Valour at home, that they can employ it no better than to sell it for a little Money to other Nations.

Their Neighbours. §. 10. This is the very Reason why the *Switzers* are the best Neighbours in the World; as being never to be feared, and always ready to assist you in case of Necessity, if you pay them for it. On the other hand they need not stand in great fear of their Neighbours. The

States

States of *Italy* are not in a capacity to do them any harm; and *Germany* is not willing to hurt them. If the House of *Austria* should attack them they are able to defend themselves; and besides this, they may in such a case be sure to be back'd by *France*. *France* alone seems to be their most dangerous Neighbour; and it has been the wonder of many, why the *Switzers* relie altogether upon the *French* Alliance and Promises, and do not in the least endeavour to secure their Country against the growing Power of *France*; and that in the last War they left the *Franche Compte* to the Mercy of the *French*, which opens the Passage into their Country, and enables the *French* to levy Souldiers on their Frontiers at pleasure. It seems therefore to be the present Interest of *Switzerland*, not to irritate the *French*, and nevertheless to take care that they do not make themselves Masters of their Frontier Places, *viz.* of *Geneva*, *Newburgh* on the Lake, the four Forest Towns, and *Constance*. They must likewise take care that they do not send too great a number of their Men into the *French* Service, whereby they may exhaust their own Stock of Souldiers; and that such as are sent into the *French* Service, may be engag'd not to be forgetful of their Duty to their native Country, so as to be ready to return home in case of Necessity. On the other hand, *France* seems to have no great reason to attack the *Switzers*, as long as they are quiet, and do not pretend to oppose the *French* Designs; it being evident, that if *France* had once obtained its aim, the *Switzers* would be obliged to submit themselves. And it seems at this time more advantageous for the *French* to make use of the *Switzers* as their Allies, than by conquering them, to make them refractary Subjects, who, by reason of their natural Stubbornness, must be bridled by strong Garrisons, which would scarce be maintained out of the Revenues of so poor a Country.

CHAP. VIII.

Of the GERMAN *Empire.*

§. 1. GErmany was anciently not one Commonwealth, but divided into a great many small States, independant of each other, most of them being Democracies; *The ancient condition of Germany.*

cies: And tho' some of them had their Kings, yet these had more Authority to Advise than to Command. These several States were at last united under the Government of the *Franks*: For the Kings of the *Merovingean* Family having undertaken several Expeditions into *Germany*, did reduce several of them under their Subjection: And *Charles the Great* reduced all *Germany* under his Jurisdiction, he being at the same time Master of *France*, *Italy*, *Rome*, and a part of *Spain*; all which Provinces he committed to the care of certain Governours who were called *Graves* or *Marc-Graves*. The *Saxons* retained more of their antient Liberty than the rest; wherefore the better to keep this then barbarous Nation in Obedience, he erected several Episcopal Sees in *Saxony*, hoping by the influence of the Christian Doctrine, to civilize this barbarous People. *Lewis* surnamed the *Pious*, Son of *Charles* the Great, had three Sons; *viz.* *Lotharius*, *Lewis*, and *Charles*, who divided the Empire of the *Franks* among them. In this Division *Lewis* got for his share all *Germany* as far as it extends on this side of the *Rhine*, and also some Countries on the other side of that River, by reason of the Vineyards, as 'tis said, which are on both sides. All which he was possess'd of as Sovereign, without being any way dependent on his elder Brother, much less the younger, who had *France* for his share: and at that time *Germany* was first made a Kingdom independent of any other.

Charles the Great. Lewis the Pious. Lewis King of Germany.

§. 2. *Carolomannus*, the Son of this *Lewis*, did, after the Death of *Charles the Bald*, who was King of *France*, and had born the Title of *Roman* Emperor, Conquer *Italy*; and took upon him the Imperial Dignity, notwithstanding that *Lewis*, Son of *Charles the Bald* and King of *France*, had, upon instigation of the Pope, assumed the same Title. After him succeeded his younger Brother *Carolus Crassus*, who maintained both the Kingdom of *Italy* and the Imperial Title. But the great Men in *Germany* having deposed the said *Charles*, they made *Arnulph*, the Son of the abovementioned *Carolomannus*, King of *Germany*; who went into *Italy*, and took upon him the Title of *Roman* Emperor, which he had contended for a good while with *Berengarius* Duke of *Frioul*, and *Guido* Duke of *Spoleto*. But after the Death of *Arnulph*, his Son *Lewis*, surnamed *the Child*, obtained the Crown of

Carolomannus. C. Crassus. Arnulph. 887. 894. Lewis the Child.

Germany,

Germany, under whose Reign the Affairs of *Germany* were in so ill a condition, that he had no leisure to look into those of *Italy*: For *Arnulph* had called to his Assistance the *Hungarians* against *Zwentepold* King of *Bohemia* and *Moravia*, that had rebell'd against him; and by their Aid reduc'd *Zwentepold* to Obedience: But the *Hungarians*, who were at that time a most barbarous Nation, having got a taste of *Germany*, made an Inroad into that Country, ravaging everywhere with an inhumane Cruelty. They also defeated *Lewis* near *Augsburgh*, obliging him to pay them a yearly Tribute; notwithstanding which, they ravag'd and plunder'd where-ever they came. This Overthrow was chiefly occasion'd by the King's tender Age and the Divisions of the Great Men among themselves, who aimed at nothing more than to establish their 911. own Authority. After the Death of *Lewis*, *Cunrad*, Duke Conrad. of *Franconia*, was elected King of *Germany*; under whose Reign, the potent Dukes of *Lorrain*, *Swabia*, *Bavaria*, and *Saxony*, did pretend to maintain the hereditary Possession and Soveraignty of their respective Countries; which *Cunrad* was not able to prevent: And because *Henry* Duke of *Saxony* was most potent, and *Cunrad* feared that at last he might quite withdraw himself from the *German* Empire, he upon his Death-bed advised the rest of the Princes of *Germany* to make him their King; which was done accordingly. And thus the Empire was transferred from the *Carolingian* Family to the *Saxons*. 919.

§. 3. *Henry*, surnamed the *Faulconer*, bridled the Fury Henry *the Faulconer*. of the *Hungarians*; for they having made a great Inroad into *Germany*, and demanded the Yearly Tribute from him, he sent them, by way of Ridicule, a Mangy Dog, and afterwards defeated them in a bloody Battle near *Merseburgh*, where he slew 80000 of them. Under the Reign of this King, the greatest part of the Cities which are situated on the sides of the *Rhine*, were either Built or else fortified with Walls. This *Henry* also did Conquer the *Serbes* and *Vandals*, a *Sarmatick* or *Sclavonian* Nation, possessed of a large Tract of Land in *Germany*, on the River *Elbe*, whom he drove out of *Misnia*, *Lusatia*, and the Marquisate of *Brandenburgh*. After he had re-establish'd the Affairs of *Germany*, he died in the Year 936. After him succeeded his Son *Otho*, surnam'd *The* Otho *the Great*. *Great*, who at first was engag'd in heavy Civil Wars a-

S 2 gainst

gainst several Princes, but especially against those who pretended to be of the Race of Charles the Great, and were extreamly dissatisfied that the Royal Dignity was transferred to the *Saxons*. He was also very fortunate in his Wars against the *Danes* and *Sclavonians*, as well as the *Hungarians*, who ventured to make another Incursion into *Germany*, and received a capital Overthrow near *Augsburgh*; since which time, they never have dared to shew themselves in *Germany*. In *Italy* there had been great Confusions for a long time, the Soveraignty having been usurped sometimes by one, sometimes by another, till at last *Otho* being call'd thither, possess'd himself both of the Kingdom of *Italy* and the Imperial Dignity, it being then agreed, That both the Imperial and Royal Dignity of *Italy* should be inseparably annexed, without any farther Election to the Royal Dignity of *Germany*, and that no Pope should be chosen without the Approbation of the King of the *Germans*. Upon this Resolve *Otho* was Crowned at *Rome*, tho' indeed this Conquest
962. has proved not very beneficial to *Germany*, the succeeding Popes having made it their Business to raise continual Disturbances, which 'twas not so easie to prevent, because these Places were not kept in awe by strong Castles or Garrisons. And for that Reason, as often as the Popes were pleased to raise new Commotions, the *Germans* were obliged to send great Armies thither, which continual Alarms consumed great Quantities of Men and Money: in lieu of which, their Kings had scarce any Revenues out of *Italy*, except that they had Free Quarters and Entertainment given them during their stay there.
974. Otho II. This *Otho* died in the Year 974, leaving for his Successor his Son *Otho* II, who at first met also with great Disturbances from some of the Princes of *Germany*. Afterwards *Lotharius* King of *France* would have made himself Master of *Lorrain*, and had very near surprised the Emperor at *Aix la Chappelle*. But *Otho* marched with an Army through *Champaigne*, to the very Gates of *Paris*; tho' in his return he received a considerable Loss At last a Peace was concluded at *Rheims*, by vertue of which *Lorrain* was left to the *Emperour*. He then undertook an Expedition into *Italy* against the *Greeks*, who had made themselves Masters of that Country. These he overthrew at first, but received afterwards a grand Defeat, because the *Romans* and those of *Benevento* immediately turned

their

their Backs; he himself fell into the Hands of the Enemy; but found means to make his Escape from them, and revenged himself against the *Romans* and *Beneventines* for their Infidelity. He died not long after, of Vexation. 983.
His Son, *Otho* III. employed a great part of his Reign in appeasing the Tumults raised in *Rome* by the Consul *Crescentius*, who aiming at the Soveraignty, was hanged for his pains by the Emperor's Order; but *Otho* was afterwards poisoned by the Widow of the said *Crescentius* with a Pair of Gloves. *Otho* having left no Children behind him, the Crown was conferred upon *Henry* II. surnamed 1001.
the Lame, Duke of *Bavaria*, who sprang from the *Saxon* Race; with whom *Egbert* Landgrave of *Hesse* did contend for the Crown, but lost his Life in the Quarrel. This Emperor was entangled in continual Troubles in *Italy*, and reduced *Boleslaus* King of *Poland*. In consideration of his being a great Benefactor to the Clergy, he was made a Saint after his Death.

§. 4. *Henry* II. having left no Children behind him, 1024.
the *German* Princes elected *Conrad Sali*, Duke of *Franconia*, Emperour in his room; which occasion'd great Jealousie in the *Saxons*, and bloody Wars in *Germany*. Conrad II.
This Emperour met with great Disturbances both in *Germany* and *Italy*, which were at last all composed. *Radolph* the last King of *Burgundy* and *Arles* dying without Issue, left him that Kingdom by his last Will, which he took Possession of, and united the same with *Germany*, having forced *Eudo* the Earl of *Champaigne*, who made a Pretension unto it, to resign his Title. He was also very 1034.
fortunate in his Wars against the *Poles* and *Sclavonians*; and died in the Year 1039. To him succeeded his Son Henry III.
Henry, surnamed *the Black*, who was continually alarm'd 1039.
by the *Hungarians* and the Pope's Intrigues, against whom he maintained the Imperial Dignity with great Bravery. He died in the Year 1056. His Son *Henry* IV.'s Reign Henry IV.
was very long, but withal very troublesome and unfortunate. 1056.
Among other Reasons, this may be counted one of the chiefest, that he being but six Years of Age when his Father died, was left to the Tuition of such as had no true care of his Education; and besides this, by selling the Church Benefices without having any regard to Deserts, had done considerable Mischief to the Empire. Wherefore *Henry* coming to his riper Years, and percei-

ving how the Ecclesiasticks had got all the best Possessions of the Empire into their Hands, he resolved to dispossess them again; whereby he drew upon himself the Hatred of the Clergy. The *Saxons* were also his great Enemies, because he had by building some Fortresses endeavour'd to restrain their Insolence; and tho' he often kept his Court in *Saxony*, yet he seldom preferr'd the *Saxons* to any Offices. Add to this, that most of the Princes were dissatisfied with him, because he rarely advised with them concerning the publick state of Affairs, but followed either the Advice of his Counsellors, who were most of them Men of mean Birth, or else his own Head. These, and some other Reasons, set the *Saxons* against him in an open Rebellion, with whom he waged long and bloody Wars, till he vanquished them at last. But Pope *Hildebrand* or *Gregory* VII. and his Successors raised a more dreadful Storm against him; for the Popes having long since been vexed to the heart, that they and the rest of the Clergy should be subject to the Emperour, *Hildebrand* thought to have now met with a fair Opportunity to set the Clergy at Liberty, at a time when the Emperour was entangled in a War with the *Saxons*, and hated by most Princes of the Empire. The Emperour had lived somewhat too free and loose in his younger Years, and the Church Benefices having been rather bestowed upon Favourites or such as paid well for them, than such as deserved them; this furnished the Pope with a specious Pretence to make a Decree, That it was not the Emperour's Right to bestow Bishopricks or other Church Benefices upon any Body, but that it belonged to the Pope. The Emperour was also summoned to appear at *Rome*, and to answer for his Misbehaviour; and in case of Failure, he was threatned with Excommunication. On the other hand, the Emperour having declared the Pope unworthy of his Office would have deposed him. So the Pope excommunicated the Emperour discharging all his Subjects from their Allegiance due to him; which proved of such Consequence in those Times, that all his Authority fell to the Ground at once among most of his Subjects, whereby he was reduced to the greatest Extremity. For the greatest part of the *German* Princes assembled at *Treves*, where they deposed *Henry*: which Sentence however, was so far mitigated afterwards, as to have it left to the Pope's Decision. *Henry* therefore

The Pope gives him great trouble.

accom-

accompanied by a few, was obliged to undertake a Journey in the midst of Winter into *Italy*; and being arrived at *Canusio*, was fain to stay three Days barefooted, in a coarse Woolen habit, in the outward Court, and in an humble Posture to beg the Pope's Absolution, which he at last granted him.

But the Emperour received no great Advantage by it; for the *Italians* were quite disgusted at this his indecent Submission and Weakness, which obliged the Emperour to make use of his former Authority to reduce them to Obedience. In the mean while the Princes of *Germany*, by instigation of the Pope, elected *Radolph* Duke of *Swabia* their King; but the *Bavarians*, *Franconians*, and the Countries next adjacent to the *Rhine*, remained in Obedience to the Emperour *Henry*. Thus a bloody War ensued, wherein *Radolph* and the *Saxons* were vanquished in two Battles, and in the third he lost his Right-hand and Life. Then *Henry* called together an Assembly of the Bishops; and having deposed *Hildebrand*, caused another to be chosen in his room; after which he took *Rome*, and banish'd *Hildebrand*. But the *Saxons* persisted in their Rebellion against the Emperour, who was again Excommunicated by the Pope, and having first set up *Herman* Duke of *Luxemburgh*, and after his Death *Ecbert* Marquiss of *Saxony* for their King, but to no purpose; they at last stirr'd up the Emperour's Son against the Father. Upon this, the Emperour raised a great Army, whom the Son met in a deceitful manner and begg'd his Pardon: Upon his Perswasions the Father having abandoned his Forces, and being upon his Journey to the Dyet at *Mayence*, accompanied by a few, this ancient Prince was made a Prisoner and Deposed. He died soon after in great misery, who in sixty six Battles which he had fought in his Life-time, generally obtained signal Victories.

1077. 1084. *His Son Rebels.* 1091.

§. 5. As soon at *Henry* V. was made Emperour, he followed his Father's Example in maintaining the Imperial Dignity; for, after settling the Affairs of *Germany*, he march'd with an Army towards *Rome*, to renew the ancient Right of the Emperors in nominating Bishops, and to be Crowned there. The Pope *Paschal* II. having got notice of the Emperour's Design, raised a great Tumult at *Rome*, where the Emperor was so closely beset, that he was fain to fight in Person for his Safety: But the Em- Henry V.

peror having got the upper hand, made the Pope a Prisoner, and forced him to give his Consent to his Demands: And tho' this their Agreement was confirm'd by solemn Oaths and Execrations, yet no sooner had the Emperour turn'd his Back, but the Pope, having declared the Agreement void, stirr'd up the *Saxons* and the Bishops in *Germany*, against the Emperour. With these *Henry* was engag'd in a very tedious War; and perceiving at last that there was no other way left to compose these Differences, he granted the Pope's Demands, by renouncing his
1122. Right to nominate Bishops, at the Dyet held at *Worms*: which Resignation, as it greatly diminish'd the Emperour's Authority, so on the other hand it strengthened the Power of the Pope. This Emperour died without Issue.
1125. Lotharius *the* Saxon. To him succeeded *Lotharius* Duke of *Savoy*, who had for a Rival in the Empire *Conrad* Duke of *Franconia*, whom he quickly obliged to beg Pardon, and sue for Peace. This Emperor having twice undertaken an Expedition into *Italy*, did with great glory restore Tranquility to that Country: and because he used to flatter the Pope, he was in great esteem among the Clergy. He died in the
Conrad III. Year 1138. After his Death *Conrad* III. obtained the Imperial Dignity, who was opposed by *Henry* Duke of *Saxony* and *Bavaria*, and his Brother *Wulff*, which occasioned bloody Wars against him. But Peace being restored among them, he took an Expedition into the Holy Land, where he underwent great Calamities; for, though he fought his way through the *Saracens*, and arriv'd safely at *Jerusalem*, yet after he had lost the greatest part of his Army, without doing any thing of moment, he was fain to return home. But whilst he was busie in making Preparations for another Expedition into *Italy*, he died in the Year 1152.

Frederick I. §. 6. *Frederick* I. succeeded him, who by the *Italians* was surnamed *Barbarossa*, Duke of *Swabia*, and who immediately, at the beginning of his Reign, having settled the Affairs of *Germany*, reduced *Italy* under his Obedience; which however was not of long continuance: for the *Milanese* quickly rebell'd, but were severely punish'd, their City being laid level with the Ground. He was also in continual Broils with the Pope, against whom and his Associates, he obtained several Victories; yet being at last tired out with so many Wars, he made Peace with

him,

him, especially since his Son *Otho* had been taken Prisoner by the *Venetians*. At the concluding of this Peace, 'tis said that Pope *Alexander* III. did set his Foot upon the Emperour's Neck, which by a great many is taken for a Fable. This Emperour was the last who maintained the Authority of the *German* Emperours in *Italy*. Last of all, he undertook an Expedition into the *Holy Land* against *Saladin* the Sultan of *Egypt*, who had taken the City of *Jerusalem*: He beat the *Saracens* several times, but endeavouring to pass over a River in *Cicilia* on Horseback, or as some will have it, intending to wash himself in the River, he was drowned. And tho his Son *Frederick*, after 1189. his Father's Death, did take a great many Cities in *Syria*, yet the whole Expedition had a very bad issue, the greatest part of the Army, together with Duke *Frederick* himself, being consumed by the Plague or Famine. *Frederick* was succeeded by his Son *Henry* VI. in the Empire, Henry VI. who, by Marrying *Constantia*, got the Kingdoms of *Sicily*, *Calabria*, and *Apulia*. This Emperour went to *Rome* to receive the Crown from Pope *Celestine*; upon which occasion the Pope sitting in his Chair, and the Emperour on his Knees, put first the Crown upon his Head, but immediately struck the same off again with his Foot, intimating thereby, as if it was in the Power of the Popes to give and to take away the Imperial Crown. He died in the Year 1198, having just then made great Preparations for an Expedition into the Holy Land, and sent his Army before, himself being ready to follow.

§. 7. After the Death of *Henry* VI. the *Germans* were Philip. miserably divided among themselves; for *Frederick* II. his Son, being then but five Years old, his Uncle *Philip* pretended to have the Tuition of his Nephew, and the Administration of the Empire, according to the last Will of the deceas'd Emperour: but this being oppos'd by the Pope, he perswaded some of the Princes to elect *Otho* Duke of *Saxony*. *Germany* was thus miserably torn in pieces, most siding with *Philip*, the rest with *Otho*. After a long War, an Agreement was made betwixt them, that *Otho* should marry the Daughter of *Philip*, but lay down the Royal Title till the Death of *Philip*, when the same was to be restored to him. Not long after, *Philip* was murthered at *Bamberg* by *Otho* the Palatin of *Wittelbach*. 1208. After his Death *Otho* obtained the Imperial Dignity, and Otho VI.

having been Crowned at *Rome*, he resolvee to re-unite such Places as were unjustly possess'd by the Popes to the Empire; which so exasperated the Pope, that he Excommunicated him, Exhorting the Princes to elect another Emperour. Most of them were for *Frederick* II. Son of *Henry* VI. which made *Otho* to hasten into *Germany*; but having in vain endeavour'd to maintain himself in the Empire, he was forc'd to render the Imperial Crown to *Frederick* II King of *Sicily* and *Naples*, and Duke of *Suabia*; who, after he had bestowed a considerable time in settling the Affairs of *Germany*, went into *Italy*, where he was Crowned by the Pope. In the Year 1228 he undertook an Expedition into the Holy Land, and retook *Jerusalem* from the *Saracens*. He was continually alarm'd by the Intrigues of the Popes, against whom he bravely maintained his Right. This occasioned several Excommunications to be thundred out against him by the Popes which raised great Disturbances. From hence rose the two famous Factions in *Italy*, whereof those who sided with the Pope, called themselves *Guelfs*, but those who were for the Emperour *Gibellins*; which two Factions, for a considerable time after, occasioned great Commotions in *Italy*: And tho' *Frederick* behav'd himself bravely against the Pope and his Associates, yet the Pope's Excommunication had such influence in that Age, that, after the Pope had solemnly deposed him in the Council held at *Lyons*, some Princes of *Germany* chose *Henry*, Landgrave
1245. of *Thuringia*, their King, who was commonly call'd the King of the Priests; but he dying in the Year next following, some princes declared *William* Earl of *Holland* their King; who was not able to establish himself as being opposed by *Conrad* Son of *Frederick* II. who was appointed to succeed his Father in the Empire. In the mean time his Father had been very unsuccesful in *Italy*, who at last died in the Year 1250. *Conrad* having left *Germany*, retired into his Hereditary Kingdoms of *Naples* and *Sicily*, where he died. *William* Earl of *Holland* was
1256. slain in a Battle against the *Frieslanders*, in the Year 1256.

Frederick II.

The Guelfs and Gibellins.

§. 8. With the Death of *Frederick* II. the Authority of the *German* Emperours in *Italy* was quite extinguish'd: And that it might not be revived again, the Pope gave the Kingdom of *Naples* to *Charles* Duke of *Anjou*, who, by the Instigation of the Pope, caused the young *Conra-*

A long Interregnum.

din

din (who being the Son of *Conrad*, was come to recover his Hereditary Kingdom, and taken Prisoner in a Battle fought betwixt them) to be executed by the hands of the Hangman; with whom was extinguish'd the Race of the Dukes of *Suabia*. In the mean time there were great Divisions among the *German* Princes, concerning the Election of a new Emperour; some of them had chosen *Richard* Duke of *Cornwal*, Son of *John* King of *England*, and the rest were for *Alfonsus* X. King of *Castile*; both were elected in the Year 1257. *Richard* came on his Journey as far as the *Rhine*, to take Possession of the Empire; but, for want of Money, was forc'd to return home again: And *Alfonsus* came not within sight of *Germany*. Then there was a long Vacancy of the Throne in *Germany*; during which time there was nothing to be seen but Confusion, every body pretending to be Master. These Civil Disorders were of the worse consequence, because that about the same time the three great Families of the Dukes of *Suabia*, the Marquesses of *Austria*, and Landgraves of *Thuringia* being extinct, a great many aspired to possess themselves of these Countries. To be short, the longest Sword was then the best Title, and he that could master another kept him under Subjection; and robbing and plundering was an allow'd Exercise at that time. Against these outrageous Proceedings several of the Cities upon the *Rhine* enter'd into a Confederacy, with whom a great many other Princes afterwards joining their Forces, they demolished the Strong holds of these Robbers, and clear'd the Highways. 1265.

Rodolph *Earl of* Habsburg. 1273.

§. 9. At last *Rodolph* Earl of *Habsburgh* and Landgrave of *Alsace* (from whom are descended the present Arch-dukes of *Austria*) was unanimously chosen Emperour; who, the better to establish himself in the Throne, marry'd his three Daughters, to three of the great Princes of *Germany*, *viz.* to *Lewis* Palatin of the *Rhine*, to *Albert* Duke of *Saxony*, and to *Otho* Marquess of *Brandenburgh*. After the Death of *Frederick* Marquess of *Austria*, who had his Head cut off at *Naples*, together with *Cunradin*, *Ottocar* the King of *Bohemia* had possess'd himself of *Austria*, *Stiria*, *Carinthia*, the *Windishmarck*, and *Portenau*. But *Rodolph*, who thought that his Family had the better Title, having retaken these Countries from *Ottocar*, gave them in Fief to his Son *Albert*; to the second Son, whose Name

Name was *Rodolph*, he gave the Dukedom of *Suabia*: and afterwards the Grandson of *Albert* brought in *Tyrol*. Thus *Rodolph* did, by obtaining the Imperial Dignity, raise his House from a moderate State to great Power and vast Riches. But tho' he was often invited to come into *Italy*, yet he could never be perswaded to it, alledging that old and notorious Saying of the Fox, *Quia me vestigia terrent*, because the Footsteps deter me: Nay, he declar'd a great many Cities there Free for Sums of Money; by which the Kingdom of *Italy*, being thus torn into a great many pieces, was quite lost; but *Germany* he took into his particular Care, and destroy'd a great many Castles there which serv'd for a Retreat for Robbers. He was the first that introduc'd the Use of the *German* Tongue in all Publick Courts and Private Transactions, whereas formerly the *Latin* Tongue had been made use of in the like cases. He died in the Year 1291.

Adolph. His Son *Albert* did lay Claim to the Empire; but by the Interest of the Archbishop of *Mayence*, *Adolph* Earl of *Nassau*, who was his Kinsman, was chosen Emperour: the Archbishop being in hopes to have, under him, the supreme Management of the Affairs; but *Adolph* not being willing to depend on the Archbishop, he conceived a Hatred against him. Some did think it unbecoming the Grandeur of the Emperour, that he engaged in a League with *England* against *France* for a Sum of Money paid to him by the *English*; but this might admit of a very good Excuse, since besides this, the *English* had promis'd the Emperor to assist him in the Recovery of the Kingdom of *Arles*, a great part of which *France* had, during the Troubles in *Germany*, taken into its Possession. On the other hand *France* sided with *Albert*; and upon their advancing near the *Rhine*, the Archbishop of *Mayence* assembled some of the Electors, who being dissatisfied with *Adolph*, depos'd him, and chose *Albert* Emperour in his stead. A bloody Battle was fought betwixt these two near *Spires*, wherein *Adolph* being slain, the Imperial Crown remain'd to *Albert*: But because he aim'd at nothing more than to enrich himself, his Reign was both very unglorious and unfortunate. His Covetousness was at last the occasion of his Death; for his Nephew *John* Duke of *Suabia*, whom he had dispossess'd of his Country,

Albert I.

1308. murder'd him near *Rhinefield*.

§. 10. After his Death, *Philip* King of *France* endeavour'd to obtain the Imperial Crown, but was prevented by the Electors; who, upon the Persuasion of the Pope, chose *Henry* VII. Earl of *Luxemburgh*. This Emperour, after he had settled *Germany*, undertook a Journey into *Italy*, with a Resolution to suppress the Civil Commotions there, and to re-establish the Imperial Authority. The Beginning of this Undertaking proved so prosperous, that every body hoped for great Success from it. But in the midst of this Prosperity he was murther'd by a Monk, who had given him a poison'd Host; he having been hired by the *Florentines*, the Emperour's Enemies to commit this Fact.

Henry VII.

Poisoned by a Monk. 1313.

The Electors were again divided in the Election of a new Emperour, some having given their Votes for *Lewis* Duke of *Bavaria*, the rest for *Frederick* Duke of *Austria*. The first was Crown'd at *Aix la Chappelle*, the latter at *Bonn*. These two carried on a War against each other for the Imperial Crown, during the space of nine Years, to the great Detriment of the whole Empire; At last *Frederick* being made a Prisoner in a Battle fought in the Year 1323, *Lewis* became sole Master of the Empire, and restored its Tranquillity. But he afterwards went into *Italy*, to back the *Gibellines*, who were of his side; and though at first he was very prosperous, yet could he not settle his Affairs to any purpose, because the Pope had Excommunicated him. Wherefore also the Pope's Associates in *Germany*, were always too hard for him; and at last, by the Persuasions of the Pope, stirr'd up the Electors against him, who chose *Charles* IV. Marquess of *Moravia*, Son of *John* King of *Bohemia*, Emperour in his stead; who, as long as *Lewis* liv'd, was not much taken notice of. He died in the Year 1347. It is observed, that the preceeding Emperours used generally to make their Progress through the Empire, and to maintain their Court out of the Revenues belonging to it. But this *Lewis* IV. was the first who kept his constant Court in his Hereditary Country, and maintained it out of his own Revenue; whose Example the succeeding Emperours follow'd, the Revenues belonging to the Empire having been by degrees extreamly diminish'd.

Lewis *the* Bavarian.

Excommunicated by the Pope.

§. 11. After the Death of *Lewis*, there were some who would have made void the former Election of *Charles*, and

Charles IV.

and had chosen in his stead *Edward* King of *England*, who did not think fit to accept of the Imperial Dignity. The same was also refused by *Frederick* Marquiss of *Misnia*: At last *Gunther* Earl of *Swartsburgh* was elected; whom *Charles* caused to be poison'd, and by his Liberality establish'd himself in the Empire. During his Reign he gave away a considerable part of the Dependencies of the Empire; and among the rest, he granted to *France* the perpetual Vicarship of the Kingdom of *Arles*; and in *Italy* he sold what he could to the fairest Bidder: But he was not so careless of his Kingdom of *Bohemia*, unto which he annex'd, among other Countries that of *Silesia*. He was a great Favourer of the Cities which he dignified with new Priviledges, that they might the better be able to maintain themselves against the Power of the Princes. The best thing that ever he did, was, that he caused first to be compiled the *Golden Bull*, wherein were set down the Rules to be observed in the Elections of the ensuing Emperours and so Divisions among the Electors were prevented for the future. He died in the Year 1378, having not long before, by great Presents made to the Electors prevailed with them to chuse his Son *Wenceslaus* King of the *Romans*: But he being very brutish and careless of the Affairs of the Empire, was deposed by the Electors, which he little regarded, but retired into his Hereditary Kingdom of *Bohemia*, where he lived for a considerable time. After *Wenceslaus* was deposed, *Jodocus* Marquess of *Moravia*, was chosen Emperour; but he happening to die, before he could take Possession of the Empire, *Frederick* Duke of *Brunswick* was elected in his stead, who in his Journey to *Francfort* was by instigation of the Archbishop of *Mayence*, murder'd by the Earl of *Waldeck*. At last *Rupert*, Palatin of the *Rhine*, was chosen Emperour, who Reigned with great Applause in *Germany*; but his Expedition into *Italy* proved fruitless. He died in the Year 1410.

The Golden Bull.

Wenceslaus. 1400.

Frederick of Brunswick.

Rupert.

Sigismund.

§. 12. After the Death of *Rupert Sigismund* King of *Hungary*, Brother to *Wenceslaus*, was made Emperour; a Prince endowed with great Qualities, but very unfortunate in his Wars, having, before he obtained the Imperial Crown, received a great Defeat from the *Turks* near *Nigeboli*; which was occasioned by the precipitant Heat and Forwardness of the *French* Auxiliaries. He caused

caused *John Huss*, notwithstanding the safe Conduct granted him, to be burnt at the Council of *Constance*; whose Death the *Hussites* did revenge with great fury upon *Bohemia* and *Germany*; insomuch that this War took up the greatest part of his Reign. He died in the Year 1437. After him succeeded his Son-in-law *Albert* II. Duke of *Austria*, and King of *Hungary* and *Bohemia*, who did not reign much above a Year. He died in the Year 1439, whilst he was very busie in making Preparations against the *Turks*. To him succeeded his Kinsman *Frederick* III. Duke of *Austria*; since which time all the succeeding Emperours have been of this House. During his Reign, several Disturbances were raised in *Germany*, which were neglected by the Emperour. He also had some Differences with *Ladislaus*, Son of *Albert* II. concerning *Austria*, and was attack'd by *Matthias Hunniades* King of *Hungary*; which War he prosecuted with more Patience than Vigour. He died in the Year 1493. To him succeeded his Son *Maximilian* I. who had the good fortune, by his Marriage with *Mary* the Daughter of *Charles* the *Hardy*, Duke of *Burgundy*, to annex the *Netherlands* to the House of *Austria*. As he was very fickle in his Undertakings, so the Success was generally answerably to it, and his Wars with the *Switzers*, and the *Venetians*, had but a very indifferent end: The chiefest thing of moment done by him is, that whereas formerly all Differences in *Germany* were decided by the Sword, he re-establish'd the Peace of the Empire. He died in the Year 1519.

Albert II. Frederick III. Maximilian I.

§. 13. To him succeeded his Grandson *Charles* V. King of *Spain*, and Sovereign of the *Netherlands*; under whose Reign the face of Affairs in *Germany* was remarkably changed; which was occasioned by the Religious Differences set on foot about that time: For the Pope had caused Indulgences to be sold here in so scandalous a manner, that the wiser sort began to be asham'd of it. Wherefore *Martin Luther*, Doctor of Divinity and Professor in the University of *Wittenbergh*, had held a publick Disputation against it; who being opposed by others, all the neighbouring Countries were alarm'd at it. *Luther* at first did submit himself to the Decision of the Pope; but finding that he favour'd the indulgent Merchants, and that he was condemn'd by him, he appealed to a free General Council, and then began to go farther, to examine the

Charles V. 1517. *The Reformation.*

the Pope's Authority; and having laid open some Errors and Abuses, which were crept in among them, his Doctrine was so approved of by some of the Princes and free Imperial Cities, that they began to banish the Priests and Monks out of several Places, and to reduce their Revenues. And though the Emperour did declare *Luther*,
1521. at the Dyet of *Worms*, an Out-Law, and endeavour'd by several Proclamations to put a stop to these Proceedings and Innovations: nevertheless, the Emperour being then engag'd in a War with *France*, and therefore not in a capacity to apply himself in good earnest to the suppressing of this Division, *Luther*'s Party grew daily stronger.

Perhaps he was afterwards not very sorry, to see the Wound encrease, that he might make the better benefit
1529. of the Cure. A Proclamation being published at the Dyet of *Spiers*, which was in no ways agreeable to the *Lutheran* Princes, they protested against the same; from whence they are called Protestants. In the Year next following they delivered a Confession of their Faith to the

The Rise of the Name of Protestants.

1530. Emperour at *Augsburgh*, and entred into a defensive Alliance at *Smalkald*; which League was renewed in the Year 1535, when a great many Princes and free Imperial Cities were receiv'd into it. This League made at *Smalkald* was a great eye-sore to the Emperour, who used all means to dissolve the same: But the Protestants, who now began to trust to their own Strength, standing by one another, the Hostilities began on both sides, and the

The League at Smalkald.

1546. Protestants did bring into the Field an Army of 100000 Men, under the Conduct of *John Frederick* Elector of *Saxony*, and *Philip* Landgrave of *Hesse*. If they had fall'n immediately upon the Emperour, whose Forces were then not joined, they might in all probability, have worsted him; but having lost the first opportunity, the Emperour so strengthen'd himself, that he forced the Protestants to quit the Field, and to disband their Forces. He also caused a Diversion to be given the Elector at home by his Kinsman *Maurice*; which had such Influence upon the free Imperial Cities, that they were obliged to submit themselves, and pay considerable Fines. In the Year next following the Emperour fell into *Saxony*, and having defeated the Elector near *Muhlberg*, and took him Prisoner, pronounced Sentence of Death against him; which, however, he changed to Imprisonment. *Philip* Landgrave of *Hesse* having submitted himself, was, contrary

trary to Agreement made a Prisoner; whereby the Protestant Religion in *Germany* was reduc'd to great Extremity. The Electorate of *Saxony* was given to *Maurice* Duke of *Saxony*, who at last being resolved not to permit any longer, that both the Religion and Liberty should be quite destroy'd, nor that his Wife's Father the Landgrave of *Hesse*, who upon his Parole had surrender'd himself to the Emperor should be detained a Prisoner, fell so suddenly with his Forces upon the Emperour that he was very near having surpized his Person at *Inspruck*. *Henry* II. King of *France*, having also made an Inroad on the other side of *Germany*, surprized *Metz*, *Toul*, and *Verdun*. Thereupon, King *Ferdinand* the Emperour's Brother interposing his Authority, a Peace was concluded at *Passau*, where the free Exercise of Religion was secured to the Protestants, till Matters could be better settled at the next ensuing Dyet. The Landgrave was released; as likewise *John Frederick* the Elector, who had been dismissed out of Prison a little before by the Emperour. At last the Religious Peace in *Germany* was establish'd at the Dyet at *Augsburgh*, where it was provided, that neither Party should annoy one another under the pretext of Religion, and that such of the Church-Lands and Revenues as the Protestants had been possess'd of before the Peace concluded at *Passau*, should remain in their possession. The Boors also in *Germany* raised a most dangerous Rebellion under the Reign of *Charles* V. of whom there were kill'd above 100000. In the Year 1529 the City of *Vienna* was besieg'd by *Solyman* the *Turkish* Emperor, but to no purpose, he being oblig'd to raise the Siege, not without considerable Loss: And afterwards the *Turks*, who were marching with a great Army into *Austria*, were beaten back again. In the Year 1534 the Anabaptists were for erecting a new Kingdom in *Munster* in *Westphalia*, under the Conduct of *John*, a Taylor of *Leyden*, and one *Knipperdolling*; who receiv'd the just reward of their Madness. At last this great Prince *Charles* V. surrender'd the Imperial Dignity to his Brother *Ferdinand* I. King of *Hungary* and *Bohemia*, who united these two Kingdoms to the House of *Austria*, he having married *Anna* Sister of *Lewis* King of *Hungary* and *Bohemia*, who was slain in the Battle fought against the *Turks* near *Mohatz*. He Reigned very peaceably in *Germany*, and died in the Year 1564. He was succeeded by his

[Margin notes: 1550. — *A Peace concluded.* — 1525. — 1555. — *An Insurrection of the Boors.* — 1525. — 1532. — *He resigns to* Ferdinand I.]

Maximilian II. Son *Maximilian* II. who also Reign'd in Peace, except that a Tumult happen'd at that time in *Germany*, raised by one *William Grumpach* and his Associates; who having first murther'd *Melchior Lobel* the Archbishop of *Wurtsburgh*, had plunder'd that City; and at the same time endeavour'd to stir up the Nobility, and to raise
1567. Disturbances in other places. This Man having been declar'd an Outlaw was protected by *John Frederick* Duke of *Saxony*, who paid dearly for it, *Gotha*, one of his best Strong holds, being demolish'd and he himself taken Prisoner. *Maximilian* died in the Year 1576. To
Rodolph II. him succeeded his Son *Rodolph* II. who Reigned also very peaceably in *Germany*, except that the *Hungarian* Wars did now and then keep the *Germans* a little in exercise; that in the Year 1609 the Right of Succession in the Country of *Juliers* was brought in question; and that his Brother *Matthias*, Archduke of *Austria*, grew impatient to possess his Brother's Inheritance before his
1612. Death. To him *Rodolphus* surrender'd *Hungary* and *Bohemia*, and at his Death left him his other Countries, and the Imperial Crown.

Matthias. §. 14. Under the Reign of *Matthias*, the Ferment did so encrease by degrees in *Germany*, that towards his latter days they caused violent Convulsions. The Origin of this War, which lasted thirty Years, was this: In the Religious Peace formerly concluded at *Passau*, two Parties were only included, *viz.* the *Roman Catholicks*
Origin of the German Wars. and those who adhered to the *Augsburgh* Confession, the free exercise of Religion being forbidden to all others. But some of the States of the Empire, among whom the chiefest were the Elector Palatine and the Landgrave of *Hesse Cassel*, having since that time receiv'd the Reform'd Religion commonly call'd the *Calvinist*, the Roman Catholicks were against their enjoying the benefit of the Religious Peace. These, on the other hand, alledged, that they did belong, as well as the rest to the *Augsburgh* Confession, and that the whole Difference did only consist in some few Heads: But the rest of the Protestants who strictly adher'd to the Words of the *Augsburgh* Confession were not for receiving them into the same Communion, tho' it was their Opinion, that they ought not to be prosecuted for the Differences that were betwixt them. But afterwards these controverted Articles were,

were, by the Heat of the Priests explain'd in so different a manner that the Name of *Calvinist* became as odious to some Protestants as, that of a *Roman Catholick*. The *Roman Catholicks* taking hold of this Opportunity, caress'd the old Protestants. especially those in the Electorate of *Saxony*, unto whom they represented the *Calvinists* as a Generation equally destructive to both Parties; whereby they hop'd to disjoyn the *Calvinists* from the rest, and after they had destroy'd them, to make the easier work with the rest of the Protestants. Those therefore of the Reformed Religion entered into a Confederacy for their common Security; into which they receiv'd a great many other Protestant Princes, and so it was call'd the *Evangelical Union*. In opposition to this Confederacy, the *Roman Catholicks* made an Alliance among themselves, which they call'd the *Catholick League*, whose Head was the Duke of *Bavaria*, a constant Rival of the Elector Palatin. There happened also some other Matters which had exasperated both Parties, *viz*. That the Protestants had reduced a great many Church Revenues, after the Peace at *Passau*; that the Cities of *Aix la Chapelle* and *Donawert* had been very hardly dealt with; and several things which were manifest Proofs of the Animosities of both Parties against one another.

The Evangelical Union.

§. 15. Both Parties being thus exasperated and prepared for War, did administer fuel to that Flame which quickly after broke out in the Kingdom of *Bohemia*. The *Bohemians* pretended, that the Emperour *Matthias* had taken from them their Privileges, and having raised a Tumult, threw three Persons of Quality, who spoke in the Emperour's behalf, out of the Castle Windows; and immediately after entered with an Army into *Austria*. In the mean while *Matthias* died, whose Nephew *Ferdinand* (who also succeded him in the Empire) the *Bohemians* had before his Death received for their King; but now, under pretence that he had broken the Contract made betwixt him and the Estates, they renounc'd *Ferdinand*, and offer'd the Crown to *Frederick* Elector Palatine. This young Prince was perswaded by some of his Friends who were of an unsettled Spirit, and not diving deep enough into a business of such consequence, to accept of this Offer, before he had laid a Foundation for such an Undertaking: For the *Bohemians* themselves were fickle and unfaithful;

The Bohemian Tumults.

1618.

Ferdinand I.

The Crown of Bohemia offer'd to the Elector Palatin.

Bethlem-Gabor, Prince of *Transilvania*, was inconstant; *England* was not for meddling in the matter, *Holland* was very backward in giving Assistance. The Union which they chiefly rely'd upon, was a Body with a great many Heads, without Vigour, or any constant Resolution. Besides, *France* endeavour'd to dissolve that League, as being not willing that the Elector Palatine and the rest of the Reformed Religion should grow too potent; for fear, that in time they might afford their Assistance to the *Huguenots*, whose Destruction was then in agitation at the *French* Court. In the Beginning of this War the Affairs of *Ferdinand* look'd with an ill Aspect, because *Bethlem Gabor*, Prince of *Transilvania*, fell into *Hungary*, in hopes to become Master of that Kingdom; and there were also great Discontents among his Subjects in *Austria*: But he having recover'd himself by the Alliance made with the Duke of *Bavaria*, the Elector Palatine, in that unfortunate Battle fought on the White-Hill near *Prague*, lost at once all his former Advantages. For *Ferdinand* soon after reduc'd *Bohemia*, *Moravia*, and *Silesia*, to Obedience, *Spinola* made an Inroad into the *Lower Palatinate*, which was deserted by the Forces of the League. The Duke of *Bavaria* got the *Upper Palatinate*, and the Electoral Dignity. The Elector of *Saxony*, who had been very instrumental in reducing *Silesia*, had for his Reward *Lusatia*, in Fief of the Kingdom of *Bohemia*.

The ill Success of the Elector Palatine.

1620.

The War spread in Germany.

In the mean time the Marquis of *Durlach*, *Christian* Duke of *Brunswick*, the Earl of *Mansfield*, and some others who were of the Elector Palatine's Party, march'd with their Armies up and down the Country; and the Emperour under pretence of pursuing them, sent his Forces into all parts of the Empire. Against these the Circle of the *Lower Saxony* arm'd it self, having made *Christian* IV. King of *Denmark* General of that Circle: But he having receiv'd a great Overthrow near *Kings Lutter*, from *Tilly* the Imperial General, the Emperour over-run all the *Lower Saxony*; and having oblig'd King *Christian* to make Peace with him at *Lubeck*, he began to get footing near the Coast of the *Baltick*.

1626.

1629.

The Proclamation concerning Church-Lands.

§. 16. The Emperour was so elated with Success, that he did not question but for the future to be absolute in *Germany*; and with that view publish'd a Proclamation, enjoyning the *Protestants* to restore to the *Catholicks* all

such

such Church-Lands or Revenues as were taken from them since the Peace made at *Passau*. Under this Pretence he hop'd quickly to subdue the rest of the Protestant Princes, not questioning but, after that, the Catholick Estates would easily be forc'd to submit themselves to his pleasure. 1629.

The Protestants, 'tis true, enter'd into a Defensive Alliance at *Leipsick*, but without any great Prospect of Success, if *Gustavus Adolphus* King of *Sweden* had not come to their assistance. This King was induc'd to enter *Germany*, partly because the Preservation of his own State seem'd to depend on the Emperour's not getting firm footing on the *Baltick*, partly because several of the *German* Princes had crav'd his Assistance, partly also because the Emperour had assisted the *Poles* against him in *Prussia*, and he stood in a good correspondence with *France* and *Holland*, who were very jealous of the Greatness of the House of *Austria*. This King came with an Army into *Germany*, and drove the Imperial Forces out of *Pomerania* and the neighbouring Countries. In the mean time the Imperial General *Tilly* had quite destroy'd the City of *Magdebourgh*, and was upon his March against the Elector of *Saxony*. But King *Gustavus* having join'd his Forces with those of the Elector of *Saxony*, defeated *Tilly* in that memorable Battle near *Leipsick*; where the Emperour lost all his twelve Years Hopes. From thence, he marched on to the *Rhine*, where he made almost miraculous Progresses; but in regard the Elector of *Saxony* had not so vigorously attack'd the Hereditary Countries of the Emperour, the Emperor had thereby leisure given him to raise another Army, under the Conduct of *Wallenstein*, against whom the King lay encamp'd for a considerable time near *Nurenburg*: and afterwards, in the Battle of *Lutzen*, tho' his Army gain'd the Victory, himself lost his Life.

Gustavus Adolphus. 1630. 1632. Gustavus's *Death.*

After his Death, his Generals and Confederates carry'd on the War, under the Conduct of *Axel Oxenstern*, Chancellour of *Sweden*, with indifferent good Success; but having receiv'd an entire Defeat in the Battle near *Norlingen*, they lost all the Fruit of so many Victories. The Elector of *Saxony* having also concluded a Peace with the Emperour at *Prague*, which was extreamly disliked by the Protestant Party, the Emperour was now again in hopes to drive the *Swedes* by force out of *Germany*;

The War continued. 1634. 1635.

many: But by the Valour and Conduct of their Generals, the *Swedish* Affairs began to look with a better face; for they carry'd the War again into the very Hereditary Countries of the Emperour. At last all Parties began to incline to a Peace; for the Emperour and the Princes of *Germany* were tired out with the War; *France* began to be divided at home by Commotions; *Holland* had made a separate Peace with *Spain*; and the *Swedes* feared that the *Germans*, of whom was compos'd the greatest part of their Army, might at last grow weary of being instrumental in the Ruin of their native Country, or that one unfortunate Blow might chance to rob them of the Fruits of their former Victories; a Peace was therefore concluded at *Osnabrug* with *Sweden*, and at *Munster* with *France*; by virtue of which the *Swedes* got a part of *Pomerania*, *Bremen*, and *Wismar*, and five Millions of Crowns, for the Payment of their Forces. *France* kept *Brisac*, *Suntgaw*, a part of *Alsace* and *Philipsbourgh*. By this Peace the Authority of the States of *Germany* and the Protestant Religion were established at once; and the Emperour's Power confin'd within such Bounds, that he could not easily hereafter attempt any thing against either of them; especially since both *Sweden* and *France* had a free Passage left them, from whence they might easily oppose him if he design'd to transgress these Limits. During this War dy'd *Ferdinand* II. to whom succeeded his Son *Ferdinand* III. who died in the Year 1657. In whose stead was, in the Year next following, elected Emperour his Son *Leopold*.

Peace of Osnabrug *and* Munster.

1648.

1637.

Ferdinand *the Third*.

Leopold.

1659. §. 19. After the *Westphalian* Peace *Germany* remained in Peace for a considerable time, except that the Emperour and Elector of *Brandenburgh* (at which time the *Swedes* were engag'd in a War with *Denmark*) fell into *Pomerania*; but these Differences were compos'd by the Peace made at *Oliva*. In the Year 1663 a War broke out with the *Turks*; in which the *Turks* took *Newheusel*, but were several times soundly beaten, especially near *St. Godhard*. Some are of opinion, that if the Emperour had at that time vigorously pursued his Victory, he might have beaten them out of *Hungary*, since the *Turks* were put into a great Consternation by the *Persians*, and some rebellious Bassa's, and the *Venetians* did so vigorously push on the Siege of *Candia*: But the Emperour

Peace of Oliva.

War with the Turks.

was

was forward in making Peace with them, because, as it is supposed, he was jealous of *France*. In the Year 1672, Germany was again entangled in a War with *France*, which was occasion'd by the great Progresses of the *French* against the *Hollanders*, who were relieved by the Emperour and the Elector of *Brandenburgh*: For tho' in the Year before the Emperour had made an Alliance with *France*, whereby he had promised not to meddle in the War in case *France* should attack one of the Triple Alliance: nevertheless he sent his Forces towards the *Rhine*, under pretence that it belong'd to him, as being Emperour, to take effectual care that the Flame which was burning in the neighbouring Countries, might not prove destructive to *Germany*: And the Elector of *Brandenburgh* made heavy Complaints, that the *French* had made great havock in his Territories of *Cleves*. The *French*, on the other side, sent an Army towards *Germany*, in hopes to oblige the Emperour not to concern himself in this War; but the *French* having committed great Outrages in the Empire, taken into possession the City of *Treves*, and made great havock in the Palatinate, the Emperour persuaded the Estates of the Empire to declare War against *France*. *Sweden* also was afterwards engag'd in the same War; which ended in the Peace made at *Nimmegen*; whereby *France* got *Friburgh* and *Brisgau*, in lieu of *Philipsburgh*; and *Sweden* was restored to those Provinces which it had lost during the War.

War with France.

Peace of Nimmegen. 1679.

§. 18. If we duly consider the Genius of the People who inhabit this great Empire, it is most evident, that this Nation, ever since the Memory of Men, has been very brave, and addicted to War; and that *Germany* has been an inexhaustible Source of Soldiers, since there is scarce ever any want of Men, who are ready to serve for Money: and if they are once well Disciplined, they are not only good at the first Onset, but are very fit to endure the Hardships and inconveniences of a long War. There are not in any other Nation so many to be met with, that are ready to list themselves in Foreign Service for Money; neither is there any Country in Christendom where greater Forces both of Horse and Foot may be raised than in *Germany*. But besides this, the *Germans* are much addicted and very fit for Commerce, and all sorts of Handicraft Trade: and not only the Inhabitants

The Genius of this Nation.

of the Cities do apply themselves with great industry to the same; but also if a Country-man gets a little before-hand in the World, he puts his Son to some Handicraft Trade or another, tho' a great many of them afterwards run into the Wars. They are generally very free and honest, very ambitious to maintain the so much praised Fidelity of the ancient *Germans*; they are not easily stirr'd up to raise Tumults, but commonly are willing to remain under the same Government where they are educated.

Nature of the Soil. §. 19. Tho' the *German* Empire has no Possessions abroad, except you would account *Hungary* to be such, which is under Subjection to the House of *Austria*; nevertheless it is a Country of a vast Extent by it self, which is full of great and small Cities, Towns and Villages: The Ground is very fertile in general, there being very few spots to be met with, of any large extent, which do not produce something or another for the Sustenance of Mankind. *Germany* also abounds in all sorts of Minerals, especially in Mines of Silver, Copper, Tin, Lead, Iron, Mercury, and other sorts. It has abundance of Springs that furnish Waters for the boiling of Salt; and those several great navigable Rivers wherewith it is adorn'd, make it very commodious to transport its Commodities from one Place to another. *Its Commodities.* The Commodities of *Germany* are these *viz.* Iron and all sorts of Instruments made of it; Lead, Mercury, Wine, Corn, Beer, Wool, coarse Cloth, all sorts of Linen and Woolen Manufacturies, Horses, Sheep, *&c.* If therefore the *Germans* would apply themselves to imitate those Manufacturies at home which are now Imported by Foreigners, the Commodities Exported out of *Germany* would much surpass the Import; and consequently it would of necessity grow very rich, especially since a considerable quantity of Silver is digged out of its Mines.

Form of Government. §. 20. As for the Form of Government in *Germany*, it is to be considered, that it is not like some Kingdoms, where the Kings have the whole Power in their hands, and according to whose Commands the Subjects are obliged to comport themselves; neither is the Sovereign Power here circumscribed within certain Bounds, as it is in some Kingdoms of *Europe*, where the Kings cannot exercise an absolute Soveraignty without the Consent of the

the Estates: But *Germany* has its particular Form of Government, the like is not to be met with in any Kingdom of *Europe*, except that the ancient Form of Government in *France* came pretty near it. *Germany* acknowleges but one Supreme Head under the Title of the *Roman Emperour*; which Title did at first imply no more than the Soveraignty over the City of *Rome*, and the Protection of the Church of *Rome* and her Patrimony. This Dignity was first annexed to the *German* Empire by *Otho* I. but it is long ago since the Popes have robb'd the Kings of *Germany* of this Power, and have only left them the bare Name. The Estates of *Germany*, some of which have great and potent Countries in their Possession, have a considerable share of the Soveraignty over their Subjects: and tho' they are Vassals of the Emperour and Empire, nevertheless they ought not to be consider'd as Subjects, or only as potent or rich Citizens in a Government; for they are actually possess'd of the Supreme Jurisdiction in the Criminal Affairs; they have Power to make Laws and to regulate Church-Affairs, (which however is only to be understood of the Protestants) to dispose of the Revenues arising out of their own Territories; to make Alliances, as well among themselves as with Foreign States, provided the same are not intended against the Emperour and Empire; they may build and maintain Fortresses and Armies of their own, coin Money, and the like. This Grandeur of the Estates, 'tis true, is a main Obstacle that the Emperour cannot make himself absolute in the Empire except it be in his Hereditary Countries; yet this has been always observ'd, the more potent the Emperour is, the more he has exercised his Authority, and the Estates have been forc'd to comply with his Commands; and it is certain, that the Grandeur of the Estates, except what is contained in the *Golden Bull* concerning the Electoral Dignity, was more founded upon ancient Customs and Precedents, than any written Constitutions; till in the *Westphalian* Peace their Rights and Authority were expresly and particularly confirm'd and establish'd.

Strength and weakness of this Empire.

§. 21. Tho' it is certain that *Germany* within it self is so potent, that it might be formidable to all its Neighbours, if its Strength was well united and rightly employ'd; nevertheless this strong Body has also its Infirmities, which weaken its Strength, and slacken its Vigour.

gour. Its irregular Constitution of Government is one of the chief Causes of its Infirmity; it being neither one entire Kingdom, neither properly a Confederacy, but participating of both kinds; For the Emperour has not the entire Soveraignty over the whole Empire, nor each Prince in particular over his Territories; and tho' the former is more than a bare Administrator, yet the latter have a greater share in the Soveraignty than can be attributed to any Subjects or Citizens whatever, tho' never so great. And this seems to be the reason why at last the Emperours did quit their Pretensions upon *Italy*, and the Kingdom of *Arles*; because these potent Princes of *Germany*, and the turbulent Bishops, who were continually stirr'd up by the Popes, used to give them so much work that they had enough to do to take care of *Germany* as the main State, without being able to concern themselves much about other Parts. Yet do I not find any Instances in History, that any of the ancient Emperours did endeavour to subdue the Princes, and to make himself absolute Master of *Germany*. But this ambitious Design of *Charles* V. as it seems, was first put upon by the *Spaniards*, or, as some will have it, by *Nicholas Perenot Granvel*.

Why the Emperour quitted the Kingdom of Arles.

And truly the Electors had the same reason not to have admitted him to the Imperial Dignity, as they had not to admit *Francis* I. King of *France*. And common Reason tells us, that no Nation that has the Power of Electing a Prince ought to choose such a one who is possess'd before of a considerable Hereditary Estate, so that he may think it his Interest to take more care of that than of the Elective Kingdom. For, he either will certainly be very careless of the Interest of the Elective Kingdom, or else he will make the Interest of the Elective Kingdom subservient to that of his Hereditary Countries, and make use of the Strength of the first to maintain the latter, and render it more Powerful; or else he will endeavour, by making himself Soveraign over the Elective Kingdom, to make it dependant on his Hereditary Estate. *Germany* found all these three Inconveniences by Experience, under the Reign of this Emperour; for he came very seldom into *Germany*, and that only *en passant*: He never made the true Interest of *Germany* the Rule of his Designs, but all was carried on for the Grandeur and Increase of his House: and at last, under pretence of Religion, he attempted to suppress entirely the antient Liberty

What is the Interest of the Electors.

The Conduct of Charles.

Liberty of the Estates. On the contrary, if *Germany* had had an Emperour at that time who had not been possess'd of any, or at least but small Countries out of the Empire, the true Interest of the Empire would have been his Rule; and it would have been his business not to side with either of these two potent and couragious Nations of the *French* and *Spaniards*, but to have look'd upon them like an Arbitrator, and whilst they had been fighting together, to have according to the Circumstances of Affairs, sometimes balanc'd one, sometimes another, so that one might not become Master of the other, and thereby gain such Advantages, as might prove prejudicial to *Germany*: For it is a far different Case, whether I come in betwixt two Parties as a Mediator, or whether I am engaged to one certain Party; for in the first Case, I can engage my self as deep as I think fit, and at last take care to come off harmless; but in the latter Case, I must needs be a Loser let things go how they will, and at last another shall reap the Fruits of my Labour.

Of the Guaranties of the Circle of Burgundy.

And to give a specious Colour to these Consequences, so prejudicial to *Germany*, *Charles* V. did gain this Point, at the Dyet of *Augsburgh*, upon the Estates, at a time when having brought the Protestants very low, no body durst oppose it, that they should take upon them the Guarantie of the Circle of *Burgundy*; whereby *Germany* was obliged to be always engaged in the Wars betwixt *Spain* and *France*, and with its Treasure and Men to assist the *Spaniards* in the Defence of the *Netherlands*. I must confess, that it is not the Interest of *Germany*, to see these Countries fall altogether into the hands of *France*; nevertheless, it is not absolutely necessary that the Estates in *Germany* should ruin themselves for their sake; since there are others, who are better able, and have the same Interest that *Germany* has to preserve these Provinces. The Attempt which *Charles* V. made against the Protestant Religion in *Germany*, was a true *Spanish* Design: For, not to mention here the notorious Falsities in the *Roman Catholick* Religion, I cannot for my life see, what could move the Emperour, if his Aim had been for the sole Interest of the Empire, to act contrary to the general Inclination of the Nation, and not rather to take hold of this so favourable Opportunity to free himself from the Tyranny of the Popes, who for several Ages together had trampled upon the *German* Empire; and with the superfluous

1548.

fluous Church-Lands, to encreaſe his own, and the Revenues of the Empire, or at leaſt to give Liberty to the Biſhops to marry without quitting their Church Benefices. If the Emperour would have given a helping hand, the Reformation would have been as eaſily ſettled in *Germany*, as it was in *Sweden*, *England*, and *Denmark*.

Ferdinand *purſues the* Spaniſh *Maxims.*

After theſe *Spaniſh* State-Maxims had laid a while dormant, they were at laſt revived, and that with more Vigour, under the Reign of *Ferdinand* II. beſides a great deal of miſery which did from thence accrue to *Germany*. This was the cauſe that the Eſtates of *Germany*, to preſerve their Liberty, were oblig'd to ſeek for foreign Aid, by which means they maintain'd their Liberty: but it had been queſtionleſs more advantageous to *Germany*, not to have wanted the Aſſiſtance of Foreigners, who were not forgetful to make their own Advantage by it. Now if it may be ſuppoſed that there are ſome Remnants of the *Spaniſh* Leaven, it may eaſily be conjectur'd what Jealouſie and Diſtruſts muſt be betwixt the Members of the Empire, and how contrary and different their Counſels and Actions muſt needs be: and tho' perhaps by ſetling a good Underſtanding betwixt the Supreme Head and the Eſtates, a Medium might be found out to obviate this and ſome other Inconveniences; yet there reign various and Great Diſtempers among the Eſtates themſelves, which ſeem to render the beſt Remedies and Counſels either ineffectual, or at leaſt very difficult: Among theſe muſt be counted the Religious Differences betwixt the Catholicks and the Proteſtants in general; which Differences do not only depend on the ſeveral Opinions in Matters of Faith, but alſo on a worldly Intereſt; the Catholicks endeavouring, upon all occaſions, to recover ſuch Poſſeſſions as were taken from them ſince the Reformation; and the Proteſtants being reſolv'd to maintain themſelves in the Poſſeſſion of them. Wherefore it has been obſerv'd, that ſometimes the *Roman Catholicks* have been more guided by their particular Intereſt, and by their Clergy, than by that of the publick: Nay, it is to be fear'd, if *Germany* ſhould be vigorouſly attack'd by a potent Foreign Enemy, that ſome of the Popiſh Bigots would not be ſo Backward in ſubmitting themſelves under the Yoke, and be willing to loſe one Eye provided the Proteſtants might loſe both.

The Difference betwixt the Proteſtants.

Beſides, the Proteſtants are again ſub-divided into two Parties;

Parties; there being among them some Differences concerning several Articles of Faith; which, by the Heat of the Clergy, were widen'd to that degree, that both Parties, were brought to the very brink of Ruin. The great number of Estates augments the Distemper, it being next to an Impossibility, that among so many, there should not be some who either prompted by their Passion and Obstinacy, or for want of Understanding, will deviate from the true Interest, or be misled by ill Counsellors to act against the same; so that it would be a Miracle to see so many Heads, of such an incoherent Body, well united. The Estates are also very unequal in Power; from whence it often happens, that some of the most potent are for being like Soveraigns; and therefore being inclin'd rather to act according to their particular Interest and Grandeur than for the Publick, they make little account how they ruin the less powerful. These therefore when they see that the Laws cannot protect them, are at last oblig'd to take more care of their own Preservation, than of the Publick Liberty, as thinking it indifferent by whom they are oppress'd. Not to mention here the Jealousie which is betwixt the three Colleges of the Empire, and the several Pretensions and Differences which are among some of the Estates.

The Neighbours of Germany.

§. 22. As to the Neighbours of *Germany*, the *Turks* border upon *Stiria*, *Croatia*, and *Hungary*: The two last do not properly belong to *Germany*, but yet belong to the House of *Austria*, and are like a Bulwark to it; so that *Germany* is much concern'd in the Preservation of them. The *Turkish* Emperour has greater Revenues out of his vast Territories, and perhaps is able to raise a greater number of Men than the *Germans* can do; nevertheless he is not so formidable to them; for the *Hungarian* Wars are very troublesome to the *Turks*, because the *Asiatick* Forces, and other Supplies of Provision and Ammunition, are not without great difficulty carried so far; neither can these Forces be put into Winter Quarters there, as being not used to so cold a Climate, the neighbouring depopulated Provinces being also not able to maintain them. The *Turks* also are in continual fear, that, as soon as they have bent their whole Force against *Hungary*, the *Persians* may fall upon them on the other side, or some of the Bassa's towards the East Revolt from them. *The Turks.*

In

In fine, a well-disciplin'd Army of *Germans* will scarce shrink before all the *Turkish* Forces; and when *Germany* is resolved to stand the Brunt, the *Turks* will, I believe, quickly be weary of attacking it. *Italy* is in no ways to be compared with *Germany* either for its Strength or number of Men, besides that it is divided into several States, by which it is disabled to attack any foreign State, much less so potent an Empire, which being possess'd of some Passes leading into *Italy*, might in time take an opportunity to renew its Pretensions upon that Country.

Italy.

The Swiss. The *Switzers* are very good Neighbours to *Germany*, as having neither Will nor Power to attack it, especially since they are destitute of good Horsemen. Neither can *Poland* compare its Strength with *Germany*; for tho' the *Poles* can bring a great Number of Horse into the Field, yet they are not to be compared with the *German* Horse; and as for their Foot, 'tis much inferiour to the *German* Infantry, and withal very unfit to attack fortified Places: so that the *Poles* can't of themselves undertake any thing considerable against *Germany*. And, if they should enter into Alliance with a Prince at War with the Empire, and give the *Germans* a Diversion, it would not be difficult for the *Germans* to be even with them, since they are not well provided with Frontier Places, or any Strong-holds within the Country, which are able to withstand an Enemy; whereas in *Germany* they would meet with Places which would give them sufficient work: And in such a case perhaps the *Muscovites* might easily be prevailed withal to fall upon the back of them. But it is not to be supposed, that such a Common-wealth as this will easily attempt an offensive War against its Neighbours. However, it is of great Consequence to *Germany*, that *Poland* should not be weakned or brought under Subjection by the *Turks* or any other Power. In fine, If these two Nations should enter into a League against the *Turks*, and attack them with joint Forces, they might do one another considerable Services.

Poland.

Denmark. *Denmark* has no Pretensions upon *Germany*, and the best Land Forces of the *Danes* being Listed in *Germany*, their Army may be ruin'd only by the Emperour's recalling the *Germans* out of that Service, if they should attempt any thing against the Empire. Neither do I believe that *Germany*, but especially the Circles of the

Higher

Higher and Lower *Saxony*, will be so careless of their own Interest, as to let *Denmark* become Master of *Hamborough* and *Lubeck*.

England cannot do any harm to *Germany*, except by disturbing the Trade of *Hamburgh*; tho' it seems to be the Interest of the *English*, rather to enjoy the Benefit of their Free Trade there. On the other hand, the *Germans* may do a Service to the *English* against the *Hollanders*, by Land, whilst these are engag'd with them in a War at Sea. England.

Holland has neither Power nor Inclination to attack *Germany*: For, if the *Germans* should be recall'd out of the Service of the *Dutch*, their Land-forces would make but a very indifferent Show: neither can they reap any Benefit by making new Conquests; but it seems rather to be for their purpose to keep fair with the *Germans*, that in case of a War with their Neighbours, they may make use of their Assistance. Holland.

Spain cannot pretend to do any considerable Mischief to *Germany*, if the Head and Members are well united; but if it should join with the Head against the Members, it may prove mischievous, especially by the assistance of their Money: but in such a case there would questionless not be wanting some that would oppose its Designs. Spain.

Swedeland alone is not so powerful as to be in any ways formidable to *Germany*: neither is this Kingdom for making any more Conquests on that side, since thereby it would lose more of its own Strength than it can gain by them: but on the other hand, it is of great Consequence to *Sweden*, that the state of Religion and of the Government remain in the same condition as it was setled in the *Westphalian* Peace: and that *Germany* be not subjected or ruled by any absolute Power. Sweden.

France has of late made it self so powerful, that this Kingdom alone may do more mischief to the *Germans* than any of the rest of their Neighbours. *France*, in consideration of its Form of Government, has a considerable Advantage over *Germany*; for the King there has all the best Men, and the Purses of his Subjects at Command, and employs them as he thinks fit. There might also be a way found out, for *Germany* to keep always a sufficient Army on foot against *France*; at least it is not easily to be suppos'd, that if *France* should attack *Germany* France.

many in good earnest, all the rest of *Europe* would be Lookers on: but if *Germany* be divided within it self, so that either one Party should joyn with *France*, or that the rest should stand Neuters till *France* has devour'd the neighbouring States, then nothing but fatal Consequences can attend it.

CHAP. IX.

Of DENMARK.

Denmark *a very ancient Kingdom.* § 1. DEnmark is one of the most ancient Kingdoms in *Europe*, which was established a great many Years before the Birth of our Saviour; but for want of good Histories, it cannot be precisely determin'd at what time it had its Beginning, or how long each of its King's Reign'd, or what were their great Deeds. We will not therefore detain the Reader by inserting here their bare Names, but only touch upon such Matters as are with some Certainty transmitted to Posterity. Among the most ancient Kings, *Frotho* III. is most famous; who, 'tis said, did Reign just before the Birth of Christ, and was a most potent Monarch, who rul'd over *Denmark*, *Sweden*, *Norway*, *England*, *Ireland*, and other neighbouring States. The Borders of his Territories were on the East-side *Russia*, and on the West-side the *Rhine*. 'Tis also related, that he Conquer'd the *Vandals*, which liv'd then in those Countries that now are call'd *Pomerania*, and *Mecklenburgh*, and that he was the first King that stiled himself King of the *Vandals*. *Gotrick*, 'tis said, did assist *Wittekind* the King of the *Saxons*, against *Charles the Great*.

Frotho. III.

Erick I. 246. *Erick* is commonly reckon'd to have been the first Christian King of *Denmark* (tho' some pretend, that his Brother *Harald*, who Reign'd before him, was the first. Under this King's Reign the Christian Religion was propagated in *Denmark* by the help of *Ansgarius* then Bishop of *Bremen*; which afterwards King *Gormo* II. endeavouring to root out again, was forc'd by the Emperour *Henry*, surnamed the *Bird-catcher*, to grant the free Exercise of the Christian Religion throughout his Kingdom. His Son *Harald* was attack'd by the Emperour *Ot*-

to I. from whom the Sea betwixt *Jutland* and *Holland* got the Name of *Otten Sound*; because the Emperor there threw in his Lance to mark the utmost Limits of his Expedition. His Son *Suen Otto* came to the Crown in the Year 980, who being taken Prisoner by the *Jutes*, was redeem'd by the Women, who gave their Gold and Silver Ornaments for his Ransom: In recompence of which he granted them this Privilege, that whereas they used only to have a small Portion in Money out of their Father's Inheritance, they for the future should have an equal share with the Males. He also conquer'd a part of *England*, and died in the Year 1012. Suen Otto.

His Son *Canute* or *Knutt* II. surnamed the *Great*, was King of *Denmark*, *Norway*, and *England*, having Conquer'd the latter of these three by Force of Arms, tho' *England* did not remain long under the Subjection of the *Danes*; for after his Death, only *Harald* and *Hardiknutt* Reign'd in *England*, the *Danes* being entirely dispossessed upon their Decease. Besides this, *Magnus* Son of S. *Olaus* King of *Norway*, made himself Master of *Denmark*; which Kingdom, after his Death, *Sueno* II. obtain'd; but he was forc'd to fight for it against *Harald Hardrode* then King of *Norway*. He died in the Year 1074. To him succeeded his Sons *Harald* VII. (who reign'd but two Years) and *Canute* IV. This King gave great Power to the Bishops in *Denmark*, and granted the Tenths of all the Revenues of the Country to the Clergy. At which the *Jutes* being exasperated, slew him at *Odensea*: But the Clergy, as an Acknowledgment of his Favours bestowed upon them, placed him in the number of Saints, and his Memory was afterwards celebrated with full Cups at their Feasts by those who call'd themselves the *Knutgylden*, from him. His Brother *Olaus* IV. succeeded him, who died in the Year 1095. and after him reigned his Brother *Erick* II. who took *Jutin*, at that time a great City in *Pomerania*. He died in the Isle of *Cyprus*, in his Pilgrimage to *Jerusalem*. Canute II. 1087.

§. 2. After his Death the whole Kingdom was in great Confusion, especially when three at once fought for the Crown, *viz.* *Sueno* III. *Canute* VI. and *Waldemar* I. These, after they had waged Wars together for many Years, did at last agree to divide the Kingdom into three parts: But *Canute* being assassinated by *Sueno*, and

Waldemar I. *Sueno* again being slain in Battle against *Waldemar*, he
1157. got the whole Kingdom into his possession. He subdued the *Rugians* and *Vandals*, who had hitherto proved
1164. very mischievous to *Denmark*: He also destroy'd the City of *Jutin*. 'Tis related that he laid the first Foundation of the City of *Dantzick*: and under the Reign of this King, *Absalom* Bishop of *Roschild* first began to build the City of *Copenhagen*. *Waldemar* died in the Year
Canute VI. 1182. To him succeeded his Son *Canute* VI. who waged heavy Wars against the *Vandals*, and at last forced their Princes to be his Vassals; taking upon himself the Title of King of the *Vandals* or *Slaves*. He took from *Adolf* Earl of *Holstein*, among other places, the City of *Hamburgh*, which however twenty seven Years after did shake off the *Danish* Yoke. He having also conquer'd *Esthonia* and *Livonia*, the Christian Faith was established in these Countries by his means. He died in the Year 1202.

After him reigned his Brother *Waldemar* II. who at the beginning was a very fortunate and potent Prince, and had under his subjection, besides *Denmark*, the Countries of *Esthonia*, *Livonia*, *Courland*, *Prussia*, *Pomerania*, *Rugen*, *Mecklenburgh*, *Holstein*, *Stormar*, *Ditmarsen* and *Wageren*, as also the Cities of *Lubeck* and *Lauenburgh*. But he lost a great part of them by the following occasion: *Henry* Earl of *Swerin* having undertaken a Journey to the Holy Land, committed during his Absence, his Lady and Country to the care of *Waldemar*: But being informed, after his Return, that the King had lived in Adultery with his Lady; he, to revenge this Affront, took him Prisoner by Stratagem; and after he had kept him three Years in Prison, dismist him, making him pay for his Ransom the Sum of 45000 Marks of fine Silver. The Countries of *Mecklenburgh* and *Pomerania*, and the Cities of *Lubeck* and *Dantzick* taking hold of this opportunity revolted from *Waldemar*: *Adolph* Earl of *Lauenburgh* took from him *Holstein* and *Stormar*; the Knights of the Cross took *Esthonia* and *Livonia*. And endeavouring to recover these Countries, he was
1227. vanquished in a Battle fought near *Bornhove*, by the Earl of *Lauenburgh*. Yet he recovered *Revel* and *Esthonia*; and died in the Year 1241.

Erick V. §. 3. His Son *Erick* V. succeeded him in the Kingdom

dom, tho' he had given ſome parts of it to his other Sons; *viz.* to *Abel*, *Sleſwick*; to *Canute*, *Bleckingen*; and to *Chriſtopher*, *Laland* and *Falſter*. These were, each of them, for being Soveraigns in theſe Countries; but *Erick* pretending that they ought to be his Vaſſals, there enſued great Commotions in *Denmark*, till *Erick* was miſerably murthered by his Brother *Abel*; and *Abel*, after he had reigned two Years, was ſlain by the *Frieſlanders* and *Ditmarſians*. To him ſucceeded his Brother *Chriſtopher* I. Againſt this King the Archbiſhop of *Lunden* raiſed abundance of Troubles, and the King having imprisoned him, he was by the reſt of the Biſhops and Clergy excommunicated, and with him the whole Kingdom. And at laſt the King was by them poiſoned, as 'tis thought, with the Hoſt.

Abel. 1250. 1252. Christoph. I. 1259.

After him reigned his Son *Erick* VI. who was at Variance with the Biſhops, and engaged in the Wars againſt *Sweden* and *Norway*; at laſt he was taken Priſoner in a Battle by *Erick* Duke of *Holſtein*, and was barbarouſly murthered by ſome of the great Men of the Kingdom. He left the Crown to his Son *Erick* VII. who immediately, had great Conteſts with the King of *Norway*, who had given Protection to the Murtherers of his Father. He alſo had ſome other Differences with ſome of the neighbouring States, and died in the 1319. To him ſucceeded his Brother *Chriſtopher* II. who got his Son Crowned in his Life-time. This King was baniſhed the Kingdom by his Subjects, who, under pretence of being oppreſſed with Taxes, elected in his ſtead *Waldemar* Duke of *Sleſwick* their King. But they grew alſo quickly weary of him, and recalled *Chriſtopher*, who afterwards in a Battle fought againſt this *Waldemar*, loſt his Son *Erick*. Under the Reign of this King, *Schonen*, being much oppreſſed by the *Holſteiners*, who were in Poſſeſſion of it, ſurrendred it ſelf to *Magnus* King of *Sweden*. And *John* Duke of *Holſtein* perceiving that he could not maintain it by force, ſold all his Right and Title to it, for 70000 Marks fine Silver. Under the Reign of this King, *Denmark* was torn into ſo many pieces, that very few places were left to the King. He died in the Year 1333. After his Death there was an Interregnum in *Denmark*, during the ſpace of ſeven Years. In the mean time the *Holſteiners* had brought the greateſt part of *Denmark* under their Subjection;

Erick VI. 1286. Erick VII. Christoph. II. 1332.

till the *Danes* making an Insurrection against them, endeavour'd to chase them out of *Denmark*, and for this purpose call'd *Waldemar* the Son of *Christopher* II. (who had been educated at the Court of the Emperour *Lewis the Bavarian*) into the Kingdom.

Waldem. III. §. 4. *Waldemar* III. did somewhat restore the decay'd State of the Kingdom, having partly forc'd and partly bought the *Holsteiners* out of *Denmark*: He sold *Esthonia* and *Revel* to the Knights of the Cross, for 28000 Marks fine Silver; most of which Sum he bestow'd upon a Journey which he undertook into the *Holy Land*. But he got *Schonen* again from *Magnus Samech* the then King of *Sweden*, by fair Promises; and by an Agreement made betwixt him and *Albert* King of *Swedeland*, *Gotland* was also surrendred to him, and some other Places belonging at that time to *Sweden*. He was frequently at wars with the *Hanse* Towns, and died in the Year 1375.

Olaus VI. After him reigned his Grandson *Olaus* VI. born of his Daughter *Margaret* and *Hacquin* King of *Norway*. During his Minority, the Mother had the supreme Administration of Affairs. Having after his Father's Death obtained the Crown of *Norway*, he laid also claim to the Kingdom of *Sweden*, because his Father was Son of *Magnus Samech* King of *Sweden*; but he died young.

In his stead the *Danes* and *Norwegians* receiv'd for their Queen, *Margaret*, his Mother; and she having declar'd *Erick Pomeran*, her Sister's Daughter's Son, her Associate in the Government, enter'd into a War against *Albert* King of *Sweden*. But the *Swedes* being in general dissatisfied with their King, deserted him, acknowledging *Margaret* for their Queen. *Albert* fought a Battle against *Margaret*, but was defeated and taken Prisoner with his Son; whom *Margaret* did not release till after seven Years Imprisonment, under condition that he should either pay 60000 Marks fine Silver for his Ransom or else resign his Pretensions to the Kingdom of *Sweden*: And he having perform'd the last, *Margaret* caused *Erick Pomeran* to be Crown'd King of *Sweden*. The next Year, the Estates of all the three Northern Kingdoms
1396. assembled at *Calmar*; where *Erick* having been declared their King, an Agreement was made among them, that these three Kingdoms, for the future, should be rul'd by one

one King. *Margaret*, who had been an extraordinary good Queen to *Denmark*, died in the Year 1412. After whose Death, *Erick* was sole King over these three Kingdoms; but he was in continual Broils with the *Holsteiners* (who were assisted by the *Hanse* Towns) concerning the Dutchy of *Sleswick*; which Differences were at last composed. He surrendred to his Cousins the Dukes of *Pomerania*, the Island of *Rugen*, which had been a considerable time under *Danish* Subjection. In the mean time the *Swedes* were grown very discontented, because *Erick* did not govern them according to his Coronation Oath, and opprest them by his foreign Officers, which obliged them to stand up for the Defence of their Liberty. The *Danes* also, seeing that he was very careless of the Affairs of the Kingdom, and always lived in *Gotland*, did withdraw themselves from his Obedience, alledging among other matters that because he had been endeavouring to establish his Cousin *Bogislaus* Duke of *Pomerania* in his Throne in his life-time, he had thereby violated their Right of a free Election: and having chosen in his stead *Christopher* Duke of *Bavaria*, *Erick*'s Sister's Son, he was Deposed, and retired into *Pomerania*, where he ended his Life. *Christopher* Reigned till the Year 1448. with whose Reign the *Danes* were very well satisfied.

Erick Pomeran. 1438. Christopher. 1439.

§. 5. After his Death the *Danes* made an Offer of that Crown to *Adolph* Duke of *Sleswick* and Earl of *Holstein*: But he being very ancient and infirm, refused to accept of it, and recommended to them *Christian*, Earl of *Oldenburgh*, his Sister's Son, whom both the *Danes* and *Norwegians* declared their King: And in this Family these two Crowns have remained ever since, by a continual Succession. This King, soon after, began a War with the *Swedes* who had made one *Charles Cnutson* their King) because they would have driven the deposed King *Erick* out of *Gotland*; but King *Christian* coming to his Assistance, made himself Master of that Island. Besides this, some of the *Swedish* Nobility, who were dissatisfied with *Charles Cnutson*, having sided with *Christian*, the War began to be carried on very vigourously betwixt these two Nations. In this War the Archbishop of *Upsal* attack'd *Charles* with such Success, that he obliged him to retire into *Prussia*, and *Christian* was Crown'd King of *Sweden*. But the *Swedes* being again

Christian I. 1458.

1463 again dissatisfied with *Christian*, recalled *Charles Cnutson*; upon which the War began afresh: and notwithstanding *Charles Cnutson* died in the Year 1470, and *Christian* came with a great Army into *Swedeland*, yet could he not maintain himself in the Throne, his Forces being defeated near *Stockholm*. In the Year 1471. the Emperour *Frederick* III. gave to him in Fief *Ditmarsen*, as also to the Country of *Holstein* the Title of a Dukedom. He married his Daughter *Margaret* to *James* III. King of *Scotland*, giving her for a Dowry the *Orkney Islands* and *Schetland*, which had hitherto been dependent on the Kingdom of *Norway*. He died in the Year 1481. the *Danes* and *Norwegians* chose his Son *John* their King, who divided the Dukedom of *Holstein* with his Brother *Frederick*. This King *John* did at last enter into a War against *Sweden*; and having defeated the *Dalekarls*, forced *Steen Sture* the Governour to surrender himself and the City of *Stockholm*, and was Crowned King of *Sweden*. But in the Year 1501, he was miserably and shamefully beaten by the *Ditmarsians*, whom he would have brought under his Subjection: and afterwards *Steen Sture* also drove him out of *Sweden*. He was in continual Broils with him and his Successor *Suant Sture*, who were assisted by the *Lubeckers*, till these Differences were at last composed, soon after which he died.

John.

1497.

1513. Christian II. §. 6. To him succeeded his Son *Christian* II. who drew upon him the Hatred of the *Danes*, partly because he entertained a Woman of mean Birth in the *Netherlands*, whose Name was *Duivecke*, to be his Mistress, and was strangely led by her Mother *Sigiberta*, a crafty old Woman; partly because he had caused *Torbern Oxe*, the Governour of the Castle of *Copenhagen*, to be, as 'tis thought, unjustly executed. In the mean time great Differences were arisen in *Sweden* betwixt *Steen Sture* the younger and *Gustavus Trolle* the Archbishop of *Upsal*, the first having destroyed the Castle of *Stoka*, which belonged to the latter. King *Christian* coming to the Assistance of the Archbishop, took him along with him into *Denmark*, where they laid the Design against *Swedeland*. A Decree therefore was obtained from the Pope, wherein he having condemned the *Swedes* to undergo great Penalties for the Violence offer'd to *Gustavus Trolle*. King *Christian*,

Christian, to put this Decree in execution, sent his Forces into *Sweden*, where *Steen Sture* being slain in an Engagement, the whole Kingdom was put into Confusion by his Death: And King *Christian*, coming at last in Person, forced *Christina* the Widow, of *Steen Sture*, to surrender the City of *Stockholm*. At last, a general Amnesty being published, he was Crown'd King of *Sweden*. But when the *Swedes* thought themselves most secure, he caused some of the chief Men, under Pretence of the former Violences committed upon *Gustavus Trolle*, to be executed by the Hangman, and committed great Cruelties. In the mean time, *Gustavus Erickson*, who had been a Prisoner in *Denmark*, having made his Escape, arrived in *Sweden*; and with the Assistance of the *Dalekarls*, whom he had stirred up, entirely drove the *Danes* out of *Sweden*, which ever since has maintained its Liberty against the *Danes*. By this time the Hatred of the *Danes* against *Christian* was mightily encreased; and the *Jutes* having withdrawn themselves from their Obedience to him, it put him into such a Consternation that he retreated with his Wife and Children into the *Netherlands*. The *Danes* chose in his stead his Uncle *Frederick* Duke of *Holstein* for their King. *Christian* having raised some Land-forces, did endeavour to regain the Throne; but they were dispersed again. *Charles* V. his Brother-in-law was so entangled in the War with *France*, that he could not send him sufficient Succours. At last he came with a Fleet into *Norway*, where he surrendred himself to *Cnut Gyldenstern*, who promised him Security. But King *Frederick* alledging that he was not obliged to keep that Promise, made him a Prisoner, and sent him to the Castle of *Sunderburgh*. But having resigned his Title to the Kingdom, he was removed to the Castle of *Callenburgh*, where he died.

Crowned K. of Sweden. 1520.

Driven thence, and afterwards out of his own Kingdom.

1532. 1546. 1559.

§. 7. *Frederick* I. entered into an Alliance with *Gustavus* King of *Sweden*, and the *Hanse* Towns, against the deposed King *Christian*; and forced the Cities of *Copenhagen* and *Malmoe*, which adhered to *Christian*, to surrender themselves to him. He also granted great Privileges to the Nobility, and died in the Year 1533, the Year after he had made *Christian* II. his Prisoner. To him succeeded his Son *Christian* III. who met with great

Frederick I.

Christian III.

great Opposition at first from *Christopher* Earl of *Oldenburgh* and the *Lubeckers*, who pretended to restore the imprisoned *Christian* to the Throne, and had brought several Provinces over to their side; but he surmounted these Difficulties with the Assistance of *Gustavus* King
1556. of *Sweden*, and made himself Master of *Copenhagen*. And because the Bishops had been all along against him, they were excluded from the general Agreement; and having been deposed in the same Year, the Protestant Religion was at the same time established in *Denmark* and *Norway*. He reigned very peaceably after that time, and died in the Year 1558.

Frederick II. 1560. §. 8. His Son and Successor *Frederick* II. subdued the *Ditmarsians*: Then he entred into a War against *Erick* King of *Sweden*, which was carried on with great Losses on both sides for the space of nine Years; at last a Peace was concluded at *Stetin*, by the Mediation of the Em-
1570. perour, and the Kings of *France* and *Poland*. He reign'd afterwards very peaceably in *Denmark* till the Year 1588. when he died.

Christian IV. Under the Reign of his Son *Christian* IV. the Kingdom was in great Tranquility till the Year 1611. when he attack'd the *Swedish* King *Charles* IX. and took from
1613. him *Calmar* and *Elfsburgh*. But he made Peace with *Gustavus Adolph* the Son of *Charles*; by virtue of which he restor'd these Places unto him, in consideration of a good Sum of Money. He was entangled in the Civil
1625. Wars of *Germany*; for being made General of the Circle of the *Lower Saxony*, he thereby came to be engaged in a War against the Emperour: in which he received a great Overthrow near *King Luttern*, and was forced to quit *Germany*, and the Imperialists enter'd *Holstein* and *Jutland* it self: Yet he recover'd all again by virtue
1629. of a Peace made at *Lubeck*, except that he lost the Advantage of some Ecclesiastical Possessions in *Germany*, which he intended for his Sons. When *Sweden* was afterwards engag'd in the *German* Wars, he offer'd his Mediation betwixt them and the Emperour, in hopes thereby to recover the Ecclesiastical Possessions, and to prevent the *Swedes* from getting a firm Footing in *Germany*. In the mean while he was very vexatious to the *Swedes*, endeavouring by all ways and means to stop the Career of their Victories in *Germany*, and to spoil their

Trade

Trade at home; till at last the *Swedes*, taking it very ill that their Ships were continually detain'd and confiscated in the *Sound*, did resolve to put an end to these Inconveniences; and after they had let the *Danes* know, that they would no longer suffer these Injuries, fell with an Army into *Holstein* and *Jutland*, and at last into *Schonen*. In this War the *Danes* were great Losers both by Sea and Land; but by the extraordinary Valour of their King they maintain'd themselves, till by the Mediation of *France* a Peace was concluded at *Bromsebroo*; by virtue of which the *Swedes* got *Gothland*, *Osel*, and *Jemperland*; and *Halland* was given them as a Pledge for the space of thirty Years. The *Hollanders* also taking hold of this Opportunity, did regulate the Toll of the *Sound*, which hitherto having been raised at pleasure, had been very troublesome to them. He died in the Year 1648.

1642.

1645.

§. 9. To him succeeded his Son *Frederick* III. who upon the Perswasions of the *Hollanders* attack'd the *Swedes*, promising himself great Success against them, at a time when he supposed that their King *Charles Gustavus* had quite weaken'd his Strength against the *Poles*; but the *Swedish* King came upon a sudden with an Army into *Holstein* and *Jutland*, and among others, took the Fortress of *Fredericksudde* by Storm; and there happening an extraordinary hard Frost at the beginning of the Year 1658, he marched over the Ice, first into *Funen*, where he surprized the *Danish* Troops, and from thence took his way over *Largeland*, *Laland*, and *Falster*, into *Zealand*. This prodigious Success obliged King *Frederick* to conclude a Peace with him at *Roschild*; by virtue of which, besides some other Advantages, he surrendred to the *Swedes*, *Halland*, *Bleckingen*, *Schonen*, *Bornholm*, *Bahus*, and *Drontheim* in *Norway*.

Frederick III. 1657. *War with the* Swedes.

But King *Charles Gustavus* being inform'd that by the Perswasions of the Emperour, the Elector of *Brandenburgh*, and the *Hollanders*, the *Danes* had resolv'd to renew the War, as soon as the *Swedes* had left the Country, or should be again engaged in a War with *Germany* or *Poland*, he resolv'd to be beforehand with them; and returning into the Isle of *Zealand*, took *Cronenburgh*, and besieg'd *Copenhagen* by Sea and Land. In the mean while the *Dutch* sent a Fleet to relieve *Copenhagen*, a-

The Siege of Copenhagen. 1659.

gainst

gainst whom the *Swedes* fought with great Bravery: But in the Year next following the *Swedes* did in vain storm *Copenhagen*, and withal lost a Battle in *Funen*: *Bornholm* revolted, and *Drontheim* was retaken. And tho' the *Danes* endeavour'd to carry on the War against the *Swedes*, hoping to have now after the Death of their King *Charles Gustavus* met with an opportunity to revenge themselves for their former Losses; yet according to a Project concluded upon by *France*, *England* and *Holland*, a Peace was made near *Copenhagen*, almost upon the same Conditions with that concluded formerly at *Roschild*, except that *Bornholm* and *Drontheim* remained in the Possession of the *Danes*, in lieu of which some Lands were assigned to the *Swedes* in *Schonen*.

A Peace concluded.

A Peace being thus concluded, the King at the Dyet held at *Copenhagen*, was declared an absolute Soveraign, and the Crown Hereditary, whereby the great Priviledges of the Nobility were abolished, and a new Form of Government introduced, by virtue of which the whole Management of Affairs depends absolutely on the King's Pleasure.

The King declared absolute, and the Crown hereditary.

This King died in the Year 1670. To him succeeded his Son *Christian* V. who after he had put his Affairs into a good Posture, entred into an Alliance with the Emperour, *Holland*, and their Confederates. And seeing that the *Swedes* had been worsted in the Country of *Brandenburgh*, he hoped to have met with a good opportunity to break with *Sweden*. He began with the Duke of *Holstein*; who, not foreseeing the Design, came to him at *Rensburgh*, whom he forced to quit all the Advantages which he had obtain'd by the Peace of *Roschild*, and to surrender into his hands the Fortress of *Tonningen*, which he caused to be demolished; and afterwards took *Wismar* from the *Swedes*.

Christian V.

1675.

In the Year next following he entred *Schonen*, where he took *Helsinburgh*, *Landscrone*, and *Christianstad*, as also the Isle of *Gothland*, with little Resistance. But he having detach'd some Troops to Invest *Halmstad*, they were surprized by the King of *Sweden*, who put most of them to the Sword, and made the rest Prisoners. Not long after, the whole *Danish* Army was beaten out of the Field in a bloody Battle fought near *Lunden*, in the Year 1677. King *Christian* besieged *Malmoe*, but having miscarried in a Storm which he made upon the

He maketh War upon Sweden.

Place, he was forc'd to raiſe the Siege, and ſoon after received another Overthrow in a Battle fought near *Landſcrone*, betwixt him and *Charles*, King of *Sweden*. In the Year next following, the *Danes* were oblig'd to raiſe the Siege of *Bahus*, and to ſurrender *Chriſtianſtad*, which was reduced to Extremity by Famine; but at Sea they had better Succeſs: yet, by virtue of a Peace made betwixt them, they reſtored all ſuch Places as they had taken from the *Swedes*. *A Peace.*

§. 10. It is evident, out of ancient Hiſtory, That this Nation has been formerly very warlike: but in our Age the Danes have loſt much of their ancient Glory, becauſe the Nobility have been rather for enjoying their Revenues in Plenty and Quietneſs, than for undergoing the Fatigues of War: and the Commonalty have followed their Example. This may alſo perhaps be alledged for a Reaſon, that they having ſeldom been engaged in any Wars but with *Sweden* (except that *Chriſtian* IV. made War in *Germany*, (which however was carried on chiefly by *German* Soldiers) which could not be of any long continuance; the *Danes* often wanted opportunity to keep themſelves in exerciſe, eſpecially ſince they had the conveniency of making uſe of the *Germans*, whom they liſted for Money: and the number of Inhabitants ſeem'd to be but proportionable to the Country, which is of no great extent. Since the King has been declar'd Soveraign, all means have been employed to improve the Military Force of the Nation; but it ſeems that the National Forces, without the help of the *Germans*, will not be of any great conſequence as to Land-Service. Neither is it the King's Intereſt to put his Nobility upon Martial Exploits, or that they ſhould grow famous in War, for fear they ſhould make an Effort to recover their former Privileges. *The Genius of this Nation.*

The *Norwegians* undergo all ſorts of Hardſhip with more Courage and Vigour, whereunto they are inured by their Climate and Air. But the *Danes*, ſince they have been Maſters of *Norway*, have always endeavour'd to keep under this Nation, by taking from them all opportunities of exerting their Vigour; and there are very few left of the ancient Nobility in *Norway*. Yet the *Norwegians* are now-a-days very good Seamen, and the *Dutch* make good uſe of them in Sea-Service; and a great *The Norwegians.*

great many of the Inhabitants of *North-Holland*, where they are addicted to Fishing, were originally of *Norway*.

Nature of the Soil. §. 11. The Country of *Denmark* is of no great Extent, yet it is generally very fertile, and fit both for Tillage and Pasturage; for a great number of Oxen and Horses are yearly Transported out of *Denmark* to other Places: And a considerable quantity of Corn is sent out of *Denmark* into *Norway* and *Iseland*. The Seas near *Denmark* are pretty well stock'd with Fish, which however are rather for the Benefit of the Inhabitants, than for Exportation. There are few or no Manufacturies there, the Inhabitants being unqualified for such Works; neither is there any Commodities fit for Exportation in great quantities. On the other hand, the *Danes* are obliged to Import Wine, Salt, good Beer, and Woollen Manufactury for Cloaths. They have begun to bring Spices themselves out of the *East-Indies*, where they have a small Fort upon the Coast of *Cormandel*. The Toll, which is paid by Foreigners in the *Sound* in ready Money, is a very good Revenue in *Denmark*: Which is the reason why the *Danes* can scarce forgive the *Swedes*, that they do not pay this tributary Toll to *Denmark*, *Norway* is for the most part an uncultivated Country, yet it produces several Commodities fit for Exportation, *viz.* dry'd and salted Fish in great quantity, Timber, Boards, Masts, Tar, Pitch, and the like. There are also in *Norway*, Silver, Copper, and Iron Mines. But it produces not Corn sufficient in quantity for the Maintenance of its Inhabitants nor to brew Beer; besides, it wants also the same Commodities which are wanting in *Denmark*. As for its Situation, it's very commodious to Export and Import Merchandizes to and from other Sea-Coasts in *Europe*. *Iceland* is stock'd with Fish, some salted Flesh, and very good Down-Feathers, which the Inhabitants are fain to exchange for such Commodities as are, besides Fish and Flesh, requisite for the Sustenance and Convenience of Life. The *Ferroe Islands* do for the most part live on their Sheep and Fish. Besides that *Denmark* cannot raise a considerable Army of its Natives, this is a great Weakness to this Kingdom, that *Its Defects.* not only *Norway* and *Denmark* are separated by the Sea, and cannot keep correspondency together but by that way;

way; but also that this Kingdom is divided into so many Islands; so that, if an Enemy once becomes Master at Sea, he must needs prove very troublesome to *Denmark*.

§. 12. As to the Neighbours of *Denmark*, it borders on one side upon *Germany*; for *Holstein*, which belongs to the present Royal Family, is a Fief of the Empire. And tho' the Land-Forces of *Denmark* do not come to any comparison with those of *Germany* and *Jutland* lies quite open on that side; yet the Islands are very secure from the *Germans*, who are not provided with Shipping, except it should happen that the *Great* and *Lesser Belt* should both be frozen, which happens very rarely. Neither is there any great probability that these two States should differ, except the Pretensions upon *Hamborough*, which the King of *Denmark* will not easily let fall, should furnish an occasion for War. But it will be a very difficult Task for the King of *Denmark* to attain his aim by open Force, except there should happen a very strange Juncture of Affairs, or that the inward Divisions, or Treachery of the Citizens, should give occasion to its Ruin. In the mean while, it is not easily to be supposed, that the neighbouring *German* Princes should suffer a City of so great consequence to fall into the Hands of a foreign Prince. In fine, it is of vast Consequence to *Denmark*, to hold a good Understanding with *Germany*, since from thence it must draw the greatest part of its Land-forces, wherewith to defend it self against *Swedeland*.

Neighbours of Denmark.

Germany.

With the *Swedes*, *Denmark* has been in continual Broils for a considerable time; and it seems that there is an old Grudge and Animosity betwixt these two Nations, arising chiefly hence, that the *Danes* have formerly always endeavour'd to make themselves Masters of *Sweden*, and to reduce this Kingdom into the same condition as they have done *Norway*. Besides that, afterwards they have made it their business, by ruining their Shipping Trade, to prevent the growing Greatness of *Sweden*: But *Sweden* has always vigorously defended it self, and in latter times has gain'd great Advantages upon *Denmark*; for the *Swedes* have not only recover'd *Schonen*, and secured *West-Gothland* by the Fortress of *Bahus*; but they have also a way open into *Jutland*, Out of their Provinces in *Germany*. On the other hand, the *Danes*

Sweden.

have

have made it their business hitherto, by making Alliances with the Enemies of *Sweden*, to get from them these Advantages. But if we consider that these two Kingdoms are now divided by their natural Bounds, to preserve which, *France*, *England* and *Holland*, seem to be mutually concern'd; and that as in humane probability *Denmark* cannot Conquer or Maintain it self in *Sweden*, so the other States of *Europe* are not likely to suffer, that *Sweden* should become Master of *Denmark*: It seems therefore most convenient, that these two Kingdoms should maintain a good Understanding, and be a mutual Security to one another against their Enemies.

Holland. From *Holland*, *Denmark* may expect real Assistance, in case it should be in danger of being Conquered, since the Prosperity of *Holland* depends partly on the free Trade of the *Baltick*; and if one should become Master both of *Sweden* and *Denmark*, he would questionless keep those Passages closer than they are now. But the *Danes* are sensible at the same time, that the *Hollanders* will not engage themselves any farther on their behalf than to keep the Balance even, for fear they should with an increase of Power, attempt hereafter to raise the Toll in the *Sound* at pleasure. But as long as *Holland* England. sides with *Denmark*, *England* will not be fond of the *Danish* Party, but rather declare for the other side; for the Preservation of *Denmark* and the Trade of the *Baltick*, is not of so great consequence to *England* as it is to *Holland*.

The Muscovites. The *Muscovites* may prove very serviceable to *Denmark*, against *Sweden*; yet cannot the *Danes* make any great account upon an Alliance with them, because it is very difficult to maintain a Correspondency with them, especially if the *Poles* should declare for *Sweden*: Besides that, the *Muscovites*, as soon as they have obtained their aim, commonly have but little regard to Alliances, or the Interest of their Allies. *Denmark* can have no Poland. great Reliance upon *Poland*, except that Crown should France. be engag'd in a War against *Sweden*. *France* has hitherto shewn no great Concern for *Denmark*, because it has always been in Alliance with its Enemies; yet *France* would not willingly see it ruin'd, because no State of *Europe* would desire the two Northern Kingdoms should be under the Subjection of one Prince: But I cannot see any reason why an Offensive Alliance with *Denmark*

should

should be profitable to *France.* *Spain* is more likely to wish well to *Denmark*, than to assist it, except it should happen that *Sweden* were engaged in a War against the House of *Austria*, or any other Ally of *Spain.*

CHAP. X.

Of POLAND.

§. 1. THE *Poles*, who anciently were called *Sarmartians*, and afterwards *Sclavonians*, derived their Name from the Nature of the Country which they possess; which lies most upon a Plain, for *Pole* signifies in their Language a *Plain*; tho' some are of Opinion that the Word *Polacki* is as much as to say the Posterity of *Lechus*. This Nation formerly did inhabit nearer to the Country of the *Tartars*; but after vast numbers out of *Germany* enter'd the *Roman* Provinces, their places were supplied by the Nations living behind them. And it seems that *Poland* being in the same manner left by its Inhabitants, which were the *Venedi* or *Wends*, they made room for the next that took their place. These then, as 'tis said, having taken Possession of this Country, about the Year 550, did under the Conduct of *Lechus*, lay there the Foundation of a new State. *Lechus* resided at *Gnesne*, being encouraged thereunto by an Eagle's Nest which he found there; and taking it as a good *Omen*, put an Eagle into the Arms of the new Common-wealth, giving to that City the Name of *Gnesne* which in the *Polish* Language signifies a Nest. This Nation first settled it self in that part of the Country which now goes by the Name of the *Great* and *Lesser Poland*; neither did their Limits extend any farther, tho' since that time they are mightily encreased.

Origin of the Kingdom of Poland.

Lechus.

§. 2. The first Governours of this Nation did not assume to themselves the Title of Kings, but only that of Dukes; and the first Form of Government was very inconstant: For after the Race of *Lechus* was extinguished twelve Governours, which in their Language

Twelve Vayvods, or Governours.

are

are called *Vayvods*, did administer the Government, who having first regulated and refined this barbarous People by good Laws and Constitutions, at last were divided among themselves. Wherefore the *Poles* elected for

700. Cracus. their Prince one *Cracus*, who having restored the Common-wealth to its former State, built the City of *Cracow*, so call'd after his own Name; which he made his place of Residence. Whose youngest Son *Lechus* II. to

Lechus II. obtain the Principality, murthered his elder Brother; but as soon as the Fact was discovered, he was banished

750. Venda. the Country. After him ruled a Virgin, whose Name was *Venda*, the only one left of the Children of *Cracus*, who having vanquish'd one *Ritiger* a *German* Prince, that pretended Marriage to her; out of a blind Superstition drowned her self in the River *Weixel*. After her Death, the Administration of the Government returned again to the Governours or *Vayvods*, which continued for some time, till the *Poles* elected again for their Prince a Goldsmith, called *Premislaus*, (who is

Lescus I. also called *Lescus* I.) in consideration of his having by a Stratagem defeated the *Moravians*, who had made an Irruption into *Poland*. But he leaving no Issue behind him, a Horse Race was instituted, with Condition that the Victor should succeed in the Government. One of the Competitors had laid Iron-hooks in the Ground, by which means the other Horses being lamed, he was the first that came to the Mark; but the Fraud being discovered, he was kill'd upon the spot: In the mean while, a certain poor Fellow on Foot had run

776. the Race, and was the next to the Impostor, whom

Lescus II. the *Poles* declar'd their Prince. His Name was *Lescus* II. and as some say, was slain in the Wars against

804. Lescus III. *Charles the Great*. To him succeeded his Son *Lescus* III. who having appeased *Charles the Great* with Presents, made Peace with him, either as an unequal Ally, or else by acknowledging himself his Vassal. He left *Poland* to his Son *Popiel*, whom he had begot in Wed-

Popiel I. lock; but to his natural Sons, he gave the neighbouring Countries of *Pomerania*, *Marck*, *Cassubia*, with

Popiel II. some others. He was succeeded by his Son *Popiel* II. an ill Man; who upon the Persuasion of his Lady murther'd his Father's Brothers: and 'tis reported, That out of their dead Bodies came forth Mice, which devoured *Popiel* with his Wife and Children.

§. 3. As-

§. 3. After his Death there was an *Interregnum* full 820.
of Troubles, till the *Poles* declared *Piastus*, a Country- Piastus.
Fellow, born at *Crusswitz*, their Prince; from whom, ever since, such of the Natives as obtain'd the Royal Dignity were called *Piasti*. His Posterity reigned for a long time in *Poland*, and from thence descended the Race of the Dukes of *Lignitz* and *Brieg* in *Silesia*, which is but lately extinguish'd. 'Tis said, that he was 120 Years old before he died. His Son *Ziemovitus* Ziemovitus.
began his Reign in the Year 895, a warlike and brave Prince: to whom succeeded his Son *Lescus* IV. a good Lescus IV.
and peaceable Prince. Much of the same Temper was 902.
his Son *Ziemovistus*, who began to reign in the Year Ziemovistus.
921. This Prince had but one Son, who being blind, was in the seventh Year of his Age (in which Year, according to the Custom of those times, his Head was to be shaved, and he to receive his Name) restored to his Sight; which was then taken for an *Omen*, that he should be enlightned with the Christian Faith. His Name was *Mieceslaus* I. and he began his Reign in the Miecessaus.
Year 962. Having a great many Wives and no Children, he had a mighty Desire to turn Christian; for some *Germans* represented to him, that if he left the Heathenish Superstitions he would certainly beget Children: and he was persuaded by them to remove his Heathenish Wives, which he did, and married *Dambrawca* the Daughter of *Bogislaus* Duke of *Bohemia*. Before he married her, he was baptized himself, and first introduced the Christian Religion into *Poland*, as also 965.
that Custom which has obtain'd since there, that at the time when the Gospel is read in the Mass, the Men half-drew their Cymeters to signifie that they were ready to fight for the Christian Faith.

§. 4. To him succeeded his Son *Boleslaus Chrobry*, 999.
who was by the Emperour *Otho* III. dignified with the Boleslaus
Title of King, who also remitted unto him all the Pre- Chrobry. *the*
tensions which the former Emperours had upon *Poland*; *first King of* Poland.
and this in consideration for the kind Entertainment he had received from *Boleslaus* in his Pilgrimage to the Grave of *Albert* Bishop of *Guesne*: which being then very famous for some Miracles, was visited by the Emperour to fulfill his Vow which he had made during a precedent Sickness. The first King of *Poland* behaved

himſelf very bravely in his Wars againſt the *Red Ruſſians*, the *Bohemians, Saxons*, and *Pruſſians*. He alſo inſtituted 12 Senators as his Aſſiſtants in the Adminiſtra-
Miecislaus II. tion of the Government. But his Son, *Miecislaus*, loſt for the moſt part his Father's Conqueſts, *Moravia* being taken from him by the *Bohemians*. He began his Reign in the Year 1025. and died in the Year 1034. leaving but one Son behind him, whoſe Name was *Caſimir*;
Caſimir I. who being an Infant, his Mother *Rixa* adminiſtred the Government for a while; but the *Poles* being diſſatisfied with her, ſhe fled with her Son into *Germany*, who aſſumed the Order and Habit of a Monk. During his Abſence there were great Diſturbances in *Poland*, *Maſlaus* having about that time made himſelf Maſter of *Maſovia*, which for a long time after remained independant of the Kingdom of *Poland*. At laſt the *Poles* prevail'd upon *Caſimir* to leave his Monaſtery and accept the Crown. And to perſwade the Pope to abſolve him from his Vow, they promiſed, that for each Head, except thoſe of the Nobility and Clergy, they would contribute yearly a Farthing towards the maintaining of a perpetual Burning Lamp in the Church of St. *Peter* in *Rome*, and cauſe their Heads to be ſhaved above their Ears, like Monks. After he came to the Crown he beat *Maſlaus* and the *Pruſſians*, and reſtored the Kingdom to its former Tranquility.

Boleslaus *the Hardy*. His Son *Boleſlaus*, ſurnamed *The Hardy*, did at firſt wage War againſt his Neighbours the *Pruſſians, Bohemians*, and *Ruſſians*, with great Succeſs; but afterwards
1058. giving himſelf over to all manner of Debauchery, and having been checked for that reaſon by *Staniſlaus*, the Biſhop of *Cracow*, who alſo at laſt excommunicated him, he cut him in pieces before the Altar. Then he was excommunicated by the Pope; and perceiving himſelf to be hated by every body, left the Kingdom, and at laſt murthered himſelf.

Uladislaus I. §. 5. To him ſucceeded his Brother *Uladiſlaus*, who ſtanding in fear of the Pope, would not at firſt take
1028. upon him the Title of King. He met with great Troubles both at home and abroad, which however he over-
Boleslaus III. came at laſt. To him ſucceeded his Son *Boleſlaus* III.
1103. a brave Soldier, who obtained a ſignal Victory over the Emperour *Henry* V. in a Battle fought in the *Hundsfeldt*,

feldt, or *Dog*'s-*Field* near *Breslau*. There was never a Prince in *Poland* more famous for Military Atchievements than himself; it being related of him that he fought 45 Battles all with good Success, except the last of all, fought against the *Red Russians*, which was lost by the Cowardice of the Vayvod of *Cracow*; unto whom the King for a Recompence sent a Hare-skin and a Spinning-Wheel, which so troubled him that he hang'd himself: But the King also was so troubled at this Defeat, that he died of Grief, leaving four Sons behind him. Among 1139. whom *Uladislaus* II. obtained a great part of the Kingdom with the Name of Prince, tho' the other Brothers also shared several great Provinces among themselves, according to their Father's last Will. This occasion'd great Divisions and Civil Wars betwixt these Brothers; and *Uladislaus*, who pretended to dispossess the rest, was himself oblig'd to quit the Country. After him *Boleslaus Crispus*, his Brother, was made Prince of *Poland*, who was forced to wage War against the Emperors *Conrade* III. and *Frederick* I. who would have restored *Uladislaus*. At last a Peace was concluded betwixt them, by Virtue of which, *Poland* remained to *Boleslaus*, but he was obliged to surrender *Silesia*, which was then dependent on *Poland*, to *Uladislaus*, which being afterwards divided into a great many Dukedoms, at last fell to the Crown of *Bohemia*. This *Boleslaus* receiv'd a great overthrow from the *Prussians*, his Army having by the Treachery of a Guide been misled into the Morasses and Boggs. He was succeeded by his Brother *Miecislaus* Senior, but he was deposed for Male-Administration, To him succeeded his Brother *Casimir*, who is only famous for that he check'd the *Prussians*. He died in the Year 1194. His Son *Lescus*, surnamed *The White*, contended with the banished *Miecislaus* for the Kingdom with various Success, till *Miecislaus* died. Whose Son, *Uladislaus*, also raised some Disturbances against him for a while, till at last he was forced to leave him in the quiet Possession of *Poland*. Under the Reign of this *Lescus* the *Tartars* made the first Inroad into *Russia*, and have ever since proved very troublesome and mischievous to *Poland*. This *Lescus* was forced to wage War with *Suentopolck*, whom he had constituted Governour of *Pomerania*; and who declaring himself Duke of *Pomerania*, did dismember it from

Uladislaus II.

Boleslaus. IV. 1146.

Miecislaus III. 1174.

Casimir. 1178.

Lescus V. 1213.

The first Inroads of the Tartars.

the Kingdom of *Poland*. *Conrade* also, the Brother of *Lescus*, had got the Possession of *Masovia* and *Cujavia*; and being not strong enough to defend himself against the *Prussians*, who were fallen into his Country, he call'd in the Knights of the Cross, who were then driven by the *Saracens* out of *Syria*. Unto these he surrendred the Country of *Culm*, under Condition, that such places as by their help should be conquer'd in *Prussia*, should be divided betwixt them; which afterwards prov'd to be the occasion of great Wars betwixt them and *Poland*.

Boleslaus V. 1226. To *Lescus* succeeded his Son *Boleslaus*, surnamed *The Chast*, under whose Reign the *Tartars* committed prodigious Barbarities in *Poland*, and from thence made an Inroad into *Silesia*, where, in a Battle fought near *Lignitz*, they slew so many of the Inhabitants, that they filled nine great Sacks with Ears which they had cut off. His reign was besides full of intestine Troubles.

Lescus VI. 1279. To him succeeded his Cousin *Lescus*, surnamed *The Black*, who was very fortunate in his Wars with the *Russians* and *Lithuanians*; he also quite routed out the *Jazygians*, who then inhabited *Podolia*; but the Civil Commotions, and frequent Incursions of the *Tartars*, occasioned great Disturbances in the Kingdom. He died in the Year 1289.

§. 6. After the Death of *Lescus*, there were great Contests in *Poland* concerning the Regency, till at last

Premislaus. 1291. *Premislaus*, Lord of *Great Poland*, got the upper-hand; who also resumed the Title of King, which the Regents *Poland* had not used during the space of 200 Years; that is, from the time that the Pope, after the Banishment of *Boleslaus the Hardy*, had forbid them to chuse a King of *Poland*: The succeeding Princes being not very ambitious of that Title, because the Country was divided among several Persons. But *Premislaus* did think himself powerful enough to make use of it. He was murthered by some *Brandenburgh* Emissaries, after he had reigned but seven Months. After him was e-

Uladislaus III. lected *Uladislaus Lecticus*, or *Cubitalis*, who did not stile himself King, but only Heir of *Poland*. But he being deposed for Male-Administration, *Wenceslaus*, King of *Bohemia*, was elected in his stead. But after his Death, which happen'd in the Year 1309. *Lecticus* was restored, who waged great Wars against the Knights of the

the Cross, whom he at last vanquished in a great Battle. Under his Reign, the Dukes of *Silesia* who were Vassals of *Poland*, submitted themselves to the Crown of *Bohemia*. He died in the Year 1333. And was succeeded by his Son, *Casimir the Great*, who having subdued all *Russia*, united it to the Kingdom of *Poland*, so as to enjoy the same Laws and Liberties. He also first introduc'd the *Magdeburg* Laws and Constitutions into *Poland*, and the Duke of *Masoria* did in his time first submit himself as a Vassal to the Crown of *Poland*. He died in the Year 1370. leaving no Issue behind him; and by his Death the Male-Race of *Piastus* lost the Crown of *Poland*. Casimir III.

§. 7. After *Casimir*, the Crown of *Poland* was devolved to *Lewis*, King of *Hungary*, the Sister's Son of *Casimir*: The *Poles* were not well satisfied with him, because he favour'd the *Hungarians* too much. He died in the Year 1382. *Sigismund*, King of *Hungary*, would fain have succeeded him in *Poland*, but the *Poles* refused him. Some proposed *Ziemovitus*, the Duke of *Masoria*, but *Hedwig*, the Daughter of King *Lewis*, for whom the *Poles* would by all means reserve the Crown of *Poland*, would not accept of him for her Husband. At last the *Poles* crowned the above-mention'd *Hedwig*, and married her to *Jagello*, Duke of *Lithuania*, under Condition that he and his Subjects should turn Christians, and *Lithuania* should be united to *Poland* in one Body. The first condition was performed immediately, for he was baptized, and called *Uladislaus* IV. But the performance of the second Article was delayed by the Kings of *Poland* for a considerable time after, under pretence that the *Lethuanians* were not well satisfied in this Point, but in effect, because the Kings were unwilling to surrender their right of Succession to the Dukedom of *Lithuania*; till at last this Union was perfected under the Reign of King *Sigismundus Augustus*. This *Jagello* defeated the Knights of the Cross in a memorable Battle, where 50000 Men having been slain, he took from them a great many Cities in *Prussia*; but they afterwards recovered themselves. He died in the Year 1434. To him succeeded his Son *Uladislaus* V. afterwards made King of *Hungary*, where he was engaged in a War against the *Turks*. In this War *John* Lewis. Jagello *or* Uladislaus IV. *How* Lithuania *was united to* Poland. Uladislaus V.

Huniades first defeated the *Turks* near the River *Moravia*, and *Uladislaus* so beat them upon the Frontiers of *Macedonia*, that they were forced to make a Truce for Ten Years. But upon the Persuasions of the Pope, who sent the Cardinal *Julian* to absolve the King from his Oath, this Truce was broken; and not long after that memorable Battle was fought near *Varna*, where the King himself was kill'd. This Defeat was very shameful and prejudicial to the Christians.

1445. Casimir IV. §. 8. In his stead *Casimir* was made King of *Poland*: And a great part of *Prussia*, which was weary of the Government of the Knights of the Cross, submitted it self to his Protection. This occasioned a heavy War betwixt them and the *Poles*, which was carried on a great while with dubious Success, till a Peace was at last concluded by the Mediation of the Pope; by vertue of which, the *Poles* got *Pomerellia*, *Culm*, *Marienburgh*, *Stum* and *Elbing*, the rest remaining under the Jurisdiction of the Knights of the Cross, under Condition, That the Master of that Order should be a Vassal of *Poland*, and a Duke and Senator of that Kingdom. Much about the same time, the Duke of *Vallachia* submitted himself as a Vassal to the Crown of *Poland*. Under the Reign of this King, the Deputies of the Provinces first appeared at the Diets of the Kingdom. *Uladislaus*, the Son of this *Casimir*, was made King of *Bohemia*, and afterwards also of *Hungary*, he defeated his Brother *John Albert* who contended with him for the latter. *Casimir* died in the Year 1492. and was succeeded by John Albert his Son, *John Albert*, who received a signal overthrow in *Vallachia* from the *Turks* and rebellious *Vallachians*. The *Turks* also fell into *Poland*, but by a sudden great Frost a great many Thousands of them were starved to Death. Under the Reign of this King, the Dukedom of *Plotzko*, in the County of *Masovia*, was united to *Poland*. He died in the Year 1501. and was Alexander. succeeded by his Brother *Alexander*, who dyed in Sigismund. the Year 1506. To him succeeded *Sigismund*, one of the most famous Princes of his time. This King was engaged in three several Wars against the *Muscovites* wherein the *Poles* always were Victorious in the Field; but the *Muscovites* who had got *Smolensko* by Treachery, kept the Possession of that place. The

War

War which he waged with the Knights of the Cross in *Prussia*, was at last composed upon these Conditions, that *Albert* Marquiss of *Brandenburgh*, who was then Master of that Order, should receive the Eastern parts of *Prussia*, as an Hereditary Fief from the King, and should acknowledge himself hereafter a Vassal of the Crown of *Poland*. Under his Reign, also the whole Country of *Masovia* was reunited to the Crown of *Poland*. He also fought very successfully against the *Vallachians*, and died in the Year 1548. leaving for his Successor his Son, *Sigismund Augustus*. Under his Reign *Livonia* submitted to *Poland*, as being not able to defend it self against the *Muscovites*, who had already taken *Dorpt*, *Felin*, and several other Places. In this publick Consternation *Estland* and *Reval* surrendred themselves to *Erick* King of *Sweden*. But the Archbishop of *Riga*, and the Master of the Teutonick Order, sought for protection of the King of *Poland*, which he would not grant them upon any other Terms, than that they should submit themselves to the Crown of *Poland*. Whereupon the Master of the Order having abdicated that Dignity, surrendred the Castle of *Riga*, and some other Places to the *Poles*. And he in recompence of his Loss was made Duke of *Curland* and *Senigal*. This occasioned a War betwixt the *Poles* and *Muscovites*, wherein these took from the former *Plotzko*. This King died without Children, and by his Death the Male Race of the *Jagellonick* Family was quite extinguished.

Sigismundus Augustus.

1552.

§. 9. After his Death there were great Contentions in *Poland* concerning the Election of a new King, and at last by the majority of Votes, *Henry* Duke of *Anjou*, Brother of *Charles* IX. King of *France*, was declared King of *Poland*, who arriving there, was crowned in the same Year. But he had scarce been four Months in *Poland*, when having notice that his Brother the King of *France* was dead, he in the Night-time, and in a thick Fog, for fear the *Poles* should detain him, relinquished *Poland*, and taking his way through *Austria* and *Italy* into *France*, took possession of that Kingdom. The *Poles* being extremely vexed at this Affront, were for electing a new King. A great many were for *Maximilian* of *Austria*; but *Stephen Batori*, Prince of *Transilvania*, being declared King by the

Henry *of* Valois *Duke of* Anjou.

Stephen Batori.

the plurality of Votes, quickly came into *Poland*, and excluded *Maximilian* by marrying *Anna* the Sister of *Sigismundus Augustus*. This King reduced the City of *Dantzick*, which had sided with *Maximilian*. Afterwards he fell upon the *Muscovites*, taking from them *Plotsko* and the neighbouring Countries. At last he made Peace with the *Muscovites*, under this Condition, that they should resign to him the whole Country of *Livonia*, in lieu of which he would restore to them such Places as he had taken from them in *Muscovy*. This King adorned the Kingdom with wholesome Constitutions, and established the Militia of Horse, these he disposed upon the Frontiers, to defend the same against the Incursions of the *Tartars*. By this means that Tract of Land which from *Bar*, *Bracklavia* and *Kiovia*, extends it self betwixt the two Rivers of the *Dniester* and the *Borysthenes*, as far as the *Black-sea*, was filled with populous Cities and Towns, and is now called the *Ukraine*, having been formerly a desolate Country. He also put into good Order and Discipline the *Cosacks*, who served as Foot-Soldiers, giving them *Techtmoravia*, situated on the River *Borysthenes*, which they made afterwards their Magazine, and the place of Residence of their Governours. Before this time the *Cosacks* were only a wild and barbarous sort of Rabble, who were gathered out of the *Polish Russia*, and having settled themselves in the Island of the River *Borysthenes* beneath *Kiow*, lived upon Robbing and Plunder. These *Cosacks*, after they were brought into good Discipline by this King *Stephen*, have been for a considerable time serviceable to the Crown of *Poland*, not only against Incursions of the *Tartars*, but also by their cruising in the *Baltick-Sea*, and so doing great Mischief to the *Turks*. For they had Courage enough to ransack the Cities of *Trebisond* and *Sinope*; nay, even the Suburbs of *Constantinople*, with other Places. This brave King whilst he was making Preparations against the *Turks*, died in the Year 1586.

The Cosacks.

§. 10. After his Death *Sigismund*, Son to *John*, King of *Sweden*, was made King of *Poland*, who had this Advantage, that his Mother *Catherine* had been Sister of *Sigismundus Augustus*, and so consequently was descended from the *Jagellonick* Race. Some of the

Sigismund III.

Poles

Poles proclaimed *Maximilian* their King, but he coming with some Forces to take Possession of the Kingdom was beaten and taken Prisoner; and before he obtained his Liberty was obliged to renounce his Title to that Crown. After the Death of *John*, King of *Sweden*, *Sigismund* went in the Year next following into *Sweden*, where he was crown'd King. But he having afterwards lost that Crown, it occasioned a War betwixt 1592. *Poland* and *Sweden*. In the beginning of this War, *Charles* IX. King of *Sweden*, took a great many Places from the *Poles* in *Livonia*, which were most of them afterwards retaken by the *Polish* General and Chancellor *Zamoiski*: Besides that, the King of *Sweden* was routed in a bloody Battle, fought near *Kirkholm* and 1605. *Riga*, where he narrowly escaped himself. But some intestine Divisions arising betwixt the King and the Nobility of *Poland*, King *Charles* got an opportunity to recover himself.

In the mean time a War broke out betwixt the *Muscovites* and *Poles*, upon the following occasion. There was a certain Person in *Poland*, who pretended that he was *Demetrius*, the Son of *John Basilowitz*, Grand-Duke of *Muscovy*, and that he was to have been murthered by the Order of *Boris Gudenow*, who hoped thereby to obtain the Succession to the Empire after the Death of *Theodore*, the eldest Son of the said *John Basilowitz*; but that another had been killed in his stead. This Man having found great Encouragement from *George Mniszeck* the *Vayvod* of *Sendomir*, promised to marry his Daughter. Upon which this *Vayvod*, with the Assistance of some other *Polish* Lords, having gathered an Army that marched with *Demetrius* into *Muscovy*; and the Grand-Duke *Boris Gudenow* happening to 1605. dye suddenly soon after, *Demetrius* was well received by the *Russians*; and having subdued such as pretended to oppose him, he came up to the City of *Moscow*, where he was proclaimed Grand-Duke: But he quickly made himself odious to the *Muscovites*, who suspected him to be an Impostor, but concealed their Resentment till the arrival of the *Polish* Bride, In the mean while the *Muscovites* (under the Conduct of the House of *Zuski*, who were by their Mother's side descended from the Family of the Grand Dukes) had under-hand got together about 20000 Men. These, at the met

The occasion of the War between Poland and Muscovy.

when

1606. when the Nuptials were celebrating with great Pomp, raised a Tumult, attack'd the Castle, and cut to pieces *Demetrius* and a great many *Poles*, who were come along with the Bride, tho' some of the chiefest defended themselves bravely and escaped their Fury.

Then *Basilius Zuski* was proclaimed Great Duke in the publick Market-place, who caused there the Body of *Demetrius* to be exposed to publick view; but he being extremely defaced by his Wounds, his Face could not be discerned by the Multitude. Immediately after, a Rumour was spread abroad, that *Demetrius* was escaped, and another appeared soon after, who pretended to be the same *Demetrius*. Whether it was the same or not is not yet determined; this is certain, that the *Poles* did acknowledge him as such, as being very desirous to revenge the former Affront, and the Death of their Friends. This *Demetrius* did march with a great

Basil *Great Duke of* Muscovy.

1608. Army, composed of *Poles* and *Cosacks* into *Muscovy*, where he several times beat *Zuski*, whom he obliged to let at Liberty the Captive Bride, and to beg the King of *Poland* to recal his Subjects. But the Bride having acknowledged this *Demetrius* for her Husband, he got a great party both in *Muscovy* and *Poland* that sided with him, and would quickly have ruined *Zuski*, if he had not been succoured by the King of *Sweden*, who sent *Pontus de la Gardie* with some Forces to his Assistance.

Sigismund in the mean time took hold of this Opportunity to try whether he could at least recover *Smolensko* and *Severia* from the *Muscovites*. With this view he besieged *Smolensko* in the Year 1609. which, however, he could not make himself Master of till the Year 1611.

Sigismund *makes his advantage of these Troubles in* Muscovy.

1609. when he took it by Storm. In the mean time, the *Poles* which had hitherto sided with *Demetrius* were recalled by *Sigismund*, who did think it not convenient that so considerable a part of his Forces should be under the Command of another. By the removal of these Forces *Zuski* had leisure given him to recollect himself, and with the Auxiliaries sent him out of *Sweden*, marched against the *Poles* who had besieged *Smolensko*; but was

1610. defeated by the *Poles* near *Clusin*. By this overthrow the Affairs of the *Muscovites* were again put into a very dangerous Condition. Upon which they took this Resolution to avoid the danger which threatn'd them from the *Polish* side. They deposed *Zuski*, who by his Misfortunes was become odious to them, and offered the Crown of *Muscovy* to *Vladislaus* the Prince of *Poland*. By this means they hoped at one stroke to ruin *Demetrius*, and to be reconciled to the *Poles*, in hopes that they might easily meet with an Opportunity hereafter, when they had once rid themselves out of the present Danger, to rid themselves also of the Prince of *Poland*. And this Project succeeded very well, for the *Polish* Troops immediately left the Party of *Demetrius*; *Zuski* was surrendered to the *Poles*, who promised to the *Muscovites*, who had sworn before Allegiance to *Vladislaus*, that he should appear in Person in *Muscovy* in the Year 1610. But King *Sigismund* by the Persuasions of some of his Friends refused this offer, thinking it more for his purpose to Conquer *Muscovy* by force of Arms; which opportunity, however, he missed of, for that he did not immediately march towards the City of *Muscow*, which he might have taken at the first Assault. But the *Muscovites* having discovered the Designs of the *Poles*, did unanimously revolt from *Vladislaus*, especially since they had in the mean while been rid of *Demetrius*, who had been murthered by the *Tartars* that were his Guards. They therefore attack'd the *Polish* Garrison in the City of *Muscow*, which consisted of 7000 Men, but these defended themselves bravely, and besides set Fire to the whole City, which before had 180000 Houses, where abundance of People were burnt. Nevertheless the *Muscovites* recover'd themselves, and besieged the *Polish* Garison in the Castle of *Moscow*. If King *Sigismund*, immediately after the taking of *Smolensko*, had sent them Relief, as he easily might have done, he questionless might have established his Affais in *Muscovy*. But he marching back with his Army into *Poland*, and sending to their Relief neither Men nor Money, the Garrison who had before plundered the Treasury of the Great Duke, to the number of 7000. leaving some to Guard the Castle, fought their way through the *Muscovites*, and came to King *Sigismund* to demand their Pay. And tho' *Sigismund* began to apply himself in good earnest to re-establish his Affairs in *Muscovy*, yet all his Designs were by the Jealousy which reigned betwixt the Generals, so long delay'd, till the *Poles* who had the Guard of the Castle of the City of *Muscow*, were forced

The Policy of the Muscovites.

The Oversight of Sigismund.

by

by Famine to surrender it. Thus all was lost in *Muscovy*; and *Sigismund* was the more troubled at it, because he made an account by the Conquest of *Muscovy* to open his way into *Sweden*.

Besides this, the *Poles* sustained in the same Year a considerable Loss in *Moldavia*. In 1617 Prince *Uladislaus* undertook another Expedition into *Muscovy*, but to no great purpose; upon which he made a Truce with them for 14 Years, wherein it was agreed, that the *Poles* in the mean time should keep in their Possession the Dukedom of *Severia*, *Zernigo* and *Novogrod*, which they had taken during these Troubles in *Muscovy*. In the mean time *George Farenbach* surrendred several Places in *Livonia* to the King of *Sweden*, *Gustavus Adolphus*; but it was suspected that he intended to betray the King; for soon after, the same *Farenbach* was reconciled to King *Sigismund*, unto whom he restored all the Places except *Pernau*.

The Poles *defeated in* Moldavia.

1617.

In the Year 1620. the *Poles* were engaged in a War against the *Turks*, that were as 'tis supposed, stirred up by *Bethlem Gabor*, Prince of *Transilvania*; for *Sigismund* having assisted the Emperour against him, *Bethlem Gabor* was for making a Diversion among them by the help of the *Turks*. Accordingly the *Turks* entered *Moldavia* with an intention to banish that Duke who sided with the *Poles*. The *Polish* General *Zolkieuski* coming to the assistance of the Duke of *Moldavia*, advanced too far into the Country, and as he was marching back was totally routed, and himself slain upon the Place. In the Year next following the *Turks* marched with their whole Force against *Poland*, and were met by the *Poles* near *Chocim*, under the Command of Prince *Uladislaus*. The *Polish* Army was about 65000 strong, but the *Turks* 392000 Men, Commanded by the *Turkish* Emperour *Osman* in Person. The *Turks* attempted three times to take the *Polish* Camp by Storm, but were as often repulsed with great Loss. But the *Poles* in the mean while suffered extremely for want of Ammunition and Provisions, and were mightily weakned by Sickness and a Mortality among their Horses. Nevertheless the *Turkish* Emperor made a very honourable Peace with them, after he had lost 60000 Men in these several Storms made upon their Camp, and a greater number in his March back to *Constantinople*.

A War betwixt the Poles *and* Turks.

In

In the mean time King *Gustavus Adolphus* falling into *Livonia*, took the City of *Riga* without any great resistance; and the rest of *Livonia*, except *Dunneburgh*, was conquer'd by the *Swedes* in the Year 1625. King *Gustavus* enter'd *Prussia* with an Army in the Year 1625. where he took the Cities of *Marienburgh* and *Elbing*, besides some other Places: This War was thus carried on without any General Engagement, till the Year 1629. when *Hans Wrangel*, the *Swedish* General, defeated the *Poles* near *Gorzno*. Then the Emperour sent some Forces to the Assistance of the *Poles*, who in a Battle fought near *Stum*, were very near having made King *Gustavus* their Prisoner. But the *Polish* Affairs after this Battle falling into great Confussion, a Truce was concluded by the Mediation of *France* and *England* till the Year 1634. the *Swedes* being in the mean while to keep in their Possession *Elbing*, *Memel*, *Braunsberg*, *Pillau*, and what else they had taken in *Livonia*; *Sigismund* died in the Year 1632.

1621. *The Invasion of* Gustavus Adolphus. 1625.

§. 11. After his Death his Son *Uladislaus* IV. was declared King, who in the Year next following, obtained a signal Victory over the *Muscovites* that had besieged *Smolensko*; for he not only forced them to raise the Siege, but also brought the *Muscovite* Army into such streights that they were forced to surrender; and the *Turks* who would have made a Diversion upon him, were also bravely repulsed. At last *Uladislaus* made a very advantageous Peace on his side with the *Muscovites*, by vertue of which, these renounced all their Pretensions upon the two large Dukedoms of *Smolensko* and *Czernicho*. This begot such a Terror among the *Turks*, that they freely made him Restitution for the Damages sustained in their last In-road, having also caused the *Bashaw* who commanded these Forces to be strangled. The Truce with *Sweden* was prolonged at *Stumdorf* in *Prussia* for 26 Years, where the Places possessed before by the *Swedes* in *Prussia* were restored to the *Poles*, because the *Swedish* Affairs in *Germany* were then, after the Battle of *Norlingen*, in a very ill Condition, and besides, the *English* and *Dutch* were extremely dissatisfied with the Tolls that were paid in *Prussia*.

Uladislaus IV. 1634. 1635.

In the Year 1637. the Foundation was laid of the War with the *Cosacks*, which has brought unspeaka-

The cause of the War with the Cosacks.

ble

ble Mischiefs upon the *Poles*. The business happen'd thus as the number of *Cosacks* was greatly increased by the great number of Boors which frequently ran into them, so the great Men in *Poland*, who had purchased great Estates in the *Ukraine*, were of Opinion that their Revenues would be considerably encreased, if the Liberties of the *Cosacks* were reduced to more narrow Bounds. Wherefore they having advised the King, that they ought to be more restrained for the future, the *Polish* General *Koniecpoliski*, caused the Fortress of *Hudack* to be built, just at a point where the River of *Zwamer* falls into the *Dnieper* or *Borysthenes*. The *Cosacks* endeavoured to prevent the perfecting of this Work by force, but being routed by the *Poles*, were obliged to surrender their General *Bauluck*, and some of their chief Men among them, who were all, notwithstanding a Pardon was promised them before-hand, beheaded. Besides, it was decreed in the Diet, that all their former Privileges, and the Fortress of *Techtimoravia* should be taken from them, and that in their stead a new Body of Militia should be settled there. To put this Decree in execution, the *Polish* Army marched into the *Ukraine*, against which the *Cosacks* fought with great Bravery, promising nevertheless that they would be faithful to the Crown of *Poland*, if their ancient Privileges were confirm'd to them, which the *Poles* did promise them, but did not perform; nay, did even treat some of them very ill. For among other oppressive Methods, they took from 'em some of their *Greek* Churches. Their General *Chmielinski* was also grosly affronted, for which he could obtain no Satisfaction. For the King having granted him a Privilege to build some Mills, a certain Gentleman, whose Name was *Jarinski*, burnt them, and withal, ravished his Wife, and afterwards killed both her and her Son.

John Casimir. 1647. § 12. In the mean time *Uladislaus* died, to whom succeeded his Brother *John Casimir*. Then *Chmielinski* to revenge himself stirred up the *Cosacks* against the *Poles*, who with Burning, Plundering and Ravishing, did what Mischief they could to the *Polish* Nobility. And the Senators having desired the King to march out into the Field against them, they were answer'd by him, That they ought not to have burnt down their Mills. Where-

at

at the *Poles* being extremely diſſatisfied, brought together an Army of 50000 Men, whom the *Coſacks* defeated, killing 10000 upon the Spot, and then taking the City of *Kiow*. To revenge this Affront, the *Poles* ſummon'd the ſeventh Man throughout the whole Kingdom, and marched againſt the *Coſacks* without the conſent of the King, but were again miſerably beaten by them. But *Chmielinski* celebrating the Nuptials of his Son with the Daughter of the Prince of *Vallachia*, at *Kiow*, the *Poles* ſurpriz'd the *Coſacks* thereabouts, plundered the City, and took the *Grecian* Patriarch Priſoner. The *Coſacks* then ſent to the King, to know whether this had been done by his Authority; and the King having anſweerd, *No, but that it had been done by the Nobility to take revenge of the* Coſacks; they joined with the *Tartars* and fell into *Poland*. Againſt theſe the King went in Perſon into the Field, at the Head of the Nobility, and defeated them in a Battle. But the King having afterwards made an Agreement with them, the Nobility was greatly diſcontented with the King's Proceedings.

The Poles *defeated by the* Coſacks.

Whilſt theſe Jealouſies reigned the *Muſcovites* fell into *Poland*, and having brought the *Coſacks* over to their Party, beſieged *Smolensko*, which they took in the Year next following, and having ravaged *Lithuania*, they took *Wilna*, and ſome other Cities, where they committed great Barbaraties.

The Muſcovites *join with the* Coſacks. 1653.

In the Year 1655, another Storm threatned the *Poles*. For *Charles Guſtavus*, King of *Sweden*, having with an Army of choſen Men enter'd that Kingdom, firſt conquer'd *Great Poland* and *Maſovia*, and afterwards the *Leſſer Poland*, with the capital City *Cracow*, from whence he marched into *Pruſſia* where almoſt all the Cities ſurrendred except *Dantzick*, in which were at firſt a great many Citizens that favoured the *Swedes*, but by the perſuaſions of ſome Miniſters were kept in obedience to *Poland*. The Reſiſtance made by this one City, was the main Reaſon why all the Advantages got by the *Swedes* proved fruitleſs at laſt, and that they could not maintain themſelves in *Pruſſia*, notwithſtanding that not only the whole Militia of *Poland*, and that part of *Lithuania* which was not under the Subjection of the *Muſcovites*, had ſubmitted themſelves to the *Swediſh* Protection, but alſo, that King *John Caſimir* himſelf had fled into *Sileſia*, For the *Poles* having recollected them-

The King of Sweden *invades* Poland.

themselves after the first Consternation was over, and being joined by the *Tartars*, fell upon such of the *Swedish* Forces as were dispersed up and down the Country. The *Lithuanians* also revolted and killed all the *Swedes* that were in Winter-Quarters with them. Add to this, that King *Charles Gustavus* had greatly weakned his Army, not only by the great March towards *Jeroslavia*, but by the opportunity given to *Czerneski* the *Polish* General to fall often with his Light-Horse upon the Rear of the Army, and so do considerable Mischief. In the mean while the *Poles* had also retaken *Warsaw*, where they made the *Swedish* Governor, *Wittemberg*, and some other great Officers Prisoners, contrary to the Articles made at the Surrender of the Place. And tho' King *Charles Gustavus* having been joined before by the Elector of *Brandenburg*'s Forces, routed the *Poles* and *Tartars* in a memorable Battle, which lasted three Days, and was fought near *Warsaw*, yet all the Princes of *Europe* began to look about them, and to consult about a Diversion to be made in *Sweden*. The *Muscovites* fell into *Livonia*, where they besieged *Riga*, but to no purpose. The *Hollanders* did give plainly to understand, that they were willing that *Prussia* should come under the Subjection of *Sweden*. And the *Danes* also began to be in motion. On the other hand, *Ragotzi* Prince of *Transilvania* enter'd *Poland* with an Army, to try whether perhaps he could obtain the Crown for himself. But the King of *Sweden* being obliged to march out of *Poland* against the *Danes*, *Ragotzi* made a bad Market of it; for before he could reach his own Country, he was totally routed, and obliged to make a shameful Accord with the *Poles*, Which misfortune however he might have avoided, if he, according to the advice of the King of *Sweden*, who promised to keep the *Poles* so long in play, till he was out of danger, would have taken his March directly over *Brescie*, *Pinsk*, and so farther towards his own Frontiers. But *Ragotzi* would by all means take his way near *Cracow*. Then the *Poles* re-took *Cracow* and *Thorn*, and chased the *Swedes* out of *Curland*, who had before taken the Duke of that name Prisoner. The *Poles* also besieged *Riga*, but were beaten from thence by the *Swedish* General *Helmsfeld*. And tho' the *Poles* by the Peace made at *Oliva* recovered all *Prussia* again, yet were they obliged to

The Battle of Warsaw.

Ragotzi *Prince of* Transilvania *invades* Poland.

1660.

to renounce all their Pretensions upon *Livonia*, and to leave the *Muscovites* in the Possession of *Smolensko*, *Severia* and *Kiow*. Neither could they appease the *Cosacks*, some of them having put themselves under the Protection of the *Muscovites*, some under the *Turks*, whereby they shewed the way to the *Turks* into *Poland*. Neither could the King put an end to the intestine Divisions and Jealousies, wherefore at last tired with these Troubles, *John Casimir* resigned the Crown, and living a retired Life in *France*, in the Abby of St. *Germain*, he there died a few Years after.

§. 13. There being now left none of the Royal Family in *Poland*, several Foreigners pretended to the Crown. But at last, a *Piastus*, whose name was *Michael Witsnowiski*, was declared King, chiefly by the Votes of the Lesser Nobility. His short Reign was full of intestine Commotions, and the *Turks* in the mean while did not cease to do considerable mischief in *Poland*; having in the Year 1672. taken *Caminieck* in *Podolia*, which Fortress having been formerly thought impregnable, serves them now for a Door, through which they may enter *Poland* at pleasure. A Peace was then concluded with the *Turks*, by vertue of which, the said Fortress remained in the Possession of the *Turks*; the *Poles* also having promised to pay to the *Turks* a yearly Tribute. The King died in the Year 1673. In whose stead in the Year next following, the *Polish* General, *John Sobieski*, was made King of *Poland*, he having in the Year before attack'd the *Turks* in their Camp with such success, that of 32000 Men scarce 1500 escaped alive. He renewed the War with the *Turks*, but concluded a Peace with them in the Year 1676. by vertue of which the *Turks* kept the Fortress of *Caminieck*, but remitted the yearly Tributes to the *Poles*.

Mchael Wisnowiski.

John Sobieski.

§. 14. It is to be considered concerning the *Polish* Nation, that whosoever is not a Nobleman in *Poland*, is esteemed a Boor. For the Inhabitants of the Cities are very little regarded, and the Tradesmen are most Foreigners. But the Boors are esteemed and used no better than Slaves, being also very raw and barbarous, both in their Life and Conversation, wherefore when we talk of the *Poles*, thereby ought only to be understood the

The Genius of this Nation.

Nobility. They are therefore commonly downright and honest, very seldom giving to the Art of Dissembling; they are of a very generous Spirit, and expect a great deal of Respect. And if you give them as much Respect as they pretend to, they are no less Courteous, and will willingly pay a Respect again to you; and their Words and Behaviour are full of Pomp and Ceremony. They are very Liberal, or rather profuse; and not given to be Parsimonious, tho' they should want the next Day. This Nation also is very fierce and Extravagant, much inclined to an uncontrouled Liberty, or rather Licentiousness and Petulancy. Wherefore Plots and Conspiracies against their Kings are frequent among them, whose Actions they canvass with a great deal of freedom being always jealous of the least Point of their Liberty. They do not want Courage, but they are more fit to Act with a sudden Heat than to endure long the Fatigues of War. And because the Nobles only apply themselves to the War, who never serve but on Horse-back, and the rest of the Inhabitants are of no great Spirit, their Infantry gathered out of the Natives is not worth much, wherefore they are obliged in their stead to make use of Foreigners listed into their Service, or of the *Cosacks* who are courageous and active.

The Nature of the Soil, &c. Its Commodities.

§. 15. This Country is of a vast extent, and very Fertile in general, fit both for Tillage and Pasture, or breeding of Cattel. For *Holland* draws most of its Corn out of *Poland*, and the *Polish* Oxen are sent in great numbers into *Germany*. The *Polish* Wooll also is in good esteem abroad. *Poland* abounds in good Horses. *Lithuania* produces abundance of Honey, which is most consumed by the Inhabitants, who make Mead of it; the rest is exported, as likewise abundance of wax, Hemp, Flax, Leather, Pot-Ashes, Salt, Wood, and the like. But on the contrary, the Commodities which are imported here are Silk, Woollen-Stuffs and Cloaths, Tapestries, Sables, *Hungarian* and *Spanish* Wines, abundance of Spice, which they use in great quantity in their Diet. If the *Poles* were addicted in the least to good Husbandry, and would apply themselves a little to Manufacturies, the Commodities fit for Exportation here, would much surpass those which need be imported.

Poland is very Populous, and full of Towns and Villages. Some have computed that the King and the Nobility have in their Possession 90000 Cities and Villages, the Bishops and Canons 100550, the rest of the Clergy, *Monks* and *Nuns* 66950, which in all amounts to the Number of 256950 Towns and Villages: But I will not be answerable for this Account.

§. 16. The chief strength of this Kingdom consists in the Nobility. The *Poles* have formerly given out that they could raise 250000 Horse, some say 300000, out of the Nobility. This seems to be a little largely spoken, except you would reckon among them their *Servants*. This is certain that in no Kingdom of *Europe* there is so great a number of Nobles. They may also find a way to raise a proportionable Infantry out of the *Cosacks*. And if they will stretch a little their Purses, they are able enough to raise sufficient Sums for the maintaining of a great Army. But here is the mischief, that the King cannot Levy any extraordinary Taxes without the consent of the Nobility; and both the Clergy and the Nobility are very backward in paying of any Taxes, or at least grow quickly weary of them, except it be in case of the highest necessity. And this is the reason why the King of *Poland* cannot carry on a War long with vigour. Besides that when the Nobles are summon'd to appear in Arms, they come slowly into the Field, and are not easily kept under Discipline. The *Polish* Armies have likewise this inconveniency in them, that where 10000 fighting Men are, at least five times the number of Servants and idle Fellows follow the Camp, which proves a Destruction to their own Country, and occasions scarcity of Provisions both for Men and Horse.

The Strength of the Kingdom.

Their Weakness.

§. 17. Concerning their Form of Government, it is to be observed that the *Poles* live under one Head, who bears the Title, and lives in the Splendour becoming a King; but if you consider his Power, which is circumscribed within very narrow Bounds he is in effect no more than the Prime or chief Regent in a Free Commonwealth. This King is always chosen by a Free Election, where every Noble Man there present has his Vote; and tho' the *Poles* have been always inclined

The Form of Government.

to keep to the Royal Race, yet have they never been for declaring a Successor during the Life of the Present King, but have always expected the vacancy of the Throne. But, that, during this Vacancy all disorders may be prevented, Justice is then exercised with more severity than at other times. The Archbishop of *Gnesna* who is the Primate of *Poland*, being in the mean while the Regent, or as it were Interrex of the Kingdom. The *Poles* have had for a considerable time this Maxim, that they would rather choose a King out of a Foreign Princely Family than out of their own Nobility; as being of Opinion that thereby the equality among the Nobility may be better preserved: for a Foreigner is no more engaged to one than to another; whereas a Native always prefers his Kindred and Relations before the rest; and this Rule they have observed ever since the time of *Jagello*, who being a *Lithuanian*, united *Lithuania* with *Poland*. But they had not the same good Fortune with *Sigismund* King of *Sweden*, partly because the situation of these two Kingdoms is such, that both cannot be well govern'd by one King; partly because they were thereby engaged in a heavy War against *Sweden*, which else might easily have been avoided; but they have been always very careful not to take their Kings out of the House of *Austria*, fearing least they should be treated like the *Hungarians* and *Bohemians*. This Elective King has a great Revenue out of the Lands belonging to the Crown, and has the sole Power to dispose of all vacant Offices, Dignities and Benefices; but he cannot make new Laws, begin a War, impose new Taxes, or undertake any other matters of great moment without the Consent of the Estates. The Estates in *Poland* are composed of the Bishops and some Abbots, of the Palatines or Vayvods, which are Governours of the Provinces, of the Castellans or Governours of Castles, and of the chief Officers of the Kingdom: These compose the Senate, which consisted formerly of 150 Persons; besides these, there are the Deputies of the Nobility out of each District, who have almost the same Power which the Tribunes of the People had at *Rome*; since one single Person among them, by entring his Protest, may annul a Decree at the Diet; and these Deputies use their Tongues very freely at the Diet, both against the King and his Ministers; from whence

The Revenues of the King.

The Estates of the Kingdom.

whence it often happens that Matters are debated here with great Confusion; especially since a certain time of six Weeks is prefixed by the Laws for the holding of the Diet which they rarely suffer to be Prorogued, and that not but for a few Days; but they call this right of contradicting, the Soul of the *Polish* Liberty. The King is also obliged to bestow all the vacant Benefices upon the Nobility, and cannot reserve any for his own use, or bestow them upon his Children without consent of the Estates; neither can he buy or take Possession of any Noblemens Lands. The King is not Master of the Judicial Courts; but there is a certain High-Court of Justice, the Judges whereof are Nobles: first Instituted by King *Stephen Batori*. These Judges are changed every Twelve Months, and keep their Sessions Six Months in the Year at *Petricovia*, and Six Months again at *Lublin*, and from these no Appeal lies to the King, except that some Cases of the greatest Consequence are determined at the Diet; but Cases belonging to the King's Exchequer, or to his Revenues, are determined by the King. The *Poles* are extremely fond of this Form of Government, as being very suitable to their natural fierce inclinations; yet the same is very improper for any sudden and great undertaking, and contributes not a little to the weakness of this vast Kingdom, especially when the Nobility is refractary and jealous of the King.

Of the Administration of Justice.

§. 18. The Neighbours of *Poland* are on one side the *Germans*, where there is an open Country upon the Frontiers; and particularly *Poland* borders upon *Silesia*, and in one corner upon *Hungary*. 'Tis true, that the *German* Empire is much superior in Strength to *Poland*; but the Interest of both these Kingdoms is such, as not to have any great occasion to differ with one another, except *Poland* should perhaps join with such Estates in *Germany*, as would upon an occasion oppose the setting up of an Absolute Sovereignty in the Empire; and in such a case, the *Poles* would not want assistance either from the *German*, or Foreign Princes, that must concur in the same Interest. The House of *Austria* alone is not powerful enough to conquer *Poland*, or to maintain a Country which is of so vast an Extent, and very Populous, and lying all upon a level is not secu-

Neighbours of Poland.

Germany.

The House of Austria *in particular.*

secured by any fortified places. If no body else should side with *Poland*, the *Turks* themselves would not easily suffer that the House of *Austria* should acquire such an advantage, and the *Turks* are the fittest Instruments to prevent it. But the House of *Austria* has often endeavoured, tho' the wisest among the *Poles* have always opposed it, to unite the Kingdom of *Poland* to their Family by an Election; but the *Poles* are conscious of the danger which might accrue from this Union to their Liberty; and besides this, they are no great admirers of the *Germans*, whose Modesty and good Husbandry they commonly despise.

The Interest of Poland *and* Germany, *with reference to the* Turks.

But it is of great consequence to *Poland*, that the *Turks* may not become quite Masters of the *Upper Hungary*, and much more that they do not get footing in *Moravia*; since thereby they would open their way into the very Heart of *Poland*. And on the other hand, it is the common Interest both of the House of *Austria*, and of all *Germany*, that the *Turks* may not become Masters of *Poland* since thereby they would open their way into *Germany* For the old Saying of *Philip Melanchton*, if the *Turk* come into *Germany* they will certainly come by the way of *Poland*, did not arise from a Prophetick Spirit, but has its good reason in Geography. And it seems to be the common Interest of *Poland*, and the House of *Austria*, to keep up a mutual good understanding, since they both cover one anothers Frontiers and *Poland* draws a great advantage from its Oxen and Salt which are sent into *Germany*. Besides, if *Poland* should engage it self in good earnest against the House of *Austria*, it ought to be jealous of the *Muscovites* who may attack it behind, except *Muscovy* were otherwise employ'd before. *Poland*, on the other hand, may be troublesome to the House of *Austria*, when that House is engaged in Wars against *France*, *Sweden* or the *Turks*. Wherefore for a considerable time the House of *Austria*, has endeavoured by Marriages to Ally *Poland* with their Family and to gain a considerable Party in the Senate. And *France* has followed the same methods to draw *Poland* from the Interest of the House of *Austria*; and the *Poles* having been caressed by both Parties, have got no small advantage by this Rivalship.

Brandenburgh.

Brandenburgh also Borders on one side upon *Poland*, and tho' he alone cannot hurt it much, yet Experi-

Experience has taught us that in Conjunction with others, he has been able to create great troubles to the *Poles*; tho, on the other hand, it is to be feared, perhaps upon a good occasion offer'd to the *Poles*, they may attempt to unite all *Prussia* to their Kingdom, as the Elector of *Brandenburgh* knew how to time it when he obtained the Sovereignty over it. As long as the Differences betwixt *Poland* and *Sweden* were on foot, *Denmark* by making a Diversion could be very serviceable to *Poland*; but since the Causes of these Differences are taken away, *Poland* need not make any particular Reflection upon *Denmark*. *Sweden* and *Poland* have all the Reason in the World to cultivate a mutual good Understanding, since they may be very serviceable to one another against the *Muscovites*. *Poland* borders upon *Muscovy* by a great Tract of Land, where the Frontiers are common to both: These two Kingdoms seem to be very near equal in Strength; and tho' the *Poles* are better Soldiers than the *Muscovites*, yet has the great Duke of *Muscovy* this advantage over them, that he is Absolute in his Dominions. And it is of great Consequence to either of them, which of these two is in the Possession of *Smolensko*, to recover which the *Poles* ought to employ all their Strength. For the rest, these two States being both obliged to have a watchful Eye over the *Turks*, can assist one another against them in case of necessity. The *Tartars* are the most pernicious Neighbours of *Poland*, for they are a Nation living by Depredations, who surprize their Neighbours and when they have loaded themselves with Spoils, return home again, where you cannot be revenged of them, they being so nimble, and having nothing worth taking from them. Against these the Country of *Modavia* used to be a Bulwark to *Poland*. For through that Country the *Tartars* have a direct Passage into the Provinces of *Poland*, which may be shut up against them by the help of that Prince. Wherefore the *Poles* do much lament the loss of this Dukedom; which having been formerly a Fief of that Crown, tho that Duke pay'd also some Tribute to the *Turks*, was brought in the Year 1612. entirely under the *Turkish* Subjection. The *Cosacks* also used to be very serviceable against the *Tartars*, as living near the *Isthmus* of the *Taurick Chersonesus*, and therefore

Denmark and Sweden.

Muscovy.

The Tartars.

Moldavia.

The Cosacks.

fore were conveniently situated to cut off their Retreat in their return Home. But the *Poles* by their ill Treatment have so exasperated the *Cosacks*, that since, they have done as much mischief to them, as formerly they used to do good.

The Turks. Lastly, The *Turk* is a dangerous Neighbour, whose Strength is much superiour to that of *Poland*, especially if the *Poles* are not assisted by the *Cosacks*, or by some Foreign State. For tho' the *Polish* Cavalry may be not inferior to the *Turks*, yet cannot I see which way they can bring into the Field such Forces as may be equal to the *Janisaries*. Tho' the Negligence and Domestick Divisions of the *Poles* have lately been the chief Inducements, which have drawn the *Turks* so deep into *Poland*. There is not any thing which would more conveniently secure the *Poles* against the *Turks*, than if the Princes of *Moldavia*, *Wallachia*, and *Transilvania*, did belong to *Poland*, they being able to hinder the Passage of the *Turks* into *Poland*. But, because the *Poles* have long ago lost this advantage, or rather neglected it, it is their business now, to take care that the *Turks* do not advance deeper into the Country. And to take away all Pretensions of a War from the *Turks*, it seems very necessary that the *Poles*, as much as in them lies, take care that the *Cosacks* do not in time of Peace commit Depredations upon the *Turkish* Subjects. For else the *Turks* are not to be blamed, if endeavouring to root out these rapacious Birds they destroy their Nest, and make the *Ukrain* a vast Wilderness. When *Poland* is engaged in a War with the *Turks*, it may expect some Subsidies from the Pope. The House of *Austria* is able, by making a Diversion to the *Turky*, to give relief to *Poland*; but this House hitherto has not been forward to attack the *Turks*, if these have not been the first Aggressors. The *Muscovites* also might contribute something this way, if there were any hopes of a true understanding betwixt these two Nations; but as the Case now stands, the *Poles* must chiefly rely upon their own Strength, and by the circumstances of their own Affairs be able to judge how far they ought to engage themselves against the *Turk*.

CHAP.

CHAP. XI.

Of MUSCOVY.

§. 1. THE first Origin of this Empire, and the Atchievements of their ancient Princes, are very uncertain and obscure, since what is to be found of this nature among an illiterate uncivilíz'd People, is all trifling and very confused. So much is certain, that this wide extended Empire was formerly divided into a great many petty Lordships, which afterwards were united in one Body. We will only relate in a few words, that the *Russians* in the year 989. first embraced the Christian Religion, at which time their Prince *Woldomir*, married *Anne*, the Sister of the *Grecian* Emperor, *Basilius Porphyrogenitus*. In the year 1237. their Prince *George* was Slain by *Battus* the King of the *Tartars*; upon which the *Russians* being brought under the Subjection of the *Tartars*, their Princes were dependent on them. After a long time they at last freed themselves from this Slavery under their Prince *John*, Son of *Basilius* the Blind, who began his Reign in the year 1450. Under his Reign *Russia* was first united into one considerable Body, he having subdued most of those petty Princes, which had divided *Russia* among them, especially the Dukes of *Tiver* and of Great *Novogrod*, in which City, 'tis said, he got a Booty of 300 Cart-loads of Gold and Silver. This Prince built *Ivanogrod*, a Castle near *Narva*.

The most Ancient State of Russia.

John.

§. 2. To him succeeded his Son *Basilius*, who, in 1509. took *Pleskow*, then a free City. From the *Poles* he took *Smolensko*; but was soundly beaten by the *Casan Tartars*, who at the same time ransack'd the City of *Muscow*. His Successor was his Son *John Basilowitz*, a cruel Tyrant, who conquer'd the two Kingdoms of the *Tartars* of *Casan* and *Astracan*, and united them to *Muscovy*. This Prince used the *Livonians* very barbarously, having killed one *Furstenburg*, the Master of the great Order of Knighthood there; which was the occasion that the City of *Revel*, and all *Esten*, surrendred themselves

Basilius.

John Basilowitz. 1533.

to *Sweden* and the rest of *Livonia* to *Poland*. He was at first Victorious against the *Poles*; but afterwards *Stephen Batori* took from him *Plotzko*, and several other Places. He died in the Year 1584. and to him succeeded his Son *Theodore Juanowitz*, a very simple Prince; against whom the *Swedes* waged War about *Ingermanland*.

Theodore Juanowitz

§. 3. This *Theodore* dying without Issue, his Brother-in-law, *Boris-Guidenow*, did by his clandestine and unwarrantable Intrigues obtain the Empire, but with very indifferent Success, especially after *Demetrius* the Impostor began to contend with him for it; during which Troubles he died. His Son *Theodore Borissowitz*, was thereupon proclaim'd Great Duke of *Muscovy*. But the greatest part of the *Muscovites* going over soon after to *Demetrius* the Impostor, he was taken Prisoner and strangled, after brooking the empty Title of Great Duke only for six Months. What became of the supposed *Demetrius*, and how *Basilius Zuski* took upon him the Imperial Dignity, we have related before. To this *Zuski*, *Charles* XI. King of *Sweden*, offer'd his Assistance against the second supposititious *Demetrius*, which he at first refused to accept of. But afterwards, when the other began to be too strong for him, he earnestly desired the same, promising to surrender to *Charles*, as an acknowledgment, *Kelkholm*. Pursuant to his Request, the King sent to his Assistance *Pontus de la Gardie* with some thousand Men, who were very serviceable to the *Muscovites*; But the *Muscovites* refusing upon several frivolous Evasions, to deliver up the Places stipulated by *Charles*, he took them by force, and by so doing, annex'd *Carelia*, and the rest of *Ingermanland* to the Kingdom of *Sweden*. How this *Basilius Zuski* was delivered up to the *Poles*; how the Impostor *Demetrius* was slain, and *Uladislaus*, Prince of *Poland*, made Duke of *Muscovy*, has been related before in the History of *Poland*.

Boris Guidenow. 1605. Thodore Borissowitz. 1606. Basilius Zuski.

§. 4. At last *Michael Fadorowitz* Son of the Patriarch *Theodore Mikitowitz*, born of the Daughter of *John Basilowitz*, maintained himself in the Empire, who having concluded a Peace with *Sweden* and *Poland*, restor'd tranquility to the *Muscovites*. He was succeeded by his Son *Alexius Michaelowitz*, who in the Year 1653, falling upon the *Poles*, took from them *Smelenzko* and *Kiow*, and com-

Michael Fadorowitz. 1613. 1645. Alexius Michaelowitz.

committed great depredations in *Lithuania*. Then invading *Livonia* he took *Dorpt*, *Kokenhusen*, and several other Places of less Note; but was oblig'd to raise the Siege of *Riga* with great Loss. And soon after a Peace ensued, by the Tenor of which he restored to *Sweden* all the Places he had taken. In the Year 1669. one *Stephen Ratzin*, a seditious Rebel, disturb'd the Repose of his Government, and made him very uneasie; for having master'd *Casan* and *Astracan*, he committed great Depredations all over *Muscovy*, till at last he was taken and brought to condign Punishment: Upon which all the Countries he had overrun return'd to their due Obedience. Soon after, many of the *Cossacks* having submitted themselves to the Protection of *Alexius*, he was thereby engag'd in a War with the *Turks*, wherein he got but little Advantage. He died in the Year 1675. leaving the Empire to his Son *Theodore Alexowitz* a young and sickly Prince, of whom we can say nothing as yet. 1661. Theodore Alexowitz.

§. 5. The Genius and Manners of the *Muscovites* afford us nothing that is very praise-worthy. For among them there is no such Politeness as among most other *European* Nations, Reading and Writing being the highest degree of Learning among them; and the Learning of their Priests themselves does not go farther than to be able to read a Chapter of the Bible, or to read a piece of a Sermon. They are also Jealous, Cruel, and Bloody-minded; insupportably proud in Prosperity, and dejected and cowardly in Adversity. Nevertheless, they have such an Opinion of their own Abilities and Merits, that you can scarce ever pay them sufficient Respect. They are very apt and cunning in the Trade of Usury, but are of a servile Temper, and must be kept under by Severity. At all sorts of Games and Sports they conclude with Blows and Fighting; so that Sticks and Whips are much us'd among them. They are of a strong Constitution, and able to undergo all sorts of Fatigue, even Famine and Thirst. In Field-Fights and Sieges they are worth nothing, because they are soon brought into Confusion, and are themselves of Opinion, that other Nations are their Masters in this Point. But they defend a Fortress to the utmost, not only in regard they are very fit to undergo Hardships and all sorts of Misery, but they endeavour to bring their Soldiers under good Discipline, *The Genius of this Nation.*

for which purpose they make use of a great many *Scotch* and *German* Officers, who instruct them in all manner of Warlike Exercises. But, they do not allow that the *Muscovites* should serve abroad and learn themselves the perfection of Military Arts and Exercises; for the Grand Duke is apprehensive, that if they should grow too knowing, they might be for making Innovations at Home.

The Nature of the Country & Commodities. §. 6. The Territories of the present Grand Duke of *Muscovy* are of a very large Extent; but then a great many Parts are meer Wildernesses scarce Inhabited at all. The *Muscovites* have at Home great plenty of Corn, Cattle, all sorts of Game, Fish, Salt, Furrs, and all other Necessaries. They have a great many Commodities fit for Exportation, especially Furrs and their precious Sables, which are esteem'd at a high Rate among their Neighbours, Salt-Fish, Cafiar, Hides, Tallow, Wax, Honey, Pot-ashes, Soap, Hemp, and the like. The Commodities which are imported to them, are Silk, Stuffs, Cloth of Gold, Cloth of Silver, Woollen Cloth, Tapestry Pearls and Precious Stones, Spices and Wines; but the latter not in any great Quantities. Tobacco is now a prohibited Commodity there. They have kept it for a constant Custom in their way of Trade, not to buy with ready Money, but to exchange Commodities for Commodities; and it is against the Laws of *Muscovy* to export any Coin. Their greatest Trade is at *Archangel*, the Navigation to which was first found out by the *English*, in the Year 1553. Before the Discovery of this way of Navigation, this Trade was carried on by the way of *Nerva* and *Revel*; but tho' this was the shorter way, yet did the Foreign Merchants not care to be so much in Subjection to the *Swedes* and *Danes*. There is also a considerable Trade carried on with the *Persians* upon the River *Wolga* by the way of *Astracan*.

Form of Government. §. 7. The Form of Government here is an Absolute Monarchy; the Grand Duke, whom they call in their Native Language *Czar*, being not tied up to any Laws or Rules, unto whom his Subjects are obliged to pay Obedience without reserve, so that they are no more than Slaves. And indeed this Condition suits best with their natural Constitution. This servile and blind Obedience *Strength of the Country.* of the People, is a great addition to his Strength, since he he cannot only raise some hundred Thousands of Men at the first Command, but enjoys immense Riches and prodigious Revenues. These accrue to him, not only out of the Taxes and Incomes of so vast a Country, but likewise from the Monopoly of Sables, which is only in his Hands; nay, if I am not mistaken, he in like manner Farms out all publick Inns, Taverns and Ale-Houses, which amounts to a prodigious Revenue in this Country, where the People are much addicted to Drinking. He makes his Presents to Foreign Princes and Ambassadors in Sables; but recieves in lieu of them Gold and Silver. Besides this, it is a common Custom with him, to set a new Stamp upon Dollars or Crown-Pieces, and to oblige his Subjects to take them for double the Value. *Muscovy* also enjoys this Advantage before other States, that it is not to be attack'd on the back-side, because its Territories are on the North-East side covered by a vast unnavigable Sea, and wide extended Desarts,

§. 8. *Muscovy* is bounded on the East by the *Persians.* These two States cannot hurt one another much; the *Caspian* Sea, unaccessable Countries, and vast Wildernesses being their common Borders: Wherefore it is not worth their while to extend their Conquests. But they may be serviceable to one another by making a Diversion to the *Turks*. The *Tartars* are troublesome Neighbours to the *Muscovites*, who make no account of Faith or Alliances, but make a Trade of Robbing and Plundring; and against whom there is no Remedy, but to kill them as fast as they can; tho' indeed that is not so easily to be done, because they are very nimble, and their Habitations are not fix'd. Of these the *Crim Tartars* are most mischievous to *Muscovy*; and to hinder their Incursions, the *Muscovites* are oblig'd to keep a considerable number of Horse upon the Frontiers; besides which, they may sometimes give them a Diversion, with the help of the *Donisque Cosacks*, and the *Nagage* and *Calmuck Tartars*. If the *Muscovites* could maintain themselves in *Kiow*, and part of the *Ukraine*, it would serve them at once to bridle these Robbers, and for a Bulwark against the *Turks*. For the *Turks* do not immediately border upon *Muscovy*, but by the Country of nhe *Crim-Tartars*, who being Vassals of the *Turks*, They make use of them like their hunt-

Neighbours of Muscovy, *the* Persians.

Tartars.

ing Dogs. Wherefore it is of great Consequence to *Muscovy*, that the *Turks* do not become Masters of the whole *Ukraine*, since therefore they would be enabled, with the help of the *Cosacks* and *Tartars*, to do great Mischief to *Muscovy*.

Poland. The *Muscovites* ought to have a watchful Eye over the *Poles*, these being so situated, that they may do the greatest mischief to *Muscovy*, especially since the *Poles* are much better Soldiers than the *Muscovites* in the Field.

Sweden. But if the *Swedes* in conjunction with the *Poles*, should attack the *Muscovites*, they would put them very hard to it. The *Muscovites* ought not to make any great account upon an Alliance with *Denmark*, because they are far distant, and therefore cannot revenge themselves upon one another: Neither have the *Muscovites* hitherto appeared at any general Treaties among the Princes of *Europe*.

CHAP. XII.

Of the Spiritual Monarchy of Rome: *Or of the* Pope.

Politick Reflections upon the Popedom.

§. 1. THE Pope may be considered two different ways: First, As far as the Articles of his Communion, which differ from those of other Christians, are agreeable or disagreeable with the Holy Scriptures, and consequently useful or prejudicial to Salvation, which Consideration we leave to Divines. Secondly. As far as the Pope is not only possess'd of a considerable Principality in *Italy*, but also pretends to be Sovereign and Supreme Head of Christendom, at least in Spiritual Matters, and in effect, exercises the said Power in those States of *Europe* which profess themselves of the same Communion with him.

This second Consideration belongs to the Politicians; for this Spiritual Sovereignty introduces great Alterations, and interferes with the Civil Supreme Power; nay, it cramps and maims it. And Religion is so interwoven with Civil Interest, that it belongs to the perfection of a consummate Politician, to be well instructed whence this Spiritual Monarchy had its Original, and by what means

means it hath so mightily increased and is still preserv'd. A just view of this Matter will at the same time let us into the Nature of the chiefest Controversies now in vogue among Christians in the Western Parts of the World, how far they are owing either to the various Interpretations of the Holy Scripture, or to Worldly Interest; so that from thence a Wise Man may easily judge, whether at any time these Controversies are likely to be composed or not.

§. 2. Now to look back to the first beginning of Things, we find, that before the Nativity of our Saviour, the Inhabitants of the whole Universe except the *Jews*, lived in ignorance as to Spiritual Affairs. For what was commonly taught concerning the Gods, was for the most part involv'd in Fables and most extravagant Absurdities. 'Tis true, some of the Learned among them have pretended to give some rational Account concerning the Nature of the Gods and the State of the Soul; but all this in so imperfect and dubious a Manner, that they themselves remained very uncertain in the Matter. They agree'd almost all of them in this Point, that Mankind ought to apply itself to the practice of Virtue; but they did not propose any other Fruits, besides the Honour and Benefits which from thence accrues to Civil Society. For what the Poets gave out concerning the rewards of Virtue and punishments of Vice after Death, was by those who pretended to be the Wisest among them, look'd upon as Fables, invented to terrify and keep in awe the common People. The rest of the People liv'd at random; and what the Heathens call'd Religion, did not contain any Doctrin or certain Articles concerning the knowledge of Divine Matters. But the greatest part of their Religious Worship consisted in Sacrifices and Ceremonies, which tended more to Sports and Voluptuousness, than to the Contemplation of Divine Things. From whence 'tis evident, that the Heathen Religion did neither give Sanctity in this Life, nor afford any Hopes of Comfort at the time of Death. *The Blindness of Heathens in Matters of Religion.*

§. 3. At that time the *Jews* were the only Nation to whom God had revealed the true Religion, which could lead Mankind in the way of Salvation. Nevertheless, *The Constitution of the Jewish Religion.*

there was a vast difference betwixt that and the Christian Religion, not only in regard the *Jewish* Religion represented the Saviour of the World and the Fountain of Salvation in Types and Promises; whereas the Christian Religion comprehends the Reality and Accomplishment of the same; but also because the *Jewish* Religion was cloathed with a great many, and those very burthensome Ceremonies: And some of these being accommodated to the natural Inclination of that Nation, proved an Obstacle to the general reception of that Religion by all Nations: This Ceremonial Part being like a Wall, whereby the *Jews* were separated from other Nations. 'Tis true, all other Nations were not excluded from receiving Salvation through the Belief in the Saviour of the World who was to come. There were also some among the *Jews*, who were very careful, and applied themselves to the Conversion of such as they kept Correspondence with. But it was not decreed by God Almighty to send all over the Earth at that time his Delegates or Apostles, instructed with peculiar Gifts to call all Nations to unite themselves with the *Jewish* Church. And what was done by some private Persons in the converting of Infidels, was of no great consequence in comparison of the whole World. Besides, the *Jewish* Nation being at that time the Select People of God, adorned with great Prerogatives, and having the possession of the only Temple of God, was grown so proud, that the *Jews* despised all other Nations besides themselves. They being also oblig'd by the Institution of their Ceremonies, not to converse too familiarly upon several accounts with other Nations; this occasioned a mutual Hatred betwixt the *Jews* and them, which was a main Obstacle to the propagation of the *Jewish* Religion. Neither could other Nations easily digest this, that as often as they were to attend the solemn and publick divine Service, they were first to travel to *Jerusalem*, as if it were not in their power to build a Temple equal to the other nearer home. Add to all this, that such as received the *Jewish* Religion, were esteemed among them one degree below the Natives; which was the reason why very few could resolve, for the *Jewish* Religion's sake, to be despised among them as Foreigners.

§. 4. The

§. 4. The Christian Religion is much clearer, and imbellish'd with greater Prerogatives than the *Jewish*; it is also freed from those Circumstances which were particular to the *Jewish* Religion, and endow'd with all Qualifications requisite for an universal Religion; so that every one is oblig'd to receive and embrace it. For here is no particular Place appointed by God Almighty for performing in public the Divine Service, nor can any Place claim a Prerogative before another; so that no Nation henceforward has any occasion to make exception about the remoteness of the Temple; but in all Places you may lift up Holy Hands unto him, no Temple in the World having any particular Promise appertaining to it that God will sooner hear your Prayers in that than in another. No Nation has, according to the Christian Religion, a Precedency before another, whereby one may claim a Prerogative above the other. Here is no *Jew*, no *Greek*, no Bond nor Freeman, but they are all one in Jesus Christ. Here is no Particular Family or Tribe appointed by God for the Publick Administration of Divine Service, as it was among the *Jews*: No one is excluded here, provided he be endowed with the necessary Qualifications. There is no Article in the Christian Religion, which forbids us to cultivate Familiarity with others, and mutually to perform the Offices enjoyn'd by the Law of Nature.

The Christian Religion is proper for all the World.

It is, purely, and by its self considered, quite remote from all worldly Ends and Interests; Her Doctrin neither changes nor opposes Civil Society or Laws, as far as they are consonant to the Law of Nature, but it rather confirms the same. There is nothing to be found in the Christian Religion, that's destructive to the ends of Civil Society, or hinders us from living honestly, quietly and securely under the protection of Civil Magistrates, or from administring all Offices, and performing such Duties without offending the Rules of Christianity, as are requisite for the maintaining a State established according to the Law of Nature. The Christian Religion rather promotes all these things, expresly commanding us strictly to observe every Commandment of the Law of Nature, and especially those upon which no Temporal Sanction could be conveniently made by the Civil Constitutions; and to perform our Duty with all

Not contrary to Civil Government.

all Faithfulness and Zeal as far as the same is consonant with Honesty and the Law of Nature.

No other Religion or Philosophy comparable to it.

Upon this Score no Philosophical Sect or Religion whatsoever can be equal to the Christian, as 'twill easily appear from a just Comparison betwixt this and all the others. For which reason, not only every one is oblig'd, as he hopes to answer for his Soul before God, to receive the Christian Religion; but even all Sovereigns and Magistrates ought, for the above-mention'd Reasons, and out of a Duty belonging to their Office, to introduce and maintain it. It is objected, that the Effects of the Christian Religion are not so visible, and that the Life and Conversation of a great many Christians is not different from that of the Heathens and *Turks*. But it is to be observed, that this Fault is not to be imputed to the Christian Doctrin, but to the Inclinations of such as profess the Name of Christians, but will not in earnest apply themselves to alter their evil Inclinations, and to live according to the wholsome Precepts of this Religion.

Concerning the outward Government of Religion.

§. 5. As what we have hitherto said, can scarce be denied by any Man of Sense, so there arises now a Question, *viz.* Whether, according to the Doctrin of the Christian Religion it is absolutely requisite, that the outward Direction or Government of the same be committed to another, besides him who has the supreme Civil Power in a State? Or, Whether, according to the Christian Doctrin, it be necessary that the outward Government of it be lodg'd with the whole Body of the Clergy, or with one of the Clergy in particular, independent of the Supreme Magistrate? Or, Whether there ought to be but one Sovereign Administrator of the Christian Religion, on whom all other Christian States ought to depend in this Point? Or, Whether every State ought to be govern'd according to its own Constitutions and Interest, or, whether all other States are oblig'd to be Slaves to one, and to promote the Interest of that one, to the Detriment and Ruin of their own?

What is meant by the outward Government of Religion

By the outward Direction of Government of the Christian Religion, we understand the Power of constituting certain Persons for the exercising of the publick Divine Service, and the supreme Jurisdiction over their Persons; the supreme Administration and Direction of such Posses-

sions

ions as are dedicated to Religious Services; the Power of making and executing Laws for the outward Safety of Religion, and the determining of such Differences as may arise among the Clergy. We make a great difference betwixt the outward Direction of Religious Affairs and the Ministry of the Church, which consists in Teaching, Preaching, and Administring the Sacraments, all which, doubtless belong only unto the Clergy. This Question is withal to be understood of a Church already planted and establish'd, not of a Church that is to be planted and establish'd. For since the Christian Religion ow'd its Original to Divine Revelation, no human Power could pretend to have any Direction in the same, before this Doctrin was throughly proposed and taught by such as had an Immediate Authority for so doing from God Almighty. For when our Saviour after his Resurrection did send his Disciples as Delegates and Apostles throughout the whole World, to publish and introduce the Christian Religion, they receiv'd their Commission for Preaching every where, not from the supreme Civil Magistrates, but from God himself: Wherefore Kings, as well as the common People, were oblig'd to acknowledge them as immediate Messengers of God, and obediently to submit themselves to their Doctrin; and it would be next to an Absurdity if any one should pretend to a Direction in such Matters as he was not instructed in before. From whence arises this Consequence, that what has been said is to be understood of such Sovereigns or supreme Magistrates as profess the true Christian Religion, but not of those who are Infidels or erroneous in the chief Articles of the Christian Faith. For to commit the Direction of Religion to the latter, would be to make the Wolf a Shepherd.

The Consideration of this Question according to the nature of Religion in general.

§. 6. This Question may be consider'd three several ways; First, Whether this Necessity arises from the Nature of Religion in general, or any Religion whatsoever? Or, Secondly, Whether it arises from the Genius of the Christian Religion in particular? Or, Thirdly, Whether the same is enjoyn'd us by Divine Institution or the particular Command of God? That it proceeds from the natural Constitution of Religion in general, I am no ways able to find out. For reason does not tell me, that if I intend to serve God, I must of necessity

make

make a division in the State, and thereby introduce tv different Powers independent of one another. The d membering of the supreme Power, or setting up such double-headed Sovereignty in a State, administers con nual Fuel, which at last breaks out into Jealousies, I visions, and intestine Commotions. On the other har it is no ways contrary to Reason to serve God, and the same time leave the supreme Direction of the o ward Matters belonging to Divine Service, to such have the supreme Power in the State; if so be, we st suppose those who have the supreme Power in their Han will not impose any thing upon their Subjects which False or Erroneous. Indeed, in the natural State, every one is bound by the Law of Nature to worst God; so it is at the same time in his Power to perfor the outward Ceremonies in such a manner as he belie they are most pleasing to God. But after the Instituti of Civil Societies, that same Power is thereby devolv to those who have the supreme Administration of Affa in a Civil Society. For the most ancient Fathers, w did not live under any regulated Government, exercis this Power in their Families, which used to be transferr to the Eldest Son, as *hæreditas eximia*, if the Brothers a ter the Father's Death resolved to live together in o Community. But when afterwards Civil Societies we instituted, the very same Power was transferred to t Heads of these Societies, and that out of a weighty Co sideration: For if every one had been left to his fr Choice in this Point, the various and different Cerem nies in the Divine Service must needs have introduc Confusion, Divisions, and intestine Commotions. A tho' among the *Jews* the publick Ministry was heredit ry to one particular Family, yet the Inspection and s preme Direction was reserved to those who had the s preme Civil Power in their Hands: As the same w practised among most other Nations.

According to the Nature of the Christian Religion in particular.

§. 7. Neither can any Reason be given why the Chr stian Religion is particularly so qualified, as to imply necessity, that the abovemention'd Direction should b committed to any other than the supreme Magistrate tho' it contains something more than is taught us by th Light of Nature; since we suppose that by virtue of th directive Power, they ought not and will not impo any thing upon us contrary to the Word of God, nor be a hindrance to the Priests in performing the Ministry according to the Ordinances of God in the Holy Scriptures. Neither can I find out any Reason, why the supreme Magistrates should want means duly to qualify themselves for this Administration or Direction. At least, they may let this Direction be exercised under their Authority by such as have acquired sufficiently Abilities for the same: In like manner as Sovereigns exercise their Power by others in Civil Affairs. No Man ever offer'd to deny Sovereigns the Power of making Laws; tho' at the same time it is certain, that a Doctor or professor of the Law, ought to be better instructed in them than is required of a King. For both in these and other Matters, Sovereigns ought to act with the Advice of such as have applied themselves throughly to such Affairs. And 'tis so far from being true, that the Male-Admininistration of this Power can intail any Advantage to a good and wise King; that on the other hand, a due and faithful Discharge of this Office will, besides the Satisfaction of Duty and Conscience, be of great Service to his Government. For the more zealous and earnest he is in maintaining the Christian Religion, the more obedient and better temper'd his Subjects are likely to be, and he may the better hope for the Blessing of God Almighty. Neither can any thing be alledged, why God Almighty should not afford his Assistance to a Christian and Orthodox Sovereign, as well as to any other Man, in order to the right direction of sacred Things. In fine, since the Christian Religion does not in any other way derogate from the Civil Ordinances and Laws, or from the Power of Civil Magistrates, as far as they are founded upon the Law of Nature; so it is not to be supposed that it disagrees in this one Point, except a positive Command of God can be alledged for the proof of this Assertion. Now, whether there be such a Command in the Holy Scriptures, which expresly forbids Sovereigns to intermeddle with this Direction, and allows the same to others in the highest degree of Sovereignty without any Dependency at all, we leave those to inquire who maintain, that there is such a Command. In the mean while we will inquire into the Rise, Progress, and Establishment of an Ecclesiastical Sovereignty of this Nature, that has fix'd itself in the Western Church.

§ 8. The

First propogation of the Christian Religion. §. 8. The Apostles having after the Ascention of o Saviour, according to the Instructions received from h own Mouth, begun to spread the Doctrin of the Chr stian Religion in far distant Countries, met with gre Approbation in short time, both among the *Jews* and ther Nations; but more especially among the Comm People, who having hitherto lived in gross Ignorance a in miserable Estate, very joyfully received this Doctri which enlightned and comforted them in the Miseries this Life. Besides, the Apostles themselves, who we of mean Extraction, and of no great Authority, used converse most among this sort of People, as having t most easie access to them as their Equals. But Men Quality and Learning, did scarce at first think it wor their while to apply themselves diligently to search in the bottom of this Religion, and very few of them woul profess it.

The Methods of God in Establishing the Christian Religion. If we may enquire into the Reasons why it was t Pleasure of the wise God to choose this way of Plantin the Christian Religion, it seems very probable, that Go was pleased not to introduce the Christian Religion b the Power and Authority of Civil Magistrates, not by t Assistance of Learned Men, that it might not be deen ed hereafter a State Trick, or a Philosophical Specul tion; but that whenever a due Comparison should b made betwixt the slender beginnings and prodigious e crease of this Religion, the World might from thence co clude, That the whole was something above human Reac In regard the Learned had proved unsuccessful with a their Subtilties in their Discoveries concerning Divin Matters; and *Socrates* and some others, who were se sible of the Vanity of the commonly received Superstit ons, and had condemn'd them as such, had not been abl to abolish those, and in lieu thereof, to introduce a be ter Religion; God Almighty was willing to convince th World of the Vanity of Worldly Wisdom, and to shew how easie it was for him to effect this great Work by th means even of poor Fishermen. Besides, the Doctri of the Apostles seem'd to be full of Absurdity to th Philosophers and Politicians, the same being founded up on, and begun with Jesus who was Crucified. For it ap peared very strange to them that the Apostles should ac knowledge him for the Son of God and their Saviou

wh

who was of a hated and despised Nation; who having lived without any great Splendour, and performed no great Heroick Actions, had not so much as made himself Famous throughout the World by long Study or Preaching, but had in his younger Years suffered a most infamous Death. And this is the Reason why the Jesuits, when they teach the Christian Religion among the refined *Chinese*, do not begin with the Doctrin of the Passion of Christ, but argue first with them from the Principles of Natural Religion and so come at last to this Article of the Christian Faith. But whether these Fathers by this Method are likely to be more successful than the Apostles, I will not here determine. It may withal be alledged, that God was pleased to deliver the common People among the Heathens, before great Men, out of their Misery and Darkness; because the first were seduced by the latter, and by them upheld in their Superstition; for the great Men, tho' sensible of the Vanity of the Pagan Religion, yet did not do their utmost Endeavours to search after a better. Wherefore God Almighty by first drawing away the common People from Paganism, did undermine the whole Structure, that so it might fall of itself; since the Simplicity and Credulity of the common People were the Foundation-Stones of the Pagan Religion.

Why the Meanest first converted.

§. 9. The Christian Doctrine being thus first propagated among the common People, it was grievously oppressed and Persecuted by the *Roman* Emperors. One of the main occasions of these Persecutions was their Ignorance of the true Nature and Precepts of this new Religion, and of the main end of it; and the Alarm they took from seeing the number of the Christians daily encrease, who all despised the Pagan Religion. The Emperors thought it below their high Station to make a due enquiry into the Foundation of this Doctrin, and there were few among the first Christians that were fitly qualified to represent their Doctrin in a polite and specious Dress to the People of Quality. So the Emperors were easily led away by the false Suggestions of the Enemies of the Christians, who insinuated to them, that the Christians in their nocturnal Assemblies, practised all sorts of Debauchery and Lewdness, much after the same manner as formerly used to be practised at the Festivals of

Persecution of the first Church.

The Calumnies against the Primitive Christians.

of *Bacchus*; or else that they were then Plotting against the State.

The Politick Reasons of the Romans against it. There were withal not a few among the *Romans*, who being averse to any Innovation whatsoever, were of Opinion, that since the *Roman* Empire had stood in a flourishing Condition several Ages past under the ancient Religion, the same ought not to be abrogated; above all they thought it no ways becoming the common People to pretend to an Innovation, and to more Wisdom than their Sovereigns. Add to this, that the Christians having among themselves a certain form of Ecclesiastical Government, this rendred them suspected to the *Romans* who look'd upon them as such as were for setting up a Faction against the State, and erecting a new Society in it, with intent to divide the Empire, and at last make themselves Masters of it. Some there were, who perceiving, that the more the numbers of the Christians encreased, the less frequented were the Temples of the Heathens, and that the *Roman* Empire began to decline and received great shocks. Upon this Observation, I say, they perswaded themselves that these Misfortunes befel them, because those Gods through whose Assistance the *Roman* Empire arrived to the Pinacle of its Grandeur, were now despised among them; and accordingly persecuted the Christians as an Atheistical Generation, endeavouring to over-turn the very Foundations of Religion. And forasmuch as the Christians refused to adore the Idols, notwithstanding the Emperor's Commands, and suffered the most prodigious Tortures and Death with Constancy and even Joy; they were treated like a perverse and obstinate sort of People by the *Romans*, who encreased their Cruelties to maintain their Authority against them. But no sufficient Reasons can be alledged for the justification of these Persecutions against the Christians, which ought to be considered no otherwise than unlawful Tyrannies, and pernicious Abuses of the Supreme Civil Power. For their Subjects had received this Religion according to the express Command of God, which could nor ought not to be opposed by the Civil Power; the Magistrates as well as the Subjects being obliged to receive it, except they would grosly sin against God Almighty. Neither could their Ignorance serve them for any excuse, since this being a new Doctrin, it was their Duty to take due Informati-

on

on concerning the same, before they had sent the Innocent Christians to Execution, only because they refused to obey the Commands of their Sovereigns, which ought not to oblige them to Obedience in this Point. For no body ought to give Sentence of Death against any one before he is duly informed concerning the nature of the Crime he is accused of.

§. 10. Forasmuch as the Sovereigns did at first not concern themselves for the welfare of the Christian Religion, the Christians did thereupon without their Assistance, constitute a Ministry and any outward Church-Government among themselves, which they maintain'd to the utmost. For this is common to all Societies instituted without the consent of the Supreme Magistrate, that the Members thereof are forced to agree among themselves, which way to order their Affairs best, and to constitute certain Rules and Governours for the managment of the Community. Indeed, according to the Rules of Policy, founded upon the Law of Nature, the outward Government of Religion belongs to the Sovereigns. But because the Magistrates would not perform their Duty at that time, the Christians were obliged to constitute Ministers of their own accord, who received their maintenance from the Charity of good Christians. And if any Errors did arise, or other Matters happen'd of such consequence, that the same could not be decided by one Assembly, several of these Assemblies used to consult among themselves concerning the Matter in question, or leave the Determination to an Assembly of such Ministers as were next at hand. Tho' it is certainly else not to be allowed in a State, that private Persons should constitute a Society among themselves, especially one consisting of a considerable number; yet the Assemblies and Synods of the ancient Christians are not therefore to be deemed unlawful Meetings; since their only aim was the exercise of their Religion, which being commanded them by God, ought not to have been opposed by any Human Power. Neither is it reasonable, that because the Magistrates are careless both of their Duty and their own Salvation, the rest who had knowledge of the true Religion, should therefore lose the benefit of their Salvation; against which no Civil Power ought to extend its Jurisdiction. And, as it is allowable for every body to defend himself

The first Church Government.

with his own Strength and Weapons, if Magistrates either can't or will not protect him: So if a Sovereign will not do his Office, as to the preservation of my Soul, I have as much more right to take care of it without him, as the Soul is dearer to me than the Body; and as by the exercise of the True Religion my Fellow Subjects are less endangered, than by a violent Defence of my own Person; for no body by becoming a Subject in a Civil Society, does thereby renounce the Privilege of taking care for his Soul and Body. Otherwise no doubt is to be made, that if it had been the Will of God to introduce the Christian Religion by the Conversion of the Emperors and Kings, these would with their Commands have assisted the Apostles in their Office, thrown down the Temples of the Idols, abolish'd the Pagan Idolatry; and would according to the instruction of the Apostles, have constituted the outward Church-Government, and maintain'd it afterwards. For it is evident enough, that such has been the manner of proceeding as to this Point, in other Countries, where the Christian Religion was first introduc'd into the State, by the Authority of their Sovereigns.

What Perswasions arise thence. §. 11. However, the first Christians being oblig'd when the Magistrates failed in their Duty, to regulate and constitute a Church-Government among themselves this occasioned the rise of several Errors, which are of no small Consequence. For some have from thence endeavoured to make this Inference, that the People, as they stand in opposition to Sovereignty, have an original and inherent Right to Elect Church Ministers. 'Tis true, a Minister ought not to be obtruded upon an Assembly against their Will, especially if they have a lawful exception against him, because he would edify but little in his Station: Nevertheless, it is not from hence to be concluded, that, because some Assemblies have been oblig'd to provide themselves with Ministers when the Magistrates neglected their Duty, therefore the same Right is ever since originally in the People. For without this supposition, an Assembly has as little Right to call and constitute a Church Minister, as to dispose of publick Offices and Employments in the State. And if in some Places the common People, or some others, have such Right, it is enjoy'd either by connivance, or a concession from the Supreme Magistrate, whom we suppose to b a Christian and Orthodox. Some also have been endeavouring to draw from thence this Conclusion, *viz.* That the outward Church-Government is separate and distinct from the Supreme Civil Power, and that it ought to be administred either by the whole Clergy, or else to depend absolutely on one single Person of the Clergy; so that according to this Supposition, there must be in each Christian State two distinct Bodies independent of one another, one of which must be called the Ecclesiastick (*Ecclesia*), the other the Politick State, (*Civitas*) and each of them must be Sovereign in its Government. But tho' this has been made use of sometimes, when Magistrates were quite negligent of their Duty, it ought not to be made a President, when Magistrates are ready duly to execute their Office. Neither does it follow, that the same Power that was Lodg'd in the Apostles at the time when the Church was first to be Established, is now devolved to the Church Ministers in an establish'd Church, who have not an immediate Vocation from God, but are ordain'd by the Hands of others. For the Office of the Apostles was particular, and very different from the Church Ministry, as it is exercised now-a-days, in like manner as the outward Church-Government is very different from the Ministerial Office: And as every lawful Church Minister is not immediately an Apostle, so the King does not become a Priest by the exercise of the Government. 'Tis true, tho' the Christian Religion ows its Original to God, and is above Human Reason, but still the Supreme Magistrate may be capable of having the outward direction over it, with the assistance of such Persons as are best vers'd in such Affairs. And from what has been said, this conclusion may be made, *viz.* That the practice of the Primitive Church as to the Point of the outward Church Government, is not to be made a perpetual and universal Rule of the Church Government in a State, which is under the Jurisdiction of a Christian and Orthodox Magistrate. For that practice was accommodated to the Circumstances of their Affairs then: But, where both the whole People and the Sovereign have received the Christian Religion, the Case is quite different, and implies not any necessity that the State should thereby become a Body with two Heads.

Constantine could not quite alter the former State of the Church. §. 12. After *Constantine* the *Great* had embraced the Christian Faith, the Church began to get another Face; the Sovereign being then fitly qualified to take upon him the outward Church Government. Nevertheless this outward Church Government could not be so regularly ordered, as if from the first beginning the Sovereigns had received the Christian Religion; For, there were a great many Remnants left of the former Provincial Church Government, which afterwards occasioned great Abuses in the Western and Latin Church. For, it was scarce possible for these Emperors, who passed then but for Novices in the Christian Religion, to make use at first of their Power in Ecclesiastical Matters, and, to bridle the Authority of the Bishops and Clergy, that were backward to part with it: They were rother obliged to keep fair with them, and to make use of their Assistance to establish themselves in the Throne, since most of their Subjects being then become Christians, paid a profound Veneration to their Priests. Add to this, that the first Christian Emperos made use of several Ministers and Officers in their Courts, who were as yet Pagans. Wherefore it seem'd not just that Matters concerning the outward Church Government, should be determined by a Council, whereof some Members were Heathens.

Of making Bishops. This was the Reason why the Vocation of Bishops and other Ecclesiasticks, was performed for the most part according to the Customs introduced before. And not only such Controversies as arose concerning certain Articles of Faith, but also such as had a relation to the outward Order and Government of the Church, and all other differences of moment among the Clergy, were brought before the Councils, or the Assemblies of the Clergy, where they claim'd the sole Right of Presiding and Voting; Tho' it is certain, that not only the right of calling them together belongs to the Sovereigns who for a considerable time have exercised their Power, *Of presiding in Counsils.* but likewise the Direction and Presidentship of such Assemblies, whatever Matter is to be debated there, does at least belong to the Prince, if their Decrees shall pass afterwards for, and have the the Power of the Law, or a definitive Sentence in the State. Indeed the supreme Magistrates can't pretend, no more than the Clergy, to a right of introducing new Articles of Faith, or of explainplaining the Scripture according to their own pleasure; Nevertheless, the whole Duty of a Christian being contained in the Holy Scriptures, which God has commanded, to be published for the benefit of Mankind, and not to be committed like Sybilline Oracles, to the custody of certain Priests; and since others, as well as the Clergy, have the opportunity to comprehend the Sense of the Holy Scripture, it seems not at all contrary to Reason, that the Civil Magistrates should have at least the supreme Direction of those Assemblies, where Matters concerning the different Interpretations of the Scriptures are to be debated. From whence also this Benfit will accrue to the Publick, that thereby the extravagant Heats and immoderate Passions, which are commonly obvious in these Disputes will be Moderated, Matters will be debated with Prudence, and not stretched too high, out of a fondness of contradicting the Slanders and Calumnies thrown upon Men by malicious Wrestling and Misinterpretation of their Words will be prevented, and the indiscreet use of Excommunication will be banish'd. In short, forasmuch as the first Christian Emperors did either neglect this their Right, or had no opportunity of exercising it, this occasioned great confusion in some Councils: And upon the same Head the People took an opportunity, after he had set himself above the Western Bishops and Councils themselves, to assume an Authority to decide Controversies even concerning Articles of Faith, to introduce such Canons or Ecclesiastical Laws in the Church, as he thought most proper for his Interest and State, and by pretending to the highest Jurisdiction, to exempt the Church from the Jurisdidiction of the Civil Magistrates; For when once this Opinion was established, that all these Matters did belong of Right to the Clergy only, without having any respect to the Civil Power, the Pope laid claim to 'em by virtue of the same Right by which he had set himself above the Clergy and the whole Church.

Abuses in the Councils.

§. 13. Besides, it was the Custom among the Ancient Christians, that pursuant to the Admonition of St. *Paul*, they very seldom pleaded their Causes before the Pagan Judges: But in case of Differences among themselves, they used to refer the same to the decision of a Bishop, that by their Contests they might not give any occasion of Scandal to the Heathens, since it might seem unbe-

Of the Episcopal Jurisdiction.

coming, That those who made profession of despising worldly Riches, should quarrel about 'em among themselves. This Custom, as it was very usefel and praiseworthy at that time; so, because it was not Abrogated, but rather confirmed afterwards by the Christian Emperors, tho' the Courts of Justice were then Governed by Christian Judges. The Bishops afterwards pretended to a formal Jurisdiction, which did not only derogate from the Authority of Temporal Judges, but diverted the Bishops from performing such Duties as properly belonged to their Office. There was likewise another Custom among the first Christians, that if a scruple arose concerning nearness of Blood in Marriages, they used to take the Opinion of the Priests in the Case; and if any Difference arose betwixt Married People, they were generally referr'd to the Arbitration of the Priests; who at the time also when the Nuptials were Celebrated, used to give them their Benediction, and Pray with them. This beginning, which in itself consider'd, was truly laudable, furnish'd an occasion of great Abuses afterwards, the Pope having from hence rais'd a pretext to subject all Matrimonial Affairs, Divorces, Nullities of Marriages, Successions, Inheritances, and the like, of the greatest Consequence, under his Jurisdiction; and to render his Pretensions the more plausible, made Marriage a Sacrament.

Concerning Marriages.

Concerning Excommunication.

Further: The first Christians were very desirous to recommend their Religion to the Heathens by a Holy and innocent Life, especially since some sort of Vices were not punishable according to the Pagan Laws. For this Reason, in the Primitive Church, if any one had given a publick Scandal by his Vicious Life, a certain Church Penance was laid upon him, which at the utmost did amount to this, that he was excluded from the Communion of the Christians. Which Custom, as it is not unreasonable, so it may be of good use in a Christian State, provided the Civil Magistrate have the Supreme Direction, and take care that such a Censure be not abused out of Obstinacy or private Ends and Passion. Especially since these Censures have had such an influence upon Civil Societies, that in the Eighth Age no body would Converse with any one that was Excommunicated. This Power ought not to be left to the absolute Disposal of any one, except the Sovereign, unless you will divide the Sovereignty. But in what manner the

Popes

Popes have afterwards abused this Censure, and extended it even to the Excommunication of Emperors, Kings, and whole Common-Wealths, and by excluding them from joyning in the Divine Service, absolving the Subjects from their Allegiance, and bestowing their Kingdoms upon others, have forced them to a compliance against their own Interest, is sufficiently known out of History. Yet in the Eastern Empire these Abuses did not grow up to the same height; for the Emperors at *Constantinople* did at least so far maintain their Authority against the Clergy, that they durst not pretend to domineer over them, Besides that, the Eastern Bishops had not the opportunity of Lording it one above the other; for that the Bishop of *Constantinople* had no other Prerogative allow'd him, but precedency of Rank above the others without his Diocess, but not any Jurisdiction.

§. 14. Indeed, in the Western Parts the Church took afterwards quite another Face, when the Bishop of *Rome* projected a peculiar sort of Monarchy, which by degrees he brought to Perfection, and which is not to be parallel'd in the Records of Time, as being founded upon quite other Principles, and upheld by very different Means from other States. The more influence this Monarchy has had for several hundred Years together upon the States and Affairs of *Europe*, and has been maintained with great Zeal by one, and opposed by the other Party, the more it will be worth our while, to dive into the first Origin and Constitution of it, and to alledge some Reason, why in the last Age this Monarchy was reduced to a tottering Condition, but has recollected its Vigour in this. From whence a wise man also may be able to judge, what Success may be hoped for from the Projects of those who are for reconciling the Dfferences betwixt the Protestants and Papists. It may be offer'd, that in promoting the increase of this Monarchy, so pernicious to the Supreme Civil Power, one great, tho' remote Instrument, was the Barbarity and Ignorance, which after the decay of the *Roman* Empire, spread itself over the Western Parts. For bad Wares are best vented in the Dark, or at least by a dim Light: And an Ignorant Person is sooner prevail'd upon to believe ridiculous Stories, than a Wise Man vers'd in all sorts of Sciences.

The Origin of the Authority of the Pope.

Barbarity and Ignorance contributed to it.

The Causes of this Ignorance. There were several Causes that gave rise to this Barbarity, which degenerated afterwards into the worst sort of idle Pedantry, (whereas the former Age had been sufficiently adorned with Learned Men.) One of the principal ones was the Invasion made upon the Western Provinces of the *Roman* Empire by those Nations, who, tho' sufficiently Brave, were ignorant of Learning; which occasioned for one or two Ages after great Changes in the Government, bloody Wars, horrible Disorders, and all sorts of Miseries in the Empire. And Learning being the product of Peace and Prosperity, it is little regarded in times of War, or during the Distractions of a State; since then there is but little leisur time given for the use of Books. The Schools are commonly destroy'd, and the Teachers oblig'd to make shift where best they can, a Musket being at such times of more use than a School Satchel. The School-Masters especially are forced to shut up Shop at such times, if the Victorious Enemy is ignorant of Learning, and makes no account of Books. There are some who affirm, that the Clergy was accessory to this Barbarism. For, in regard the Philosophers had under the Reigns of the Pagan Emperors proved very mischievous to the Clergy, and afterwards under the Christian Emperors continued to oppose them, these had conceived such a hatred against Philosophy, and against all such as professed it, that they not only infused the same into their Auditors, but also removed out of the Schools, and took from the young Students, who were committed to their care, the Pagan Authors, under pretence that they might otherwise be again infected with erroneous Principles of the Pagans, and that it could not but be sinful for Christians to read such Books as were filled every where with the Names of Pagan Idols, which they would not have so much as named by Christians. *St. Hierom's Dream.* They related a Story concerning St. *Hierom*, how that he was whip'd in a Vision with Rods, because he used frequently to Read the Works of *Cicero*; and about the Year 400, after the Birth of our Saviour, the Council of *Carthage* forbid the Bishops the reading of Pagan Authors. Now Learning being in those miserable Times become almost useless, except to those who intended to profess Divinity, and the remains of Learning being by that means lodg'd among the Clergy, the main Institution in the Schools was only directed for that purpose, and the rest of the

young

young Disciples were not very forward to dive much into the Secrets of Ancient Learning. That this Ignorance and Barbarism have greatly promoted the Establishment of Popery is evident enough to those, who will consider that in a Learned Age, those Decretals which are ascribed to the first Popes, could never have passed Muster; which nevertheless have been made use of to persuade the People that the Bishops of *Rome* have exercised an Authority from the very beginning of Christianity, to prescribe Laws to the Christian World.

But when afterwards the Times proved more favourable in *Europe*, and the Popes perceiv'd that some among the most considerable Nations of *Europe*, could not be longer kept in gross Ignorance, they introduc'd into the Schools, over which they had assumed the Supreme Direction, the most wretched sort of trifling noisy Pedantry, which is maintain'd by their Votaries in the Schools with great earnestness to this very day. But above all things it appears, that the Ignorance of the true Principles of Policy, has had a main stroke in laying the Foundation of Popery, for want of being duly instructed concerning the Foundation, Nature and Perfection of the Supreme Civil Power, and taught that no State could be esteemed well Established, where the Supreme Civil Power was either divided or mained. For the *Grecian* and *Roman* Politicians themselves had divulged most pernicious Doctrins concerning the Division and Mixture of the Supreme Power, whereby they had enamour'd the People with an Aristocratical or Democratical sort of Government, infused into them such a hatred against Monarchy, that it was a common Maxim among them, that the more they could incroach upon the Authority of the Prince, the more it must turn to the Advantage of the State. In this pernicious Opinion a great many were confirm'd by the Tyrannical Proceedings of the Emperors, who were mortally hated by most of their Subjects. It was therefore no great wonder, that at the time of this general Ignorance the knowledge of true Policy was not taught among the Christian Clergy, since it seem'd to them to be repugnant to their Profession. From hence it was, that, when by degrees the Foundation of the Ecclesiastical Sovereignty was laid, few did throughly understand of what Consequence this undertaking was, and how prejudicial it would prove to the Supreme Civil Power, whenever it could be brought

The Pedantry introduced into the Schools.

The Greek and Roman Politicians prejudicial to Monarchy.

to

to perfection. And we see even to this Day, that in those Schools, which are under the care of the Popish Clergy, the Principles of true Policy are either neglected, or at least so disfigured, that they may not be hurtful to the Authority of the Popes, but rather serve to support it.

Why Rome *was made the place of Residence of the Ecclesiastical Monarchy.*

§. 15. But the chief reason, why *Rome* was chosen for the place of Residence of the Ecclesiastical Monarchy, seems to be, that this City had a particular Prerogative of being the Capital City of the *Roman* Empire, where the Christian Religion had at first its Rise and Increase. For what is related concerning St. *Peter*'s Chair, is nothing but a vain Pretence, which may be easily seen from hence, that afterwards the Bishop of *Constantinople* had the next place assign'd him after the Bishop of *Rome*, only because that City was then the place of Residence of the Emperor, and *New Rome*. And when afterwards the Western *Roman* Empire was come to decay, and the City of *Rome* had lost its former lustre, the Bishop of *Constantinople* disputed the Precedency with the *Roman* Bishop. After the Persecutions, which the Christians endur'd under the Pagan Emperors, were ceased, and they enjoy'd their full Liberty, the Clergy began under pretence of introducing a wholsome Order in the Church, to Establish a particular sort of Government of Hierarchy; the Bishops having then begun to claim a great Prerogative above the Priests. The Bishops were also made subordinate to one another; so that commonly the Inspection over the Bishops in a certain Province, was committed to the Bishop of the Capital City of the same Province, who being then called Metropolitans, did afterwards, *viz.* about the Eight Century, most of them, assume the name of Archbishops. Four of them were most eminent above all the rest, *viz.* The Archbishops of *Rome*, *Constantinople*, *Antioch* and *Alexandria*, these being then the four Principal Cities of the *Roman* Empire; and the Archbishop of *Jerusalem* was added to their number, because of the Ancient Holiness of that City. And tho' the Emperor *Phocas*, out of spite to the Patriarch of *Constantinople*, who would not approve of the Murther committed upon *Mauritius*, granted the Precedency to *Boniface* III. the then Bishop of *Rome*, who thereupon took upon him the Title of Oecumenical Bishop; yet this Prerogative did not extend further than to bare Precedency,

Metropolitans.

Patriarchs.

cedency, nor did it imply any Power or Jurisdiction over the rest; for the other Patriarchs never acknowledg'd any. And in former times, when the Bishop of *Rome* pretended to put his Commands upon the Bishops of *Africa*, and for that purpose alledged a Canon of the Council of *Nice*, which was corrupted, they sent him back a very smart Answer.

Upon the whole, here is no Footsteps of Divine Institution to be met withal, the Institution being purely Human; nor can any Reason be alledged, why the Bishop of *Rome* possesses the first Rank, other than why he of *Antioch* has the third among them. And since one State cannot prescribe Laws to another, if any Prerogatives have been granted to the Bishop of *Rome*, by the *Roman* Emperors, or the Ancient Councils, (which were nothing formerly but an Assembly of the Clergy of the *Roman* Empire, the same do not oblige any other State, nor can they extend beyond the Bounds and Jurisdiction of the ancient *Roman* Empire. But if we put the Case, that some Christian Princes or States have afterwards allow'd to the Pope a certain Power over the Church in their Dominions; this was done, because they either understood not the true nature of this Power, or because they were deceiv'd by the Popes. In the first Case, the Allowance is to be deem'd nothing else but a Treaty of Alliance with the Pope, the better to Administer the Church Affairs with the Pope's Direction. Such a Treaty or Alliance, as it originally proceeds from the Consent of that State; so the same may be Annulled again, in the same manner as other Alliances are, whenever it proves prejudicial to the State, or the Pope begins to abuse the Authority granted him by the State. But if the Pope has either by Fraud or Imposition obtained his Power over other States, these so misguided and thus surprized States, have a Right as soon as they have discovered the Fraud, and are convinced of their Error, to shake of such an unjust Usurpation, and besides to demand satisfaction for the Damages sustained by these Impostures.

Of the Pope's Power.

§. 16. Neither could the Bishops of *Rome* extend their Power over the Western parts all at once, but it was introduc'd from time to time, by degrees, and by various Artifices, and under several Pretences. For, when they

Further increase of the Ecclesiastical Sovereignty.

they had once fastned their Paws, they did not retreat till they had obtain'd their Pretentions, tho' they were several times deny'd admittance. They very wisely took hold of that Opportunity which presented it self, and was the chiefest of all in my Judgment, when the Emperors began to choose other places of Residence besides *Rome*, since by their constant presence there they might easily have kept under the ambitious Designs of the Bishops. For the Bishops of *Constantinople*, who questionless were no less proud and ambitious than those of *Rome*, could never gain this Point. The next thing which mainly contributed to this Power, was, that afterwards the Western Empire was divided into several new Kingdoms, erected by several barbarous and pagan Nations; and these having been converted to the Christian Faith by the direction of the *Romish* Church, thought themselves oblig'd to pay to her a profound Respect, and to honour her as the most ancient, and the principal of the Western parts.

What contributed to it.

To recite all the particulars here is not for our purpose; it will be sufficient to touch upon some of the main Points: It is therefore to be remarked, that since the Fifth Century the Bishops that liv'd on this side of the *Alps* began in the Fifth Century to go to *Rome* to visit the Sepulchres of S. *Peter* and S. *Paul*, out of a sort of Superstition or Devotion very common in those Days, or with intent to testifie their firm Adherence to the Christian Faith. This voluntary Devotion was afterwars by degrees changed into a necessity, and such as neglected it, used to receive severe rebukes. From hence it was easie for the Popes afterwards to pretend that the Bishops ought to receive their Confirmation from *Rome*. Besides, some other Bishops and Churches that were Novices in comparison of the ancient *Roman* Church, used to refer themselves to, and ask the advice of the Church of *Rome*, concerning some Matters of great Consequence, and the true use and interpretation of the Canons. And when they once perceiv'd at *Rome* that their Answers were taken as Decisions, they begun to send their Decrees before they were demanded, under pretence that *Rome* being the first Seat of the Christian Bishops, it ought to take effectual Care that the Canons and Ecclesiastical Laws were duly put in Execution. Under the same pretence they made themselves immediate

The Pope's Confirmation of Bishops.

Judges

Judges of the Differences arisen betwixt the Bishops, and encroaching upon the Right and Jurisdiction of the Metropolitans, used to depose such Bishops, as according to their Opinion had not a right Ordination; or such as were accused of some enormous Crimes they suspended, and oblig'd to appear before them at *Rome* to plead their Cause. And if there were any that desir'd an Exemption from the Canons, they travel'd to *Rome*, where they were kindly receiv'd and encourag'd in their Demands; for that thereby the Staple of Dispensations and Favours to be granted, was establish'd at *Rome*. If any one had lost his Cause before the ordinary Judge, he used to appeal to *Rome*, where he was kindly receiv'd and encourag'd. The *French* Historians relate, that, because the Emperor *Henry* had made the City of *Arles* the Capital City over seven Provinces, the Pope Constituted the Archbishop of the said City his Vicar in *France*, for fear lest the said Archbishop might by degrees attempt to make himself Patriarch of *France*. And this Archbishop chose rather to have the Inspection, tho' precariously over seventeen Provinces, into which *France* was divided at that time, than to be the Head only of seven in his own Right; and accordingly, to add the more Authority to his Commission, did as much as in him was, endeavour to Establish the Pope's Authority there.

In the Eighth Century, when great Disorders and Debaucheries were become frequent among the Monks and Clergy, an *English* Fryar, whose name was *Winifred*, and who afterwards called himself *Boniface*, did out of a particular Zeal, take upon himself the Reformation of the Manners and Lives of the Clergy; and endeavour'd to Establish the Christian Religion in several Parts of *Germany*, but especially in *Thuringia* and *Friezland*. This Man, to acquire the greater Authority to himself, had entirely devoted himself to the Interest of the *Roman* Chair, from whence he receiv'd the Episcopal Pall, and the Title of Archbishop of *Mayence*, having also been Constituted by Pope *Gregory* III. his Vicar, with full Power to call Councils, and to constitute Bishops in those places which were by his means Converted to the Christian Faith, and with ample Recommendations to those Nations, and particularly to *Charles Martel*, the then Grand Master of *France*, requiring that he should take him into his Protection, which he

Of the Monk Winifred.

he very willingly did. And when afterwards his Son *Carlomannus* shew'd a great forwardness to have the Church Discipline regulated, *Boniface* was very willing to take upon him this Office to the great advantage of the *Roman* Chair. At the request of *Carlomannus* he call'd a Council in *Germany*, and upon the demand of *Pepin*, several Synods in *France*, where *Boniface* was always present in the quality of Legat of the *Roman* Chair. In the first Council the Clergy sign'd a certain Confession of Faith, whereby they oblig'd themselves, not only to maintain the Catholick Faith, but also to remain in constant Union with the *Roman* Church, and to be obedient to the Successors of St. *Peter*. This *Boniface* also was the first who put it upon the Bishops of *Germany* to receive the Episcopal Pall from the Pope, and sent it to the Bishops of *France* without their request, thereby to increase their Obligation to the *Roman* Chair. And when once these Ornaments were become customary amongst them, they were put upon them afterwards as of absolute Necessity, and the Episcopal Function was forbidden to be exercised by them before they had receiv'd these Ornaments.

Further: The Popes assum'd to themselves an Authority of giving leave to the Bishops to remove from one Episcopal See to another, and oblig'd all the Western Bishops to receive the Confirmation from *Rome*, for which they were oblig'd to pay a certain Sum of Money as an *Annals.* acknowledgment, which was since converted to Annals. At the same time the Popes, by making void the Decisions of the provincial Synods or Assemblies, sunk their Authority; so that, when every Body plainly perceiv'd that the Decrees of these Assemblies could produce no other Effect, but to be continually annulled by the Popes, without as much as hearkning to any Reasons, they were by degrees quite abolish'd. Add to this, that Pope *Gregory* VII. forc'd the Bishops to swear an Oath of Fealty to the Pope, and by a Decree enacted, that none should dare to condemn any one that had appeal'd to the Pope. They were also not forgetful in sending Legates or Nuncio's to all Places, whose Business was to exercise in the name of the Pope, the same Authority which had formerly belong'd to the Bishops, Metropolitans and Provincial Assemblies.

§. 17. This growing Ecclesiastical Sovereignty was the more prejudicial to the Supreme Civil Power, so that the Church daily increas'd both in Numbers and Riches. The first Foundation of the Wealth of the Church was laid by the Liberality and Charity of Princes and other great Men, who were of Opinion, that they did a very agreable Service to God Almighty if they were liberal and bounteous towards his Church and the Clergy. And after they had once persuaded the People, that by doing good Works, among which the Gifts and Donations for pious uses had the first Place, they could and must deserve Heaven from God Almighty; this Liberality was increas'd to a high degree. Yet the voluntary Contributions of the People not being able to satisfy the Avarice of the Clergy, which increas'd with their Riches, other Ways and Artifices were found out to empty the People's Purses, and a great many unnecessary Institutions introduc'd, which were to be purchas'd for Money. Then it was that the saying of Masses for the Living and the Dead, Purgatory, Indulgences, Dispensations, Pilgrimages, Jubilees, and the like, were introdu'd without measure. They had withal, a watchful Eye over such as were at the point of Death, as knowing that Men are commonly not so much addicted at that time to their Worldly Riches, especially if they foresee they are to leave 'em to Heirs which will rejoice at their Death: Nay, they were not asham'd to make a Profession of Begging. *Riches of the Church.*

Among other Tricks, the Popes did in the Eleventh and the following Century, turn the Croisadoes to their great Advantage. For in these Expeditions after the People had once receiv'd the sign of the Cross to assist in the recovery of the Holy Land, the Popes pretended to the supreme Command and Direction; they took the Persons and Estates of such as had receiv'd the Cross under their particular Protection, exempting them thereby from the Civil Jurisdiction both in Civil and Criminal Causes, and rendring their Dispensations and Indulgences more frequent and flourishing than before; the Pope's Legates dispos'd of such Alms, Collections and Legacies as were given for that purpose, and under the same pretext receiv'd the Tenths from the Clergy; nay, they even pretended to put their Commands upon Princes to receive the Cross themselves. This sacred Militia they employ'd *The Policies of the Popes in the Croisade.*

employ'd afterwards against such as were declar'd by them Schismaticks or Hereticks, whose Possessions they us'd to confiscate and bestow upon those who had prov'd serviceable to them, without asking the Advice of the Sovereign, who durst not but invest them with such Countries as were presented to them by so high a Hand.

Multitude of Ecclesiasticks. §. 18. At the same time the number of Ecclesiasticks increas'd proportionably to the increase of the Riches of the Church, for there were not wanting such as were willing to have a share of their Wealth without taking much Pains. For it was not thought sufficient to have an ordinary Minister, Chaplain and others, necessary for the exercising of Divine Service, always belonging to each Church, but each Cathedral had a Chapter of Canons, and there were great numbers of Persons of high and low Quality that were forward in taking upon them these profitable and in no ways burthensome Functions, because the inconveniency of Celibacy, which the Pope in the Tenth and following Century forc'd upon the Ecclesiasticks, not without great trouble and reluctancy, was sufficiently recompenc'd by the Honours and Revenues which they enjoy'd quietly in their several Stations.

Friars and Nuns. Besides, an innumerable multitude of Friars and Nuns settled themselves all over Christendom. This sort of People began first to appear in the World at the time of the great Persecutions, but in the Fourth and following Centuries muliply'd their numbers to a prodigious degree. In the beginning they liv'd upon what they could get by their Handy-work; a great many us'd to give their Goods voluntarily to the Poor, and liv'd under the Direction of the Bishops, according to a Discipline prescrib'd in the Canons. In the Seventh Century, especially, Friars and Nuns were much in vogue in the Western Parts, which were every where provided with Monasteries and Nunneries, built by the encouragement of Princes and other great Men, that endow'd them with great Revenues. But when the Charity and Liberality of the People seem'd almost to be exhausted by the great Charges bestow'd upon so many rich Monasteries, and yet there were not enough to contain all such as were desirous to enter into this sort of Life; at last in the Thir- *Mendicants.* teenth Century, the order of the Mendicant Friars was erected:

erected: These made a great shew of Holiness, because they would not be taken for such as were forward to choose a Monastick Life to live in plenty, but for such as had taken a Resolution to bid farewel to all the Pleasures of this World, and at the best, maintain themselves by Alms. A great many have embrac'd this severe Order, out of an Opinion of a particular Holiness and Merit, which they believ'd did belong to this Order, or rather an Ecclesiastick Ambition; the Pride of Mankind being so great and natural to some, that they did not think the Commands of God sufficient, but would receive Heaven from God Almighty, rather as a Desert than as a Gift, and were ambitious of having a Preference before others, even in the other Life. Some there are who embrace a Monastick Life out of Despair, some out of Laziness: A great many are by their Parents and Relations sent into a Monastry out of Superstition or Poverty, and to prevent the ruin of a Family by the division of the Estate among a great many Children. And out of these Friars the Pope has chosen his Regiment of Guards; which he posts in Garrison, not only to plague the Laity, but also to curb the Bishops and the rest of the Clergy. It was for this reason, that the Pope supported the Friars with so much Zeal against the Bishops, in the Tenth Century, especially, when they withdrawing themselves from the Jurisdiction of the Bishops, submitted themselves to the immediate Authority of the Pope. And the Popes know so well how to manage them, that tho' there are great Jealousies on foot betwixt their several Orders, as for Example, betwixt the *Franciscans* and *Dominicans*; they nevertheless keep so even a Ballance betwixt them, and so equally dispose of their Favours towards them, that one Order shall not oppress another, and that none of 'em shall have any reason to complain of the Pope's Partiality.

The Motives to embrace this manner of Life.

These Friars us'd to interfere often with the regular Clergy, as pretending to a great share in the Legacies and Burials of the richer sort, to the direction of Consciences and the administration of the Sacraments. From hence arose a continual Envy and Hatred from the Bishops and regular Clergy against the Friars, who being buoy'd up by the Pope's Favour, were not concern'd at their Anger. And for that Reason, whenever a Bishop attempted any thing against the Pope's Authority, the Fri-

Friars prejudicial to the regular Clergy.

ars with their Clamour and Noise, pursu'd him every where like so many Hounds and rendered him odious to the Common People, amongst whom they were in great Veneration, through their outward appearance of Holiness; and from thence it came to pass, that the Bishops who opposed the Pope's Authority never could make a great Party among the common People. Moreover the Friars kept always a watchful Eye over the Actions of the Bishops, giving continual Advices of them to their Generals residing at *Rome*, whereby the Popes were enabled to make a timely Opposition to any Design intended against their Authority. In fine, these Friars prov'd the main Obstacle, why the Bishops could not so effectually oppose the Authority that the Pope assum'd over them; so that being destitute of means to help themselves, they were forc'd to give way to the Current. Tho' it is equally certain, that some of them were very well satisfy'd with it, as believing that they participated of the Grandeur of their Supreme Head, and that thereby they should be exempted from the Jurisdiction of the Civil Magistrates, which was more dreadful to them than a foreign Jurisdiction, exercis'd by those of their own Order, from whom they had all the Reason to expect more Favour. But after all, 'tis undeniable, that a great many Bishops, especially among those on this side the *Alps*, bear a grudge to the Pope's Authority to this very Day, which evidently appear'd at the Council of *Trent*, where the *French* and *Spanish* Bishops insisted very closely to have it decided, that Bishops are oblig'd to Residence by the Law of God, which is also the Opinion of the *Jansenists*. The more refin'd sort did easily perceive what their Intention was by making this Proposition. For if God had commanded them this, it must also be a consequence that he had given them means, and instructed them with sufficient Power (*qui dat jus ad finem, dat jus ad media*) and that therefore they were not oblig'd to go to *Rome* first, and to purchase an Authority to exercise their Function. The Pope met with great Difficulties before he could surmount this Obstacle at the Council of *Trent*, wherefore it is very likely that this will be the last Council, since the Pope will scarce hereafter put his Grandeur to the hazard and the decision of such an Assembly: Not to mention that now they are of no further use, since the Jesuits and some others have

have taught, that the Pope is Infallible and above Councils, from whom these ought to receive a Confirmation, and a binding and obligatory Power. But let this be as it will, the Bishops are for their own sakes oblig'd not to withdraw themselves from the Pope's Subjection, since thereby they would fall under the Jurisdiction of the Civil Power, and would be oblig'd to seek for Protection from their Sovereigns, who must be potent Princes if they should protect them against the Pope; and so they are now forced to choose the least of two Evils.

§. 19. Tho' the Church had abounded never so much in Riches and in great numbers of Ecclesiasticks, yet was it absolutely necessary, that the Pope, if he intended to establish an Ecclesiastical Monarchy, should not be any ways dependent on any Temporal Prince; that he should reside in a Place which was free from all Subjection to any Civil Power but himself; that he also should be possess'd of such an Estate as might be sufficient to maintain his Grandeur, and not to be liable to be taken away from him upon any pretence whatsoever; and where his Adherents might find a safe Retreat whenever they should be pursu'd by the Civil Power. To establish this, was a Business of a considerable Time and Labour, neither could it be effected without great Opposition, and that by a great many Artifices and knavish Tricks. And it is certain, that as long as there was an Emperor in the Western Empire, and as long as the Empire of the *Goths* lasted in *Italy*, the Bishops of *Rome* could not so much as think of this Greatness. But this having been destroy'd under the Emperor *Justinian*, and *Rome* and *Italy* made a Province of the *Grecian* Empire, then it was that the Popes took their opportunity to exempt themselves from the Jurisdiction of these Emperors, whose Authority was mightily decay'd in *Italy*, partly by the ill management of their Governors at *Ravenna*, partly by their own Weakness and want of Strength; at the same time that the *Lombards* taking advantage of the Divisions and Confusion of the Empire under *Justinian* II. inlarg'd their Strength to a great degree, and became Masters of *Italy*. Besides this, some of the Emperors were against the adorning of Images, and *Leo Isaurus* quite ejected them out of the Churches, because this Adoration was wholly degenerated into Idolatry

How the Church was free'd from all Power over it.

How the Popes withdrew themselves from their subjection to the Emperors.

latry; and as to the outward Appearance, the Saints were more regarded than God himself. Now this Undertaking was very vehemently oppos'd by Pope *Gregory* II. who stood up for the Images, partly because the *Roman* Chair found this Superstition very advantageous; partly because the Pope took it very ill that the Emperor should undertake a Reformation in Matters of Religion without his Knowledge and Consent; and, that at that time when he was busie to introduce the Ecclesiastical Monarchy in the Western parts; or else, because he thought this a fair Opportunity to shake off the Jurisdiction of the *Grecian* Emperors. The better to obtain his Aim, he stir'd up the *Romans* and *Italians*, who hitherto had been under the Obedience of the Emperors, to refuse to pay them Tribute; and the Governor residing at *Ravenna*, endeavouring to maintain the Emperor's Right, was slain in a Tumult. By this means the Jurisdiction and Power of the *Grecian* Emperors was abolish'd in those parts of *Italy*, and these Countries began to be free and independent on any foreign Jurisdiction.

The Pope seeks for protection in France. § 20. The Pope having thus freed himself from the Jurisdiction of the Emperors of *Constantinople*, he was not long after threatned by another Enemy, who being nearer at hand, was likely to prove more troublesome to him than formerly the Emperors who liv'd at so considerable a distance. For the Kings of the *Lombards* endeavour'd first to make themselves Masters of those parts which were fallen off from the Emperor, and afterwards of all *Italy*. They had already taken *Ravenna*, and there was none left in *Italy* who was able to stop their Victories. The Popes were then hard put to it, and knew not where to seek Protection, except of the Kings of *France*, who at first endeavour'd to put an end to these Differences by an amicable Composition; but the *Lombards* not being willing to rest satisfied therewith, they resolv'd by force of Arms to maintain the *Italian* Liberty and State of *Italy*. This Resolution they were the more confirm'd in upon the consideration Pope *Zachary* had approv'd of the proceedings of *Pepin*, who having abdicated the Lawful King, was from a Grand-Marshal become King of *France*; and withal, that by this Interposition, *France* had an opportunity offer'd them to make Conquests in *Italy*, whereof the *French* Nation has been

always

always very ambitious. In fine, *Pepin*, and afterwards *Charles* the Great, being so fortunate in their Wars against the *Lombards*, as to Conquer their whole Kingdom, they gave to the Papal Chair all that Tract of Land which had been formerly under the Jurisdiction of the *Grecian* Governors. There are some who are of Opinion, that to obtain this Gift, the Pope made use of the fictitious Donation of *Constantine* the Great, which in those barbarous Times was easily impos'd upon the ignorant World. However, the *French* Kings had great Obligations to the Pope for the above mention'd Reasons, and were also fond of acquiring the name of pious Princes, by bestowing liberal Presents out of other Men's Possessions. For, it was in those Days a common Custom, that Men of all Degrees made it their business to outdo one another in Liberality towards the Clergy. Nay, the Princes us'd to make such Grants without any Incumbrances or Restrictions, that thereby the Ecclesiasticks might be sure to enjoy free possession of what they had bestow'd upon them. These extravagant Donatives were none of the least Causes that put the Clergy afterwards upon labouring with so much vehemency to withdraw themselves from the Jurisdiction of Kings and the Civil Magistrates, as fearing that these extravagant Donatives and Grants might be recall'd and declar'd void by their Successors. To this purpose it has been been always a Maxim of Wise Men, that Princes by granting extravagant Privileges and Gifts, made their Subjects rather Enemies than Friends; since those who have obtain'd them living always in fear that the same either in part, or wholly, may be taken away again, employ all means so to establish themselves as to be in a Capacity to maintain themselves therein in spite of the Prince. Those Learned Men who are of an impartial Judgment, take it for granted, that the Pope pretended to exercise a Soveregn Power over the Countries thus granted to him by the *French* Kings, but that the People refus'd the same, as being desirous to maintain their Liberty, and thinking it very odd, that the Pope, who was an Ecclesiastical Person, should pretend to be at the same time a Worldly Prince. When therefore the *Romans* mutinied against Pope *Leo* III. he was forc'd to seek for Assistance from *Charles* the Great, who restor'd the Pope. But on the other hand, the Pope and People of *Rome* Proclaim'd

Charles Emperor, whereby he was put into possession of the Sovereignty over that part of *Italy*, which formerly belong'd to the Jurisdiction of the Governors at *Ravenna*, and the other remnants of the Western Empire; so that the Pope afterwards enjoy'd these Countries under the Sovereign Jurisdiction of the Emperor, who therefore us'd to be call'd the Patron and Defender of the Church, till the Reign of the Emperor *Henry* IV.

The Pope withdraws himself from the Obedience of the Emperors, and establishes an Ecclesiastical Sovereignty.

§. 21. But the Popes began at length to grow weary of the Imperial Protection, because the Emperor's Consent was requir'd in the Election of a Pope, and if they were mutinous, the Emperors us'd to check them, and sometimes turn them out of the Chair. To exempt themselves from the Power of the Emperors over them, the Popes did for a long time together employ all their Cunning and Labour before they could obtain their Aim. They us'd to make it their constant Business to raise intestine Commotions against the Emperors, sometimes in *Germany*, sometimes in *Italy*, in order to diminish their Power and Authority. The Bishops, especially in *Germany*, were always very busy, as being dissatisfy'd that they were dependent on the Emperors, who nominated the Bishops; and accordingly they joyn'd with the Pope to assist him in setting up the Ecclesiastical Sovereignty. Now, the Reign of the Emperor *Henry* IV. furnish'd them with an Opportunity to put in execution their Design: For this Emperor by his Debaucheries and ill management of Affairs, liv'd in Discontents and continual Broils with the Estates of *Germany*; and as soon as *Gregory* VII. who was before call'd *Hildebrand*, a proud, resolute and obstinate Man got into the Chair, he began to exclaim against the Emperor, that the granting of Church-Benefices did not belong to him, since he made a Traffick with them, and sold them to all sorts of People whom he enstall'd before they had taken Holy Orders: Nay further, when the Emperor offer'd to maintain his ancient Right and Title, he Excommunicated him, and stirr'd up the Bishops and Estates of *Germany* against him, who rais'd such a Hurricane in the State, that he was oblig'd to resign his Right of the Constituting of Bishops. The Pope under this pretext, did not only intend to exempt the Bishops from the Emperor's Jurisdiction, but the main point was to make him-

Pope Gregory Ex*communicates* Henry *IV.*

self

self Sovereign over *Italy*, and to make all the other Princes submit to the Popes Authority. And some are of Opinion, that this Design might have been put in Execution, considering that *Europe* was at that time divided into so many Principalities, and most of these Princes being not very Potent, might either out of Devotion, or to avoid falling under the Jurisdiction of more potent Princes, submit themselves to the Pope's protection, and pay him Tribute. It is therefore not improbable, that if three or four Popes had succeeded one another, qualify'd with sufficient Capacity to cover their Design with the Cloak of Holiness, and in the mean while to maintain the Interest of the People against the Oppressions of their Princes, the Popes might have made themselves absolute Sovereigns both in Temporal and Spiritual Affairs.

The Pope endeavours to subject the Emperor.

Neither did the Pope only pretend to free himself from the Emperor's Jurisdiction over him, but also endeavour'd to make him his Subject; for he pretended to be his Judge, he summon'd him before him to make answer to the Complaints of his Subjects, excommunicated him, and declar'd him to have forfeited his Right and Title to the Empire. And tho' his Son, the Emperor *Henry* V, endeavour'd to recover what was forcibly taken away from his Father, and made Pope *Paschal* a Prisoner, whom he forc'd to restore to him the Right of Constituting Bishops, yet were the whole Clergy in *Europe* so dissatisfy'd, at this Adventure, and raised such Commotions, that at last he was oblig'd to resign the same Right again into the Pope's hands. 1122.

Disputes in England about the investiture of Bishops.

Much about the same time, there were great Disputes concerning this point in *England*, which were compos'd in such a manner, that the King should not pretend to the power of investing Bishops, but that these should do Homage to him. The last of which the Pope was very unwilling to grant, who would fain have had the Bishops to be quite independent of the King, which was the reason why he expresly forbid the Bishops in *France* to follow this Example; but King *Lewis* VI. and his Successors, maintain'd their Right with so high a Hand, that the Popes were never able to establish their pretended Right in *France*. Neither did the Popes think it advisable to fall out at once with the Emperor and *France*, but that it would be more secure to have one at hand to uphold them against the other; above all, the Popes were not so much for weakning *France*, because they were not so nearly concern'd with that Kingdom, as for humbling the Emperor's that were potent in *Italy*, and pretended to the Sovereignty over the City of *Rome*. Neither was *Germany* so entirely united as *France*, and most Princes of *Europe* being then very jealous of the Grandeur of the Empire, were very willing to join with the Pope against the Emperors, under pretence of maintaining the Authority of the Holy Church and Papal Chair. 'Tis true, the two Emperors, *Frederick* I. and II. did afterwards endeavour to restore the ancient and Imperial Right, but were not able to maintain their Aim, especially since *Italy* was divided into the two Factions of the *Guelfs* and *Gibellines*, the first whereof were for the Pope, the latter for the Emperor, which caused such Confusion in *Italy*, that the Emperors could never afterwards reduce *Italy* to an entire Obedience. And forasmuch as after the Death of the Emperor *Frederick* II. the whole Empire was, during that long vacancy of the Throne, put into great Confusion and Disorders, the succeeding Emperors found so much Work in *Germany*, that they were not in a Condition to look after *Italy*, whereby the Pope had sufficient leisure given him to make himself Sovereign, not only over his own Possessions, but over all Possessions retaining to the Church.

The Pope pretends to a Power over Princes, even to depose them

§. 22. But the Pope not being contented to have attained this degree of Grandeur, quickly set on foot another Doctrin, which was of far greater Consequence, viz. That the Pope had an indirect power over Princes; that it belong'd to him in his own Right to take care how they govern'd and manag'd their Affairs. For tho' they did not expresly pretend in gross Terms; that Princes did depend on them in Civil Affairs, yet they believ'd that the Supreme Ecclesiastical Power did intitle them to an Authority to judge concerning the Actions of Princes, whether the same were good or bad, to admonish them, to correct them, and to command what was fitting, and to forbid what was unfitting to be done. If therefore Princes waged War against one another, the Pope pretended to have an Authority to command a Truce to be made betwixt them, to bring their Differences before him, and refer them to his Decision, not without Threatnings that he would not only Excommuncate them in their

their Persons, but also forbid the exercise of Divine Service and Administration of the Sacraments throughout their whole Kindom: They likewise gave out, that it belong'd to their Office to obviate all publick Scandals, to defend such as were oppress'd, and to see Justice done to all the World. It was from this pretention, that they receiv'd the Complaints of all such as pretended to be oppress'd; nay, they went further, for they sometimes took Information concerning the Injuries done by Princes to their Subjects, and concerning some Impositions laid upon the People, whereby the People thought themselves aggriev'd, which they forbid to be levy'd upon them under the penalty of Excommunication. Sometimes they us'd to declare the Possessions of such as were Excommunicated, forfeited, exposing their Persons to danger, and releasing the Subjects from their Oaths of Allegiance, under pretence that the Government of a Christian People ought not to be trusted to the management of such as had rebell'd against the Church. This has been attempted against a great many Crown'd Heads, and put in Execution against some of them.

This abominable Pretention (as they perswaded the ignorant) was founded upon their fictitious Decretals; and accordingly upon these they built their Canon Laws, which grants to the Pope an unlimited power over Christians, by virtue of which, he may as the Common Father, send out his Commands to all Believers, and admonish them concerning all such Matters as belong to Religion and their Salvation, and in case of Disobedience, inflict Punishments upon them. That the Predecessors of *Gregory* VII. did not make use of this Power, (they say) was, because the preceding Emperors, either kept themselves within their Bounds, or else the Popes liv'd an ungodly supine Life. To give specious Colours to these Pretentions, they made use of the Example of *Ambrose* and *Theodosius*; they us'd to relate how the *Spanish* Bishops had oblig'd King *Wamba*, by way of Penance, to lay down the Crown: As also how the Bishops of *France* had depos'd *Lewis*, Sirnam'd the *Pious*, who afterwards could not recover his Crown without the Consent and Authority of another Assembly of Bishops. They alledg'd for another Example, how *Fulc*, then Archbishop of *Rheims*, had threatned *Charles*, Sirnamed the Simple, to absolve his Subjects from their Oaths

How they colour over his Power.

Oaths of Allegiance, if he made an Alliance with the *Normans*, who were then Pagans. They suppos'd it without Question, that the Pope's Power extended it self beyond that of all other Bishops, since it was not limited by any thing, except by the express Canons of Councils and Decrees of the Popes, wherein nothing was contain'd against this Power of deposing Kings, and (they say) it was not to be suppos'd that they could have been forgetful of this point. And in regard they had assum'd a power to give a Name and Title of a King to some, who are either prompt'd by their Ambition, or Superstition, had begg'd the same from them; they suppos'd that by the same Right, they might take away the Crown from such as they esteem'd unworthy of wearing it.

They also had forbid to Marry within the seventh degree of Consanguinity, and the fourth of Affinity, whereby they often met with an Opportunity to be troublesome to Princes: For as it seldom happen'd among those of so high a Rank, but that one side or other was within one of these Degrees, so they stood in continual fear lest the Pope should disturb their Negotiations, unless they humbly begg'd for a Dispensation; and in both Cases the Popes knew how to make their Advantage of them. Lastly, the Popes having abundance of Business to dispatch, did thereby draw the best and most refi'd Wits to their Courts, who us'd to go thither to look for Imployment, and to perfect themselves in the great School of *Europe*. These were always for promoting the Pope's Interest and Designs, from whom they expected their Promotion; besides that, the whole Clergy adher'd to him as to their supreme Head. Pope *Boniface* VIII. did clearly give us to understand his meaning at the *Jubilee* kept in the Year 1300. when he appear'd sometimes in the Habit of an Emperor, sometimes in that of a Pope, and caus'd two Swords to be carry'd before him as the Ensigns of the Ecclesiastical and Civil Power.

The Papal Authority oppos'd.

§. 23. But the Popes could not long enjoy this unsufferable Usurpation in quiet; for it was so often call'd in question, 'till they were oblig'd to draw in their Horns, and to make their Pretensions a little more plausible. 'Tis true, in the business with the Emperors, the *Henrys* and

the

cily; to the latter, the Emperor *Frederick* I. all *Germany*, and the Clergy of *Rome*. And after the Death of *Victor*, those of his party chose three successive Popes, all whom *Alexander* out liv'd. These used to make a common Trade to excommunicate and revile one another, and each of them were fain to behave themselves towards their Protectors, more like a Client than a Master. But much greater was the Schism after the Death of *Gregory* IX. when again two Popes were elected at once, whereof one resided at *Rome*, the other at *Avignon*. This Schism lasted through several Successions, near the space of Forty Years; during which time, both parties excommunicated one another very frequently, and committed great [illegible] *France*, *Scotland*, *Castile*, *Savoy* and *Naples*, [illegible] of the side of the Pope that resided at *Avignon*, but all the rest of Christendom declar'd for the other at *Rome*. Both parties took great pains to set out the great numbers of Saints that were of their party, and what Miracles and Revelations were made concerning their Approbation. And both sides knew how to produce such Reasons, that at last there was no other Remedy left them, but to force both the Anti-Popes to resign at the Council of *Constance*, and to choose a new one in their stead. The last Schism of all arose when the Council of *Basil* having deposed *Eugenius* IV. did in his stead elect *Felix* V. Pope, unto whom the former would not submit. And these Dissentions were continu'd till after the Death of *Eugenius*, when *Nicholas* V. was chosen in his stead, unto whom *Felix*, consulting his own Repose and Tranquillity, resign'd the Chair upon very advantageous Terms in the Year 1438.

Hence an occasion taken to bridle the Pope's Power by general Councils.

It is very easily to be imagin'd how these Divisions did expose to publick view the Secrets of these Fathers. Since from hence an opportunity was taken to make use of the Assistance of the Councils to bridle the Popes, and to appeal from the Popes to these; so that Councils were now made use of to terrify the Popes, whenever they pretended to transgress their Bounds. The Popes could the less refuse to acknowledge the Power of the Councils at that time, because *Gregory* VII. himself, after the quarrel betwixt him and the Emperor was renewed, had proposed to call a Council to be held in a place of Security, where both Friends and Foes, both the Clergy and Laity, might meet to judge whether he or the Emperor

peror had broke the Peace, and to concert Measures how to re-establish the same. *Gelasius* II. who had Differences with *Henry* V. made the same Declaration, adding withal, that he would rest satisfied with what Judgment his Brothers the Bishops should give, who were constituted Judges in the Church by God Almighty, and without whom, he could not decide a Business of this nature. So *Innocent* III. had inserted in his Rescript, that he would not undertake to decide the Marriage Controversie betwixt *Philip Augustus* and *Engebourgh* of *Denmark* without consulting a general Council; for if he should attempt any such thing, he might thereby forfeit his Office and Dignity. Which words seemed to intimate, that a Pope for mismanagement might be Deposed. And when afterwards these, and the like words were made use of against the Popes, it was then too late to endeavour to make them pass for Compliments; since it proves often dangerous to be too modest in matters of such consequence. Wherefore the Council of *Pisa* in the Year 1409. did depose the two Anti-Popes, *Benedict* XII. and *Gregory* XII. in whose stead they chose another, *viz.* *Alexander* V. In like manner the Council of *Constance* did not only confirm the deposition of these two Popes, but also turned out *John* XXIV. who was made Pope after the Death of *Alexander* V. In the same manner the Council of *Basil* did with *Eugenius* IV. and besides this made a Decree that neither at the Court of *Rome*, nor in other Places, any Mony should be taken for the dispatches of Ecclesiastical Affairs. All which, as it shook the very Foundation of the Papal Chair, so it was not to be admired that the Popes were very averse afterwards to call the Council of *Trent*, and were forced to make use of all their Cunning, that nothing might pass there to the prejudice of their Grandeur, and that, since that time they have bid farewel to Councils for ever.

Concerning the Seat of the Popes, its being transferred to Avignon.

§. 24. Among other divisions, this has proved very prejudicial (as it seems) to the Authority of the Popes, that *Clement* V. did transfer the Papal Chair from *Rome* to *Avignon*, as I suppose, upon instigation of *Philip* Surnamed the Handsom, King of *France*, who having had great differences with *Boniface* VIII. was Excommunicated by him. To render this Excommunication ineffectual, he thought the Residence of the Pope in *France*, the

the most proper Expedient; hoping withal, by the sa
means to prevent the like for the future; since it was very probable that the greatest part of the Cardinals he
after would be taken out of the *French* Nation. Th
Popes made this City their constant place of Residen
for seventy Years together, not to mention that some
the Anti-Podes did likewise Reside there. This chang
of the Seat carry'd along with it several Inconvenienc
which proved very prejudicial to the Ecclesiastical M
narchy. For the Pope's Authority was among ot
things founded upon this Belief, that St. *Peter* had be
at *Rome*, and by his Presence had communicated a par
cular Prerogative and Holiness to that Chair, and wh
ther the same could be transferred to *Avignon*, seem
somewhat doubtful to a great many; besides, the Po
was then for the most part obliged to comply w
France, and to live as it were at the Discretion of t
French Kings: Tho' indeed the *French* who then thoug
they had a great Catch, have since complained, that th
got little else by the presence of the *Roman* Court, th
Simony, and another abominable Vice not fit to be n
ed. Add to this, that the Court of *Rome* being th
kept among Strangers, and as it were, out of its Na
ral Element, its Faults were the sooner discovered,
the whole the more despised. This removal of
Court of *Rome* proved likewise very prejudicial to
Revenue of the Church in *Italy*. For after the Autho
of the Emperors in *Italy* came to decay, each State
for living free, and being Sovereign it self, and the
ctions of the *Guelfs* and *Gibellines* caused most horrid
stractions: And the Authority of the Pope being vanis
by his absence, they made bold with the Church Pos
sions. Most Cities of the Ecclesiastical State, upon
persuasions of the *Florentines*, had sent away the Po
Legats, and acknowledged no Sovereign; and so
fell to the share of the petty Lords. The Emperor *Le*
Surnamed the *Bavarian*, who was at Enmity with
Pope, but in great esteem among the Inhabitants of
Ecclesiastical State, pretended to the Sovereignty over
same, as being a Fief of the Empire, which he gran
to such as upheld his party against the Pope. The
trimony of the Church was then but very slender,
tho' the Popes recovered part of it afterwards, they w
obliged to leave most in possession of what they had got

Bu

But after all, the City of *Rome* was after a long Resistance, forced to submit to the Pope's Power, when *Boniface* IX. in the Year 1393. put on the Bridle, by building the Castle of St. *Angelo*. And *Alexander* VI. was the chief cause that the Ecclesiastical State was reduced under the Obedience of the Popes. This Pope had a natural Son, whose Name was *Cæsar Borgia*, but who commonly is called Duke of *Valence*, from the Dukedom of *Valence*, which he got with his Lady *Charlotte d' Albret*. The Pope being very ambitious to make this his Son a great Prince in *Italy*, proposed this Expedient to him, that he must drive out these petty Lords, which were then in Possession of the Ecclesiastical State, promising that when he had made himself Master of these Places, he would confirm him in the possession of them for ever. He succeeded very well in this Enterprise, having made away with most of these petty Lords, some by Force, some by Treachery; for he used to stick at nothing, alledging, That whatever he did could not be done amiss, since he had received his Commission from his Father, who was endowed with the Holy Ghost. And being reduced to the utmost want of Mony, wherewith to pay his Soldiers, he and his Father agreed to Poison the richest Cardinals, at a Feast intended for that purpose; some of whom they also knew to be averse to their Designs. But the Servant who had the management of the business, having out of carelesness fill'd the Pope and his Son a Cup out of the poison'd Flasks, the Father died immediately, the Son narrowly escaping by the help of some Sudorificks. And *Cæsar Borgia* not being able so to influence the next Election, as to get one chosen fit for his purpose, his whole Project came to nothing. For after the Death of *Pius* III. who sat but a few Weeks in the Papal Chair, *Julius* III. a most mortal Enemy of *Borgia*, was chosen in his stead, who having taken into his possession all what he had got before, banish'd him out of the Country. Neither did this Pope rest satisfy'd, till he recover'd all what formerly belong'd to the Church, except *Ferrara*, which was not re-united with the Papal Chair, till about the latter end of the last Age, when the Legitimate Race of the Dukes of *Este* was extinct. This Pope also prevented the *French* from becoming Masters of *Italy*.

§. 25. But

Luther gives a great Blow to the Grandeur of the Pope.

§. 25. But when the Ecclesiastical Monarchy seem to be come to the very Pinacle of its Grandeur, when the Western parts were either in Communion with, or Obedience to the Church of *Rome*, except some Remnants of the *Waldenses* in *France*, and of the *Huss* in *Bohemia*; and just when the Differences arose betw Pope *Julius* II. and *Lewis* XII. which easily might ha occasion'd another Schism, were after the Death of first happily Composed by *Leo* X. and all the Complai against the Ambition of the Court of *Rome*, were alm extinguish'd; In this their happy, flourishing, and pe able State, there happen'd a Revolt from the Chair *Rome*, which tho' first started from a trifling Occasi came to such a Head that a great part of *Europe* wi drew it self from the Obedience of the Pope, who thereby put in danger of losing all. We will in this, we have done in all other Matters, only relate how, human Counsels and Helps were concern'd therein. F the hidden Counsels and Works of God Almighty, oug in our Judgment, rather to be receiv'd with Admirat and Submission, than to be div'd into with Presumpti And what *Tacitus* says, in a certain place, may conve ently be apply'd here: *Abditos numinis sensus exq illicitum, anceps, nec ideo assequare*, i. e. To search, the hidden Designs of God is unlawful and uncerta nor are they to be be penetrated by us.

The Virtues and Faults of Leo.

Pope *Leo*, of the House of *de Medici's* was an aff and magnificent Man, very Liberal towards all hon and learned Men, who might have made a very go Pope, if he had but had an indifferent knowledge of ligion and an inclination to Piety, whereas he was carelesss of both. He having liv'd very splendidly, by his Liberality and Magnificence exhausted the A stolical Chamber, and not being acquainted with Arts of acquiring Riches, made use of the Cardinal *rence Puccius*, who at last, when all the other Gold M were emptied, propos'd the way of raising Mony by dulgencies. These Indulgencies were therefore Abroad all over Christendom; and not only Absolu was sold both for the Dead and the Living; but E Milk and the like were allow'd to be eaten on Fast D The several Sums of Mony by this Fund to be r were beforehand allotted to certain Uses: All that w to be Collected in *Saxony* and thereabouts, as far as to the Sea-side, having been granted to *Magdalen* the Pope's Sister; She, to make the best of the Pope's Grant, had committed the whole management of her share to one *Arcimbold*, a Bishop by his Title and Coat; but one who was most experienc'd in all the *Genoese* Tricks and Shams in the way of Merchandizing. He again employ'd such as profer'd the most, and had no other Prospect than the getting of Mony. It had been formerly a Custom in *Saxony*, that the Hermits of the Order of St. *Austin* us'd to proclaim the Indulgencies. But *Arcimbold*'s Commissioners did not think fit to trust them at this time, as knowing them to be expert in that Trade, and fearing that they might not deal fairly with them, or at least that they would not bring in more Mony than us'd to be gather'd at other times. They chose therefore the *Dominicans* to preach up the Indulgencies, which the *Austin* Friars took very ill, as being thereby defrauded of their Authority, Right and Profit. The *Dominicans* in the mean while, to shew themselves well qualify'd for this new Employment, magnify'd their Wars to that extravagant degree, that their Auditors were extremely scandaliz'd at it; especially since the Commissioners liv'd in continual Debaucheries, and spent with great Infamy, what the poor Country Fellows spar'd out of their Bellies, to redeem their Sins. This oblig'd *Luther*, a Friar of the Hermits Order of St. *Austin*, to oppose these impudent Merchants of Indulgencies; and having duly weigh'd the matter himself, he in the Year 1517. did affix 95 Theses concerning this Point at *Wittenberg*, and *John Tezel*, a *Dominican* Friar, publish'd some other Theses in opposition to those at *Frankfort*. The Dispute being thus set on foot, each of them began to enlarge himself upon the above-mention'd Theses. *Luther* having both Reason and Scripture upon his side; his Adversary had nothing to alledge for himself, but the Authority of the Pope and the Church. Wherefore *Luther* was oblig'd to make an enquiry, upon what Foundation the Authority of the Pope was built, and in what condition the Church was at that time; which led him by degrees unto the discovery of the Errors and Abuses which were crept into the Church, and to an invective against the Impostures, and scandalous Lives of the Monks and Priests, and that it was a Duty incumbent

Luther *opposes Indulgences.*

Afterwards the Pope's Power.

upon the Magistrates to abolish these Abuses. And t
this purpose, as also to oblige the Magistrates to uphol
his Doctrin, he spoke very magnificently concerning t
Nature and Grandeur of the Civil Power, which
Priests hitherto had represented as despicable. By wh
means he at first got a great Party, and his Doctrin
spread abroad every where.

The Circumstances of these Times.

§. 26. But that we may the better understand
Reason; how a poor Friar was able to give such a Bl
to the Chair of *Rome*, we must, next to the Supreme D
rection of God Almighty, consider the Circumstances
these Times, and what Disposition there was at that j
cture of time in the Minds of the People in Gene
First then, *Luther's* Propositions concerning the Ind
gences were very good and reasonable, and a great m
ny Divines, which afterward oppos'd his Doctrin w
at first of his side, as were also some Cardinals, a
George Duke of *Saxony* himself. His Adversaries we
so perverse, that every body lamented their Folly a
Perverseness. Neither was it at first in the least
spected, that Things would go so far as they did.
ther himself had at first not the least Thoughts of
ling off from the Pope. The Emperor *Maximilian*
no Aversion to the Doctrin of *Luther*; and it is credi
related, that, when he first heard of him, he did sa
that this Friar ought to be kept safe, since good use mi
be made of him. Some Monks only, and these Co
missioners, who were likely to be the Losers by it,
make such a Clamour, and rais'd such Tumults by blow
ing up the Coals, that this small Spark broke out into
great Flame. All Christendom was at the same time
a miserable Condition, as being quite overwhelm'd w
Ceremonies; the perverse Monks did what they plea
and had entangel'd tender Consciences in their Snar
All Divinity was turn'd into Sophistry. New Doctr
and Propositions were broached, without any rega
how they ought to be prov'd and maintain'd. And
whole Clergy of all Degrees had rendred their Lives a
Conversations odious and despis'd to the World. T
late Popes, *Alexander* VI. and *Julius* II. had been in
mous for their Pride, Treachery, turbulent Spirit,
other such like Vices, as were very ill becoming Eccle
astical Persons. Such Bishops as were good for any thing
had

ıad quite entangled themſelves in worldly Buſineſs; a ;reat many of them led a moſt ſcandalous Life, and were more expert in Hunting, than skill'd in the Bible. The Prieſts and Monks were over Head and Ears in Ignorance, and ſcandaliz'd the Common People by their Debaucheries, and their Avarice was grown unſupportble to every Body.

The Ignorance of Luther's *Adverſaries.*

Add to all this, that thoſe who firſt pretended to oppoſe *Luther*, were a ſort of ſimple, miſerable, and ſome f them debauch'd Wretches; theſe, when they ſaw *Luther* maintain his Arguments in a manner which was not ommon at that time, were ſoon confounded and put to *nonplus*, not knowing where to begin or to end. 'Tis true, in former Ages all the Clergy had not been free rom Vices, but the Ignorance of thoſe barbarous Times ad ſerv'd them for a Cloak. But after *Europe* began to e reſtor'd to its flouriſhing Condition, and all ſorts of earning began to diſpel the former Darkneſs, it was hen that theſe abominable Spots became more conſpicuus to the Eyes of the World. As the Ignorant Prieſts nd Monks, who could not bear the Glance of this bright hining Light, were ſtark mad at thoſe who had reſtor'd earning to *Europe*, and did them all the Miſchief they ould, and when they found themſelves worſted by hem, us'd to make a point of Religion of their different Diſputes, and to accuſe thoſe of Hereſie that were nore Learned than themſelves: So theſe us'd to expoſe heir Folly, and as much as in them lay to diſcover their gnorance to the World. 'Twas upon this Account, the mpudent Monks pick'd a Quarrel with *John Reuchlin*, vhom they fain would have made a Heretick; from vhence that learned Gentleman, *Ultrick van Hutten*, (if remember right) took an Opportunity to expoſe them noſt in *Epiſtolis obſcurorum virorum*. While the War bewixt the Lovers and Perſecutors of Learning was cary'd on with great Heat on both ſides, *Luther*'s Doctrin ppear'd in the World. And becauſe the Monks made their Buſineſs to bring the moſt Learned Men into the ame Quarrel which they had againſt *Luther*, in hopes to trike them both down at one Blow; this prov'd the Ocaſion that moſt of the Learned Men in *Germany* did actully ſide with *Luther*.

Erasmus favour'd by Luther.

It is also undeniable, that *Erasmus* of *Rotterda* considerable share in the Reformation; for he had discover'd, and reprehended a great many Abu Errors; he had rejected the School Divinity, commended the reading of the Bible and Fathe had ridicul'd the Barbarity and Ignorance, whi upheld by the Monks, and approv'd at first Cause, tho' he always excepted against his viol biting way of Writing: Nay, his Silence alone very prejudicial to *Luther*'s Adversaries. For being then esteem'd the most Learn'd Divine of every Body took his Silence for a kind of an A tion of *Luther*'s Cause. And when he afterwar lish'd his Treatise *de libero Arbitrio*, it made no gi pression upon the Minds of the People, since it su ly appear'd, that it was rather writ to please othe of his own Inclination. Besides, that this was main Point in Dispute, and *Luther* did refute su his Propositions.

The Princes of Germany *dissatisfied with the Pope.*

At the same time the Princes and Estates of being sufficiently convinc'd, that heavy Impositi been laid upon them of late, under several Prete the Court of *Rome*, for no other Purpose but to the Grandeur of the Ecclesiasticks at *Rome*, treamly dissatisfy'd with the Pope. And furthe general Fear which was then in *Germany* of an by the *Turks*, and the Differences arising betwixt V. *Francis* I. and *Henry* VIII. contributed very promote the Reformation, since there was but li for to think much of these Disputes. Some are nion, that *Charles* V. conniv'd at the spreading Doctrin of *Luther* throughout *Germany*, hoping Divisions to get an Opportunity to suppress the Liberty of the Estates, and to make himself S over *Germany*. For else (they say) he might ea quench'd the Fire at first, *viz.* in the Year 1521. had *Luther* in his Power at *Wormes*, where he mi put him to Death, which would have pass'd well for a State Trick. But it is not so evident, whet *Luther* had been murther'd against the Public granted him, his Doctrin would thereupon h rooted out; it is more probable that the Empero then but young, did not at that time foresee Consequence this Business might prove afterwar that he did not think it advisable at that juncture of Time to break with the Elector of *Saxony*, who was then in great Authority. Neither could he pretend at the same time, when he was engag'd in a War against *France* and the *Turks*, to attack the Princes of *Germany* that were then courted by *France*, and who began to make Alliances with them. Yet it is certain, that under the Pretence of Religion he afterwards made War upon the Protestant Estates of *Germany*, and intended by their Ruin to open himself the way to the absolute Monarchy over *Germany*. And tho' he was very successful in the War against the League made at *Smalkald*, he could not accomplish his projected Design, because he stood in need of the Assistance of the *German* Princes against *France*, and the *Turks*, and to obtain the Imperial Crown for his Son *Philip*. Nay, *Paul* III. himself dreaded the growing Greatness of the Emperor, to that Degree, that he stir'd up the *French* to oppose his prevailing Power, and to prevent the intire Ruin of the Protestants, allow'd them to make use of the Alliance with the *Turks*, against the Emperor, who he fear'd intended a thorough Reformation of the Court of *Rome*, and the reducing of it to its ancient State of Simplicity and Integrity.

The ill Conduct of Leo *and Cardinal* Cajetan.

Upon the whole, the ill Conduct of the Pope did great Mischief to the *Roman* Catholick Party. For it was a grand Mistake in *Leo* X. that he with so much Violence declar'd himself for these Merchants of Indulgences, and by this Bull of the 9th of *November* in the Year 1518. decided the Points in Controversie betwixt them, whereby he cut off all Hopes and Means for an Accommodation. It would questionless have been better for him to have stood Neuter, and to have impos'd Silence upon both Parties, and in the mean while to have found out an Expedient to appease *Luther*. And Cardinal *Cajetan* did in the Year 1519. act a very imprudent part at *Ausburg*, when he dealt so very rudely with *Luther*, and refus'd to accept of his Proposal, *viz.* That he would be silent, provided his Adversaries would do the same. For by this Refusal made to so resolute a Man, whom he would have oblig'd to make a Recantation, he forc'd him to do his utmost, and to fall directly upon the Pope himself. It would have been no difficult Matter to have granted him, that some corrupt Manners were crept into the Church, to keep him from medling with the Reformation of the Doctrins. But on the contrary, making continual Instances at the Elector of Court, to have *Luther* deliver'd up to him. *L* thereby oblig'd to shew the Unreasonableness of and to demonstrate that his own Doctrin was b a very solid and good Foundation. And the dred his Cause very suspicious, that he, when *L* peal'd to a Council, did by making a great m sions delay to call one: From hence it was evi he did not trust much to the Goodness of his Ca were to be debated before impartial Judges. I so an unlucky Hit for the Pope, when he fell *Henry* VIII. who to spite the Pope, did open for the Protestant Religion to be settled in *Eng* like manner the House of *Navarre* propagated tected the Protestant Religion in *France*, out o as some say, against the Pope, who had shewn *nand* the Catholick way into that Kingdom. Be there were abundance of good Men of the *Ro* tholick Religion, who were glad to see that *L* wash the scabby Heads of the Monks with so Lye, as he did. So that every thing seem'd to promote the Decree of God Almighty.

Why the Doctrin of Luther *was not spread farther.*

§. 27. But why the Doctrin of *Luther* was n farther, and the Ecclesiastical Monarchy was r over turn'd, several Reasons may be alledg'd. is to be consider'd, that, in those States, wher Doctrin was receiv'd, the Supreme Direction i astical Affairs came necessarily to be devolv'd o vil Magistrates. For if any of these States w pretended to this Direction over the others of Communion, these, who would have thought t no less capable, would never have acknowl same. Which did not a little weaken their U Strength, and was the main Occasion, that th not act so unannimously and vigorously against t as he against them. It is also to be consider'd, Reformation was not undertaken after mature tion, and as it were on purpose to form or set State; but this great Revolution happen'd up den and unexpectedly, so that the whole Work ry'd on as Occasion offer'd and by Degrees. *Luther* was the first that gave the Alarm, yet the not think themselves oblig'd to follow precisely his Opinion, but were also ambitious of having contributed something towards the Reformation. This occasion'd Disputes among themselves; and because no Body had an Authority among them to decide these Controversies, each party persisted obstinately in their Opinion; from whence arose such Schism, that they became neglectful of the Common Enemy, and fell upon one another. This furnish'd the Popish party with a very feasible Argument, who cry'd out aloud, the Hereticks were faln into Confusion among themselves, as not knowing what to believe; and since they had left the Church of Rome, they were brought into an endless Labyrinth. There were also a great many of the Protestants, who under the profession of the Gospel led an impious and scandalous Life, as if by the Liberty of the Gospel they had obtain'd a License to abandon themselves to all sorts of Vices. This gave further Occasion to the Papists to defame the Doctrin of *Luther*; especially since he had with great Severity reproved the Licenciousness of the Clergy, and had been generally applauded for it. Another great Detriment to *Luther*'s Doctrin, was, that immediately after whole Swarms of Fanaticks, Anabaptists, and the like appear'd in the World, and that the Boors in *Germany* run as it were mad, and made a most dangerous Insurrection. When some Princes took this Point into Consideration, the Doctrin of *Luther* began to become suspicious to them, as if thereby the Licenciousness of the Common People was Taught and Authorised; which they looking upon as a greater Evil than what Oppression they were likely to suffer from the Clergy, did with all their Power oppose the Doctrin of *Luther*.

Divisions among the Protestants

The Licenciousness of some Protestants.

Some will have it, that the University of *Paris* had a share in retarding the Progress of the Reformation. For *Luther* having perswaded himself, that this University was dissatisfied at *Leo* X. because he had abolished the Pragmatick Sanction relating to the Investiture of Bishops; and that therefore the Members thereof would be glad of an Opportunity to revenge themselves, he submitted his Disputation with *Eckius* to their Judgment; but these gave their Judgment against him, and that in very hard Words. Add to this, that the Kings of *Spain* with this View did afterwards consider that it was for their purpose to take upon them the Protection of the

The University of Paris.

Roman Chair; again they oppos'd the Protestant Do
with all their Might, and so powerfully assiste
League in *France*, that *Henry* VI. if he would mai
his Crown, was obliged to leave the Protestant
gion.

Zwinglius and Calvin.

Some have observed; that when *Zwinglius* and
wards *Calvin*, began all upon a sudden to introdu
rapid a Reformation, not only as to the Essential M
ries of our Religion, but as to the External Form o
Church and Manner of Worship, and thereby fell
one Extreme to another, this proved a main Obsta
the Increase of the Protestant Religion. For *Luthe*
hitherto made very little Alteration in outward M
He had left in the Churches the Ornaments, Clocks
gans, Candles, and such like; he had retained the
est part of the Mass, but had added some Prayers
Native Tongue, so that he was look'd upon by so
a Reformer of the Abuses only. But when it seem'
this Revolution was likely to become Universal Zi
lius appear'd in *Switzerland*, as did *Calvin* afterwa
France; and these, instead of following the Footste
Luther, began to Preach against the Presence of th
dy of Christ in the Sacrament of the Lord's Supper,
lish'd all sorts of Ceremonies and Ornaments, de
all Reliques, broke the Altars and Images, abolish
Order of the Hierarchy, and despoiled Religion
such things as did most affect the Eyes and exte
Senses of the People. This caused an Aversion and
mosity in the common People against them, an
creas'd a Zeal for that Religion which they ha
ceived from its Ancestors. The Riches of the C
had a various Influence in promoting or thwartin
ther's Doctrin according to the different Circumstan
Persons: For on the ones Hand a great many gladl
hold of the Opportunity to possess themselves of
Ecclesiastick Revenues, by departing from the R
Church: On the other hand the ample Ecclesiasticl
venues kept a great many Prelates under the Obec
of the *Roman* Chair, who, if they had not been afr
losing their Rich Benefices, would not have been so
ward to side with *Luther*'s Party. This was mani
to be seen in *France*, where both the Prelates an
Common People had made no great Account o
Pope's Authority before the Reformation, but wher

ſaw that thoſe of the Reformed Religion were for breaking into their Quarters, they agreed better afterwards with the Court of *Rome*, and the Commonalty turn'd very Zealous againſt the Reformed Religion.

The Popiſh Sovereignty recovered.

§. 28. In ſhort, the Pope, as ſoon as his Adherents had recovered themſelves from their firſt Conſternation, and his Enemies were faln out among themſelves, has ſince ſettled his Affairs in ſuch a manner, that the Proteſtants in all likely-hood will not only not be able to hurt him for the future, but himſelf by degrees gets ground of them. For thoſe things wherewith *Luther* upbraided the Church of *Rome*, and did the moſt Miſchief to them, they have either quite aboliſh'd, or at leaſt they are tranſacted in a more decent manner, *Si non caſte, tamen caute.* They have alſo made uſe of the ſame Weapons, with which *Luther* attackt them. For the Popes now adays do not inſult with ſo much Haughtineſs over Princes, but treat them with more Civility and Lenity. It is true, in the laſt Age *Paul* IV. behaved himſelf very imprudently towards *Spain* and in our Age *Paul* V. did the ſame with *Venice*. But by the Mediation of wiſer Heads, theſe Differences were Compoſed, before they came to any great Head; and the Popes ever ſince have been ſufficiently convinced, that theſe hot headed Proceedings are in no ways ſuitable to their preſent Condition. For *Paul* V. ſoon gave fair Words, when the *French* Ambaſſador made him believe, that the *Venetians* had ſent for ſome Miniſters from *Geneva*, to be inſtructed in the Principles of the Reformed Religion. Neither has the Papal Chair of late Years been fill'd with ſuch *Debauches* as *Alexander* VI. or ſuch Martial Popes as *Julius* II was; but of late they have endeavour'd to carry on the Intriegues under hand, whilſt they in outward Appearance pretended to be Promoters, and Mediators of Peace. That moſt ſcandalous Trade of Indulgences, and that groſs ſort of Simony they have ſet aſide, whilſt they make it their Buſineſs to conjole the People out of their Mony in a handſomer way.

The Biſhops, Prieſts, and Monks, more Regular and learned than heretofore.

The Biſhops are now of another Stamp, and carry it on with much more Gravity than before the Times of *Luther*, nay, there are now among the Prelates excellent and well qualified Men. The Ordinary Prieſts and Monks alſo are much reformed in their Manners, and have

have been obliged to lay aside their former brutish I rance. *Luther* and his Adherents did at first gain tily upon the People by their most excellent and lea Sermons, and by their Books which they publish'd, t by to excite the People to Piety, Prayers, Godly Me tions and Exercises. Both which the Papists have tated since, for among them now adays are to be f most excellent Preachers, and very good Prayer-Bo so that the Protestant Clergy has now not much to o against them, as to their Ability or outward Behav They have also got a very good Insight into all the troverted Points, and have a dozen or more Distinct at hand against any Objection. For Example, whe nothing seems more ridiculous, than that the Pope sh grant his Indulgences for twenty or thirty thousand Y to come, they know how to give this a fine Colou the whimsical Distinctions of *Intensive* and *Extensive*, *tentialiter* and *Actualiter*, which relish strangely young Students, and the Ignorant suppose them t Terms full of Mysteries. And because the Ignoranc the Clergy, and the hatred conceived against Lear and learned Men, have proved very prejudicial to Popish Monarchy, the Popish Clergy, and especially Jesuits have since altered their Course, and having t upon them the Education of Youth, have pretende the Monopoly of Learning among the *Roman* Catholi so that since that time Learning has not only not prejudicial but very profitable to them.

How they make Converts. Lastly, Now adays they do not make use of Fire Sword to propagate the *Roman* Catholick Religion, the chief Men among the Protestants are inticed to c over to their Party with fair Words, great Promises, actual Recompences. If any one who is well qual will go over to their Party, he may be sure to make Fortune, since the Wealth of their Church furnishes t with sufficient Means to maintain such a Person, tho Merits were not extraordinary. Whereas on the cor ry if any one goes from them to the Protestant Relig and either has not wherewithal to live, or is not dow'd with extraordinary Qualifications, he must ex nothing but Want. *The House of* Austria *most zealous for Popery.* Last of all, the House of *Au* promoted the Popish Interest mightily, when they d the Protestants out of the Hereditary Countries in *many*, out of the Kingdom of *Bohemia*, and the C tries belonging thereunto, and lately did the same to the Protestants in *Hungary*, except to a very few; or else forc'd them to profess themselves *Roman* Catholicks.

§. 29. From what has been said it may easily be understood, in what manner this Ecclesiastical Sovereignty has extended her Power over the Western Parts of *Christendom*. But in order to understand throughly the whole Structure, and Composure of his Engine, and by what Means it is sustained, it will not be improper to consider the Pope in two different Capacities; first as a Prince in *Italy*, and secondly as the Spiritual Monarch over the Western Church. As to the first it is be observed, that the Pope may be reckon'd a Potent Prince in *Italy*, but is in no ways to be Compared with the other Princes in *Europe*. The Countries under his Jurisdiction are the City of *Rome*, with her Territories situated on both sides of the River *Tyber*; the Dukedom of *Benevento* in the Kingdom of *Naples*, the Dukedoms of *Spoleto*, *Urbino* and *Ferrara*, the Marquisate of *Ancona*, several places in *Tuscany*, *Romaniola* or *Flaminia*, where are situated *Bologna* and *Ravenna*. In *France* the Country of *Avignon* belongs to him. *Parma* is a Fief of the Church, which *Paul*. III. granted to his Son *Lewis Farnese*. But since that time a Constitution has been made, that it shall not be in the Power of any Pope to Alienate any Fief, or to grant any of the Countries belonging to the Church in Fief to any Person whatsoever. This was done, to prevent the Ruin of the Ecclesiastick State, and, that, in case the Revenues from Abroad should fail, the Pope nevertheless might not want means to maintain himself and his Court. The Kingdom of *Naples* is also a Fief to the Church, in acknowledgment of which the King of *Spain* every Year presents the Pope with a white Horse and some thousands of Ducats. What other Pretensions the Court of *Rome* makes are out of date. For the rest, these Countries are indifferently populous and Fertile, having several Cities of Note, out of which the Pope receives a Revenue of two Millions *per Annum*. And the Pope's Ministers take effectual Care, that their Subjects may not be overgrown in Riches.

The Temporal State of the Pope.

His Dominions.

Perhaps there might be a considerable Number of good Soldiers maintain'd out of the Ecclesiastick State, but his Military Strength is scarce worth taking Notice of, since he

His Forces.

he makes use of quite other means, to preserve his S than other Princes do. He maintains about twenty lies which have their Station at *Civita Vechia.* chief State Maxim of the Pope, as a Temporal Prin that Peace may be preserv'd in *Italy*, and that *Italy* ma main in the same State as it is now, and especially, there may not be introduced any other Sovereign Po which might prove so formidable as to domineer the rest. He must take great Care that the *Turks* not get footing in *Italy*, and in case of an Invasion the *Turks*, not only *Italy* would be oblig'd to join ag them, but all *Christendom* would be confederate to e or chase out these Barbarians, since no Christian P would be contented that this delicious Country sh fall into their Hands.

How he stands with Relation to Germany, Spain and France. The Pope has nothing more to fear from the *Ger* Empire, as long as it remains upon the same Founda But if it should fall under the Government of an A lute Monarch, it is likely he might attempt to renew Ancient Pretensions. *Spain* and *France* are the two K doms, which are most formidable to the Pope. Ag them the Pope makes Use of this Maxim, that he e sets them together by the Ears, or at least keeps up Ballance betwixt them, that one may not become q Master of the other. I am apt to believe that the would be glad with all his Heart, that the *Spaniards* driven out of *Italy*, especially out of the Kingdo *Naples.* But it is scarce to be suppos'd, that he shoul able to do it by his own Strength; and to make u the *French* in this Case, would be to fall out of the ing Pan into the Fire. Therefore all the Pope can is, to take Care, that *Spain* may not incroach upon ot in *Italy*; and there is no question but if the *Spani* should attempt any such thing, *France* and all the o *Italian* States would be ready to oppose their De Neither can it be pleasing to the *Pope*, if the Kin *France* should get so much footing in *Italy*, as to be to sway Matters there according to his pleasure, wh the Pope ought to prevent with all his Might. The P need not fear much from the other States of *Italy.* tho' some of them are under hand his Enemies, and dr his Spiritual Power, and some of them have been sev ly chastised by the Court of *Rome*; nevertheless, t must at least in outward Appearance pay to the *Pop* due Veneration, neither dare they as much as devise to make any Conquests upon the Pope. Notwithstanding which, they would not look with a good Eye upon the Pope, if he should pretend to make any Conquests upon his Neighbours, and enlarge his Dominions; this wise Nation being extremely jealous, and desirous to keep up the Ballance betwixt the States of *Italy*.

§. 30. But if we consider the Pope, secondly, as the Spiritual Monarch of *Christendom*, and the Vicar of Jesus Christ upon Earth, we meet in his Spiritual State with such surprising and subtile Pieces, that it must be confessed, that since the Beginning of the World, there has not been set up a more Artificial Fabrick than the Popish Monarchy. It has required the more Sagacity to erect and sustain this Structure, the more the ends of this Sovereignty are quite different from the ends of all other States in the World, and the more feeble the Title appears upon which it is founded: For it is the main end of other Commonwealths, to live in Security and Peace; for the maintaining of which, the Subjects contribute a Share out of their Goods and Possessions, nay, venture their Lives that they may sufficiently provide against the Attempts of malicious People, and live in Security and without Danger from their Enemies. And besides this, it is the Duty of every Subject, to take Care that he may be able to maintain himself out of his own Revenues, or by his Labour and Industry. But the Popish Monarch's chief Design is, that the Popes and the Clergy may live in Plenty and Splendour in this World, all which is to be maintain'd at the Cost and Charge of other People, who must be perswaded to part with their Money by several shining Arguments, and Artificial Perswasions. Whereas other States are fain to maintain their Forces and Garrisons with great Expences, the Pope on the contrary entertains his Militia without any Charge, nay, rather with Profit to himself. And whereas it is a State Maxim among the wiser Princes, not to extend their Conquests too far, the Pope has no Occasion to imitate them in this Point, since it is neither dangerous nor troublesome to him, tho' he extends his Jurisdiction over the *East* and *West-Indies*. The Rights of Sovereignty are founded upon evident and undeniable Principles and Divine Institution, since without it, it is impossible that Mankind should live honestly,

Particular Constitution of the Popish Monarchy as Spiritual.

neſtly, ſecurely, commodiouſly, and decently. But to find out the ſame Neceſſity and Foundation of the Pope's Sovereign Authority, and to demonſtrate that as the Peace and Welfare of Mankind, cannot ſubſiſt without a Supreme Civil Power, ſo the Chriſtian World cannot be without a Supreme Eccleſiaſtical Power, is in my Mind impoſſible to be done. He that is unwilling to believe this, let him find out a Demonſtrative Proof, and he will be the Miracle of the World. But if the Pope's Champions pretend to a poſitive Command from God Almighty, they are oblig'd to prove by clear and evident Proofs, and that in all its Clauſes and Determinations, out of the Holy Scripture; that our Saviour when he ſent his Diſciples all over the World to Preach the Chriſtian Faith not only gave them full Power to propagate the Chriſtian Doctrin among all Nations; and be independent on any Humane Power in their Office, ſo they can't be hindred from Preaching, or forc'd to add or retrench any thing from their Doctrin (which Power is unqueſtionable): But likewiſe granted them a Commiſſion, to put into the Miniſtry of the Goſpel, and that without the Conſent of the Magiſtrates (tho' profeſſing the true Chriſtian Religion) as many, and whom they pleas'd; and to inveſt theſe again with full Power to increaſe their Order to ſuch a Number as they ſhould think fit themſelves, without having any Regard to the Civil Power or Magiſtrates, whoſe Right and Title is thereby impaired. He muſt prove that ſince they can't live upon the Air, they have a Power granted them to ſeek out all ways and means not only for their Subſiſtence, but alſo for carrying on their Pride and Extravagancies. They muſt alſo have a Prerogative granted them of being exempted from the Civil Juriſdiction both in their Perſons, and ſuch Poſſeſſions as they have acquired to themſelves, tho' the ſame appertain to the Revenues of the Commonwealth, are ſituated in the Territories, and enjoy the Protection of the Sovereign; who is to have no Power to lay Taxes upon ſuch Poſſeſſions, or imploy them to any other Uſes. Further, they muſt prove that the Supreme Direction over this Order with Relation not only to their Office, but their Poſſeſſions, belong to one of the ſame Order, on whom the reſt depend as their Sovereign, and that the Civil Magiſtrates can't pretend to any Superiour Juriſdiction over them, tho' the Ecclesiastical Order either by its Number or Misbehaviour should prove pernicious to the State, and tho' the State could not be maintain'd without the Revenues of the Ecclesiasticks, which must not be imployed for the Benefit of the Publick, without the Consent of him, who has the Supreme Direction over this Order. Besides all this, they are oblig'd to prove some other *Hypothesis* of theirs, which run upon Matter of Fact. Particularly, that our Saviour granted the Spiritual Sovereignty over the Church to St. *Peter* only, without allowing the least Share to the rest of the Apostles. That he granted this Prerogative, not only to St. *Peter* for his own Person, but as a perpetual Inheritance to such as should succeed him in that Place where he resided as Bishop. They must prove that St. *Peter* was actually Bishop of *Rome*, that he exercised the same Power there, and granted the said Prerogative to no other Place where he used to Preach, besides *Rome*. And because these Points are so very hard to be prov'd, the Popish Doctors are oblig'd to be very cautious in proposing these Questions distinctly to the World, and rather treat of them confusedly and superficially. It is rather their Business to fill the Peoples Heads with far-fetched Arguments that do not so nearly touch the Point, *viz.* concerning the great Promises, that the Gates of Hell shall not prevail against the Church, concerning the great Authority and Prosperity of the Church, her Antiquity, the Succession of the Popes, the Holy Fathers and Councils, the Authority of so many Ages and Nations, Miracles and such like Stuff fit for a Declamation. They also make use of another Expedient, *viz.* That if any one dares to contradict these things, he is immediately without hearing his Reasons, branded with the Name of a Heretick, and esteemed as one that being a Novice, and ignorant in his Trade, ought not to be so bold as to contradict his Master, but deserves to be burnt.

Why the Popish Sovereignty was to be exercised in the Form of a Monarchy

§. 31. It is easily to be imagin'd, that this Spiritual Sovereignty was of Necessity to be establish'd in the Form of a Monarchy, since it was in no ways suitable to a Democratical or Aristocratical Government, not only by Reason of several Inconveniencies which would have attended it, but more especially, because that so many different Heads as sway a Democratical and Aristocratical

ſtocratical Government, would even by the moſt Laws never have been kept in ſuch an Union, b by raiſing of Factions and Diſſentions, they wou eaſily overturn'd a Work built upon ſo ſlight a F tion. But among the ſeveral ſorts of Monarchi vernments, they have choſen ſuch an one as that the Art of Men, there could not have been inven more ſuitable to their Purpoſe; it being moſt cert all the ſpeculative Inventions of the moſt refined cians, are not in the leaſt to be compared to wh be met withal in this Popiſh Monarchy. 'Ti ſome Princes have gain'd to themſelves and their ment a great Authority, by pretending to be t ſpring of the Gods, and that they had laid the Fc on of their Government, by the expreſs Comman Gods, and by their peculiar Approbation; wh they uſed to be after their Death plac'd in the Nu the Gods, and were ador'd as ſuch. But the P gone farther, and perſwaded the People that h Lieutenant of Jeſus Chriſt, who has all Power in and Earth, and his Vicar in the World, and th more exalted Senſe than it is ſpoken of the Mag that they are Miniſters of God's Juſtice upon Ear he pretends that he has the Power of diſpenſing t rits of Jeſus Chriſt, and that ſuch as refuſe to a ledge this Prerogative, are not capable of obtain vation. And ſince there is nothing more powerfu World, to induce People to a profound Venerati the Divine Majeſty, and no Motive more ſtron force from them an obedience and an entire Subm all ſorts of Hardſhip, than the Fear of God's Wr Eternal Damnation; it is evident that if this Point gain'd, and the People throughly perſwaded, the no further Proof of the reſt of their Articles o than that αὐτὸς ἔφη, the Pope has determin'd it ſo

Why it muſt be an Elective Monarchy.

Further, moſt Nations eſteeming an hereditary ment the moſt convenient and leaſt dangerous, ha duc'd that Form into their States; but this Form vernment could not ſuit with the Intention of thi tual Monarchy. For in thoſe States where the C Hereditary, it muſt of Neceſſity ſometimes happ the ſame is devolv'd to Princes who are Minors: would be an odd Sight, that a Child that rides tl by-Horſe, ſhould be taken for the Vicar of Chr that the Protector of *Christendom* should want a Tutor. Neither is it to be suppos'd, that young Princes could behave themselves so gravely and wisely, as seems to be requisite for a Person of his Station; neither can it so much be hop'd, that a whole Succession of Princes should be inclinable to such a Function. In a word, an Hereditary Succession would have made it the same with a Temporal State, which could never have been maintain'd long upon so awkard and slight a Foundation. For the great Ministers themselves would have been for putting by the Pope, that they might succeed in his stead; whereas these seeing they cannot possess themselves of the Papacy by open Force, are now very obedient, in hopes that either they themselves, or at least their Friends, may one time or another attain to this Dignity by Election. Besides, it might easily have happen'd, that in case the Royal Family should have been extinguish'd, such Dissentions might have arisen concerning the Succession, that the whole Frame of the State would thereby have been disjoynted.

Why the Pope was to live in a State of Celibacy.

It was also thought convenient this Spiritual Sovereign should be oblig'd never to Marry, which seem'd most suitable to the Gravity of this Court, since a great Train of Ladies living in great Splendor and Plenty would have made such a Figure, as must needs appear but little suitable to excite others to a Holy Life and Devotion. Upon this Consideration, the main Design was, by a feigned Hypocrisie, to impose a Belief upon the People, as if the Court of *Rome* was so wholly taken up with Spiritual Affairs, that there was no room left for worldly Pleasures. It was also reasonably suppos'd, that a Prince who had Wife and Children might sometimes be led away to take more to Heart the private Interest of his Family, than the publick Good of the State, since there can scarce be any thing more prevailing upon a Man, than the Consideration of the Welfare and Preservation of Wife and Children. And what *Alexander* VI. and *Paul* III. did with their Bastards, have been convincing Instances of the Importance of this Position to the Court of *Rome*. It is possible likewise they took this into Consideration, that if a Temporal Foreign Prince should obtain this Dignity, he would entail it upon his House, which Inconveniencies are now avoided by the Obligation laid upon the Pope never to Marry.

The Conclave is in like manner a most admira vention to bridle the immoderate Ambition, and those Schisms, which us'd formerly miserably to the See, and weaken the Authority of the Popes; that, thereby a long Vacancy of the Chair is pre and by means of this Election, it is much easier out one that is fitly qualify'd to represent the gr artificial Hypocrite, and afterwards to make Peo lieve, that are ignorant of the Intrigues of the Co that it was by the particular Providence of God A ty, that such a Person was chosen as was the most to be God's Vicar upon Earth. Thus much at lea be obtain'd by an Election, that such a Person is, as is well vers'd in the Arts of Policy and their tious Designs, and one whose Age being above th ard Extravagancies of young Men, may by his and long Experience appear more venerable in hi ction. It is also a very wise Order touching the E of a Pope, that he is to have two third Parts of th in the Conclave, which seems to have been intr that the new Pope might not be unacceptable to number of Cardinals. Now adays it is a general im in the Choice of a Pope, to Elect an *Italian*, w done not only because they rather will bestow this ty and ample Revenue upon a Native of *Italy* than Foreigner, but also because the Security and Prese of the Papal Chair depends in a great Measure, Balance which is to be kept betwixt *France* and which is not to be expected from a *French* or S Pope, who would quickly turn the Scale, and by ing too great Prerogatives to his Country-men, vour to exclude others from the Papal Chair. chuse commonly a Pope who is pretty well in Yea very seldom a young one, that others may be in hc attaining the same Dignity, and that a young Pop ing a long Regency may not undertake to alter the stoms and Maxims, or to make his Family so Ri Potent, and set up so many Creatures of his o thereby to entail the Papal Chair upon his House. sides that, in this Station where the Pope need not to the Field, there is more Occasion for a grave a Man than a vigorous young Person. It is also a Maxim among them, to take care that he may too near a Kin to the deceas'd Pope, to the end th

What Qualifications are necessary for one that is to be chosen Pope.

vacant Church-Benefices may not fall into the Hands of one Family; and that the new Pope may be the sooner prevail'd upon to mend the Faults of his Predecessor. It often so happens, that one is chosen Pope of whom no Body thought before; and this comes to pass when the Cardinals are tired out by so many Intriegues, and are glad to get out of the Conclave. It is also often observ'd, that a Pope proves quite another Man after he has come to sit in the Chair than he was before, when yet a Cardinal. The Pope at his entring upon the Government, is not tied to any certain Rules or Capitulations, since it would seem very unbecoming to controul by human Laws and Contracts the Power of him who is pretended to be endow'd with the Holy Ghost.

But the College of Cardinals is as it were the standing Council of the Ecclesiastical State, in like manner as the Chapters of the Cathedrals are to the Bishops in *Germany*. With those the Pope advises concerning Matters of the greatest Moment; tho' indeed it often happens, that the Popes and their Nephews make but little Account of their Advice, but act as they please. The chief Prerogative of the Cardinals consists in that they have the Power of chusing a Pope, and that out of their own Body, they being suppos'd to be the next to him, and best acquainted with the Affairs of the Court of *Rome*, which is one necessary Qualification of a Pope. Their ordinary Number is Threescore and Ten, which is seldom compleat. Now a-days they are distinguish'd by the Title of your Eminency, according to a Decree of Pope *Urban* VIII. whereas they were formerly call'd most Illustrious (*Illustrissimi*) which Title was grown very common in *Italy*. And because the Cardinals had got a new Title, the Princes of *Italy* pretended in like manner to be dignify'd by the Title of your Highness (*Altazza*) whereas formerly they were very well satisfy'd with the Title of your Excellency (*Excellenza*.) The Election of the Cardinals depends absolutely on the Pope's Pleasure, who nevertheless, constantly takes notice of such as are recommended to that Dignity by *France*, *Spain* and other Princes. The Parasites of the Court of *Rome*, are not asham'd to maintain that the Cardinal's Cap is equal in Dignity to a Crown'd Head, and to this Day they pretend to have the Precedency before the Electors of the Empire.

College of the Cardinals.

The Popes enrich their Kindred.

Ever since the time of Pope *Sixtus* IV. that is, since the Year 1471. the Popes have made it their Business to enrich their Families out of the Church-Revenues, of which there are very remarkable Instances. For it is related that *Sixtus* V. during his Regency of five Years, did bestow upon his Family above three Millions of Ducats; and *Gregory* XV. had in two Years and three Months got together the value of three Millions in Lands, without reckoning what he left in ready Money. It is reported of the House of the *Barbarini*'s, that at the Death of *Urban* VIII. they were possess'd of 227 Offices and Church Benefices, most of them reckon'd at three, five, eight and ten Thousand *Schudi* a piece, whereby 'tis said, that they got together a Treasure of 30 Millions of *Schudi*. This has been represented as a very scandalous thing by some, but if duly consider'd, it is a great Folly to suppose, that since the main Intention of the Popish Soveraignty is to enrich the Clergy, the Popes should stifle their natural Inclination towards their Kindred, and not make Hay whilst the Sun shines. 'Tis known to be a common thing, that Favourites and others, whilst they are Fortunate, are envy'd by others, who are vex'd, because Fortune is not so favourable to them. Besides, the Revenues of the Church are so great, that the Popes, since they need not entertain any considerable Army, scarce know how to employ them better.

Cardinal Patroon.

Since the time of Pope *Urban* VIII. a Custom has been introduc'd, to make one of the Pope's Nephews Chief Minister of the Ecclesiastical State, whom they call Cardinal Patroon (*Cardinal Patrono.*) Among other Reasons, why the Pope commits the Management of Affairs to one of his Nephews, this is alledg'd for one; that by the nearness of Blood, he ought to be preferr'd before others, and that by so doing, the Pope's Person is better secur'd against any Attempts, which are more likely to be made upon his Life than upon any other Hereditary Princes, whose Death their Successors are able to revenge. How fearful the Popes are of Poison, may be judg'd from thence, that as often as the Pope receives the Sacrament, his Chaplain, who is to administer the Bread and Wine, is oblig'd to taste of both before the Pope. It is also pretended, that by the Ministry of the Nephews, this Advantage is obtain'd, that the other Ministers and Governors have not so much Opportunity to

enrich

enrich themselves, and to put one another out of Place, which is the common Custom in Elective States. For their Nephews are few in number, and therefore sooner to be satisfy'd; neither will they easily suffer that others should enrich themselves, since they are sensible that all the Hatred falls upon themselves. They are also very serviceable to the Pope, in that they more freely can disclose the Interests of the several Princes to him, than other Ministers who are not so nearly allied to him, and that they are fain to be more circumspect in their Management of Affairs, for fear lest they may one time or another be call'd to an Account; for which Reason it is their Business, so to oblige one Prince or another, that they may upon all Occasions be sure of his Protection. Besides, that by their Assistance, Affairs may be carry'd on with much more Secrecy than otherwise. And if the Pope were destitute of their Counsel, he would be oblig'd to have recourse to the Cardinals, who most commonly are very partial, being most of them engag'd to Foreign Princes either by Pensions or Benefices.

Concerning the Celibacy of the Popish Clergy.

§. 32. The Subjects of this Ecclesiastical Monarchy may properly be divided into two several Sorts; the first comprehends the whole Clergy, the second all the rest of *Christendom*, as far as they profess the *Roman* Catholick Religion, which is commonly call'd the Laity. The first may be compar'd to the standing Army of a Prince, who thereby maintains his Conquests; the rest are to be deem'd as Subjects that are Tributaries to the Prince, and are oblig'd to maintain those standing Forces at their Charge. The first have this particular Obligation upon them, that they must abstain from Marriage. This is done under pretence of a special Holiness, and that thereby they may be the more fit to perform their Duty without any hindrance; but the true Reason is, that they should not prefer the Interest and Welfare of their Wife and Children, before that of the Church, and in Consideration thereof, not side with those Princes, under whose Jurisdiction they live, or that they should not enrich their Children with the Revenues of the Church, but be the more ready upon all Occasions to execute the Pope's Will, especially against such Princes, under whose Protection they live. For since Wife and Children are esteem'd the dearest Pledges, not to be left to the Discretion of an enrag'd Enemy, they could the easier despise the Anger their Princes, if they had no other Care to take but themselves, a single Man not needing to fear a Livelihc in any Place whatever. And it has been the main I deavour of the Popes to exempt the Clergy by all me from the Jurisdiction of the Civil Magistrates, and make them only dependent on himself. But those w have been so busie to force Celibacy upon the Cler were forgetful in not prescribing them at the same tim *Recipe* against Incontinency, which they seem to stand great need of. How vast a Number there is of this of People, may be best judg'd out of what is related Pope *Paul* IV. who us'd to brag, that he had 2880 Parishes, and 44000 Monasteries under his Jurisdicti if he did not mistake in his Account, especially as to Monasteries. The Clergy may again be subdivided in two sorts, *viz.* those who are bare Priests and Eccle sticks, and those who have engag'd themselves by a p ticular Vow, as the *Monks* and *Jesuits*, who are to esteem'd the Pope's.

Their Number.

The Popish Doctrin suted to the State.

§. 38. The Pope makes Use of this Artifice to keep Laity in Obedience, that he perswades them to rece and consider his Ecclesiastical Troops, as the Chief P moters of their Salvation, and Masters over their Co sciences; which serves like a Bridle to lead and tu them about according to the Will of the Clergy. A that every thing may be accommodated to the Interest his Spiritual Monarchy, several Articles of the Christi Religion have been by Degrees stretched or patched with new Additions; and any one that will duly wei these Matters, wherein they differ with their Adversari will soon find that in those Points there is generally Mixture of Interest, as to the Authority, Power and R venues of the Clergy. Among those in the first Plac to be reckon'd the Doctrin concerning the Authority a Power of the Pope, whereby they pretend to set h above the Councils, and make him Infallible; wh Point is stretched to the utmost by the Jesuits, becau if that stand fast, all the rest is soon prov'd. So t what has been taught formerly, and if I am not mis ken, is taught even unto this Day, by the Doctors the *Sorbon*, *viz.* that the Councils are equal to, or rat above the Pope, is destructive to the very fundamen

As that of the Pope's Power.

Constituti

Constitution of the Popish Monarchy, since this Doctrin smells strongly of a Democracy, which is directly contrary to a Monarchy. And, indeed it is not easily to be reconcil'd, how the Pope, who pretends to have such great Prerogatives above all others, should be subject to the Censure of his Creatures and Vassals. For as they will have it, whatsoever either the Holy Scripture, or the Ancient Fathers have attributed to the Church, ought altogether to be apply'd to the Pope; in like manner, as what is spoken of a whole Kingdom, is commonly to be understood of the King.

The Prohibition of the Laity's reading the Scriptures.

The Laity are debarred from Reading the Holy Scripture, by which means not only the Authority of the Clergy, is maintain'd among the People, as if the Priests were the only Men that have a Priviledge to approach to the Divine Oracles; but also the Laity is thereby prevented from finding out those Points in the Scripture, which are repugnant to the Interest of the Clergy. For if the People should once get a true Understanding of the Scripture, they would not be so forward to follow so blindly the Instructions of the Priests. By the same means they prevent the Laity from diving too deeply into Divinity, which they pretend belongs only to the Clergy; and for this Reason it is that they attribute the Power of Explaining the Scripture to the Pope only, that nothing may be brought to Light, which may in any ways be prejudicial to the Spiritual Monarchy. For the same Reason the Pope pretends to have the Sole Authority of deciding all Controversies whatsoever.

Traditions.

It is also given out among the People, that the Holy Scripture is imperfect, which Defect must be made up by Ancient Traditions; whereby they gain this Point, that if they invent any Doctrin for the Interest of the Spiritual State, whereof there is not the least Footstep to be found in the Holy Scripture, they without any other Proof, may have recourse to the Ancient Traditions alone.

Venial and Mortal Sins.

The Distinction betwixt Venial and Mortal Sins, as also what is alledged *de casibus reservatis*, is barely invented for the Benefit of the Clergy. The infinite Number of Books of Confession, enough to fraight whole Fleets withal, is not publish'd with an Intention to correct Vices, but that by laying a Tax upon the Expiation, the Clergy may the better be able to maintain their

Grandeur, and satisfy their Avarice. The most comfortable Doctrin of Remission of Sins, has wholly been accommodated to the Interest of the Clergy. For, in regard it would not have turn'd to the Profit of the Clergy, if every one who truly repented should obtain Remission of his Sins, only by Faith in the Merits of Christ; it has been the Doctrin of the Church of *Rome*, that it is an essential Piece of Penitence, and the means to obtain Forgiveness of Sins, that a most exact and precise Account of every individual Sin committed, should be given to the Priest. By which means, they not only keep the People at their Devotion, and make such Impressions upon them, as are fitting for their Purposes, but also come to the Knowledge of all the Secrets, Councils, Designs and Inclinations of the People, which they make good Use of for their own Benefit; notwithstanding, that they are under an Obligation not to reveal any thing that is told them by way of Confession; for, else it would be impossible for them to perswade the People to act against the natural Inclination of all Mankind. The Priest has also a Power to command Works of Satisfaction to be done, by which he commonly gains very handsomely. For tho' certain Prayers, Pilgrimages, Fasts, Flagellations, and the like, are often impos'd upon them for Penances, yet they also very often condemn some, and especially the richer sort, in a good Sum of Money, to be given instead of a Penance to a certain Monastery, Church, or the Poor, in which Number they reckon the Mendicant-Fryars. These honest Fellows call themselves *Minimos Fratrum*, according to Chap. 25. of St. *Matthew*, that they may, have a fair shining Pretence to fill their Purses. For by this Interpretation, the Christians have got this Benefit, that they are oblig'd to feed and maintain one hundred thousand lazy idle Fellows. Add to this, that the first sort of Penance may be redeemed with Money, if you think it too hard to be performed. And who that is wealthy, would not be civil and liberal to his Father Confessor, to oblige him to a Mitigation of the Penance, or to repay his former Favours of that kind.

Penance.

With what View good Works have been made meritorious, and the means of obtaining Salvation from God Almighty, is easily to be guessed. For when they gave

Merit of good Works.

a De-

Definition of good Works, they were sure to put in the first Place, that the People ought to be liberal towards the Clergy, Churches and Monasteries, and to perform every thing commanded them by the Pope and his Adherents, tho' never so full of Superstition and Hypocrisie. Neither must this be forgot, that they likewise taught, that the *Monks* are not only able to perform good Works sufficient for themselves, but have an Overplus of Merits, or expiatory Works of Supererogation, which they can sell to the Laity. And out of this Overplus, they have laid up an inexhaustible Store very profitable to the Clergy, which cost them nothing, and does not grow musty nor ever decays, neither can it be turn'd upon their Hands, when the Buyer finds out the Cheat.

Ceremonies

Their Religious Exercises are full of Ceremonies, many superfluous Festivals, and Processions are instituted, numerous Chapels and Altars erected, only to imploy so great a Number of Clergy-men, who else would appear like so many idle Fellows. And withal to find some profitable Account for themselves, for the Clergy still gets by all manner of Services; which is also the Reason why they have encreas'd the Number of the Sacraments to Seven, since they know that none of them can be administred, but the Priest who never works *Gratis*, must needs get by it. The Mass without Communicants has been introduc'd and proclaim'd a Sacrifice, both for the Dead and Living, that they might have an Opportunity to put both the Dead and Living under Contribution. For no Body undertakes any thing of Moment, but he has a Mass sung first, for the good Success of the thing in Hand. No Body of Wealth dies, but he orders a good Store of Masses to be sung for his Soul, all which brings Grist to the Priest's Mill.

Half Communion.

On the other Hand, an abusive Custom having once prevail'd, that the Laity received the Sacrament without partaking of the Cup, it was made into a Law. And tho' the contrary was very evident both by the Institution of Christ, and the Practice of the Church, for a great many Centuries, yet did they persist with great Obstinacy, because it should not seem that the Clergy had committed an Error; and also that they might have a Prerogative before the Laity in this Sacrament. And to ridicule the more impudently both God and Men, they give to the Laity a Chalice, which is not Consecrated,

crated, which in very despicable Terms, they rinsing Chalice, as People when they have eate clean thing, use to rinse their Mouths.

Marriage made a Sacrament. Marriage must likewise come in for a Sacran nothing is more absurd and ridiculous, that th might have an Opportunity to hook all Ma Causes into their Jurisdiction, which are often ficable, very various, and of the greatest Con for as much as the Welfare, Inheritance and of most People, nay, even of whole Kingdom thereon. This oblig'd *Mary* Queen of *Englan* deavour the Re-establishment of Popery in t dom; for without the Pope's Authority, she pass'd for a Bastard. And *Philip* III. King was among other Reasons oblig'd to the Pope, f a Dispensation to his Father to Marry his ow Daughter, of whom *Philip* was Born, which could not easily have been approv'd by other C There are also so many prohibited Degrees, in on purpose, that the Clergy may have frequen tunities to give Dispensations, in the Manag which they know how to feather their Nest.

Extreme Unction. Extreme Ointment the Priest takes an Occasi hort the dying People, to leave Legacies for pi which they commonly know how to apply to vantage of their own Order.

Purgatory. Purgatory was for no other Purpose, but that the dying Man that time is not so greedy of Worldly Goods, is to leave to others, might be liberal towards th men, in hopes, by their Intercession, and a good of Masses, to get the sooner out of that hot Pla

Reliques. Veneration paid to the Reliques, has also been ve ficial to the Clergy; these are employ'd, besic uses, to reward People of Quality, that have d Services to the Pope, with a Piece of an old Bor of a better Present.

Prayers to Saints. The Adoration of the Sai for a Pretext to build the more Churches, instit Holy-days, and employ, and feed a greater N Priests.

Canonization. The Power, which the Pope has assum nonization, gives him a considerable Authority a People; as if it were his Prerogative to besto ties and Offices upon whom he thinks fit, even in and as if God Almighty could not but accept of fetendaries, as the Pope is pleas'd to represent him.

y this means he makes himself Master of the Inclinati-
ns of the People, tho' living in far distant Places, unto
hom he proposes this as a Recompence of their Credu-
ty, and Ambition, if they stick at nothing to promote
s Interest. And ever since this, Superstition has taken
oot in Christendom, those who have been Canonized,
ave for the most part been Clergy-men, who either by
new invented Hypocrisie, or outward Appearance of
Holiness, had made themselves famous in the World. Or
f by Chance one Layman or another has attained to this
Dignity, either he himself, or at least those that interceed
or him, have been fain to deserve very well of the Pa-
al Chair. Here I forbear to mention, in what manner
y fictitious Miracles, several sorts of Images, Apariti-
ns, exorcisms, Indulgences, Jubilees, prohibition of di-
ers sorts of Victuals, and such like Tricks, they us'd to
ool the People out of their Money.

§. 34. Next to the Particulars mention'd but now, which have partly been Instituted by the Popes Autho-rity, partly by other States, yet so that most of them have been Confirmed by the Popes, who at the same time claim'd the Supreme Direction over them; These Universities, I say, have been mainly Instrumental in maintaining the Popish Sovereignty. It is evident e-nough of what Consequence this Direction must needs be to the Pope. For in the Universities Men are first tinc-tur'd with such Opinions, as they afterwards are to make use of during their whole Life, and instil them into o-thers: And 'twas for this Reason that the Universities, and Sciences there to be taught, were sure to be accom-modated to the Popes Interest. Neither were the Pro-fessors of Divinity here, who claim'd the Precedency be-fore all others, the only Creatures of the Pope, but al-so the Professors of the Canon Law, who were as busie as any to palm his Decrees upon the World, and to maintain his Authority. For the World may thank the Canon-Law for the first Introduction of those long Law-suits, which the Clergy pretended to belong to their Jurisdiction, that by receiving of Bribes, they might the sooner gratify their Avarice. The greatest part of the Philosophers were likewise the Popes Slaves, and if one or t'other attempted to dive into the true Causes of Things, he was sure to be kept under by all the rest.

The Universities have promoted the Popish Sovereignty.

The

The Divinity and Philosophy profess'd in these Universities were not taught with an Intention to make the young Students more Learned aud Understanding, but that the Ingenious by these confus'd and idle Terms, might be diverted from throughly canvising those Matters, which would have led them to the whole Discovery of the Popish Intrigues. For their Scholastick Divinity is not employ'd in searching and explaining the Holy Scripture, but for the most part entangled in useless Questions, invented chiefly by *Peter Lombard*, *Thomas Aquinas*, *Scotus*, and the other Patriarchs of Pedantry. And what they call Philosophy, is nothing else but a Collection of foolish Chimera's, empty Terms, and very bad Latin, the Knowledge of which is rather hurtful than profitable, if you have not been better Instructed otherwise. So that all their Aim was, to take care that the Sciences should not be fundamentally taught to the Students. With this Trumpery the Universities were not only over-run during the former barbarous times, but continue in the same forlorn State; and tho' most Sciences are so much improved, the old Leaven is with great Industry preserved and propagated: On the contrary, all the solid Sciences, especially such as are instrumental in discovering the Vulgar Errors of the World, are suppress'd. Above all the rest, the most useful of all, the Doctrine of Morality is much mis-interpreted and entangled in an endless Labyrinth, that the Fathers Confessors may not want means to domineer over the Lay-men's Consciences, and to entangle them with so many dubious and double-meaning Insinuations, that they are thereby rendred incapable to examine and rule their Actions according to solid Principles, but are oblig'd to be guided blindfold at the pleasure of their Fathers Confessors.

Why the Jesuits have taken upon them the Education of the Youth.

§. 35. But, in regard Learning gave the main Blow to the Pope, at the time of *Luther*'s Reformation, the Jesuits, who may well be call'd the Pope's Guard de Corps, have since taken upon them the management of the Youth; for they not only teach publickly in the Universities, but they have hlso engross'd to themselves the Instruction of the Youth in the Schools, that they may have all the Opportunity so to guide and direct them in their Studies, that they may not only not prove

pre-

453

Licensing of Books. Neither ought it to be pass'd by in Silence, that th Pope and his Adherents pretend to have a right of Cen suring and Licensing all Books whatsoever, by whic Claim, they may easily hinder any thing to come t light, that may prove prejudicial to them. And in th Censuring of Books, they are so impudent, as not onl to strike out of the ancient Authors, when these are t be Reprinted, even such Passages as they dislike, but t insert such new Passages as are suitable to their Schemes If any one Book is to be publish'd in their Territorie first the same is exactly Revis'd and Corrected. And i it should happen by chance, that something should b overseen in the first Edition, which does not suit wit their Interest, it is mark'd in an Index made for tha Purpose, that it may be omitted in the next Edition. But the Books of their Adversaries are prohibited; nay the reading of them is not allow'd, but to some particu lar Persons, and that not without special Leave, and these are such as they know to be thorow-pac'd, and in tirely devoted to their Interest. By so doing, they may lay to their Adversaries Charge what they please, since their Subjects never get sight of the others Refutation. It has been a general Observation, that since the scanda lous Lives of the Monks had not only been very prejudi cial to the Popish Monarchy, but also that the Prote stants had set out their Vices in their natural Colours; The Papists had bespatter'd the Protestant Ministers with the same Vices as they were charg'd withal, and have not only represented the Infirmities of some particular Per sons to the World, but also have laid to their Charge the most heinous Crimes they could invent; and afterwards have chaleng'd their Adversaries to prove the contrary; which Calumnies have such Influence, at least upon the simple and common sort of People, that it gives them a great Aversion to the Protestants. They also do not want Impudence to set out at a high rate their Miracles, Mar tyrdoms, and other great Feats, which generally are transacted in far distant Countries; by which means they gain a great Credit, at least by the inconsiderate Multitude. Among others, *Edwin Sandys*, an *English* Knight, had discover'd abundance of these Tricks, in his Treatise concerning the State of Religion.

§. 36.

§. 36. But the Pope makes use of yet more violent Means to maintain his Authority. In former Ages his Excommunication was a most terrible thing, when whole Countries were forbidden the Exercise of Religious Worship, by which means the Popes have often oblig'd Emperors and Kings to come and creep to the Cross. But now-a-days this Weapon is not frightful to any Body, except to some petty States in *Italy*. However, in *Spain* and *Italy* they have set up a certain Court, which is call'd, The Office of the Holy Inquisition, where Information is taken, and all such proceeded against as have in any ways rendred themselves suspected of Heresie: And it is counted the worst sort of Heresie, if any one attempts any thing against the Popish Law and Doctrin, or against the Pope's Authority. This serves for a Bridle to curb the People with, and to the Inhabitants of those Countries is as terrible as the Plague, since Matters are transacted with so much Severity in this Court, that scarce any Body, that falls under the Inquisition, escapes their Hands without considerable Loss.

Excommunication and Inquisition.

§. 37. Though the Supreme Direction and Administration of the *Romish* Religion, together with their other Rules, which serve to uphold it, and have been alledg'd by us here, are a sufficient Awe upon the People; and besides this, the Popish Clergy know how to manage their Affairs with that Dexterity as to give some Satisfaction to every one; so that I am apt to believe, that a great many who live under the Popish Subjection, are verily perswaded to believe what the Priests tell them to be real, since they want Means and Opportunity of being better Instructed: Nevertheless it is very probable, that a great many of the more Learned and Wiser sort, are sufficiently convinc'd, in what manner Things are carry'd on among them, and that therefore it is in respect of some particular Considerations, that they do not free themselves from this Yoke. I am apt to believe, that most are kept back, because they do not see how to remedy this Evil; And yet they are unwilling to ruin their Fortunes, by going over to the Protestant side, where they are not likely to meet with so plentiful a Share. These Temptations are not easily to be

Some Reasons why the People remain in the Communion of the Church of Rome.

be resisted, whereby they think it sufficient for the ob-taining of Salvation, if they believe in Jesus Christ, an trust upon his Merits, but for the rest, think it of great Consequence, if in some Matters, which are th Inventions of Priests, they by conforming themselve play the Hypocrite, and believe as much concernin them, as is suitable with their Opinions. They suppo it to be of no great Consequence, that perhaps the male Sex and the Vulgar sort of People that are alway fond of Extravagancies, do believe these things in goo earnest. There are also questionless, not a few, who having sufficient Capacity to distinguish betwixt su Points in Religion, as are commanded by God, and twixt such as are invented by the Clergy for priva Ends, and perhaps coming afterwards to the Knowled of some of these Frauds they take all the rest for fab lous Inventions, only covering their Atheistical Prin ples with an outward decent Behaviour to save the selves the Trouble of being question'd and disturb Every Man of Sense, may without Difficulty imagine ho easily a sensible *Italian* or *Spaniard*, that has never re the Bible, or any other Protestant Book, may fall in this Error, if he once had an opportunity to take noti of the Intrigues of the Clergy; tho' it is certain, th since the Reformation of *Luther*, the Church of *Ro* has chang'd her Habit, and her Garment appears more decent than before. But besides this, there ar great many Persons of Quality, as well as of a mean Condition, who make their Advantage of the *Romi* Religion, in which they have an Opportunity to pro vide for their Friends, by putting them either into som Order or other of Knighthood, or into that of Monks, or other Ecclesiasticks, by which means a gre many Families are eas'd of a great Charge, and som times are rais'd by it. At least the Superstitious Pare are well satisfy'd when they see their Children are come such Saints: And those that cannot make th Fortunes otherwise, run into a Monastery, where they sure to be provided for. All these Conveniencies wo be taken away, if the *Popish* Monarchy should fall, the Church Revenues were not apply'd to the use of State. The *Popish* Doctrin has also got so firm Footing those Countries where it now rides Triumphant, that any of their Princes should endeavour to root it out,

wou

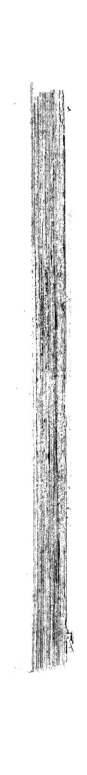

Bishops ond Prelates stand firm to the Popish Interest in *Germany*, since they find it more advantageous to be great Princes than poor Preachers. Besides, they have been deterr'd from undertaking any Reformation of the Church Discipline, by the Example of two Electors of *Cologne*, which they in the last Age did begin with a very unfortunate Success in their Dominions. After *Charles* V. (influenc'd by the *Spanish* Counsels) let slip the Opportunity of settling the Protestant Religion throughout the Empire; the Emperors have ever since that time, for Reasons of State, not been able to disentangle themselves from the Popish Sovereignty, if they had been never so willing. For as the Case now stands, the Ecclesiastical Princes of the Empire, are tied to the Emperor's Interest, from whom they hope for Assistance against the Secular Princes, in case of Necessity. But if the Emperor should abandon the Church of *Rome*, the whole Clergy would be against him; and he could not promise himself any certain Assistance from the Secular Princes, especially since some of the most Ancient Houses of those Princes, that now have laid aside the hope of attaining the Imperial Crown, by Reason of Difference in Religion, would then pretend to have the same Right to this Dignity, with the House of *Austria*. The Pope also upon such an Occasion, would not cease to stir up Heaven and Earth against him; and the King of *France* would not let slip this Opportunity, but would with all his Might endeavour to obtain the Imperial Dignity, in which Attempt he perhaps might meet with Encouragement from the *German* Clergy.

Spain. The *Spaniards* pretend to be the greatest Zealots, for the *Romish* Religion, because they stand in Need of the Pope's Fovour, to assist them in the Preservation of the Kingdom of *Naples* and the State of *Milan*; and they commonly use to lay their Designs under the Cover of preserving and maintaining the *Roman* Catholick Religion, tho' indeed they have for the most part miscarried; not to mention here, that the Clergy is very Potent in *Spain*, and that the common People, thro' the false Perswasions of the Priests, have imbib'd great Aversion against the Protestants.

France. *France* does outwardly shew itself not so fond of the Popish Interest, nor has the *Gallick* Church ever acknowledged the Pope's absolute Power over her. And whatever

ſtred from the Church of *Rome*. On the other hand, the Pope is heartily afraid of a *French* Monarchy, as being fully convinc'd, that it would endeavour a thorough Reformation of the Church of Rome, and that his Wings would be clipt to that Degree, that in effect he would be no more than a Patriarch. Neither ought he to expect any better Treatment, if the *Spaniſh* Monarchy had been brought to perfection: Tho' at the ſame time 'tis equally true, that either of theſe muſt needs have been deſtructive to the Proteſtant Religion.

The main Pillar of the Popiſh Monarchy.

It may therefore be taken for granted, that one of the main Pillars of the Popiſh Monarchy, is the Jealouſy and Ballance, which is to be kept up betwixt theſe two Crowns; and that it is the Pope's Intereſt, as much as in him lies, to take care that one of theſe Crowns do not ruin the other, and ſet up for an Univerſal Monarchy. If we look into the Tranſactions of former times, we will find that the Popes have long ſince obſerv'd this Maxim. 'Tis true, after the Death of King *Henry* II. when *France* was extreamly weaken'd the Popes were forc'd to ſide with *Spain*, whether they would or no, the *Spaniards* having then found out the way to oblige them to it, by fair or foul Means. They knew how to Influence the Popes by their Nephews, who were for ſettling and enriching their Families, whilſt their Kinſmen were alive. Thoſe they brought over to their Party by granting to them Penſions, Church-Benefices, large Poſſeſſions, great Offices, and advantagious Matches: Who in acknowledgment of the ſame, us'd often to make the Pope good *Spaniſh*, even againſt his Inclination; but if they reſiſt theſe Temptations, the *Spaniards* us'd to proſecute theſe Nephews with a Vengeance, after the Pope's Deceaſe. And it was their conſtant practice, in thoſe Days to exclude thoſe from the Papal Chair, as they thought were againſt their Intereſt. But as ſoon *France* began to recover its Strength, the Popes manag'd themſelves with more Indifferency, and ſhew'd no more Favour to either ſide, than they thought was ſuiting with their preſent Circumſtances. It is remarkable that the Jeſuit *Guiciardin* in a Sermon preach'd at *Paris*, in the Year 164[illegible] in the Month of *July*, did ſay, that the War which the then King of *France* wag'd againſt the *Spaniards*, was to be deem'd a Holy War, carry'd on for the preſervation of the Holy Religion. For if the King of *France* had

not

vours to start and keep up Controversies among them. By these Artifices the Popish Clergy has got very visible Advantages in this Age over the Protestants, and are likely to get more every Day, since they see with the greatest Satisfaction, that their Adversaries do weaken themselves by their intestine Quarrels and Divisions.

No Peace is to be expected betwixt the Roman *Catholicks and Protestants.*

§. 40. From what has been said, it is easily to be judg'd, whether those Differences which are on foot betwixt the Roman Catholicks and the Protestants, may be amicably compos'd, either so that both Parties should remit something of their Pretensions, and agree to one and the same Confession of Faith, leaving some By-Questions to be toss'd in the Universities; or so that both Parties may retain their Opinions, and notwithstanding this Difference, treat one another like Brethren in Christ, and Members of the same Church. Now if we duly weigh the Circumstances of the Matter, and the Popish Principles, such a Peace is to be esteem'd absolutely impossible; since the Difference does not only consist in the Doctrin, but both Interests are absolutely contrary to one another. For first, the Pope is for having the Church Possessions restor'd; but the Protestants are resolv'd to keep them in their Possession. The Pope pretends to be the Supreme Head of Christendom, but the Protestant States will not part with their Prerogative of having the Direction *circa Sacra*, which they look upon as a precious Jewel belonging to their Sovereignty. And to pretend to live in Communion and Amity with the Pope, and not to acknowledge his Sovereignty in Ecclesiastical Affairs, is an absolute Contradiction. In the same manner, as if I would be called a Subject in a Kingdom, and yet refuse to acknowledge the King's Authority. Further, the Infallibility of the Pope, is the Foundation-Stone of the Popish Sovegeignty, and if that is once remov'd, the whole Structure must needs fall; wherefore it is impossible for the Pope, and that for Reasons of State, to abate any thing from his Pretentions, wherein he differs from the Protestants. For if it should be once granted that the Pope had hitherto maintain'd but one single erroneous Point, his Infallibility would then tumble to the Ground; since, if he has err'd in one Point, he may be equally erroneous in others. On the other gand, if the Protestants should allow the Pope's Infallibility, they must of Conse-

quence

quence acknowledge that all his Dogmata and Sacred Rites are just and true: But it seems not probable that the Protestants can ever be brought to contradict and at once to recal their Doctrin concerning the Vanity of the Popish Tenets. Nay, if it might be suppos'd that the Laity should do it, what must become of the Clergy? Where will they bestow their Wives and Children? Wherefore, how good so ever the Intention may have been of those that have propos'd a way of Accommodation, betwixt the Papists and Protestants, which is commonly call'd, Syncretism, 'tis certainly nothing else but a Scheem of very simple and Chimerical Inventions, which are ridiculed by the Papists; who in the mean while are well satisfied to see that the Protestant Divines bestow their Labour in vain as to this Point, since they (the Papists) are no Losers, but rather the Gainers by it. For this Syncretism does not only raise great Animosities among the Protestants, but at the same time does not a little weaken their Zeal against the Popish Religion. It is easy to be imagin'd, that some who do not throughly understand the Differences, and hear the Divines talk of an Accommodation, betwixt both Religions, are apt to perswade themselves, that the Difference does not lie in the fundamental Points; and if in the mean while they meet with an advantageous Proffer from the Roman Catholicks, are sometimes without great Difficulty prevail'd upon to bid farewel to the Protestant Religion. It is taken for a general Rule, that a Fortress and a Maiden-head are in great Danger, when once they begin to parly.

§. 41. But if the Question were put, Whether the Pope with all his Adherents be strong enough to reduce the Protestants under his Obedience by force, it is evident enough that the Joynt-Power of the Papists, is much superiour to the Strength of the Protestants. For *Italy*, all *Spain* and *Portugal*, the greatest part of *France* and *Poland*, adhere to the *Pope*, as also the weakest part of the *Swiss Cantons*. In *Germany*, those Hereditary Countries which belong to the House of *Austria*, the Kingdom of *Bohemia*, and the greatest part of *Hungary*, all the Bishops and Prelates, the House of *Bavaria*, the Dukes of *Newburgh*, and Marquisses of *Baden*, besides some other Princes

Strength of the Protestants and Papists.

Princes of less Note; some Counts, Lords, and others of the Nobility, and some Imperial Cities, besides others of the the *Roman* Catholick Communion, that live under the Jurisdiction of the Protestant States; all which according to my Computation, make up two Thirds of *Germany*. There are also a great many Papists in *Holland*, and in *England* there are too many of that sort of Kidney, for the Reliques of the old Leaven, if I may so speak, are still to be seen there. But of the Protestant side are *England*, *Sweden*, *Denmark*, *Holland*, most of the Secular Electors and Princes, and of the Imperial Cities in *Germany*. The *Hugonots* in *France* are without Strength, and the Protestants in *Poland* being dispers'd throughout the Kingdom, are not to be feard. *Courland* and the Cities of *Prussia*, may rest satisfied, if they are able to maintain the free Exercise of their Religion; neither is *Transilvania* powerful enough to give any considerable Assistance to the Protestant Party. The Papists also have this Advantage above the Protestants, that they all all acknowledge the Pope for the Supreme Head of their Church, and, at lest to outward Appearance, are unanimous in their Faith; whereas on the contrary, the Protestants are not joyn'd under one visible spiritual Head, but are miserably divided among themselves. For not to mention those Sects of lesser Note, *viz*. The *Arminians*, *Socinians*, *Anabaptists*, and such like, their main Body is divided into two Parties, of very near equal Strenth, *viz*. Into the *Lutherans* and those of the Reformed Religion, a great many of which, are so exasperated against one another, that they could not be more against the Papists themselves.

Divisions of the Protestants.

Other Inconveniencies.

Neither are the Protestants united under one Church-Government or Liturgy, but each of the respective States regulate that according as they think fit. Neither can it be denied, but that the *Roman* Catholick Clergy in general, is more zealous and industrious in propaging their Religion than the Protestants; For the Monks and Jesuits gain great Applause by their Missions in the *East* and *West-Indies*; and though perhaps they brag more than is true of their great Success there, yet is this Institution in the main, very praise-worthy. Besides this, there is such an

implacable

the Religion and Liberty of the Protestants of Germany. But suppose they should compass their Design; it is most certain that those Two Houses by the Addition of those Countries, would be much less formidable to the Emperor, than they were at that time, when they were held by Sweden. And it is a great Mistake if they persuade themselves that what Assistance they may expect from Denmark and Holland, can countervail what they had from France and Sweden. If the Emperor should obtain his Ends and drive those Two Nations out of Germany, and restore the Spanish Interest, and then tire out the Circles by keeping up great Armies, it would be a very difficult Question, who would be able to oblige the Emperor in such a Case to disband his victorious Forces? Whether the Emperor might not under some pretence or other keep his Army on foot, and oblige the Circles to provide for them in their Territories? Whether Brandenburgh and Lunenburgh would be able themselves to oppose the Emperor's Design? But if the Protestant States should find themselves not strong enough to resist his Power, it would be a Question whether the Crowns would be immediately ready at their Demand, or whether the Circumstances of their Affairs would be such, as to be able to undertake such a Task? Or whether at the time of imminent Danger such a one as Gustavus Adolphus, would be sent down from Heaven, who could act with the same Fortune and Success? For he that believes, that the Reform'd Religion is sufficiently secured by Seals and Deeds, or that the Emperors have laid aside all Thoughts of making themselves Sovereigns of Germany, if an Occasion should present it self, especially since Religion and the Recovery of the Church Possessions furnishes them with so specious a Pretence, must needs have lost the Memory of all past Transactions. But the last Peace made at Nimeguen has sufficiently convinc'd the World, that such Designs could not be put in Execution: Those Protestant States therefore that are Independent on other Princes, need not fear the Power of the Roman Catholicks. For, as two States that are of the same Religion, differ in State Interests, and are jealous of one another, which is plainly to be seen betwixt France and Spain, and betwixt England and Holland; so tho' States are of a different Religion, it is not from hence to be concluded, that if a potent Prince of the

Catholick Perswasion should attempt to ruin a Pro-
State, the other *Roman* Catholick States would
prevent it, if it was for their Interest to see that
testant State preserv'd.

The best way then to preserve the Protestant Religion is, that each of these States take effectual Care, how the same may be well preserv'd in their respective Territories. And this may be done without any crafty Inventions, such as the *Roman* Catholicks are oblig'd to make use of, and only by plain and simple Means. One of the main Points is, that both the Churches and Schools may be provided with Persons fitly qualify'd for that Purpose; That the Clergy by their wholsome Doctrin and a good Life, may shew the way to the rest: That the People in general, but more especially such as are in all Likelihood one time or another may have a great sway in the State, be well instructed in the true and fundamental Principles of the Protestant Religion, that thereby they may be Proof against the Temptations of the Court of *Rome*, especially when they are to travel in Popish Countries. That the Clergy may be so qualify'd as to be able to oppose the Devices and Designs of their Enemies, who every Day busie themselves in finding out new Projects against them.

The best way to preserve the Reformed Religion.

Some are of Opinion, that the Protestant Party would be mightily strengthned, if the two chief Factions among the Protestants, who, besides the Difference in their Doctrin, are also of a different Interest, could be reconcil'd to one another; and they believe this not impracticable, if the old Hatred, Animosities, Pride and self-conceited Opinions could be laid aside. But if we duly take into Consideration the general Inclinations of Mankind, this seems to be a hard Supposition. For those who peruse the Writings of both Parties without Partiality; cannot but admire how their Authors are often oblig'd to rack themselves, that they may maintain their Advances, whether they be consonant to the Scriptures or not: As likewise how they bring to light again the old Arguments, which have been refuted a thousand times before. Neither will this do the Business, if one Opinion should be suppos'd as good as the other; since such an Indifferency would be a shrewd Sign, that the whole must needs be very indifferent to us. Neither can we without danger declare some Points, in which we differ, problematical,

Whether the Lutherans and those of the Reformed Religion are likely to agree.

since

since I do not see how we can pretend to have a Powe to declare a certain Article either necessary or fundamen tal, or problematical. Some therefore have thought up on this Expedient, to make a Tryal, whether out of th Articles, wherein both Parties agree, could be compos'd a perfect System of Divinity, which might be link'd to gether like one Chain according to Art. If this coul be affected, tho' some different Opinions remain'd, long as this Chain was kept intire, we might be assur that we did not differ in the fundamental Points necess ry to the obtaining of Salvation; and what remain'd u decided, would not be of such Consequence as to hi der us from being united into one Body or Church. B before a true Judgment can be given of this Propositi it would be requisite that such a System, compos'd a cording to Art, were propos'd to the World. For m part, I know no better Advice, than to leave it to th Direction of God Almighty, who perhaps one time other will put us in the way of finding out a good Ex pedient. For untimely Remedies may prove the Occa sion of new Divisions. In the mean while it behov both Parties, notwithstanding these Differences, to mindful of their joint Interest against their Comm Enemy, since they may verily believe that the Pope h no more kindness for the *Lutherans*, than for those wh follow *Calvin*.

Socinians *and* Anabaptists.

As for the other Sects of less Note, *viz.* The *Socinian Anabaptists*, and such like, it is evident, that their Prin ciples cannot possibly be reconcil'd with our Religion For those who adhere to the first, do not consider th Christian Doctrin otherwise than a Moral Philosoph and the latter scarce know what to believe themselve The *Anabaptists* have hatch'd out I know not what Rul of Policy and Schemes of Government, which if not su press'd in time, must prove destructive to the State. B whether the *Socinians* also have any such monstrous Pr jects in their Heads, I am not able to determine, sin hitherto they have not been powerful enough to ra any Disturbance in the State.

CHA

CHAP. XIII.

Of Sweden.

§. 1. THE *Swedish* Historians have out of their antient Monuments shewn the World, that the Kingdom of *Sweden* is the most antient Kingdom in *Europe*, and that this Country, was after the Deluge, sooner stor'd with Inhabitants than the other Parts of *Europe*. But it is very uncertain who were the first Inhabitants, and at what time they first settled there; as likewise whether they were immediately govern'd by Kings, or whether the Fathers of Families had the chief Sway among them, till the Regal was grafted on the Paternal Power. The Names and Actions of their Kings, and the time of their Reigns, are also not easie to be determin'd; for the List that has been publish'd of these Kings, is not so Authentick, but that it may be call'd in question; And, as to the Transactions of those Times, they are most of them taken out of antient Songs and Fabulous Legends, and some of them out of the Allegorical Traditions of their antient Poets or Scalders, which have perhaps been too much wrested and strain'd by some Authors. *Johannes Magnus* makes *Magog*, the Son of *Japhet*, Grandson of *Noah*, the first Founder of the *Scythick* and *Gothick* Nations, and says, that from his two Sons, *Sweno* and *Gather*, or *Geg*, the *Swedish* and *Gothish* Nations had their Names. He relates, that after this Family was extinguish'd, *Sweden* was, during the space of four hundred Years, under the Government of certain Judges; and that about eight hundred Years after the Deluge, both the Kingdoms of the *Swedes* and *Goths* were united under *Bericus*, who in Person planted a Colony of the *Goths* beyond the Seas, after having Conquer'd the *Ulmirugii*, who then inhabited *Prussia*, from whence he extended his Conquests over the *Vandals*. A considerable time after, these Nations settled themselves not far from the Mouth of the River *Danube*, near the Black Sea, from whence having undertaken several Expeditions both in *Asia* and *Europe*, at last in the third and fourth Centuries after the Birth of Christ, they enter'd

Sweden the most antient Kingdom in Europe.

First Founders of the Gothick Nation.

the

the *Roman* Provinces on the South-side of the *Danub* and carry'd their Conquering Arms into *Italy* and *Spai* where they erected two Kingdoms. But the greate part of this Relation is contradicted by *Messenius*, wh also rejects the List, that *Johannes Magnus* has given u of the Kings before our Saviour's Birth, alledging th the Times before Christ's Nativity, are all involv'd i fabulous Narrations, as to those Northern Parts, an that most of these Kings liv'd after the Birth of our Sa viour. However, since even the Chronology of the fir Centuries after Christ's Nativity, under the Genealog of those Kings, is somewhat uncertain in these Coun tries, it will suffice to mention here some few of th most Famous among them, till the latter Times furni us with an Opportunity to relate things with more Ce tainty.

Sweden the most ancient Kingdom in Europe.

Othin *or* Woden.

§. 2. Sixty Years before the Birth of Christ, the fa mous *Othin* or *Woden*, being driven by *Pompey* out of *A sia* with a great Number of People, first Conquer'd *Ru sia*, afterwards the *Saxons* and *Danes*, and last of all *Norwa* and *Sweden*, about twenty four Years before the Birt of Christ. *Othin* kept for himself *Sweden* only, yet fo that all the other *Scandinavian* Princes should own hi as their Supreme Lord, from whence came that Custor which was us'd for several hundred Years after, *viz* That at the great and general Meetings of these Nati ons, the King of *Denmark* us'd to hold the Bridle of th King of *Sweden*'s Horse, whilst he mounted it, and th King of *Norway* the Stirrup. He was succeeded by *Fr tho* surnam'd *Forgo*, who cover'd the Temple at *Upsa* with Gold, and surrounded its Pinacle with a Golde Chain. After him were these following Kings, *Nior Sigtrug, Asmund, Uffo, Hynding, Regner, Halvard, Helg Attilus, Hother, Roderick*, surnam'd *Singabond, Hogne Hogrin, Erick, Haldan, Sivand, Erick, Haldan, Ungrin Regnald*. About the Year 588. *Rodolph* was King of th *Goths*, but being vanquish'd by the *Angles*, whom he le in possession of that Kingdom, he himself fled into *Italy* where he sought Sanctuary of *Theodorick* the King o the *Goths*. At that time *Frotho*, either the Son, or else Kinsman of *Regnald*, was King of *Sweden*, to whon succeeded these following Kings, *Fiolmus, Swercher, Va lander, Visbur*, who was burnt by his own Sons, *Damal*

Frotho.

der

King refusing to hearken to his Doctrin, was by th *Swedes* banish'd the Kingdom, together with his Fathe
Amund. *Regner.* His Successor *Amund* did also Rule but a ver few Years, for he having rais'd a most horrible Persecu tion against the Christians, was in like manner banish' the Kingdom. The *Swedes* being quite tired out wit *Amund's* Tyrannical Government, call'd in *Olaus*, out o
Olaus. *Wermeland*, to be their King, who, to establish himsel in the Throne, marry'd the Daughter of *Regner* to hi Son *Ingo*, and thereby obtain'd the quiet Possession o
A.C. 853. the Two Kingdoms of the *Swedes* and *Goths*. Not ma ny Years after *Ansgarius* return'd into *Sweden*, and Con verted *Olaus* (who then resided at *Birca*, a most popu lous City) to the Christian Faith. *Olaus* then march' with a potent Army into *Denmark*, and having committe the Administration of that Kingdom to his Son *Ennige rus*, return'd into *Sweden*; where he was by his Heathe
Ingo. Subjects Sacrific'd to their Idol at *Upsal*. His Son *Ingo*
A.C. 890. the better to Establish himself in the Throne, marry'd th King of *Denmark's* Daughter, and afterwards was kill'
Erick. in the War against the *Russians*. To him succeeded hi
Erick Segherfell. Son *Erick*, surnam'd *Weatherhat*, famous for his Skill i Witchcraft, who was succeeded by his Son *Erick*, sur nam'd *Segherfell*, who Conquer'd *Finland*, *Curland*, *Livo nia* and *Esthen*. From *Denmark* he re-took *Holland* an *Schonen*, and at last drove the *Danish* King *Sweno* out o *Denmark*, who could not recover his Kingdom till afte the Death of the former. His Son *Stenchill*, surnam'
Stenchill *the* Mild. the *Mild*, was Baptiz'd at *Sigtuna* (a great City at tha time) and having destroy'd the Idol at *Upsal*, and forbi his Subjects upon pain of Death to Sacrifice to the Idols the Pagans were so enrag'd thereat, that they slew an burnt him near *Upsal*, and with him the two Christia Priests that were sent to him by the Bishop of *Hambur*
Olaus. His Brother *Olaus* nevertheless obtain'd from King *Ethel red* of *England* several Christian Priests, who not only preach'd the Gospel in *Sweden*, but also the King, and a great number of People were Baptiz'd by one of them call'd *Sigfred*, in a Fountain call'd *Husbye* which is call'd St. *Sigfred's Kalla Well* to this Day. This *Olaus* was sur nam'd *Skotkonung*, *i. e.* King of Tribute, because upon the Perswasion of the *English* Priests he granted to the Pope a Yearly Tax against the *Saracens*, which was call'd *Romskot*. He took from *Oluf Triggeso* the Kingdom of

Norway,

Norway, which however the latter recover'd afterwards. This *Olaus Skotkonung* was also the first who made a perfect Union betwixt the two Kingdoms of the *Swedes* and *Goths*, who had hitherto been often at great Enmity with one another.

To *Olaus* succeeded his Son *Amund*, under whose Reign the Christian Religion encreas'd very successfully in *Sweden*; after him Reign'd his Brother *Amund*, surnam'd *Slemme*, a Man very negligent both in maintaining Religion and Justice. He was slain with the greatest part of his Army by *Cnut* King of *Denmark*, near a Bridge call'd *Strangepelle*. After his Death the *Goths* and *Swedes* disagreed about the Election of a new King, the first choosing *Haquin*, surnam'd the *Red*, the latter *Stenchill* the younger. At last it was agreed betwixt them, that *Haquin* being pretty well in Years should remain King during his Life, and should be succeeded by *Stenchill*. After the Death of *Haquin*, who Reign'd thirteen Years, *Stenchill* the younger, *Olaus Skotkonung*'s Sister's Son, began his Reign, who vanquish'd the *Danes* in three great Battles. To him succeeded *Ingo*, surnam'd the *Pious*. This King utterly destroy'd the Idol at *Upsal*, which so enrag'd his Pagan Subjects, that they Banish'd him the Kingdom, and afterwards murther'd him in *Schonen*: He was buried in a Convent call'd *Wamheim* in *West-Gothland*. After him Reigned with great Applause his Brother *Halstan*, to whom succeeded his Son *Philip*. *Ingo*, *Philip*'s Son, and his Queen *Ragvild*, were also very famous for their Piety and other Virtues: She was after her Death honour'd as a Saint, and her Tomb frequently visited at *Talge*. This King left no Sons, but two Daughters, *Christina* and *Margret*; the first was marry'd to St. *Erick*, the second to *Magnus*, King of *Norway*. He was Poison'd by the *East Goths*, who were grown weary of the *Swedish* Government. Under the Reign of these five last Kings there were Golden Times in *Sweden*; the Christian Faith was then Establish'd, and the Subjects liv'd in Peace and Plenty.

The Swedes and Goths united in one Kingdom

Amund.

Amund-Slemme.

Haquin the Red.

Stenchill.

Ingo the Pious.

Halstan.

A.C. 1086

Philip.

Ingo.

A.C. 1138

§. 4. After the Death of *Ingo*, the *East Goths*, without the Consent of the other Provinces, made one *Ragwald Knapholfde*, a Man of great bodily Strength, but of no great Wisdom, their King, who was slain by the *West Goths*. In his stead the *East Goths* chose *Swercher* II. *Swer-*

Ragwald Knaphofde.

a very good King, who nevertheless was murder'd by one of his Servants. After the Death of *Swercher*, the *East Goths* chose his Son *Charles* for their King; but the *Swedes* at their General Assembly at *Upsal*, Elected
Erick *the* Holy. *Erick* the Son of *Jesward*, he having Marry'd *Christin*, the Daughter of *Ingo*, surnam'd the *Pious*. But both the *Swedes* and *Goths*, considering afterwards, how necessary it was to keep up the Union betwixt these two Kingdoms, made an Agreement, that *Erick* should remain King over both Kingdoms, and that *Charles* should suceed him, and that afterwards their Heirs should Rule the Kingdom in the same manner alternatively. This *Erick* having reduc'd the *Finns* to their former Obedience, oblig'd them to receive the Christian Doctrin. He also order'd
A.C. 1154. the ancient Constitutions of the Kingdom to be Collected into one Book, which was call'd after his Name, St. *E-*
1160. *rick*'s Law. He was slain in the Meadows near *Upsal*, by *Magnus* the King of *Denmark*'s Son, who having first defeated his Army, was proclaim'd King. But the *Swedes* and *Goths* under the Conduct of *Charles* the Son of *Swercher*, fell again with such Fury upon the *Danes*, that they kill'd all the *Danes* with their King and his Son
Charles *the Son of* Swercher. upon the Spot, and out of the Spoil built a Church near *Upsal*, which they call'd *Denmark*. Thereupon *Charles*,
1168. the Son of *Swercher*, became King of *Denmark*, who
Cnut E- *rick's Son.* Reign'd with a general Applause; till *Cnut* the Son of *Erick*, return'd out of *Norway*, and under pretence that he had abetted his Father's Death, surpriz'd and kill'd him. His Lady and Children fled into *Denmark*, where having got some Assistance, they joyn'd with the *Goths* under the Conduct of *Koll*, the Brother of *Charles*, to recover the Kindom; but their General was Kill'd upon the spot, and their Forces dispers'd by *Cnut Erick's*
Swercher *III.* *son*. After which he Reign'd very peaceably for the space of twenty three Years. After the Death of *Cnut*, *Swercher*, the Son of *Charles* was made King of *Sweden*, but had for his Rival *Erick*, the Son of the last deceased King. At last the Difference was thus compos'd, that *Swercher* should remain King during his Life, but should be succeed by *Erick*. But *Swercher*, who notwithstanding this Agreement, was for settling the Crown upon his
1207. Family, did barbarously Murther all the Sons of *Cnut* except *Erick*, who escap'd into *Norway*; from whence he return'd with some Forces, and being assisted by the

the *Swedes*, vanquish'd *Swercher*, who fled into *West Gothland*. *Swercher* having obtain'd Succours of sixteen thousand Men, from *Waldemar*, the King of *Denmark*, attempted to recover his Kingdom, but was miserably beaten by *Erick's* Army, he himself narrowly escaping into *Denmark*; from whence he not long after fell again 1208.
into *West Gothland*, but was again defeated and slain in 1210.
Battle, leaving *Erick Cnutson* in the quiet Possession of the Throne, who renew'd the former Agreement made betwixt these two Families, and constituted *John*, the Son 1219.
of *Swercher*, his Successor in the Kingdom. He Marry'd *Ricknot*, the Sister of *Waldemar*, King of *Denmark*, and died in *Wisingsoe*. To him succeeded according to Agreement, *John*, the Son of *Swercher*, who Reign'd but three Years, and died also in the Isle of *Wisingsoe*, which was the general place of Residence of the *Swedish* Kings in those Days.

Erick Cnutson.

§. 5. After the Death of *John-Erick*, the Son of the former King *Erick*, became King of *Sweden*, who being lame, and besides this lisping, was Sirnam'd the *Lisper*. There was about that time a very potent Family in *Sweden*, call'd the *Tolekungers*, who aim'd at the Crown. To bring these over to his Party, the King had Marry'd three of his Sisters to three of the chiefest among them, he himself having marry'd *Katherine*, the Daughter of *Sweno Tolekunger*. But these being grown more Potent by this Alliance, *Cnut Tolekunger* rebell'd against the King, and having worsted him, oblig'd him to fly into *Denmark*; from whence he soon return'd with a strong Army and vanquish'd *Tolekunger*, and having caus'd him and *Halingar* his Son to be slain, restor'd the Peace of the Kingdom. Under the Reign of this King it was, that *Gulielmus Sabinensis*, the Pope's Legat, did first forbid the Priests in *Sweden* to Marry, whereas before that time, it had been a common Custom among the Priests there to Marry, as well as Lay-men. This *Erick*, by the Conduct of his Brother-in-law *Birger*, forc'd the *Finnes* to return to Obedience, and to receive the Christian Faith, and built several Fortresses upon their Frontiers. 1250.
He died without Issue in *Wisingsoe*. Whilst *Birger Yerl* was absent in *Finland*, the States made *Waldemar*, the eldest Son of *Birger Yerl*, their King, as being the deceas'd King's Sister's Son: Who being Crown'd in the Year 1251
next ensuing, the Administration of the Kingdom was

Erick Lisp.

Celibacy of the Clergy introduc'd in Sweden.

Waldemar.

committed, during his Minority, to his Father *Birger*, who augmented the Law-Book, and deserv'd so well of the Publick, that upon the request of the Estates, he was created a Duke, whereas before he had been only an Earl, or as it is in their ancient Language, *Jerl*. He met with great opposition from the *Tolekungers*. But the Duke, under pretence of making an Agreement with them, after having granted them a a safe Conduct, perswaded them to give him a Meeting, where having made them all Prisoners, he caus'd them to be Executed, except *Charles Tolekunger*, who fled into *Prussia*, and re-
1263. main'd there all his Life-time. Things being thus setled, he Married his Son to *Sophia*, the Daughter of *Erick*, King of *Denmark*, and laid the first Foundation of the Castle and City of *Stockholm*; and tho' his Son was become of Age, yet he did never surrender the Government to him as long as he liv'd. He died after he had
1266. been Regent fifteen Years, leaving four Sons, *Waldomar*, King of *Sweden*, *Magnus*, Duke of *Sudermanland*, *Erick* of *Smaland*, and *Benedict* of *Finland*, who afterwards rais'd great Disturbances: For *Waldomar* having, during his Pilgrimage to *Rome* and *Jerusalem*, left the Administration of the Kingdom to his Brother *Magnus*, at his return accus'd him of having aim'd at the Crown.
1275. The States of *Sweden* held an Assembly at *Strengness*, to to compose these Differences if possible; but met with so much Difficulty, that it was impossible to be effected. Upon which, *Magnus* and *Erick* retiring into *Denmark*, soon return'd from thence with a considerable Force; and having routed the Vanguard of King *Waldemar*, made him their Prisoner. Whereupon *Magnus* call'd together the Estates of the Kingdom; who being most of them in his Party, adjudg'd the whole Kingdom to Duke *Magnus*, except only East and West *Gothland*, *Smaland*, and *Dahl*, which the King was to have for his share. But this Ageeement lasted not long; for the *Danes*, who had not receiv'd their Subsidies promis'd by *Magnus*, siding with *Waldemar*, the War was renew'd, which was carry'd on with various Success; till at last the *Danes* having receiv'd Satisfaction for the Money due to them, left *Waldemar* in the lurch, who in the Presence of the Estates, resign'd the Kingdom to *Magnus*.

§. 6. *Wal-*

§. 6 *Waldemar* having resign'd the Kingdom, *Magnus* Magnus,
was crown'd at *Upsal*; who resum'd the Title of *King* 1219.
of the Swedes *and* Goths, which had not been us'd by his Predecessors never since the time of *Olaus Skotkonung*, but is since retain'd by the Kings of *Sweden* to this Day. Under this King's Reign the Family of the *Tolekungers* began to raise new Commotions, and being assisted by some of the Nobility, murthered *Ingemar Danschkep*, the King's Favourite, and took *Gerhard*, the Earl of *Holstein*, and Father-in-law to the King, Prisoner, laying also close Siege to the Castle of *Joncoping*; which oblig'd the King to appease them for that time by fair Promises; But not long after the Earl was releas'd, the King accus'd them before the Assembly of the Nobility, of High-Treason, and caus'd them all to be Executed at *Stockholm*, except *Philip* of *Runby*, who was fain to redeem his Life at a very dear Rate. With this Stroke the Greatness of the Family of the *Tolekungers* was quite laid in the Dust. Having thus settled his Affairs, he got his Lady *Hedwig* Crown'd at *Suderasping*; and with
the Advice of the Senators, made King *Waldemar* a Pri- 1288.
soner in the Castle of *Nicoping*, where he died four 1290.
Years after. *Magnus* died in *Wisignoic*, and was Buried at *Stockholm* in the Church of the *Grey Friars*, having left the Tuition of his Son *Birger*, who was but Berger II,
Eleven Years of Age, and the Care of the Kingdom to *Torckel Cnutson* the Rix-Marshal. *Torckel Cnutson* was Regent for the space of Thirteen Years, during which time he Imprison'd King *Waldemar*'s Sons; but after their Decease, he sent an Army into *Carelia*, and induc'd them to receive the Christian Faith; he built on their Frontiers the Fortress of *Wibourgh*, and took from the *Russians Kelkhelm*. King *Birger* being by this time come
to the Years of Maturity, Married *Mareta*, the Daughter 1292.
of *Erick*, King of *Denmark*; and having sent new Forces into *Carelia* and *Ingermania*, built the Fortress of 1298.
Norburgh, on the Frontiers of *Russia*, which however a few Years after was re-taken and demolish'd by the *Rus-*
sians. Soon after he declar'd his Son *Magnus*, who was 1303.
but three Years old, his Successor in the Kingdom, which was confirm'd by the chief Men of the Kingdom, and especially by his Brothers. But this solemn Transaction was of no long Continuance, for his Brothers quick-

ly fell into Divisions, among themselves, and the younger growing mistrustful of the King, the Marshal tired first into *Denmark*, and from thence into *Nor* to make use of that King's Intercession to recover t Inheritance, which King *Birger* had seiz'd upon ; bu this proving ineffectual, they made several Inroads West *Gothland*, and kill'd and dispers'd the *Swe* Troops that were sent to oppose them. The King v at last in Person with an Army, and was met by Brothers with some Forces, which they had obtain' the King of *Norway* ; when by the Intercession of s Senators, the Differences betwixt the Brothers were c pos'd, aud the two younger restor'd to their Estate

1305. *Sweden*. This Agreement cost the old *Torckel* his H who, under pretence of having upheld the Animo betwixt the Brothers, and some other Matters laid to Charge, was Beheaded at *Stockholm*. But no sooner this Wise Man dead, but the two younger Brothers gan to aim again at the Crown, and having surpriz'c King and Queen at their Country Seat, call'd *Hat* forc'd him to resign the Kingdom, and to surrender Crown and City of *Stockholm* to his Brother *Erick*, made the King a Prisoner in the Castle of *Nicoping* ; his Son *Magnus* was, during this Tumult, carry'd *Denmark*. The King of *Denmark* undertook three s ral Expeditions to relieve his Brother-in law and Si but to no great purpose, only that at last it was agr That the King, Queen, and their Children, should b at Liberty, and the Matter decided in the Assembl the Senate of the Kingdom. The Senate being acc ingly call'd together at *Arboga*, it was there conclu that in case King *Birger* would Pardon all past Inju and be contented with what part of the Kindom sh be assign'd to him, he should be at Liberty ; which perform'd accordingly, the Senate and his Brothers ving again sworn Fealty to him. Thus Matters see to be compos'd for the present. But not long after *E*

1308. King of *Denmark*, having made an Alliance with *Haq* King of *Norway*, came with an Army of 60000 Men *Sweden*, to assist King *Birger* in bringing his Brot under his Subjection ; their first Success was answer to their great Preparations, having taken *Joncoping*, forc'd the Duke's Forces to fly before him ; but the *D* who began to be in want of Provisions, being mo

them gone home, there was a Meeting appointed betwixt the Brothers at *Halsingburg*, where the former Agreement made at *Arboga*, was renew'd; by Virtue of which, Duke *Erick* was to have West *Gothland, Daht, Halland, Wermeland* and *Smaland*: Duke *Waldemar* was to have for his share, *Upland, Oeland* and part of *Finland*; the rest to remain under the King, and the Dukes to hold their Possessions in Fief from him. Thus all Animosities seem'd to be laid aside, and the three Brothers liv'd in great Splendor, striving to out-do one another in Magnificence; which occasioning some new Taxes, prov'd also the occasion of some Insurrections in the Kingdom, which were nevertheless happily appeased, and Peace restor'd to the whole Kingdom.

In the mean while, Duke *Waldemar* in his Journey from *Calmar* to *Stockholm*, gave a Visit to the King at *Nicoping*, who not only treated him with extraordinary Civility, but also desir'd him to return and bring his Brother along with him, *by which means he hop'd that the very Seeds of their former Animosities betwixt them, might be rooted out.* *Waldemar* overcome by these fair Promises, over-persuaded his Brother *Erick*, who was very averse to it at first, but at last consented. Being arriv'd in the Castle where the King was, they were kindly receiv'd, and splendidly entertain'd at Supper; but they had not been long in Bed, and most of their Servants dispers'd into several Quarters of the Town, when they were made Prisoners, beaten, abus'd, and half Naked loaded with Irons, thrown into a strong Tower, their Servants being all either Kill'd or taken Prisoners. This done, the King march'd directly for *Stockholm*, in hopes to surprize the City; but the News of this barbarous Act having been already carry'd thither, they not only repuls'd, but pursu'd him to *Nicoping*. The King perceiving that they intended to Besiege *Nicoping*, retir'd to *Streckeburgh*; but before his departure having caus'd the Doors of the Prison to be barricado'd up, he threw the Keys into the River, and commanded upon pain of Death, not to open the Doors till his return. Soon after *Nicoping* was Besieg'd, but before it could be forc'd, both the Brothers died with Famine. King *Birger* having by this treacherous Fact, animated the whole Kingdom against him, sought for Aid in *Denmark*; and having obtain'd some Forces, shifted with them from Place

1317.

to Place, till some of them were surpriz'd at *Su ping*; and the *Danish* Horse having also left *Nyc* the King destitute of all, retir'd with the Quee *Gothland*, leaving his Son *Magnus* in the Castle of S *burgh*. The *Swedes* having immediately after in the Place, forc'd it to surrender by Famine, an
1319. *Magnus* Prisoner to *Stockholm*. There the Senate c Kingdom made *Matthew Ketelmundson* Regent o *den*, who vigorously prosecuted the remains of the Party, which oblig'd King *Birger* to seek for shelt *Christopher*, King of *Denmark*.

Magnus Smieck.

§. 7. After King *Birger* had left *Gothland*, the assembled at *Upsal*, chose for their King *Magnu* Son of Duke *Erick* who was then but three Years The next Year *Magnus*, the Son of King *Birger* withstanding that the Senate and Estates of the Kin had sworn Fealty to him as to their future King villanously Sentenc'd to Death, and Beheaded accor ly; and King *Birger* and his Queen died soon aft Grief. But the *Swedes*, who had conceiv'd great of their new King, found themselves extreamly de in their Expectation after the Death of *Ketelmu* who at first manag'd Affairs with great Prudence. the King being now of Age, marry'd *Blanch*, the D ter of an Earl of *Namur*; and laying aside the old cellors, made use of the Advice of his young Favo among whom one *Benedict*, born in West *Gothland* the Chief Place. The Inhabitants of *Schonen* bei verely oppress'd by the *Holsteiners*, put themselves his Protection, which was afterwards confirm'd by *demar*, King of *Denmark*, and the *Sound* by co Consent, made the common Borders of these two doms on that side. After he had Ruled twelve Ye Peace, he undertook an Expedition against the *Ru* which succeeded very ill, he being oblig'd to buy by the Surrender of a part of *Carelia*. His Tre being mightily exhausted, he not only impos'd ne heavy Taxes upon the People, but Pawn'd a great of the Crown Lands. Soon after, Pope *Clemer* Excommunicated him, because he had apply'd th venues of St. *Peter*, given to the *Roman* Chair by *Skotkonung*, to the use of the *Russian* War. The P being extreamly discontented at these Proceeding

King, at the persuasion of the Senate, caused his two Sons to be declar'd Kings, *viz.* *Erick* of *Sweden*, and *Haquin* of *Norway*. The Nobility being now Headed by a new King, began to withdraw their Obedience from the old, and kill'd his Favourite *Benedict*. The King, who now began to see his Error, sought for Aid from the King of *Denmark*, which so exasperated the Nobility, that they oblig'd the young King *Erick* to take up Arms against his Father, which occasion'd a bloody War, till at last the Kingdom was divided betwixt them, the Father having allotted him *Upland*, *Gothland*, *Wormeland*, *Dahl*, *North-Halland*, *West-Gothland*, and *Oeland*. 1357.
But *Schonen*, *Blackingen*, *South-Halland*, *East-Gothland*, *Smaland* and *Finland*, fell to the Son's share.

Notwithstanding this Agreement, the Jealousie continued betwixt the Father and the Son; and not long after, the Father having sent for his Son, under pretence of some Business of great Moment, he was there Poysoned by his Mother. King *Magnus* by his Death, being put again into the possession of the whole Kingdom, studied nothing but Revenge against the Nobility. The better to compass his Design, he made an underhand Alliance with the King of *Denmark*, unto whom he surrendred *Schonen*; who not only took Possession of it, but also by the Connivance of King *Magnus*, fell into 1361.
Gothland and *Oeland*, where he Kill'd a great many Boors, plunder'd the whole Country, and demolished *Borgholm*. The *Swedes* being thus put to a *Nonplus*, submitted themselves to the Protection of *Haquin* King of *Norway*, who made his Father *Magnus* a Prisoner in the Castle of *Calmar*. The Senate of the Kingdom then perswaded King *Haquin* to Marry the Daughter of *Henry*, Earl of *Holstein*, which he seemingly consented to at that time. But the Bride in her Voyage into *Sweden* being driven on the Coast of *Denmark*, was detain'd by *Waldemar* King of *Denmark*, who intended to marry his Daughter to King *Haquin*. Thereupon *Albert*, Duke of *Mecklenburgh* aud the Earls of *Holstein*, denounc'd War against the King of *Denmark*, if he did not release the Bride; but King *Waldemar* had in the mean time so well concerted Affairs with *Haquin*, that he resolv'd to Marry *Margaret* his Daughter; so the Bride was set at Liberty: But being arriv'd in *Sweden*, was so slightly receiv'd by King *Magnus*, who in the mean time had ob-

tain'd

tain'd his Liberty. That she retir'd into a Nunnery; those Senators who urg'd King *Haquin* to perfor[m] Marriage contract, were by *Magnus* banish'd the King who soon after Married his Son to *Margaret*, ther[n] eleven Years old. At this Wedding held at *Copenh*[agen] *Waldemar* caused the Parents of *Haquin* to be Poy[son'd]. Queen *Blenha* died immediately, but King *Magnus* preserv'd by the Skill of his Physician.

§. 8. Those *Swedish* Lords that were banish'd by [King] *Magnus*, having for some time lived in *Gothland*, d[id at] last agree among themselves to elect *Henry* Earl of [Hol]*stein*, King of *Sweden*. But he being a Man in Y[ears] and not willing to entangle himself in those trouble[some] Affairs, recommended to them *Albert* Duke of *Mec*[klen]*burgh*, King *Magnus*'s Sisters Son. The banish'd L[ords] therefore having chosen his second Son, whose name [was] likewise *Albert*, their King, carry'd him into *Gothl*[and] and from thence to *Stockholm*, which they easily t[ook] being assisted by a strong Party within the City. [Hav]ing then call'd together such of the Nobility as they k[new] to be Enemies to King *Magnus*, they Proclaimed [Al]*bert* King in the City of *Stockholm*. *Magnus* [and]
1364. his Son, with a very considerable Army, Mar[ched] against King *Albert* into *Upland*, and were met [by] him near *Encoping* where a bloody Battle ensued; the Victory inclining to *Albert*'s side, King *Magnus* [was] taken Prisoner, and *Haquin* wounded, but escap'd [the]
1365. Hands of his Enemies. During the Imprisonmen[t of] K. *Magnus*, *Sweden* was reduced to a most miserable [con]dition by the Wars that were carried on betwixt K[ing] *Albert*, *Haquin* and *Waldemar*, the two last sending [con]tinual Supplies into *Sweden* to uphold their Party, [till] *Haquin* being grown so strong that he defeated King [Al]*bert* in a Battle, and besieged *Stockholm*. At last it [was]
1371. agreed that King *Magnus* should have his Liberty, p[ay]ing a Ransom of 12000 Marks of fine Silver, and re[sign] the Crown of *Sweden* and *Schonen* to King *Albert*, w[hich] was perform'd accordingly. King *Magnus* retir'd [into] *Norway*, where he was drown'd by accident. King [Ha]*quin* did not long survive his Father, and his Son *O*[laus] dying very young, Queen *Margaret* his Mother after [his] decease was sole Queen of *Norway*. By the Death of *Olaus*, the ancient Race of the *Swedish* Kings were ex[tin]guish'd, which ever since the time of St. *Erick*, *viz*.

e space of 200 Years had ruled in *Sweden*. Not long ter, *Waldemar* King of *Denmark*, died without leaving 1376.
y Male Heirs behind him. In whose stead the *Danes* unite *Norway* with *Denmark*, declar'd his Daughter *argaret* their Queen. King *Albert*, by the Death of s Enemies, being now establish'd in the Throne of *Swe-n*, began to slight the *Swedish* Nobility, and to em-oy the *Germans* in his Service; and his Treasury be-g exhausted by the War which was carried on a-inst *Denmark*, he demanded from the States that part the Revenues of the Clergy, and some of the Lands hich belong'd to the Nobility, should be incorporated ith the Crown; which they refusing to consent to, he vertheless pursued his Intentions by open Violence. In ie, whilst some sided with the King, the rest were con-ring how to deliver themselves from these Oppressions, d having renounc'd their Obedience to King *Albert*, ught for Protection from *Margaret*, Queen of *Denmark*, Margaret.
hich she granted them, upon Condition that if she de-ver'd them from King *Albert*, she should be Queen of *veden*. which the *Swedes* being forc'd to accept of, she as proclaim'd Queen of *Sweden*. This prov'd the oc-sion of unspeakable Miseries, both Parties committing eat Outrage in the Country, that had been quite exhau-ed before by K. *Albert*; who at last was forced to Pawn e Isle of *Gothland* for 20000 Nobles to the *Prussian* 12 *Sett.* 1388.
nights of the Cross. But after all, being not able to efray the Charges of the War, he Challeng'd Queen *Margaret* to a Battle, to be fought in the Plains of *Tal-ping* in *West-Gothland*. The appointed Day being come, *The Battle of* Talcoping.
bloody Battle was fought in the beforemention'd Plain, here the Queen's Forces at last obtain'd the Victory, ing *Albert* and his Son being taken Prisoners. But is Victory, rather increased than diminished the Mise-es under which the Kingdom had groaned before, be-use the Dukes of *Mecklenburgh*, Earls of *Holstein*, and e *Hanse* Towns, sided with King *Albert*'s Party, and nt constant Supplies from *Rostock* and *Wismar*, by Sea, *Stockholm*, *Calmar*, and other strong Holds in their ossession, from whence the *German* Garisons made Mi-rable Havock all round the Country. And the Sea-oasts were extreamly infested by Privateers, which uite ruined the Trade of the Kingdom.

This

This pernitious War having thus lasted Seven Yea
1394. a Treaty of Peace was set on Foot at *Helsingburgh*, whi
1395. proving fruitless, another Meeting was appointed at *A*
holm, where it was agreed, That the King and his So
and the rest of his Prisoners of Note, , should be set
Liberty, upon condition, that within the space of th
Years he should resign all his Pretentions to the Kin
dom into the Hands of Queen *Margaret*, or else retu
to Prison; and that in case of failure, the Cities of *L*
beck, *Hamburgh*, *Dantzick*, *Thorn*, *Elbingen*, *Saralsu*
Stetin and *Campen*, *should oblige themselves to pay* 60
Marks of fine Silver to the Queen. Thus King *Al*
returned into *Mecklenburgh*, after he had Reigned
Years in *Sweden*. But notwithstanding this, did not l
aside the hopes of recovering his Kingdom, for which
had made great preparations, if his Son had not di
two Years after; Upon which, he at the appointed ti
resign'd his Pretensions, and the Places as yet in his P
session, to the Queen, and at last ended his Days in
Native Country of *Mecklenburgh*. Thus *Margaret*
came Queen over all the three Northern Kingdoms, wh
she Govern'd with extraordinary Wisdom; yet so, t
the *Danes* were much better satisfied with her Gove
ment than the *Swedes*.

Erick, *Duke of* Pomerania.

§ 9. Queen *Margaret* having restor'd Peace to
Northern Kingdoms, her next care was to Unite th
three Crowns for ever under one Head. For which p
pose she sent for *Henry* the young Duke of *Pomera*
her Sister's Son, whose Name, to please the *Swedes*
chang'd into that of *Erick*. This Prince, tho very you
was in the second Year after the releasing of K
Albert, proclaimed King. In the next Year, the Se
tors and Nobility of all the three Kingdoms being ass
bled at *Colmar*, where also the young *Erick* was Crow
the Union of the three Kingdoms was propos'd, wh
at last was perfected and confirm'd by Oath, and by
Hands and Seals of the States of the three Kingdo
which might have tended to the great Advantage of th
three Nations, if the *Danes* had not afterwards b
this Union, and endeavour'd to make themselves M
sters of *Sweden*, which proved the occasion of blo
1396. Wars betwixt these two Kingdoms. But because K
Erick was but very Young, Queen *Margaret* had the A

Union made at Calmar, *betwixt* Sweden, Denmark, *and* Norway.

ministratio

1410.
1412.

all his Forces against the *Swedes*. And this for a great part destroy'd by Storm, he arriv rest at *Stockholm*; but not being able to c great a Multitude as *Engelbrecht* had rais'd ag was fain to make a Truce with them for twel In the mean while he retir'd into *Denmark*, l a Garison of 600 Men in the Castle of *Stockhol* departure, *Engelbrecht* was declar'd *Generali* the Forces of the Kingdom, who, at last, up suasion of the Archbishop *Oluf*, agreed to be set on foot betwixt the King and his Subj it was agreed that the *Swedes* should again a him for their King, provided he would stand on; which the King at that time consente ving only to his free disposal, the three Castl *holm*, *Calmar*, and *Nycoping*, all the rest being mitted to the Government of the Natives Thus things seemed to be restored to the anc but no sooner had the King got the afore into his Possession, but he began to retract, left a Garison of 500 Men in the Castle of retir'd upon a sudden into *Denmark*, King E thus left the Kingdom a second time, the S tors, who feared that he might soon return w er Force, being assembled at *Arboka* call'd t the whole Nobility, and a Burger-Master, City, to consult about the present exigency, but before they could come to any steady *Engelbrecht*, by the assistance of some of the *Stockholm*, had made himself Master of that besieg'd the King's Lieutenant in the Ca Treaty being thus broke off, and the Flame o

Charles Cnutson. again re-kindled, the Marshal *Charles Cnut* clar'd Governor and General of the Kingd was like to have occasion'd great Disturbance *berche*, who pretended to be injur'd by this not been first appeased with great Promises wards Murther'd by one *Benedict Suenson*, he had an old Quarrel. But *Erick Puke*

1436. Companion of *Engelbrecht*, taking up his Frie rel against his Murtherers that were protecte *Cnutson*, it occasion'd great Jealousies bet The Castles of *Stockholm* and *Calmar*, being

King's Possession, and some of the chiefest of the Kingdom grown very jealous of the greatness of the Marshal, the Treaty was renewed with the King at *Calmar*, who came thither in Person, and promis'd to put into all Offices and Places of Trust, Natives of *Sweden*; and having made *Benedict Suenson* Governor of the Castle of *Calmar*, appointed an Assembly of the Senate and Nobility to be held in *September* following, when he would be ready to surrender all the Strong-holds into the Hands of the Natives of *Sweden*. Soon after, the King in his Voyage from *Gothland* to *Sudercoping*, was overtaken by a violent Storm, wherein most of his Ships being lost, he narrowly escap'd Drowning. As soon as the *Swedes* got Notice of this Misfortune, not knowing whether the King was alive or Dead, it was resolv'd, that the last Treaty made at *Calmar*, would remain in force. Pursuant to this Decree, the Marshal having partly by great Promises, partly by Threats, got into the Possession of all the Castles of the Kingdom, seem'd to want nothing to accomplish his Designs, but the Title of King; whereat *Erick Puke* being disgusted, rais'd a great number of Boors against him, who having defeated the Marshal and his Forces, would quickly have put an end to his Greatness, if under pretence of Reconciliation, he had not invited *Erick Puke* to an Interview, and notwithstanding his Faith given, sent him to *Stockholm*, where he was Beheaded. In the mean while the Senators of the Kingdom having got Notice that the King was alive, appointed an Assembly to be held at *Calmar*, where the King was to fulfil the former Treaty; but the King not coming at the appointed time, 1437. Commissioners were sent into *Denmark* to treat with him about the performance of the Agreement made at *Calmar*, which he refusing to do, they made an under-hand League with some of the Great Men in *Denmark*, against K. *Erick*, the Effects of which he felt soon after. Whilst these Things were Transacting in *Denmark*, the Marshal had by his Cunning, got the whole Power of the Kingdom into his Hands, and influenced the Senate of *Sweden* to appoint a certain Day for the King to appear in *Sweden*, and put an end to those Differences betwixt him and the Estates, and in case of refusal, they renounced their Allegiance to him.

But

But the Archbishop *Oluf*, and some of the chief M
of the Kingdom, that were dissatisfy'd at the Marsh
Proceedings, did so far prevail by their Authority, tha
General Assembly of all the Senators of the three N
thern Kingdoms should be held at *Calmar*, which in
likelihood might have had better success than before,
the Archbishop had not been poison'd in his Journey
ther by the Marshal. Notwithstanding this, the rest
the Senators appear'd at *Calmar*, but the King's Co
missioners refusing to acknowledge and to confirm
Treaty made at *Calmar*, which the *Swedes* insisted up
the whole meeting prov'd fruitless. In the mean ti
King *Erick* was retir'd with all his Treasure out of D
mark into *Gothland*, and the *Danish* Senators who as w
as the *Swedes* had been dissatisfy'd with the King for
considerable time before, agreed with the *Swedes* to
nounce their Allegiance to him, and to chuse one in
stead, that would maintain the Union betwixt these Ki
doms. In pursuance of this agreement the *Danes* sent
Christopher Duke of *Bavaria*, who being King *Eri*
Christopher Duke of Bavaria. Sisters Son, had for some time liv'd in *Denmark*; desir
him to accept of that Crown. As soon as he was arri
in *Denmark*; Ambassadors were sent to the Marshal a
the other Senators of *Sweden*, that were then at *Calm*
to notifie the arrival of the Duke of *Bavaria*, and to u
with them to receive him also for their King, as the o
1439. means to maintain the Union and Peace betwixt th
Kingdoms. The Marshal and his Party were not a li
surpriz'd at this Proposition; but perceiving that at t
Dyet held at *Arboga*, most of the Estates were inclin'd
maintain the Union, and receive *Christopher* for th
King, they also agreed with the rest of the Estates, a
Christopher was receiv'd by the Marshal and the Senat
with great Pomp at *Calmar*, from whence being co
ducted to *Stockholm*, and from thence to *Upsal*, he w
there Crown'd King of *Sweden*, and soon after retur
into *Denmark*. After he had Reign'd four Years,
marry'd *Dorothee* the Daughter of *John*, Marquis
Brandenburgh; and King *Erick*, who was yet in
Possession of *Gothland*, doing considerable damage to
Swedish Ships, *Christopher* was prevail'd upon by the S
nate to undertake an Expedition into *Gothland*. Wh
every Body was in great expectation of the success of t
Enterprise, he on a sudden clapt up a Peace with Ki

Erick

Erick, leaving him in the quiet Possession of Gothland. He died at Hilsingburgh in his Journey to Joncoping, whither he had call'd together the Senate and Nobility of Sweden, having left great Legacies to several Churches in Sweden; but the Danes, who had all his Ships, Amunition, rich Furniture, and ready Mony in their Hands, would not pay one Groat of it. 1448.

After the Death of King Christopher, the Estates of Sweden, that were assembled at Stockholm, were divided into two Parties, some of them being for deferring the Election of a new King, till such time as the Senators of the three Kingdoms could, at a general Assembly, chuse a King, according to the Union agreed upon betwixt them; but the Marshal and his Party, which was the strongest, were for chusing immediately a King of their own: This Contest lasted for several Days, and that with such Heats that they were ready to come to Blows, till at last the Marshal Charles Cnutson's Party prevail'd, and he was chosen King of Sweden. But the Danes offered the Crown of Denmark to Adolph Duke of Holstein, and he, by reason of his old Age, having refused to accept of it, they made Christian Earl of Oldenburgh, the Duke's Sister's Son, their King. Charles, at the very beginning of his Reign, besieg'd King Erick in the Castle of Wisby, who having deluded the Swedish Generals with a Truce, did, in the mean while provide himself with all Necessaries, and was at last relieved by Christian, King of Denmark; who sent him into Pomerania, where, in the City of Rugen, he ended his Days, without making any further pretention to the Crown. Charles Cnutson.

In the mean while the Norwegians, some of the Nobility excepted, made Charles also their King, which occasion'd almost a continual War betwixt him and Christian King of Denmark, in which King Charles was pretty successful at first; but after the Death of the Brave Thord Bonde his General, who was barbarously Murther'd; King Christian, with the assistance of the Archbishop of Sweden, and several others of the Swedish Nobility, who were Enemies to King Charles, prov'd too hard for him; for the Archbishop having surpriz'd the King's Forces at Strengness, besieg'd him in the City of Stockholm; so that King Charles finding himself reduc'd to the utmost Extremity, resolv'd to Embark with all his Treasure, for Dantzick, where he arriv'd safely after a

Voyage of three Days, in the tenth Year of his Reign. No sooner had King *Charles* left the Kingdom, but the
1458. Archbishop having got all the strong Holds of the King-
Christian I. dom into his Hands, sent to *Christian* King of *Denmark*, to invite him to *Sweden*; who being arriv'd with a considerable Fleet at *Stockholm*, was by the Senate and Nobility declar'd King of *Sweden*, and Crown'd at *Upsal*. He Reign'd at first with the general satisfaction of the *Swedes*; but some Years after, by his Cruelty and heavy Impositions laid upon the People, became odious to them; for he not only caused some of the Great Men to be Tortur'd to Death, but also exercised great Cruelty upon a great number of Boors, that were risen in Arms against him, and caused the Archbishop to be carry'd Prisoner to *Copenhagen*. This so exasperated *Katil* the Bishop of *Lyncoping*, that he made an Insurrection against the King, and forc'd him to retire to *Denmark*: And tho' the King return'd the next Year with a considerable Army, yet being defeated by the Bishop's Forces, he was forc'd to leave the Kingdom a second time, and the Bishop having laid Siege to the City and Castle of *Stockholm*, where King *Christian* had left a Garrison, sent for Assistance to King *Charles*, who being glad of this
1464. opportunity, came with some Forces (which he had gather'd in *Poland* and *Prussia*) into *Sweden*, where he was no sooner arriv'd, but the City of *Stockholm* was surrender'd to him, and he again receiv'd as King of *Sweden*. But this Joy was of no long continuance; for a difference being arisen betwixt him and Bishop *Katil*, about the exchanging of the Archbishop that was Prisoner at *Copenhagen*, the said Bishop did underhand agree with King *Christian* to restore him to the Kingdom of *Sweden*, upon condition that he should set the Archbishop at Liberty. According to this Agreement, a Reconciliation being made, betwixt King *Christian* and the Archbishop, the latter was receiv'd very splendidly by the Bishop, and was no sooner arriv'd in *Sweden*, but he defeated King *Charles* in a bloody Battle fought upon the Ice, near *Stockholm*, and forc'd him to abjure his Right and Pretentions to the Kingdom. After the King's Resignation, the Archbishop made himself Master of all the Strong-holds of the Kingdom, without any Opposition, except that one *Nils Sture*, a particular Friend of King *Charles*'s, travers'd sometimes his Designs. This *Nils* *Sture*

Erick Axelson.

1466.

1468.

1470.

1471.

general Applause; so that King *Christian* during his Regency, never durst return into *Sweden*, but died in *Denmark* in the Year, 1481.

1481. After the Death of King *Christian*, the *Danes* and *Norwegians* having made *John*, the Son of *Christian*, their King, the *Swedes* also agreed with King *John* upon certain Articles, and he was declar'd King of *Sweden*. But the Regent *Steen Sture*, notwithstanding this solemn Transaction, remain'd in the possession of the Kingdom for fourteen Years after, under pretence that the *Danes* had not fulfill'd their Promise; during which time, the Kingdom was miserably afflicted by intestine Divisions, and the Wars which were carry'd on against *Denmark* and *Russia*. The Senators therefore of *Sweden*, having in vain endeavour'd to perswade *Steen Sture* to lay down his Office, at last depos'd him from the Regency, and crav'd

John II. Assistance from King *John*, who having defeated *Steen Sture* and his Party, near *Stockholm*, was by the Senate and Regent himself, receiv'd as King of *Sweden*, and his

1497. Son *Christian* declar'd his Successor after his Death, in that Kingdom. This King Reign'd very peaceably for a while; but after some Years, fell into the same Error which had been the undoing of his Predecessors: For under pretence that the Revenues of the Crown were extreamly diminish'd, he oblig'd *Steen Sture* and several others, to surrender the Fiefs belonging to the Crown, which they were in Possession of; some of which he bestow'd upon the *Danes* and *Germans*; besides, his Governors committed great Insolencies in their Provinces, which so exasperated the People, that as soon as the News of his Defeat in *Ditmarsen* was spread over *Sweden*, the *Swedes* headed by *Steen Sture*, assembled at *Wadstana*, where having renounc'd their Allegiance, they bid open Defiance to him, alledging, that he had not fulfill'd the Articles of the Treaty made at *Calmar*.

The King at this unexpected News, sail'd forthwith for *Denmark*, leaving the Queen with a good Garrison at *Stockholm*; which City was thereupon Besieg'd by *Sture*; who being soon after again constituted Regent of the Kingdom, forc'd the Castle of *Stockholm* to surrender, and got almost all the rest of the strong holds in *Sweden* into his Possession; notwithstanding which, the *Danes* burnt *Elfsburgh* and *Offesteen*, and committed great Cruelties in *West-Gothland*, under the Conduct of *Christian*,

King *John*'s Son, who had done the like not long before in *Norway*, where he had rooted out almost all the Noble Families. But in regard the Queen was as yet in *Sweden*, the Fury of the *Danes* was for a while appeas'd by the Intercession of the *Lubeckers*, and the Cardinal *Raimond*, who having procur'd Liberty for her to return into *Denmark*, she wcs conducted by the Regent to the Frontiers of *Smaland*. But in his return to *Joncoping*, he died suddenly, and his Death having been kept secret for a while, there was a strong suspicion that he had been Poyson'd by *Mereta*, the Widow of *Cnut Alfson*; thereby to open the way for her Bridegroom *Suante Sture*, to the Regency of the Kingdom. As soon as the 1503. News of the Regent's Death was known, the Estates assembled at *Stockholm*, where it was disputed for some time, whether King *John* should be recall'd, or *Suante Nilson Sture* be made Regent: And the latter prevailing, the said *Sture* was made Regent of the Kingdom. Then the War being renew'd with King *John*, was carry'd on 1504. with various Success, both Parties committing great Devastations, without any other remarkable Advantage. The *Danes* having at first stirr'd up the Emperor, the Pope, and the *Russians*, against the *Swedes*, did considerable Mischief; but the Regent having made a Peace with the *Russians*, and set the *Lubeckers* against *Denmark*, e-took *Calmar* and *Bornholm*, and would in all likeliood have made greater Progresses, if he had not soon fter died at *Westeraos*, in the eighth Year of his Regeny. After the Death of this Regent, there were again 1511. reat Divisions in the Senate about the Election of a ew Regent; the younger sort were for *Steen Sture*, the Steen eceas'd Regent's Son: But the Arch-bishop and Bishops, Sture *the* nd the rest of the Ancient Senators, for electing *younger.* *ustavus Trolle*, an ancient wise, and experienc'd Man. fter several Prorogations and very hot Debates, at last *teen Sture*, who was favour'd by the common People, 1512. nd had most of the Strong-holds of the Kingdom in his ands, was declar'd Regent, and King *John* died the ext Year at *Ahlburgh* in *Jutland*. After his Death, the 1513. *anes* and *Norwegians*, declar'd *Christian* his Son, their ing; but the *Swedes*, who had not forgot his Cruelties ormerly committed in *West-Gothland*, desir'd time to conder of a thing of such Importance. King *Christian* findg himself after four Years Tergiversation, frustrated in his Hopes, and that the Regent would not part with his Power by fair means, did not only stir Pope *Leo* X. up against him, but also brought *Gustavus Trolle*, the new Arch bishop, by great Presents, over to his side, and perswaded the *Russians* to make an Inroad into *Finland*. *Steen Sture* soon convinc'd of the Arch-bishop's sinister Intentions, tender'd the Oath to him, which he refusing to take, was besieg'd by the Regent in his Castle of *Stecka*. Then it was' that the Arch-bishop call'd King *Christian* to his Assistance, who took some Ships loaden with Amunition belonging to the Regent, and in vain endeavour'd to relieve the besieg'd Castle. And thus the War was begun on both sides. The Arch-bishop being forc'd to surrender the Castle and his Office, Pope *Leo* thereupon Excommunicated the Regent, laying a Fine of 100000 Ducats upon the *Swedes*, and enjoyning the Execution thereof to King *Christian*. Pursuant to this Decree, the King of *Denmark* fell with a great Army into *Sweden*, and was met by the Renget and his Forces in *West-Gothland*; but the Regent receiving a Wound there, of which he died soon after at *Strengness*, his Army first retreated, and being depriv'd of a Leader, afterwards dispers'd. Then King *Christian* dividing his Army, sent one part into *West* and *East-Gothland*, which were soon subdu'd, and march'd with the rest to *Strengness*.

1520. The Arch-bishop taking hold of this Opportunity, reassum'd his Archi-episcopal Dignity, and being assisted by the two other Bishops, and seven of the Senators of the Kingdom, declar'd *Christian* King of *Sweden*, in the name of the Estates, at *Upsal*. The King having been Crown'd by the Arch-bishop *Trolle*, and receiv'd into his Hands the City of *Stockholm* by Surrender, treated the *Swedes* at first with abundance of Humanity, but soon after found out a Weapon wherewith to destroy his Adversaries, *viz.* The Plea of the Degradation of the Arch-bishop, and the ruining of his Castle of *Stecka*. For, tho' the King by an Amnesty, had pardon'd all past Offences, yet no Satisfaction having been given to the Pope, the Arch-bishop in his Name demanded a Million of pounds of Silver, in reparation of the Damages done to the Church at *Upsal*, and his Castle of *Stecka*. And to make up the Matter, it was pretended that Gunpowder had been convey'd into the King's Palace to blow him up. *Steen Sture*'s Widow, his Mother-in-Law, and fifteen

uftav. I.

1523.

the Kingdom, re-took *Oeland* and *Borkholm*, but also re-cover'd the Castle and City of *Calmar*, and made *Gustavu* K. of *Sweden*; who threupon immediately summon'd *Stock-holm* to surrender, and the Garrison being without hope of Relief, surrendred the City and Castle to the *Lubeckers*, who gave up the same to K. *Gustavus*. In the mean whil K. *Christian* was retir'd with his Queen into the *Nether-lands*, and the *Jutlanders* having made *Frederick* I. K. *Chri-stian*'s Uncle, their King, would fain have perswaded t *Swedes* to follow their Example; but these being not ambi-tious of continuing the Union with *Denmark*, had refu their proffer, and chosen *Gustavus* their King. But K. *Gu-stavus* finding the Treasury mightily exhausted by the long intestine Wars, he not only tax'd the Clergy to rai considerable Sums towards the pay of his Soldiers, but al so made bold with the superfluous Ornaments of the Chur-ches; upon which *Brask*, the Bishop of *Lincoping*, havin protested and made Complaint thereof to *Johannes Mag-nus*, the Pope's Legate, *Peter*, Bishop of *Westeras*, en-deavour'd to raise an Insurrection among the *Dalkerls*.

But whilst these Bishops were employ'd in maintainin their Privileges, the Protestant Religion had begun t spread all over the Kingdom. The same was by some Mer-chants and *German* Soldiers first introduc'd into *Sweden* and some *Swedish* Students, that had studied at *Witten-burgh*, had brought along with them into their Nati Country, both the Doctrin and Writings of *Luther*. A-mong these, one *Olaus Petri* was the Chifest, who havin been an Auditor of *Luther*, at his return into *Sweden*, wa made a Canon and Protonotary to the Bishop of *Strengnes* this Man after the Death of the Bishop, having broug *Lars Anderson* the Arch-deacon over to his Opinion, be-gan not only to defend *Luther*'s Doctrin publickly in th Schools, but also to publish the same from the Pulpi The Bishoprick being vacant, Dr. *Nils*, Dean of th Chapter, with all his might oppos'd this new Doctrin which being come to the King's Ears, he advis'd with *La Anderson*, who having instructed him in the chief Points o it, and in what manner a great many *German* Princes ha taken away the superfluous Riches of the Clergy, bega to hearken to his Opinion, and resolving nevertheless t go on Cautiously in this Business, and to see how som Princes in *Germany* would proceed in the Affair, as al so how the Bishops in *Sweden* would relish this Doctri

Reformati-on began in Sweden.

In

In the mean while Pope *Hadrian* IV. had sent his Legate into *Sweden*, to endeavour the Extirpation of this Heresy, and the Clergy of *Sweden* grew every Day more refractory, refusing to pay the Taxes impos'd upon them, as being contrary to their Privileges. On the other hand, *Olaus Petri* being encourag'd by the King, defended his Cause both by Dispute and Writing, with such Success, that the King not only constituted him Minister in the great Church of *Stockholm*, and put into other vacant Church-Benefices, such Ministers as had studied at *Wittenberg*, but also constituted over the Dominicans and Black-Fryers, such Priors as he knew to be faithful to him, and such of them as were Foreigners he banish'd the Kingdom; and told unfeignedly to Bishop *Brask*, That he could not deny Protection to the *Lutherans*, as long as they were not convicted of any Crime or Error.

All this while one *Soren Norby*, who still adhered to King *Christian*, had *Gothland* in his Possession, and did considerable Damage to the *Swedes* in their Trade; but King *Gustavus* having sent *Bernherd van Melan* with some Forces to reduce the said Island, *Norby* finding himself too weak, put himself and the Island under the Protection of *Denmark*, which occasion'd some Differences between these two Northern Kings, who had been very good Friends ever before. About this time *Olaus Petri* was publickly Marry'd in the great Church at *Stockholm*, and the King had not only demanded the Tenths of the Clergy towards the Maintenance of his Forces, but also Quarter'd some of his Horse in the Monasteries, which so incens'd Bishop *Brask*, that he forbid his whole Diocess so much as to name the Doctrin of *Luther*. The King having understood that *Olaus Petri* was busie in Translating the New Testament into the *Swedish* Tongue, Commanded the Arch bishop, to take care that the *Roman* Catholicks also should make a Translation, which though it relish'd very ill with the Bishops, yet were they fain to comply with the King's Command, who to mortify them the more, also order'd a Disputation to be held at *Upsal*, betwixt Dr. *Pieter Galle* and *Olaus Petri*, concerning the chiefest Points in question betwixt the *Roman* Catholicks and *Lutherans*, where *Olaus Petri* had much the better, and his Translation was approv'd of before the others, which had been patch'd up by so many Translators. In the mean time the *Danish* Clergy gave a considerable

Subsidy

Subsidy to their King, to be employ'd against King *Christian*; upon which King *Gustavus* taking hold of this Example, demanded a considerable Supply from the *Swedish* Clergy; but these objecting that it was against their Priviledges and Rights, he order'd the Point to be examin'd in another Dispute betwixt *Olaus Petri* and Dr. *Pieter Galle*, and because they were not able to prove their Title out of the Holy Scripture, the King at the Dyet held at *Westeraos*, not only demanded a Supply from the Clergy, but also propos'd that the superfluous Bells should be taken out of the Churches, and be employ'd towards the Payment of the Debt due to the *Lubeckers*. And because the Arch-bishop grew more troublesome every Day, the King first took him into Custody, and afterwards sent him Ambassador into *Poland*, from whence he never return'd into *Sweden*. He also commanded another Disputation to be held concerning the chief Points in question betwixt the *Lutherans* and *Roman* Catholicks, which however met with great Opposition from Bishop *Brask* and the rest of the *Roman* Catholick Clergy, who set up a Country Fellow against *Gustavus*. This Fellow pretended to be the Son of *Steen Sture* (notwithstanding he was
1527. dead a Twelvemonth before) and having got a Party among the *Dalekerls*, and being upheld by Bishop *Brask* and the Bishop of *Druntheim* in *Norway*, and encouraged in his Undertaking by King *Frederick* of *Denmark*, laid open Claim to the Crown, threatning all the *Lutherans*, and especially the City of *Stockholm*, with Fire and Sword, that City being the most forward in settling the Protestant Religion.

About the same time the Emperor besieged Pope *Clement* VII. in the Castle of St. *Angelo*, and King *Gustavus* taking hold of this Juncture, appointed a Dyet to be held at *Westeraos*: And in his Declaration he profess'd, *that the* Roman *Catholick Clergy had made it their Business to charge him with making Innovations in Religion, for no other Reason, but that he would not let them domineer over the Laymen, and had forced them to submit to the Civil Power, and to give part of their superfluous Riches, some of which they had got by Fraud, towards easing the common People of those burthensome Taxes (which he hitherto had been forced to impose upon them) and that for the same Reason the Emperor himself had been forced lately to teach the Pope his Duty.* The same thing was proposed by the King to the

whole

the *Dalkerls*, who had made an Insurrection, were frigh ned by the King to comply with his Commands, and send away their Leader the suppositious *Sture*; and *Sigismund* King of *Poland*, unto whom the dissatisfy'd Par had proffered the Crown, did not think fit to accept of i so that Bishop *Brask*, despairing of the *Roman* Catholic Cause, under pretence of a Journey, retir'd to *Dantzick*

1528. The King having surmounted all these Difficulties, h Coronation was solemnized at *Upsal* with the usual Ce remonies, and then summoned the rebellious *Dalkerls* t appear before him at *Thuana*, threatning them with Fir and Sword if they did not appear at the appointed Tim The Rebels being frighten'd by the King's Severity, ap peared without Arms at the appointed Place, where h caused several of the Ringleaders to promise to be obe dient for the future. In *Helsingland* he appeased the tu multuous Multitude with Threats, and fined their Lea ders, and having called together a Synod of the Clergy a *Orebro*, the chiefest Points of the Popish Doctrine wer there abolished, and the Protestant Religion introduced and it was also ordered, that a Protestant Professor of Di vinity should be constituted in each Cathedral. This wrought in a manner Miracles among the inferior Cler gy and Monks, who left their Monasteries, were married and became Ministers in the Protestant Churches. But the Bishops and their Party entred into an Association with some of the dissatisfy'd Lords in *West Gothland* who accused the King of Heresy and other Crimes, re nouncing their Allegiance to him. These were headed by *Thuro Johanson*, the Rix-Marshal, who made an In surrection among the *Dalkerls*, and endeavoured also to stir up the *West* and *East Goths*, whom he persuaded to make *Magnus Brynteson*, a Man in great Authority among them, their King. But the King having again appeased this Tumult, by granting his Pardon to most of the Re bels, *Magnus*, the Bishop of *Skara*, and *Thuro Johanson* fled into *Denmark*, but *Magnus Brynteson*, *Nils Oloffson* and *Thuro Erickson*, being convicted of High Treason a the Dyet held at *Strengness*, the Two first were Execu ted, and the Third paid a considerable Fine. Then the King, to settle the Minds of his Subjects, renewed his Pardon, and caused the superfluous Bells to be taken out of the Steeples, according to a Grant made by the Estates towards the Payment of a Debt due to the *Lubeckers*

The Protestant Religion established in Sweden.

Thi

This proved a new Subject for an Insurrection; for the Dalkerls not only seized upon some of these Bells, but also pretended to hold an Assembly at Arboga, to consult about the deposing of King Gustavus, which obliged the King to call together the Estates at Upsal, whither he came in Person with a good Army, and meeting with great Opposition from the mutinous People, ordered his Soldiers to fire among them, which so terrify'd them, that upon their Knees they begg'd his Pardon, promising to be more obedient for the future. Things being thus pretty well settled, the King marry'd Katherine, the Daughter of Magnus Duke of Saxon Lauenburgh, and receiving Intelligence that King Christian was landed in Norway with a considerable Force, he sent some Troops under the Command of Lars Sigeson, the Rix-Marshal, to the Frontiers of Norway, who, being joined by some Danes, forc'd King Christian to raise the Siege of Bahus, who at last surrendering himself to the Danes, was by Frederick King of Denmark committed to Prison, where he died after Twenty Seven Years Imprisonment. 1533. But no sooner was this Storm over, but the Lubeckers raised another against Sweden. For having demanded of the King to grant them the sole Right of Trading on his Northern Sea-Coasts, he refused to consent to it, upon which they peremptorily demanded their Debt, and joyning with a great many Refugees of King Christian's Party, made John Earl of Hoya, who had marry'd King Gustavus's Sister, their Head, and proposed to themselves no less than the Conquest of the Northern Kingdoms, having enticed some Citizens of Stockholm, under pretext of making that City a free Hanse-Town, to promise to lay violent Hands on the King: and after the Death of Frederick King of Denmark, when that Kingdom was divided into several Factions, persuaded the Senate of Copenhagen and Malmoe to enter into the Confederacy of the Hanse-Towns. Being thus strengthened by a considerable Party within that Kingdom, they had great Success against the Danes, till these having declared Christian III. their King, and being assisted with Money, Ships, and Forces, by King Gustavus, beat the Lubeckers near Helsinburg, and afterwards in a Sea-Fight defeated their whole Fleet, and carried a great many of their Ships into Denmark. Soon after King Gustavus, to strengthen himself the better at Home, married Margaret the Daughter of Abraham Erickson, Governor of West

Gothland, which Alliance stood afterwards his Son D
John in great stead against King *Erick*. King *Gust*
having conceiv'd a jealousie against the Emperor *Cha*
the V. whom he suspected to be for making *Pals* G
Frederick, Son in Law of the imprison'd King *Christ*
King over the Northern Kingdoms, took a resolution
strengthen himself with the Alliance of *France*. To
this design in execution, he sent his Secretary into *Fra*
who having first made a Treaty of Commerce betw
1542. these two Crowns, did afterwards conclude a defen
Alliance with them.

1544. *Gustavus* having thus settled his Affairs, called a D
to be held at *Westeraas*, where the Estates of the Ki
dom declar'd the Succession Hereditary for the fut
Constituting *Erick Gustaveson*, who was then but ele
Years old, his Father's Successor. At the same Dyet
Popish Religion was quite abolish'd, and the *Luthe*
Religion Establish'd in *Sweden*, the King and the Est
having obliged themselves by a Solemn Oath to maint
the same with all their Power. In the Year 1551. Ki
Gustavus, after the Death of his Queen *Margaret*, r
the Kingdom of *Sweden* with great Tranquility, exc
that the *Russians* fell into *Livonia* and *Finland*, with wh
having made a Peace, and being now grown very old,
by his Testimony gave to *John* his second Son the Du
dom of *Finland*, to the third Son *Magnus* the Duked
of *East Gothland*, and to *Charles*, the youngest of all,
Dukedom of *Sundermanland*, *Nerick* and *Wermeland*, wh
Countries they were to hold in Fief from the Cro
But his Eldest Son *Erick*, who was to succeed him in
Kingdom, being persuaded by his Tutor *Dionysius B*
raeus a Frenchman, to make his Addresses to *Elizab*
Queen of *England*, sent the said *Dionysius* into *Engla*
who having writ to his Master, that nothing was want
to make up the Match but his presence, the Prince wo
have gone forthwith into *England*, if his Father had
opposed it, who sent in his stead his second Son *John*
Steen Sture. These being very civilly entertain'd
Queen *Elizabeth*, at their return Home told the Pri
that they believed nothing to be wanting to compleat
Marriage but his presence, which was very joyfully
ceived by the Prince. But the old and wise King, wh
soon perceiv'd, that they had mistaken Compliments f
Realities, thought it adviseable to communicate the busi-

The Kingdom of Sweden made Hereditary and the Popish Religion abolish'd

ness with the Estates Assembled at *Stockholm*, who after having confirm'd the Hereditary Succession, and the King's Testament, at last gave their consent to this Marriage, granting a considerable Supply towards the defraying of the Charges of this Marriage. But whilst the Prince was preparing for his Voyage, part of his Baggage having been sent before, he being ready to follow in Person, King *Gustavus* died at *Stockholm*, and King *Erick*, not thinking it adviseable to trust his Brother with the Kingdom, was forc'd to put off his Journey into *England*. 1559.

§. 10. King *Erick* was twenty seven Years of Age when he succeeded his Father in the Kingdom. His first Business was to enter into certain new Articles with his Brothers, thereby to maintain the Royal Authority against them, which tho' sorely against their Will they were forc'd to subscribe at the Dyet held at *Arboga*. At his Coronation he first introduc'd the Titles of Earls and Barons into *Sweden*, alledging that in an Hereditary Kingdom there ought to be also Hereditary Dignities among the Nobility. At his very first Accession to the Crown, he was engag'd in the Troubles, which then sorely afflicted the *Liflanders*. For some of them having put themselves under the protection of *Denmark*, some under the Crown of *Poland*, those of *Reval* and the Nobility of *Esthenland*, that were nearest to *Sweden*, sought for Protection from King *Erick*. Hereupon the King having sent an Army under the Command of *Claes Horn*, (who was joyfully receiv'd at *Reval*) took them into his Protection, and confirm'd to the City and Nobility their former Privileges. The *Poles* upon the Arrival of the *Swedish* Army at *Reval*, sent an Ambassador to demand *Reval* from the *Swedes*, who having receiv'd no other Answer, but that the *Swedes*, had at least as good a Title to *Reval*, as the *Poles*, return'd Home again, and the *Swedish* Garrison in *Reval*, that was besieg'd by the *Polish* Forces, forc'd them to quit that Enterprize. Soon after, the King being fully resolv'd to pursue his Intentions of the Marriage with Queen *Elizabeth* of *England*, Embark'd at *Elsborgth* to go thither in Person, but was by a violent Tempest forc'd to return. As he was very inconstant in his Temper, and very superstitious, being much addicted to Astrology, so after this Misfortune, he laid aside the thoughts of his Marriage for a while, making his Addresses by his Ambassadors,

Erick XIV.

1561. *The Titles of Earls and Barons introduced.*

Ambassadors, and with great Presents, to *Mary* Queen of *Scotland*, and the Princess of *Lorrain*, both at one time, and not long after to *Katherine* the Daughter of the Landgrave of *Hessen*, but succeeded in neither. In the mean while his Brother *John* marry'd *Katherine*, Daughter of *Sigismund* King of *Poland*, which being done without King *Erick*'s Approbation, put him into such a Rage, that he besieged his Brother in the Castle of *Aboa*, and taking him by Stratagem caused him to be sentenced to Death, which Sentence he however changed into a perpetual Imprisonment for that time, but seemed to repent of it afterwards, when the *Russians* demanded the said *Katherine*, his Brother's Wife, in Marriage for their Great Duke. The *Poles* to revenge this Affront, stir'd up the *Danes* and *Lubeckers* against the *Swedes*, and the *Danes* having affronted the *Swedish* Ambassadors at *Copenhagen*, soon broke out into a War, wherein the *Swedes* routed the *Danes* and *Lubeckers* in several Sea Engagements, but lost their Admiral Ship (which carried Two Hundred Brass Guns) and by Land there was great Havock made on both sides, with almost equal Fortune, except that the *Swedes* had pretty good Success in *Livonia*. Whilst King *Erick* was engaged in War with all his Neighbours, the inward Discontents began to encrease more and more among his Subjects, by the ill Management shewn both in his Affairs and Amours, being surrounded with a Seraglio of Mistresses (among whom one *Katherine*, an ordinary Country Wench, had the greatest Sway, whom he also married afterwards, and thereby lost his Authority among the Nobility.) Besides, he was guided in most Concerns of Moment by one *Joran Peerson*, his Favourite, and his former Tutor, *Dionysius Beurræus*, who fomented a continual Jealousy betwixt him and the Family of the *Stures*, which at last broke out into a fatal Revenge. For there having been Witnesses suborned against *Stuarte Sture* and his Son *Erick*, they were, with several others of that Family, not only committed to Prison, and miserably murthered, by the King's Command, but he also with his own Hands stabb'd *Nils Sture*; and repenting soon after of so barbarous a Fact, caused his former Tutor *Dionysius*, who advised it, to be slain by his Guards.

much longer against the Duke's Forces, and beside were Favourers of their Party, would have persu ded the King to Surrender; which Proposition bei rejected by the King, they, whilst the King was Church, open'd the Gates to his Enemies, so that narrowly escap'd into the Castle. Then the Duk Forces laid close Siege to the Castle; so that Ki *Erick* having first receiv'd Hostages, was forc'd come out, and after having resign'd the Crown, Surrender himself a Prisoner to his Brother Du *Charles*. The Estates then assembled at *Stockho* having also jointly renounced their Obedience to hi he was made a close Prisoner, and committed to Care of some of the Friends of the Murther'd Lor who us'd him most barbarously.

John III. 1568. §. 11. After the Deposition of King *Erick*, *Jo* was by the Estates proclaim'd King of *Sweden*, w having caus'd some of those who had been instrum tal in the Murther of the Estates at *Upsal*, to be E ecuted; sent his Ambassador to treat with the Ki of *Denmark*, either concerning a Peace, or at least prolongation of the Truce; but these Ambassad having exceeded their Commission, the whole Tr saction was declar'd void at the next Diet, and Ki *John* sent other Ambassadors to desire more mod rate Propositions of Peace; ond put his Broth *Charles* into the Possession of *Sudermannia*, *Neri* ond *Wermeland*, which Provinces were granted h before, pursuant to his Father's Testament. Then was Crown'd at *Upsal*; and having sent back *Russian* Ambassadors, he sent some of his own i *Muscovy*, to prolong the Truce betwixt them; but *Muscovites* took them into Custody, and perceiv that the *Liflanders* would in no wise submit th selves under their Yoke, they found out this Expe ent, to put *Magnus* Duke of *Holstein*, into the Po sion of that Country, with the Title of an Heredit King, paying only some small acknowledgmen the Grand Duke of *Muscovy*. This Proposition ving been approv'd of by the King of *Denmark*, Duke of *Holstein*, and the *Liflanders* in general, w were very willing to live under the Jurisdition a German Prince. The *Muscovites*, to put their Design in execution, advanc'd with a great Army, which oblig'd King *John* to make Peace with the *Danes* at *Stetin*, upon very disadvantagious Terms. But whilst the *Muscovites* employ'd all their Forces in *Livonia* and *Finland*, the *Tartars*, set on by the *Poles*, fell into *Muscovy*, and having taken and burnt the City of *Moscow*, cut above thirty Thousand of the Inhabitants to Pieces. But the *Muscovites* having made a Truce with the *Tartars* and *Poles* for some Years, they again entred *Livonia* with 80000 Men, and committed most inhumane Barbarities. But a *Swedish* Party of 600 Horse and 1000 Foot, that were fallen in with the *Muscovites*, having routed 16000 of them upon the Spot, the *Czar* of *Muscovy* was so dismay'd thereat, that he, of his own accord, offer'd a Treaty of Peace to be set on Foot at *Newgarten*; which Place being dislik'd by King *John*, the War began a-fresh, and was carry'd on with very indifferent Success on the *Swedish* side, they being repuls'd before *Wesenburgh* and *Telsburg*. Besides this, the *German* Horse and *Scotish* Foot that were in the *Swedish* Service, came to handy Blows, upon some distaste taken against one another, wherein 1500 *Scotish* Foot were all cut to pieces by the *Germans*, except 80 that escap'd their Fury; and the *Russians* not long after surpriz'd the *Swedes* and *Germans* that were drunk in their Camp, and kill'd a great many of them upon the spot; but on the other side, the *Swedes* making frequent Inroads into the *Russian* Territories, a Truce was concluded betwixt them for two Years. Most of the *Swedes* are of Opinion, that King *John* might have prosecuted this War with more Vigour, if he had not been more intent upon a Religious Design, than upon Warlike Preparations.

1571.

War with the Muscovites.

The Business proceeded thus: King *John*, tho' educated a Protestant, yet having been very conversant with a great many Learned *Roman Catholicks*, and influenc'd by his Queen, had resolv'd to restore by degrees the *Roman* Catholick Religion, under pretence of making a Reformation in the lately introduc'd Protestant Religion, after the Model of *Gregorius Cassander*, that was employ'd by the Emperors

Ferdinand I. and *Maximilian* II. to unite an
pose the Religious *Differences* in *Genmany*, and
call'd in some Jesuits disguis'd in Laymens H
at the Convocation of some of the Bishops an
gy at *Stockholm*, propos'd to them a new for
Liturgy, wherein a great many of the Popi
monies were to be restor'd in the Administra
the *Sacraments* and Consecration of Bisho
Priests, as well as the Mass, which was agai
duc'd; which new Lituigy being subscrib'd
new Consecrated Bishops and some of the
Clergy, was call'd the Liturgy of the *Swedish*
conform to the Catholick and Orthodox Churc
Liturgy being publish'd under the new Arch
Name, in the *Swedish* and *Latin* Tongues, t
and other *Roman* Catholick Hymns were ag
in the *Swedish* Churches (except in the Te
belonging to Duke *Charles* the King's Broth
the Celibacy of Priests ond other Popish
were extoll'd in the Pulpits by these Disguis'
Catholicks. Then he sollicited his Brother
by his Delegates, to introduce this Liturgy i
ritories; and he making Answer, that it
cording to their Father's Testament) neither i
in the King's Power, to make any Innovation
gion; this prov'd the Subject of a great M
standing betwixt them. Next the King had
to the Pope, who also disapproving his Unde
he demanded of the Clergy of *Stockholm*,
their Approbation of the said Liturgy; but t
swer'd, that thereby a Door was open'd for
man Catholick Religion to be re-establish'd
den; and having made their Appeal to a
Sgnod of that Clergy in the Kingdom, a Co
1577. *New Liturgy induc'd.* on of the Clergy of the Kingdom (except
the Dukes Territories) was held by the Ki
thority, where the King's Party prevail'd so
the Liturgy was confirm'd, not only by
Clergy, but also by the Temporal Estates,
clar'd all such Traiters, as should for the fu
pose it. The King having gain'd this poi
ish'd and Imprison'd some of those that w
conform to the said Liturgy, notwithstandin

a great many of the Clergy, upheld by Duke *Charles*, did not only boldly discover the deceitful Snares of the adverse Party, but also sent their Remonstranses to the *German* Universities of *Wittemberg*, *Leipsick*, *Helmstadt*, *Francfurt*, and others, where their Zeal for the *Augsburgh* Confession was approv'd, and the said Liturgy condemn'd as dangerous to the Protestant Religion. Hitherto King *Erick* had suffer'd a very hard Imprisonment during the space of nine Years. But King *John* now fearing that these Intestine Divisions might furnish him with an opportunity to make his Escape, gave him Poyson in a Pease-Soop. The King being rid of this Danger, began now to act more barefac'd than before; for now the Invocation of Saints was publickly taught in the Pulpits; those that oppos'd it were Imprison'd; a new University of Papists was to be Erected at *Stockholm*, and he sent his Ambassador to reside at *Rome*, and the Pope had his Nuncio at *Stockholm*; and to compleat the Matter, a great many young Scholars were sent to the Jesuits abroad to be duly instructed in their Principles. In the mean while, the War betwixt the *Swedes* and *Muscovites* was carry'd on without any remarkable Advantage on either side, till it was agree'd betwixt the Kings of *Poland* and *Sweden*, that each of them should act seperately against the *Muscovites*, and what either of them could gain by his Sword, should remain in his Possession. All this while, the Misunderstanding betwixt the King and his Brother *Charles* being not remov'd, the King call'd a Dyet at *Wadstena*, and sent a Summons to the Duke to appear there in Person. The Duke on the other hand having assembled some Forces in his Territories, did not appear at the said Dyet, but Lodg'd himself in some of the adjacent Villages; tho' at last, by the Mediation of some of the Senators, the Brothers were reconcil'd, the Duke having begg'd the King's Pardon, and referr'd the Differences concerning the Liturgy, to the decision of his Clergy, who at an Assembly held at *Strengness* rejected the aforesaid Liturgy. In the mean while died *Stephen* King of *Poland*, and his Widow *Anna* being Aunt of Prince *Sigismund*, the 1587.
Son of King *John*; she prevail'd with some of the

Great Men in *Poland*, to make him their King,
not without great difficulty on the *Swedish* side,
could not for a great while agree to the several
positions made to them by the *Poles*, and King *Si*
mund himself seem'd soon after to repent of it.
soon as *Sigismund* had left *Sweden*, his Father K
John began to renew his Care for establishing the r
Liturgy in the Duke's Territories; but the Cle
there trusting to the Duke's Authority and Protecti
and remaining stedfast in their Opinion, the King
last, tired out by their Constancy, sent for his Brot
Charles to *Stockholm*, where a hearty Reconcilia
being made betwixt them, *Charles* was so dear to
ever after, that he did nothing without his Adv
and Consent; which Friendship continu'd till a li
before the King's Death, when *Charles* having M
ry'd *Christina*, the Daughter of *Adolph*, Duke of *H*
1592. *stein*, the former Jealousie was renew'd in some m
sure in the King, tho' soon ceas'd by his Death, wh
happen'd a few Months after at *Stockholm*.

§. 12. King *John*'s Death having been notify'd
Duke *Charles*, he forthwith came to *Stockholm*, a
Sigismund sent a Messenger to King *Sigismund* in *Poland*, but
the mean while took upon him the Administration
the Government, with the Consent of the Senate, wh
was confirm'd to him by King *Sigismund*. Soon af
he call'd together the *Swedish* and *Gothick* Cler
at *Upsal* (the *Finns* refusing to appear) where the *Au*
burg Confession was confirm'd, and the Liturgy a
Popish Ceremonies lately introduc'd, were quite ab
lish'd. This Decree being approv'd of by the Estat
they also made another, wherein it was declar'd, Th
no body should Appeal out of *Sweden* to the King
Poland, and that the King should subscribe these D
crees before his Coronation. But the King unde
standing what had Pass'd at *Upsal*, declar'd, That
being an Hereditary Prince in *Sweden*, would not
blige himself to any thing before his Coronatio
which the Estates look'd upon as an ill Omen for t
Protestant Religion in *Sweden*. Their Jealousie w
not a little augmented, when they saw King *Sigi*
smund come into *Sweden*, accompanied by the Pope
Nunci

Nuncion, by whose Advice the King demanded a Church for the *Roman* Catholicks in each City; that the new Archbishop should be Depos'd, and that he should be Crown'd by the Pope's Nuncio; which oblig'd the Estates to send their Deputies to Duke *Charles*, to desire him to interpose his Authority with the King. *Charles* having in conjunction with the Estates, in vain endeavour'd to persuade the King to a Compliance with the Estates, entred into an Association with them for the Defence of the Protestant Religion, and muster'd his Troops near *Upsal*. The King perceiving them to be in earnest, consented to most of their Propositions, the same morning when he was to be Crown'd, and the Coronation was to be perform'd by the Bishop of *Strengness*. But soon after took a Resolution quite contrary to his Promise, 1594. with an intention to obtain by force what he could not get by fair means. And having sent for some Forces out of *Poland*, he hop'd to terrify the Estates into a Compliance at the next Dyet; but these being back'd by Duke *Charles* and the *Dailkerls*, remain'd stedfast in their Resolution. The King seeing himself *disappointed*, resolv'd, by the Advice of the *Poles*, to leave the Kingdom and the Government in an unsettled Condition, hoping thereby to oblige them to be more pliable for the future. But as soon as the Senators understood that he was sail'd towards *Dantzick*, they in Conjunction with Duke *Charles*, took upon themselves the Administration of the Government, depos'd the King's Governor at *Stockholm* (he being a Papist) and forbid the exercise of the *Romish* Religion. And soon after a Peace being concluded with the *Muscovites*, a Dyet was held at *Sudercoping*, where after the Estates had justify'd their Proceedings in a Letter to the King, the *Augsburgh* Confession was again confirm'd, the Popish Religion abolish'd, all *Swedes* that adher'd to the same, were declar'd incapable of any Employments in the Kingdom; and several other Decrees made against the Papists, and for maintaining the Privileges of the Subject. Then they constituted D. *Charles* once more Regent of the Kingdom, in conjunction with the Senate: And this whole Transaction was publish'd in the *Latin*, *Swedish*, and

German Tongues. This having occasion'd a ge
flight among the *Roman* Catholicks out of *Sw*
King *Sigismund* quickly sent some Commissi
out of *Poland*, to dissuade the Duke from these
ceedings ; but their Dissuasives proving ineffe
he writ a Letter to the Estates, in which he
mitted the whole management of Affairs to th
nate, excluding the Duke from the Regency. I
mean while, some Senators, declined to appe
the Dyet, which was appointed to be held unde
Dukes Authority at *Aboga*. Notwithstanding w
the few Senators and the Estates there present
again confirm the Decrees lately made at *Upsa*
Sudercoping; declaring Duke *Charles* sole Rege
Sweden. But *Niclaco Flemming*, the King's Ge
having lately kill'd a great number of Boor
Duke also gather'd what Troops he could, and
sessed himself first of *Gothland*, and not lon
ter, of the whole Kingdom of *Sweden*, the
Governors, and those of the Senators, that ha
appear'd at the last Dyet held at *Arboga*, flyi
great numbers to the King of *Poland*. King
1598. *mund* then resolv'd to go into *Sweden* in Person
6000 Men; which the Duke being appriz'd of,
together the Estates of the *Gothick* Kingdom at
stena: It was there unanimously resolv'd to mee
King with an Army near *Calmar*. But the
Goths and *Smalander's* having taken up Arms fo
King, and the *Finns* equipped some Ships for his
vice, the former were beat back by the Boors, l
ed by two Professors of *Upsal*, and whilst
Charles was sail'd with his Fleet to reduce the I
which he did with good Success, the King wi
any Oposition, arriv'd at *Calmar*. Several Tr
were then set on foot to endeavour the Settleme
the Kingdom ; which proving ineffectual, both
ties had recourse to Arms. The first Encounter
pen'd near *Stegeburg*, where the Duke's Forces
surrounded, were quickly put to the Rout ; but
ing down their Arms, obtain'd Pardon from
King ; but the Duke soon after having Surp
part of the King's Army at *Strangben*, he k
2000 of them upon the spot, with the loss o

Men only on his side. This Defeat occasioned an Agreement betwixt the King and Duke upon certain Articles, of which the Estates were to be Guarantees; and the King promised to come forthwith to *Stockholm*, to settle the Affairs of the Kingdom, whither he would needs go by Sea, though it was in *October*: but in lieu of sailing to *Stockholm*, directed his Course from *Calmar*, (where he was droven in by contrary Winds) to *Dantzick*. The Duke hereupon called together the Estates of the Kingdom, who having once more constituted him Regent of *Sweden*, at their second meeting, renounced their Obedience to King *Sigismund*, offering at the same time the Crown to his Son *Uladislaus*, in case he would come within 12 Months time into *Sweden*, and be educated in the *Lutheran* Religion, but in case of failure he and his Heirs to be excluded from the Crown. Duke *Charles* thereupon marched against the *Finns*, whom he quickly forced to Obedience, and having made an Alliance with the *Russians*, convened the Estates of the Kingdom in the next following Year at *Sincoping*, where some of the Lords that were fled into *Poland* were condemned of High-Treason, and executed accordingly, and not only King *Sigismund* declared incapable of the Crown, but also his Son *Uladislaus* excluded from the Succession.

1599

1600

Sigismund *deposed.*

About the same time the Duke being assured that the *Eastlanders*, and especially those of *Reval*, were inclin'd to his side, he marched thither with a great Army, and being received very joyfully by the Inhabitants of *Reval*, the *Polish* Governors left the rest of the Places of *Esthland* voluntarily to the Disposal of *Charles*. In *Livonia* he took also several Places of Note without much Opposition, but was forced to raise the Siege of *Riga* upon the Approach of the *Poles*, who retook *Kakenhausen*, and some other Places thereabouts. *Charles* having in the mean time got Notice how the *Poles* had set up the false *Demetrius*, and assisted him against the *Muscovites*, under pretence of being afraid of the Designs of the *Poles* against *Sweden*, desired to resign. But these having first offered the Crown to *John*, King *Sigismund*'s half Brother, who refused to accept of the same, they bestowed

1604. ftowed it upon *Charles*, and his Heirs, e
Charles IX. Females. No fooner was *Charles* declared
he undertook an Expedition into *Livonia*,
received a fignal Overthrow from the *P*
Sigifmund was prevented by the inteftine
ons of the *Poles* to purfue his Victory. T
alfo having flain the falfe *Demetrius*, mad
their Grand Duke, and craved Affiftance
Charles, who fent fome Thoufand Auxili
the Command of *James de la Gardie*,
fuccefsful againft the *Poles*. But in *Liflan*
got the better of the *Swedes* in feveral

War betwixt the Swedes *and* Poles *in* Livonia.

and the *Danes* feeing the *Swedes* engaged
began to make great Preparations for
Mufcovites alfo had delivered their G
Suski up to the *Poles*, and offered that
Uladiflaus, the Son of *Sigifmund*, fo tha
difh Affairs looked with an ill Face at th
Prince *Guftavus Adolphus*, King *Charles*'
not upheld their drooping Courage. Fo
1611. 1500 Horfe not only furprized their chief
in *Blekinyen*, but alfo took from the *Danes*
Oeland and the Caftle of *Borkholm*; and
his Father King *Charles* died at *Nicoping*
Year of his Age.

Guftavus Adolphus.

§. 13. *Guftavus Adolphus* was then fcarc
of Age, but the *Swedifh* Affairs being mu
at that time, it was concluded at the Dy
ping that he fhould take upon himfelf the
tion of Affairs. The new King immediat
all his Care to the *Danifh* War, which w
on but with indifferent Succefs on the *S*
efpecially by Sea, the *Swedifh* Fleet bein
very ill Condition; and the *Danes* having
fides *Calmar*, *Rubyfort* and *Elffesburgh*, two
ble Places in *Sweden*. King *Guftavus* findin
1613. very grievous to the Kingdom, a Peace was
with the *Danes*, the *Swedes* being obliged to
Million of Crowns for thefe 3 Places above.
In the mean while *James de la Gardie* h
managed his Affairs in *Mufcovy*, that the
mong them defired King *Guftavus Adolph*
Brother *Charles Philip* to come into *Mufco*

other Places in *Prussia*, before the *Poles* had Notic
his Arrival. Soon after the *Poles* sent 8000 H
and 3000 Foot into *Prussia*, who formed a Desig
surprize *Marienburg*, but were repulsed with the
of 4000 Men, and were also forced to raise the Sieg
1627. *Meve.* In the next Spring the *Swedish* King inten
to attack *Dantzick*, but having received a Shot in
Belly before one of their Out-works he desisted for
time, but soon after made himself Master of the
Fort. Soon after both Armies encamped at *Dirsh*
where King *Gustavus* did not think fit to attack
Poles in their advantageous Camp, but when t
drew off fell on their Rear and killed them a g
Number of Men. But some Days after attacking
in their Camp he received a Shot in his Left Shoul
with a Musket Bullet. Towards the latter end of
Year a new Treaty being set on foot betwixt the t
Kings, but was soon broke off. King *Gustavus*,
fore his Army went into Winter-Quarters, took seve
Places from the *Poles*, and at the beginning of the Y
next following attack'd a Fort near *Dantzick*, but
repulsed with Loss; and after a smart Engagement w
the *Poles*, wherein 3000 of them were killed, the K
advanced nearer to *Dantzick*, having sent 8 Men
War to block up that Harbour; but the *Dantzic*
with 10 Men of War attacked the *Swedish* Squadr
killed the *Swedish* Admiral *Nils Sternshield*, took
Ship, forced their Vice-Admiral to blow up his o
Ship, and put the rest to Flight. King *Gustavus*
ving detached 1000 Foot Soldiers they surprized M
burg, a Magazine of the *Poles*, where they took n
of their Baggage and 600000 Crowns in Money.
1629. next Year *Herman Wrangel* raised the Blockad
Brodznitz, where 3000 *Poles* were killed, 1000 ta
Prisoners, with 5 Pieces of Cannon, and 2000 W
gons with Provision. But the *Poles* being joined
7000 Imperialists under *Arnheim* encamped near *G*
dentzi, and King *Gustavus* with an Army of 5
Horse and 8000 Foot near *Quidzin*, both Armies
after having met near *Stum* there happened a b
Engagement betwixt them, wherein the *Swedish* H
were first repulsed, but the King coming up in

on soon forced the *Poles* to retreat, and King *Gusta-*
vus endeavouring to cut off their Retreat the Fight
was renewed on both sides with great Fury, so that
he King venturing himself too far, was twice in most
minent Danger of being either taken Prisoner or
ain. In this Action the *Swedes* got 17 Colours and
Standards, the Imperial Forces having received the
reatest Damage. Not long after the *Poles* were again
vorsted in another Engagement. The *Poles* imputed
hese Losses chiefly to *Arnheim*, the Imperial General,
who being a Vassal of the Elector of *Brandenburg*, was
uspected by them to hold a Correspondence with the
aid Prince, and being grown quite weary of the Im-
erial Forces, and withal pestered with Famine and
he Plague, by the Mediation of *France*, *England*, *Bran-*
denburg and *Holland*, a Truce was concluded for 6
Years, by virtue of which King *Gustavus* was to re-
tore to *Poland*, *Brodnitz*, *Wormdit*, *Melsack*, *Stum*,
nd *Dirshaw*; *Marienburg* was committed to the Cu-
tody of the Elector of *Brandenburg*. King *Gustavus*
ept the Castle and Harbour of *Pillaw* and *Memel*, as
lso *Elbingen* and *Braunsburg*, besides all what he was
ossessed of in *Livonia*; so that King *Gustavus Adol-* *Truce with*
hus put a glorious End both to the *Russian* and *Polish* Poland.
War.

§. 14. But it was not long before he performed *German*
much greater Actions in *Germany*, where he had been *War.*
nvited by the Protestants long before, but he being
t that time entangled in the *Polish* Affairs was not at 1626
eisure to engage himself with them. But *Christian* IV.
King of *Denmark* having in the mean while received a
great Defeat from the Imperialists, who since that had
made themselves Masters of the *Lower Saxony*, and got
footing on the *Baltick*. King *Gustavus* pressed the har-
der upon the *Poles* to oblige them to a Peace or Truce, 1628
nd having called together the Estates of *Sweden*, he
epresented to them the Danger which threatned *Swe-*
den from the Imperialists, who had not only got foot-
ng on the *Baltick*, but also made themselves Masters
of a part of *Denmark*; whereupon it was resolved to
meet the Enemy abroad, and to keep him from get-
ing footing on the Borders of the *Baltick*. *Albert*
Wal-

Wallenstein, Duke of *Friedland*, the Imperial
having not long after laid a Design against
of *Strahlsund*, the King, who was then in *Pr*
only sent them some Ammunition, but also en
an Alliance with them, and sent some of his
their Assistance, who were very instrument
fending that City against the Imperialists,
did not think fit to attempt any thing furthe
time, because *Wallenstein* and *Tilly* were wi
siderable Armies not far off. But as soon as t
War was ended, he with all Expedition pre
the next Campaign, and having droven the I
1630 ists out of the Isle of *Rugen*, and settled his
Home, he embarked with 92 Companies of
16 of Horse (which were however considera
mented afterwards by some Regiments raised
sia) and landed the 24th of *June* at *Usedom*.
his Arrival the Imperialists having left thei
thereabouts and at *Wollin*, he re-embarked h
ers, with a Train of Artillery, in some smal
and directly took his Course towards *Stetin*,
ving obliged the Duke of *Pomerania* to rec
and his Forces into that City, he made a
Alliance with him. From hence he marched
gard, *Anclam*, *Uckormund* and *Wolgast*, all whi
he took without much Opposition. And whi
Gustavus acted with such Success against the
alists in *Pomerania*, *Christian Wilhelm*, Admi
of *Magdeburg*, (who had been deposed by the
had got again into the Possession of the City
ritories of *Magdeburg*. In the mean while se
giments of *Liflanders* and *Finlanders* arrived u
Command of *Gustavus Horn*, and these bein
by such Troops as were lately come out o
the King left his Camp near *Stetin*, and marc
that Army into *Mecklenburg*. In his Absence th
rialists had endeavoured to force the *Swedi*
near *Stetin*, but were vigorously repulsed, a
return he also beat them out of the furtherm
of *Pomerania* and the *New Marck*, and then
into an Alliance with the Archbishop of *Breme*
George of *Lunenburg*, and *William* Landgrave

Charles Gustavus *lands with his Forces in* Germany.

And at the beginning of the next ensuing Year concluded also the so long projected Alliance with *France*, by virtue of which he was to receive a yearly Subsidy of 400000 Crowns from the *French* King. Having thus strengthened himself, he, notwithstanding the Winter Season, took *Lokenitz*, *Prentzlew*, *New Brandenburg*, *Clempenow*, *Craptow*, and *Leitz*, without much Opposition. *Demmin* also, where the Duke of *Lavilli* was in Garison with 2 Regiments, was surrendred after a Siege of 3 Days, and *Colberg* surrendred after a Blockade of 5 Months. The Emperor in the mean while gave to *Tilly*, the *Bavarian* General, the supreme Command over his Forces, who being an ancient, experienced, and renowned Captain, marched directly to the Relief of *Demmin*, but the Place being surrendred before, he fell with great Fury upon *Kniphausen*, who lay with 2 Regiments of *Swedes* at *New Brandenburg*, which being a Place of no Defence he forced, after a brave Resistance, killing most of the common Soldiers. But perceiving that King *Gustavus* being strongly entrenched, was not to be forced in his Camp, he directed his March upwards to *Magdeburg*, whilst King *Gustavus* marched directly towards *Frankfort* upon the *Oder*, which he took by Storm after a Siege of 3 Days, slew 700 of the Enemies, and took 800, among whom were a great many Officers of Note. About the same time a general Meeting of the Protestant *German* Princes was held at *Leipsick*, where a League was proposed to be made, in Opposition to the demanded Restitution of the Church-Lands. Thither *Gustavus* sent some of his Ministers to demand some Assistance of Men and Money. But the Elector of *Saxony* was very backward, intending to make himself Head of the Protestant League, and in the mean while to take this Opportunity of putting the Protestants in a good Posture, to keep the Ballance betwixt the Emperor and the *Swedes*. King *Gustavus* perceiving that the Protestants in *Germany* were so over cautious, did not think fit to advance to the Relief of *Magdeburg* before he had secured his Retreat, and therefore marched with his Army streight to *Berlin*, and having obliged the Elector of *Brandenburg*,

1631

Alliance made with France.

burg, partly by fair Words, partly by put into his Hands the Forts of *Spandau* a for the Security of a Retreat over the T of the *Havel* and *Oder*, he would have st marched to the Relief of the City of *Ma* the Elector of *Saxony* would have joyned whilst the said Elector made a great many sations, the City was taken by Storm b *Tilly*, who burnt the City, and kill'd most habitants. After this Disaster, King *Gusta* cleared the whole *Pomerania* of the Impe divided his Army, and having sent part of to the Assistance of the Duke of *M* marched with the rest into *Mark*, and en *Werben*, near the River *Elbe*, to observe having received Intelligence of the Kin near that River, was obliged to alter (which he intended to have directe *Saxony*) in hopes to force the King to a B the King surprized and totally ruined T ments of his Horse. Notwithstanding approached near the King's Camp at *We* the King refusing to fight, and he not da tack him in his Camp, he was, for want obliged to march back to his former Cam *merstadt*. In the mean while the Duke o *burg* had, with the Assistance of the *Swedi* aries, driven the Imperialists out of his except *Domitz*, *Wismar*, and *Rostock*, wh they kept block'd up. And about the *James* Marquis of *Hamilton* came with 60 and *Scots* into *Pomerania*, but stood the great stead, most of them dying in the sam several Diseases. *Tilly* seeing that he coul tack the King near *Werben*, marched to from thence to *Halli*, and from thence w Men to *Leipsick*, which he took soon after.

The City of Magde-burg *taken by the Imperialists* May 10.

The Elector of *Saxony* being thus put to a nonplus, was then forc'd to desire King *Gustave*, to joyn his Army, which lay encamp'd near *Torgawe*; the King who had foreseen what would befal him, being already advanc'd near *New Brandenburgh*: Now after having entred into certain Articles with the Elector, he pass'd the River *Elbe*, near *Wittenbergh* with 13000 Foot, and 9000 Horse, and joyn'd the Elector near *Dieben*. Here a Council of War having been call'd, the King, who did not expect that the old cunning General would give them any opportunity to Fight, was for acting very cautiously; but the Elector of *Saxony*, was not for protracting the War, telling them, that if the rest refus'd, he would fight alone: This Opinion at last prevail'd, and the King then thought it most convenient to attack him immediately, before he could be joyn'd by the General *Altinger* and *Tieffenbach*, Thereupon the Command of the right Wing being left to the King, and that on the left to the Elector, they march'd towards the Enemy. *Tilly* was no sooner inform'd of their Approach, but he began to fortifie himself in his Camp near *Leipzick*. But *Pappenheim* and the rest of the Imperial Generals, trusting too much to the Bravery of their *Veteran* Bands, and despising the new Levies of the *Saxons* and the *Swedes*, would by all means Fight the Enemy in the Plains near *Braitenfield*, where *Tilly* lost the Fruits of his former Victories. He had possess'd himself of all the rising Grounds; but King *Gustavus*, who had put some Battalions of Foot, among the Squadrons of Horse, by wheeling about, having oblig'd the Imperialists to open their left Wing, *John Banner* fell in among them and put them into Confusion. But the greatest force of the Imperialists fell upon the *Saxons*, whose Infantry and some of the Militia Horse were put to flight, which oblig'd the King to fall with his Wing upon the Enemy's Horse that were in pursuit of the *Saxons*, whom he quickly forc'd to fly. But the Imperial Infantry still held out, till *Gustavus's* Horse, with some Squadrons of the right Wing fell into their Flank; and the King about the same time having taken all the Enemy's Artillery, they were put to an entire Rout, leaving 7600 Men dead upon the spot, besides what was kill'd in the pursuit, and 5000 Prisoners that took Service under the King. *Tilly* himself, who refus'd Quarter, was likely to have been kill'd by a Captain of Horse, if *Rodulph Maximilian*, Duke of *Saxon*

Battle near *Leipzick*, 7 *September*.

Lauenburgh, had not deliver'd him by ſhooting the Captain through the Head. The *Swedes* loſt 2000 Men; moſt of them Horſe; and the *Saxons* 3000. However, the *Saxons* quickly retook *Leipzick*, whilſt the King march'd towards *Merſeburgh*, where he cut to pieces 1000 of the Enemies, and took 500 Priſoners. Then it was reſolv'd at a Council of War held at *Halle*, not to follow *Tilly*, who was retir'd towards the River of *Weſer*, but to carry their victorious Arms into the Emperor's Hereditary, and other *Roman* Catholick Countries. Purſuant to this Agreement, the King march'd towards *Erffurt*, (where *William* Duke of *Weimar* was receiv'd without oppoſition, and from thence into *Franconia*, where he took *Koningſhofen*, and *Sweinfurt* without any oppoſition, and the Caſtle of *Wurtzburgh*, after ſome Reſiſtance. In the mean while *Tilly* the Imperial General having been reinforc'd by ſeveral Troops, was march'd toward the River of the *Tauber*, to cover the *Bavarian* and the Emperor's Hereditary Countries on that ſide; but in his March, the *Swedes* falling into his Rear, cut off four entire Regiments. The King having then made an Alliance with the Marquiſs of *Anſpach*, march'd towards the *Rhine*, ſurpriz'd *Hanaw*, *Frankfort* on the River *Mayn* ſurrendring voluntarily, and having poſſeſſed himſelf of the whole Country of *Ringaw*, directed his March into the *Palatinate*, then in the Poſſeſſion of the *Spaniards*. Soon after entring into the *Bergſtrate* he took *Gerſheim*, and paſs'd the *Rhine* near *Stockſtadt*, having defeated the *Spaniards* that would have diſputed his Paſſage. The Garriſon of *Mayence* ſurrendred upon Articles, and *Landau*, *Spires*, *Weiſenburgh*, and *Manheim*, fell ſoon after into the King's Hands. *Roſtock* alſo and *Wiſmar* having in the mean while ſurrendred, the *Baltick* Sea-Coaſt was clear'd from the Imperialiſts, and the Members of the Circle of the *Lower Saxony*, at an Aſſembly held at *Hamburgh*, had reſolv'd to levy 6000 Foot, and 500 Horſe for the Defence of that Circle. The Elector of *Saxony*, in the mean while having refus'd the Offers made to him by the *Spaniſh* Ambaſſador, had ſent his Army under the Command of Lieutenant-General *Arnheim* into *Bohemia*; where among other places, they took the City of *Prague*; but conceiving a Jealouſie againſt the King (whom he ſuſpected to aim at the Imperial Crown) he could not be prevail'd upon to march further into *Moravia* and *Auſtria*. The Imperial Court now reſolv'd solv'd to give the supreme Command of the Imperial Forces to *Wallenstein*, who being an old experienc'd Soldier, and in great Authority among the Soldiers, had besides this, gather'd such Riches, that he was able to raise an Army at his own Charge. Accordingly *Wallenstein* rais'd an Army of 40000 Men against the next Spring. But whilst these Preparations were making at *Vienna*, the King's 1637. Forces, notwithstanding the Winter Season, having beaten the *Spaniards* upon the *Moselle*, had taken *Creutznack*, *Braunfels*, *Kobenhausen*, and *Kirchbergh*; and the King having left the supreme Direction of Affairs on the *Rhine* to *Axel Oxenstirn*, he himself towards the Spring march'd into *Franconia*. And *Tilly* at his approach, retiring on the other side the *Danube*, the King possess'd himself of all the Places along that River as far as *Ulm*, from whence he march'd towards the River of *Lech*, where *Tilly* had entrench'd himself in a Forest on the other side of that River. Here General *Tilly* being wounded by a Cannon-Bullet, of which he died in a few Days after at *Ingolstadt*. His Army left their advantageous Post, and the *Swedes* having cut 1000 of them in pieces in their Retreat, march'd straightways into the Country of *Bavaria*, where they took Possession of *Rain*, and *Newburgh* upon the *Danube*. *Augsburgh* surrendred without much Resistance. But their design upon *Ingolstadt* and *Ratisbon* miscarry'd; for they were repuls'd at the first, where the King's Horse was shot under him, and *Christopher*, the Marquiss of *Baden* kill'd by his side; and the latter the Elector of *Bavaria* had secur'd by throwing some of his Forces into the Place. Upon this the King returning into *Bavaria*, put that Country under Contribution, and the City of *Munick* open'd its Gates to him. In the mean while General *Wallenstein*, having left the Elector of *Bavaria* a while to shift for himself, had driven the *Saxons* out of *Bohemia*, by the Treachery of their General *Arnheim*, who was an utter Enemy to King *Gustavus*, and the Imperialists under Lieutenant-General *Pappenheim*, had made considerable Progresses in the Circle of the Lower *Saxony*. General *Wallenstein* being join'd by the Elector of *Bavaria*, King *Gustave* encamp'd under *Neurenbergh*; whereupon *Wallenstein* made a shew as if he would turn his Arms against the Elector of *Saxony*, thereby to draw the King out of his advantageous Post near that City; but the King remaining in his Post he march'd towards him, spreading his Cavalry all round about, which occasion'd a great scarcity of Forage in the King's Camp, but as for Provisions he was sufficiently supply'd from *Nurembergh.* Whilst the King was reduc'd to these Straits, he receiv'd a Reinforcement of 15000 Foot, and 10000 Horse from several Places; so that now being superior in number, he attack'd *Wallenstein* in his Camp, who being strongly entrench'd, repuls'd the *Swedes* with the loss of 2000 Men. In the mean time the Imperial General *Pappenheim* had beat the *Hessians* near *Volckmarsen*, had forc'd the Duke of *Lunenbergh* to raise the Siege of *Callenbergh*, had beat General *Baudiss* from before *Paterborn* and *Hoxter*, had reliev'd *Wolffenbuttel*, and taken *Hildersheim*, from whence he was march'd into *Thuringia*, to joyn *Wallenstein*. Whilst on the other hand the *Saxons* had entred *Silesia* with an Army of 16000 Men, where meeting with no Opposition, they might have carry'd all before them, if their General *Arnheim* had not been treacherous. The King therefore, not to lose any more time, having put a strong Garrison into *Nurembergh*, resolv'd to send part of his Army into *Franconia*, and with the main Body to return towards the *Danube* into *Bavaria*, where he had taken several Places on the River of *Lech*. But whilst he was carrying on his victorious Arms among the *Roman* Catholicks, frequent Messengers were sent to him by the Elector of *Saxony*, craving his Assistance against *Wallenstein*, who was with all his Forces entred into *Misnia*. The King, though he had great reason to be dissatisfy'd with the Elector, yet fearing he might be forc'd to make a separate Peace with the Emperor, if he did not come to his Assistance, left some Forces in *Bavaria*, *Swabia*, and *Alsatia*, (where *Frankendale* was surrendred to them,) and himself march'd with the Army towards *Misnia*. Being arriv'd at *Naumburgh*, he receiv'd Information, that the Enemy had detach'd *Pappenheim*

Battle near *Lutzen*. *Nov. 6.*

with some Forces upon some Design. Having therefore resolv'd not to stay for his Conjunction with the Duke of *Lunenbergh*, but to fight the Enemy before he could be rejoyn'd by *Pappenheim*. He march'd to the great Plains near *Lutzen*, where a most bloody Battle was fought betwixt them, in which the *Swedish* Infantry fell with such Fury upon the Imperial Foot, that they routed them, and made themselves Masters of their Cannon. But the *Swedish* Horse being stopt by a broad Ditch, (that was cut cross the Plains for the conveniency of the floating of

Wood)

Wood) the King put himself at the Head of the *Smaland* Regiment of Horse, and thus furiously advancing before the rest, being only accompanied by *Francis Albert*, Duke of *Saxon Lauenburgh*, and two Grooms, he there lost his Life. Concerning his Death there are different Opinions, but the most probable is, that he was shot by the said Duke of *Lauenburgh*, who was set on by the Imperialists that had their only Hopes in the King's Death. The *Swedes* were so far from being dismay'd at the King's Death, that they fell with greater Fury again upon the Enemy, whom they routed on all sides. The Imperialists being re-joyn'd by *Pappenheim*, rally'd again; but *Pappenheim* having also been kill'd, they were routed a second time, leaving an entire Victory to the *Swedes*; which was nevertheless dearly purchas'd by the Death of so great a King. King *Gustavus Adolphus* kill'd.

§ 15. The Death of this great King caus'd great Alterations in *Europe*; the Imperialists being now in no small Hopes that the *Swedish* Affairs would now sink under their own Weight, and with that Prospect made great Preparations against them the next Campaign. The Protestants in *Germany* were by his Death divided into several Factions, and the *Swedes* overwhelm'd with Troubles, his Daughter *Christiana* being then but six Years of Age. Nevertheless, having setled their Affairs at home, and committed the Administration of the Kingdom to the five chief Officers of the State, the chief Management of the Affairs in *Germany* was committed to the Care of the Lord Chancellor *Oxenstiern*, who having been sent by the King's Order into the higher *Germany*, receiv'd the sad News of his Death at *Hanau*. The Chancellor did not so much fear the Power of his Enemies as their Constancy and unanimous Resolution, whereas the Protestants were not likely to follow his Directions after the King's Death; nevertheless he thought it not adviseable to ruin at once the Protestant Cause, and the Interest of *Sweden*, but rather to endeavour, by a brave Resistance, to obtain an honourable Peace. Having therefore sent some Regiments back into *Sweden*, he divided his Army, and sent 14000 Men under the Command of *George* Duke of *Lunenburgh* into the lower *Saxony* and *Westphalia*, the rest were order'd into *Franconia*, and some Forces were also detach'd towards *Silesia*. These Forces acted with good Success against the *Christiana* 1631.

Imperialists especially in *Westphalia*, where the Duke of *Lunenburgh* took several Places, defeated the Earl of *Mansfield* near *Rinteln*, and besieg'd the City of *Hamelen*. But in *Silesia* there being a Misunderstanding betwixt the *Swedish* and *Saxon* Generals; these left the *Swedes* in the lurch, who were at last miserably beaten by the said *Wallenstein*. But in all other Places they had better Success, and the Duke of *Lunenburgh* had also retaken the strong City of *Hamelen* by Capitulation, after having defeated 15000 Imperialists that were coming to its Relief, whereof 2000 were kill'd upon the spot, and as many taken Prisoners. Thus the *Swedish* Army were every where flourishing but in *Silesia*; nevertheless the Burthen of the War grew heavier upon them every Day, most of their Confederates being grown weary of the War, and willing to be rid of the *Swedes*. Whilst they labour'd under these Difficulties, *Wallenstein* being kill'd by the Emperor's Order, they hop'd to reap some Advantage by this Change: But the Emperor had made the King of *Hungary* (his Son) General of his Army, who having taken *Ratisbon*, and being joyn'd by the *Spanish* Forces that were marching towards the *Netherlands*, besieg'd *Nordlingen*, whilst the *Swedish* Van-Guard intended to possess themselves of a Hill near that City, they were engag'd with the Imperialists, which occasion'd a Battle betwixt the two Armies, and the *Swedish* left Wing being put into Disorder by the *Polish*, *Hungarian* and *Croatian* Horse, was forc'd back upon their own Infantry, which were also put into Confusion, and totally routed, 6000 being slain upon the spot, a great Number taken Prisoners, among whom was *Gustavus Horn*, and 130 Colours lost, besides the whole Artillery and Baggage. After this Battle the whole upper *Germany* being overrun by the Imperialists, and the Elector of *Saxony* having made a separate Peace with the Emperor, the *Swedish* Affairs seem'd to be reduc'd to a very ill Condition, especially since the Elector of *Brandenburgh* also had sided with the *Saxons*, and the Truce with the *Poles* was near expir'd about the same time, which made the *Swedes* very desirous of a Peace; but the same not being to be obtain'd in *Germany*, they were fain to prolong a Truce with the *Poles* for twenty six Years, and to restore to them their so dearly belov'd *Prussia*, and to draw *France* to their Assistance, and to put it in possession of *Philipsburgh*. Thus having in a manner setled their Affairs, the Wars broke out be-

1634. *Aug.* 27. Battle of *Nordlingen*.

Truce prolong'd with the *Poles*.

betwixt them and the Elector of *Saxony*, who offer'd them a Recompence of Money for the Arch-bishoprick of *Magdeburgh*, which the *Swedes* refusing to accept of, there happen'd a sharp Engagement betwixt them near *Allenburgh*, upon the *Elbe*, where, of 7000 *Saxons*, one half were kill'd, and the rest taken Prisoners. Notwithstanding this Advantage, the *Swedes* had no small Obstacle to surmount, since the Emperor was in possession of the whole upper *Germany*, and had besides this, set the Elector of *Saxony* upon their Back, which oblig'd the *Swedes* to take new Measures, and being now left by all their Confederates, they were at liberty at least to act more unanimously, though perhaps with less Force, the Effects of which appear'd soon after; for though the Elector of *Saxony* had the good Fortune to retake *Magdeburgh* from the *Swedes*, yet they soon after reveng'd this loss near *Perlebergh*, where they attack'd the said Elector with a less Number in his fortify'd Camp, and having routed his Army, kill'd 5000 upon the spot, besides what were kill'd in the pursuit; 1100 being kill'd on the *Swedish* side, and 3000 wounded. Having soon after droven the Imperialists out of *Hessia* into *Westphalia*, and regain'd *Erffurt*, they were again in a fair way to get footing in upper *Germany*. They had also in the next ensuing Year several Encounters with the Imperialists and *Saxons*, which prov'd much to their Advantage, *Banner* having defeated eight *Saxon* Regiments near *Eldenbergh*, and soon after 2000 more near *Pegau*; and when the Imperialists thought to have got him with his whole Army into their Clutches near *Custrin*, he got off with great Dexterity, but could not prevent the Imperialists taking several Places in *Pomerania*, as well as near the Rivers of *Havel* and *Elbe*; *George* Duke of *Lunenburgh* having also declar'd against the *Swedes*, who at the same time began to be extreamly jealous of *Brandenburgh*, by reason of his Pretensions upon *Pomerania*. After the Death of *Ladislaus* XIV. the last Duke of *Pomerania*, (who died this Year) an Alliance was concluded betwixt them and *France* for three Years.

War betwixt the *Swedes* and Elector of *Saxony*.

1637.

1638. Alliance with *France*.

The *Swedes* having been somewhat straiten'd the Year before, they now, after having receiv'd fresh Recruits, began to recover what they had lost the Year before, *Banner* having driven *Gallas* the Imperial General back, even into the Hereditary Countries of the Emperor. And *Bernard* Duke of *Weimar* having besieg'd *Rhinfelden*, he fought

twice with the Imperialists, that came to its Relief, and having routed them in the second Engagement, took *Rhinfelden*, *Kuteln*, and *Fryburgh* in *Brisgau*. After this Exploit, having besieg'd *Brisack*, which suffered greatly by Famine, the Place surrendred to the Duke. The Imperialists being thus routed both near the *Rhine*, and in the lower *Saxony*, the Duke and *John Banner* did take a Resolution to carry on the War into the Emperor's Hereditary Countries, and *Banner* march'd straight (after several Defeats given to the Imperialists and *Saxons*) into *Bohemia*, where he in all likelihood might have had great Success, if the untimely Death of Duke *Bernhard*, (who was to joyn him) had not broke his Measures. This Duke being sollicited by the *French* to surrender *Brisack* into their Hands, (which he refus'd) was poison'd by them, and his Army with great Promises and Money, debauch'd to submit under the *French* Command. The Imperialists then growing too strong for *Banner* alone in *Bohemia*, he march'd back into *Misnia* and *Thuringia*, and being joyn'd by the Duke of *Longueville*, who commanded the Army of the lately deceas'd Duke of *Weimar*, and by some *Hessians* and *Lunenburghers*, near *Erffurt*, (which made an Army of 21 Brigades, and 2000 Horse) he would fain have fought the Imperialists, but these avoiding to come to a Battle, the Campaign was mostly spent in marching
1641. up and down the Country. In the beginning of the next ensuing Year, *Banner* had very near surpriz'd the City of *Ratisbon*, where the Emperor and the Estates of the Empire were then assembled, if the Ice, which was by a sudden Thaw loosen'd in the River, had not hindred them from laying a Bridge of Boats. This Design miscarrying, *Banner* resolv'd to carry the War again into *Moravia*, *Silesia*, and *Bohemia*. But the *Weimarian* Forces under the Command of the *French* General having left him, the Imperialists did so closely beset him, that there was no way left to retreat, but through the Forest of *Bohemia*, which was done with all expedition, by leaving behind him Colonel *Slange* with three Regiments of Horse, who after a brave Resistance, were all made Prisoners of War, but sav'd the *Swedish* Army. Not long after died the famous
May 10. *Swedish* General *John Banner*, whose Death caus'd some dissatisfaction in the Army; notwithstanding which they beat the Imperialists near *Wolffenbuttel* two several times, and *Torstenson*, (who was made General) directed his

March

March into *Silesia*, where he took *great Glogau* with Sword in Hand, and a great many other Places, the chiefest of which was *Sweinitz*, where he defeated the Imperialists, that came to its Relief, under the Command of *Francis Albert* Duke of *Saxon Lauenburgh*, who was kill'd himself and 3000 Horse, but was prevented from marching into *Bohemia*. Wherefore having pass'd the River *Elbe* at *Torgaw*, he straightways went to besiege the City of *Leipzick*. But the Imperialists under the Command of the Arch-Duke, and General *Piccolomini*, coming to its Relief, a bloody Battle was fought in the same Plains near *Breitenfield*, where King *Gustavus Adolphus* had obtain'd a signal Victory against the Imperialists. In this Battle the left Wing of the Imperialists having been put in Confusion, the left Wing of the *Swedes* underwent the same Fate; but the *Swedes* left Wing rallying again and falling into the Flank of the Imperialists right Wing, they put them to the rout, 5000 being kill'd upon the spot, and 4500 taken Prisoners. The *Swedes* lost 2000 Men, and had a great many wounded. After the loss of this Battle, *Leipzick* was soon forc'd to surrender, but *Fribergh* defended it self so well, that the *Swedes*, upon the approach of the Imperial General *Piccolomini*, were forc'd to raise the Siege with the loss of 1500 Men. And the *Weimarian* Army under the Command of the *French* General *Gebrian*, was for the most part ruin'd by the *Bavarians*.

1642. Battle fought near *Leipzick*. *Oct.* 23.

In the mean while, the *Swedes* being provoked to a War by the *Danes*, *Torstenson* march'd with great secresie into *Holstein*; beat their Troops in *Jutland* and *Schonen*, and ruin'd their Fleet, and made themselves Masters of the whole Bishoprick of *Bremen*, and the Isle of *Bernholm*; which oblig'd the *Danes* to make a disadvantageous Peace with them at *Bromsebroo*, giving to the *Swedes Jempteland* and *Herndalen*, *Gothland* and *Oesel*, besides other Advantages. *Torstenson* having then made a Truce with the Elector of *Saxony*, march'd again into *Bohemia*, where another Battle was fought near *Janewitz*, betwixt the Imperialists and *Swedes*, wherein the first were routed with the loss of 8000 Men, one half of whom were kill'd, the rest taken Prisoners. The *Swedes* had 2000 Men kill'd. The *Swedes* then march'd through *Bohemia* into *Moravia*, and from thence into *Austria*, where having been joyn'd by *Ragozi*, they were in a fair way of making greater Progresses, if *Ragozi*, who had receiv'd satisfaction from the

War with *Denmark*, 1644. 1645. Peace with *Denmark*.

Empe-

Emperor, had not march'd Home with his Forces. At the same time the *French* under the Command of *Turenne*, having been again routed by the *Bavarians*, *Torstenson* march'd back into *Bohemia*, and left the Supreme Command of the Army to *Wrangel*, who finding the Enemy too strong for him thereabouts, march'd further back into *Misnia*, and from thence towards the *Weser*. But, being not long after joyn'd by *Turenne* near *Giessen*, they attack'd *Ausburgh*, but were forc'd to quit the Siege upon the approach of the Imperialists, who also retook several Places in the Hereditary Countries of the Emperor. Not long after *Wrangel* made a Truce with the Elector of *Bavaria*, which however lasted not long, the said Elector having, upon the Persuasion of the Emperor, broke the same a few Months after, and joyn'd his Forces with the Imperialists.

1648. But *Wrangel* marching early out of his Winter-Quarters in conjunction with *Turenne*, press'd so hard upon the *Bavarians*, that they were forc'd to retire to *Saltzburgh*, leaving a great part of the Country to the Discretion of the Allies.

July 16. About the same time *Koningsmark* surpriz'd the Suburbs of *Prague*, where he got a prodigious Booty in the Imperial Palace, and other Noble-mens Houses, which are all built on that side of the River, but could not take the City, which was defended by 12000 Citizens. And in the mean time receiv'd the News of a Peace being concluded at *Munster*.

Peace made at *Munster* and *Osnabrug*. This Peace had been long in agitation before it was brought to Perfection, the Imperialists having endeavour'd after they saw the *Swedes* recover themselves so bravely after the Battle of *Nordlingen*, to persuade them to a separate Peace, without including the Protestant Estates in *Germany*. But the *Swedes* having refus'd these Offers, seven Years were spent in concerting the Preliminaries, and these being adjusted, the Treaty it self was begun at *Osnabrug* and *Munster*. The *Imperial*, *French*, *Spanish* and *Dutch* Ambassadors, as also those of most of the *Roman* Catholick Estates, and the Pope's *Nuncio*, met at *Munster*, and the Imperial Ambassadors also, and those of most of the Protestant Estates assembled at *Osnabrug*. So that at last a Peace was concluded, by virtue of which *Sweden* got the Dukedoms of *Bremen*, and *Veerden*, the greatest part of *Pomerania*, the Isle of *Rugen*, and the City of *Wismar*, under condition of holding these Countries in Fief of the Empire, with all the Privileges thereunto belonging, and five Millions of Crowns towards the Payment of their Armies. Besides this, they had the Honour of having been Instrumental in re-establishing several *German* Princes in their Territories, and setling both the Quiet and Protestant Religion in *Germany*. The War being thus ended to the great Honour of the *Swedes*, the Queen, who had already taken a Resolution of surrendring the Crown to her Nephew *Charles Gustavus*, would willingly have put an end to the Differences betwixt *Sweden* and *Poland*, which were likely to revive again after the Truce expir'd; but the *Poles* were so haughty in their Behaviour, that no Peace could be concluded at that time. Having therefore setled her Affairs, and reserv'd a certain yearly Allowance for her self, during her Life, she surrendred the Crown to the said *Charles Gustavus* her Nephew, at the Dyet at *Upsal*, where he was Crown'd the same day that she resign'd the Government. *1654. June 6.*

§ 16. *Charles Gustavus* obtain'd at the first Dyet from the Estates, that the fourth Part of such Crown-Lands as had been granted away since the Reign of *Gustavus Adolphus*, should be re-united to the Crown; and having again setled the Military Affairs, resolv'd to force the *Poles* to an honourable Peace. Accordingly he march'd in Person into *Poland*, where after having defeated some that would have oppos'd his Passage, not only the *Poles*, but also the *Lithuanians*, submitted voluntarily, swearing Allegiance to him; and *John Casimir*, their King, was forc'd to fly into *Silesia*. But whilst the King of *Sweden* was march'd into *Prussia*, the *Poles*, with the Assistance of the House of *Austria*, having with the same readiness again forsaken his Interest, fell upon the *Swedes* in their Quarters, of whom they kill'd a great many, especially in *Lithuania*, forcing the rest to seek for shelter in some Strong-holds that were in their Possession. The King having put an end to the Differences betwixt him and the Elector of *Brandenburgh* concerning *Prussia*, in conjunction with the said Elector, march'd back towards *Warsaw*, where he obtain'd a signal Victory over the *Poles* and *Tartars*; and being in the beginning of the next Year joyn'd by *Bogislaw Radzivil*, Prince of *Transylvania*, would in all likelihood have humbled the haughty *Poles*, if the *Danes* had not threatned a dangerous Diversion near Home, and actually denounc'd War against *Sweden*. *1656.*

Charles Gustavus.

The War with *Poland* renewed.

This

War with *Denmark*. 1658. This oblig'd the King to draw his main Army that way, where he not only made great Progresses both in *Holstein* and *Bremen*, but also by a Prodigy scarce to be believ'd by Posterity, march'd over the Ice into the Island of *Thunen*, and from thence to other Islands, and at last into *Zealand*, where he carry'd all before him; which reduced the King of *Denmark* to such Distress, that he was forc'd to clap up a sudden Peace at *Roeshild*, giving to the *Swedes*, *Schonen*, *Halland* and *Bleckingen*, and the Isle of *Bernholm*, besides several other Possessions in *Norway*. But this Peace was of no long continuance; for the King having again conceiv'd a Jealousie at the *Danes*, embark'd his Forces in *Holstein*, and under pretence of going towards *Dantzick*, landed in *Zealand*, and besieg'd *Copenhagen*; Siege of *Copenhagen*. whilst *Wrangel* reduc'd the strong Fortress of *Cronenburg*. But the *Danes* being chiefly encourag'd by their King's Presence, defended themselves bravely, till the *Dutch* Fleet gave them Relief, which oblig'd the King, after having attempted in vain to take it by Storm, to raise the Siege. But the greatest Misfortune befel the *Swedes* in the Island of *Thunen*, Battle in *Tounen*. where being out-numbred by the joynt Forces of the Imperialists, *Poles*, *Brandenburghers*, and *Danes*; 1666. they were totally routed near *Nyborg*, their Infantry being most cut to pieces, and the rest made Prisoners. The King being busie in repairing this loss, was seiz'd with an Epidemical Fever, of which he died on the 23d. of *February*.

Charles XI. § 17. *Charles* XI. being but five Years old when his Father died, the *Swedes* apply'd all their care to obtain an honourable Peace, Peace made with the *Poles*. *May* 3. which was concluded with the *Poles* in the Monastery call'd *Oliva*, near *Dantzick*, wherein were also included the Emperor and Elector of *Brandenburgh*, and King *John Casimir* resign'd his Pretension to the Crown of *Sweden*, and the *Poles* to *Livonia*. *May* 23. Peace made with *Denmark*. In the same Month a Peace was concluded with *Denmark*, much upon the same Conditions, which were agreed on formerly at *Roeshild*; except that the *Danes* kept the Isle of *Bornhelm*, and *Drunthein* in *Norway*. For the rest, the *Swedes* were for preserving Peace with their Neighbours, during the Minority of the King, 1674. The *Swedes* routed by the Elector of *Brandenburgh*. till having broke off the Triple Alliance made betwixt them and the *English* and *Dutch*, they sided with *France* against the Elector of *Brandenburgh*, but the Elector having routed the *Swedish* Army, took all what the *Swedes* were possess'd of in *Pomerania*, as the *Lunenburghers* got into their possession the Dukedoms of *Bremen* and *Veerden*, and the King of *Denmark* the City of *Wismar*, and several considerable Places in *Schonen*: However the *Danes*, being at last routed in two Battles in *Schonen*, the King, after the Treaty of *Nimeguen*, by a particular Peace was put again into the possession of his Countries in *Germany*, very few excepted; and *Denmark* was forc'd also to restore the Places taken from the *Swedes* in *Schonen*. Thus Peace being again setled in *Sweden*, the King marry'd *Ulrica Eleanora*, the present King of *Denmark*'s Sister, since which time the King has chiefly apply'd himself to settle his Military Affairs and Revenues, and to maintain Peace with his Neighbours. 1678.

The Nature and Qualification of the *Swedish* Nation.

§ 18. The *Swedish* and *Gothick* Nation has anciently been famous for Warlike Atchievements, and is very fit to endure the Fatigues of War; tho' in former Times their chiefest Force consisted only in the Boors, till *Gustavus* and his Successors, with the Assistance of some *Scotch* and *German* Officers and Soldiers, introduced such a Discipline, as that now they do not stand in so much need of Foreign Soldiers, except it be to make up the number of Men, wherewith they are not overstock'd, especially since the late great Wars. As in most other Kingdoms of *Europe*, by reason of the multitude of their populous Cities, the Estate of the Citizens is the fundamental part of the State, so is in *Sweden* that of the Boors, who enjoy more Liberty in *Sweden* than in other Kingdoms, and also send their Deputies to the Dyet, where their Consent is requisite to any new Taxes to be levy'd upon the Subjects.

This Nation loves to shew a great deal of Gravity and Reservedness, which if not qualify'd by Conversation of other Nations, often degenerates into Mistrustfulness: They generally are apt to think very well of themselves, and to despise others. They have sufficient Capacity to attain to the first Principles of any Art or Science, but commonly want Patience to attain to the Perfection of it. Their Inclination is not much to Trade or Handy-work, and therefore Manufactures are but little encourag'd among them.

Condition of the Country, and its Strength.

§ 19. The Kingdom of *Sweden* is of a great Extent, but full of great Forests and innumerable Lakes, and the Sea-

Coast surrounded with many Rocks. But deeper into the Country, there are a great many fertile Tracts of Ground; the Forests furnish them with Fuel, and the Lakes with great store of good Fish, which also contribute much to the easie Transportation of the Native Commodities from one Place to another. The Country produces Corn sufficient for its Inhabitants, neither is there any want of Cattle or Horses. *Sweden* produces more convenient Mines of Copper and Iron than any other Kingdom in the World, being surrounded with Woods and Rivulets. There is a Silver Mine in *Westmanland*. *Finland* brings forth Pitch and Tar, and Deal; and *Wermeland* good store of Masts. The Native Commodities of *Sweden*, are Copper, Iron, Tar, Pitch, Masts, Boards, *&c.* In lieu of which, *Sweden* receives from abroad, Wine, Brandy, Salt, Spices, Cloaths, Silk and Wollen Stuffs, fine Linnen-Cloath, *French* Manufactures of all sorts, Furs, Paper, and such like, all which in some Years surpasses in Value the Commodities fit for Exportation here. To recompence this, Navigation and Commerce has been encourag'd of late Years among the Natives and several sorts of Manufactories, whereof those made of Copper, Iron and Brass, would questionless turn to the best Account, if Artists were duly encourag'd to settle themselves in this Kingdom, Copper and Iron being the Foundation of the *Swedish* Commerce abroad.

APPEN-

APPENDIX:

Containing an

INTRODUCTION

TO THE

HISTORY

Of the Principal

Sovereign States

OF

ITALY,

VIZ.

Venice,	*Florence,*
Modena,	and
Mantua,	*Savoy.*

LONDON:
Printed, for *Benj. Tooke*, at the *Middle-Temple-gate Fleet-street*; *Daniel Midwinter*, at the *Three Crowns*, and *Maurice Atkins*, at the *Golden-Ball*, in St. *Paul's* Church-yard. 1711.

...PENDIX:

Containing an

...RODUCTION

TO THE

...STORY

Of the Principal

...ereign States

OF

...ALY.

VIZ

...ia,		Florence,
...ena,		and
...tua,		Savoy.

LONDON:
... Tooke, at the Middle-Temple-gate Fleet-street;
...ers, at the Three Crowns, and Edward Atkins, at
..., in St. Paul's Church-yard. 1711.

APPENDIX.

VENICE.

§ 1. THE first Inhabitants of the Isles of the *Lagunes*, amongst which *Venice* is now seated, are by some said to come from *Vannes* in *Britany*, called by *Cæsar Veneti*. Others derive 'em from the *Heneti*, who after the Destruction of *Troy*, came with *Antenor* into *Italy*, and landing in those Marshes of the *Adriatick* Sea, inhabited the adjacent Country. But without entring into that Dispute, this is certain, that they were only Inhabited by poor Fishermen till the beginning of the fifth Century; at which time, the *Rialto* being declared a place of Refuge, by the *Paduans* who were Lords of the Islands of the *Lagunes*, the Conveniency of a safe Retreat in a time of Calamity and Distress, gave rise to this Republick, that has since prov'd the Ornament of *Italy*. 'Tis well known that after the Emperor *Constantine* the Great had remov'd the Seat of the Empire to *Constantinople*, *Italy* was afflicted with a long chain of Misfortunes, and frequently plagu'd with the Invasions of the *Barbarians*. And 'twas the misery and desolation that the *Goths*, *West-Goths*, and *Huns*, made one after another in the space of half a century of Years, that put the Inhabitants of the Country adjacent to the *Lagunes*, under a necessity of flying to take shelter in these Marshes, where, after they had felt the Benefit of a safe Protection from such dismal Inundations, they settled, and by degrees formed a very Potent and well constituted Republick. Upon the first Invasion of the *Goths* under their King *Radagaisus*, in the Year 407, the Neighbouring Inhabitants of the *Terra firma* resorted thither with their Goods and Treasure; but soon after, upon the defeat of

The Nativity of the Republick of Venice.

Radagaisius by the two Generals of the Emperor *Honori* they returned to their Habitations. But in the Year 4 the Incursions of the *West-Goths* under *Alarick*, and t horrible Ravages they committed all over *Italy*, made t same People betake themselves to the Sanctuary that h protected them but six Years before. And *Alarick* maining longer in *Italy* than *Radagaisius*, they then beg to build Houses of Wood and Reeds for their own Co veniency. At that time the *Paduans* having a Port at t Island of *Rialto* (one of the *Lagunes*) where their Ri then terminated, resolv'd upon making this a considera Place, not only as an *Asylum*, but likewise to protect th
421. Commerce at Sea. To which purpose in the Year 4 the Senate of *Padua* sent three Consuls, and declared *R alto* a place of Refuge to all sorts of People; which occasio ed it to be Peopled in a very little time. But the third I ruption of the *Barbarians* under *Attila* King of the *Hu* compleated at once the misery of *Italy*, and the peopli of *Rialto* and all the Islands of the *Lagunes*; for after t Destruction of *Pavia*, *Milan*, *Padua*, *Aquileia*, and sev ral other famous Cities, the miserable remains of so ma populous Places having now no hopes of returning to the former Habitations, begun to lay the Foundations of the future Abodes in the *Lagunes*, fetching away the Ston and Marble of the demolish'd Palaces upon the *Terra fi ma*, to build themselves others more safe in these Island So in about fifty Years time, both the People of Qualit and those of an Inferiour Degree, were conveniently a commodated according to their respective Conditions.

The first Government under *Tribunes*.

§ 2. The Senate of *Padua*, perceiving the *Rialto* to be come considerable thro' the Multitude of Inhabitants, se down Consuls to govern 'em. Soon after, observing th Inconveniency of Governing so many Populous Islands b Consuls residing only at *Rialto*, they appointed Yearly Tribune for each Island; and a general Council for the joint Concerns, consisting of the respective Tribunes an some of the more noted Citizens. Such as were mo Powerful and Rich in these Islands, were in process time acknowledged as Protectors of the People, by reaso of the occasion they had for their assistance. And in th manner each Island had their particular Tribunes, wh continuing to increase their Authority, came in time t be the little Potentates of these very mutinous Bodies; an 'tis alledg'd that the Family of the *Badouaires* continued successive *Tribunes* at the *Rialto*, from those times to the sinking of that Office. However, under the Government of the Tribunes, this Commonwealth began to build Ships both for War and Traffick, and to enrich themselves by Trade, particularly by Fishing; so that in process of time they came to make a great Figure in the Defence of *Italy*. For in the time of the Emperor *Justinian*, when *Bellisario* besieged the *Gothish* King *Wittige* in *Ravenna*, they fitted out Ships and Boats upon the *Po*, with which they defeated part of the *Gothick* Army. Again, joyning their Ships with those of *Valeriano* Governour of *Ravenna*, they shar'd in the Glory of taking and sinking most of King *Totila*'s Fleet before *Ancona*. By such means they at once rendered themselves considerable, and gain'd respect and favour from the Emperor and his Generals. *Narses*, partly to thank 'em for their good Services, and partly to gratifie his Curiosity in seeing their City and Oeconomy, went in Person to the *Rialto*; and while he was there, the *Paduans* sent an an Embassy to him, to complain that the *Venetians* (so I choose to call 'em, tho' they had not yet received that Name) had usurp'd those Marshes and Islands, which had been theirs time out of Mind. But the Tribune of the *Rialto* made such a Satisfactory reply, that *Narses* declining to enter upon the Merits of the Cause, exhorted the *Paduans* to shew the same Diligence and Loyalty in the Defence of their Country, that the *Venetians* had done. In fine, they continued for near 300 Years under the Government of the Tribunes, without any remarkable Accident, except that the Bishops (afterwards made Patriarchs) of *Aquileia* on the main Land, and of *Grado* one of the *Lagunes*, had frequent Differences relating to their respective Jurisdictions. At last the Calamity of *Italy* still continuing, and Persons of Interest and Fortune still flocking to the *Lagunes* as to an Ark to save them from the Inundation, so that *Rialto* (*Venice*) increased prodigiously in Wealth, Power and Number of Inhabitants; *Luipandro* D. of *Friuli*, whether dreading their growing Power, or envying their Prosperity, animated some of his Neighbours to curb them, and for that end, having provided a competent number of Boats, assaulted *Grado*, *Heraclea* and *Rialto* in the Night, and seiz'd upon some Merchant Men: But the Alarm being given, they were pursued, and most of the Spoil recover'd. However, this Alarm made ſuch an impreſſion upon the Inhabitants of the *Lagunes*, that they began to diſlike the *Tribunitial* form of Government, and judging it neceſſary to enter into a better Method of governing theſe Iſlands, that were grown ſo extremely Populous, thought fit to compoſe a Republick, and to chooſe one amongſt them for Chief. Upon which occaſion, as 'tis recorded, the Patriarch of *Grado*, an Ancient Man of great Learning and Reputation, made a long Oration, importing that Concord was Inconſiſtent with plurality of Heads, and that without fixing the Hinge of their Government upon one Will and one Voice, neither Wealth, nor Populouſneſs, nor Advantage of Situation, nor Valour of Inhabitants, could be improv'd to any Advantage. However, the Tribunes of the twelve Principal Iſlands, recollecting that they could not make ſuch a Change, without infringing the Rights of the City of *Padua* in theſe Places to which they had reſorted for ſafety, ſent Deputies to the Emperor, who was Sovereign Lord of the Country, as alſo to Pope *John* V. to obtain permiſſion of chooſing a Prince, to whom they gave the Name of Duke or Doge.

709. The firſt Doges who were deſpotick.

§ 3. After the Tribunes had obtain'd this Grant, they met in *Heraclea*, (a City of the *Lagunes*, of which there remains only ſome Ruins near the place where the River *Piave* diſcharges it ſelf into the *Lagunes*) and there elected *Paul Lucio Anafeſte* for their firſt Doge A. D. 709, being 288 Years after the proclaiming of the *Rialto* by the *Paduans* for a City of Refuge. Tho' it ſeems but juſt that the *Republick* of *Venice* ſhould date her Nativity from the day of this Election; the *Venetians* do nevertheleſs compute it from the Proclamation as above. And accordingly upon that day do ſolemnize the Nativity of the *Republick*.

Paolo Lucio Anafeſte. 709.

§ 4. *Paolo Lucio*, reſiding in *Heraclea* the firſt ſeat of the *Republick*, made it his firſt Care to reconcile ſuch of the Inhabitants as were at variance, and to appoint Forts and Watches for guarding the Mouths of the Rivers. He ordered every Town to have a certain number of Boats in readineſs upon a Call, inlarged the *Venetian* Dominions, made an Advantageous Peace with *Luipandro*, and cultivated Friendſhip with *Ariperto*, King of *Lombardy*. But the moſt Memorable of all his Actions, was the reforming of the Laws, and digeſting them in ſuch a conciſe plain

Me-

Method, that every Man might be his own Lawyer, without having recourse to Mercenary Council. Imperial Laws, they had none, and their Municipal Written Laws were very few; so that where these were not express, they were determin'd by the natural Principles of Equity and Justice. After him was elected *Marcello*, another Citizen of *Heraclea*, far short of his Predecessor in Vigilancy, and Care. To *Marcello* succeeded *Orso*, who first introduc'd the Custom of bringing up the Youth to the Exercise of Arms, and rais'd the Reputation of his Country by reinstating *Paolo*, the Grecian Emperor's Captain, in his Government of *Ravenna*; but was murthered by the People for his Cruelty, or else for being deem'd the Author of an unhappy Quarrel between the Inhabitants of *Heraclea*, and those of *Equilo*. Upon his Death, the Patriarch of *Aquileia* took from 'em the Towns of *Messone* and *Centenara*: Tho' afterwards, thro' the menaces of *Gregory* Bishop of *Rome*, he restor'd *Mossone* when he had utterly destroy'd *Centenara*.

Marcello. 717.

Orso. 716.

§ 5. The People being thus weary of their Princes, whose absolute Power easily degenerated to Tyranny, an *Interregnum* of five Years insued, during which, the *Republick* was govern'd by the oldest Knights Annually elected; the Seat of Election and Residence, being then translated to the *Lido* of *Malomoco*, which at that time was become very Wealthy and Populous; not to mention that the uneasie People were dissatisfyed that *Heraclea* alone had enjoyed that Honour so long. This *Lido* of the old *Malomoco* was half a League further into the Sea, than the present *Malomoco*; and is since totally swallow'd up, without leaving the least Appearances where it was. (*Malomoco* continued to be the Place of Residence till *Pepin* visited the *Lagunes*.)

An Interregnum.

§ 6. But after all, the People tyr'd with that Ambulatory Form of Government, came to desire a Doge again; and accordingly *Deodato*, the Son of *Orso*, was Elected at the *Lido* of *Malomoco*; but *Galla* a Citizen of *Malomoco*, put out his Eyes, and for Retribution lost his own, and his Life into the Bargain. The next Doge was *Domenigo*, who strugling for absolute Power was degraded, and had his Eyes put out. Next to him was *Mauritio*, in whose time they assisted *Charlemaigne* in the Siege of *Pavia*, when he

Deodato. 737.

Galla.

Domenigo. 747.

Mauritio. 752.

he took *Desiderio* King of *Lombardy* Prisoner. To him s
Giovanni. 768. ceeded *Giovanni* his Son, who had ruled seven Years joy
ly with his Father, and was afterwards forced to fly
Obelerio. 788. *Mantua* with his Son and Collegue *Mauritio.* (While t
Despotick Power was lodg'd in the Doges, they freque
ly made their Brothers or their Children to be elected
their Collegues or Successors.) The next Doge Elect
was *Obelerio*, in whose time the Difference reviving
tween the Inhabitants of *Heraclea*, and those of *Equi*
both the Towns were destroyed, and the Inhabitants tra
sported to *Malomoco* and *Rialto*. At that time *Pepin*, est
blished King of *Lombardy* by his Father *Charles* the Gre
who had destroyed the Kingdom of the *Lombards*, requi
passage and Provisions of the *Venetians* in order to assa
the Coast of *Dalmatia*, and *Obelerio* leaning to *Pepin*'s i
Angelo Particiaco, or Participatie. 792. terest, was forced to fly to him, *Angelo Particiaco* being
lected in his Room: For the *Venetians* resolv'd that th
would not violate the Ancient Alliance of the *Greek* E
K. Pepin attacks the Republick. perors, to gratify a Stranger; notwithstanding that, *Pep*
being possess'd of *Ravenna*, might have ruin'd their mai
tim Commerce. Upon which, *Pepin* irritated, took sev
ral Towns, and forced the Inhabitants of *Malomoco* to fl
to *Rialto* with their Families and Riches; but approachin
to *Rialto*, was defeated (as some say) by *Nicaa* the Impe
rial General, who had been sent both to succour the *Vene
tians*, and to defend *Dalmatia*. Upon which a Peace in
sued between *Pepin*, the Emperor, and the *Venetians*
Some relate that *Pepin* was the Sovereign of all these Pro
vinces, in which Quality, the Republick pay'd him a
Annual Tribute; and resolving to visit the Maritim Island
within the Jurisdiction of his *Demesne*, was refus'd en
trance by the Doge; whereupon he attack'd *Malomoco*
and upon the retreat of the Inhabitants to *Rialto*, imbark'd
his Forces upon Floats to transport 'em thither by Night
but there rose so great a storm that it broke his Floats, and
drown'd most part of his Soldiers. Which bad success so
alter'd the Courage of the King, that he resolved to leave
those People in quiet. But desiring to see the *Rialto*, wa
received there with such Demonstrations of Joy, and so
many Marks of Honour, that in a pure Sentiment of Affection for those People, he threw his Scepter into the Sea
with this Imprecation, *Thus may they Perish who attempt
the Peace of this* Republick. The *French* Writers will
have it, that *Pepin* was receiv'd at the *Rialto*, rather as a
ge-

generous Conqueror, than a Prince ill treated by Fortune, to whom the *Republick* would not have consented, after the loss of his Army, what they had obstinately refus'd when he was in a Condition of getting it by Force. That he exercised all Acts of Sovereignty, leaving several Marks of Liberality to the Doge and the Publick, as likewise discharging the *Republick* of the Tribute they annually pay'd him; and presented them with five Miles of extent on the *Terra firma* against the *Lagunes*, with ample Liberty of Trafficking both by Sea and Land. That *Pepin* observing the Doge to wear no external Mark of Dignity, took off one of the Sleeves of his Vest, and put it upon the Doge's Head in the form of a Bonnet, from whence comes the Original of the Ducal *Horn*, so named from the pointed End of this Sleeve upon his Head. That it was then that *Venice* received the first time this Appellation, for *Pepin* would have the Isle of *Rialto*, with the other Neighbouring Islands, to bear the Name of *Venice*, which was then that of the whole Neighbouring Province to the *Lagunes*, and that the *Rialto* should be from thence forwards the Residence of the Doges and Senate of the *Republick*. *Venice when so call'd.*

§ 7. To *Angelo Particiaco* who rebuilt *Heraclea*, Christening it *Citta Nuova*, succeeded *Giustiniano*, in whose time they assisted the Emperor by Sea, in defending *Sicily* from the *Turks*; and some *Venetian* Merchants brought the Body of St. *Mark* (as 'tis said) from *Alexandria*, upon which the Church of St. *Mark* was founded, and that Saint made Patron of the City. The next Doge was his Brother *Giovanni*, who warr'd with *Narona* in *Dalmatia*, took *Veglia*, an Island upon the Coast of *Dalmatia*, beheaded *Obelerio*, and burnt *Malomoco*, because some of *Obelerio*'s old Friends fled thither for Refuge. At last a Conspiracy obliging him to turn Friar, *Gradenico* joyn'd with his Son succeeded, and at the desire of the *Grecian* Emperor, sent 60 Armed Vessels against the *Saracens* that had then landed near *Rome*, which Vessels were all taken or Sunk; upon which the Doge was murdered in Church at the Vespers. This black Action gave rise to the Office of *Avogadori*, for prosecuting Murder and Manslaughter, which is still of great Authority at *Venice*. The next Doge routed the *Saracens* who had taken *Candia* a little before, and insulted the Coasts of *Dalmatia*; and presented the Emperor *Basilio* (who had done him much Honour) with *Giustiniano Participatio.* 810. *Giovanni or John.* 813. *Pietro Gradenico.* 826. A loss at Sea. Office of *Avogadori*, its rise. *Orso Particiaco.* 865.

12 Brass Bells, which are said to be the first that were
Giovanni, Particiaco, 884. ver used among the *Greeks*. His Son and Successor to
Commacchio, and falling sick, and considering he had
Brother for his Collegue that was not qualified for G
Candiano, 890. vernment, generously mov'd the Senate to elect a ne
Duke, who beat the *Slavonians* twice. After the Death
this last, *Giovanni* was chosen again, and after putting
PietroTribuno, 891. end to the *Slavonian* Wars, resign'd. The next Dog
Tribuno, routed the *Hungarians*, after they had defeat
the Emperor *Berengario*, over-run all *Italy*, and approach
so near to *Venice*, that they had master'd *Heraclea*, *Equi*
Orso Baduaro, 915. and *Capo d' Aggere*. His Successor was the first that coin
Money in *Venice*. *Candiano*, the next Doge, conquer
Pietro Candiano, 938. part of *Istria*, defeated *Alberto* Lord of *Ravenna*, who in
terrupted the *Venetian* Commerce, and made the *Slavoni*
Pietro Candiano, 958. *ans* Tributary. He banish'd his Son for his dissolute Life
who was Elected Doge after his Father's Death, notwith
standing he had joyn'd with *Alberto di Ravenna* against hi
Native Country. But the People incens'd by his Conduc
when Doge set fire to his Palace, and kill'd him as he fled
with his Son in his Arms. But the fire they had kindled
was not so soon extinguish'd, as their fury was appeas'd;
for it burnt a great part of the Church of St. *Mark*, with
two other Churches, and above 300 Houses. The three
succeeding Doges resign'd one after another, and turn'd
Friars; and in that time the most remarkable Transaction
was, that the *Venetians* succoured *Bari* (a Maritim Town
in the Kingdom of *Naples*) then besieged by the *Saracens*.
Pietro Orseolo. 987. The next after them, a particular Favourite of the Emperor's, conquer'd *Dalmatia* with the adjacent Islands;
Dalmatia conquer'd. and so was the first that obtain'd the title of Duke of *Dal-
matia* and *Venetia*. After his Death, his Son *Otho*, out of
Ortone Orseolo. 1007. regard to his Father's Merits, was Elected Doge at the
Age of 18. He overcame the City of *Adria*, with the
King of *Croatia*; and falling into the hands of Conspira-
Domenico Flabenio. 1031. tors died in *Greece*. The three succeeding Doges did no-
thing remarkable. The next after them made a Law that
Contarini. 1042. no Doge should have a Collegue. His successor reduc'd
Zara a Maritim Town in *Dalmatia*, that had rebell'd,
worsted *Roberto Guistando* in *Puglia*, and rebuilt the City
of *Grado*, that had been half destroyed by the *Patriarch* of
Dominico Sylvio, 1068. *Aquileia*. To him succeeded *Domenico Sylvio*, a Man of
greater Reputation and Honour than any of his Prede-
cessors, who married the Emperor *Nicephorus*'s Sister, and
upon

upon the ill success of his Army, against Robert Duke of Puglia and Calabria, was deposed. His Successors Army *Vitale Faletro,* was worsted in the same Cause, but prov'd very successful *1082.* in Dalmatia. The next Doge was Vitale Michele, a Person *Vitale Michele, 1095.* admirably well versed in Naval Affairs, in whose time the Venetian Navy was reckon'd 200 Sail of Arm'd Ships and Galleys; which being sent into Asia upon the holy War, under the Command of his Son, took 22 Galleys from the Pisans near Rhodes; and afterwards took Brundizi and several other places in those Seas. His Army had good Success against the Infidels, and master'd Smyrna, Soria and Jerusalem. After him Ordelaffo Faletro was created Duke, *Ordelaffo Faletro, 1098.* in whose time they assisted again in the holy Wars; a great part of Venice was burnt down by an Accidental Fire; and the Paduans, after being soundly beaten, came to an accommodation with the Venetians about their Limits, by the Mediation of the Emperor. This Duke reduc'd Zara upon a new Rebellion, and gloriously repulsed the Hungarians in Croatia. But upon their second Invasion was kill'd in Battle; upon which, his Army giving way, the Venetians were forced to sue to the Hungarians for a Truce, which they obtain'd with much ado for five Years. The next Doge upon the Sollicitation of Pope Ca- *Domenico Michelo, 115.* lixto went with 200 Sail and reliev'd Joppa, then besieged by 700 Sail of Infidels. Pursuing his Victory, he took Tyre, and gave it to the Patriarch of Jerusalem. Emmanuel Emperor of the Greeks alarm'd at his Victories, injoyn'd him to make no farther Progress. Upon which the Doge turning his Arms against the Emperor, took the Islands of Scio, Rhodes, Sannos, Metellino and Andre. His Successor *Pietro Polano, 1130.* conquer'd the City of Fano, and defeated the Armies both of Pisa and Padoua. He recover'd Corfu for the Emperor, and over-run and sack'd all Sicily, in opposition to Roger *Domenico Morosini, 1147.* Duke of Puglia. The next Doge made Pola and Parenzo Tributary; and obtain'd from William K. of Sicily divers *Vitale Michele, 1154.* Privileges in the way of Trade. The next to him was Vitale Michele, in whose time Verona, Ferrara and Padoua, at the Instigation of the Emperor Frederick Barbarossa, did no small damage to the Venetians. But he took the Patriarch of Aquileia Prisoner, and made him Tributary. The Emperor having taken from the Venetians, Spolato, Trau and Raugia in Dalmatia, he made Head against him and recover'd them; but upon the perswasion of the Governour of Negropont, concluded a Peace with the Emperor; for

for which, and for bringing home the Plague in his Army, the *Venetians* kill'd him at his return. Some say, that this Sickness fell upon his Army before *Constantinople*, by reason of the Waters which the Emperor *Emmanuel* had caus'd to be poysoned.

The Despotick Power Limited.

§ 8 From the first Election of *Paolo Lucio*, *A. D.* 709. to the Death of *Vitale Michele*, *A.* 1171. the Doges reign'd with an absolute Authority. The whole Body of the People was their Electors, and as Tyranny is frequently usher'd in by Confusion and Tumult, so the Doges being once Elected by the People, they acted as Monarchs, were sole Masters of their own Council, and accountable to none for their Administration. In short, they had a *Despotick* Power both in Peace and War. And this perhaps was the occasion of the frequent Insurrections, and Conspiracies of the People, who oftentimes murdered their Dogues, there being no other way provided for redressing the grievances of Tyranny, but the Justice of the Mob. In short, the absolute Authority of the Prince having oftentimes exposed the State to many dangerous Accidents, and the Tumultuary Elections of the People frequently ending with the greatest Inconveniencies. The Principal Citizens met together upon the death of their Prince *Vitale Michele*, to consult how they might prevent those Disorders before they proceeded to the Election of a new Doge. To which purpose they devolv'd the Power of Election upon a Council of Eleven (some Writers say ten) Persons of Probity, who retiring into the Church of St. *Mark*, Elected *Sebastian Ziani*. And to take for the future from the People, the right they had of choosing the Doge, and at the same time to moderate the great Authority of the Prince, they Establish'd an independant Council, from which should be drawn by Election, the Electors of the Doge. An alteration of this Consequence that establish'd an entire new Method of Government, would without dispute have caused a Revolution in the State; if in imitation of the Ancient Government of *Rome*, they had not pleas'd the People, by allowing them in exchange the Liberty of nominating twelve Tribunes, whose consent should be necessary to the Validity of the Prince's Orders. Those Tribunes, who were two in each of the six Wards of the City, had moreover a right of choosing every Year, at the Feast of St. *Michael*, Forty Persons out of each Ward or Quarter, to com-

compose the great Council they then establish'd, consisting of 240 Citizens, chosen without distinction, out of the three different Estates, *viz.* Nobility, Citizens, and Tradesmen. As this Council was to be renewed every Year, so every one was to be of it in his Turn, or at least had the right of pretending to it.

§ 9. *Zebastian Ziani*, the first Doge upon this new Method of Government, siding with the Pope *Alexander* III. against the Emperor *Frederick Barbarossa*, took Prisoner *Otho*, the Emperor's Son, upon which a Peace insued. *Zebastian* triumphing upon this Naval Victory, first introduc'd the Custom (that every Doge does still observe upon his Election) of throwing among the People Gold and Silver Medals with proper Inscriptions. He thought it necessary to shew this Liberality to the People, as the sweetest Charm, and most proper Remedy to allay their Indignation for being deprived of their Right of Electing the Prince, which they had alone injoyed for several Ages. The Pope rewarded the Doge, with License for him and his Successors to Seal in Lead, to have a Canopy or Ombrella carryed over him, a Wax Taper before him with Trumpets and Standards, and once a Year to espouse the Sea with throwing a Gold Ring into it, all which Ceremonies the *Venetian* Dukes use to this Day; and when the Doge throws the Gold Ring into the Sea, he pronounces these Words. *Desponsamus teo Mare, in signum veri & perpetuii Dominii.* Some *Historians* insinuate, that tho' the Command of the *Adriatick* Sea belonged to the *Venetians* by the Right of Conquest and Arms, yet it was the Pope that gave the *Venetians* the actual Soveraignty of it. But 'tis certain that the Commonwealth does not at all found their Right upon the Pope's Gift. The next Duke did little remarkable, but turn'd Friar. The next after him excluded *Verona* from Trading with *Venice*, upon which, *Verona* stop'd their Passage upon the *Adige*. He humbled *Pisa*, made all *Istria* Tributary, recover'd *Zara*, and put *Dalmatia* under Contribution. Joyning his Army with the *French*, he took *Constantinople*, and restor'd *Isaac*, and his Son *Alesso* to the Empire; and the latter being murder'd, retook it again from the Usurper, upon which the *Venetians* and the *French*, divided the Empire between them, *Baldewine* representing the latter, and *Morosini* the former, with the Title of Patriarch, who annexed *Candia*

Zebastian Ziani, 1171.

Arrigo or Henry Dandolo, 1194.

They take *Constantinople.*

and the other Islands of the *Jonian* and *Ægean* Sea to the *Venetian* Territories. This Duke dying at *Constantinople* the *Venetians* Elated with their new Empire, began to dispute among themselves, whether they should remove the Seat of their Commonwealth to *Constantinople*, in pursuit of a further accession of Power and Glory: But the Wiser part over-rul'd and carry'd it, that it was better for 'em to trust in the Perpetuity and Situation of *Venice*, that had prov'd to them and their Ancestors so safe a Sanctuary, than to expose the being and Welfare of the *Republick*, to the hazard and uncertainty of an Imperial Seat.

Pietro Ziani, 1203. § 10. The next Doge was *Peter Ziani*, who recruiting his Army in *Greece*, took *Corfu*, *Modon*, *Coron*, *Gallipoli*, *Nassr*, *Paro*, *Melo*, *Erma* and *Andro*; defeated the *Genouese*, made *Negroponte* Tributary, sent a Colony to *Candia*, conquered *Padua*, and at last retir'd to a Monastery. His *Tiepolo*, 1225. Successor rescued *Candia* from the *Greek Corsairs*, rais'd the Siege of *Constantinople*, war'd successfully against *Frederick Barbarossa*; taking *Terma*, *Campo*, *Marino* and *Bestice*, and burning his Capital Ship in the Haven of *Manfredonia*; he recovered *Pola* a Maritim Town in *Istria*, and *Zara* that had so often rebell'd, stipulating from the King of *Hungary*, that from thenceforth he should never lay claim to it. But in his time *Tzelino di Romano* took *Padua* from the *Venetians*, and penetrated into the *Venetian* Marshes as far as St. *Ellero* and the *Bebbe*. After *Tiepolo* came *Morosini*, 1249. *Marino Morosini*, who recover'd *Padua*, while *Tzelino* lay before *Mantua*; for which *Tzelino* in a rage cut to pieces 12000 *Paduans* of his own Army; a piece of Barbarity that Story can't match. This *Tzelino* dying of Vexation soon after, put an end to the cruellest and most Inhuman Race (Originally *German*) that every *Italy*, or perhaps the *Renneri Zeno*, 1250. World saw. The next Doge beat the *Genouese* at Sea, between *Ptolemais* (now *Acre*) and *Tyre*. But *Baldewin* and the *Venetian* Patriarch at *Constantinople* being betrayed by the *Greeks*, and *Paleologo* possessing himself of the City and Empire of *Constantinople*, and afterwards taking many Islands, and extending his Conquest towards the *Morea*, by the help of the *Genouese*: *Zeno* attack'd the *Genouese* again upon the Coast of *Sicily*, and gain'd a notable Victory, which put the Emperor *Paleologo* into such a Consternation, that he sued for a Truce, which he obtained for five Years. In the mean time the charge of the War, and the necessi-

necessity of laying on fresh Taxes, occasioned a Mutiny at *Venice*. After that, *Zeno* fought the *Genouese* again with success. In his Successor's time there was a great Dearth *Lorenzo* of Corn at *Venice*, their Neighbours not suffering any to *Tiepolo*, come to them. Upon this the *Venetians* enacted that all 1267. Merchant Ships passing between the Gulf of *Fano*, and the Mouth of the River *Po*, should pay Toll to them; which prov'd a very profitable Revenge. The *Bologniaus* disputing this Order were beat, and forced to ask Peace, as well as to demolish a Castle at *Primano* on the *Po*, and to grant the *Venetians* free entry into their Rivers. In this Doge's time *Venice*, *Genua*, and *Pisa*, entered into a mutual League by the Mediation of *Philip* King of *France*. Next to him was *Contarini*, in whose time *Istria* revolt- *Jacopo Contarini*, ing at the Instigation of the Patriarch of *Aquileia*, was 1273. reduced by Force of Arms; and *Ancona* besieged for their Depredations, but the Siege was raised upon the Intercession of the Pope. The next Election fell upon *John Dan-* *John Dandolo*, 1281. *dolo*, in whose time the Water in *Venice* swell'd so high, that the City was in a manner drown'd; and after that followed a terrible Earthquake. Upon the Desire of the Pope, he made Preparations for sailing to *Soria*, in defence of *Ptolemais*; but the King of *Babylon* prevented him, in taking and sacking *Ptolemais*, and leveling it with the Ground. He was the first Duke that coin'd Ducats of Gold.

§ 11. With his Death ended that Method of Govern- 1289. ment, that was introduced at the Election of *Sebastian Zi-* *Peter Gradenigo*. *ani* 117 Years before. For *Peter Gradenigo* being elected Doge, took upon him the entire Alteration of the Form *A fresh Reformation of the Government*. of this Republick, and established a perfect Aristocracy, in fixing the great Council for ever to a certain number and their Descendants, who taking upon themselves for the future the whole Cognisance of all Matters of State, were invested with the Soveraign Administration, exclusive to all other Families. The Method proposed was, that all such as had been Members of the great Council for the four preceding Years should be balloted, and those who had twelve favourable Balls should be Hereditary Members of this new great Council, which is called *Il serrar* *Il serrar del Consiglio*. *del Consiglio*. This Doge, whether to be reveng'd on his Enemies, or totally to abolish the Democracy, managed the Balloting so dextrously, that he excluded all such as

were

were disaffected to him; leaving the Nobility nothing fo their share but a Passive and blind Obedience. Question less, several Noble Families were irritated to see their Inferiors prefered before them, and could not but forese the mighty consequence of this Exclusion. In resentmen of which, *Bagamonte Trepolo*, head of one of the first an Ancientest Families of the *Republick*, joyn'd by the *Quirini*, and some other Illustrious Families, entered into Conspiracy to assassinate the Doge and all his Party. Bu the Plot being discovered, he with several of his Confederates was put to Death between the Pillars of St. *Mark* This gave occasion to the erecting of that Powerful an Formidable Tribunal call'd the Council of Ten; a Cour of such ample jurisdiction in all Criminal Matters, tha it keeps the Nobles and the Commonalty equally in awe In fine, however unjust *Gradenigo*'s innovation may seem with respect to several considerable Families, yet the *Republick* owes its preservation to it, to this day.

Under the Administration of this Doge, the *Venetian* fitted out the greatest Force that ever they had befor Upon his first Accession to the Ducal Dignity, the Truc with the *Genouese* being expir'd, they fitted out a Fleet under the Conduct of *Proveditor Morosini*, who took *Per* and *Castello del Foglie Vecchie*; and wintring there, the were reinforc'd with 25 Galleys, and took the City of *Ca fa* in the *Chersonesus*. In the mean time, the *Genouese* entred the *Adriatick* Sea with a Fleet of 70 Galleys, an tho' they retir'd at first upon sight of the *Venetian* Flee they engaged them afterwards upon the Coast of *Dalmati*, defeated them, and took Prisoner *Andrea Dandolo* Proveditore, who was so galled with the bitter Thoughts of h misadventure, that he dashed his Head against the Plank of the Galley, and so expired. Tho' the loss of this Fle and Army was of great Importance to the *Venetians*, the speedily refitted and reinforced their Fleet, and puttin to Sea again, ingaged the *Genouese* once more in the Streigh of *Gallipoli*, but came off with Disadvantage. Howeve these Victories cost the *Genouese* so dear, and exhauste their strength to that Degree, that they were glad to dro the pursuit of 'em, and clap up a Peace with the *Venetian* No sooner was an end put to this foreign War, than Civ Dissentions arose at *Venice*, a Conspiracy being formed a gainst the Doge and Senate by one *Marino Bacconio*; bu a seasonable discovery being made, he and several of his Accomplices were put to death between the Pillars of St. *Mark*. At the same time the *Venetians* had the Mortification to see the *Padouans* fortify a place call'd *Petabubula*, between *Chiozza* and *Albano*; but in process of time they found means to redress themselves. Sometime after they made sufficient Reprisals upon the *Grecian* Emperor, for a Sum of Money that they had lent him a long time before. For *Belletto Justiniano* being sent with a Gallant Fleet to *Greece*, made himself Master of all that Coast, and returned home fraighted with 15000 Prisoners and a large Sum of Money. At that time *Azo d' Este* was put in possession of *Ferrara* by the Assistance of the *Venetians*, for which *Clement* Bishop of *Rome* excommunicated them, and by Publick Letters gave their Goods as a lawful Prey to all Men; by which they sustain'd no small Loss. To add to their Calamity; towards the latter end of this Doge's Administration, *Zara* renewed its wonted Rebellion. While Preparations were made for reducing that Place, *Gradenigo* dyed, and was succeeded by *Marino Georgio*, who lived but ten Months after. *Marino Georgio,* 1312.

§ 12. The next was *Soranzo*, who reduced the troublesome City of *Zara*; and added to the *Venetian* Dominions, several Towns in *Dalmatia*, particularly *Nona*, *Spalatro*, *Traw*, and *Sebenico*. In the mean time, their Ambassador did so soften the Pope, that the Sentence of Excommunication against them was taken off, and the *Republick* entituled to the Priviledge of a future immunity from such Thunder-claps. The *Genouese* having under the shelter of the above-mentioned Excommunication, made drepredations upon the *Venetians*, these sent out 50 Galleys to make Reprisals, who returned satisfied upon Promise of Restitution. About that time *Candia* rebell'd, but Proveditore *Justiniano* by his wise Conduct quieted the Minds of the People. And the *Padouans*, threatned with Oppression from *Mastino della Scalla*, were preserved by Succours from *Venice*. *Soranzo* dying, was succeeded by *John Soranzo,* 1319.

§ 13. *Francis Dandolo*, in whose time the City was very much straitned for want of Corn, but received a seasonable supply from *Sicily*. This Duke annexed *Polat* and the *Valais* to the *Venetian* Dominions, and defended them from the Power of the Patriarch of *Aquiliea*. The *Turks* having *Francis Dandolo,* 1329.

having expelled the Christians from *Soria*, he sent an Army which engaged and defeated them. After that he waged a successful War with *Mastino*, the head of the Family *della Scala*, who having dispossessed the *Rossi* of *Parma* had made themselves Masters of *Feltro*, *Belluno*, and *Ceneda* which the *Rossi* had formerly taken from the King of *Bohemia*. The War was occasioned by the *Seignori della Scala* building of Fortresses about *Petabubula*: For upon that the *Venetians* entred into a League with the King of *Bohemia*, and most of the States of *Italy*; and their Confederate Army commanded by *Peter Rosso*, Head of the League, routed *Mastino* in two several Battles. Upon which a Peace was made, stipulating to *Charles*, Son of the King of *Bohemia*, *Feltro*, *Belluno*, and *Ceneda*; to *Visconti* Duke of *Milan*, *Bergamo*, and *Brescia*; to the *Florentines* four Castles; and to the *Venetians*, *Treviso*, *Castelbaldo*, and *Bassano*.

Bartholomeo Gradenigo, 1360. § 14. *Dandolo* dying, was succeeded by *Bartholomeo Gradenigo*, in whose time *Venice* was in great danger of being laid under Water, the Water swelling for three days together, four Yards higher than usually. At the same time the *Candians* revolted, but were soon reduc'd. *Gradenigo*

Andrea Dandolo, 1343. dying, his Successor was *Andrea Dandolo*, a mild and wise Prince, in whose time they defeated the *Turks*, and took *Smyrna*: But not long after, were routed by the *Turks* as well as those of *Cyprus* and *Rhodes*. The King of *Hungary* having taken *Zara* by surrender, a considerable Force was sent out, which defeated that King at the Head of 120000 Men, and recovered *Zara*. This Duke procured of the King of *Babylon* free Liberty to the *Venetian* Merchants to trade into *Egypt*; and erected the Office of the three *Auditors*, for easing the *Avogadori*, who had too great a charge upon their Hands. In his time *Venice* was alarm'd with a Scarcity and Dearth of Corn, an Earthquake and a dismal Plague. To remedy the first he sent six Bishops into *Sicily*, two of whom died by the way, but the other four returned with Supplies. The Earthquake threw down three or four Steeples, with divers other Buildings; and the Pestilence laid the City in a manner desolate. Notwithstanding the Weight of this Calamity they raised an Army against the *Genouese*, and at *Carist* near *Negroponte*, the *Genouese* were beaten, but the *Venetians* had soon after the same Fate. At last the *Genouese*

wer

Durazzo, with some other Towns about *Ceneda* and *Trevi-so*, that he had lately mastered. After the Death of *Delfino*, *Lorenzo Celso* then Captain of the Fleet, and Army upon the Gulf, was elected Doge. In his time the Duke of *Austria*, and the King of *Cyprus*, coming at separate times to *Venice*, were splendidly received. *Candia* revolting upon account of the heavy Taxes laid upon them, was at last reduced, but with great difficulty and expence of Blood. *Celso* dying, and *Cornaro* succeeding, *Candia* revolted again, but were reduced and severely punished, the Bishop of *Rome* having granted Pardon and Remission of Sins, to all that should bear Arms on the *Venetian* behalf in that Enterprize.

Lorenzo Celso, 1360.

Marco Cornaro, 1365.

Andrea Contarini, 1367.

§ 16. *Cornaro* dying, the Election fell upon *Andrea Contarini*, who then accepted of the Dignity, tho' he had often refus'd it before. In his time *Trieste* assisted by the Duke of *Austria* rebell'd, and after a very sharp Engagement, were reduced to their wonted Obedience. A new Quarrel was started between the *Carrari* Lords of *Padoua*, and the *Venetians*, about the adjusting of their Confines; and after many Skirmishes in which the *Venetians* had still the better, the *Padouans* drew into their Alliance the King of *Hungary*, the Duke of *Austria*, the *Genouese* and the *Patriarch* of *Aquileia*; and then the *Venetians* were attacked on all sides both by Sea and Land. In the mean time, the *Venetians* in conjunction with the King of *Cyprus*, defeated *Andronico*, the Son of the Emperor *Calojanni* with the *Greeks*, in the *Isle* of *Tenedo*; and worsted the *Genouese* at Sea. And at Land, being assisted by *Bernardo Visconti*, they defeated the *Paduans*, and made themselves Masters of some Towns. But these Advantages were more than sufficiently repaid, when they lost at *Pola* fifteen Galleys in one Engagement, and were gradually dispossessed of *Umago*, *Grado*, *Caorle*, *Chiozza*, *Loreo*, *Le Bebbe*, *Capo d' Aggere*, *Malomoco* and *Paviglia*; and expected every minute to see *Venice* it self attacked. In this forelorn condition, they sent a Chart Blank to *Peter Doria*, then General of the *Genouese* Army. But *Doria* elated with Prosperity, would grant them no other Terms than surrendring at Discretion. And by this his inconsiderate Presumption, he gave the *Venetians* time to recover out of their Consternation, and inspired 'em with fresh Courage and Resolution. In the mean time, *Carolo Zeno*, with the

The War with the *Carrari* of *Padua*, and the *Genouese*.

Venice reduced to great *Straits*.

Ve-

Venetian Fleet scoured the *Levant* Seas, took many Rich Ships of their Enemies, and with the Slaughter of 300 *Genouese* restored the Fortress of *Constantinople* to *Calojanni* the *Grecian* Emperor, and besieged *Pera.* In short, after many signal Victories obtained in those parts, receiving advice of the Danger that *Venice* was in, he returned home, and joyned *Vittorio Pisani*, Commander of the rest of the *Venetian* Fleet. These two Commanders scoured the Seas near *Brondolo*, *Chiozza* and those other Places; and after several Engagements with various Fortune, recovered *Chiozza* by Famine, and took 80 *Paduans* Boats, and 19 *Genouese* Galleys, besides some Ships laded with Salt and a great number of Prisoners. But the Remains of the *Genouse* Fleet thus defeated at *Chiozza*, went from thence to *Trieste*, where they caused a Revolt, and then leaving *Istria* under the Inspection of the *Patriarch* of *Aquileia*, returned again to attempt the Recovery of *Brondolo* and *Chiozza*: But finding that impracticable, they made the like Attempt upon *Pirano* and *Parenzo*, which proving equally successless, they retired to the Haven of *Marano*. In the mean time, the *Venetians* recovered *Bebbe*, and the other Places about them, excepting *Capo d' Aggere* which remained still in the Hands of the *Carraro*. But soon after *Pola* and *Arbe* in the Isle of *Scardona* were taken by the *Genouese*. Upon which the *Venetians* fitted out a fresh Force, which passing to *Istria*, sack'd *Justinopoli*, and besieged *Zara*. In this Enterprize *Vittorio Pisani* died, so that *Carlo Zeno* had then the sole Command; who with 8 Galleys scoured the Coasts of *Dalmatia* again, took 12 *Slavonian* Ships, and infested the *Genouese* River very much; whilst the *Genouese* and their Confederates on the other side sacked *Capo d' Istria*, took *Conigliano*, and *Novale*, *Treviso* surrendred to the Duke of *Austria*, and in the Bay of *Pesaro* 14 *Venetian* Ships were taken by the *Genouese*. Thus did they wage War one upon another, till at last both Parties were tired, and by the Mediation of the Duke of *Savoy*, came to an Accommodation, in which the *Venetians* gave up to the *Genouese* the Isle of *Tenedos*, which had formerly come into their Hands by means of the Emperor *Calojanni*. Not long after the King of *Hungary* being dead, the *Carraro* of *Padoua* took *Treviso* by Force from the Duke of *Austria*, and the Doge *Contarini* died.

Michel Morosini, 1383. § 17. After *Contarini*, a new Doge was elected, who lived but four Months, and did nothing remarkable, unless it be a new Law for the Trial of Murder. His Successor *Antonio Veniero*, was a Person that had formerly distinguished himself by his Prudence and Conduct in the Governourship of *Tenedos*. He observed the greatest niceties of Justice, insomuch that a Complaint being lodged against his own Son for being guilty of some Indecencies before a Man's Door, with whose Wife he was inamoured, the Doge sent him to Goal; and the Infection of the Plague having reach'd the Goal, upon which the young Man's Friends interceded for his being removed to another Prison, the Father (with a stubborn Ostentation of Vertue) denied to his own Son the Concessions that would readily have been granted to any other Prisoner, and so suffered him to die in misery. About this time, the *Venetians* entred into a League with *John Galeas Visconti* Duke of *Milan*, and with the Marquis *d'Estè* of *Ferrara*, against *Carraro* of *Padoua*, and so the Territory of *Carraro* was divided between these three Potentates; that is, the *Venetians* had *Treviso*, the Marquis of *Estè* had some Castles that he had lost before; and *Visconti* had *Padua*, *Feltro* and *Belluno*, which with *Vicenza* and *Verona*, that he had got a little before, did so aggrandize the Duke of *Milan*, that he made War with the *Bologneſe* and the *Florentines*. Upon this, all the Neighbouring States conceived such a Jealousy of his Greatness, that the *Venetians*, the *Mantuans*, the *Ferrareſe*, *Carlo*, *Malatesta*, and Robert Duke of *Bavaria*, (to whom the young *Novello Carraro* was fled for Succour) entered all into a League against him; the consequence of which was, that *Verona* was sacked, *Padua* besieged, and the Duke of *Milan* reduced to that Extremity, that he was fain to sue for a Truce, which was granted him for ten Years.

Antonio Veniero, 1383.

Michele Steno. 1400. § 18. After the Death of *Veniero*, *Steno* was elected Doge, in whose time four *Venetian* Galleys richly Laden, were lost in the *Archipelago*. The *Genoueſe* having infested *Soria*, sack'd *Baruiti*, and taken some *Venetian* Ships; the *Venetians* sent out *Zeno* with eleven Galleys, who falling in with the *Genoueſe* Fleet between *Modone* and *Giunchio*, put them to flight, notwithstanding they were double his number. In the mean time, the young *Carraro* (partly

thro'

thro' the Favour of the Venetians) restored to the Dominion of *Padua*, besieged *Vicenza*; which thereupon threw it self into the Hands of the *Venetians*. At the same time, the *Venetians* were mightily dissatisfyed with *Carraro*, upon the Consideration that he was the Person that had instigated the *Genouese* against them, and advised *William Scala* to take upon him the Dominion of *Verona*. And accordingly in pursuit of their resentment they fell first upon *Alberto d' Este* of *Ferrara*, who had joyned with *Carraro* in promoting his Designs; and at last took by open Force *Padua* and *Verona*; and carryed this *Novello Carraro* with his two Sons Prisoners to *Venice*; where they all three were strangled in the Night time. Thus were the tedious *Padouan* Wars put to an end, in which the *Venetians* had expended above two Millions of Ducats; and they were so overjoyed with their Conquest, that forgetting all their vast Charge, they triumphed with Festivals and Bonfires, till they set the top of St. *Mark*'s Steeple on fire; which was afterwards rebuilt and gilded over at no small cost. But tho' they had thus happily put an end to the heavy *Paduan* Wars, they did not long enjoy the repose of Peace: For *Ladislaus* King of *Naples* and *Hungary* fell upon them in *Dalmatia* and took *Zara*; which they redeemed of him for the Sum of 100000 Ducats, and clapped up a Truce for five Years. *Steno* dying, *Mocenigo* was elected, who reformed some Offices in the *Rialto*, recovered some Towns in *Friuli* that the *Hungarians* had taken in the former War, and was the Author of the rebuilding of the Palace of St. *Mark*, making a voluntary offer of 1000 Ducats, which by an ancient Law were a Penalty fixed upon the Person that should first motion the altering of the Form and Structure of that Palace.

The Venetians conquer Padua.

§ 19. To *Mocenigo* succeeded *Foscaro*, who upon the solicitation of the *Florentines*, entered into a League with them against *Philip* Duke of *Milan*, and sent General *Carmignuola* to take *Brescia*, which he did; while the *Florentines* under the command of *Nicholas d' Este*, Marquis of *Ferrara* ravaged the *Genouese* Territories, and carried off a great Booty. Upon this, Duke *Philip* fearing least the Country of *Romagnia* should return to the Hands of the *Florentines*, delivered it into the Hands of the Legate of *Bononia*, for the use of the Church of *Rome*; and by the Mediation of the same Legate, obtained a Peace at *Ferrara* af-

Francis Foscaro. 1424.

Notwithstanding this Peace, the Duke of *Milan* galled with the loss of *Brescia*, without ever dismissing his Army fell more hotly upon the *Venetians* than before, tho' with no better Success; for, after much treasure spent to no purpose, instead of having the first Peace confirmed with the loss only of *Brescia*, he was obliged to buy a second at the expence of giving up *Bergamo*. But not long after *Philip* encouraged with the Money, and large Offers to the *Milanese*, violated against the Articles of the Treaty and invaded the *Mantuan* Territory. One would not have thought that after the Duke of *Milan* had smarted so severely before, he would have offered another Breach: But the natural Inconstancy of that Prince, never suffered him to live at ease. And the *Venetians* on the other hand understanding perfectly well with whom they had to deal made as if they were afraid of his Power, that so they might incourage him to a Rupture, being sure always to gain somewhat by falling out with the Duke of *Milan*. In fine, the *Venetians* and their Confederates took the Field, and managed their Matters so well, by the help of *Nicolaus* Marquis of *Ferrara*, as to sow Seeds of Jealousie betwixt the Duke and his General, *Francis Sforza*. This *Sforza*, who was one of the most renowned Commanders of his time, came thereupon over to the *Venetians*, and with him the Duke's Fortune: For under the Command of *Carmignuola*, they gave the Duke a signal Overthrow near *Terentiano*, taking his Baggage, Plate and Treasure; and if he had pursued the Victory, had gone near to have driven him out of his Dutchy. In fine, after several Agreements and Violations, a full and solid Peace was concluded; by Vertue of which *Bergamo* and *Brescia* were to remain in the Hands of the *Venetians*. The *Cremonese* was to be given to *Sforza* the Duke's late General for the Dowery of his Wife, Daughter to Duke *Philip*; all the Fortresses of *Giera d'adda* (excepting *Peschiera* and *Lanado*) were restored by the *Venetians* to the Duke of *Milan*; *Gonzaga* had the rest of the *Mantuan* Territories; and *Legniago*, *Porto*, *Riva*, *Torboli*, *Penetra*, and *Ravenna*, remained in the *Venetian* Hands. By that same Treaty *Nicolas Piccinino* the Duke of *Milan*'s new General was to restore *Bononia* to the Church within the space of two Years; *Astorre di Faenza* was to deliver to the *Florentines* their Fortresses; and the Duke of *Milan* was obliged not to disturb the *Genouese*. This Treaty gave full Satisfaction to all

They take *Brescia* and *Bergamo*.

The Duke of *Milan* beat.

all the Parties concerned, excepting the Pope's Legate, who thought the parting with *Bononia* would look dishonourable on his side. While these Transactions happened in *Lombardy*, the *Turks* took *Thessalonica*, a City belonging to the *Venetians* in *Macedonia*. About the same time the Waters swelled so high at *Venice*, that their loss was computed at a Million of Gold. *Alphonsus* King of *Naples* having betrothed his Daughter to *Leonel d'Estê* Marquis of *Ferrara*, she was brought in the *Venetian* Galleys to *Venice*, where the Doge and Senate took occasion to express their Respect to King *Alphonsus* and the Marquis, in the great State with which they received her; but the People crouding to see her, broke down the Bridge of the *Rialto*, and several were killed and wounded. Not long after, Pope *Eugenius* impatient upon *Piccinino*'s keeping *Bononia* so long, entered into a League with *Alphonsus* King of *Naples*, and *Philip* Duke of *Milan* against *Sforza*, and the Wars being thus renewed, the *Venetians* and *Florentines* assisted the *Bolognese* in the recovery of their Liberty, and mastered several of the Enemies Forts and Castles. Upon which Duke *Philip* engaged the *Venetians* and *Florentines* near *Casal Maggiore*, where he was routed, four thousand of his Horse being taken, and himself pursued to the Gates of *Milan*. In fine, *Philip* reduced to that Extremity that he had nothing left besides *Milan* and *Crema*, and *Lodi*, sued for Peace, and by the Mediation of *Leonel* Marquis of *Ferrara*, a Negotiation was set on Foot at *Ferrara*; but the Death of *Philip* Duke of *Milan*, in whom the race of *Visconti* failed, put a stop to all their proceedings, the Duke leaving things in that Confusion, as if he had designed to intail upon *Lombardy* the Divisions which he had all his Life fomented. Then the City of *Milan* weary of absolute Government, inclined to form it self into a *Republick*, and several other Places submitted to Neighbouring Princes, particularly *Lodi* and *Vicenza* to the *Venetians*. *Leonel* Marquis of *Ferrara* promoted the Interest of *Sforza*, Son in Law to the late Duke, insomuch that, when several Towns offered to throw themselves upon his Protection, he recommended 'em to *Sforza*. The *Venetians* in the mean time, having so fair an Invitation to enlarge their Dominions on the *Terra firma*, pleaded that the Duke dying, their declared Enemy, they had a right to seize upon what they could. In earnest, *Sforza* had no Title to the Dutchy by his Wife, she being a Bastard; however to get some

The Battle of *Casal Maggiore*.

The Race of *Visconti* extinct.

footing in it he offered to be General of *Milan*, against all who had any design upon it, expecting under that plausible pretence to establish himself Duke. Being invested with the Quality of General he marched with an Army to *Vicenza*, and took and sack'd it. On the other hand *Atlendulo* the *Venetians* General laid waste a great part of the *Milanese*. The Dutchess Dowager of *Milan* knowing *Sforza*'s Ambition, endeavoured to cross him to the utmost of her Power, and threatned to call in *Savoy* and *France* to oppose him. Upon which the *Venetians* jealous of the Power of *France*, came to an Accommodation with *Sforza*, upon the Terms, that *Venice* was to assist *Sforza* with 4000 Men and 13000 Ducats every Year, till he got full Possession of the State of *Milan*; and when he should come to be Duke, he was under Promise to renounce and resign to them all that Duke *Philip* had on their side the *Adda*. Soon after *Sforza* being made Duke of *Milan*, performed his Promise accordingly; and the *Venetians* in an Engagement with the *Genouese* and *Sicilians* burnt 47 of their Ships; upon which a general Peace insued for a time. But after some Years, the *Venetians* took the Alarm, observing that *Sforza* was now more considerable than every the late Duke of *Milan* had been; for tho' he had not inlarged his Dominions, yet being the greatest General of his Age, and one who had raised himself to this height merely by his Virtue, he made all *Italy* sensible of the Power of *Milan* under such a Duke. The *Florentines* dreading his Power sided with and assisted him; and the *Venetians* who were not so easily over-awed, enter'd into a Confederacy (against *Sforza*) with the King of *Naples*, the *Sienese*, the Duke of *Savoy*, the Marquis of *Monsferrat*, and the Lords of *Corregio*. In pursuance of this Treaty the King of *Naples* invaded *Tuscany*, and the Army of the other Confederates took *Lodi*, *Gotolengo*, *Manerbio*, and *Pontoglio*, and penetrated even to the Gates of *Milan*. In this War, 'tis plain that *Sforza* and the *Venetians* fought for no less Prize, than the Sovereignty of *Lombardy*; the Ruin of either Party, as Cases then stood, making it sure for the other. But in the mean time, while they who might have saved *Greece* and *Christendom* from Bondage and Infidelity, were sheathing their Swords in one another's Sides, *Mahomet* seiz'd upon the Imperial City of *Constantinople*. Upon the news of which, the Pope dispatched Legates to *Naples*, *Venice* and *Milan*, conjuring those

Treaty betwixt *Venice* and *Sforza*.

Confederacy against *Sforza*.

Constantinople taken by the *Turks*.

those Princes and States to take pity on the dangerous State of Italy, that so composing all Differences, they might make head against the Common Enemy. This Proposal was not unacceptable to the Venetians, who were apprehensive of the Turks above all others. In fine, by the Mediation of Borsias Duke of Ferrara a Peace was speedily concluded, in which 'twas agreed, that Sforza should restore to the Venetians all he had taken from them in this War, except the Castles of Giera d'Adda; that the King of Naples should do the like to the Florentines, Castiglione excepted; that the Florentines should do the like to the Sienese; and that when any controversy arose among them, it should be left to the amicable determination of the Pope. By the Interest of the King of Naples, the Genouese were left out of this Peace. This done, Frederick the Emperor required Ambassadors from all the Princes of Europe, to make a new League against the Turk. But in the mean time, the Turks sent an Ambassador to Venice, with a Proposal of certain Articles of Agreement; which the Venetians accepted, and so confirmed Peace with the Turks.

Peace betwixt Venice and the Turks.

Such were the Publick Transactions during the Administration of Foscaro, whose own Son was twice confined to Candia for some Misdemeanours, and there dyed. In this Doge's time a certain Greek called Stamato, robbed the Treasure of St. Mark's Church, after he had been two Years in cutting a Hole thro' a very thick Stone Wall; and being betrayed by a Taylor, the Treasure was recovered, and he hanged with a Golden Chain, in Memory of his Ingenuity and Patience in the unwarrantable pursuit of Riches. In the same Doge's time the King of Bosnia sent the Venetians a Present of several Vessels of Silver, a great many Hawks, and four Goodly Horses. And Frederick the Emperor returning to Germany from his Coronation at Rome, passed by the way of Venice; were the Senate presented the Empress with a rich Crown set with Jewels, among which one Stone was valued at 3000 Ducats; and with two Coverings for a Cradle, richly embroidered with Stone and Pearl; she being at that time big with Child.

§ 20. The next Doge was Maripietro, of whom I find nothing of importance, unless it be that in his time happened the terrible Earthquake that did so much harm

Pasquale Maripietro. 1457.

in

Christophoro Moro. 1462. in *Italy*. After him came *Moro*; in whose time the *Turks* mastered and levelled to the Ground the *Venetian* Wall upon the Isthmus of the *Morea*, (or *Peloponnesus*) and over-

Morea over-run by the *Turks*. ran all that Noble Country. This Wall, which was not above six Miles long, was a great Security to the *Venetian* Subjects; and might easily have been defended against a much greater Power. But the *Venetians*, being the first Christian State that entred into Alliance with those Infidels, relyed too much upon their new Alliance, and were more intent upon ruining their Christian Neighbours at home, than guarding so fine a Country from the Irruptions of a puissant and barbarous Enemy. Soon after the

Battle of Parasso. loss of that Wall they were shamefully beaten at *Parasso*, and lost *Negroponte*, where the *Turks* made a terrible Effusion of Christian Blood. At the same time, the Infidels marched with another Army by Land towards *Dalmatia*; and the Senate was fain to give the King of *Hungary* a very large Sum of Money to ingage him to oppose their Passage.

Nicolaus Trono. 1471. § 21. The next Doge was *Nicolaus Trono*, who entred into a League with the King of *Persia* against the *Turks*. In his time the *Venetians* got the Kingdom of *Cyprus*, and that by this means, *James*, the last King of *Cyprus*, considering the entire Friendship that had been kept up between his Ancestors and the *Venetians*, came to *Venice* and desired the Senate to single out one of the Noblemens Daughters, and adopt her as Daughter of the Commonwealth, in order to be his Wife. Accordingly they gave him in Marriage one *Katharine Cornaro*, a very beautiful young Lady; upon which he returned home and lived in Peace. At his Death, leaving his Wife big with Child, he ordained that she and her Child should enjoy the Kingdom. However, the Child dyed soon after 'twas born; and the *Venetians* hearing of the King's Death, sent some armed Galleys under the command of her Brother, *George Cornaro*, with the pretence of a compliment of Condolance in the Name of the Senate. Pursuant to the Instructions given by the Senate, *Cornaro* came no sooner before *Famagosta* (the *Metropolis* of *Cyprus*) than he feigned himself sick, so that he could not go ashoar; upon the News of which, the Queen with some of her Courtiers came on Board to visit her Brother, where she and her Train was secured, and the *Venetians* surprising the City, subdued it

and

and the whole Kingdom. Such was the Stratagem that gain'd them *Cyprus*, tho' in it self but an unnatural consequent of the Confidence that King *James* reposed in them, and the strict Amity that had continued so long between the *Republick* and his Ancestors. After *Trono* followed *Nicolus Marcello*, in whose time the only remarkable thing was the brave and resolute defence of *Scodra* in *Albania*, against a numerous Army of *Infidels*. The next was *Mocenigo*, Commander at Sea; who had just before his Election suppress'd a Powerful Rebellion in *Cyprus*, preserved *Scodra* from the fury of the *Turks*, and restored the King of *Caramannia* to his Territories. In his time *Loredano*, who commanded at Sea relieved *Lepanto* when besieged by the *Turks*, and with great diligence covered the Country of the *Morea*.

Nicolas Marcello, 1473.

Peter Mocenigo, 1474.

§ 21. After *Mocenigo*, *Vendramino* was elected Duke, in whose time the *Turks* returning into *Albania* came first before *Croja*, and then over-ran all the the Country between that and the River of *Taglіamente* in *Friuli*; so that the *Venetians* were fain to recal General *Montone*, whom they had dismissed long before, who was then in *Tuscany*. This Duke set on Foot a Negotiation of Peace with the *Turks*; but it was interrupted by the Interest of the Kings of *Hungary* and *Naples*. After *Vendramino* followed *John Mocenigo*, Brother to *Peter* mentioned above. This Doge made Peace with the *Turks*, and so put an end to a seventeen Years War. The Conditions of the Treaty, were, that the *Venetians* should deliver to the *Turks* *Scodra* the chief City of *Albania*, with the Islands of *Corfu*, *Tenaro*, and *Lemnos*; and withal pay them 80000 Ducats a Year. In consideration of which the *Turks* on the other hand agreed to grant to the *Ventians* free passage for Traffick into the *Euxine* Sea, and to allow 'em a *Venetian Bailo* or *Consul* at *Constantinople*. Not long after this Treaty, the *Venetians* conquered the Island of *Corcyra* in *Dalmatia*. A Dispute arising between the *Venetians* and the Duke of *Ferrara* about the Confines of *Rovigo*, the Duke proffered to leave the Matter in contest to any two Princes; and both *Ferdinand* King of *Naples*, and *John Galeazzo* Duke of *Milan*, imployed their Ambassadors to accommodate the Matter. But notwithstanding all their Remonstrances, the *Venetians* declared War against him, being sure of the Pope's Countenance, because he hated the Duke ever since the

Andrea Vendramino. 1476.

John Mocenigo, 1478.

Peace with the *Turks*.

War between *Venice* and *Ferrara*.

the War of *Florence*, in which he assisted the *Florentines* against the King of *Naples*, after the Pope had excommunicated them. *Galeazzo* and *Ferdinand* declared for *Hercules*, and *Frederick* Duke of *Milan*, who was reckoned the greatest General in *Italy*, after the Death of *Francis* of *Milan*, undertook the Conduct of his Army. The *Venetians* at first carried all before 'em, as having a very numerous Army; and the Pope denyed passage to the *Neapolitan* Troops. But thro' the Solicitation of the Kings of *Hungary* and *Spain*, who were both related to the Dutchess of *Ferrara*, the Pope departed from the *Venetian* Interest; upon which the Duke of *Calabria*, (the King of *Naples* his Son) advanced to *Lombardy* with his Army, but was defeated by the *Venetians*. In fine, the *Venetians* took *Commacchio*, and put the Duke to very great Streights. But what by the Intercession of other Princes, and what by a prospect of a more dangerous War just ready to break out in *Italy*, both Parties chose to forbear acts of Hostility. The next Doge was *Barbarico*, a very peaceable Man, who never studyed Revenge, affirming that a Wise Prince ought to rest satisfyed in having the Power to resent, which is a sufficient cause of Fear to his Enemy. Pursuant to this Maxim he never punished any private Offences against his own Person, but was very severe in inflicting the due Penalty upon all Transgressors of the Laws of the *Republick*.

Venetians defeat the Duke of Calabria.

Marco Barbarico, 1485.

§ 23. In the time of his Successor, *Venice* was intangled in several Wars, particularly with *Edmund* Duke of *Austria*, with *Charles* VIII of *France*, who then invaded *Italy*, and above all with the *Turks*, who coming to a Rupture with them, over-ran all their Countries as far as *Tagliamente*, slew above 70000 Subjects of *Venice*, and took from them *Lepanto*, *Modone*, *Corone*, and *Durazo*. In the mean time, notwithstanding all these Diversions, the *Venetians* got *Cremona*, and divers other Towns in *Italy*; for they always chose rather to bend their Force in dispossessing their Christian Neighbours, than in screening their remoter Countries from the Barbarity of the Infidels.

Augustino Barbarico, 1486.

About this time *Lewis Sforza*, Uncle and Tutor to *John Galeas* Duke of *Milan*, having laid the Foundation of his greatness by a Confederacy with *Ferdinand* of *Arragon*, King

1491. *Charles VIII. invades Italy*

King of *Naples*, the *Venetians* and the Pope; began to perceive that the Pope and the *Venetians* had different Intentions from his, and being withal jealous of, not only his own People, but of the *Arragons* and *Peter de Medicis*, thought it his Interest to bring in a Foreign Force. With which view he called in *Charles* VIII. of *France* to attempt the Kingdom of *Naples*, to which he had a Title by the Ancient Rights and Conveyances of the House of *Anjou*. In this Juncture, while the other Potentates of *Italy* were divided into the *French* and the *Neapolitan* Parties, the *Venetians* only remained Neuters; whether it was that they confided in their own Greatness, or that they waited for an Opportunity of enlarging their Dominions when their Neighbours should be tyred out with a Foreign War; or else that the Suspicion they had of the *Turks*, obliged them to reserve their Force for the War with them. King *Charles* VIII solicited their Amity, but they wisely declined any other than what admitted of Neutrality. But after he had made such progresses as alarmed all *Italy*, and extended to *Florence*, *Rome*, and *Naples*, the Senate wisely observing that his Design extended farther than the Kingdom of *Naples*, in regard he had made himself Lord of *Pisa* and other Fortresses of the *Florentines*, and had left Garrisons in *Sienna*, and in the State of the Church; they listened to the Solicitation of *Lewis Sforza*, who then began to have his Eyes opened, and to desire a Confederacy against the Prince that himself had call'd in. In short, a Confederacy was concluded at *Venice*, between the Emperor, the King of *Spain*, the Pope, the *Venetians*, and the Duke of *Milan*: But the Duke of *Ferrara* and the *Florentines* would not come into it. In pursuance of this Confederacy, the Confederate Army drew together about the Borders of *Parma*, the Flower and Sinews of which, were the *Venetian* Forces commanded by *Francis Conzagua* Marquis of *Mantua*, a young, but a brave and an aspiring General. At that time the King of *France* was in full March to return to *France*, his interest in *Naples* having suffered a great Declension; and 'tis certain, that if he had not dallyed by the way at *Pisa*, *Sienna*, and other Places, without any pressing occasion, he might have passed without meeting his Enemy. But the Confederates having time to post themselves in his way, as he descended from the *Apennine*, a bloody Engagement insued at *Fournoue* upon the Banks of the *Taro*; each Party appro- Battle of Fournoue.

priating

priating to themselves the Glory of the Victory, tho' the most impartial gave it to the *French*. However, the Duke of *Milan*, and the *Venetians* laid Siege to *Novaro*, with great alacrity, incouraging their numerous Army with double Pay and other Largesses. At last the *French* being obliged to abandon *Novaro*, a Peace was concluded between the Confederates and the King of *France*; and that King returned to his own Country. Thus was *Italy* restored to Tranquility, chiefly by the Power and Valour of the *Venetians*. But it did not last long, for soon after the Duke of *Milan* violated the Treaty in assisting the King of *Naples*, and the *Venetians* took into their Protection *Pisa*, which had revolted from the *Florentines*. *Ferdinand* having taken *Nocera* from the *French*, reduced them to great Streights; and the *Venetians* took up Arms for the Defence of the Duke of *Milan* their Confederate, and made offers to the King of *France*, on the behalf of *Ferdinand*. The *Pisans* offered to subject themselves to the Duke of *Milan*; but that Duke being doubtful and apprehensive, the *Venetians* openly declared they were under their Protection. 'Tis certain, that 'twas not so much the desire to preserve the Liberty of their Neighbours, nor any regard to the common Benefit and safety, as the eager prospect of being Lords of *Pisa*, that made the *Venetians* so resolute in defending it, at a time when 'twas denied Succours by the other Confederates. Many of the *Venetian* Senators declaim'd warmly against the Protection and Defence of *Pisa*, as being a Place remote from their Confines, and from the Sea: But the Doge *Barbarino*, a Person of great Authority and Interest, over-perswaded them to endeavour the keeping of *Pisa*, and to repress the arrogance of the *Florentines*, who had upon several occasions done the *Venetians* more harm than any other Neighbouring Potentate. In the mean time, *Ferdinand* of *Arragon* made a League with the *Venetians*; by which several cautionary Ports were put into the Hands of *Venice*, as Pledges for the Money and Forces with which they assisted him. These Ports being in the upper Sea, and lying conveniently for *Venice*, contributed much to inlarge their Power and Splendor, which now began to display it self in all the Corners of *Italy*. The Duke of *Milan* solicited the Pope, and the Kings of *Spain* and *Naples*, for the restitution of *Pisa* to the *Florentines*, who by his Instigation insinuated, that if *Pisa* were restored to them, they would

The *Pisan* War.

joyn with the Confederates in the mutual Defence of *Italy* against the *French*. But the *Venetians* would by no means consent to it, alledging that 'twas not proper to trust the *Florentines* with the accession of a Place of such Importance, since they adhered so inviolably to the King of *France*. While the War was carried on betwixt the *Florentines* and *Pisa*, (which the *Venetians* were still careful to succour.) *Lewis* XII. of *France* (claiming a Title to the Dutchy of *Milan* by the Succession of the Lady *Valentina* his Grandmother, Daughter of *John Galeas Visconti*, married to *Lewis* Duke of *Orleans*, Brother to *Charles* VI.) made War against the Duke of *Milan*, against whom the *Venetians* had conceiv'd an incredible hatred; and solicited the *Venetians* to joyn with him, offering to reward them with the City of *Cremona* and all *Guera d'adda*. Many of the Senators represented very warmly, and with great weight of Reason, the danger that might accrue to their State from the Power of *France* in *Italy*. But the hatred they bore to the Duke of *Milan*, and the alluring prospect of the Districts of *Cremona* and *Guera d'adda*, which carried their Dominions to the *Po*, and brought in a large Accession of Revenue, bore down all other Considerations, and Influenced them to enter into an Alliance with the *French* King, in hopes to have some time or other an Opportunity of fetching in all the Dutchy of *Milan*, when the *French* King should be employed on the other side of the Mountains. In short, *Lewis* assisted by the *Venetians*, possessed himself of the Dutchy of *Milan*, and compounded with all the Potentates of *Italy*, excepting *Frederick* King of *Naples*. In the same Year, the *Venetians*, and indeed all *Italy*, received a terrible blow from the *Turks*, which we mentioned above. In the next Year happened the beginning of the War betwixt the Pope and the *Vicars* of *Romagna*; and tho' the *Venetians* were possessors in that Country of *Ravenna* and *Cervia*, which they had many Years before taken from the Family of *Polenta*, yet such respect was shewn to their Power, that their Title was not disputed. In the mean time died the Doge *Augustin Barbarini*, whose Government was attended with such Prosperity, that he extended his Authority far beyond that of his Predecessors. But the Power of his Successors being limited by new Laws,

Lewis XII. takes *Milan*. 1499.

§ 22.

Leonardo Lorendano, 1501.

§ 22. *Leonard Loredano* was elected in his Place; in the beginning of whose Government the *French* and the *Spaniards* were busie in dividing *Naples* between them; and the *Florentines* in indeavouring in vain to reduce *Pisa*. About the same time, Pope *Alexander* dying, the *Venetians* aspired to the Dominion of all *Romagna*, and took *Faenza* and *Rimini* notwithstanding the Remonstrances of the new Pope, and *Cæsar Borgia*. At the same time they took in *Romagna*, *Montefiora*, St. *Archangeo*, *Verrucque*, *Gattere*, *Savignano*, and *Meldole*, the Haven of the Country of *Cesena*. And in the Territory of *Imola*, *Tossignara*, *Solaruolo*, and *Montbattaille*. So that *Cæsar Borgia* held in *Romagna*, only the Castles of *Forly*, of *Cesena*, of *Forlimpople*, and of *Bertinoire*. In 1504 a Peace was concluded betwixt *Bajazet Ottoman* and the *Venetians*, which both Parties embraced with equal desire; for this *Turk* was of a mild peaceful Temper, (quite contrary to his Father's) and withal had the Mortification to see the Pope, the King of *Bohemia* and *Hungary*, and the *French* and *Spanish* Kings, send Succours several times to the *Venetians*. And on the other hand the *Venetians* had been often worsted by the *Turks*, and were much straitened for want both of Corn and of Traffick, the *Portuguese* having gotten the Spice Trade from them. By this Peace the *Turk* kept all he had got; and the *Venetians* reserving only the Isle of *Cefalonia*, yielded him St. *Maura*. After this the Republick, and indeed all *Italy* were in a State of Tranquility for three or four Years, excepting that the Wars between the *Florentines* and the *Pisans* were still on Foot. But this Calm was followed by a dismal Storm; and the *Venetians* had the Mortification to see the Republick reduced to the lowest ebb of Distress, by the blow they received from the League of *Cambray*, in which the Emperor, the Pope, the Kings of *France* and *Spain*, and the Dukes of *Mantua* and *Ferrara* combined to dispossess the *Venetians* of the *Terra firma*. The King of *France* began the War, and gave the *Venetian* Army, which was commanded, or rather divided, by two Generals of quite different Tempers, so great an Overthrow at *Guera d'adde* (which the *Venetian* Writers call a *Cannæ* to them) that it animated the other Confederates to vye for a share in the Spoil. The *Venetians* seeing themselves in no condition of defence, wisely made a Vertue of Necessity, and allowed their Subjects the Liberty to make the

The League of *Cambray*, 1509.

Battle of *Guerad'adda.*

The State of *Venice* at a low Ebb.

the best terms they could with the Enemy, for they presumed, that this instance of their Tenderness, would invite them home to their ancient Masters as soon as the Storm was over. In fine, the torrent was so rapid, that in a short time the *Venetians* had nothing left on the *Terra firma* but *Treviso*, all their Possessions being divided among the Confederate Princes. The *French* King had for his share *Brescia*, *Bergamo*, *Cremona* and *Crema*; the Emperor *Maximilian*, *Verona*, *Vicenza*, *Padua*, and part of *Friuli*; the King of *Spain* their Cities and Ports in *Puglia*; the Pope *Arimino*, *Faenza*, *Ravenna* and *Cervia*, with the rest of *Romagna*; and the Duke of *Ferrara*, *Rovigo*, *La Badia*, with *Monfelice*, *Estè*, and other Places which formerly belonged to his Family. The *Venetians* had so little left on the main Land, that the Emperor *Maximilian* came to *Maestre*, (five little Miles from *Venice*) as near as the Sea would suffer him to approach; and there with an insulting sort of Triumph discharged his Artillery towards *Venice*, tho' he could not hurt it. The *Venetians* provoked to a degree of Despair, and animated by an Oration pronounced by the Doge, conjuring them rather to die like Men, than to sit tamely under such inglorious Contempt; mustered up a Land Army, surprized *Padua*, which the Victors glutted with Success, and wrapt up in Security, had but carelesly guarded, and fortified both it and *Treviso*.

The Duke of *Ferrara* being then declared General of the Church, they discharged all their Fury upon him, and sent 17 Galleys and 400 Boats to attack the *Ferrarese* by the River *Po*. But as some Writers say, such was their ill Success, that their very Navy became a Prey to the Duke, that had no Ships; for having chain'd them up by Night within the Mouth of the River, where they thought themselves secure, he burnt some, and took others, and returned to *Ferrara* in a sort of Naval Triumph upon one of their best Galleys. But let that be as it will, they behaved themselves so that they broke the League: Whether it was that the League consisted of so many different, or rather incompatible Interests; or that the *French* King being at that time possess'd of the State of *Milan* and *Bononia*, besides other Places, was become formidable to his Allies. In fine, the *Venetians* granting a full Title to the Pope of all the Places in *Romagna*, he joyn'd with them, and soon after the King of *Castile* did the same, in order to drive *Lewis* XII. of *France* out of *Italy*. The Duke of *Ferrara* adhering stifly to the King of *France*; the Pope excommunicated both the one and the other. The City of *Brescia* returned to the *Venetian* Obedience, and *Andrea Gritti*, with several other Noble *Venetians* and Officers, with a competent number of Soldiers, being sent to defend it, a very sharp Engagement insued between them and the *French*, in which they were all either kill'd or taken, and *Andrea Gritti* sent Prisoner to *Lewis*. The *Venetians* alarmed with this great Loss, fitted out a Naval Force, with which they sack'd *Argenta*, took *Mirandola* and infested the *Ferrarese* Territories. The joynt Land Army of the King of *Spain*, the Pope and the *Venetians* which lay before *Bononia*, retired from thence to *Ravenna* and the French Army under the Command of *Gaston de Foix*, Duke of *Nemours*, joyn'd by the Duke of *Ferrara* advanced from *Milan* in pursuit of them. In fine, the two Armies met near *Ravenna*; and after a very obstinate and bloody Fight the *French* obtain'd the Victory, sack'd *Ravenna*, and took divers other Towns in *Romagna*; but after all, their Victory cost 'em very dear, *Gaston* falling in the Action; and from that Hour the *French* Arms declin'd in *Italy*, leaving those at last, whom they had beaten, in Possession of what they fought for.

The End of the *Cambray* War.

Thereupon followed the Peace of *Brussels* betwixt *Francis* King of *France*, and *Charles* Duke of *Burgundy*, and Grandson to the Emperor *Maximilian*; and a Truce was concluded with the Republick, by vertue of which the *Venetians* had *Verona* of the Emperor for a great Sum of Money. Such was the Conclusion of that *Cambray* War, which made *Italy* a Scene of Blood and Confusion for eight Years; and in which the *Venetians* gave a lasting Proof of their invincible Prudence, Fortitude and Constancy, which remained unshaken, while all *Europe* made head against 'em.

Antonio Grimani. 1521.

§ 23. After the Death of *Loredano*, who had thus saved his Country when reduced to the last extremity, and left it in a peaceable and flourishing State, *Antonio Grimani* was elected Doge, who reigned but 22 Months. His Successor was *Andrea Gritti*, who had formerly been Prisoner in *France*, and had done great Services in the *Cambray* War. He made Peace with the Emperor *Charles* V. and afterwards entered into a League with the *French* King, assisted him to recover *Milan*, and to make a great Progress in

Andrea Gritti, 1523.

in *Naples.* But soon after the *French* lost all, and *Francis* I. was taken Prisoner. In fine, this Doge by practising sometimes with *France*, sometimes with the Emperor, and sometimes with the Bishop of *Rome*, left the Commonwealth in a flourishing State of Tranquility and Peace, and dyed much lamented by the Citizens. Towards the latter end of his Administration, the *Venetians* growing jealous of the *Turks*, made Preparations for War, and fitted out a Fleet under the Command of *Pesareus.* They refused to suffer this Fleet to joyn that of the Emperor *Charles* V. (which he earnestly solicited) whether it was that no Hostilities being yet committed against them, they were loth to pull a heavy War upon their own Heads; or that they were influenced by the Solicitation of *Francis* King of *France* to the Contrary. However soon after Hostilities commenced, and the *Turks* making a Descent upon *Corcyra*, over-ran the Island with Fire and *Sword.* This Island lying between the *Adriatick* and *Ionian* Sea, is very convenient for either Defending or Invading not only *Greece* and *Epirus*, but even *Italy.* Upon this Alarm, the *Venetians* pressed anxiously for a Confederacy of the Christian Princes against *Solyman*; which accordingly was Proclaim'd by the Pope in the begining of 1537. In the mean time, the Imperial Admiral, *Andreas Auria* refused to joyn the *Venetians*, who had so lately given him the like Denial. However, the *Turks* were forced to break up the Siege of the Town of *Corcyra*, and were defeated at Land by the Imperialists. Peace being concluded betwixt the Emperor and the *French* King; the Senate entred into a League with *Charles* V. and the Pope against *Solyman*, and endeavour'd to have brought in *Henry* King of *England*; but he declin'd it, whether it be that he took it ill that he was not mentioned in the Treaty, or that he was supicious of the over-grown Power of the Emperor. The Confederates carried on the War with various Success till the End of the Year 1540, in which the *Venetians* concluded a Peace with the *Turks*, giving up to them *Napoli di Romania* and *Raguza*, which they had taken in the War. This was under the Administration of *Peter Landi*, who had succeeded *Gritti* in 1538. In his time the Citizens underwent a great Famine, which he with his Prudence, Vigilancy and Liberality remedied as much as was possible. *Charles* V. passing thro' *Italy* in order to his *African* Expedition, the Senate renewed their Alliance

Pietro Landi, 1538.

with him; and soon after the Emperor and the King of *England* having fallen upon *France*, they solicited and obtain'd a Peace between the Emperor and the *French* King.

Francis Donato, 1545. The next Doge was *Franciscus Donatus*, who cultivated Peace while the rest of the World was involved in War. *Antonio Trivisano*, 1553. The next after him liv'd but a Year after his Election; then *Venerio* was chosen, who in Imitation of the three preceding Dukes, liv'd in Peace, the Seat of the Wars being then transfer'd beyond the Mountains. *Francesco Venerio*, 1554. The *Turks* having infested the Coast of *Apulia*, the Knights of *Jerusalem*, under pretence of pursuing the Infidels, rifled some *Venetian* Ships and took some *Turkish* Vessels in the *Venetian* Ports; Upon which the Senate ordered, that by way of Reprisal, their Rents in the *Venetian* Territories should be confiscated, till due reparation were made. The Knights made heavy complaints of this Usage as an Incroachment upon the Dignity, and an unsuitable Reward of the Merit and great Services of their Order. The Original of the Knights of *Jerusalem*. The Original of the Order was this, upon the Declension of the *Roman* Empire, the Kingdoms of *Jerusalem*, *Syria*, and *Egypt* falling into the Hands of the *Persians*, some Christians were still left in *Jerusalem*, and permitted to live in that Quarter of the City where our Saviour's Sepulcher is placed. This Sepulcher was frequently visited by Strangers, who repaired to *Jerusalem* either upon a religious Errand, or in the way of Traffick: And especially the Merchants of the Coast of *Amalfi* in the Kingdom of *Naples*, who gaining the good Will of the Infidels and their King, by importing to them Foreign and unknown Commodities, obtain'd leave to lodge and live in the City. Upon which they built a Monastery, and an Hospital for Pilgrims, dedicated to St. *John*, in the same Quarter with the Sepulcher; and about the Beginning of the 12th Century, in the celebrated Expedition of *Godofred*, *Gerandus*, the Master of that Hospital, and some of his Associates, assumed the Habit of the Order; which being confirm'd, and approv'd by the Patriarch of *Jerusalem*, and the Pope of *Rome*: Persons of Quality and Merit that afterwards had occasion to visit the Holy Sepulcher, listed themselves in the Order, vowing implacable hatred to the Enemies of Christianity. The Liberality of Princes inlarged the Treasury of the Order, and the Kings of *Jerusalem* were glad to make use of their Valour. But when *Jerusalem* was taken by *Saladin*, the Emperor of the *Turks*, they retir'd to *Acre* and *Tyre*, and

from

from thence to the Island of *Rhodes*, which they took by force in 1308. This Island they defended against the *Turks* for 214 Years, during which time it proved a Bulwark for the Christians to keep off the *Turkish* Invasions upon *Italy*: But then being dispossess'd, they had *Malta* granted 'em by the Emperor *Charles* V. Such was the Origin and Progress of that Order, which has produced many brave and famous Men. To return, they were so dissatisfied with the *Venetians* for confiscating their Rents, that they appeal'd to Pope *Paul* IV. who shew'd such regard to the Benefit of Society, and the Preservation of Peace, that he prohibited them to search the *Venetian* Vessels, or scour their Seas; lest the rifling of a small Ship should cost the Christians the loss of Kingdoms. At that time the difference hapned between the *Pope* and the *Columna*'s; *Henry* King of *France* siding with the former, as the King of *Spain* did with the latter; but *Venerio* would by no means enter into any Measures that might disturb the Peace of his Country, tho' warmly solicited on both sides. Upon which *Venerio* merited the Appellation of *Princeps Pacis*. In 1556. *Bona Sfortia* the Daughter of *John Galeas*, formerly Duke of *Milan*, and Queen of *Poland*, returning to *Puglia* by the way of *Venice*, was received by the Doge and Senate with such Pomp and Splendor, as spoke a flourishing Peaceful State.

§ 24. The next Doge encounter'd at once the hardships of Famine and Pestilence. The one he guarded off by seasonable Constitutions and Orders, particularly the *Lex Agraria*, injoyning the manuring of all Lands that lay uncultivated, as being cover'd with Pools, &c. and the other by Diligence and Care. After which he gave the City the agreeable Diversion of the Coronation of his Dutchess; after the manner of their Ancestors; a splendid Solemnity that *Venice* had not seen for many Years before; for from the time of the Doge *Paschal Marepietro*, till this time, there had been no Dutchess of *Venice*. In his time a Truce was concluded between *Philip* of *Spain* and the Pope, by Vertue of the unwearied Solicitation and Mediation of the *Venetians*, who look'd upon that War as highly pernicious not only to *Italy*, but to all Christendom. The *Turks* made great devastations upon the Coasts of *Naples*; and the *Venetians* apprehensive for their own Territories inlarged their Fleet, and fortifyed *Cyprus*, and *Corcyra*.

Laurentio Prioli. 1556.

Charles V. dying, his Son *Philip* yielded to the Solicitation of the Senate, in making Peace with *Henry* of *France* at *Lisle*. The Ambassador of *Spain* disputing the Precedency with the Ambassador of *France* at *Venice*, the Senate gave it for the latter. This Doge dying was succeeded by his Brother *Hieronymo Prioli*, in whose time the Pope gave the Senate leave to choose the Patriarch of *Venice*, with a perpetual Right of Patronage; in consideration of their Zeal against the Doctrine of *Luther* and *Calvin*. He adorn'd the Ducal Robe with precious Jewels, and the two Crowns of *Cyprus* and *Candia* in wrought Gold.

Hieronymo Prioli, 1559.

§ 25. The next Doge was *Loredano*, Elected at the Age of 86, after great Dissentions about other Candidates; for he was not so much as proposed at first, till the discording Parties relinquishing their respective Favourites, agreed to sink all their jarring Pretensions in a Person of his Age and Experience... He had the Mortification to see the State attack'd at once by War, Fire, and Famine. In the height of a great Famine, that affected both it and all *Italy*, the *Arsenal* took Fire, and was levell'd with the Ground. Then insued the Invasion of *Cyprus* by *Solyman* the *Turkish* Emperor, who thought this a favourable Opportunity, not only on account of the Destruction of their Naval Stores, but in regard that the other Christian Powers, *France* and *Spain* being then imbroiled in Civil Wars, could spare no assistance against the common Enemy. This *Cyprus* lying near the Coast of *Asia*, and at a great distance from *Venice*, was very serviceable for infesting the *Asiatick* Coast, and sheltering the Christian Ships. The *Venetians* in the mean time made all necessary Preparations with wonderful Alacrity, and animated the other Christian Princes to joyn with them. But *Loredano* dying, *Mocenico* was Elected Doge, in the beginning of whose Administration the *Venetians* took *Suppotum*, and some other Places; the *Turks* took several Places in *Dalmatia*; and seiz'd three rich *Venetian* Merchant Ships at *Cyprus*, which were nevertheless blown up by the unwonted Courage of a Noble Matron. Then they took *Leucosia* and *Famagusta* the chief Town, after a resolute Defence; and contrary to the Capitulation, flea'd alive *Bragadeno* the Governour. Before this Town they lost above 60000 Men. *Cyprus* being thus lost, the *Venetians* entring into Alliance

Pietro Loredano, 1468.

The *Cyprian* War.

Aloysius Mocenicus, 1570.

Cyprus taken by the *Turks*.

Alliance with Pope *Pius* V. and *Philip* II. of *Spain*, fitted out a Confederate Fleet which engaged the *Turks* in the Gulf of *Lepanto*, and gain'd a very considerable Victory, 1571.
which Galled the *Turks* extreamly, and made them aban- Battle of
don *Cyprus*. But the Dissensions between the Christian *Curzolary.*
Victors were such, that after a few inconsiderable Efforts, the *Venetians* were fain to clap up a Peace with the *Turks*, by Vertue of which, the *Venetians* gave up *Suppotum*, and all the Towns and Territories in *Dalmatia* and *Epirus*
were put upon the same Foot, as before the Commence- 1573.
ment of the War. In 1574 *Henry* King of *Poland* taking *Venice* in his Way to *France*, upon the Death of *Charles* IX. was received at *Venice* with all Splendor and Demonstrations of Joy, and advis'd by the Doge to sink the civil Dissentions of *France* by Lenity and Moderation, in order to promote the Grandure of his Kingdom, and inable it to assist and protect their Allies. Which *Henry* readily engaged to do: Soon after the City was humbled with repeated Fires, and with a dismal Plague, the progress of which was imputed to the Ignorance of the *Pedouan* Physicians.
Venerio the next Doge (who had commanded the *Sabastiano*
Fleet in the Battle of *Lepanto*) lived but 9 Months after his *Venerio,*
Election, and was succeeded by *Nicolaus de Ponte* a cele- 1577. *Nicolaus de*
brated Philosopher, who studying peaceful Arts, adorned *Ponte,*
the City with handsome Fabricks, restrain'd Prodigality 1578.
by Sumptuary Laws, composed a Difference between the Pope and the Senate, about a small Fief claim'd by the Patriarch of *Aquileia*, whose cause the Pope espoused; gave the Ambassadors of the King of *Japan* a suitable Reception; and reformed the Power of the *Decemviri*. In his time the *Maltese* and the *Uscochi* committed several Piracies and Depredations, but were check'd for their Insolence. The next Doge was much respected for his Piety, *Pascalis Ci-*
Prudence, and Humanity. He preserved Peace tho' the *conia,*
rest of *Europe* was ingaged in War, made a Bridge over 1585.
the *Rialto*, punished the *Uscochi* for their Depredations, own'd *Henry* IV. of *France*, notwithstanding the Remonstrances of the Pope, and made Preparations to oppose
the *Turk* upon occasion. His Successor *Marino Grimani* *Marino Gri-*
fitted out a Fleet to suppress the *Uscochi* or Pyrats, whom *mani,*
they beat in an Engagement, and so cleared the Seas. In 1595.
his time Pope *Paul* V. in vindication of his Pontifical Authority, required the Senate to disanul their Decrees relating to Ecclesiastical Persons and their Estates; and the Se-

nate insisting on their Civil Power and Authority over all their Subjects, he issued forth a Bull of Excommunication against them. In this Doge's time the Senate entered into a League with the *Grisons*, *A.* 1603. His Successor, *Donato* protested publickly against the Pope's Bull, and caused the Protestation to be dispersed in all the *Venetian* Dominions. The Subjects of *Venice*, and the very Clergy, excepting the *Jesuits*, appeared much incensed at the Pope's Invasion of the Civil Right; and the *Jesuits* were banished *Venice*. Thus was every thing ready to break out into War, when *Henry* IV of *France* sent Cardinal *Joyeuse* to make up the difference; by whose Mediation 'twas agreed, that the Imprisoned Ecclesiastical Persons should be given up to the Pope, and the Pope should recal his Interdict. Both *Spain* and *France* interceded for the Pardon of the *Jesuits*, but the Senate flatly refused it. Peace being thus restored, the Doge applyed his Mind to the Suppression of the Pyrates, particularly the *Usocchi*. His Successor was *Antonio Memo*, who made vigorous Preparations to suppress the *Usocchi*, a barbarous and perfidious sort of Pyrates; who had treated the *Venetian* Governours and Præfects with the utmost Indignity and Cruelty, and had barbarously infested the Coast of *Illyricum*, &c. But in 1613 *Ferdinand* Arch-duke of *Austria*, ingaging to keep them in order, and to prevent their being harboured in Maritim Places, the Matter was taken up. In the mean time, *Emmanuel*, Duke of *Savoy* laying claim to the Principality of *Montferrat* upon the Death of the Duke of *Mantua*, some Commotions insued, which ended in Peace at *Asti*, by the Intercession of *Spain* and *Venice*, who espoused the Cause of the House of *Gonzaga*; and studyed by all means to preserve the Peace of *Italy*.

Leonardo Donato, 1605.

Jesuits banished.

Antonio Memo, 1612.

§. 26. After the Death of *Memo*, *John Bembo* was Elected Duke; who bent his force against the Pyrates, who were grown more impudent than ever, and were favoured by their Prince, the Arch-duke of *Austria*. He took some of the Arch-ducal Towns, the Governors of which had favoured and sheltered the Pyrates, and besieged *Gradisca*, a Town in *Stiria*, belonging to the Arch-Duke. In the mean time, *Toledo* Governour of *Milan*, and the Duke *de Ossuna* Viceroy of *Naples*, started a fresh War against the *Venetians*; and the *Spaniards* took several loaden Ships, homeward bound from *Syria*. However *Gradisca* was re-

Giovanni Bembo, 1615.

reduced to that Extremity, that 'twas upon the point of surrendring, when by the Mediation of *Lewis* XIII King of *France*, and *Charles* Duke of *Savoy*, a Peace was concluded between the Arch-Duke and the *Republick*, in the Island of *Veglia*, by Vertue of which, Commerce was restored, most of the *Usocchi* transported to *Carlistot* and other Frontiers of the *Turks*, further from the Sea; the Pyratical Barks were burnt, and in them the very Name of the *Usocchi*; by which means the *Republick* was rid of an Inconveniency that had gall'd 'em very much for many Years. For these *Usocchi* living on the Coast that runs from *Dalmatia* to the Gulf of *Quarnaro*, full of dangerous Rocks, Flats and Islands, and subject to the Arch-Duke of *Austria*, as being part of *Hungary*, had a strong Garrison in *Segna*, which was given to them as a Frontier against the *Turks*; and from thence infested both the *Turks* and *Venetians* with their Depredations and Pyracies. The *Turks* pressed the *Republick* to whom the Dominion of the Sea belonged, to Curb and Punish them, threatning to take revenge of their insolence upon all Christendom; and accordingly declared War in *Hungary* against the *Austrians*. The *Republick* made repeated Complaints to their Prince, *Ferdinand* of *Austria*, but he still connived at their Insolence; whether it was that the Arch-Duke could not be at the Charge of a *German* Garrison in *Segna* to suppress them, or that he was influenced by the *Spaniards*, who loved to see *Venice* imployed, that they might not be at leisure to oppose their Designs in *Italy*. At last the matter was composed as above. The next Doge *Donato*, detected and prevented the designs of the Count *d'Ossuna* and *Alphonsus Quera*, the *Spanish* Ambassador, to surprize the Fleet by Treachery; and again to set fire to the Magazin, cut down the Bridges, and Master the City. Two of the Accomplices having discovered the Conspiracy, the rest were taken and brought to condign Punishment. To this discovery, and the contemporary Commotions in *Bohemia*, was owing in a great measure the Peace of *Italy*; *Spain* being obliged to assist the Emperor, and *France* involved in Domestick Broils. This Doge reigning only 40 Days, he was succeeded by *Antonio Prioli*. In his time the Senate perceiving the Design of *Spain*, to establish a predominancy in *Italy*, entered into a League of Defence with *Charles* Duke of *Savoy*, whom they had assisted with Men and Money; and invited into it the Dukes of

Nicolas Donato. 1618. The Peace of *Madrid.*

Antonio Prioli. 1618.

Man-

Mantua, *Parma*, *Modena*, and *Urbino*; but these had nc courage to own their Consent, tho' they all applauded i as the only only Defence of the common Safety. At th same time, they were tied in a League with the *Swis*, And being thus pretty secure by Land, they fortifye themselves at Sea, by a defensive Alliance with the State of *Holland*. The Duke *d' Ossuna*, under the pretence c guarding off the *Turks*, kept Armed Vessels in the Gulpl and took some *Venetian* Ships, for which the *Venetiar* made suitable reprisals. At last the Court of *Spai* thought fit to remove that Seditious Duke from his Ty rannical Government, and recaling him to *Spain*, punish ed him with Death. Soon after the *Valteline* revoltin from the *Grisons*; and being as 'twere a Gallery, whic uniting the Countries of *Germany* with those of *Spain*, s parates the *Venetians* and *Italy* from the Assistance of tl Strangers; the *Venetians* were very much alarmed, foreseeing that the Emperor and the *Spaniard*, who we then involably linked together, would by mastering th *Valteline* hem them in from all foreign Levies. To ave this Blow, they animated the *Grisons* and the *Swiss*, an supplyed them with Money, Arms and Men; they solic ted the Kings of *France* and *England*, and the Duke c *Savoy*, to assist in vindicating the Liberty of the *Grison* against the Power of the *Austrians*. The Duke of *S voy* having form'd a Design to suppress *Geneva*, the Se nate interposed and perswaded him to drop the D sign. In the beginning of 1623. the Senate confederate with *France* and *Savoy*, to procure a restoration of the Pl ces taken by the *Austrians* in the Valteline and the *Grison* Country, and a diversion of the *Austrians*, by *Mansfelt* i *Alsace*.

The War of the *Valteline*.

Francesco Contarini, 1623.

§ 27. *Prioli* dying, was succeeded by *Francesco Contar ni*, under whose Administration the Senate confederate with *France* and *Savoy*, pursued the Restitution of the *Va teline*, solliciting the Pope, into whose Hands the For had been delivered by the *Austrians*, to make an end the Affair: For they perceived plainly that the design the *Austrians* and *Spaniards* was to subject both *Italy* ar *Germany*, by uniting their Countries, and so opening Door to over-run the one or the other at Pleasure. Tl Senate continuing to employ all their care to unite tl Princes of *Italy*, made a perfect Accommodation betwee

th

the Dukes of *Savoy* and *Mantua*, upon the Difference so long in Question. The King of *France* and the Duke of *Savoy* having formed a Design upon *Genoua*, as an Inlet to *Milan*, the *Venetians* generously represented it as an inglorious design of revenging the provocations of the House of *Austria*, upon an innocent State. The Conferences at *Rome* proving ineffectual, the Army of the League made such progress in the *Valteline*, that in a little time they took possession of the whole Country, except *Riva*; and the Ancient Alliances of the *Grisons* with *France* and the *Swiss*, were restored to their former Splendor. The *Venetians* flattered by the *Austrians*, scorn the dishonour of deserting the League; and refuse to endanger Christendom by the proffered assistance of the *Turks*. They advise the King of *France* to invade the *Milanese*, rather than the *Genouese*, tho' that Prince egged on by the Ambition of the Duke of *Savoy*, would not listen to their wholesome Advice. In the mean time, *Contarini* dying, *Giovanni* *Giovanni*
Cornaro was chosen Duke; and *Carlos* Duke of *Savoy*, with *Cornaro*,
the *French* General *Lesdiguieres* being obliged to retire 1625.
from the *Genouese* without carrying their point, the Senate wisely foreseen they had no Succours near 'em, refus'd to comply with the repeated Request of these Princes, that they should invade the *Milanese*, to divert the Destruction of *Piemont*, then threatned by *Feria* Governor of *Milan*. They interposed (tho' in vain) their most effectual Offices for Peace betwixt King *Charles* I. of *England*, and the King of *France*. The Pope declaring for the House of *Austria* in the *Valteline* Affair; Cardinal *Richelieu* Sacrificing all considerations to appease a furious Treaty of
Storm that threatned a civil War, and the downfal of his *Monzone*.
Authority; claped up a separate Peace with *Spain* upon that Head, to the great surprize of the *Republick* and the Duke of *Savoy*. However, the Senate joyning Prudence with Necessity, approved of the Peace; and *Carlos* agreeing to a Suspension of Arms with the *Genouese*, Peace was restored to *Italy*, tho' at the same time it saw it self
big with fiercer Storms, by the Succession of *Mantua*, the 1626.
House of *Gonzagua* being then without Hopes of Issue Male. *Rhetel* Son to the Duke of *Nevers*, marrying the Niece of *Vincenzo*, Duke of *Mantua*, at the very hour of his Death, declared himself Duke; and *Savoy* making Pretensions with the Countenance of *Spain*, as well as the House of *Guastala*, the Senate was at a Loss, how to pre-

serve

ſerve the Peace of *Italy*, *France* being then ingaged in a Civil War. Both the *Republick* and the Pope leaned to *Nevers's* ſide, he being the lawful Heir; but the Former ſtood true to their ſetled Maxim, not to declare themſelves but in Conjunction with *France*; and indeed not then, till they ſaw the *French* Troops enter *Italy*, for the *French* had frequently indeavoured to bring them to a Rupture with *Spain* without caring to ſecond it. *France* could give nothing but Promiſes till the Affair of *Rochel* was over; and ſo the Hopes of *Italy* were refered to that one Iſſue. At laſt *Lewis* XIII of *France*, having taken *Rochel*, and made Peace with *England*, croſſed the *Alpes* with 30000 Men, and concluded a Treaty of Peace with the Duke of *Savoy* at *Suſa*; and an Alliance offenſive with the *Republick* and the Duke of *Mantua*. Soon after both the King and Cardinal *Richelieu* returned with the greateſt part of the Army, to the no ſmall Mortification of *Venice* and *Mantua*. The *Spaniards* willing to improve this Opportunity in *Italy*, offered a Truce to the *United Provinces* of *Holland*, which the *Venetians* found means to avert, in order to continue the Diverſion on that ſide. In the mean time the Emperor marching with a Gallant Army towards the confines of *Italy*, and afterwards to the *Milaneſe*; the Senate made Vigorous Preparations; aſſiſted *Mantua* with Men, Ammunition and Money; Garriſoned and reliev'd *Mantua*, but afterwards it was taken by Treachery and ſack'd. In the mean time, the Duke *Cornaro* dyed; and a diſmal Peſtilence raged all over *Italy*.

Mantua taken.

Nicolo Contareni, 1630.

§ 28. *Nicolo Contareni* the next Doge, had the Mortification to ſee the *Republick* deploring the Loſs of ſo much Treaſure ſpent, and 14000 of their beſt Troops that periſhed by Slaughter or Sickneſs in the ſucceſsleſs Defence of *Mantua*. But the Senate, accommodating themſelves to Fortune and Time, purſued the common Intereſt of *Italy* with their wonted Steadineſs. The King of *Spain*'s Siſter being betroth'd to the King of *Hungary*, the *Spaniards* propoſed to carry her from *Naples* to *Trieſte*, on Board the *Spaniſh* Fleet; but the *Venetians* denying them Paſſage, they were forced to accept of the Offer the Senate made of conveying her on Board the *Venetian* Fleet; which accordingly they did with great Splendor, and for ſo doing, had the Thanks of the Emperor and the Catholick King. In the mean

mean time, a Peace was clapped up at *Ratisbon* between the Emperor (then apprehensive of the *Swedes*) and the *French* King, by which the Affair of *Mantua* was setled; tho' not with due regard to the *Republick*, that had stood alone the heaviest Shocks of the War. However, in pursuance of this Treaty, the Peace of *Italy* was in ample Form ratifyed by all Parties at *Chievastro*. And thus was the *Republick* and all *Italy* restored to Peace, to which the Commotions in *Germany* contributed not a little. *Gustavus Adolphus* having by a rapid Progress in *Germany*, advanc'd towards *Italy*, and sent an Embassy to the Senate, demanding Money and Assistance, upon the Plea that having rescued the Liberty of *Germany*, he had it in his Power to advance the Peace and Security of *Italy*: The Senate apprehensive of the Approach of an Ambitious and Fortunate Prince, made Answer, that the Liberty and Honour of *Italy* always had been, and still was their Care.

§ 29. *Francesco Erizzo* the next Doge, succeeded to a peaceable Calm, after so long a Series of Care and Calamity. *Francesco Erizzo, 1631.* Pope *Urban* having by a Bull given Cardinals the Title of Eminence, annexed *Urbino* to the Holy See, incouraged his Nephew *Barberino* to take Precedency of Ambassadors as Prefect of *Rome*, and incroached upon the *Venetian* Confines adjacent to *Ferrara*; the Senate refus'd to comply, and some Jealousies arose between them and his Holiness, which through the Intercession of the *French* were stifled. *France* and *Spain* coming to an open Breach, the *Venetians* still preserved a Neutrality, notwithstanding the Vigorous Solicitations of the *French*; only they continued to garrison *Mantua*, and guard their own Confines. *Charles* Duke of *Mantua* dying, and some Jealousies arising between the Princess and the *French*, the Senate interposed. In 1638 the *Barbary* Pyrates, who were now very numerous and strong, infested the Coasts of the *Adriatick* Gulph; and had a design, as 'twas thought, to plunder *Loretto*: But putting into *Valona* were pursued thither, and their Galleys taken and sunk by the *Venetian* Fleet. *Victory of Valona.* The *Turk* then ingaged in the *Persian* War, ordered the *Venetian* Consul to be taken up, and Reparation to be demanded for the *Corsaires* Galleys. Soon after, *Amurath* having taken *Babylon*, and returned to *Constantinople*, made great Preparations against the Republick; who were

not

not backward in the necessary Preparations on their sid but foreseeing they could have no Assistance from oth Christian Princes, (who were imbarqued in the quarr of *Piemont)* agreed to give *Amurath* some Money by wa of Reparation. The *Republick* thus happily rid of the Fears in the *Levant*, cast their Eyes upon *Italy*; for the Pr servation of which, they entered into a League with Po *Urban*, being much alarm'd at the *Spaniards* investir *Casal*. But their Fears on that side were soon dispele when they saw *Casal* relieved, and *Turin* taken by t *French*. They maintained an exact Neutrality betwee the two Contending Crowns. In 1641 a differen happening between the Duke of *Parma*, and the *Ba berins*, Nephews to Pope *Urban*, who exerted the

1641. Power and Authority to a Licentious Degree, to the gre Provocation of the Princes of *Italy*: A War broke ou the *Barbarins* taking *Castroe*, &c. which did not a litt perplex the Senate, whose chief study was to continue th Peace of *Italy*. The Senate resolving to make open For the last Remedy, interposed their utmost Efforts by wa of Mediation; but finding after many fruitless Conferen ces, that Pope *Urban* was stiff, and the *Barberins* elate with Success, they entered into a League with the grea

1642. The Pontifical and Confederate War. Duke of *Tuscany*, and the Duke of *Modena*, for the mu tual Defence of themselves, and of other *Italian* Princes particularly for the Protection of *Edward* Duke of *Parm* This done, the War (the greatest Burden of which fell o the *Venetians*) was carried on with various Success, be tween the Pontifical and the Confederate Army, till 164 by the diligent and effectual Mediation of Cardinal *Rich* Minister of *France*, Peace was concluded, to the mutu Satisfaction of the contending Parties. Pope *Urba* dying, his Successor, *Innocent* X. renewed the Inscrip tion in the Ambassadors Hall, in the *Vatican*, commem rating the glorious Merit of *Venice*, in having alone de fended Pope *Alexander* III. against *Frederick Barbaros* the Emperor, which Inscription Pope *Urban* had altere to the disadvantage of the *Republick*.

Francesco Molino, 1645. § 30. In the mean time *Francesco Molino* having ascen ed the Ducal Chair, the *Turks* starting new Pretensio upon the Kingdom of *Candia*, sent out a numerous an potent Fleet with 60000 Men, and took *Canea* by Tre

War of *Candia*. chery. Now *Candia* being conveniently situated for gre

In

Interprizes, as lying at equal distances from *Italy*, *Egypt*, and *Syria*, the *Republick* made vigorous Efforts to save it. But the *Turk* prevailing there, they made a strong Diversion in *Croatia* and *Dalmatia*, and after taking several Places, made themselves Masters of *Clissa*, that was reckoned invincible. This noble Victory was followed by the Accession of *Novogrod*, *Harissa*, *Tinus*, *Nadinus*, *Sassus*, *Viana*, and the Towering Castle of *Salo*, all which made sufficient Reparation for the loss of *Canea*. At Sea the *Turkish* Fleet was burnt by a *Venetian* Fireship sent in upon 'em in the Haven of *Foggium*. *Molino* dying, was succeeded by *Carlo Contareni*, who lived after his Election but 35 Days. *Carlo Contareni.* In which time, *Lazaro Mocenigo* gain'd an Important Victory over the *Turks* at *Sestos* and *Abydos*. The next Doge survived his Election but 20 Days. After him came *Bertuccio Valerio*, under whose Administration *Laurentio Mercelli* gain'd a compleat Victory at Sea, over the *Turks* at the *Dardanels*; and being shot with a Cannon Ball, his Command was taken up by *Badouaire*, who redoubled the Victory, and took *Tenedos*, and the *Cyclades*, to the great Consternation of the *Turkish* Emperor. *Francesco Cornaro, 1655. Bertuccio Valerio, 1655.* Mean time, upon the earnest Solicitation of Pope *Alexander* VII. the *Jesuits* were restored and kindly entertained in *Venice*, after they had been kept out above fifty Years: *Jesuits restored.* By which means the *Republick* hoped to ingage his Holiness in the Defence of *Candia*. *Valerio* dying, was succeeded by *Giovanni Pisauro*, who survived his Election but a Year and a half. *Giovanni Pisauro, 1658.*

§ 31. To him succeeded *Domenico Contareni*, who upon his Accession to the Ducal Chair, had the Satisfaction to see a Peace concluded betwixt *Spain* and *France*, and all Christendom in Tranquility. *Domenico Contareni, 1659.* He renewed the Alliance of the *Republick* with the Duke of *Savoy*, stipulating that the Duke should not assume the Title of King of *Cyprus*, which was then in the *Ottoman* Hands, and had been lawfully possessed by the *Venetians* for many Years. During his Administration, the War with the *Turks* was carried on with various Success. Notwithstanding the several Victories obtain'd by Sea and Land over the *Turks*, they over-ran the Island of *Crete*, and in 1667 laid Siege to the important Fort of *Candia*. The Pope suppressing three Ecclesiastical Orders, gave their Indowments to the *Republick* towards the Charge of the War. In 1669 *Lewis*

XIV.

XIV. King of *France* sent 7000 Foot, and 500 Horse, in the Pope's Name to the relieve of *Candia*, who mounting the Trenches with a precipitant Heat, and assuring themselves of the Victory, of a sudden gave way, upon the firing of a Barrel of Gunpowder, as apprehending the Ground to be all Undermined: Upon which the *Turks* pursued, and the *French*, who were run down by their own Men, left above 1000 Men upon the Spot, among whom was their General *Beaufort*. Upon this a Council of War being call'd, the Generals resolved, for the last Relief of the Besieged, to cut off part of the Town, and cover it with new Fortifications, that so the Infidels might have a new Town to take after the other part. But this not being agreed to by the *French* General, he shipp'd his Men and put to Sea. The *Turks* having Advice of the Departure of the *French*, made a fresh Attack upon the Besieged, but were so warmly received, that they were obliged to retire. After some Weeks the Besieged wanting both Men and Ground to stand upon, and despairing of Relief, enter'd into a Treaty with the Infidels *Sept.* 1669. by which 'twas provided, That the *Turks* should keep all the Island of *Candia*, excepting the Castles of *Suda*, *Garabusæ*, and *Spina Longa*; and make to the *Venetians* a Cession of *Clissa*, and all the Towns they had taken in *Dalmatia* and *Albania*. In this triennial Siege the Christians lost 29000 Soldiers, and 38000 Boors and Slaves that were employed in the Trenches and Mines. And thus did the Kingdom of *Candia* fall after a Twenty-five Years War; in which were buried 150 Millions of Gold, and 100000 Men.

Treaty of *Candia*.

The Humour and Genius of the *Venetians*.

§ 22. Having thus run thro' the Principal Heads of the *Venetian* History, concluding about the same Period of Time, with which *Puffendorf*'s Account of the other Nations terminates: We come now in pursuance of that Author's Method, to give some short hints of the Humour and Genius of the People, the Nature of the Soil, the Strength or Infirmity of the State, and the Relation they stand in to other Nations. The *Venetians* are a grave Prudent People, uniform in their Actions (at least to external appearance) and as firm and steady in the Prosecution of their Resolves, as they are slow in forming them. Their outward Appearance is always Serene, let the inward

inward Disquiet be never so great; and even in extream Difficulties their Constancy and Patience is invincible. The Authority of their Laws is kept up with a steady and equal hand, and has held an uninterrupted Course through all the Convulsions of the State. Their Friendship (in private Cases) is as firm, as its easily obtained by those who know how to manage them; and their Secrecy is inviolable not only in Affairs of State, but in ordinary Concerns. They live with great Oeconomy and Frugality in their private Families, and for that end seldom receive Visits, or entertain in their own Houses; transacting all their private Concerns in publick Places of Meeting, so that they can't readily form a Faction against the Government. Tho' they are very temperate in the use of Liquors, (whether through Vertue or Parsimony) they are strangely addicted to their Pleasures. Their Wives they treat like Servants, and watch them with the highest degree of Jealousie: And at the same time know no bounds to Whoredom. Notwithstanding their strict Jealousy with respect to their Wives, (whom they sometimes Stab upon the slenderest Suspicion) they readily agree to a Mistress in common; and this community of Embraces, which in all other Countries is the Subject of Discord and Hatred, is among them the firmest Bond of Union and Amity: Insomuch that the Senators do generally form and propagate their State Designs, at the interviews of these their Joint Amours. But above all, the Licentiousness of the Youth is without a Parallel; the Fathers and Mothers being so infinitely fond of their Children, that they never lay any restraint upon them, nor deny them any thing they desire; by which means, in conjunction with the sordid Flattery of their Domestick Servants, they become haughty, imperious, lascivious, and violent in all their Passions. Their Knowledge is confin'd to Affairs of their own Republick, and the Intrigues of the *Broglio*, where they meet publickly every Day. They read no Books but those of their own History and Customs; and, abating for such as have been Ambassadors at foreign Courts, they are very ignorant of Foreign Affairs. They are so wrapt up in their own Constitution, that they think the Government of *Venice* a just Standard and Model for all others. Dissimulation they practise to Perfection, and know admirably well how to cover the most inveterate Hatred with Flattery and Praise; Nay, some observe of them, that the more complaisant they appear, the keener is their Envy. Where they have done the least Injury, they bear eternal Enmity, as reckoning a true Reconciliation impossible. As they are implacable in their Hatred, they are cruel to the last degree in their Revenge: For 'tis one of the Ancient Maxims of their State, That it is a dangerous thing to shew Clemency to those they have injur'd, or to take Vengeance only by halves. Above all, their Silence upon the receiving of an Affront, is most to be suspected, for the more they conceal their Resentment, the more irreconcileable they are; choosing only to stifle it for a time, in order to discharge it with more fury thereafter. Ambition and Pride is the Predominant Quality of the *Venetians*; and yet the greatest of their Senators are observ'd to lay down the highest and most distinguishing Posts, without the least Reluctancy: And perhaps, one principal Cause of the long duration of their Republick, is, its consisting of Members that know so well how to obey; for no Place can give greater and more pregnant Instances of a perfect Submission to the Laws. Some observe that they are Timorous, Superstitious, and Credulous, and oftentimes let slip the fairest Opportunities for want of firm Courage, and a ready Presence of Mind: But that I take to be owing rather to the Constitution of their Government, which consists of so many Heads, and the affected slow-paced Gravity of their Counsels. Tho' they make a great shew of Piety and Devotion, are very Magnificent in their Churches and Hospitals, and seem inviolably to adhere to all the rigid Forms of the Church of *Rome*; yet, they have shewn upon several Occasions how little they regard either the Political or Spiritual Capacity of his Holiness, especially when any Incroachment is offered to the Measures of their State.

The Government of Venice.

§ 33. The Government of *Venice* is chiefly *Aristocratick*, the whole Authority being lodg'd in the hands of a certain number of Families written in the golden Book, which is a Register of the *Venetian* Nobility. This Nobility or Gentry pretend to be of more ancient Descent than any other in *Europe*; nay, many of 'em have run the merit of their Antiquity so far, as to think themselves equal with Sovereign Princes. And indeed it must be own'd, own'd, that some of 'em have unquestion'd Proofs of an Antiquity, not only equal with, but even Prior to, the Time of the first Foundation of the Republick. This Nobility is divided into three Orders. The First consists of those Twelve Families that were the Twelve Tribunes, who elected the first Doge of the Republick, *Anno* 709; including likewise Twelve more, whose Antiquity is in a manner Parallel to that of the first Twelve, as being very considerable, long before the *Il Serrar del Consiglio*. The Second Order consists of those who are declar'd Hereditary Members of the great Council, call'd *Serrar del Consiglio*, erected *Anno* 1289, and Thirty Families more that were admitted about 100 Years after, for their good Services in the *Genouese* War. The Third Order comprehends Sixscore Families, who purchas'd their Nobility with Money, upon the pressing Exigencies of the *Candian* War, which exhausted the Treasure of the Republick. These three Orders compose that August Number, in whom the Political Power is lodged. The Nobility or Gentry of the *Terra firma*, that is, out of *Venice*, and within the Dominions of the Republick, are not admitted to any Share in the Political Government; but compose the *Councils* of the Cities where they live, which have a limited Power of Regulating some Inferiour concerns. The Doge has only Precedency before the other Magistrates; but his Robes and Habits are so rich and distinguishing, that they give a Majestick Air in Publick Ceremonies, if the Sword which the Senate orders to be carried behind him, were not a mark of his dependance. This slender share of Authority is recompenc'd by the continuance of his Dignity, which is during Life; with this restriction, that if old Age or Sickness render him incapable of performing his Function, the Senate has Power to depose him. In fine, the Doge is only an Image and Shadow of Majesty, while the Senate reserves the Power to themselves only; for since the Republick has been govern'd by Doges, there has happen'd no Alteration in their Method of Government, which did not tend to the Diminution of the Prince's Authority. The Senate knowing perfectly well, that the Liberty of the Republick is inconsistent with the Libertine Power of a Prince. All the Majesty of this Prince resides in the *College*, a Court compos'd of the Doge and Twenty six Assistants, who give Audience to Ambassadors, dispatch Letters, receive

Petitions, and in fine, prepare Matters to be debated and regulated by the *Pregadi*. This *Pregadi* is the Senate, in which resides the Authority of the Republick. They consult of Peace and War, Leagues and Alliances, the disposal of all Posts of Honour and Trust, the Nomination of Ambassadors, the Laying on of Taxes, the Nomination of the Members of the College; and in fine, are the very Soul of the State, and consequently of all the Actions in the Body of the Republick. 'Tis compos'd of Sixscore Senators (nominated by the great Council) who are always of an advanc'd Age, known Merit, and antient Nobility. Tho' the *Pregadi* regulates without controul the Affairs of State, yet the *Great Council*, which is the Assembly General of all the Nobility, is the first Tribunal, and indeed the Basis and last Court of resource in the Government. For the *Great Council* hath Power to Enact new Laws, choose Senators, confirm the Transactions of the Senate, and in fine to rectify and regulate all manner of Mismanagements. Besides these, there is a very considerable Council, call'd the *Council of Ten*, who have the Cognizance of all Criminal Matters, both in the City and State of the Republick. They are called the Inexorable Judges, and are chang'd every Year, and have such Power, that they can condemn even the Doge to Death without acquainting the Senate. To conclude, the Government of *Venice* has all its Springs chain'd together in perfect good Order: In it we see so just a Temperament, such an admirable Reciprocation of Superiority and Dependance, that from thence results a perfect Union, and a fervent Zeal for the common Welfare, which are the lasting Foundations of the Power and Strength of the Republick. In it, we have a perfect appearance of *Monarchy*, *Aristocracy*, and *Democracy*; for the Majesty of a Sovereign shines in the Person of the Doge, in whose Name all Dispatches and Negotiations run: The *Pregadi* represents a real *Aristocracy*, as the great Council does a *Democracy*. The most peculiar thing in the Government of *Venice*, is, That all the Nobles that turn Ecclesiasticks, are excluded for ever from any Charge in the State; by which Maxim they keep the Ecclesiasticks in dependance, and are as Absolute in the Ecclesiastical Government as that of the State; insomuch that they would never permit the common Ecclesiastical Jurisdiction to be establish'd in their State, with the same Authority that all other Chri-

stian

stian Princes allow. As for the Provinces of the Republick, they are govern'd by *Proveditors*, who have Absolute Power in the Affairs relating to Peace and War; besides which, they have a *Podestate* to Administer Justice, and a Captain of Arms to Command the respective Guards and Garrisons. They are likewise visited once in five Years by three Senators, call'd the Inquisitors of the *Terra firma*, who Hear and Redress the Peoples Complaints, examine into the Administration of the *Podestates*, Captains, and other Officers, *&c.* These Magistrates execute Justice with great Severity; by which means the Senate keeps the Officers to their Duty, and the Country Nobility in Fear and Submission; and insinuates into the People, the Mildness and Equity of the Government under which they live. In the City of *Venice*, besides the Nobility describ'd above, and the common People, there is a Midling State, call'd the Citizens of *Venice*; which are divided into two Classes. The first are originally Citizens by Birth, as being descended from those Families which had a share in the Government before the Establishment of the great Council, upon the Election of Doge *Gradenigo*; and these would not yield either in Birth or Riches to the best Houses in *Venice*, if they liv'd without the Dominions of the Republick. The Second Order of *Citizens* consists of such, as have either by Birth or Money obtain'd that Privilege in the Republick. The Privilege of Citizens consists in wearing Vests as well as the Nobles, and being Candidates for all such Posts and Places as are thought below a Noble *Venetian*, the highest of which is that of Great Chancellor of the Republick. To conclude, the Government of *Venice* are very frugal Managers of their Revenues, but affect a wonderful Splendidness in their Embassies: Foreign Ambassadors they treat with great Respect, but are mighty careful in not leting them into the Secrets of their Affairs.

The most considerable part of their Trade lies to *Persia*, *Constantinople*, and *Germany*, whether they send an incredible Quantity of Brocades, Damasks, and Cloths of Gold. For the Preservation of this Trade, they grant great Privileges and Immunities to each respective Nation inhabiting among them. Trade.

Venice is naturally defended against all the Attacks of a Naval Force, since Ships of Burthen can't approach nearer than the Port of *Malomoca*; for those that pass up The City of *Venice*, its Strength.

up to *Venice* by the *Lagunes*, are obliged to be first Unladed, and then towed up through certain Passages, where the deepness of Water sufficient for Ships of Burden is mark'd out by great Piles; or else to return to Sea, taking the same Course that the Galleys do, and come in through the Port of *Lido*, where the great Current of Water has preserved a deeper Channel than in any other part of the *Lagunes*. Now this Port of *Lido* is very well fortify'd, and the Entrance is nothing near a Musquet-shot over. On the other hand, it is of the highest importance to *Venice*, to secure and defend these two Ports or Entrances; for if an hostile Army should get Possession of one of 'em, the City would quickly be reduc'd to the last Extremity. On the Land side they are yet more Secure, in regard the few Roads or Causeys that lead to *Venice*, are easily cut in any pressing Necessity, so as to render the City inaccessible on that Side, considering the shallowness of the *Lagunes*, running about fives Miles from the City to the *Terra firma*; in which course the smallest Boats must now and then run aground. As their principal Strength consists in the shallowness of the *Lagunes*, so it sometimes Alarms the Republick in a very sensible manner: For the Ground rising continually higher and choaking the Entrances of the Ports, they fear it may at last become dry, or at least inaccessible to Ships of Burthen; and for that Reason are put to an inexpressible Charge in clearing the *Lagunes*. The Populousness of *Venice*, the great resort to it from all Parts, the Conveniency of its Situation by vertue of adjacent Rivers and Canals, which convey all things to it in great plenty, we pass over as being commonly known; as well as their Possessions in the *Terra firma* and *Dalmatia*, and their Islands in the *Mediterranean*.

The Interest of *Venice*.

§ 35. The Interest of *Venice* seems now to consist in Preserving, rather than in enlarging her Dominions; and that by Treaty and Alliances, rather than by open War. She has smarted sufficiently for fomenting and improving to her own Advantage the Divisions of her Neighbours, and establishing her Greatness upon their Ruins. As she has of late Years, so it still behoves her to endeavour, by all means, to preserve the Peace and Tranquility of *Italy*, and maintain a perfect good Understanding with all the *Italian* Princes. *Italy* (the Gar-

With respect to the Princes of *Italy*.

den

tion of Europe) must needs prove an alluring Bait to a foreign Power, if their intestine Divisions furnish the Opportunity. The *Venetians* ought to cultivate Peace with the Pope, and maintain his temporal Sovereignty; since the conveyance of the Holy Patrimony into powerful and active Hands, would overturn the Ballance of Power in *Italy*; not to mention, that his Holiness may be of great use to the *Venetians* in case of a Rupture with the *Turks*, by gaining them Confederates. Their Alliance should be inviolable with the Duke of *Savoy*, who keeps the keys of *Italy*, and through whose Territories the *French* can only molest it: And on the other hand, that Duke can best, and most securely, rely upon the Alliance of the *Venetians*, and the other States of *Italy*, to maintain the Possession of his Country, that lies wedged in between the Territories of the House of *Austria*, and those of the House of *Bourbon*. As for the *Turks*, there's no Enemy the *Venetians* ought more to dread; they have already receiv'd many and severe Blows from them; under the Weight of which, the Republick bends to this day. The most beneficial Branch of their Trade, is that to *Constantinople* and the East: So that 'tis by no means their Interest, to be the first Aggressors with the *Turks*. On the other hand, if he should invade *Italy*, or their Dominions, he can't but expect, that the Pope, and all the *Italian* Princes, will joyn in the mutual Defence. Considering, that *Spain* is now no more in a Condition to threaten the Liberty and Peace of *Italy*, 'tis the interest of *Venice*, that *Milan* and *Naples* should continue in its hands. When the House of *Austria* was formidable, and had projected the Conquest of *Italy*, the Senate did wisely side with the *French*, &c. to retrieve a just Ballance of Power: But now that this House is in a declining Condition, 'tis their reciprocal interest to support it; lest the *French* King, gaining Possession of *Milan*, should over-run *Italy*. But withal, if the House of *Austria* should ever offer to inlarge their Territories in *Italy*, *Venice* and all the *Italian* States will take the Alarm, and oppose them, even at the hazard of calling in *France* to their assistance. As for *France* it self, as long as he keeps on the North side of the *Alps*, the *Italian* States will scarce care to meddle with him; tho' they can't but entertain a just Jealousy of his growing Power. The Security of the Republick, lyes in keeping an even hand between the Houses of *Austria* and *Bourbon*; and when either

The Pope.

The Duke of Savoy.

The Turks.

Spain.

France.

ther of 'em is exorbitant, to make use of the Alliance the other, to recover a just Ballance. With the *Swiss* a the *Grisons*, the *Venetians* will always cultivate Frier ship; from them they can have Mercenary Troops up a Call, without the difficulty of marching thro' an inte vening Country: Besides that, the *Grisons* Country is t only interjacent Bulwark that dis-unites *Germany* fro *Milan*, and the *Venetians* will always be jealous of seei the Territories of the Imperial Branch of the House *Austria*, joyn those of the *Spanish* Branch in *Italy*: Wi ness their vigorous Efforts in the Affair of the *Valteline*, the beginning of the Seventeenth Century. 'Tis high the Interest of *Venice*, to cultivate Peace and Allian with the Imperial Court, upon the account of the Neighbourhood to the *Turks*, whom the Imperialists ca effectually divert, when they offer to Attack the Repu lick. At the same time, they will scarce care to see th Emperor possess'd of considerable Territories in *Italy*, c to see the House of *Austria* inlarge their Power to an great heighth in that Country. In fine, considering wha a beneficial Trade the *Venetians* have to *Germany*, an how near their Territories are to the Hereditary Coun tries, they must study, by all means, to cultivate Peac with the Emperor. From the *Barbary* Shoar they have no thing to fear, if they keep but a few Galleys to scour the Gulf, and defend their Shiping from the *Corsaires*. As for the two Maritim Powers, (*England* and *Holland*) 'tis absolutely the Interest of *Venice* to cultivate Peace with them, both upon the score of the Trade of these two Nations to *Venice*, and upon the account of the vast Superiority of the *French* Naval Force in the *Mediteranean*, which must ever range there without controul, unless these Northern Maritim Powers send Fleets into those Seas.

Swiss and *Grisons*.

Germany.

Coast of *Barbary*.

England and *Holland*.

MO-

MODENA.

§ 1. MODENA, the chief Town of the Country nam'd *Modena* in *Italy*, with a Bishoprick, Suffragan to *Bologna*, was anciently better known by the Name of *Mutina*, and famous in those Times for the first Battle between *Anthony* and *Augustus Cæsar*; in which *Hirtius* and *Pansa*, the *Roman* Consuls, lost their Lives, and *Augustus* gain'd the principal Step to his future Greatness. 'Twas then a *Roman* Colony, but afterwards shar'd in the common Calamity of *Italy*, arising from the Northern Inundations; being ruin'd by the Fury of the *Goths* and *Lombards*, though afterwards new Built at the Charge of the Citizens, in the Reign of *Charlemaigne*'s Sons. In the Distractions of *Italy*, between the Emperors and the Popes, *Guido* the Pope's Legate, and then Bishop thereof, consign'd it to *Azo*, Lord of *Ferrara*, of the House of *Estè*; in which Family it still continues, with the Countries and Territories bearing the same Name. Now of this Family of *Estè*, which claims the greatest Antiquity of any in *Italy*; the first remarkable Person, was *Forestus* of *Estè*, who appearing very forward at the general Rendezvous at *Padua*, was made Commander of the Forces sent to relieve *Aquileia*, and forcing his Way thro' *Attila*'s Army, enter'd the City and made a vigorous defence; but was unfortunately kill'd in a Sally, being drawn into an Ambush by the Treachery of his Soldiers. His Son *Acarinus* brought fresh Supplies to the City, and when he found it reduc'd to the last Extremity, retir'd with the besieged to *Grado*. After that he supplied *Altinum* in like manner, notwithstanding *Attila*'s vigorous Efforts to prevent him; and when he could hold out no longer, convey'd the Inhabitants in Boats to the Islands of *Boran*, *Mazorbo*, and *Torcella*. At the same time he advis'd the Inhabitants of *Treviso*, *Padua*, and *Vicenza*, to retire to *Malomoco*, and the other little Islands in the *Adriatick* Sea, which gave rise to the famous City and Republick of *Venice*, that has since prov'd the greatest Ornament of

The Condition of the Family of *Estè* before the Invasion of the *Lombards*.

Acarinus.

of *Italy*, and the Wonder of the World. His own People, (I mean those of *Esté*) he conducted to *Palæstrina* and *Chiozza* near the Mouth of the *Po*, *An.* 461. The *Alains*
461. making an Incursion into *Italy*, *Severianus* the Emperor raised an Army to expel 'em, and made *Acarinus* General of Horse; who distinguished himself so much by his Bravery and Conduct in the decisive Battle of *Borgamo*, that shook off the Yoak of the *Alains*, that he was made Go-
471. vernour of all the Parts that lie beyond the River *Adige*, as being the fittest Person to guard the Frontiers against the Barbarous Nations, which commonly made their Inroads that way. This great Trust he injoyed till the Battle near *Lodi*, in which *Acarinus* was defeated and kill'd by *Odoacer* King of the *Hercules*, upon which the Western
Azo. Empire was entirely abolished. *Azo* and *Constantius* the two Sons of *Acarinus* retired to *Germany*, where *Azo* mar-
481. ried the Daughter of *Theodo* Duke of *Bavaria*. After that they served with distinguishing Characters under *Theodorick* King of the *Ostrogoths* against *Odoacer*, and having done great Services in the three several Battles where *Odo-*
491. *acer* was defeated, and at the Siege of *Ravenna*, where he was forced to surrender part of his Kingdom to save the rest. *Theodorick* treated 'em during his whole Reign with very particular Marks of his Favour and Bounty. And after *Theodorick*'s Death, when *Theodatus* imprisoned and
Constantius, put to Death his Daughter *Amalasuntha*. *Constantius* mind-
534. ful of his obligations to *Theodoricks* Family, resented the
539. Murder of the Innocent Queen, by inviting and assisting *Justinian* to dethrone *Theodatus*. *Constantius* dying not
Boniface. long after, *Basilius* his Son, and *Boniface* his Cozen had the Honour of pursuing the War, (thus begun by *Constantius*) both under *Belisarius* and *Narses*, and assisted in that great Battle where the *Goths* were over-thrown, in which
553. *Boniface* was mortally wounded. But *Basilius* survived the Victory, and saw the War put to an end in the Extirpation of the Eastern *Goths*: Upon which insued the Invasion of the *Lombards*.

§ 2. In the time of the *Lombards*, this Family continued
574. to make a considerable Figure. The Kingdom of *Lombardy* being divided into thirty Dukedoms, *Basilius* and
585. *Valerian* (the Son of *Boniface*) ingaged and defeated the Duke of *Friuli*. *Valerian* dyed, fighting with the *French*
Aldoardus, Auxiliaries against the *Lombards*. *Aldoardus* his Son, Heir
626.

to

to his Father's Courage as well as Fortune, bravely defended *Monfelice* his Patrimonial Possession against the Duke of *Friuli*, to whom he was afterwards reconcil'd. His Cozen and Heir *Eribert* liv'd and dyed in Peace, who *Eribert.* was succeeded by his Son *Ernestus*, who was general for 694. the *Lombards* against the *Sclavonians*, whom he brought to *Ernestus.* reasonable Terms; but in the business of *Ravenna* he stood 718. by the Emperor, defended that Town twice at the Head 740. of a *Venetian* Army, saved *Rimini*, and was shot in the third Siege of the former. *Charles* the great coming into 770. *Italy* to finish the Destruction of the *Lombard* Monarchy, *Henry* the Son or Grandson of *Ernestus*, appeared at the *Henry.* Head of the *Venetian* Troops sent to assist the *French*, and behaved himself so well, that *Charles* added to his former Possessions *Treviso* and *Scodosia* with the Title of Count. 774. *Henry* being murdered by the Instigation of the Duke of First Count of *Estè.* *Friuli*, who lost his Head for it, his Son *Berengarius* headed the Army of the Emperor *Lewis* VII. against *Bernard* *Berengarius.* King of *Italy*, and perswaded *Bernard* to surrender himself to his Uncle, tho' he had no hand in his Uncle's Cruelty towards him. After that he still stood by the Emperor and shared in his Misfortunes, and died at *Paris*, with the Repute of one of the wisest and greatest Captains of his Age. His Son *Otho*, General of Horse to the Emperor 840. *Lewis* XI. gave him the City and Territory of *Commachio*, *Otho.* as a Reward of his own and his Father's Services to the Imperial Crown: Upon which the *Venetians*, ever jealous of their growing Neighbours, took Possession of it, complaining that *Marinus*, *Otho*'s Son, had affronted their Ambassador in his way to *Rome*, in seizing him and making him swear never to attempt any thing to the prejudice of *Commachio*. But by the Emperor's Intercession *Otho* got *Commachio*, and the Ancient Friendship betwixt the Republick and the Family of *Estè* was renewed. *Ubertus* 887. the Son of *Otho* was very serviceable to *Berengarius* King of *Ubertus.* *Italy* in all his Troubles, and had a large share in his Bounty and Affection: His Brother *Sigfred* was chosen Governour or Prince of *Parma* and *Lucca*: *Almericus* his Brother's Son was chosen first Rector, and then Prince of *Ferrara*: *Albertus* his own Son, married *Gisela*, King *Berengarius*'s Daughter. *Hugo* and *Azo*, the two Sons of *Alber-* 903. *tus* distinguished themselves on several Occasions, particu- *Albertus.* larly *Hugh* delivered *Adeleidis*, *Lotharius*'s Widow (be- *Hugo* and *Azo.* trothed to *Otho* King of *Germany*) from the Tyranny and 892.

Cru-

Cruelty of *Berengarius*, and made way for *Otho's* Possessing himself of the Imperial Crown: For which Services he was made Governour of all that Tract of Country, that is now known by the name of *Milan*, *Montferrat*, *Piemont*, and *Genoua*. *Hugo* dying, and *Berengarius* returning again to *Italy* with the Title of King, *Azo* was by him turned out of all he had, and forced to fly with his Son to *Germany*, from whence neither of 'em ever returned.

960.

Azo III. *Vicar of* Italy, 970.

§ 3. With them must the Family of *Este* have perished, had not the hopeful Issue of *Sigfred*, Prince of *Parma* supported it: for his eldest Son *Azo* took possession of the Estate in spite of the Tyrant, and confirmed his younger Brothers in theirs at *Parma* and *Lucca*. This *Azo* being declared General of the Emperor's Army, obtained signal Victories, reduced several Places to the Emperor's Obedience, accepted of the Offer made by *Piacenza* and *Reggio* to come under his Protection, and was by the Emperor made Vicar of *Italy*. *Albertus* the eldest Son of *Azo* succeeding to vast Possessions by the Death of his Father and Uncle, was created Marquis of *Este* by the Emperor, who likewise gave him his Daughter in Marriage. He was intrusted in the chief Posts of Government by the succeeding Emperors, *Otho* II. and *Otho* III. having been eminently Instrumental in setting the Imperial Crown upon their Heads. His Son *Hugh* having discovered a Conspiracy of the *Romans* against *Otho* III. for puting to Death *Crescentius*, and narrowly saved him, was by the Emperor created Marquis of *Italy*, a Title never given to any other. Upon the Death of *Otho* III. *Hugh* Marquis of *Italy* finding *Henry* Duke of *Bavaria* chosen Emperor, whose Father had been opposed by his Father *Albertus*, put up *Ardoinus* for King of *Italy*, and *Henry* proving successful, was taken Prisoner with his three Sons; but thro' the Emperor's Clemency, and his Regard to Merit, was restored to his former Dignity, and did the Emperor considerable Service in advancing his Authority, without invading the Rights of the People. *Azo* the Son and Successor of *Hugh* married the Duke of *Bavaria's* only Daughter, whose Son *Welpho* falling Heir to his Grandfather the Duke of *Bavaria*, gave the first Rise to the Illustrious Family of *Brunswick* and *Lunenburgh*, which is thus descended of the Family of *Este*. By a second Marriage to the Emperor's Daughter, Niece or Grandchild, *Azo* had a Son, *viz*. *Azo*

Albertus.

First Marquis of *Este*.

993. *Hugo*, II.

Marquis of *Italy*, 1000.

1026 *Azo*, IV.

The rise of the *Lunenburg* Family.

zo V. who, if the Pope had not shewed himself most unjust in the matter of his Marriage with his Cousin, the Countess *Matildis*, was in a fair way to have been one of the richest Princes of that Age; for *Matildis* being the only Daughter of *Boniface*, Son to *Theodald*, Uncle to the great *Hugo* of *Est* became Heir to *Tuscany*, *Ferrara*, *Modena*, *Mantua*, *Regio*, *Lucca*, *Parma*, and *Verona*; and married first to the Duke of *Lorain*, upon whose Death she married her Cousin *Azo*; but he favouring the Emperor against Pope *Gregory* VII. the Pope divorced her from him, after which she married her Cousin *Welpho* Duke of *Bavaria*; but her love to her Husband was always grounded on their Devotion to the Pope, and she spared no Cost, Pains nor Danger to advance the Papal Authority in opposition to the Imperial. *Matildis* dying, left to the holy See what we now call the Patrimony of St. *Peter*, and several Cities in *Tuscany*; and 'tis certainly her whom *Rome* must chiefly thank, and others blame, for the Pope's bearing such a Figure since, among the temporal Princes of *Italy*. *Matildis* having by this her unnatural Conduct almost destroyed the Family that gave her a Being. *Azo* dying, his Brother *Bertoldus* had a great Hand in reconciling the Emperor and the Pope; and after that living privately upon his Patrimonial Lands, left his Son *Rinaldus*, who proved a great General in the War of *Milan* against *Frederick Barbarossa*. For *Rinaldus* disgusted for not having a share of *Matildis*'s Estate, and being chosen General by the Confederates Cities against that Emperor, brought 10000 of his own Men into the Field, and being joyned by the respective *Quota*'s of the Cities, made a Review of 50000 Men well armed at *Milan*; before which, the Emperor with the Kings of *Bohemia*, *Denmark*, and *Norway*, sate down with 110000. *Rinaldus* finding his Army moulder by Famine and Sickness, marched out to give Battle to the Enemy, and after a Bloody Engagement in which the King of *Bohemia* was wounded, gain'd a compleat Victory, the Emperor escaping narrowly: But his Son *Azo* being taken Prisoner in the Battle, and *Barbarossa* obstinately refusing to set him at Liberty while his Father lived; *Rinaldus* drop'd the Pursuit of so glorious a Victory, and threw up his Commission, for fear of exasperating the Emperor, while he had such an Hostage from his Family. Upon this ensued the Destruction of *Milan* and the Submission of all the other Cities. Soon after the Cities grow-

[Margin notes: 1037. Azo, V. — The odd Conduct of Matildis. — 1105. — 1115. — Bertoldus. — Rinaldus 1137. — Battle of Milan. — Rinaldus's Son taken.]

1161. growing uneasy under the Yoak of the Imperial *Podesta's*, they sollicited *Rinaldus* to be their General, but his Tenderness to his Son made him deaf to all Perswasion; and 1174. in 1174 he died.

1175. *Azo*, VI. § 3. *Rinaldus* dying, his Son *Azo* VI. who was in the Emperor's Custody, was honourably dismiss'd by him, that the World might see he would not revenge the Father's Guilt upon the Son; and the Government of *Milan* was added to his Patrimonial Possessions. But he dying *Opizo*. soon after, was succeeded by his Cousin *Opizo*; whose Rise begat great Emulation in the Breasts of two powerful Neighbours, and the most dangerous Enemies the Family of *Estè* ever dealt with, *viz. Salinguerra*, *Taurellus* of *Ferrara*, and *Actiolinus* of *Onara*, who had married *Azo's* Sister. The former stir'd up the People of *Ferrara* against *Opizo*; but he having obliged them by procuring from the Emperor *Henry* VI. some Privileges, which they had lost by being undutiful to his Father, this friendly Act did so affect them, that they obliged the Marquis to send his Son *Azo* to live among them: And from that Instant we date 1184. the House of *Estè's* taking sure footing in *Ferrara*. In the mean time *Actiolinus* had seiz'd upon *Rovigo* (belonging to the Marquis) claiming a Title by his Wife; and the *Guelph* and *Gibelline* Factions being then spread all over *Italy*, the former declaring for the Emperor, and the latter for the Pope; *Actiolinus* to secure the Emperor's Favour, and to strengthen his Party against *Opizo*, declared himself Head of the *Gibellines*, which obliged *Opizo* to take upon him *Azo*, VII. the Protection of the *Guelphs*. Soon after *Opizo* died; but 1193. a few days before his Death, his Son *Azo* heading the *Veronese* and *Ferrarese* defeated *Actiolin* at *Bachilio*. *Azo* marrying a Nobleman's Daughter of *Ferrara*, was received there with all the Formalities of a Prince. *Salinguerra* and *Actiolin* having conspired to be absolute in *Verona*, *Azo* 1200. upon the request of the Citizens, encountered them in the Market-place, took the latter Prisoner, while the other escaped, and restored the City to its Ancient Freedom; af-1209. ter which he did the like to *Pescera*. His Cousin *Otho* being made Emperor, gave him the Principality of *Verona*, the Government of the Mark of *Ancona*, and several Castles belonging to *Vicenza*: Notwithstanding which, *Azo* afterwards joyn'd with the Pope's Sentence against *Otho*, declaring for *Frederick* II. and made a considerable Figure

at

at the Head of the *Guelphs*. *Azo* dying, was succeeded by his Son *Aldobrandin*; who being opposed by *Salinguerra*, *Aldobrandin.* and assisted by the *Bolognese*, took *Ferrara*, and by the Intercessions of the *Bolognese*, suffered *Salinguerra* to live there. Soon after he rais'd the Siege of *Este*, and drove the *Gibellines* from the Mark of *Ancona*; for which the Pope made him Marquis of *Ancona*.

§ 5. *Aldobrandin* dying, his Brother *Azo*, a Person well 1216. versed both in Peaceful and Military Arts, succeeded and *Azo* VIII. setled at *Ferrara*; but a Civil War arising there between the *Guelphs* and the *Gibellines*, the former headed by *Azo*, and the latter by *Salinguerra*, the City was reduced by the various Insurrections to a heap of Rubish; after which *Salinguerra* and *Azo* came to an Accommodation, stipulating that all, whether *Guelphs* or *Gibellines* should return, and *Azo* should not come to *Ferrara* above twice a Year. These Concessions *Azo* gave out of tenderness to Count 1226. *Boniface* the Pope's Legate, whom *Salinguerra* had perfidiously detain'd. The *Guelphs* headed by *Azo*, and the *Gibellines* under the Command of *Actiolin*, (the Son of the *Actiolin* above-mentioned) having tired out and almost ruined the Country; a welcome Peace was concluded and sealed with the Marriage of *Actiolin's* Niece to *Rinaldus*, 1237. *Azo's* Son. But the Peace signified little, for Hostilities still continued between *Azo* and *Actiolin*. In the mean time *Salinguerra* falling out with the *Venetians*, upon the score of the Toll that they demanded on the *Po*, and having expell'd the *Gibellines* from *Ferrara*, contrary to his Treaty with *Azo*; *Azo* being chosen General of the *Guelphs*, and assisted by the *Venetians*, took *Ferrara* after an obstinate Resistance of four Months, and the City unanimously declared him their Prince. *Salinguerra* was sent Prisoner to *Venice*; the *Venetians* in consideration of their Charge *The House of Este Princes of Ferrara.* were allow'd to settle a Magistrate in *Ferrara*; and the Pope's Legate, who was likewise concerned in the Expedition, took upon him, in his Master's Name to confirm the City's Choice of the Marquis of *Este* for their Prince, which at first seem'd to be only Matter of Ceremony, but was strangely made use of afterwards, to prove the Pope's Title to that City. After that *Azo* and *Actiolin*, the one at the Head of the *Guelphs*, and the other of the *Gibellines*, 1245. pursued one another with alternative Success again and again, and made *Italy* a Scene of Blood and Confusion,

and

and Treachery and all manner of Barbarity. *Actiolin* or
1256. *Ezelino* the Head of the *Gibellines* being then terrible to his Neighbours, by reason of his unparrallel'd Cruelty, the *Venetians*, the Pope and the Marquis entered into a League against him, and took or rather relieved *Padua*, which had for some time been the unhappy Scene of *Actiolin*'s Cruelty. Soon after the Marquis gave battle to *Actiolin*, and took him Prisoner, upon which he died of Grief and Vexation. *Azo* being again declared General of a new *Croisado*, he besieged *Albericus*, *Actiolin*'s Brother, in the Castle of St. *Zeno*, and put him with his Wife, six Sons and two Daughters, to miserable Deaths; thus extirpating that Family of *Onara*, that had for several Ages aimed at an absolute Dominion over that part of *Italy*, and rendered their Memory odious to all Posterity by their insupportable Tyranny and Barbarity. This done, the Marquis check'd the Insolence of *Mastino* *Scaliger* *Podesta* of *Verona*, and died soon after much lamented by the *Guelphs*.

The fall of the House of *Onara*.

Opizo II. 1266. § 6. He was succeeded by his Grandchild *Opizo*, who in Conjunction with his Guardians promoted the Accession of *Charles* of *Anjou* to the Crown of *Naples*. When he came to be of Age, he maintain'd a strict Union with *Charles*, which drew upon him the Displeasure of Pope *Nicolaus* III. and engaged him in a War with *Scaliger* of *Verona*, and the *Gibellines*, which ended in a favourable Peace.
1276.
1286. In short, *Opizo* marrying the Prince of *Verona*'s Daughter, instead of heading the Faction, applyed himself to the composing of the unhappy Animosities that had so long rent *Italy*; and *Modena* and *Reggio* chose him for their Prince. By thus promoting the Peace of *Italy*, he got more in a few Years, than his Father had done all his time by Fomenting their unnatural Divisions. His Successor was *Azo* IX. who began a War with *Bologna* in resentment of their ill Offices, in diswading *Parma* from choosing him for their Prince; which terminated in Peace by the Intercession of the Pope and the *Florentines*. Being declared General of the Confederacy against *Visconti* of *Milan*, he managed the War successfully, and upon the Conclusion of Peace married his Sister to *Galeazzo*, *Visconti*'s Son. *Visconti* being a little depressed, *Azo* was absolutely the greatest Prince in *Lombardy*; for besides *Ferrara*, *Modena*, *Reggio*, *Rovigo*, *Commacchio*, with several other Places of less note, all his

The House of *Este* Princes of *Modena*.

Azo IX. 1297.

own

own; *Bergamo*, *Cremona*, *Crema*, and *Pavia* lived under his Protection. He married the youngest Daughter of *Charles* II. King of *Naples*; and this Alliance added to his Greatness, made his Neighbours jealous of him, insomuch that *Verona*, *Mantua*, *Parma* and *Bologna* by the Instigation of the Pope declared War against him, and took *Modena* and *Reggio*. For such was the State of Affairs in *Lombardy* in that Age, that when any one Potentate grew too great, the rest combined to humble him. At the same time, his Brother *Francis* rebelled, and *Azo* dying, got himself declared Marquis of *Ferrara*, to the prejudice of *Friscus*, *Azo*'s Son, who fled to *Venice* and there dyed. *Francis* thus raised by the help of the Legate of *Bologna*, was soon after murdered by his Order at *Rovigo*. By this means the Pope got *Ferrara*, and to keep it from the Emperor as well as to humour the People, consigned it into the Hands of *Robert* King of *Naples*, Brother-in-Law to *Azo* IX. But the Inhabitants disobliged by their Governor, made an Insurrection, and called home *Azo* the Son of *Francis*. *Azo* dying soon after, was succeeded by *Rinaldus* his Cousin, the Son of *Aldobrandin*, Brother to *Azo* IX. and *Francis*. The Pope having excommunicated the Prince and the City, *Milan*, *Verona*, and *Lucca* entered into an Alliance for their Defence; upon which the Pope took off the Sentence. But not long after, the Legate of *Bologna* unexpectedly invested *Ferrara* with 30000 Men; upon which *Milan*, *Mantua*, and *Verona*, without distinction of *Guelphs* or *Gibellines*, in this common danger sent Forces to relieve it. Upon their approach the Marquis went out to lead 'em, and the City sallying out at the same time, the Pope's Army was surprised, and received such a total Overthrow, that very few escaped being killed or taken Prisoners.

Modena and *Reggio* taken, 1308.

Francis.

Ferrara lost and recovered.

Azo X.
Rinaldus II.

1327.

§ 7. *Rinaldus* dying, was succeeded by his Brother *Opizo*, who retook *Modena*, and bought *Parma* of *Azo* of *Correggio*; but soon after perceiving how *Visconti* and *Gonzagua* lay both in wait for it, and considering that it lay at a distance from his other Territories, he parted with it upon the same Terms that he bought it. *Opizo*'s Successor was *Aldobrandin* the second, who bafled the Attempts of his Uncle *Francis* upon *Ferrara*, and relieved *Modena* when besieged by *Visconti* of *Milan*, the War betwixt *Venice* and *Genua* having then divided the Princes of *Italy* into two

Opizo III.
Modena retaken.

Aldobrandin II. 1336.

Factions. *Aldobrandin* dying young, was succeeded l Brother *Nicolaus*, who defeated *Barnabas Visconti* of M and obliged him to Peace. But *Visconti*, possessing which of right belonged to *Nicolaus*, he retook it, then was contented to stand on his own Defence. *laus* left but one Son, who entring into a Religious O resigned all to his Cousin *Albertus*; who apprehensi *Galeazzo*'s Power cultivated Peace with him, and fou the University of *Ferrara*. But when he thought to dedicated the rest of his time, and no small part of hi venue to the *Muses*, his sudden Death deprived the l ed of the best Patron of that Age. He left his Son N *us*, yet a Child, to the tuition of the chief Families o *rara*, empowering them to administer by turns; th having some share in the Government, they might the heartily espouse their young Prince's Interest. Duri Minority, *Azo* the Son of *Francis*, and a Crandch the Family of *Visconti*, giving frequent Alarms, they fain to pawn *Rovigo* to the *Venetians* for a Sum of M By the Interest of the *Venetians* a Match was conclude twixt *Nicolaus* and the Daughter of *Francis Carrara*, of *Padua*, &c, who, next to *Visconti* was then the powerful Prince in those Parts. Upon the Death of *Galeazzo*, who had threatned all *Lombardy*, *Nicolaus* declared General of the Church against his Son; bu War was prevented by the Condescension of the Dut *Dowager* of *Milan*. The Friendship betwixt the *Ven* and *Carrara* ending in a bloody War, *Nicolaus* to av own Ruin, was forced to make Peace with the *Vene* and tamely to see the miserable end of his Father-in- Family. *Ottobon* of *Parma* having seized *Regio*, *Ni* with the Duke of *Milan* and others declared him a d ber of the Peace of *Lombardy*, and call'd by his desi an Interview in order to adjust Differences, perce *Ottobon*'s Design to surprize and kill him, prevented by the Assistance of *Francis Sforza* (afterwards Du *Milan*) in killing *Ottobon* first. In few days after bo *gio* and *Parma* were delivered to him; and the M sold *Parma* to the Duke of *Milan*, who at the same renounced all his Pretensions to *Regio*. *Philip* Duke *lan* having seiz'd *Genua*, and threatned *Florence*, *N* entred into a League with the *Venetians*, and acted su fully as their General; that Republick giving up t Marquis *Rovigo*, without requiring the Sum borrow

Margin notes: *Nicolaus*, 1356. *Regio* retaken, 1379. 1387. *Albertus*. *Nicolaus* II. 1396. 1406. 1416.

on it. Soon after *Nicolaus* mediated Peace betwixt the Duke and the Republick, and died at *Milan* with the Reputation of the wisest Prince of that Age. He was succeeded by his Son *Leonel*, who married the Daughter of *Alphonsus* King of *Naples*, and sent *Hercules* and *Segismond*, his two Brothers by another Mother to be bred at the Court of *Naples*. His Neighbours being all involved in War, he observed a perfect Neutrality, and upon all occasions acted as Mediator; whence *Ferrara* was called the *House of Peace*. Upon the Death of *Philip* Duke of *Milan*, he quitted his own Interest to befriend *Forza*, prefering Peace and ease to new Conquests, and loving the Patronage of Learning. And soon after he dyed with the Reputation rather of a good than an active Prince. *Leonel.*

§ 8. *Leonel's* Successor was his Brother *Borsius*, who had been bred to Arms both in the *Venetian* and the *Milanese* Army. The City of *Lucca* seizing upon some Castles belonging to *Modena*, he soon recover'd 'em, and thro' the intercession of the *Florentines*, accepted a proffer'd Reparation, without further resentment. *Frederick* III. being invited to *Ferrara* in his passage from *Rome*, declared *Borsius* Duke of *Modena* and *Reggio*, and Earl of *Rovigo*; giving to the Family a new Coat of Arms, and leave to seal in white Wax, a punctilio much observed among the Princes of *Italy*. *Mahomet* seizing upon *Constantinople*, *Borsius* mediated a Peace betwixt the Duke of *Milan* and the King of *Naples* with the *Venetians*, in order to a Confederacy against that Tyrant. His two Brothers *Hercules* and *Sigismond* being discountenanc'd at the Court of *Naples*, he sent for them home, and to shew he had no Jealousie of either, made the one Governour of *Modena*, and the other of *Regio*. Being invited to *Rome* by Pope *Paul* II. he was there created Duke of *Ferrara*; and in a few days after his return died, with the Character of a just and a generous Prince, beloved not only by his own People, but by all the Potentates of *Europe*. He was succeeded by his Brother *Hercules*, who ought to have succeeded at his Father *Nicolaus*'s Death, and married the Daughter of the King of *Naples*. *Nicolaus* the Son of *Leonel*, and a Grandchild of the House of *Mantua*, made an Insurrection in *Ferrara*, but not being seconded by the People was taken and beheaded, and a *German* Soldier that had followed him, chose rather to die with his Master than to accept of the Duke's Pardon.

Borsius the first Duke of *Ferrara* and *Modena*.

1452.

1459.

1470.

Hercules I.

Two days after a List being brought to the Duke of a[ll] that were privy to the late Design, *Hercules* burnt it without Opening; generously declaring, he did not desire t[o] know who had been his Enemies, lest he should be tempted to bear them a Grudge. A War breaking out betwee[n] *Florence* and the Pope joyn'd by the King of *Naples*, *Hercules* was made General of the *Florentine* Army; but soo[n]
1479. after a Peace ensued. The *Venetians* declaring War against *Hercules* upon some contests relating to the Confines of *Rovigo*, he was assisted by *Milan* and *Naples*; and the *Venetians* being much Superior in Power, Peace was solicited an[d]
1489. obtained by the Kings of *Hungary* and *Spain*. *Charles* VII[I] having over-run *Italy*, not without the Countenance of th[e] Duke of *Ferrara*; when the Confederacy was formed against the King, the Duke refused to enter into it, and b[y] his Mediation obtain'd honourable Articles to the *Fren[ch]* at *Navarre*. In the succeeding War betwixt *Lewis* XII
1500. and *Sforza* of *Milan*, the Duke's own Son-in-law, he observed a perfect Neutrality: But when the *French* Troop[s] march'd again to the Conquest of *Naples*, none was mor[e] forward than the Duke to assist them. This *Hercules* wa[s] complemented with the Order of the Garter by *Henry* VI[I] of *England*.

Alphonsus I. § 9. His Son and Successor *Alphonsus*, was married first to the Duke of *Milan*'s Daughter, and then by the interest of *Lewis* XII to *Lucretia Borgia*, Pope *Alexander* the Sixth's Daughter. *Cæsar Borgia* being ruined, he defended *Bologna* for *Julius* II. and defeated *Bentivoglio*. Not long after he joyned in the League of *Cambray*, to dispossess the *Vene-*
1509. *tians* of the *Terra firma*; and for his share was once in Pos-
1510. session of *Rovigo*, *La Badia*, *Monfelice*, *Estè*, and other Places: But soon after Pope *Julius* resenting his refusal to abandon the Confederacy, excommunicated him, order'd those of *Romagna* to seize his Places, and exhorted the *Venetians* to fall upon him. By which means the Duke in a short time lost *Rovigo*, all the *Polecine*, *Monfelice* and *Estè*, all the places of *Romagna*; and what grieved him most, *Modena* and *Sassuolo*, with several Castles near him. Some time after, the *French* Army under *Gaston de Foix* lying in *Romagna*, the Duke recovered his Places from *Julius*; and commanded the Artillery in the memorable Battle near *Ravenna*. After the Retreat of the *French* Army, Pope *Julius*, thro' the Intercession of *Fabricius Colonna*, whom

War with the Pope and the *Venetians*.

the Duke had taken Prisoner and generously set at Liberty, was invited to *Rome*, where he was absolved from his Censures; but apprehending the Pope would detain him, was privately conveyed out of *Rome* by *Colonna*, who thought his Honour concerned in the Duke's Safety. But before he could arrive at his own Territories, the Pope's Officers took not only the places in *Romagna*, but *Regio*, *Brescello* and *Carpi*: All which must have ended in the Duke's utter ruin, if Pope *Julius* had not died in the mean time; whose Successor *Leo* X. absolved him anew, and promised to restore what his Predecessor had taken. But after all, *Leo* was so far from performing that Promise, that he watched every Opportunity to fall upon him, and suborn'd an Assassin to kill him; but at last *Francis* I. of *France* being sensible that his Losses proceeded from his adhering to the *French* Interest, obliged the Pope to comprehend him in their Joynt Treaty, and to do him justice. Then *Alphonsus* was a third time Married (as 'tis said) to one *Laura Eustochia*, a Gentlewoman of *Ferrara*, who bore to him *Alphonsus* the Father of Duke *Cæsar*; of whom more hereafter. *Adrian* VI. prov'd his sincere Friend; but *Clement* VII laid Claim to *Modena* and *Regio*, offering the Emperor large Sums for that end. The Emperor being unwilling to advance the House of *Medici* by an Act of injustice to that of *Este*: *Clement* resenting the Refusal, brought upon himself and the City of *Rome* a dismal Scene of Calamities. While the Pope lay in Prison, *Alphonsus* forgetting his former Injuries, got a League of most of the Christian Princes to be concluded at *Ferrara* for the Pope's releasement. By vertue of this League *Alphonsus*'s Son *Hercules*, was married to a Daughter of *Lewis* XII. Not long after *Charles* V. coming to *Bologna*, decided the Difference between Pope *Clement* and the Duke, in favour of the latter: And at the desire of the Duke, crown'd *Ariosto* the Duke's Subject with Laurels at *Mantua*, as a second *Virgil*.

1520.

1530.

§ 10. *Hercules* II. his Son and Successor went to *Rome*, where Pope *Paul* III. absolved him from all Censures, renounced what Pretensions the late Popes had made to *Modena*, and granted him the Investiture of the Dutchy of *Ferrara*. He narrowly escaped being assassinated, and the Assassin flying to *Venice*, was sent back to *Ferrara* in Chains; but in remembrance of ancient Friendship, only doomed to perpetual Imprisonment by the Duke. His Dutchess being

Hercules II.

1540.

1550.

being suspected of favouring *Calvin* and the reformed Religion, was confined by the Interest of the Jesuits to a few Rooms in the Palace. Pope *Paul* IV. being assisted by *France* in opposition to *Philip* II. of *Spain*; the Duke's Son *Alphonsus* was declared General of the *French*, and the Pope's Forces; and after a Signal Defeat of the *French* at St. *Quintin*, a Peace was concluded. *Hercules* dying, was
Alphonsus II succeeded by his Son, *Alphonsus* II. then at the Court of *France*, who made haste to arrive at *Ferrara*, and married the Daughter of *Cosmo* Duke of *Florence*, who died in 14
1560. Months after. His Brother *Lewis* was created a Cardinal, as his Father's Brother *Hippolytus* had been before. *Alphonsus*'s second Dutchess was a Daughter of the Emperor *Maximilian*; and to assist his Father-in-Law against the *Turk*, the Duke made a Splendid and chargeable March to *Hungary*, and was afterwards a Candidate for the Crown
1570. of *Poland*. The succeeding Years he spent at home in Peace; and having to preserve the Game of his Country, hung up several Highway-men (sentenced for other Crimes) in the Fields, with Partridges, Pheasants, &c. about them, as if they had been executed for spoiling the Game; the People took up such a firm Opinion of his Cruelty, that no after-discovery could root it out of their Minds. He married a third time to a Daughter of the House of *Man-*
1580. *tua*. *Italy* being then disturb'd by the *Banditi*, who put the Country under grievous Contributions, *Alphonsus* sent out Count *Monteeuculi* with a strong Party to suppress them. The Duke growing old, and having no hopes of Children, got the Emperor to renew the Investiture of *Modena* and *Regio* to himself, and to *Cæsar* his Uncle, *Al-*
1590. *phonsus*'s Son, who was his next Heir: But Pope *Clement*
1597. VIII put him off with delays till 1597. that *Alphonsus* died, declaring by his Will his Cousin *Cæsar* to be Successor.

Cæsar Duke of *Modena*. § 11. *Cæsar* being declared Duke, the Court of *Rome* alledged, that the Dutchy of *Ferrara* came by Devolution to the Pope, upon the Plea that the present Duke's Father, namely, *Alphonsus* the Son of Duke *Alphonsus* I. by *Laura Eustochia*, was a Bastard, *Alphonsus* I. being never married to *Laura*. The Partisans of the House of *Este* say that *Laura* was actually married, only 'twas kept private to humour *Hercules* the Son and Successor of *Alphonsus* I. by his former Dutchess, who had no Kindness for *Laura*, and afterwards incouraged the report of her being not married,

in

in resentment of the Grants made by his Father of independant Jurisdictions to her Sons. They add farther, that *Ferrara* was never held of the Church as a feudal City. However, the Pope having excommunicated *Cæsar* and his Adherents, and ordered his Troops to march; and *Cæsar* having thro' a Mistake of Politicks sent the chief of the Nobility, whose Loyalty and Interest could have done him best Service at Home, to compliment foreign Princes upon his Accession to the Ducal Dignity: The Pope's Emissaries made a Party in the City; upon which *Cæsar* growing jealous lest *Modena* and *Regio* might be lost, while he laboured in vain to preserve *Ferrara*, took a sudden resolution to capitulate, and so parted with *Ferrara*, removing his Court to *Modena*, to the vast Improvement of the latter, and the irretrievable Detriment, or rather Ruin of the former. After this Mortification *Cæsar* liv'd in Peace, without embarquing in the Quarrels that in his Time prevail'd among his Neighbours. The Dispute between Pope *Paul* V. and the *Venetians*, the War of the *Valteline*, and that upon the Succession of *Montferrat* and *Mantua*, were the Troubles that plagu'd *Italy* in his Time; and notwithstanding the vicinity of the Flames, he still observ'd a Neutrality. It being concerted betwixt the Prince of *Piedmont*, and *Ferdinand* Duke of *Mantua*, that *Margaret* the Dutchess Dowager, and her Daughter *Mary*, should retire to *Modena*, and be under *Cæsar*'s Care: *Cæsar* considering the weight of the Charge, refus'd it. The Great Duke of 1613. *Tuscany* offering to send Troops to the Assistance of the Duke of *Mantua*, *Cæsar* deny'd them Passage thro' his Territories, as well as the *Genouese* and the Pope. The Republick of *Venice* invited him to take part in the League they concluded with the Duke of *Savoy*, for the Defence of *Italy* against the predominant Power of *Spain*: But he 1618. refus'd to engage, for want of Heart, as well as Force.

Ferrara annexed to the Holy See.

§ 12. *Cæsar* dying in 1628, was succeeded by his Son *Alphonsus* III. who, when the *Germans* block'd up *Mantua*, 1629. sav'd his Country from being ravag'd, by disbursing Money among them, and receiving *Colalto* the General with his Guards in *Reggio*. After the Death of his Wife *Isabella* of *Savoy*, he took upon him the Habit of a *Capuchine*, and was succeeded by his Son *Francis*. A fresh War breaking out between *France* and *Spain*, both Parties made great 1635. Proffers to the several Sovereigns of *Italy*, to retain them

Alphonsus III.

Francis.

on their side. To the Duke of *Modena*, *Spain* offer'd the Delivery of *Coreggio*, a little Sovereign State; which had been Pawn'd to the *Spaniards* by the Emperor. Accordingly, the Duke after amusing *France* for some time, to try how high they would bid, entred into a Treaty with *Spain*, engaging to adhere to their Party, and to send the Prince *Rinaldo*, his Brother, with Three Thousand Foot into the *Milanese*, in recompence of the Garrison which he was permitted to bring into *Coreggio*. Thereupon the *French* and the Duke of *Parma* fell on a sudden into his Country, and made great Devastations. *Modena* then unprovided for Defence, had recourse to the *Venetians*; but they observing a perfect Neutrality, refus'd to be concern'd; only they suffer'd their General, Prince *Louis d' Estè*, Uncle to the Duke, to go and Head his Troops. Upon this he was forc'd to address himself to *Leganes*, Governor of *Milan*; who lent him Two Thousand Foot and Eight Hundred Horse; and these, in conjunction with Four Thousand Country Militia, made an Inroad into *Parma*, where the *French* engag'd and defeated them. In fine, through the Intercession of the Pope, the two Dukes (of *Modena* and *Parma* ty'd by Inter-marriages) agreed to a tacit Suspension of Hostilities, as to their own particular; and about a Year after, the former delivering *Rossena* to the latter, all Mis-understandings between them ceas'd. Not long after, a Rupture happening between the Pope and the Duke of *Parma*, with reference to the Dutchy of *Castro*, the Duke of *Modena* interpos'd, by his Minister the Marquis of *Montecuculi*: But, finding the Court of *Rome* did but trifle with him, he recall'd his Minister. While things were thus preparing for the Eruption of the Pontifical and Confederate War in *Italy*, the Duke of *Modena* was charg'd with Inventing, or at least countenancing a Rumour; that, in order to a suppos'd Marriage of a Daughter of the Prefect with the Duke of *Mirandula*, then under Age, an Ecclesiastical Garrison was to be brought into that place: And the rumour being false, the Guardians of that young Prince suspected, that as the Duke of *Modena* had given being to the Report, so he might aim to intrude himself into that Place by an Imperial Decree, which he pretended to have, with power to put a Garrison into it. Soon after, an Express came from that Prefect to the Duke of *Modena*, demanding Passage for the Pontifical Army thro' his Territories; and after putting it off as long as he cou'd, the

Coreggio given to the Duke.

His difference with the Duke of *Parma*.

1636.

1641.

the Duke being altogether unprovided, as having not above 1000 Foot in Pay, and being openly threatned with immediate hostile Invasions, was forc'd to consent to it upon some Conditions for a Month. However, this being extorted from him by necessity, he did not drop his Resentment, but entring into a League with *Venice* and the Grand Duke, gave the Prefect to know, that he could no longer dispose of his Country, or of Himself, without the consent of his Allies. The Articles of the Confederacy were, to have an Army of Twelve Thousand Foot, and one Thousand Eight Hundred Horse; the *Venetians* furnishing one half, the Duke two thirds of the other half, and *Modena* the remainder: With a provisional Clause of inlarging their Forces in the same proportion, for the defence of the other Princes of *Italy*. To this was added, a secret Article, to assist the Duke of *Parma*, if there should be occasion, and admit him into the League if he desir'd it. This done, the Duke of *Parma* obtaining Passage of the Duke of *Modena*, invaded the Ecclesiastical State, and the Confederate Army entred the *Modenese* to cover it, in case of *Parma*'s Disaster, which was much fear'd. *Parma* meeting with Success, the Duke of *Modena* solicited the *Venetians* to give him leave, with their Troops, which he had in his Country, to enter into the *Ferrarese*; which being all in Confusion and without a Garrison, an opportunity was offer'd of considerable progress, in recompence of the large Sums he pretended to be due to him from the Pope. But the Senate deny'd to comply with his Request, and rather earnestly disswaded him from adding Embroilments to the Business, and Fire to the Flame, which it was studiously endeavour'd to adjust and extinguish. Soon after a Treaty was as good as concluded between the contending Parties, by which all the Possessions of *Parma* were to be deposited in the Hands of the Duke of *Modena*; but the Treaty was eluded by the Artifices of the Court of *Rome*. The Duke of *Modena* thought to have march'd with some of the Regular Troops into the Ecclesiastical State, having laid a Correspondence in *Ferrara*, for the surrender of that Town when he came before it; but the Plot being discover'd, he put off the March. After that, several Treaties were set on foot to no effect, and the Duke of *Modena* mov'd to the Senate of *Venice*, to have his Pretensions with the Pope included in the League; but such a Precedent as that cou'd not be allow'd of. The

War

1642. *Modena* in League with *Venice* and *Florence*.

1643.

War going on, with various success, the *Modenese* was [in]vaded, and several Places taken by the Pontifical Ar[my] but soon after, they abandon'd 'em. And 'tis observ'[d by] some Writers, that the Duke of *Modena* was more a [bur]den than any advantage to the League; for that he ha[d not] in the Field above 1000 Foot and 500 Horse; and [the] whole Army of the Confederates was employ'd in def[end]ing his Country. In fine, Peace was concluded at *Ve[nice]*

1644. Treaty of Venice. by the Mediation of the Minister of *France*. Tho' the [Prin]ces of *Italy* were thus at Peace with themselves, the [War] continued in *Italy*, between the *French* and *Spaniards*;

1656. *Francis* deserting *Spain*, espous'd the Cause of *France*, at the head of the *French* Troops took *Valence* upon th[e Po]. He died in 1658, leaving behind him the Character [of a] very prudent Prince. He had three Wives, the first v[vas a] Daughter of *Rainutio*, Duke of *Parma*; the second wa[s her] Sister, and the third a Daughter of the Son of *Palest[rina]*.

Alphonsus IV. 1658. *Alphonsus* IV his Son and Successor, surviv'd his Succ[ession] to the ducal Dignity only four Years, in which space [we find] nothing material, unless it be, that he was a Gener[al in] the *French* Service; he married Cardinal *Mazarine*'s [Niece], by whom he had (besides a Daughter that married *Jam[es II.]*

Francis II. 1662. King of *England*) *Francis* II. who succeeded his Father [un]der the Regency of his Mother at Two Years of Age.

§ 13. Tho' the Inhabitants of the *Modenese*, can't [free]

The Genius of the People. themselves from the predominant Vices of *Italy*, *viz.* [Jea]lousy, Revenge, Lust and Swearing; they are said [to be] better Natur'd than most of *Italy*, very Civil, Affabl[e and] Hospitable to Strangers; of unshaken Loyalty to [their] Prince, and more capable of warlike Expeditions than [their] Neighbours. The Country of *Modena* lyes in that p[art of]

The Soil. *Lombardy*, call'd *Cis-Padana*; and is very fertile in Corn, Rice and Pulse, being well water'd with the [Secchia] and the *Panaro*. That part call'd *Coreggio* is richly [stock'd] with Cattle; and that call'd *Frignano* with Metallick [Mines]. The Territory of *Reggio*, is blam'd for a thicker Ai[r than] that of *Modena*, but its Fertility is not much inferior. [The] *Modenese*, or the Dominions subject to the Duke of [Modena,] contains the Dutchies of *Modena* and *Reggio*, the Pri[ncipa]lities of *Coreggio* and *Carpi*, and the Territories of C[arfag]*nano*, *Frignano*, and *Sassuolo*. The chief City whe[re the] Duke resides is *Modena*, a populous and pretty large [City],

City of Modena. not very stately in its Buildings, excepting the Pala[ce and] Churches; nor much enrich'd with Trade, but na[...]

strong, tho' its artificial Fortifications are neglected. *Estè* (anciently *Ateste*) which gave denomination to the illustrious House, lies in the Country of *Padua*, between that City and *Verona*, near the *Euganean* Hills. 'Tis very ancient, being mention'd by *Pliny*, *Tacitus*, *Ptolemy*, &c. but suffer'd extreamly in the time of *Actiolin*, or *Ezzelin*, the Tyrant, that headed the *Gibellines* in the beginning of the Thirteenth Century, and is now an inconsiderable Place, under the Dominion of *Venice*. To return to *Modena*; the Court of *Modena* appears with as much splendor as it can well bear; and 'tis observ'd of the Family of *Estè*, that they have all along endeavour'd to exceed in Magnificence and Hospitality. However, the Revenues of the Duke of *Modena* are but small, and his Forces scarce worth mentioning. In the Pontifical and Confederate War, about the middle of the Seventeenth Century, he was scarce able to maintain a Thousand Foot and Five Hundred Horse; tho' oblig'd in the Treaty of Confederacy, to raise and pay a Sixth part of the whole Confederate Army: And considering that the Dukes of *Modena* have had no accession of Territories since, nor any visible encrease of Riches, as being Land-lock'd from Navigation and Trade, we may conclude the same still. As for what relation he stands in to his Neighbours, it may suffice to observe, that considering the Danger that *Italy* may apprehend from foreign Powers, it is the joynt Interest of the Princes of *Italy*, to Unite for their mutual Defence. Besides, *Modena* is in no capacity by himself, to molest any of his Neighbours; and if he offer'd to do it by a foreign Force, the rest of the Princes of *Italy* would declare against him. Tho' his Family may retain some Resentment against the Papal Chair, for turning them out of the *Ferrarese*, yet 'tis not his Interest to disoblige his Holiness, nor in his Power to Injure him: And on the other hand, he can apprehend no Danger from any of his *Italian* Neighbours, whose chief aim must be to preserve the intrinsick Peace of *Italy*, lest their domestick Dissentions, should call in a foreign Power to the equal ruin of 'em all. When *Austria* was great, they found it their Interest to Confederate among themselves, and to League with *France*, for putting a stop to the incroaching Power: And now, that nothing is to be fear'd from the House of *Austria*, and that *France* extends its Arms with a most equal Ambition and Success, 'tis indispensibly incumbent upon them to Confederate with *Spain*, for reducing that exorbitant Power.

Estè describ'd.

Court of *Modena*.

The Duke's Strength.

The Interest of *Modena*.

MANTUA.

The Revolutions of *Mantua* before its Accession to the House of *Gonzaga*.

§ 1. THE City which gives Name to this Dukedom, is said by the best Antiquaries, to have been Founded by the *Tuscans* (that came from *Lydia* in *Asia*) above 300 Years before the Building of *Rome*: Their Leader *Ogno*, giving it the Name of *Mantua*, alluding to his own Expertness in what they call'd the Science of Divination. Some indeed derive the Origin of this City from *Oenus* the Son of *Manto* the Prophetess, the Daughter of *Tiresias*, after his Mother's Name; but that we wave, as not so well attested. Upon the Declension of the *Roman* Monarchy, it follow'd the Fate of the Western Empire, being sack'd and destroy'd no less than four Times; namely, by *Attila* King of the *Huns*, about the middle of the Fifth Century; by *Agilulphus* King of the *Lombards*, towards the beginning of the Seventh; by *Cagianus* King of the *Avares*, and by the *Hungarians*. After these repeated Disasters, it was rebuilt, and given by *Otho* II. to *Theobald*, Earl of *Canoss*, for the many good Services he had done him. *Boniface* who succeeded him, was Lord of great Territories; enjoying then, besides *Mantua*, *Lucca*, *Parma*, *Reggio*, and *Ferrara*, call'd altogether, at that time *Il Patrimonio*. He married *Beatrix*, the Sister of *Henry* II. who outliv'd him, and govern'd his Dominions Fifteen Years after his Death. From this Marriage sprung *Matildis* the famous Warriouress, that made so great a Figure in the World. *Matildis* dispossess'd of her Estate, by the Emperor *Henry* III. joyn'd with the Popes against the Emperors, recover'd all her own Estate, and dismembred from the Empire many goodly Territories; leading her Armies oftentimes in Person, to the great reputation of her Courage and Conduct. She show'd an invincible Partiality to the Popes, and was charg'd with a Criminal Familiarity with Pope *Gregory* VII. upon whose Death she was like to have receiv'd a severe Blow, but by her Resolution and Conduct prevented it. She had three Husbands, namely, *Godfrey* Duke of *Lorrain*, *Azo* V. of *Este* her own Cousin, and *Welpho* Duke of

Margin notes: *Theobald.* — *Boniface.* — 1040. — *Beatrix.* 1063. — *Matildis.* — 1084.

of *Bavaria*. The first she got rid off by Death, and the other two by kind Divorces from the Popes. In the 76 Year of her Age, *An.* 1115 she died, without Issue by either Husbands or Popes; leaving all her Territories to the Holy See. After her Death, the City of *Mantua* continued under the Protection of the Empire, being govern'd by *Roman* Vicars and Legates for about a Century of Years; till one *Sordello*, a Person mightily fam'd for an uncommon Strength of Body, found means to be Principal Governor of it. This *Sordello* married a Daughter of *Actiolin* (or *Ezzelino*) of *Onara*, who in resentment of his Son-in-Law's Refusal to betray the City into his Hands, besieg'd it, but in vain. Upon the Alarm of this Siege, the *Mantuans* added New Fortifications to their City, and fell into a dispute with the *Cremonese*. In this Juncture, the greatest Families in the City, strove to outvie one another in bearing the most distinguishing Figure: And among these, the most Puissant was that of the *Bonacelsi*; the Head of which, namely, *Pinamonte*, being chosen Chief Judge, with a Collegue, slew his Collegue, and usurp'd the Dominion of the City by Force; and continu'd in it Eighteen Years, leaving it then to his Son *Bardalio*, and he to *Botticello*, and he again to *Passavino*, the last of that Tyrannical and much hated Family, who was kill'd in the Market-place by the People, under the Command and Conduct of *Lewis de Gonzaga*, a Noble *Mantuan*; who thereupon, with great Applause, assum'd the Government.

1115. 1220. *Sordello*. *Bonacelsi* Family, *Pinamonte*. The Exit of the Family of *Bonacelsi*. 1328.

§ 2. This Family of *Gonzaga*, derives it Origin (according to some) from one *Lewis Tedesco*, an *Allemain* of great Extraction, who setled with his Family at *Mantua*, when the great Armies were about *Rubicon* (now *Piscatello*.) *Schowart* says, one *Hugo*, who married one of the *Gonzaga's*, a Family of a Noble Extraction in *Lombardy*, had a Son *Gerhard*, who was Invested with *Mantua* by his Cousin *Adelbert*, as an immediate Feudatory of the Empire; and assum'd the Name of *Gonzaga*. This *Hugo* is said to have been the Son of another *Hugo*, who was Earl of *Provence*, and King of *Italy*, and Son to King *Lotharius* III. Grandson to King *Lotharius* II. and Great-Grandson to *Lotharius* the Emperor. The eleventh in Descent from the before mention'd *Gerhard*, was this *Lewis de Gonzaga*, that headed the Insurrection of the *Mantuans*, and was Confirm'd Lord, or Governor of *Mantua*, by the Empe-

The Family of *Gonzaga*. *Lewis Gonzaga*, 1329.

ror *Charles* IV. in 1329. *Lewis* had Nine Sons by Three Wives: And *Philippino* the Second Son of the First Marriage, did good Service in the War of the King of *Hungary*, against the King of *Naples*. The Wife of *Visconti* of *Milan* making a sham Progress, and coming to *Mantua* to gratify her unlawful Passions for *Ugolino* the Son of *Guido*, the eldest Son of *Lewis*, was innocently entertain'd in the House of the *Gonzaga* Family; in Resentment of which Affront, *Visconti* laid Siege to *Mantua*, which might have prov'd of fatal Consequence, if the Demonstration of the Innocence of all *Ugolino*'s Friends (who knew nothing of the Intrigue) had not influenc'd *Visconti* to raise the Siege. *Lewis Gonzaga* joyn'd in the League with the Republick of *Venice* and *Florence*, against *Scaliger* of *Verona*; but after a short time, a mutual Peace was concluded. He Entertain'd at *Mantua*, the Emperor *Charles* IV. who afterwards
1366. befriended his Family. *Lewis* dying after a great Age, in which he had seen his Posterity very numerous in all its Branches, to the Fourth Generation, was succeeded by his
Guido. Son *Guido*, who oppos'd and confin'd to *Ferrara*, *Opizo* Marquis of *Ferrara*; and by the help of his Brother *Philippino*, got *Lamporeggio*. He had three Sons, the two Younger of which slew the Eldest. *Bernardo Visconti*, Uncle in Law to the Eldest, revenged his Death, by besieging *Mantua*; but *Guido* having Recourse to the Emperor *Charles* IV. the Matter was accommodated through his Intercessi-
Lewis II. 1369. on. *Guido* was succeeded by his Son *Lewis*, who built a
Francis I. 1382. noble Palace, and was kill'd by an Insurrection, upon the open commission of Adultery. His Son and Successor *Francis*, a Prince highly extol'd for his Wisdom and Learning, married the Daughter of *Bernard Visconti*. He courted Peace in the beginning of his Administration, and refused to enter into Confederacy with *John Galeazo*. *Galeazo* resenting this Indifferency of *Lewis*, razed out of his Coat of Arms the Adder that had formerly been Quarter'd in it, for a Mark of inviolable Amity, between the Houses of *Visconti* and *Gonzaga*. *John Galeas* besieg'd *Mantua* for a whole Year; in which Siege a Noble Defence was made, many fine Gentlemen falling on *Francis*'s side, especially of the *Gonzaga* Family; and among them *Galeas Gonzaga*, the greatest Champion of his Age: But at length the Difference was taken up, and *Francis* joyning with *John Galeas*, declared War against the *Bolognese* and *John Bentivoglio*. In the Heat of this War, he took Prisoner, and carried

carried to *Mantua*, *James Carrara* of *Padua*, who being allow'd too much Liberty, made his Escape: This done, and *John Galeas* dying, *Francis* was chosen General of the *Venetians*, in the War with the *Carraro's*, and after gloriously reducing to the *Venetian* Subjection *Padua* and *Verona*, died, leaving his Possessions to his Son *John Francis*, who giving an honourable Reception to the Emperor *Sigismund*, (whose Relation, a Daughter of the Marquis of *Brandenburg*, was married to his Son *Lewis*) was by the Emperor declared Marquis of *Mantua*. After that he was thrice General of the *Venetians*, and acted with Reputation and Success; but soon after forsook 'em, and joyning with *Philip* Duke of *Milan*, occasion'd (in part) their loss of *Verona*, and many other Towns in the *Brescian* and *Vicentine*. At his Death, he divided his Possessions between his Four Sons, leaving to *Lewis* the Eldest, the City of *Mantua* and his Territories about *Verona*. *Lewis* was soon after his Accession molested by his Brother *Carlo*, to whom his Father had left *Lucera* and his other Possessions in the *Cremonese*. This *Carlo* was a very Turbulent Man, and was sufficiently Punish'd for his Unquietness, by his Brother *Lewis*, who dispossess'd him of his Patrimonial Lands. Thereupon *Carlo* fled to the *Venetians*, and after serving them some time, obtain'd of 'em a Body of Men to invade the *Mantuan*, which reduced *Lewis* to extream Difficulties. But in the end, *Lewis* prevailing, *Carlo* dy'd very Meanly in Exile. *Lewis* having thus surmounted his Difficulties, and composed his Affairs, gave a magnificent Reception at *Mantua*, to the Emperor *Frederick* III. and the King of *Denmark*; and being then a Widower by the Death of his first Wife, married the Emperor's Kinswoman, a Daughter of the Duke of *Bavaria*. This *Lewis* was a valiant Prince of a very large Stature, and perfectly well skill'd in the Sciences of Arms, Liberal and Courteous, and a Lover of Wit and Learning. These engaging Qualities gain'd him the Love of all Men, and in a particular manner, of the three Dukes of *Milan*, *Philip*, *Francis*, and *Galeas*. Being a Prince that loved his Pleasure, he hasten'd his Death by his Disorders.

1400. 1407. *John Francis*. 1433. First Marquis of *Mantua*. *Lewis* III. 1444.

§ 3. He was succeeded by *Frederick* his Son, who was afterwards General to the Duke of *Milan*; and in the *Venetian* Wars against the Duke of *Ferrara* got *Asola*, but was constrain'd by Force to restore it; upon which he

1478. *Frederick*.

1484. *Francis* II. he died of Grief. His Son and Successor *Francis* was made General of the *Venetians*, and in that Post did very great Services, especially in the Battle against *Charles* VIII. near the *Taro*, and afterwards with the *French* Army in *Puglia*: In fine, the King of *France* courted him with great Offers, but could not obtain his Service. He joyn'd in the League of *Cambray* against the *Venetians*, and being taken Prisoner by the Treachery of his Forces, and kept some time in *Venice*, found Means to procure his Liberty by the Intercession of the Pope, in whose Hands he left his Son as a Hostage; or else, by Vertue of a stern Message to the Republick on his behalf, from *Bajacet* the *Ottoman* Emperor, with whom the Marquis had entertain'd a long Correspondence, and whom he had obliged by several

Frederick II. 1519. Presents. He was succeeded by his Son *Frederick*, who commanded the Armies of *Leo* Xth, *Adrian* VIth, and *Clement* VII, as well as that of the *Florentines*. He enter-

First Duke of *Mantua*. 1530. tain'd with great Solemnity *Charles* V. and was then created Duke of *Mantua*, and Marquis of *Montferrat*, that Principality devolving to him by the Right of his Wife *Mar-*

The Accession of *Montferrat*. *garet*, Daughter and Heir of *William Paleologus*, late Marquiss of *Montferrat*. This *Montferrat* was a considerable Addition to the patrimonial Fortune of the Family of *Mantua*; and wou'd have been much more so if it had lain more Conveniently, of which more hereafter. His Son

Francis III. 1540. and Successor *Francis* III. being at his Father's Death but 14 Years of Age, his Mother and his Uncle *Hercules* the Cardinal, were appointed Guardians by the Father's

1549. Will. In 1549 this *Francis* married *Catharine*, the Daughter of *Ferdinand* the Emperor, the Lady being accompany'd to *Mantua* by *Ferdinand* Arch-duke of *Austria*, her

William. 1550. First Duke of *Montferrat*. Brother. But next Year the Death of *Francis* made way for *William* his Brother, who was created first Duke of *Montferrat* by the Emperor *Maximilian* in 1573. He married *Leonora*, Daughter of the Emperor *Ferdinand*, amassed vast Treasures, and recovered several Castles former-

1587. *Vincent*. ly alienated. He was succeeded in 1587 by his Son *Vincent*, the fourth Duke of *Mantua*, and the second of *Montferrat*. He married *Leonora di Medici*, Sister to *Mary* Queen of *France*; and left Issue *Francis*, *Ferdinand*, and *Vincent* Cardinal; *Leonora* the Empress, and *Margaret* Dutchess of *Lorrain*. His first Successor was his Son

Francis IV. 1612. *Francis*, who married *Margaret* the Daughter of *Charles Emmanuel*, Duke of *Savoy*; but died in the Flower of his Age,

Age, leaving Issue only a Daughter *Mary*, and his Dukedom to his two Brothers Cardinals. His dying without Male Issue occasion'd great Commotions in *Italy*: For the Duke of *Savoy* thereupon reviv'd his old Pretensions to *Montferrat*, which were grounded upon the ancient Right of the *Paleologi*; for *Montferrat* had first its own Marquisses, till the Reign of *Rodolph* of *Hapsburg*, in which it devolved by Marriage to the Imperial Family of *Constantinople*, of the Race of the *Paleologi*, who possess'd it to the Extinction of the Male Line in the Person of *John George* in 1445. Upon which, *Aimon* Count of *Savoy* having formerly Married *Joland*, Daughter of one of the Marquisses of *Montferrat*, stipulating that if the Male Issue of the *Paleologi* fail'd, the Dukes of *Savoy* should succeed to *Montferrat*: Upon this Plea, I say, *Charles* III. Duke of *Savoy* put in his Claim; but *Charles* V. as Sovereign of the Fief, adjudged the Succession to *Frederick* II. of *Mantua*, who had married the Daughter of the last Marquis: And this Sentence rather fomented than extinguish'd the jarring Pretensions which at last broke out in a Flame. The War of *Montferrat*.

§ 4. *Ferdinand* the Cardinal succeeded his Brother, and disputed the Matter with the Duke of *Savoy*, being favoured by the *Venetians* and the Grand Duke. Several Places in *Montferrat* were seized by the *Savoyards*; and the Armies of the two contending Crowns of *France* and *Spain* were almost equally Pernicious to it; but *Savoy* was forc'd to desist by the Interest of *Spain*. Both the *Spaniards* and the *Savoyards* contended mightily to have the Cardinal's Niece, *Mary*, in their Custody; but the Cardinal resolutely oppos'd it, knowing that both he and his Brother *Vincenzo* were without Hopes of Children; and though Princess *Mary*, as a Woman, was excluded from the Investiture of the Dutchy of *Mantua*, she had some Reason, though doubtful, to pretend to that of *Montferrat*. Many propos'd for her Husband *Charles* Duke of *Rhetel*, Son of *Charles* Duke of *Nevers*, descended of *Lewis Gonzagua*, the Son of *Frederick* I. Duke of *Mantua*, who had setled in *France*, and married the Heiress of *Nevers*, &c. This the *Spaniards* vigorously opposed, looking upon the Duke of *Rhetel* as a perfect Frenchman, and dreading to introduce the *French* into the Heart of *Italy*, and into two Countries that have the *Milanese* in the middle. With this View they used many Artifices, though in vain, to *Ferdinand*. 1612.

get the young Niece into their Hands, and propos'd her Marriage to the Prince of *Guastala*, a remoter Branch of the House of *Gonzagua*. The *French* and the *Venetians* were for *Rhetel*. In the mean time *Ferdinand* dying, was

1526. *Vincenzo.* succeeded by his Brother Cardinal *Vincenzo*, who profess'd to break his preceding Marriage, and by a Dispensation from the Pope marry his Niece. But every Body concluded the old lewd Cardinal was not fit for new Adventures; so he sent privately for *Rhetel* to *Mantua*, to have him married to his Niece before himself died. *Rhetel* came, but the Pope's Dispensation did not arrive till the

1628. very Minute the Duke expired. However, the Marriage was immediately Consummated; the Corps of *Vincenzo* being yet warm, who, it was given out, had by his last

Charles I. Words Ordain'd it. Thereupon *Charles Gonzagua* Duke of *Nevers*, Father to *Rhetel*, assumed the Ducal Dignity

Mantuan War. of *Mantua* and *Montferrat*. He had none to Protect him but the *French*, who were then engag'd in the Business of *Rochel*, unless we reckon in the *Venetians* and the *Pope*, who were both apprehensive of the Power of *Spain*, and the Intrigues of the Duke of *Savoy*. In fine, the *Spanish* and *Austrian* Family over-run all; they took and sack'd *Mantua* in the most barbarous Manner, distress'd *Casal* to the last Extremity, and in a manner ruin'd both the Countries of *Mantua* and *Montferrat*. The Pillaging of *Mantua* lasted three Days, but will remain (says *Baptista Nani*) Infamous to all Ages; for there was seen a direful Representation of all sorts of Calamity, with all the Excesses which Cruelty and Licence suggested to Conquerors. The City for many Years habituated to Idleness and Pleasures, became the Spectacle of deplorable Misery; Boys and Virgins were abused and ravished, Churches robbed, Houses pillaged, Fire and Sword every where; heaps of dead Bodies and Arms appearing at every Step, with Torrents of Blood and Tears. The Duke had, in a long Peace, made a Collection of Precious things with so much Pomp, that Treasures having been profusely expended for Ostentation, it seemed now that Luxury serv'd for nothing but the Funerals of Fortune. The Palace was given to Plunder, and so many Rarities and so much Wealth were every where found, that the Value of the Prey exceeds the Memory of all other Spoils whatever. In this calamitous Distress the Duke retir'd by Capitulation to the Country of *Ferrara*, where he was supply'd ply'd with Money to maintain him by the Republick of Venice. Some charg'd this Prince with Irresolution and Distrust, which perhaps was only owing to the Apprehension he had of the Infidelity of his People. However it be, soon after a Peace ensu'd at Chievasco, by which the Emperor acknowledged and invested the Duke of Nevers as Duke of Mantua, and that Duke made a Cession to the Duke of Savoy of some Places in Montferrat, in consideration a Sum of 494000 Crowns. And on the other hand, the Duke of Savoy yielded to the King of France Pignerol, on the Condition of his paying the 494000 Crowns to the Duke of Mantua. Peace being thus happily concluded, the Duke of Mantua return'd to the dismal Remains of his City and Country, enter'd into a League with France, and was supported by the Venetians; and about six Years after his Death, made way for his Grandson Charles III. his own immediate Son Charles II. mention'd above under the Name of Rhetel, dying in his Father's Life time, and leaving Mary of Gonsaga a Widow, whom Charles I. her Father-in-law would thereupon have married, if the Pope had not deny'd him a Dispensation. Of this Prince Charles I. 'tis said, that whilst he liv'd privately he had several Thoughts and Designs of a great Prince; but having attain'd the Principality with great Hazard, govern'd himself amidst great Troubles with the Spirit and Manners of a private Man. He left his Grandson then a Child, under the Regency of his Mother, and under the Protection of the French and Venetians. This Charles III. Married a Sister of the Count of Tirol in 1649, and dying in 1665, left his Son Ferdinand Charles under the Regency of his Mother.

Peace of Chievasco. 1631.

Charles III. 1637.

Ferdinand Charles. 1665.

§ 5. The Soil of Mantua is like the rest of Lombardy, very Fertile; but some reckon the Inhabitants more Clownish than their Neighbours. The Mantuan Territories include, besides the Dutchy of Mantua, properly so call'd, and what they possess in Montferrat, several Lordships that have been dismember'd in this Dutchy in Appennage to younger Sons. The City of Mantua is built in the middle of the Lake made by the River Mincio, so that 'tis accessible only by two Bridges built upon the Lake, which makes it very Strong. The Duke's Palace, Famous for its rich Furniture, is the greatest Ornament of the City. To conclude, his Revenues are but small, not above 500000

The Strength, Interest, &c. of Mantua.

Ducats, tho' perhaps if the Country was put to it, they are able to raise more. His Interest lies in being contented with what he has, and placing his Felicity in the general Tranquility of *Italy*.

TUSCANY or *FLORENCE*.

THAT part of the ancient *Tuscany*, which is now known by the Name of the Dominions of the Great Duke, being first brought into one Body after the Distractions of *Italy* by the *Florentines*, we stand oblig'd in the Sketch now propos'd, to trace the Thread of the History by the successive Revolutions, Actions and other Circumstances of the City of *Florence*.

Of the Condition of *Florence* to the Division of *Guelphs* and *Gibellines*.

§ 1. *Florence* standing on a Plain on the River *Arno*, sprung from the Ruins of the ancient City of *Fiesole*, which stood two Miles distant on the top of an Hill, and so had not the Conveniency of easie Water-carriage. 'Twas first enlarged by *L. Sylla* the Dictator, and then by the *Triumviri*, *Augustus*, *Antonius* and *Lepidus*. It took the Name of *Florentia* from its flourishing Condition. Upon the Declension of the Empire it was destroyed by *Totila* King of the East *Goths*, but rebuilt by *Charlemaigne*, to whose Successors it continu'd Faithful as long as they had any thing to do with the State of *Italy*. But the War arising between the Emperor *Frederick*, and Pope *Alexander* III. and the *German* Factions, known by the Name of the *Guelfs* and *Gibellines*, invading *Italy*, they screw'd up Sedition to that Height, that they divided the whole Nation, put all the Families at Variance with one another, and the Citizens to Civil Wars within themselves, and even Brothers against Brothers, without any regard to the Ties of Nature: And among others, *Florence* felt the unhappy Effects of the Divisions. The *Guelfs* were the Assertors of the Power of the Bishop of *Rome*, as the *Gibellines* were of the Emperor's Right of Sovereignty. They rag'd with incredible and dismal Fury in *Italy* above 300 Years; and yet we are at a loss to known certainly the De-

Derivation of the Names by which they distinguish themselves. Some give the following Reason: In 1130 there happen'd a Schism in the Church, through the Concurrence of *Innocent* II. and *Anacletus*; the first favour'd by the Emperor; the other, by *Roger*, Count of *Sicily* and *Naples*, an Active and Warlike Prince, who drew to his side *Guelfe*, Duke of *Bavaria*. The Emperor *Conrad* III. entring *Italy* with a *German* Army, and follow'd by Prince *Henry* his Son, who was brought up at a place in *Germany* call'd *Gibelline*, *Guelfe*, Duke of *Bavaria*, march'd to the Assistance of his Ally; and it fortun'd, as both Armies were ready to Engage, that the *Bavarians* cried in their Language, *Hier. Guelfe*: Which being answer'd, by the Troops commanded by the Prince, by *Hier Gibellines*, the *Italians* retained the Words, to distinguish the different Parties, and call'd the Factions by them. Others say, the Name of *Guelfs* and *Gibellines* owes its Rise to two *German* Brothers, the one nam'd *Ghibeli*, the other *Guelfi*, who falling out upon the Controversy of the Pope's Authority in comparison with the Emperor's, fought openly in Vindication of their respective Opinions. But let that be as it will, the City of *Florence* continu'd Flourishing and United in it self till the Year 1215. that it was miserably rent by these Factions.

The Origin of the Name of *Guelphs* and *Gibellines*.

1215.

§ 2. But before we proceed beyond that Period, let's take along with us the general State of the Province of *Tuscany* to that Time. For the purpose, the ancient *Tuscany* (of which the Dukedom now before us is the greatest and goodliest part) was properly and originally call'd *Tyrrhenia* from *Tyrrhenus* the Son of *Atys*, King of *Lydia*, who came and planted in those Parts about the time that *Gideon* judg'd the Tribes of *Israel*. The Name of *Tuscany* is but an accidental Name from θύειν, *Sacrificare*, alluding to their extream addictedness to Superstitious Rites. Not to mention their wasting 300 Towns of the *Umbri* their neighbouring Nation, and Building 12 other Cities in the other side of the Mountains, they stood up most stifly in Defence of their Liberties against the *Romans*, and were not conquer'd till *A. U. C.* 455. In the Declension of the *Roman* Empire, *Tuscany* became a Member of the Kingdom of *Lombardy*, then of the *French*, and finally of the *German* Empire; during which times, it was govern'd by an Officer of Trust and Power, whom I find sometimes

The Antient State of *Tuscany*.

call'd the Marquis, sometimes Duke of *Tuscany*; who had here more or less Authority, as they could work on the Necessities of their several Princes. *Desiderius* the last King of the *Lombards*, had been Duke of *Tuscany*, and so was *Albericus* in the time of the *Berengarii*; and *Guido* is call'd Marquis of it, under the Reign of *Henricus Auceps* the *German* Emperor. Afterwards, as the Popes grew in Power and Greatness, so they made bold to intermeddle in the Affairs of this Province; giving it one while to the Kings of *Naples*, another while to the Dukes of *Anjou*, they making some Claim to that Kingdom.

The Origin of the Divisions of *Florence*. At last a Division happen'd in the City of *Florence* upon the Heir of the House of *Bendelmonti*, the principal Family of the City, his falsifying a Promise of Marriage to a Lady of the Family of *Amidei*: And the latter assisted by the House of *Uberti*, another principal Family, slew the Heir of the former as he was going to Church. The Interest of the two Families of *Bendelmonti* and *Uberti* divided the whole Town into two Factions, who having strong Houses and Towers, especially in the Country, continued mutual Hostilities for many Years with various Success; till 1240. the Emperor *Frederick* II. King of *Naples* joyn'd with the *Uberti* to enlarge the Interest of the *Gibellines*, who thereupon expell'd the *Bendelmonti*, now call'd *Guelfs*. But that Emperor dying, the two Parties were reconciled, and before the new Emperor's Power could reach 'em, joyntly drew up a Form of Commonwealth for the Preservation of their Liberty; appointing Twelve yearly Governors for the City, which they divided into six Parts, allotting two of 'em a Part; and two separate Judges for Civil and Criminal Matters. They order'd Twenty Standards or Banners for the City, and Seventy six for the Country, upon which were written the Names of the Able-bodied Men in the respective Districts; and these Men were to repair to an Engin covered with white drawn with two Oxen, carrying all the Standards, whenever it was drawn out in Publick View; that being the signal of their Rendezvous. By observing these Constitutions they got great Reputation, and brought in *Pistora*, *Arezzo*, *Sienna* and *Volterra*. But soon after the *Gibellines* finding the People more inclined to take the Advice and Direction of the *Guelphs*, as reckoning their Liberties less in danger from the Pope than from the Emperor; the *Gibellines* form'd a Plot with *Manfred* King of *Naples*, which being discovered

The Commonwealth of *Florence*. 1250.

ed, they were expell'd the City, and withdrew to *Sienna.* But receiving Succors from *Manfred*, they gave the *Guelphs* such a total Rout, that they took *Florence*, turn'd out the Magistrates, and left no face of Liberty; and if it had not been for the Interest of the Head of the *Uberti*, who openly opposed it, they had certainly raz'd *Florence.* Mean time the *Guelphs* who fled to *Lucca*, did good Service, particularly under *Charles of Anjou*; and by way of reward from the Pope, had the Ensign of the Church granted them, which is still used at *Florence.* Count *Guido Novello* having impos'd a Tax upon the People, they rose and expell'd both him and the *Gibellines*, confiscating their Estates. But the *Guelphs* growing too apt to make Insurrections, the Bishop of *Rome* interposed, so that the Commons were bridled, the Pride of the Nobility was abated, and the Division of *Guelphs* and *Gibellines* seem'd to cease. Not long after 'twas like to have reviv'd again through a Quarrel of two Young Noblemen, one of whom was hurt in the Action, and the other had his Hand chop'd off by the other's Father; had not *Charles of Valois* come thither in Person and appeased the growing Tumult, banishing the most Contentious. Thus they persecuted one another with repeated Revivals; the People or Commons still falling upon the Incroachers of their Liberty, particularly upon *Corso Donati*, a Head of a great Family whom they slew. But after that they lived in 1308.
Peace till *Henry* the Emperor besieged them, though in vain, they being assisted by *Robert* King of *Naples.* Soon after they received such severe Blows from the *Gibelline* Lords of *Pisa* and *Lucca*, that they were not able to make the least Resistance, but left the Country to be overrun and destroyed by *Castruccio Castracani.*

Florence besieged.

§ 3. In this Distress they were forced to sue for relief to *Robert* King of *Naples*, who forced them to accept of his Son *Charles*, Duke of *Calabria* for their Lord. But *Charles* prov'd as odious to 'em as their Enemy, for he levied of the 1326.
City in one Year 400000 Florins, and left *Pistoia* to the mercy of *Castruccio.* But soon after both *Charles* and *Ca-* 1328.
struccio died, and the *Florentines* were well rid (as they thought) both of their Tyrant and of their Enemy. Not long after some of the Emperor's Retinue having taking *Lucca*, offer'd it to the *Florentines* for 20000 Florines; which being refus'd, they sold it to a *Genouese*

Charles Duke of *Calabria* Lord of *Florence.*

for 30000; and the *Florentines* were thereupon so incensed, that they spent more Money than the Sum demanded, in endeavouring to take it by open force; though in the end all their Endeavours prov'd successless. After the

1340. Death of *Castruccio* they lived in Peace till 1340, when a Tumult arose about bringing Strangers into Offices.

Lucca bought and lost.

Not long after the *Pisans* bidding Money to *Mastino Della Scala* for *Lucca*, which was then in his Possession, *Florence* over-bid them, and purchas'd it; upon which the *Pisans* assisted by *Visconti* of *Milan* besieg'd it and took it by Force, in spite of all the Succours of *Florence*, so that *Florence* lost both their Money and their Honour in that Adventure. In this their low condition they renew'd their wonted Petition to the King of *Naples*, who sent them the Duke of *Athens* to be their Captain; but the Remedy prov'd as bad as the Disease, the Duke broke through all the Measures of their Government, he violated the Rights both of Nobles and Commons, loaded them with arbitrary Impositions; and making use of mercenary Troops fill'd the City with *French*, who ravish'd the Women without controul, and committed all manner of Abuse. This Tyranny they bore for ten Months; at the end of which, the Nobles, Commons and Artificers rose in three distinct Bodies, and forc'd the Duke to renounce his Title and depart the City. This done they introduc'd a new Form of Government, Lodging an unwonted Power in the Nobles; but the Commons exasperated by the Arbitrary Proceedings of the Nobles, stood up in defence of their Liberty, and after many Skirmishes, much Bloodshed and repeated Fire, brought them so low that they never dar'd to make head against them since.

The Duke of *Athens* Captain of *Florence*.

The Nobility suppress'd.

1353. In 1353. they were visited with that dismal Plague which swept off above 96000 Souls. No sooner was its Rage abated, than that of Contention broke out in fresh Flames, reviving the old Division of *Guelfs* and *Gibellines*, by virtue of a Quarrel between the two Families of *Albizi* and *Ricci*, who to gratify their private Spleen, adopted the same Plea, and set up the same Banners that the *Bendelmonti* and *Uberti* had done before: The Consequence of which was, that the Severe Laws against the *Gibellines* were repeal'd, and the *Gibellines* took the favourable Opportunity to retrieve their lost Interest by stirring up the People against the Lords, who were thereupon forc'd to

Gibellines restor'd.

1357. abandon both the Palace and the Reins of Government

to

to the Fury of the People. So precipitant was this their Fury, that one *Michel Di Lando*, a Wool-Carder, clad in Rags without either Shoes or Stockings, mounted the great Hall with his Standard in his Hand, and harangu'd the Multitude; who thereupon gave Acclamations to him as their Lord. *Michel* fond of the Upstart Dignity, with a surprizing Presence of Mind thought of a Stratagem to pacify the Mob, by sending them to find out one *Nuto* that had been a Judge before, whom he caus'd to be hang'd by the Heel in the Market-place, and there torn to pieces. After proceeding upon several Reformations, the People smelling that *Michel* (out of a principle of Politicks) preferr'd the Chief Men to Dignities and Offices, made a fresh Insurrection against him; but *Michel*, a Man of great Natural Capacity and Resolution, dispers'd them, though all he could do could not sink their fatal Divisions. While they were thus quarrelling and fighting among themselves, a Discovery was made of a Plot to deliver up the Gates of the City to one *Salerno* at the Head of the *Florentine* Exiles: Upon which they executed some suspected Persons, and retain'd one *John Sharpe* an *English* Captain or Leader, who in those Days had such Reputation in *Italy*, that he could take a Town or two when he pleas'd, and sell it next Day. About that time the common People were entirely manag'd by one *Scali* and one *Strozzi*, who upon a certain Occasion exerted their Power so indiscreetly, that they rescued a Criminal from Justice and sack'd the Palace; but this being resented by all the Magistrates, the inconstant Mob suffer'd him and his Friends to be Beheaded. When he was condemn'd, most of the City was in Arms to Guard the Execution of Justice; but when the Execution was over, they were not so easily disarm'd; for the Feuds between the better sort of People and the lower did so flame, that for the space of a whole Year they had Skirmishes every Day; the Consequence of which was, that by the Agreement of both Parties the *Gibelline* Magistrates were depos'd, and the *Guelfs* restor'd to their wonted Posts of Honour and Power; and even *Michel Lando*, whose Virtue and Merit were indeed conspicuous to a surprizing degree, could not scape the Fury of the People. The *Guelfs* rul'd the City and its Territories in Peace, till 1387. that *John Galeas Visconti* Duke of *Milan* made War upon the *Florentines*. In this War, which lasted 12 Years, *John Galeas* took *Bologna*,

A Wool-Carder Lord of *Florence*.

John Sharpe an *English*-man of great Reputation.

The *Guelfs* revive again.

1381.

1387.

logna, Pisa, Perugia and Siena, and had he taken Florence bid fair to be King of Italy. During the Flames of this War, the Commons of Florence mutinying against the Lords, offer'd the Government of the City to Veri di Medici, a Citizen, who declin'd the Offer, and by his Prudence and the weight of his Counsel stifled the Tumult. The Duke of Milan frustrated in his Attempts upon Florence died soon after, and so the Milanese War ending the Florentines retook Pisa. But they were no sooner rid of John Galeas, than yet a more formidable Enemy gave a new Alarm, namely Ladislaus King of Naples; who being Master of Rome, Siena, La Marca and Romagna, wanted only Florence to gain a full March into Lombardy. But Poyson administred to him by his Physician (perhaps by their Instigation) made an end of Ladislaus, as a Natural death had lately done of John Galeas: And so to the death of a King and a Duke, the Florentines owed a Safety which all their Force could not have insur'd. However a fresh War insued with Philip D. of Milan, in which they expended 3500000 Ducats, and besides the Defeat of their Army at Zagonora, lost most of their Towns of Romagna, though soon after they recover'd them by engaging Venice in a League against Duke Philip. This done, a War broke out between Florence and Lucca, the latter being headed by Nicolas Piccinino, a General sent 'em by the D. of Milan, who defeated the Florentine Army. But the space of three Years concluded this War, and then began Domestick Feuds, occasion'd by the great and popular Interest of Cosmo di Medici.

Veri di Medici invited to be Lord of Florence. 1400. 1405. 1414. 1428.

§. 4. This Cosmo di Medici was descended of an Ancient Family, esteemed the Chief of the Popular Nobility; that is, such of the Ancient Nobles, as, to be capable of the Magistracy and Publick Offices, (then wholly shar'd among the Commons) had as it were degraded themselves and become part of the Commonalty. John de Medicis, Father of Cosmo, maintained the Peoples Liberties, and so far won their Hearts that he almost gain'd the Sovereignty. Cosmo having the Management of Affairs, a Faction rose against him, by whom he was first imprison'd and then banish'd. But being recall'd next Year, he acted as Sovereign of the State, and reformed the Civil Government with wonderful Prudence. In his Time the Florentines made a fresh but successless Attempt upon Lucca. Then follow'd the

The Rise and Progress of the Family of Medici. *Cosmo de Medicis.* 1434. 1438.

Council

Council of *Florence*, at which the Emperors of *Greece* and the *Greek* Church came to an Accommodation with the *Roman*: and a War with *Piccinino*, whom the *Florentines* in Conjunction with the Pope's Forces defeated at *Anghiari*, taking likewise *Poppi* from the Count of that Name, and buying *Borgo St. Sepulchro* of the Pope for 25000 Ducats. In the mean time they were still in League with the *Venetians* against *Philip* Duke of *Milan*; and to favour the Duke of *Milan*, *Alphonsus* King of *Naples* invaded *Tuscany*, but his Disappointment at the Siege of *Piombino* oblig'd him to retire. And some Years after he renewed the War, upon the score of their siding with *Francis Sforza* in Opposition to the *Venetians*; though they scap'd this as 1464. well as the former. In 1464. *Cosmo* died after a Government of 31 Years, which he managed without assuming any other Character than that of a private Citizen, to the infinite Satisfaction of all the People. He was succeeded in the direction of Affairs by his Son *Peter*, whose whole time was imployed in suppressing Domestick Insurrections, and at his Death left all his Power and the great Wealth which he had gotten (but with a greater measure of his Father's Virtues) to *Lawrence* and *Julian* his two 1472. Sons. The Archbishop of *Pisa*, at the Instigation of the Pope who hated the House of *Medici*, form'd a Faction with the *Salviati* and *Pazzi*, two Potent Families in *Florence*, who took occasion to surprize *Lawrence* and *Julian* at Mass, and kill'd *Julian*, *Lawrence* making his escape. The Archbishop and the Conspirators being hang'd for this horrid Crime; Pope *Paul* II. in resentment of the death of the Archbishop, excommunicated the *Florentines*, and *Ferdinand* King of *Naples* invaded them. Being reduc'd to great Extremity by the Joint-Arms of the King and the Pope, *Lawrence* went in Person to *Naples* to deprecate the King's Enmity, and to the surprizal of all, return'd soon after with the Conclusion of a lasting Peace between *Florence* and *Naples*. This done he softened the Pope with Embassies, and obtain'd the Absolution of the *Florentines*, to which the Dangers that then threatned *Italy* from the Invasion of the *Turks* contributed not a little. 1486. Some Years after the *Florentines* ingaged in a War with the *Genouese*, and took from 'em *Pietra Santa*, and other Towns. At last *Lawrence di Medicis*, the Father of *Catherine de Medicis*, the *French* Queen, the most renown'd Private Man of his Time, and a great Advancer of Learning 1492.

Peter de Medicis.

Lawrence de Medicis.

ing

Peter de Medicis. 1495 The Family of *Medicis* banish'd. 1512. Pope *Leo* X. his Brother. 1529. ing in *Italy*, died, leaving his Estate and Government to his Son *Peter*: Who departing from the Moderation, Liberality and Prudence of his Ancestors, and having imprudently delivered up *Pisa*, *Legborn*, and other Places, to *Charles* VIII. of *France*, was by the People banish'd with his whole Family. *John de Medicis* Brother of *Peter* being made Pope by the Name of *Leo* X. restor'd the House of *Medicis* again; but after his Death their Exile recommenced. In resentment of this Disgrace, *Julio di Medicis* Son to *Julian* the Brother of *Lawrence* abovemention'd, being declar'd Pope by the Name of *Clement* VII. *Florence* besieg'd by the Emperor, and taken. instigated the Emperor *Charles* V. to besiege *Florence*. The *Florentines* tho' destitute of all Assistance, made a long and a memorable Resistance for a Year, and then surrendred, 1531. thro' Famine rather than want of Force. The Emperor being Master of *Florence*, gave it to *Alexander* Nephew to Pope *Clement*, who had married the Emperor's Natural Daughter.

The first Dukes of *Florence*. Duke *Alexander*. 1532. 1534. § 5. *Alexander* having taken upon him the Government with the Title of Duke granted him by the Emperor, disoblig'd the People by his Arbitrary Government, by his wanton Carriage, and by his Building a Cittadel to overawe the City. Upon the death of Pope *Clement* VII. the disaffected People sent Deputies to the Emperor to complain of Duke *Alexander*'s Cruelty, and intreat Redress: But the Deputies missing the Emperor, Duke *Alexander* D. *Alexander* stabb'd. was stabb'd by *Laurence di Medici*, a particular Favourite of his own, as he lay in bed in *Laurence*'s own House. *Laurence* fled to *Venice*, where he was afterwards kill'd by Surprize; and the House of *Medici* and their Party, hearing that the three *Florentine* Cardinals that were then at *Rome* were marching with an Army towards *Florence*, found it proper to prevent the Ruin of their Party by the *Cosmo* II. 1538. early Election of *Cosmo di Medici* for their Duke, a Young Man of 20 Years of Age descended from *Laurence* Brother to the first *Cosmo*, and next Male-Heir of that Line. This done, they sent Deputies and pacify'd the Cardinals with fair Promises; which at first influenced 'em to separate their Army, but afterwards finding the Promises not perform'd, they sent an Army against 'em commanded by *Peter Strozzi*, who were to favour the Execution of a Conspiracy laid in the City. But *Strozzi* being defeated, the Conspiracy took Air; and the Conspirators were brought

brought to condign Punishment. All this while the Citadel of *Florence* was in the Hands of the Emperor; for that *Alexander Vitelli*, an experienc'd Imperial General, had possess'd himself of the Citadel by Surprize upon the death of Duke *Alexander*; and it was this *Vitelli* who defeated the Troops of *Strozzi* mentioned but now. However Duke *Cosmo* having thus settled himself in the City, married a Daughter of the Viceroy of *Naples*, by whose intercession he soon after redeem'd the Citadel of the Emperor for 400000 Ducats. Then *Cosmo* rul'd for many Years with great Reputation, to the Satisfaction of all the People. He was afterwards deeply concern'd in the Wars between the *French* and the Imperialists, for tho' he endeavour'd to stand Neuter, he was forc'd to side with the Emperor, in Consideration of *Siena*, of which he became Master in 1557. by driving the *French* out of it. In fine, *Cosmo* prov'd such an excellent Statesman and fortunate Commander, that he had a great Sway in the Affairs of *Italy*, and *Philip* II. of *Spain*, spar'd nothing to insure his Friendship. *Pius* IV. had an Intention to have crown'd him King of *Tuscany*; but *Philip* of *Spain* (tho' otherwise his particular Friend) oppos'd it, as being unwilling to see any Kings in *Italy* besides himself. However in the Year 1570. Pope *Pius* V. crown'd *Cosmo* at *Rome* with the Title of *Great Duke* of *Tuscany* for him and his Heirs for ever. *Cosmo* dying was succeeded by his Son *Francis*, Father to *Mary* Wife of *Henry* IV. of *France*, who reigned Thirteen Years in Peace; only having instituted the Order of St. *Stephen*, he bent all his Care to inrich his Subjects by making depredations upon the *Turks*; of which the *Turks* made loud Complaints to the *Venetians*, threatning to Revenge it upon the Christian Princes in General. Having no Male Issue, his Succession devolv'd to his Brother *Ferdinand*, a Cardinal; who thereupon quitted his Cardinal's Cap at 50 Years of Age. In the differences of *Italy* relating to the *Spaniards* and the *French*, he inclin'd to the former, and deliver'd up to them that *Don Sebastian* that call'd himself K. of *Portugal*. He married *Christian* the Daughter of *Charles* Duke of *Lorain*, and by her had besides *Cosmo* his Successor, several Children. *Ferdinand* having bent all his Care to inlarge the Wealth and Commerce of his People, died, leaving his Inheritance to his Son *Cosmo* the Third of the Line, but the Second Great Duke, who married *Magdalen* of *Austria*, Sister to the Emperor *Ferdinand*

Becomes Master of *Siena*. 1557.

Created *Great Duke*. 1570.

D. *Francis*. 1574.

Duke *Ferdinand*. 1587.

Duke *Cosmo* III. 1609. *nand* II. *Cosmo* assisted his Couzen the Duke of *Mantua* in the difference then started between him and the Duke of *Savoy*, relating to the Succession of *Montferrat*. He was a very sickly Prince, but Meek, Affable and Liberal, and a Prince that neglected nothing to preserve the Peace and Tranquillity of his Subjects. He died in 1620, and was succeeded by his Son *Ferdinand* II. then Seven Years old; who in the beginning of his Reign interpos'd, tho' a Youth, in the behalf of the Duke of *Mantua* with the Emperor, who had then put him to the Imperial Ban; but his Negociations were frustrated by Force. In the Pontifical War he assisted *Parma* and *Modena* in the most effectual manner; and next to the *Venetians*, not only bore the heaviest Burthen, but was the most Active in the Confederacy; in pursuance of which, he carried his Arms with Success into the Ecclesiastical State, and made Conquests in *Peruggia*; and when Attack'd in several Quarters defended himself every where and retir'd with Advantage. That War ending soon after in a seasonable Peace, which he cultivated with all his Neighbors, and imploy'd the Remainder of his long and happy Reign in improving the Tranquillity and Wealth of his Subjects. He died in 1670. leaving for his Successor his Son *Cosmo* the Fourth, or rather the Third Great Duke, who married a Daughter of the Duke of *Orleans*.

Duke *Ferdinand* II. 1621.

1645.

Duke *Cosmo* IV. 1670.

The Nature of the Soil, *&c.*

§ 6. The Inhabitants of the Dominions of the Great Duke are reckon'd a cunning industrious People and well train'd to Manufactures. They are stingy, tenacious, jealous, and in such other things of the like temper with the other *Italians*. The *Pisans* were formerly noted for good Soldiers, but that Character is now neglected among them. The *Sienese* are a more generous People, and have struggled hard for their Liberty. The Soil of *Florence* is very fertile, it bears Oil, Corn, Wine and Pulse in a great Abundance; the *Sienese* Land lies much of it Uncultivated, as being less fertile. The Air is wholsome, abating for the Parts that lie upon the Sea. The Country possess'd by the Great Duke is of a considerable Extent, taking in *Siena*, *Pisa*, *Florence*, part of the Isle of *Elbe*, *Pontremolis*, &c. and in all that Tract of Land he has but one considerable Port on the main Land, namely *Legborn*, so that his Strength in Shipping is not very great; for his whole Fleet consists ordinarily but of twelve Galleys, two Gallions, and five Galli-

The Naval and Land Force.

Galliasses. But if his Subjects, who are wholly taken up in Manufacture, took care to export their Commodities upon their own Bottoms, and not sell 'em to Strangers in foreign Vessels, that one Port might be of much greater Benefit to 'em. However as it is, the Great Duke has thereby an Advantage beyond his Neighbours who are Land-lock'd. His Force by Land is very considerable, being 16000 Foot and 500 Horse, besides many numerous Garrisons, as well as in time of Peace as War. His Revenue is very great, some compute it at 150000 Ducats; besides his Land Tax, he lays an Excise upon all Commodities, even to Herbs and Sallades; he keeps his Money-stock circulating among the Bankers, Merchandizes very much himself, and is the only Corn-merchant in his Country, others not being permitted to sell till he has sold out. The Customs of *Leghorn* amount yearly to 1300000 Ducats, not to mention many other Branches. In fine, the Great Duke has vast Treasures in his Coffers, and is still accumulating more, tho' his Subjects must needs be very Poor. As to the Relation he stands in to his Neighbours and other foreign Princes, it is perfectly the same with that of *Venice*, to which we refer the Reader.

His Revenue.

His Interest.

S A V O Y.

§ 1. Upon the Declension of the *Roman* Empire under *Honorius*, that Part of *Gallia Narbonensis* call'd *Savoy*, shared in the common Calamity of being left a Prey to several barbarous Nations. After that, becoming a Part of the Kingdom of *Burgundy*, it passed with the other Rights of that Kingdom into the Hands of the Emperor of *Germany*; and continued so till the Year 999. that *Berold* or *Bertold*, setled here under the Title of Earl of *Maurienne* (a Part of *Savoy*.) This *Bertold*, the Founder of the Illustrious Family that is still possess'd of the Sovereignty, was the great Grandson of *Wittekind* the Saxon King, and Son to *Hugo* Marquis of *Italy*; and in reward of his faithful Service presented by *Rodolphus* King of *Burgundy*, with a Piece of Land then called the Earldom of *Maurienne*. Some *French* Authors call this Genealogy in question; but we chose to follow it as being the most approved.

The Ancient Condition of Savoy.

999.

Bertold first Earl of Maurienne.

This

This *Beroldus* died Marquis of *Italy* and Earl of *Maurienne*, *A. D.* 1023. His Son and Successor was *Humbert* I. call'd *White-hands*, who was presented with the Countries of *Chablais* and *Wallis*, and obtain'd the Earldom of *Savoy* in Fief. Marrying the Heiress of the Marquis of *Suse*, he thereby added that noble Marquisate to his Patrimonial Fortune, as *Humbert* II. who came after two *Amadeus*'s, did by Conquest the Town and Territory of *Tarentaise*. After the Death of *Humbert* II. in 1103. his Son *Amadeus* the third succeeded, and died at *Nicosia*, upon an Expedition to the Holy Land, *An.* 1149. His Son and Successor was *Humbert* III. sirnamed the *Saint*; who had War with the Princes of *Dauphiny*, and sided with Pope *Alexander* III. against the Emperor *Frederick* I. *Humbert*'s Son and Successor was *Thomas* I. who gain'd a great Part of *Piemont* by Conquest, and was succeeded by his Son *Amadeus* IV. who added to his Patrimonial Territories the Countries of *Vaud* and *Chablais*, and was created Vicar General of the Empire by *Frederick* II. This *Amadeus* IV. was the eldest of four Sons left by *Thomas* I. the other three being named *Thomas*, *Peter*, and *Philip*. *Amadeus* left a Son, namely *Boniface* who died without Issue, and was succeeded by his Uncle *Peter*. This *Peter*, sirnamed the little *Charlemaigne* for his many brave Actions, had been originally design'd for a Churchman, and accordingly was made a Canon and a Provost, but that Profession did not suit his Spirit, and so in 1234. he desired of *Amadeus* IV. his eldest Brother, to assign him a Fortune suitable to his Birth. At that time he gave Proof at once both of his Courage and of his Probity, by protecting the Churches and Prelates from ill Usage and Oppression. In 1241. he took a Journey to *England*, where King *Henry* III. received him very kindly, gave him several Lands, made him a Knight, and imployed him to Negociate some Affairs in *France* and elsewhere. In 1263 he succeeded his Nephew *Boniface*, to the Prejudice of the Children of *Thomas* his elder Brother, and annex'd to the Family the rest of *Piemont* that Earl *Thomas* had not reach'd; and ever since the eldest Son of *Savoy* is stil'd Prince of *Piemont*. *Peter* dying without Issue in 1268. was succeeded by his Brother *Philip*, likewise a Churchman, Bishop of *Valence*, and Archbishop of *Lyons*, who then quitted the Ecclesiastical Order and married the Daughter of *Otho*, Count of *Burgundy*. Besides the beforenamed *Philip* and *Peter*, there

[Margin notes: 1023. *Humbert* I. first Earl of *Savoy*. 1027. *Amadeus* I. *Humbert* II. — *Humbert* III. 1149. — *Thomas* I. 1586. *Amadeus* IV. 1233. — *Boniface*. *Peter*. 1263. — *Philip*. 1268.]

there was a third Brother, namely *Boniface* (Uncle to the *Boniface* above-mentioned) who was Archbishop of *Canterbury*. *Philip* dying likewise without Issue, the Succession devolved at last to the Posterity of *Thomas* the elder Son of *Thomas* I. whose Right had been thus infringed. *Thomas* (the Second of that Name) had three Sons, namely *Thomas* (the Third of that Name) *Amadeus* V. and *Lewis*. *Lewis* had *Vaud* given him out of the Inheritance, of which he was made Baron: But his Posterity failing in another *Lewis*, it returned to the principal Stem in 1350. *Thomas*'s Son, namely *Philip*, had a Partition made for him of all *Piemont*, excepting the Marquisate of *Susa*; and his Posterity continued to Inherit it in a separate Line from the Principal till 1418. that it became Extinct in Prince *Lewis* of *Savoy*. The Estate being thus mangled, the County of *Savoy*, with the remaining Appendages were alloted to *Amadeus* V. whom we now consider as immediate and direct Successor to *Philip* I. in 1285. *Amadeus* V. for his many Valiant Exploits was firnamed *the Great*, and is said to have made 32 Sieges. He was a Prince of singular Prudence, and highly esteem'd by the Emperor *Henry* VII. He made considerable Additions to the Dutchy of *Savoy*, and died at *Avignon*, whither he went to perswade Pope *John* II. to undertake a Croisade against the Infidels, in favour of *Andronicus*, Emperor of the East, who married his Daughter. His Successor was *Edward* his Son, who at 20 Years of Age carried Succours to *Philip* the *Fair*, who Knighted him at the famous Battle of *Mont en Puele*. Afterwards he accompanied *Philip* of *Valois* into *Flanders*, and appear'd in the Battle of *Mont Cassel* in 1328. He died without Issue in 1329, and was succeeded by his Brother *Aymon*, firnamed the *Peace-maker*. *Aymon* did nothing remarkable that we can meet with. He died and was succeeded by his Son *Amadeus* VI. call'd the *Green Count*, because at a Tournament he appear'd all in Green Armour, with his Horse capparison'd in the same Colour. He assisted *John* of *France* against *Edward* of *England*, fought the Prince of *Achaia*, and instituted the Order of the *Anunciade*. In 1356 he assisted and saved the Emperor of *Greece*. In 1383 going to assist *Lewis* of *Anjou* in the Conquest of *Naples*; he died of the Plague after he had reign'd 40 Years, and by his distinguishing Merit made himself Arbiter of all the Grand Affairs of his Time.

Vaud and *Piemont* in separate Branches.

Amadeus V.

Edward 1323.

Aymon 1329.

Amadeus VI. 1342.

Amadeus VII. 1383.

His Son and Successor *Amadeus* VII. sirnamed *the Red*, enlarg'd his own Dominions with the Conquest of *Nice*, assisted *Charles* VI. of *France*, and died by a Fall from his Horse in pursuit of a Wild Boar.

Amadeus VIII. The first Duke of *Savoy*. 1397.

§ 2. He was succeeded by *Amadeus* VIII. who in 1416. was created Duke of *Savoy* by the Emperor *Sigismond*, and in 1434. resigned to his Children and retired to the Priory of *Ripaille*, where he Founded the Order of St. *Maurice*. He was after that elected Antipope to *Eugenius* IV. by the Name of *Felix* V. But at the Request of *Charles* VII. of *France* resigned the Pontificate to *Nicholas* V. in 1449. However Pope *Nicholas* sent him a Cardinals Cap, made him Dean of the Sacred College, and Legate of *Germany*. He was a Generous Prince, and for Wisdom and Equity esteemed the *Solomon* of his Age. Soon after *Amadeus* assumed the Ducal dignity, *viz.* in 1418. *Piemont* returned

Piemont re-annex'd to *Savoy*. D. *Lewis* 1434.

to the principal Line upon the Death of his Cousin *Lewis* without Issue. Upon the Resignation of *Amadeus* VIII. in 1434. his Son *Lewis* assum'd the Government. This *Lewis* gave signal instances of his Courage and Prudence from his very Youth; having acted as Lieutenant-General of *Savoy* in his Father's time. He appeared at *Basil*, when his Father was chosen Pope by the Name of *Felix* V. made his Entrance there in

Assists the *Milanese*. 447.

1440. Upon the death of *Philip Maria* Duke of *Milan* 1447. he sided with the People of *Milan*, on the behalf of *Francis Sforza* Son in Law to the deceased *Philip*, in opposition to the Pretensions of the Duke of *Orleans* Nephew to the said *Philip*, of the Emperor who claim'd it as a Fief by way of devolution, and of *Alphonsus* V. King of *Arragon*, who alledged a Will made by *Philip* in his Favour. In the first Attempts of the *Savoyard* or Confederate Army in this Quarrel, it was defeated near the River *Sezia*; but proving Victorious in another Battle, they procured a Peace, leaving *Francis Sforza* in peaceable Possession; which could not have been so easily effected, if *Charles* the VIIth. and *Lewis* the XIth. of *France* had not thwarted the Pretensions of the House of *Orleans*. *Lewis* of *Savoy* entred into a strict League of Friendship with

Keeps in with *France*.

Charles VII. of *France*; and when the Dauphin of *France* (who was afterwards *Lewis* XI.) took up Arms against his

his Father, and retiring into *Dauphiny*, made a League with the Duke, and married his Daughter *Charlotta*; the Duke neverthless observ'd the Articles of his Treaty with *Charles* the VIIth, and prevented that Prince's Resentment, by declaring that the Marriage was concluded without his Consent, and by denying Succours to the Dauphin. After his Son in Law became King, he gave him a Visit in *France*, and dyed at *Lyons* in 1465, and was Buried at *Geneva*.

§ 3. *Lewis* was succeeded by *Amadeus* IX. an inactive, but devout Prince, who married *Isabel* of *France*, and left to her the sole Government of his Territories. His Nobles taking the Advantage of his slack Government, made an Insurrection and seized *Montmelian*; but were soon reduced by the Assistance of *Lewis* the XIth. of *France*. At last this Poor Prince dyed after a Reign of Seven Years, leaving the Government to his Son *Philibert*. But before we enter upon the Reign of *Philibert*, 'twill be proper to acquaint the Reader, that Duke *Lewis* the Father of *Amadeus* the IXth. was married to *Anne* the Daughter of *Janus* or *John* the First King of *Cyprus*, and of *Charlotta* of *Bourbon*; by whom, he had besides *Amadeus* many Sons, particularly *Philip* (who came afterwards to the Ducal dignity) and *Lewis*. Now, this *Lewis* married *Charlotta* the Daughter of *John* II. King of *Cyprus*, who coming to dye without Male Issue, bequeath'd his Kingdom to his Daughter; though She nor her Husband *Lewis* never came to the Possession of it, by reason that *James* the Natural Son (as it is said) of *John* II, and a Clergyman, usurpt it from her, marrying *Catherine Cornaro* of *Venice*, whom the Senate had Adopted, as we intimated above in our Introduction to the History of *Venice*, as well as that it fell into the Hands of the *Venetians* by the Consequence of that Marriage, and afterwards into those of the *Turks*. However *Lewis* and *Charlotta* dying without Issue, the House of *Savoy* have since assum'd the Title of the Kings of *Cyprus*. To return to *Philibert*, he was Sirnamed the Hunter, and succeeded his Father at Six Years of Age. During his Minority, his Mother *Isabel* declared her Self Regent; but her Regency was disputed by *Lewis* the XIth. her Brother,

Amadeus IX. 1465.

The Occasion of the Title of Kings of *Cyprus*.

Philibert. 1472.

the Duke of *Burgundy*, and several other Lords, whi
proved very Calamitous to the Country. He kill
himself with Hunting, and dyed at the Age of Eig
Charles. 1482. teen. He was succeeded by his Brother *Charles*, wl
was then but Fourteen Years of Age. He was br
up in *France* at the Court of *Lewis* the XIth. H
paid such Respect to the See of *Rome*, that he ref
sed to enter into the League with the *Italian* Princ
against *Innocent* VIII. This *Charles* was married to
Daughter of the Marquis of *Saluces*, and the Ma
quis dying without Male Issue, the Marquisate fell
the Daughter; and though there was no Issue by th
Marriage, the Dukes of *Savoy* have ever since laid Clai
Marquisate of *Saluces* annex'd. to it. 'Tis true, an Insurrection headed by the Ma
quis of *Saluces* was troublesome to him for a tim
but he soon put an end to it by taking *Saluces* an
Carmagnole, and striping the Marquis of his Estat
Charles II. 1489. *Charles* dying in 1489, was succeeded by his Son *Charl*
II. or *Charles John Amadeus*, an Infant of a Year ol
who dyed in Seven Years after. Upon this the Suc
cession fell to his Grand-Uncle *Philip*, Brother to *Ama*
Philip. 1496. *deus* IX. as we intimated above. This *Philip* wa
Fifty Eight Years of Age, when he came to be Duke
and brook'd his Government but one Year. He wa
Nick-named *Sans Terre*, in his Youth at the Court o
France, because he had then no Inheritance, nor an
other Title besides *Philip Monsieur*. It is said his Fa
ther sent him to *France* to be out of the way, upo
the Apprehension that his pregnant and early Qualitie
which drew to him the Eyes and Affection of th
Court of *Savoy*, might either eclipse, or influence him
to despise his elder Brothers; for he was but the fifth
Son. In 1460. his Father gave him the Earldom of
Beauge, and the Title of Count of *Bresse*. Having
stood in Opposition to the Favourites of his Mother
Anne of *Cyprus*, *Lewis* XI. threw him in Prison; but
upon the intercession of *Philip the Good* Duke of *Burgundy*, he was released; and thereupon *Lewis* gave him
the Order of St. *Michael*, and the Duke of *Burgundy*
the Order of the *Golden Fleece*, with the Government
of the two *Burgundies*. After that he accompanied
Charles VIII. to the Conquest of the Kingdom of *Naples*,
and upon his return was made Governour of *Dauphiny*,
where he continued till the Death of *Charles John Amade-*
us,

us. After he became Duke, he drop'd the resentment of all past injuries, and was very obliging and kind to his Subjects.

§ IV. His Son and immediate Successor was *Philibert* II. Sirnamed *the Handsom*, then but Seventeen Years of Age; though before that he had accompanied his Father, when Count of *Bresse* in the Expedition of *Charles* VIII. to the Conquest of *Italy*. He sided with *Lewis* XII. of *France* in his Pretensions to the Dutchy of *Milan*, and after adjusting by Treaty the Condition of the March of the King's Troops through his Territories, accompanied him in his Expedition for the Conquest of that Dutchy. Though *Italy* was then involved in the greatest Calamities of War, he maintained his own Dominions in Peace by a prudent Management. He was a Prince of a generous complaisant Temper, and a Pursuer of Virtue: But was taken off by an immature death, at the Age of Twenty four, by drinking too much iced Wine, after being over-heated in Hunting. To him succeeded his Brother *Charles* III. at the Age of Eighteen, a Learned, Just, and Virtuous Prince, but unhappily singled out for a Throne, for which he was by no means qualifyed. He was miserably toss'd between the *French* and the *Austrians*, who in his time disputed warmly for the Dutchy of *Milan*: For endeavouring to accommodate the Differences between *Francis* I. his Nephew, and *Charles* V. his Brother-in-Law, and neither of 'em allowing of a Neutrality, his Country became a Prey to both Parties, for the *French* Plunder'd *Turin* in 1536, and *Nizza* in 1543, and struck Terror over all *Piemont* after they had won the Battel of *Cerisoles* in 1544.

Philibert II. 1489.

Charles III. 1504.

K. of *France* seizes upon *Piemont*, &c.

Besides, *Francis* I. charged a Debt upon him, for the Dowry of *Louise* the Duke's Sister and his Mother: Nor had *Louise* failed to start some Pretensions to the Ducal dignity it self, upon the Plea that their Father *Philip* being twice Married, *Charles* III. sprung from the Second Marriage, *Philibert* and she being the only Children of the First, from whence she would have concluded an imaginary Right of Primogeniture after the Death of *Philibert*. In fine, the King of *France* possessed himself of almost all his Country: And after all, to add to his Affliction, the City of *Bern* declar'd against him, and took Possession of the *Vaude*, a fine Country adjacent to the Lake of *Geneva*. Duke *Charles*, seeing himself thus stripp'd of his Countries, dyed of Grief at *Vercelli*, An. 1555. after a long but unfortunate Reign.

Emanuel Philibert. 1555.

§ 5. The Son and Successor of *Charles* the Unfortunate was *Emanuel Philibert*, Sirnamed *Iron-head*; who was Bred from his very Youth under *Charles* V. who made him a Knight of the Golden Fleece in 1548. He behaved himself so well in all the Steps of the Military Profession, that he was entrusted with the Command of the Imperial and *Spanish* Army, and was General of it at the Siege of *Metz*, and in the Memorable Battle of St. *Quintins* in 1557. in which he gained such a Compleat and Signal Victory over the *French*, that had he marched directly for *Paris*, he had gone near to carry all *France* before him; and *that* he had certainly done, if King *Philip* had not given Orders to the contrary, upon the Apprehension that good Offers from the *French* might have mollifyed, and gained *Emanuel*, at a time when they were Masters of his Country. However, this Battle proved an Advantagious Peace, both for *Spain* and the Duke, for by the Peace of *Cambray* which thereupon insued, Duke *Emanuel* was restored to his Territories. After that, *Emanuel* married *Margaret* the Daughter of *Francis* the First, and living peaceably at home, governed his Countries with Equity, Prudence and Fortitude; and distinguished himself by his Piety, and the Regard he had for Learning and learned Men. Having accompanied King *Philip* into *England*, he was then installed Knight of the Garter; and in his own Country he instituted the Orders of St. *Maurice* and St. *Lazarus*. He dyed in 1580.

He gains the Battle of St. *Quintins*.

Is restor'd to his Territories.

Charles Emanuel. 1580.

§ 6. To *Emanuel Philibert* succeeded *Charles Emanuel*, in the Nineteenth Year of his Age, a Prince, of whom all Writers give the highest Character that can be, abating for some Faults which appeared but too evidently in his Conduct, and brought such repeated Misfortunes upon him, that his Reflection upon these accelerated his End. Generosity and Courage were his inseparable

parable Companions from his Birth; but they were blended with a boundless desire of Dominion. He was a Prince of Sublime Parts and happy Memory: He was witty in Conversation, and could Speak *French*, *Italian* and *Spanish* to Perfection; the Readiness of his Apprehension did not baulk his Judgment: He was very well versed in many Parts of Learning, especially the Mathematicks: He could read Men happily, and Pump their Secrets with great dexterity; though on the other hand he was himself so reserved and close in his Designs, that it was commonly said of him, That more Mountains covered his Heart than his Country. In fine, the lustre of so many Virtues was in some measure eclipsed by many considerable Faults. Not to mention his Irregular Passion for Women, he was Jealous and Suspicious to a dishonourable degree, and was no strict Observer of his Word. He played fast and lose, sometimes in with *Spain*, sometimes in with *France*, as he found them disposed to gratify his Ambition. His unlimited Ambition put him upon making himself Count of *Provence*, in 1590; Upon Aspiring to the Kingdom of *France* during the League; Upon Pretending to the Imperial Crown after the Death of the Emperor *Matthias*; Upon entertaining the Thoughts of conquering the Kingdom of *Cyprus*, and accepting the Principality of *Macedonia*, offered him by the People of that Country driven to Despair under the *Turkish* Tyranny.

He married a Daughter of *Philip* II. and espoused with her a Partiality to that Crown and the Maxims thereof, in hopes that their Favour joyned to the Divisions of *France*, would open a Way to the Execution of his Ambitious Designs. Accordingly, while *France* was imbroiled, he seized upon the Marquisate of *Saluces*; but not being able by himself to make head against *France* and stand his Ground, he lost several Battles in engaging with *Lesdiguieres* the *French* General, who at the same time seized a great Part of his Country, that was not re-delivered but by the Peace of *Vervain*, concluded between *France* and *Spain*. When that Peace was concluded, the Duke refusing obstinately to deliver up the Marquisate of *Saluces*, the Decision of the Matter was left to the Pope; but

War with *France*. 1588.

Peace of *Vervain*. 1598.

the Pope unwilling to disoblige either Party, drilled on the Matter so long, that *Henry* the IVth. made a positive Resolution to force the Duke to a Compliance. The Duke went in Person to have an Interview with *Henry*, and in Order to an Accommodation promised full Satisfaction for the Marquisate. But the Duke had not Regard to his Promise, as being buoyed up with Hopes, that either *Spain* would stand by him, or Marshal *Biron*, with whom he kept a private Correspondence, would raise such Intestine Commotions, as would give him an Opportunity of lopping off some Part of *France* for himself. In fine, *Henry* did Actually declare War against him a second time, and seized upon a great Part of his Country, and at last forced him to conclude Peace at *Lyons*, and make a Cession of the Province of *Bresso* in Exchange for the Marquisate of *Saluces*; which *Henry* the IVth. did always look upon as a Door through which he could march his Forces into *Italy* at pleasure. This done, the Duke turned his Ambition another way, *viz.* upon *Geneva*; upon which he had some Old and not ill-grounded Pretensions: His Plea is thus grounded. The Earls of *Savoy* were anciently called in to Assist and Protect the Earls of *Geneva* against the incroaching Power of the Bishops, and *Thomas* Earl of *Savoy* married *Beatrix* a Daughter of the Earl of *Geneva*, by Virtue of which, all the Power of the Earls devolved to him. Add to this that the Emperor *Charles* the IVth. granted to *Amadeus* the Fifth, Earl of *Savoy*, a Patent to be Vicar-General of the Empire in that Country, which gave him a Command over the Bishops; and in fine, Pope *Martin* gave to *Amadeus* the VIIIth. the first Duke of *Savoy*, a full Grant of all the Temporal Jurisdiction of *Geneva*, in pursuance of which, all the Money of *Geneva* was stamped with his Name and Figure, all Sentences were executed in his Name, and the very Keys delivered to him when he called for them: And thus it continued till 1528. that both the Civil and Ecclesiastical Government were altered. This, I say, is the Plea of the Dukes of *Savoy* relating to *Geneva*. But however the Justice of it may lie, *Charles Emanuel* had Ambition enough to attempt the taking of it by Scaling; for which End he had prepared such Ladders as might easily be joyn'd

Peace of *Lyons*. 1601.

The Scaling of *Geneva*. 1603.

or inchased in one another without any great Noise. The Stratagem took so well, that two Hundred Men actually got into the Town in the Night time; but before the *Savoyards* could open the Gate, upon which by chance one of the *Geneva* Soldiers had left down the Port-Cullis, the Alarm Bell was rung, and the Burghers rising immediately fell upon the *Savoyards*, who made but a sorry defence, and threw most of 'em headlong over the Wall, and what Prisoners they took, they immediately hang'd.

The Mountferrat War. 1612.

Charles Emmanuel being thus baulk'd, found still a fresh Opportunity for his Ambition to work upon. After the Death of *Francis* III. Duke of *Mantua*, he started Pretensions to the Dutchy of *Montferrat*, the Ground of which Pretensions we mention'd above in our Introduction to the History of *Mantua*. But *Spain* interpos'd on the behalf of D. *Ferdinand* Brother of D. *Francis*, and roundly gave him to know, they would force him to Disarm. This *Charles Emmanuel* resented with such fury, that he sent his Badge of the Order of the Golden Fleece to *Philip* the Third, made Preparations for a vigorous resistance to the *Spaniards*, and call'd in the *French* to his Assistance: Upon which ensued a very sharp War, and some bloody Encounters between the Armies of the two Crowns. But not long after it terminated in Peace; by Vertue of which, Duke *Charles Emmanuel* stood obliged to make a Cession of the Dutchy of *Montferrat* to Duke *Ferdinand*. 1618.
After that, he renewed his Pretensions to *Montferrat*, a new War breaking out in *Italy* upon the Death of *Vincent Gonzagua* Duke Regent of *Mantua*, and endeavour'd to trim with the *French* and *Spaniards* in declaring for neither, but suffered extreamly for it; for having denied the *French* Passage thro' his Country, Cardinal *Richelieu* with the *French* Army advanced and took *Pignerol*, with the adjacent Country. The Duke disturb'd both for the Loss and the 1630.
Insult, roll'd in his Mind the most violent and vexing Thoughts; for having from his younger Years proposed to himself great Undertakings and Victories, with increase of State and Glory, and being now reduced to an unhappy Old Age, he saw his Maxims ill-grounded and his Hopes defeated. He had in his Bosom an Enemy implacable, and a Conqueror, and saw no other Refuge but recourse to the

Austrians,

Austrians, who he knew would be almost equally oppressive and Burdensome, there being a Necessity of receiving *Germans* and *Spaniards* into his Towns. In fine, after wavering between various Thoughts, between making his Country a Theater of War, and despairing to pacify the *French*, he threw himself into the Arms of the *Austrians*, who accordingly succour'd him with a Body of *Germans*, tho' at the same time it was very doubtful whether they contributed most to the Defence or to the Desolation of the Duke's Country. In the mean time, the King of *France* over-run all the Dutchy of *Savoy*, taking *Chamberry* and every place but *Montmelian*, and the Cardinal took Possession of the Marquisate of *Saluzzo*; and on the other hand, *Spinola* the *Austrian* General laid Siege to *Cassal*. In fine, the Duke's Country was nothing but a Scene of Misery, both the Invading and the Protecting Armies being equally Cruel and Oppressive. Amidst so many and so grievous Accidents, Duke *Carlo Emmanuel* bending under 69 Years of Age, Dyed of an Apoplexy, *Anno* 1630.

Victor Amadeus. 1630.

§. 7. His Son and Successor was *Victor Amadeus*, Born 1587. a Prince of a more compos'd Ambition than his Father, and one that seem'd to incline to Peace. Immediately after his Accession to the Ducal Dignity, a Negociation was set on Foot and a Treaty concluded, by which the Duke of *Mantua* yielded to the Duke of *Savoy* several Places in *Montferrat* in consideration of the Sum of 494000 Crowns. And the Duke of *Savoy* made a Cession of *Pignerol* to the *French* for Paying the said Sum to the Duke of *Mantua*. Duke *Victor* gave Proof of his Valour on several Occasions; he was wounded at the Siege of *Verue*, and commanded the *French* Armies. A fresh War breaking out in *Italy* and *Germany* between the two Crowns, *Victor* sided with *France*. He married a Daughter of *Henry* IV. and appear'd always in the *French* Interest, notwithstanding that in his Youth he had been chief Commander of the King of *Spain*'s Galleys, with a Pension of 100000 Crowns *per annum*; and at the same time all his Brothers subsisted by *Spain*. He died in 1637. leaving the young Prince an Infant to the Guardianship of his Dutchess *Christina*, Sister to the King of *France*, with an exclusive Clause against his

Peace of Chierasco, 1631.

his own two Brothers, *Maurice* and *Thomas*. The two Brethren opposed the execution of the Will, and being both in the *Spanish* Service, ingaged that Crown to back 'em. On the other hand, *France* sent Succours to the Dutchess Dowager, under the Command of the Marquis of *Harcourt*; and so a new War broke out in *Savoy*, in which the *Spaniards* had the Disadvantage, being beaten under the Duke of *Leagues* before *Cassal*. But soon after the Difference was accomodated between the two Brothers and the Dutchess, and Prince *Thomas* quitting the *Spaniards* entred into the *French* Service. When Duke *Victor Amadeus* died, his immediate Successor was *Hyacinth* the Eldest Son; but he dying in a Year's time, the Succession came to *Charles Emmanuel* II. in 1638. who was then but four Years of Age. He continued under the Guardianship of his Mother till 1648. that he was declared of Age. He sided most with the *French*, and in the *Pyrenean* Treaty demanded restitution of the *Spaniards*, for the Losses he had sustain'd thro' their means. In 1654. and 1655. thro' a religious Zeal he fell with incredible Fury upon the Inhabitants of the Valleys of *Piemont*, commonly call'd the *Vaudois*, in order to make 'em Roman Catholicks by Compulsion. Upon the intercession of *Oliver Cromwel*, he granted them Peace, but *Oliver* was no sooner Dead, than he renewed his Cruelty to a very barbarous degree; the Circumstances of which (as related) are almost incredible. Having by this violent Persecution dispeopled his Country, he invited those who had fled to come Home again, promising not to disturb 'em in the exercise of their Religion; but they were no sooner return'd, than he recommenced the former Persecution in a very deplorable manner. Upon this they took up Arms in their own Defence; and being perfectly well acquainted with all the Avenues and Places of Access in that rugged and impracticable Country, bafled all the Attempts of the Duke's Troops to dislodge 'em. The *Suiss* Protestant Cantons, and most of the Protestant Princes in *Europe* interceded on their Behalf; but all in Vain, till the two Dutchesses of *Savoy* died, upon which the Protestant *Vaudois* had a general Indemnity granted by the Duke, and so they returned peaceably to their ancient Habitations. Some will have it that the Severities of the Duke to these Protestants have been industriously magnified beyond Matter of Fact; and that the

Charles Emanuel II. 1638.

1658.

Persecutes the Vaudois.

1662.

the Matter was not taken up, till the King of *France* interpos'd his Mediation, upon the Desire of the *Suiss* Cantons. After that, they continued in Peace during the Life of this Prince, who liv'd only to 1675. He was a graceful Person, and a Prince very well vers'd in all Gentlemanny Accomplishments, particularly in Riding; for the Improvement of which, he caused an Academy to be open'd at *Turin*. He loved Learning, and was a Prince of Spirit and Sense. His first Dutchess was a Daughter of the Duke of *Orleans*, and the second a Daughter of the Duke of *Nemours*. The Son of the last, *Victor Amadeus Francis* succeeded him in 1675. being then Nine Years of Age.

Victor Amadeus II.

The Soil, &c. of Savoy.

§. 8. The Dukes of *Savoy* are possess'd of a Country Important for Situation, Plentiful by its Fertility, and for its extent Considerable. *Piemont* is a very fertile Country and wonderful Populous, and contains 160 Castles and Wall'd Places. It abounds with Corn, and Wine, and all sorts of tame and wild Animals; Fruit, Hemp, and Minerals, *&c.* When the *French* and *Spanish* Armies made it the Seat of War for 27 Years together, it still found Provisions for 'em both. The County of *Nice* indeed is a little rugged, but it is very well cultivated. The Inhabitants of *Piemont* are very true to their Prince, and make good Soldiers, only they love their Pleasure as all the *Italians* do. The Dutchy of *Savoy* properly so call'd, is for the most party Hilly and Mountainous, but it has very fruitful Valleys, and a fertile open Plain extending towards the Lake of *Geneva*. The Inhabitants of it are charged with dull gross Understandings, and an Unmilitary Temper; but considering that the Nature of their Country makes them hardy and fit to undergo Fatigue, there's no question to be made but Discipline and Experience will conquer all that natural Dulness, and render them perhaps fitter for Military Exploits, than those who boast of a natural Disposition for 'em. The Country is naturally Strong and the Passes easily defended, not to mention that the Forts which are there are next to impregnable if well provided, witness *Montmelian*. In *Montferrat* the Duke of *Savoy* possesses all that lies North of the *Po*, and the Territory of the *Canavese*; where he has very considerable Forts, and a very fertile tho' a hilly Soil. He has that Advantage beyond

many

many Princes that what by Art and what by Nature his Country is guarded on all Hands; and his Capital perhaps is one of the noblest Fortifications in *Europe*. He may conveniently raise above 30000 good Soldiers in his own Territories; his yearly Revenue amounts to above 1800000 Crowns, which Sum he may inlarge, without displeasing his Subjects, upon a pressing Occasion; he has the Mortification to be environ'd with two such Powers as the *Austrian* and the *Bourbon* Houses, which must always keep him upon his Guard. In case of a Rupture between *France* and *Spain*, his Country must be a continual thorough-fare, and be equally expos'd to the Insults of both Armies. Upon such Occasions the Dukes of *Savoy* have frequently attempted to stand Neuter, but besides that neither of the contending Parties will readily allow of such a Neutrality; 'tis infinitely more the Interest of the *Savoyard* to join his Forces with one to keep out the other, that so his Country may not be exposed to be a Theater of War (as it has been so often) nor his own Property left to the Discretion of a Conqueror, whose down-weighing Power he might have prevented by joyning his Force with the Weaker. *Milan* watches him on the one hand, and *France* on the other; and since *Milan* is in the hands of the *Spaniards*, who are in no Capacity to attempt further Conquests, 'tis absolutely his interest it should continue so, for should the House of *Bourbon* be possess'd of *Milan*, they'll never suffer his Country to remain long a Partition Wall to intercept the Communication of their Territories: Besides, he will then live precariously, and be almost block'd up from Foreign Relief. 'Tis true, while the two Parties are contending, he may happen to be expos'd to Danger as lying next, and sometimes to be surpriz'd; which perhaps has been in part the occasion of the frequent shifting of Hands observable in his Ancestors. But the best Security he can have against such Inconveniences, is a firm Alliance with the *Suiss* Cantons and the Princes of *Italy*, whose Interest is the same with his. For the *Italian* Princes have always look'd upon the Keys of *Italy* as in his Hands; The *Suiss* Cantons can succour him at all times; and will doubtless be unwilling to see an overgrown Power spread all round 'em. On the other hand, the *Austrians* and all the *Italian* Princes will be glad of his Alliance; neither can they lye under any Temptation of Invading his Territories while he continues firm to their Interest

The Neighbours of Savoy.

tereft and Skreens them from the Irruption of the Enemy. Only he muft take care not to think of inlarging his Conquefts on their Side; he is in no Capacity to make Conquefts or to keep them when made, confidering how he is fituated. He will do well to keep in with the Northern Maritim Powers, who in cafe of Diftrefs, can Succour him by the way of *Nizza* and *Villa Franca*; not to mention that mercenary Troops may be found in *Switzerland* to joyn him, if Money, the Sinews of War, be but found.

INDEX.

INDEX.

Battle

INDEX.

INDEX.

I N D E X.

Pope

Her

INDEX.

Philip

INDEX.

blow

Of

Sharpe,

T

V

FINIS.

[illegible]

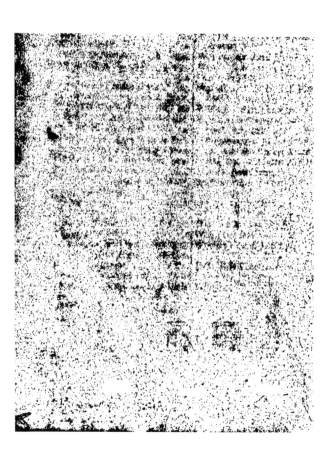

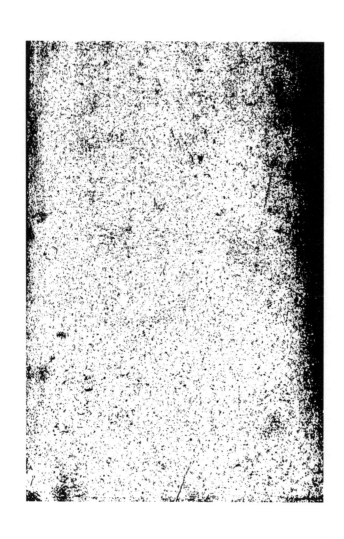

Lightning Source UK Ltd.
Milton Keynes UK
UKHW010608011218
333025UK00006B/776/P

9 780265 599686